REVISED
COMMON
LECTIONARY

Adapted For
THE CHURCH OF ENGLAND

❧ REVISED ❧
COMMON
LECTIONARY

Adapted For
THE CHURCH OF ENGLAND

NEW INTERNATIONAL VERSION

Hodder & Stoughton
LONDON SYDNEY AUCKLAND

The Church of England Lectionary (RCL adapted)
NEW INTERNATIONAL VERSION

First published in Great Britain in 1997 by Hodder & Stoughton

10 9 8 7 6 5 4 3 2 1

British Library Cataloguing in Publication Data
A record for this book is available from the British Library

ISBN 0 340 71003 9

Typeset by Best-set Typesetter Ltd, Hong Kong
Printed and bound by Clays Ltd., St. Ives plc.

Hodder & Stoughton Ltd
A Division of Hodder Headline PLC
338 Euston Road
London NW1 3BH

CONTENTS

Introduction and how to use
Calendar
Dates of Festivals transferring from Sunday
The Lectionary Year

THE SEASONS	YEAR A	YEAR B	YEAR C
Advent 1	1	232	389
Advent 2	2	234	390
Advent 3	5	236	392
Advent 4	7	239	394
Christmas Eve	9	9	9
Christmas Day, Set I	11	11	11
Christmas Day, Set II	13	13	13
Christmas Day, Set III	15	15	15
Christmas 1	18	242	396
Christmas 2	20	20	20
Epiphany - 6 January	22	22	22
Baptism of Christ	25	243	398
Epiphany 2	26	245	400
Epiphany 3	29	247	401
Epiphany 4	31	249	404
Presentation of Christ - 2 February	33	33	33
Proper 1	35	250	406
Proper 2	38	253	409
Proper 3	40	255	411
Second Sunday Before Lent	41	257	413
Sunday Next Before Lent	45	259	415
Ash Wednesday	48	48	48
Lent 1	52	260	417
Lent 2	55	262	419
Lent 3	56	264	422
Lent 4	59	266	424
Mothering Sunday	62	62	62
Lent 5	65	268	426
Palm Sunday	68	270	428
Monday of Holy Week	77	77	77
Tuesday of Holy Week	79	79	79
Wednesday of Holy Week	81	81	81
Maundy Thursday	83	83	83
Good Friday	85	85	85
Easter Eve	93	93	93

Easter Vigil	96	279	437
Easter Day	112	280	437
Old Testament Readings for Sundays in Eastertide	116	284	442
Easter 2	121	290	448
Easter 3	123	291	450
Easter 4	125	293	453
Easter 5	126	294	455
Easter 6	128	296	457
Ascension Day	130	130	130
Easter 7	133	297	458
Pentecost - Whit Sunday	135	299	461
Trinity Sunday	139	303	464
Thanksgiving for Holy Communion	141	141	141
Proper 4	142	305	466
Proper 5	146	308	470
Proper 6	149	312	473
Proper 7	152	314	477
Proper 8	156	319	482
Proper 9	159	323	485
Proper 10	162	326	489
Proper 11	166	329	492
Proper 12	169	332	495
Proper 13	173	335	499
Proper 14	175	339	502
Proper 15	179	341	506
Proper 16	181	344	509
Proper 17	185	347	512
Proper 18	188	350	515
Proper 19	191	353	518
Proper 20	195	356	521
Proper 21	198	359	524
Proper 22	202	363	527
Proper 23	206	366	531
Proper 24	209	369	534
Proper 25	213	373	536
Bible Sunday	215	376	540
Dedication Festival	217	378	542
All Saints' Day	219	380	544
1 November	221	221	221
4 before Advent	223	382	546
3 before Advent	225	383	548
2 before Advent	227	385	550
Christ the King	229	386	551

ALTERNATIVE PSALMODY FOR
THE PRINCIPAL SERVICE LECTIONARY 554

FESTIVALS AND HOLY DAYS

The Naming and Circumcision of Jesus -
1 January   555
The Conversion of Paul - 25 January   556
Joseph - 19 March   559
The Annunciation - 25 March   560
George - 23 April   562
Mark - 25 April   564
Philip and James - 1 May   565
Matthias - 14 May   567
The Visit of Mary to Elizabeth - 31 May   570
Thanksgiving for Holy Communion   *see above*
Barnabas - 11 June   572
The Birth of John the Baptist - 24 June   575
Peter and Paul - 29 June   577
Peter (alone) - 29 June   580
Thomas - 3 July   582
Mary Magdalene- 22 July   583
James - 25 July   585
The Transfiguration - 6 August   586
The Blessed Virgin Mary - 15 August   588
Bartholomew - 24 August   590
Holy Cross Day - 14 September   592
Matthew - 21 September   593
Michael and all Angels (Michaelmas) -
29 September   595
Dedication Festival   *see above*
Luke - 18 October   597
Simon and Jude - 28 October   599
All Saints' Day   *see above*
1 November   *see above*
Andrew - 30 November   600
Christmas Eve - 24 December   *see above*
Stephen - 26 December   602
John - 27 December   603
Holy Innocents - 28 December   604

HARVEST

Year A   607
Year B   610
Year C   612

THE CHURCH OF ENGLAND LECTIONARY
(RCL adapted)
New International Version

INTRODUCTION AND HOW TO USE

Depending on which part of the Anglican tradition you, the reader, come from or currently worship among, will determine the expectations you have of Sunday morning or evening worship - the principal service. In some practices, Holy Communion or the Eucharist is the principal service each Sunday; in others, the preaching and teaching from the Bible, the Word of God, is the focus. Whatever the service, a central or *the* central ritual act (alongside Holy Communion) of Sunday worship is the public reading of Scripture.

> "The Scripures themselves are in origin a collection of hand-written texts designed, either by original intent or by inclusion within the canon, to be heard by the gathered people of God. This corporate reception in the Christian assembly—and its priority over private Bible-reading—is important to the proper interpretation of Scripture." [1]

How this public reading of Scripture is arranged within each service and within the broader Church Year, is of vital significance so that the different seasons of the Church's Year and the nature and scope of the different books and collections of books of the Bible are recognised and addressed. The characteristics of the new Church of England lectionary which has been adapted from the *Revised Common Lectionary* (published in 1992), is important.

1)   Unlike the *Alternative Service Book 1980*, the new lectionary is not thematic but uses a semi-continuous pattern of readings which highlights the narrative aspects of Scripture as the stories of the Old and New Testaments unfold over a number of weeks, together with the argument and teaching in the letters;

2)   Unlike the *Alternative Service Book 1980*, the cycle of readings is arranged over three years not two. This exposes congregations, preachers and individuals to a much wider range of Scripture than previously, a provision which some consider:

> "may be the most important gift of [the system] for the public proclamation of the word of God. At last we have recovered a liturgical way to lead the faithful followers of Christ through his birth, baptism, ministry, death, and resurrection,". [2]

This volume contains the full text of the readings for the principal Sunday service (Years A, B and C) and for the major festivals, that is, the most commonly observed of the holy days not the lesser festivals (such as The

Beheading of John the Baptist) and the commemorations (such as Saints and Martyrs of England).[3] The Bible text used is the New International Version of the Bible (1984 and Anglicised). Rather than appearing in two-columns, the Bible text runs across the page for ease of use and readibility. The usual sectional headings which appear in NIV Bibles are not included as these are not part of the translation itself but are a helpful way of breaking up the text into digestible sections, a device which is not needed in a book of relatively short readings such as this. Where a suggested reading is from the Apocrypha, only the reference is given as the NIV does not include a translation for these texts. The user is encouraged to use the alternative reading provided or to use a modern English Bible translation which includes the Apocrypha.

Alternative readings are clearly marked and where optional additional verses are set, the reference and the text are placed in square brackets. Where shorter psalm readings are possible, this volume highlights this by use of an asterisk at the opening Bible reference which refers the reader to the table of alternative psalmody provided at the back of the book. Where "Selah" is usually part of the Bible text, this "word of uncertain meaning"[4] has not been included.

Where Old Testament readings may be required for Sundays in Eastertide, they appear in the body of the text after the readings for Easter Day rather than at the back of the book, the aim of the publishers being to minimise page-turning and confusion.

For ease of use, a table is included which lists the dates for Easter and other major festivals as well as indicating the Lectionary Year (A, B or C) for each Church Year from now, 1997/1998, until 2024/2025. A table of transference is also included for a few years (1997/1998 to 2001/2002) to inform the user of the date to which a saint's day or major festival should be transferred if they should fall on a Sunday. The rubrics are as detailed as possible, space permitting, to enable accurate and informed use of these readings.

[1] Michael Vasey, Better Than Trainspotting, INTRODUCING THE NEW LECTIONARY, Grove Booklet No. 141, (c) Michael Vasey, Jane Sinclair, Trevor Lloyd, Peter Moger, Grove Books 1997
[2] THE REVISED COMMON LECTIONARY THE CONSULTATION ON COMMON TEXTS, The Canterbury Press, Norwich, 1992.
[3] For information about what constitutes a Festival or a Lesser Festival, see THE CHRISTIAN YEAR: CALENDAR, LECTIONARY AND COLLECTS, pp 243-245.
[4] See the Translators' Preface to any Anglicised NIV Bible, 1984 or later.

Year	Ash Wednesday	EASTER DAY	Ascension Day	Pentecost (Whit Sunday)	Advent Sunday
1997	12 February	30 March	8 May	18 May	30 November
1998	25 February	12 April	21 May	31 May	29 November
1999	17 February	4 april	13 May	23 May	28 November
2000	8 March	23 April	1 June	11 June	3 December
2001	28 February	15 April	24 May	3 Jun	2 December
2002	13 February	31 March	9 May	19 May	1 December
2003	5 March	20 April	29 May	8 June	30 November
2004	25 February	11 April	20 May	30 May	28 November
2005	9 February	27 March	5 May	15 May	27 November
2006	1 March	16 April	25 May	4 June	3 December
2007	21 February	8 April	17 May	27 May	2 December
2008	6 February	23 March	1 May	11 May	30 November
2009	25 February	12 April	21 May	31 May	29 November
2010	17 February	4 April	13 May	23 May	28 November
2011	9 March	24 April	2 June	12 June	27 November
2012	22 February	8 April	17 May	27 May	2 December
2013	13 February	31 March	9 May	19 May	1 December
2014	5 March	20 April	29 May	8 June	30 November
2015	18 February	5 April	14 May	24 May	29 November
2016	10 February	27 March	5 May	15 May	27 November
2017	1 March	16 April	25 May	4 June	3 December
2018	14 February	1 April	10 May	20 May	2 December
2019	6 March	21 April	30 May	9 June	1 December
2020	26 February	12 April	21 May	31 May	29 November
2021	17 February	4 April	13 May	23 May	28 November
2022	2 March	17 April	26 May	5 June	27 November
2023	22 February	9 April	18 May	28 May	3 December
2024	14 February	31 March	9 May	19 May	1 December
2025	5 March	20 April	29 May	8 June	30 November

DATES OF FESTIVALS TRANSFERRING FROM SUNDAY

Year	Festival	Date	Transferred Date
1997/1998	Andrew	Sunday 30 November	Monday 1 December
	Holy Innocents	28 December	Monday 29 December
	Conversion of Paul	25 January	Monday 26 January
	Visit of Mary to Elizabeth	31 May	Monday 1 June
	Barnabas	11 June	Friday 12 June
	(if Thanksgiving for Holy Communion celebrated)		
	Luke	18 October	Monday 17 October
1998/1999	John	27 December	Friday 12 June
	James	25 July	Monday 26 July
	The Blessed Virgin Mary	15 August	Monday 16 August
1999/2000	Stephen	26 December	Wednesday 29 December
	Joseph	19 March	Monday 20 March
	George	23 April	Tuesday 2 May
	Matthias	14 May	Monday 15 May
	Barnabas	11 June	Monday 12 June
	The Transfiguration	6 August	Monday 7 August
2000/2001	The Annunciation	25 March	Monday 26 March
	Birth of John the Baptist	24 June	Monday 25 June
	Mary Magdalene	22 July	Monday 23 July
	Simon and Jude	28 October	Monday 29 October
2001/2002	Michael and All Angels	29 September	Monday 30 September

THE LECTIONARY YEAR

Church Year (Advent to Advent)	Lectionary Year
1997/1998	C
1998/1999	A
1999/2000	B
2000/2001	C
2001/2002	A
2002/2003	B
2003/2004	C
2004/2005	A
2005/2006	B
2006/2007	C
2007/2008	A
2008/2009	B
2009/2010	C
2010/2011	A
2011/2012	B
2012/2013	C
2013/2014	A
2014/2015	B
2015/2016	C
2016/2017	A
2017/2018	B
2018/2019	C
2019/2020	A
2020/2021	B
2021/2022	C
2022/2023	A
2023/2024	B
2024/2025	C

CHURCH OF ENGLAND LECTIONARY FOR THE PRINCIPAL SUNDAY SERVICE (RCL AMENDED)

Year A

THE SEASONS: ADVENT

First Sunday of Advent

Isaiah 2:1–5   This is what Isaiah son of Amoz saw concerning Judah and Jerusalem:

> In the last days
>
>> the mountain of the LORD's temple will be established
>>> as chief among the mountains;
>> it will be raised above the hills,
>>> and all nations will stream to it.
>
> Many peoples will come and say,
>
>> "Come, let us go up to the mountain of the LORD,
>>> to the house of the God of Jacob.
>> He will teach us his ways,
>>> so that we may walk in his paths."
>> The law will go out from Zion,
>>> the word of the LORD from Jerusalem.
>> He will judge between the nations
>>> and will settle disputes for many peoples.
>> They will beat their swords into ploughshares
>>> and their spears into pruning hooks.
>> Nation will not take up sword against nation,
>>> nor will they train for war any more.
>
>> Come, O house of Jacob,
>>> let us walk in the light of the LORD.

Psalm 122   I rejoiced with those who said to me,
> "Let us go to the house of the LORD."
Our feet are standing
> in your gates, O Jerusalem.

Jerusalem is built like a city
> that is closely compacted together.
That is where the tribes go up,
> the tribes of the LORD,
to praise the name of the LORD
> according to the statute given to Israel.
There the thrones for judgment stand,
> the thrones of the house of David.

Pray for the peace of Jerusalem:
"May those who love you be secure.
May there be peace within your walls
and security within your citadels."
For the sake of my brothers and friends,
I will say, "Peace be within you."
For the sake of the house of the LORD our God,
I will seek your prosperity.

Romans 13:11–14 Understand the present time. The hour has come for you to wake up from your slumber, because our salvation is nearer now than when we first believed. The night is nearly over; the day is almost here. So let us put aside the deeds of darkness and put on the armour of light. Let us behave decently, as in the daytime, not in orgies and drunkenness, not in sexual immorality and debauchery, not in dissension and jealousy. Rather, clothe yourselves with the Lord Jesus Christ, and do not think about how to gratify the desires of the sinful nature.

SECOND READING

Matthew 24:36–44 Jesus said: "No-one knows about the day or hour, not even the angels in heaven, nor the Son, but only the Father. As it was in the days of Noah, so it will be at the coming of the Son of Man. For in the days before the flood, people were eating and drinking, marrying and giving in marriage, up to the day Noah entered the ark; and they knew nothing about what would happen until the flood came and took them all away. That is how it will be at the coming of the Son of Man. Two men will be in the field; one will be taken and the other left. Two women will be grinding with a hand mill; one will be taken and the other left.

"Therefore keep watch, because you do not know on what day your Lord will come. But understand this: If the owner of the house had known at what time of night the thief was coming, he would have kept watch and would not have let his house be broken into. So you also must be ready, because the Son of Man will come at an hour when you do not expect him."

GOSPEL

Second Sunday of Advent

Isaiah 11:1–10 A shoot will come up from the stump of Jesse;
    from his roots a Branch will bear fruit.
The Spirit of the LORD will rest on him –
    the Spirit of wisdom and of understanding,
    the Spirit of counsel and of power,
    the Spirit of knowledge and of the fear of the LORD –
and he will delight in the fear of the LORD.

He will not judge by what he sees with his eyes,
    or decide by what he hears with his ears;
but with righteousness he will judge the needy,
    with justice he will give decisions for the poor of the
        earth.

FIRST READING

He will strike the earth with the rod of his mouth;
  with the breath of his lips he will slay the wicked.
Righteousness will be his belt
  and faithfulness the sash round his waist.

The wolf will live with the lamb,
  the leopard will lie down with the goat,
the calf and the lion and the yearling together;
  and a little child will lead them.
The cow will feed with the bear,
  their young will lie down together,
  and the lion will eat straw like the ox.
The infant will play near the hole of the cobra,
  and the young child put his hand into the viper's
    nest.
They will neither harm nor destroy
  on all my holy mountain,
for the earth will be full of the knowledge of the Lord
  as the waters cover the sea.

In that day the Root of Jesse will stand as a banner for the peoples; the nations will rally to him, and his place of rest will be glorious.

Psalm 72:1–7, 18–19* Endow the king with your justice, O God,   P
  the royal son with your righteousness.   S
He will judge your people in righteousness,   A
  your afflicted ones with justice.   L
The mountains will bring prosperity to the people,   M
  the hills the fruit of righteousness.
He will defend the afflicted among the people
  and save the children of the needy;
  he will crush the oppressor.

He will endure as long as the sun,
  as long as the moon, through all generations.
He will be like rain falling on a mown field,
  like showers watering the earth.
In his days the righteous will flourish;
  prosperity will abound till the moon is no more.

Praise be to the Lord God, the God of Israel,
  who alone does marvellous deeds.
Praise be to his glorious name for ever;   S R
  may the whole earth be filled with his glory.   E E
                              Amen and Amen.   C A
                                                  O D
Romans 15:4–13 Everything that was written in the past was written to N I
teach us, so that through endurance and the encouragement of the Scrip- D N
tures we might have hope.   G

May the God who gives endurance and encouragement give you a spirit of unity among yourselves as you follow Christ Jesus, so that with one heart and mouth you may glorify the God and Father of our Lord Jesus Christ.

Accept one another, then, just as Christ accepted you, in order to bring praise to God. For I tell you that Christ has become a servant of the Jews on behalf of God's truth, to confirm the promises made to the patriarchs so that the Gentiles may glorify God for his mercy, as it is written:

> "Therefore I will praise you among the Gentiles;
> I will sing hymns to your name."

Again, it says,

> "Rejoice, O Gentiles, with his people."

And again,

> "Praise the Lord, all you Gentiles,
> and sing praises to him, all you peoples."

And again, Isaiah says,

> "The Root of Jesse will spring up,
> one who will arise to rule over the nations;
> the Gentiles will hope in him."

May the God of hope fill you with all joy and peace as you trust in him, so that you may overflow with hope by the power of the Holy Spirit.

Matthew 3:1–12 John the Baptist came, preaching in the Desert of Judea and saying, "Repent, for the kingdom of heaven is near." This is he who was spoken of through the prophet Isaiah:

> "A voice of one calling in the desert,
> 'Prepare the way for the Lord,
> make straight paths for him.'"

John's clothes were made of camel's hair, and he had a leather belt round his waist. His food was locusts and wild honey. People went out to him from Jerusalem and all Judea and the whole region of the Jordan. Confessing their sins, they were baptised by him in the Jordan River.

But when he saw many of the Pharisees and Sadducees coming to where he was baptising, he said to them: "You brood of vipers! Who warned you to flee from the coming wrath? Produce fruit in keeping with repentance. And do not think you can say to yourselves, 'We have Abraham as our father.' I tell you that out of these stones God can raise up children for Abraham. The axe is already at the root of the trees, and every tree that does not produce good fruit will be cut down and thrown into the fire.

"I baptise you with water for repentance. But after me will come one who is more powerful than I, whose sandals I am not fit to carry. He will baptise you with the Holy Spirit and with fire. His winnowing fork is in his hand, and he will clear his threshing-floor, gathering his wheat into the barn and burning up the chaff with unquenchable fire."

GOSPEL

Isaiah 35:1–10
The desert and the parched land will be glad;
  the wilderness will rejoice and blossom.
Like the crocus, it will burst into bloom;
  it will rejoice greatly and shout for joy.
The glory of Lebanon will be given to it,
  the splendour of Carmel and Sharon;
they will see the glory of the LORD,
  the splendour of our God.

Strengthen the feeble hands,
  steady the knees that give way;
say to those with fearful hearts,
  "Be strong, do not fear;
your God will come,
  he will come with vengeance;
with divine retribution
  he will come to save you."

Then will the eyes of the blind be opened
  and the ears of the deaf unstopped.
Then will the lame leap like a deer,
  and the mute tongue shout for joy.
Water will gush forth in the wilderness
  and streams in the desert.
The burning sand will become a pool,
  the thirsty ground bubbling springs.
In the haunts where jackals once lay,
  grass and reeds and papyrus will grow.

And a highway will be there;
  it will be called the Way of Holiness.
The unclean will not journey on it;
  it will be for those who walk in that Way;
  wicked fools will not go about on it.
No lion will be there,
  nor will any ferocious beast get up on it;
  they will not be found there.
But only the redeemed will walk there,
  and the ransomed of the LORD will return.
They will enter Zion with singing;
  everlasting joy will crown their heads.
Gladness and joy will overtake them,
  and sorrow and sighing will flee away.

FIRST READING

Alternative Psalm or Canticle

Either **Psalm 146:5–10**

Blessed are those whose help is the God of Jacob,
whose hope is in the LORD their God,
the Maker of heaven and earth,
the sea, and everything in them –
the LORD, who remains faithful for ever.
He upholds the cause of the oppressed
and gives food to the hungry.
The LORD sets prisoners free,
the LORD gives sight to the blind,
the LORD lifts up those who are bowed down,
the LORD loves the righteous.
The LORD watches over the alien
and sustains the fatherless and the widow,
but he frustrates the ways of the wicked.

The LORD reigns for ever,
your God, O Zion, for all generations.

Praise the LORD.

Or Canticle: **Magnificat**

Luke 1:466–55

Mary said:

"My soul glorifies the Lord
and my spirit rejoices in God my Saviour,
for he has been mindful
of the humble state of his servant.
From now on all generations will call me blessed,
for the Mighty One has done great things for me –
holy is his name.
His mercy extends to those who fear him,
from generation to generation.
He has performed mighty deeds with his arm;
he has scattered those who are proud in their
inmost thoughts.
He has brought down rulers from their thrones
but has lifted up the humble.
He has filled the hungry with good things
but has sent the rich away empty.
He has helped his servant Israel,
remembering to be merciful
to Abraham and his descendants for ever,
even as he said to our fathers."

James 5:7–10   Be patient, brothers and sisters, until the Lord's coming. See
how the farmer waits for the land to yield its valuable crop, patiently wait-

ing for the autumn and spring rains. You too, be patient and stand firm, because the Lord's coming is near. Don't grumble against each other, brothers, or you will be judged. The Judge is standing at the door!

Brothers, as an example of patience in the face of suffering, take the prophets who spoke in the name of the Lord.

Matthew 11:2–11   When John heard in prison what Christ was doing, he sent his disciples to ask him, "Are you the one who was to come, or should we expect someone else?"

Jesus replied, "Go back and report to John what you hear and see: The blind receive sight, the lame walk, those who have leprosy are cured, the deaf hear, the dead are raised, and the good news is preached to the poor. Blessed is the man who does not fall away on account of me."

As John's disciples were leaving, Jesus began to speak to the crowd about John: "What did you go out into the desert to see? A reed swayed by the wind? If not, what did you go out to see? A man dressed in fine clothes? No, those who wear fine clothes are in kings' palaces. Then what did you go out to see? A prophet? Yes, I tell you, and more than a prophet. This is the one about whom it is written:

"'I will send my messenger ahead of you,
who will prepare your way before you.'

I tell you the truth: Among those born of women there has not risen anyone greater than John the Baptist; yet he who is least in the kingdom of heaven is greater than he."

(margin: GOSPEL)

Fourth Sunday of Advent

Isaiah 7:10–16   The LORD spoke to Ahaz, "Ask the LORD your God for a sign, whether in the deepest depths or in the highest heights."

But Ahaz said, "I will not ask; I will not put the LORD to the test."

Then Isaiah said, "Hear now, you house of David! Is it not enough to try the patience of men? Will you try the patience of my God also? Therefore the LORD himself will give you a sign: The virgin will be with child and will give birth to a son, and will call him Immanuel. He will eat curds and honey when he knows enough to reject the wrong and choose the right. But before the boy knows enough to reject the wrong and choose the right, the land of the two kings you dread will be laid waste."

(margin: FIRST READING)

Psalm 80:1–7, 17–19*   Hear us, O Shepherd of Israel,
you who lead Joseph like a flock;
you who sit enthroned between the cherubim, shine
forth
before Ephraim, Benjamin and Manasseh.
Awaken your might;
come and save us.

(margin: PSALM)

Restore us, O God;
> make your face shine upon us,
> that we may be saved.

O Lᴏʀᴅ God Almighty,
> how long will your anger smoulder
> against the prayers of your people?
You have fed them with the bread of tears;
> you have made them drink tears by the bowlful.
You have made us a source of contention to our
>   neighbours,
> and our enemies mock us.

Restore us, O God Almighty;
> make your face shine upon us,
> that we may be saved.

Let your hand rest on the man at your right hand,
> the son of man you have raised up for yourself.
Then we will not turn away from you;
> revive us, and we will call on your name.

Restore us, O Lᴏʀᴅ God Almighty;
> make your face shine upon us,
> that we may be saved.

Romans 1:1–7   Paul, a servant of Christ Jesus, called to be an apostle and set
apart for the gospel of God – the gospel he promised beforehand through
his prophets in the Holy Scriptures regarding his Son, who as to his human
nature was a descendant of David, and who through the Spirit of holiness
was declared with power to be the Son of God, by his resurrection from the
dead: Jesus Christ our Lord. Through him and for his name's sake, we
received grace and apostleship to call people from among all the Gentiles
to the obedience that comes from faith. And you also are among those who
are called to belong to Jesus Christ.

SECOND READING

To all in Rome who are loved by God and called to be saints:

Grace and peace to you from God our Father and from the Lord Jesus
Christ.

Matthew 1:18–25   This is how the birth of Jesus Christ came about: His
mother Mary was pledged to be married to Joseph, but before they came
together, she was found to be with child through the Holy Spirit. Because
Joseph her husband was a righteous man and did not want to expose her to
public disgrace, he had in mind to divorce her quietly.

GOSPEL

But after he had considered this, an angel of the Lord appeared to him in
a dream and said, "Joseph son of David, do not be afraid to take Mary home
as your wife, because what is conceived in her is from the Holy Spirit. She
will give birth to a son, and you are to give him the name Jesus, because he
will save his people from their sins."

All this took place to fulfil what the Lord had said through the prophet: "The virgin will be with child and will give birth to a son, and they will call him Immanuel" – which means, "God with us."

When Joseph woke up, he did what the angel of the Lord had commanded him and took Mary home as his wife. But he had no union with her until she gave birth to a son. And he gave him the name Jesus.

CHRISTMAS

Christmas Eve

(Readings for Years A, B, C are the same)

2 Samuel 7:1–5, 8–11, 16 After King David was settled in his palace and the LORD had given him rest from all his enemies around him, he said to Nathan the prophet, "Here I am, living in a palace of cedar, while the ark of God remains in a tent."

Nathan replied to the king, "Whatever you have in mind, go ahead and do it, for the LORD is with you."

That night the word of the LORD came to Nathan, saying:

"Go and tell my servant David, 'This is what the LORD says: Are you the one to build me a house to dwell in?

"Now then, tell my servant David, 'This is what the LORD Almighty says: I took you from the pasture and from following the flock to be ruler over my people Israel. I have been with you wherever you have gone, and I have cut off all your enemies from before you. Now I will make your name great, like the names of the greatest men of the earth. And I will provide a place for my people Israel and will plant them so that they can have a home of their own and no longer be disturbed. Wicked people shall not oppress them any more, as they did at the beginning and have done ever since the time I appointed leaders over my people Israel. I will also give you rest from all your enemies. "'The LORD declares to you that the LORD himself will establish a house for you:

Your house and your kingdom shall endure for ever before me; your throne shall be established for ever.'"

Psalm 89:2, 21–27 I will declare that your love stands firm for ever,
that you established your faithfulness in heaven itself.

My hand will sustain him;
surely my arm will strengthen him.
No enemy will subject him to tribute;
no wicked person will oppress him.
I will crush his foes before him
and strike down his adversaries.
My faithful love will be with him,
and through my name his horn will be exalted.
I will set his hand over the sea,
his right hand over the rivers.

He will call out to me, 'You are my Father,
   my God, the Rock my Saviour.'
I will also appoint him my firstborn,
   the most exalted of the kings of the earth.

Acts 13:16–26   Paul motioned with his hand and said: "People of Israel and s
you Gentiles who worship God, listen to me! The God of the people of Israel E
chose our ancestors; he made the people prosper during their stay in C
Egypt, with mighty power he led them out of that country, he endured their O
conduct for about forty years in the desert, he overthrew seven nations in N
Canaan and gave their land to his people as their inheritance. All this took D
about 450 years.

   "After this, God gave them judges until the time of Samuel the prophet. R
Then the people asked for a king, and he gave them Saul son of Kish, of the E
tribe of Benjamin, who ruled for forty years. After removing Saul, he A
made David their king. He testified concerning him: 'I have found David D
son of Jesse a man after my own heart; he will do everything I want him to I
do.' N

   "From this man's descendants God has brought to Israel the Saviour G
Jesus, as he promised. Before the coming of Jesus, John preached repentance and baptism to all the people of Israel. As John was completing his
work, he said: 'Who do you think I am? I am not that one. No, but he is coming after me, whose sandals I am not worthy to untie.'

   "Brothers, children of Abraham, and you God-fearing Gentiles, it is to
us that this message of salvation has been sent."

Luke 1:67–79   John's father Zechariah was filled with the Holy Spirit and G
prophesied: O
                                                                              S
   "Praise be to the Lord, the God of Israel, P
      because he has come and has redeemed his people. E
   He has raised up a horn of salvation for us L
      in the house of his servant David,
   as he said through his holy prophets of long ago,
   salvation from our enemies
      and from the hand of all who hate us –
   to show mercy to our ancestors
      and to remember his holy covenant,
      the oath he swore to our father Abraham:
   to rescue us from the hand of our enemies,
      and to enable us to serve him without fear
      in holiness and righteousness before him all our days.

   And you, my child, will be called a prophet of the Most High;
      for you will go on before the Lord to prepare the way for him,
   to give his people the knowledge of salvation
      through the forgiveness of their sins,

because of the tender mercy of our God,
>   by which the rising sun will come to us from heaven
> to shine on those living in darkness
>   and in the shadow of death,
>   to guide our feet into the path of peace."

Christmas Day – 25 December

(Readings for Years A, B, C are the same)

Any of the following sets of readings may be used on the evening of Christmas Eve and on Christmas Day. Set III should be used at some service during the celebration.

CHRISTMAS, SET I, YEARS A, B, C

Isaiah 9:2–7   The people walking in darkness   F
>   have seen a great light;   I
> on those living in the land of the shadow of death   R
>   a light has dawned.   S
> You have enlarged the nation   T
>   and increased their joy;
> they rejoice before you   R
>   as people rejoice at the harvest,   E
> as men rejoice   A
>   when dividing the plunder.   D
> For as in the day of Midian's defeat,   I
>   you have shattered   N
> the yoke that burdens them,   G
>   the bar across their shoulders,
>   the rod of their oppressor.
> Every warrior's boot used in battle
>   and every garment rolled in blood
> will be destined for burning,
>   will be fuel for the fire.
> For to us a child is born,
>   to us a son is given,
>   and the government will be on his shoulders.
> And he will be called
>   Wonderful Counsellor, Mighty God,
>   Everlasting Father, Prince of Peace.
> Of the increase of his government and peace
>   there will be no end.
> He will reign on David's throne
>   and over his kingdom,
> establishing and upholding it
>   with justice and righteousness
>   from that time on and for ever.

The zeal of the LORD Almighty
   will accomplish this.

Psalm 96   Sing to the LORD a new song;   P
      sing to the LORD, all the earth.   S
   Sing to the LORD, praise his name;   A
      proclaim his salvation day after day.   L
   Declare his glory among the nations,   M
      his marvellous deeds among all peoples.

   For great is the LORD and most worthy of praise;
      he is to be feared above all gods.
   For all the gods of the nations are idols,
      but the LORD made the heavens.
   Splendour and majesty are before him;
      strength and glory are in his sanctuary.

   Ascribe to the LORD, O families of nations,
      ascribe to the LORD glory and strength.
   Ascribe to the LORD the glory due to his name;
      bring an offering and come into his courts.
   Worship the LORD in the splendour of his holiness;
      tremble before him, all the earth.

   Say among the nations, "The LORD reigns."
      The world is firmly established, it cannot be moved;
      he will judge the peoples with equity.
   Let the heavens rejoice, let the earth be glad;
      let the sea resound, and all that is in it;
      let the fields be jubilant, and everything in them.
   Then all the trees of the forest will sing for joy;
      they will sing before the LORD, for he comes,
      he comes to judge the earth.
   He will judge the world in righteousness
      and the peoples in his truth.

Titus 2:11–14   The grace of God that brings salvation has appeared to all   S R
   men. It teaches us to say "No" to ungodliness and worldly passions, and to   E E
   live self-controlled, upright and godly lives in this present age, while we   C A
   wait for the blessed hope – the glorious appearing of our great God and   O D
   Saviour, Jesus Christ, who gave himself for us to redeem us from all   N I
   wickedness and to purify for himself a people that are his very own, eager   D N
   to do what is good.   G

Luke 2:1–14 [15–20]   In those days Caesar Augustus issued a decree that a
   census should be taken of the entire Roman world. (This was the first census that took place while Quirinius was governor of Syria.) And everyone
   went to his own town to register.

So Joseph also went up from the town of Nazareth in Galilee to Judea, to Bethlehem the town of David, because he belonged to the house and line of David. He went there to register with Mary, who was pledged to be married to him and was expecting a child. While they were there, the time came for the baby to be born, and she gave birth to her firstborn, a son. She wrapped him in cloths and placed him in a manger, because there was no room for them in the inn.

And there were shepherds living out in the fields near by, keeping watch over their flocks at night. An angel of the Lord appeared to them, and the glory of the Lord shone around them, and they were terrified. But the angel said to them, "Do not be afraid. I bring you good news of great joy that will be for all the people. Today in the town of David a Saviour has been born to you; he is Christ the Lord. This will be a sign to you: You will find a baby wrapped in cloths and lying in a manger."

Suddenly a great company of the heavenly host appeared with the angel, praising God and saying,

"Glory to God in the highest,
and on earth peace to those on whom his favour rests."

[When the angels had left them and gone into heaven, the shepherds said to one another, "Let's go to Bethlehem and see this thing that has happened, which the Lord has told us about."

So they hurried off and found Mary and Joseph, and the baby, who was lying in the manger. When they had seen him, they spread the word concerning what had been told them about this child, and all who heard it were amazed at what the shepherds said to them. But Mary treasured up all these things and pondered them in her heart. The shepherds returned, glorifying and praising God for all the things they had heard and seen, which were just as they had been told.]

CHRISTMAS, SET II, YEARS A, B, C

Isaiah 62:6–12   I have posted watchmen on your walls, O Jerusalem;
  they will never be silent day or night.
You who call on the LORD,
  give yourselves no rest,
and give him no rest till he establishes Jerusalem
  and makes her the praise of the earth.

The LORD has sworn by his right hand
  and by his mighty arm:
"Never again will I give your grain
  as food for your enemies,
and never again will foreigners drink the new wine
  for which you have toiled;
but those who harvest it will eat it
  and praise the LORD,
and those who gather the grapes will drink it
  in the courts of my sanctuary."

Pass through, pass through the gates!
  Prepare the way for the people.
Build up, build up the highway!
  Remove the stones.
Raise a banner for the nations.

The LORD has made proclamation
  to the ends of the earth:
"Say to the Daughter of Zion,
  'See, your Saviour comes!
See, his reward is with him,
  and his recompense accompanies him.'"
They will be called the Holy People,
  the Redeemed of the LORD;
and you will be called Sought After,
  the City No Longer Deserted.

Psalm 97   The LORD reigns, let the earth be glad;
  let the distant shores rejoice.

Clouds and thick darkness surround him;
  righteousness and justice are the foundation of his throne.
Fire goes before him
  and consumes his foes on every side.
His lightning lights up the world;
  the earth sees and trembles.
The mountains melt like wax before the LORD,
  before the LORD of all the earth.
The heavens proclaim his righteousness,
  and all the peoples see his glory.
All who worship images are put to shame,
  those who boast in idols –
  worship him, all you gods!

Zion hears and rejoices
  and the villages of Judah are glad
  because of your judgments, O LORD.
For you, O LORD, are the Most High over all the earth;
  you are exalted far above all gods.

Let those who love the LORD hate evil,
  for he guards the lives of his faithful ones
  and delivers them from the hand of the wicked.
Light is shed upon the righteous
  and joy on the upright in heart.
Rejoice in the LORD, you who are righteous,
  and praise his holy name.

Titus 3:4–7   When the kindness and love of God our Saviour appeared, he saved us, not because of righteous things we had done, but because of his

mercy. He saved us through the washing of rebirth and renewal by the
Holy Spirit, whom he poured out on us generously through Jesus Christ our
Saviour, so that, having been justified by his grace, we might become heirs
having the hope of eternal life.

Luke 2:[1–7] 8–20   [In those days Caesar Augustus issued a decree that a
census should be taken of the entire Roman world. (This was the first
census that took place while Quirinius was governor of Syria.) And everyone went to his own town to register. So Joseph also went up from the
town of Nazareth in Galilee to Judea, to Bethlehem the town of David,
because he belonged to the house and line of David. He went there to
register with Mary, who was pledged to be married to him and was expecting a child. While they were there, the time came for the baby to be born,
and she gave birth to her firstborn, a son. She wrapped him in cloths and
placed him in a manger, because there was no room for them in the inn.]

And there were shepherds living out in the fields near by, keeping watch
over their flocks at night. An angel of the Lord appeared to them, and the
glory of the Lord shone around them, and they were terrified. But the angel
said to them, "Do not be afraid. I bring you good news of great joy that will
be for all the people. Today in the town of David a Saviour has been born to
you; he is Christ the Lord. This will be a sign to you: You will find a baby
wrapped in cloths and lying in a manger."

Suddenly a great company of the heavenly host appeared with the angel,
praising God and saying,

"Glory to God in the highest,
   and on earth peace to those on whom his favour rests."

When the angels had left them and gone into heaven, the shepherds said
to one another, "Let's go to Bethlehem and see this thing that has happened,
which the Lord has told us about."

So they hurried off and found Mary and Joseph, and the baby, who was
lying in the manger. When they had seen him, they spread the word
concerning what had been told them about this child, and all who heard it
were amazed at what the shepherds said to them. But Mary treasured up
all these things and pondered them in her heart. The shepherds returned,
glorifying and praising God for all the things they had heard and seen,
which were just as they had been told.

CHRISTMAS, SET III, YEARS A, B, C

Isaiah 52:7–10   How beautiful on the mountains
               are the feet of those who bring good news,
            who proclaim peace,
               who bring good tidings,
               who proclaim salvation,
            who say to Zion,
               "Your God reigns!"

Listen! Your watchmen lift up their voices;
    together they shout for joy.
When the LORD returns to Zion,
    they will see it with their own eyes.
Burst into songs of joy together,
    you ruins of Jerusalem,
for the LORD has comforted his people,
    he has redeemed Jerusalem.
The LORD will lay bare his holy arm
    in the sight of all the nations,
and all the ends of the earth will see
    the salvation of our God.

Psalm 98

Sing to the LORD a new song,   P
    for he has done marvellous things;   S
his right hand and his holy arm   A
    have worked salvation for him.   L
The LORD has made his salvation known   M
    and revealed his righteousness to the nations.
He has remembered his love
    and his faithfulness to the house of Israel;
all the ends of the earth have seen
    the salvation of our God.

Shout for joy to the LORD, all the earth,
    burst into jubilant song with music;
make music to the LORD with the harp,
    with the harp and the sound of singing,
with trumpets and the blast of the ram's horn –
shout for joy before the LORD, the King.
Let the sea resound, and everything in it,
    the world, and all who live in it.
Let the rivers clap their hands,
    let the mountains sing together for joy;
let them sing before the LORD,
    for he comes to judge the earth.
He will judge the world in righteousness
    and the peoples with equity.

Hebrews 1:1–4 [5–12]   In the past God spoke to our forefathers through the prophets at many times and in various ways, but in these last days he has spoken to us by his Son, whom he appointed heir of all things, and through whom he made the universe. The Son is the radiance of God's glory and the exact representation of his being, sustaining all things by his powerful word. After he had provided purification for sins, he sat down at the right hand of the Majesty in heaven. So he became as much superior to the angels as the name he has inherited is superior to theirs.

[For to which of the angels did God ever say,

"You are my Son;
today I have become your Father"?

Or again,

"I will be his Father,
and he will be my Son"?

And again, when God brings his firstborn into the world, he says,

"Let all God's angels worship him."

In speaking of the angels he says,

"He makes his angels winds,
his servants flames of fire."

But about the Son he says,

"Your throne, O God, will last for ever and ever,
and righteousness will be the sceptre of your kingdom.
You have loved righteousness and hated wickedness;
therefore God, your God, has set you above your companions
by anointing you with the oil of joy."

He also says,

"In the beginning, O Lord, you laid the foundations of the earth,
and the heavens are the work of your hands.
They will perish, but you remain;
they will all wear out like a garment.
You will roll them up like a robe;
like a garment they will be changed.
But you remain the same,
and your years will never end."]

John 1:1–14   In the beginning was the Word, and the Word was with God, and the Word was God. He was with God in the beginning.

Through him all things were made; without him nothing was made that has been made. In him was life, and that life was the light of all people. The light shines in the darkness, but the darkness has not understood it.

There came a man who was sent from God; his name was John. He came as a witness to testify concerning that light, so that through him all might believe. He himself was not the light; he came only as a witness to the light. The true light that gives light to everyone was coming into the world.

He was in the world, and though the world was made through him, the world did not recognise him. He came to that which was his own, but his own did not receive him. Yet to all who received him, to those who believed in his name, he gave the right to become children of God – children born not of natural descent, nor of human decision or a husband's will, but born of God.

The Word became flesh and made his dwelling among us. We have seen his glory, the glory of the One and Only, who came from the Father, full of grace and truth.

First Sunday of Christmas

Isaiah 63:7–9	I will tell of the kindnesses of the Lord,	F
	the deeds for which he is to be praised,	I
	according to all the Lord has done for us –	R
	yes, the many good things he has done	S
	for the house of Israel,	T
	according to his compassion and many kindnesses.	
	He said, "Surely they are my people,	R
	children who will not be false to me";	E
	and so he became their Saviour.	A
	In all their distress he too was distressed,	D
	and the angel of his presence saved them.	I
	In his love and mercy he redeemed them;	N
	he lifted them up and carried them	G
	all the days of old.	

Psalm 148*	Praise the Lord.	P
	Praise the Lord from the heavens,	S
	praise him in the heights above.	A
	Praise him, all his angels,	L
	praise him, all his heavenly hosts.	M
	Praise him, sun and moon,	
	praise him, all you shining stars.	
	Praise him, you highest heavens	
	and you waters above the skies.	
	Let them praise the name of the Lord,	
	for he commanded and they were created.	
	He set them in place for ever and ever;	
	he gave a decree that will never pass away.	

Praise the Lord from the earth,
  you great sea creatures and all ocean depths,
lightning and hail, snow and clouds,
  stormy winds that do his bidding,
you mountains and all hills,
  fruit trees and all cedars,
wild animals and all cattle,
  small creatures and flying birds,
kings of the earth and all nations,
  you princes and all rulers on earth,
young men and maidens,
  old men and children.

Let them praise the name of the LORD,
>   for his name alone is exalted;
>   his splendour is above the earth and the heavens.
He has raised up for his people a horn,
>   the praise of all his saints,
>   of Israel, the people close to his heart.

Praise the LORD.

Hebrews 2:10–18   In bringing many sons to glory, it was fitting that God, for whom and through whom everything exists, should make the author of their salvation perfect through suffering. Both the one who makes men holy and those who are made holy are of the same family. So Jesus is not ashamed to call them brothers. He says,

>   "I will declare your name to my brothers;
>   in the presence of the congregation I will sing your praises."

And again,

>   "I will put my trust in him."

And again he says,

>   "Here am I, and the children God has given me."

Since the children have flesh and blood, he too shared in their humanity so that by his death he might destroy him who holds the power of death – that is, the devil – and free those who all their lives were held in slavery by their fear of death. For surely it is not angels he helps, but Abraham's descendants. For this reason he had to be made like his brothers in every way, in order that he might become a merciful and faithful high priest in service to God, and that he might make atonement for the sins of the people. Because he himself suffered when he was tempted, he is able to help those who are being tempted.

Matthew 2:13–23   When the Magi had gone, an angel of the Lord appeared to Joseph in a dream. "Get up," he said, "take the child and his mother and escape to Egypt. Stay there until I tell you, for Herod is going to search for the child to kill him."

So he got up, took Jesus and his mother during the night and left for Egypt, where he stayed until the death of Herod. And so was fulfilled what the Lord had said through the prophet: "Out of Egypt I called my son."

When Herod realised that he had been outwitted by the Magi, he was furious, and he gave orders to kill all the boys in Bethlehem and its vicinity who were two years old and under, in accordance with the time he had learned from the Magi. Then what was said through the prophet Jeremiah was fulfilled:

>   "A voice is heard in Ramah,
>   weeping and great mourning,
>   Rachel weeping for her children
>   and refusing to be comforted,
>   because they are no more."

After Herod died, an angel of the Lord appeared in a dream to Joseph in Egypt and said, "Get up, take the child and his mother and go to the land of Israel, for those who were trying to take the child's life are dead."

So he got up, took the child and his mother and went to the land of Israel. But when he heard that Archelaus was reigning in Judea in place of his father Herod, he was afraid to go there. Having been warned in a dream, he withdrew to the district of Galilee, and he went and lived in a town called Nazareth. So was fulfilled what was said through the prophets: "He will be called a Nazarene."

Second Sunday of Christmas

(Readings for Years A, B, C, are the same)

Alternatives provided for the first reading and its complementary Psalm or Canticle

Either **Jeremiah: 31: 7–14**

This is what the LORD says:

Sing with joy for Jacob;
    shout for the foremost of the nations.
Make your praises heard, and say,
    'O LORD, save your people,
    the remnant of Israel.'
See, I will bring them from the land of the north
    and gather them from the ends of the earth.
Among them will be the blind and the lame,
    expectant mothers and women in labour;
    a great throng will return.
They will come with weeping;
    they will pray as I bring them back.
I will lead them beside streams of water
    on a level path where they will not stumble,
because I am Israel's father,
    and Ephraim is my firstborn son.
"Hear the word of the LORD, O nations;
    proclaim it in distant coastlands:
'He who scattered Israel will gather them
    and will watch over his flock like a shepherd.'
For the LORD will ransom Jacob
    and redeem them from the hand of those stronger
        than they.
They will come and shout for joy on the heights of Zion;
    they will rejoice in the bounty of the LORD –
the grain, the new wine and the oil,
    the young of the flocks and herds.
They will be like a well-watered garden,
    and they will sorrow no more.

Then young women will dance and be glad,
    young men and old as well.
I will turn their mourning into gladness;
    I will give them comfort and joy instead of sorrow.
I will satisfy the priests with abundance,
    and my people will be filled with my bounty,"
                      declares the Lord.

and **Psalm 147:12–20**
Extol the Lord, O Jerusalem;
    praise your God, O Zion,
for he strengthens the bars of your gates
    and blesses your people within you.
He grants peace to your borders
    and satisfies you with the finest of wheat.

He sends his command to the earth;
    his word runs swiftly.
He spreads the snow like wool
    and scatters the frost like ashes.
He hurls down hail like pebbles.
    Who can withstand his icy blast?
He sends his word and melts them;
    he stirs up his breezes, and the waters flow.

He has revealed his word to Jacob,
    his laws and decrees to Israel.
He has done this for no other nation;
    they do not know his laws.

Praise the Lord.

Or **Ecclesiasticus 24:1–12**

and Canticle: **Wisdom of Solomom 10:15–21**

Ephesians 1:3–14
Praise be to the God and Father of our Lord Jesus Christ, who has blessed us in the heavenly realms with every spiritual blessing in Christ. For he chose us in him before the creation of the world to be holy and blameless in his sight. In love he predestined us to be adopted as his sons through Jesus Christ, in accordance with his pleasure and will – to the praise of his glorious grace, which he has freely given us in the One he loves. In him we have redemption through his blood, the forgiveness of sins, in accordance with the riches of God's grace that he lavished on us with all wisdom and understanding. And he made known to us the mystery of his will according to his good pleasure, which he purposed in Christ, to be put into effect when the times will have reached their fulfilment – to bring all things in heaven and on earth together under one head, even Christ.

In him we were also chosen, having been predestined according to the plan of him who works out everything in conformity with the purpose of his will, in order that we, who were the first to hope in Christ, might be for the praise of his glory. And you also were included in Christ when you heard the word of truth, the gospel of your salvation. Having believed, you were marked in him with a seal, the promised Holy Spirit, who is a deposit guaranteeing our inheritance until the redemption of those who are God's possession – to the praise of his glory.

John 1:[1–9] 10–18   [In the beginning was the Word, and the Word was with God, and the Word was God. He was with God in the beginning.

Through him all things were made; without him nothing was made that has been made. In him was life, and that life was the light of all people. The light shines in the darkness, but the darkness has not understood it.

There came a man who was sent from God; his name was John. He came as a witness to testify concerning that light, so that through him all might believe. He himself was not the light; he came only as a witness to the light. The true light that gives light to everyone was coming into the world.]

The Word was in the world, and though the world was made through him, the world did not recognise him. He came to that which was his own, but his own did not receive him. Yet to all who received him, to those who believed in his name, he gave the right to become children of God – children born not of natural descent, nor of human decision or a husband's will, but born of God.

The Word became flesh and made his dwelling among us. We have seen his glory, the glory of the One and Only, who came from the Father, full of grace and truth.

John testifies concerning him. He cries out, saying, "This was he of whom I said, 'He who comes after me has surpassed me because he was before me.'" From the fulness of his grace we have all received one blessing after another. For the law was given through Moses; grace and truth came through Jesus Christ. No-one has ever seen God, but God the One and Only, who is at the Father's side, has made him known.

(right margin: GOSPEL)

EPIPHANY

The Epiphany – 6 January

(Readings for Years A, B, C are the same)

Isaiah 60:1–6   "Arise, shine, for your light has come,
and the glory of the LORD rises upon you.
See, darkness covers the earth
and thick darkness is over the peoples,
but the LORD rises upon you
and his glory appears over you.
Nations will come to your light,
and kings to the brightness of your dawn.

"Lift up your eyes and look about you:
All assemble and come to you;

(right margin: FIRST READING)

your sons come from afar,
 and your daughters are carried on the arm.
Then you will look and be radiant,
 your heart will throb and swell with joy;
the wealth on the seas will be brought to you,
 to you the riches of the nations will come.
Herds of camels will cover your land,
 young camels of Midian and Ephah.
And all from Sheba will come,
 bearing gold and incense
 and proclaiming the praise of the Lord."

Psalm 72: [1–9] [Endow the king with your justice, O God,
10–15 the royal son with your righteousness.
He will judge your people in righteousness,
 your afflicted ones with justice.
The mountains will bring prosperity to the people,
 the hills the fruit of righteousness.
He will defend the afflicted among the people
 and save the children of the needy;
 he will crush the oppressor.

He will endure as long as the sun,
 as long as the moon, through all generations.
He will be like rain falling on a mown field,
 like showers watering the earth.
In his days the righteous will flourish;
 prosperity will abound till the moon is no more.

He will rule from sea to sea
 and from the River to the ends of the earth.
The desert tribes will bow before him
 and his enemies will lick the dust.]
The kings of Tarshish and of distant shores
 will bring tribute to the king;
the kings of Sheba and Seba
 will present him gifts.
All kings will bow down to him
 and all nations will serve him.

For he will deliver the needy who cry out,
 the afflicted who have no-one to help.
He will take pity on the weak and the needy
 and save the needy from death.
He will rescue them from oppression and violence,
 for precious is their blood in his sight.

Long may he live!
 May gold from Sheba be given to him.
May people ever pray for him
 and bless him all day long.

P
S
A
L
M

Ephesians 3: 1–12   I, Paul, am the prisoner of Jesus Christ for the sake of you ꜱ
Gentiles – ᴇ

Surely you have heard about the administration of God's grace that was ᴄ
given to me for you, that is, the mystery made known to me by revelation, ᴏ
as I have already written briefly. In reading this, then, you will be able to ɴ
understand my insight into the mystery of Christ, which was not made ᴅ
known to men in other generations as it has now been revealed by the Spirit
to God's holy apostles and prophets. This mystery is that through the ʀ
gospel the Gentiles are heirs together with Israel, members together of ᴇ
one body, and sharers together in the promise in Christ Jesus. ᴀ

I became a servant of this gospel by the gift of God's grace given me ᴅ
through the working of his power. Although I am less than the least of all ɪ
God's people, this grace was given me: to preach to the Gentiles the ɴ
unsearchable riches of Christ, and to make plain to everyone the adminis- ɢ
tration of this mystery, which for ages past was kept hidden in God, who
created all things. His intent was that now, through the church, the mani-
fold wisdom of God should be made known to the rulers and authorities in
the heavenly realms, according to his eternal purpose which he accomplished in Christ Jesus our Lord. In him and through faith in him we may
approach God with freedom and confidence.

Matthew 2:1–12   After Jesus was born in Bethlehem in Judea, during the ɢ
time of King Herod, Magi from the east came to Jerusalem and asked, ᴏ
"Where is the one who has been born king of the Jews? We saw his star in ꜱ
the east and have come to worship him." ᴘ

When King Herod heard this he was disturbed, and all Jerusalem with ᴇ
him. When he had called together all the people's chief priests and teach- ʟ
ers of the law, he asked them where the Christ was to be born. "In
Bethlehem in Judea," they replied, "for this is what the prophet has written:

"'But you, Bethlehem, in the land of Judah,
   are by no means least among the rulers of Judah;
for out of you will come a ruler
   who will be the shepherd of my people Israel.'"

Then Herod called the Magi secretly and found out from them the exact
time the star had appeared. He sent them to Bethlehem and said, "Go and
make a careful search for the child. As soon as you find him, report to me,
so that I too may go and worship him."

After they had heard the king, they went on their way, and the star they
had seen in the east went ahead of them until it stopped over the place
where the child was. When they saw the star, they were overjoyed. On coming to the house, they saw the child with his mother Mary, and they bowed
down and worshipped him. Then they opened their treasures and presented him with gifts of gold and of incense and of myrrh. And having been
warned in a dream not to go back to Herod, they returned to their country
by another route.

The Baptism of Christ

The First Sunday of Epiphany

Isaiah 42:1–9   "Here is my servant, whom I uphold,
  my chosen one in whom I delight;
I will put my Spirit on him
  and he will bring justice to the nations.
He will not shout or cry out,
  or raise his voice in the streets.
A bruised reed he will not break,
  and a smouldering wick he will not snuff out.
In faithfulness he will bring forth justice;
  he will not falter or be discouraged
till he establishes justice on earth.
  In his law the islands will put their hope."

This is what God the LORD says –
he who created the heavens and stretched them out,
  who spread out the earth and all that comes out of it,
who gives breath to its people,
  and life to those who walk on it:
"I, the LORD, have called you in righteousness;
  I will take hold of your hand.
I will keep you and will make you
  to be a covenant for the people
  and a light for the Gentiles,
to open eyes that are blind,
  to free captives from prison
  and to release from the dungeon those who sit in darkness.

"I am the LORD; that is my name!
  I will not give my glory to another
  or my praise to idols.
See, the former things have taken place,
  and new things I declare;
before they spring into being
  I announce them to you."

(margin: F I R S T   R E A D I N G)

Psalm 29   Ascribe to the LORD, O mighty ones,
  ascribe to the LORD glory and strength.
Ascribe to the LORD the glory due to his name;
  worship the LORD in the splendour of his holiness.

The voice of the LORD is over the waters;
  the God of glory thunders,
  the LORD thunders over the mighty waters.
The voice of the LORD is powerful;
  the voice of the LORD is majestic.
The voice of the LORD breaks the cedars;
  the LORD breaks in pieces the cedars of Lebanon.

(margin: P S A L M)

He makes Lebanon skip like a calf,
    Sirion like a young wild ox.
The voice of the LORD strikes
    with flashes of lightning.
The voice of the LORD shakes the desert;
    the LORD shakes the Desert of Kadesh.
The voice of the LORD twists the oaks
    and strips the forests bare.
And in his temple all cry, "Glory!"

The LORD sits enthroned over the flood;
    the LORD is enthroned as King for ever.
The LORD gives strength to his people;
    the LORD blesses his people with peace.

Acts 10:34–43 Peter began to speak: "I now realise how true it is that God
does not show favouritism but accepts men from every nation who fear
him and do what is right. You know the message God sent to the people of
Israel, telling the good news of peace through Jesus Christ, who is Lord of
all. You know what has happened throughout Judea, beginning in Galilee
after the baptism that John preached – how God anointed Jesus of
Nazareth with the Holy Spirit and power, and how he went around doing
good and healing all who were under the power of the devil, because God
was with him.

"We are witnesses of everything he did in the country of the Jews and in
Jerusalem. They killed him by hanging him on a tree, but God raised him
from the dead on the third day and caused him to be seen. He was not seen
by all the people, but by witnesses whom God had already chosen – by us
who ate and drank with him after he rose from the dead. He commanded us
to preach to the people and to testify that he is the one whom God appointed
as judge of the living and the dead. All the prophets testify about him that
everyone who believes in him receives forgiveness of sins through his
name."

Matthew 3:13–17 Jesus came from Galilee to the Jordan to be baptised by
John. But John tried to deter him, saying, "I need to be baptised by you, and
do you come to me?"

Jesus replied, "Let it be so now; it is proper for us to do this to fulfil all
righteousness." Then John consented.

As soon as Jesus was baptised, he went up out of the water. At that
moment heaven was opened, and he saw the Spirit of God descending like
a dove and lighting on him. And a voice from heaven said, "This is my Son,
whom I love; with him I am well pleased."

Second Sunday of Epiphany

Isaiah 49:1–7 Listen to me, you islands;
            hear this, you distant nations:

Before I was born the Lord called me;
    from my birth he has made mention of my name.
He made my mouth like a sharpened sword,
    in the shadow of his hand he hid me;
he made me into a polished arrow
    and concealed me in his quiver.
He said to me, "You are my servant,
    Israel, in whom I will display my splendour."
But I said, "I have laboured to no purpose;
    I have spent my strength in vain and for nothing.
Yet what is due to me is in the Lord's hand,
    and my reward is with my God."

FIRST READING

And now the Lord says –
    he who formed me in the womb to be his servant
to bring Jacob back to him
    and gather Israel to himself,
for I am honoured in the eyes of the Lord
    and my God has been my strength –
he says:
"It is too small a thing for you to be my servant
    to restore the tribes of Jacob
    and bring back those of Israel I have kept.
I will also make you a light for the Gentiles,
    that you may bring my salvation to the ends of the
        earth."

This is what the Lord says –
    the Redeemer and Holy One of Israel –
to him who was despised and abhorred by the nation,
    to the servant of rulers:
"Kings will see you and rise up,
    princes will see and bow down,
because of the Lord, who is faithful,
    the Holy One of Israel, who has chosen you."

Psalm 40:1–11   I waited patiently for the Lord;
    he turned to me and heard my cry.
He lifted me out of the slimy pit,
    out of the mud and mire;
he set my feet on a rock
    and gave me a firm place to stand.
He put a new song in my mouth,
    a hymn of praise to our God.
Many will see and fear
    and put their trust in the Lord.

Blessed are those
    who make the Lord their trust,

PSALM

who do not look to the proud,
　　to those who turn aside to false gods.
Many, O Lord my God,
　　are the wonders you have done.
The things you planned for us
　　no-one can recount to you;
were I to speak and tell of them,
　　they would be too many to declare.

Sacrifice and offering you did not desire,
　　but my ears you have pierced;
burnt offerings and sin offerings
　　you did not require.
Then I said, "Here I am, I have come –
　　it is written about me in the scroll.
I desire to do your will, O my God;
　　your law is within my heart."

I proclaim righteousness in the great assembly;
　　I do not seal my lips,
　　as you know, O Lord.
I do not hide your righteousness in my heart;
　　I speak of your faithfulness and salvation.
I do not conceal your love and your truth
　　from the great assembly.

Do not withhold your mercy from me, O Lord;
　　may your love and your truth always protect me.

1 Corinthians 1:1–9　Paul, called to be an apostle of Christ Jesus by the will of
God, and our brother Sosthenes,

To the church of God in Corinth, to those sanctified in Christ Jesus and
called to be holy, together with all those everywhere who call on the name
of our Lord Jesus Christ – their Lord and ours:

Grace and peace to you from God our Father and the Lord Jesus Christ.

I always thank God for you because of his grace given you in Christ
Jesus. For in him you have been enriched in every way – in all your speaking and in all your knowledge – because our testimony about Christ was
confirmed in you. Therefore you do not lack any spiritual gift as you
eagerly wait for our Lord Jesus Christ to be revealed. He will keep you
strong to the end, so that you will be blameless on the day of our Lord Jesus
Christ. God, who has called you into fellowship with his Son Jesus Christ
our Lord, is faithful.

John 1:29–42　John saw Jesus coming towards him and said, "Look, the Lamb
of God, who takes away the sin of the world! This is the one I meant when I
said, 'A man who comes after me has surpassed me because he was before
me.' I myself did not know him, but the reason I came baptising with water
was that he might be revealed to Israel."

Then John gave this testimony: "I saw the Spirit come down from heaven as a dove and remain on him. I would not have known him, except that the one who sent me to baptise with water told me, 'The man on whom you see the Spirit come down and remain is the one who will baptise with the Holy Spirit.' I have seen and I testify that this is the Son of God."

The next day John was there again with two of his disciples. When he saw Jesus passing by, he said, "Look, the Lamb of God!"

When the two disciples heard him say this, they followed Jesus. Turning round, Jesus saw them following and asked, "What do you want?"

They said, "Rabbi" (which means Teacher), "where are you staying?"

"Come," he replied, "and you will see."

So they went and saw where he was staying, and spent that day with him. It was about the tenth hour.

Andrew, Simon Peter's brother, was one of the two who heard what John had said and who had followed Jesus. The first thing Andrew did was to find his brother Simon and tell him, "We have found the Messiah" (that is, the Christ). And he brought him to Jesus.

Jesus looked at him and said, "You are Simon son of John. You will be called Cephas" (which, when translated, is Peter).

Third Sunday of Epiphany

Isaiah 9:1–4   There will be no more gloom for those who were in distress. In the past the LORD humbled the land of Zebulun and the land of Naphtali, but in the future he will honour Galilee of the Gentiles, by the way of the sea, along the Jordan –

> The people walking in darkness
>> have seen a great light;
> on those living in the land of the shadow of death
>> a light has dawned.
> You have enlarged the nation
>> and increased their joy;
> they rejoice before you
>> as people rejoice at the harvest,
> as soldiers rejoice
>> when dividing the plunder.
> For as in the day of Midian's defeat,
>> you have shattered
> the yoke that burdens them,
>> the bar across their shoulders,
>> the rod of their oppressor.

Psalm 27:1, 4–9*   The LORD is my light and my salvation –
> whom shall I fear?
> The LORD is the stronghold of my life –
>> of whom shall I be afraid?

FIRST READING

PSALM

One thing I ask of the LORD,
   this is what I seek:
that I may dwell in the house of the LORD
   all the days of my life,
to gaze upon the beauty of the LORD
   and to seek him in his temple.
For in the day of trouble
   he will keep me safe in his dwelling;
he will hide me in the shelter of his tabernacle
   and set me high upon a rock.
Then my head will be exalted
   above the enemies who surround me;
at his tabernacle will I sacrifice with shouts of joy;
   I will sing and make music to the LORD.

Hear my voice when I call, O LORD;
   be merciful to me and answer me.
My heart says of you, "Seek his face!"
   Your face, LORD, I will seek.
Do not hide your face from me,
   do not turn your servant away in anger;
   you have been my helper.
Do not reject me or forsake me,
   O God my Saviour.

1 Corinthians 1:10–18 I appeal to you, brothers, in the name of our Lord S
Jesus Christ, that all of you agree with one another so that there may be no E
divisions among you and that you may be perfectly united in mind and C
thought. My brothers, some from Chloe's household have informed me that O
there are quarrels among you. What I mean is this: One of you says, "I fol- N
low Paul"; another, "I follow Apollos"; another, "I follow Cephas"; still D
another, "I follow Christ."

Is Christ divided? Was Paul crucified for you? Were you baptised into R
the name of Paul? I am thankful that I did not baptise any of you except E
Crispus and Gaius, so no-one can say that you were baptised into my name. A
(Yes, I also baptised the household of Stephanas; beyond that, I don't D
remember if I baptised anyone else.) For Christ did not send me to baptise, I
but to preach the gospel – not with words of human wisdom, lest the cross N
of Christ be emptied of its power. G

For the message of the cross is foolishness to those who are perishing,
but to us who are being saved it is the power of God.

G

O

Matthew 4:12–23 When Jesus heard that John had been put in prison, he S
returned to Galilee. Leaving Nazareth, he went and lived in Capernaum, P
which was by the lake in the area of Zebulun and Naphtali – to fulfil what E
was said through the prophet Isaiah: L

"Land of Zebulun and land of Naphtali,
   the way to the sea, along the Jordan,
   Galilee of the Gentiles –
the people living in darkness
   have seen a great light;
on those living in the land of the shadow of death
   a light has dawned."

From that time on Jesus began to preach, "Repent, for the kingdom of heaven is near."

As Jesus was walking beside the Sea of Galilee, he saw two brothers, Simon called Peter and his brother Andrew. They were casting a net into the lake, for they were fishermen. "Come, follow me," Jesus said, "and I will make you fishers of men." At once they left their nets and followed him.

Going on from there, he saw two other brothers, James son of Zebedee and his brother John. They were in a boat with their father Zebedee, preparing their nets. Jesus called them, and immediately they left the boat and their father and followed him.

Jesus went throughout Galilee, teaching in their synagogues, preaching the good news of the kingdom, and healing every disease and sickness among the people.

Fourth Sunday of Epiphany

1 Kings 17:8–16   The word of the LORD came to Elijah: "Go at once to Zarephath of Sidon and stay there. I have commanded a widow in that place to supply you with food." So he went to Zarephath. When he came to the town gate, a widow was there gathering sticks. He called to her and asked, "Would you bring me a little water in a jar so I may have a drink?" As she was going to get it, he called, "And bring me, please, a piece of bread."

"As surely as the LORD your God lives," she replied, "I don't have any bread – only a handful of flour in a jar and a little oil in a jug. I am gathering a few sticks to take home and make a meal for myself and my son, that we may eat it – and die."

Elijah said to her, "Don't be afraid. Go home and do as you have said. But first make a small cake of bread for me from what you have and bring it to me, and then make something for yourself and your son. For this is what the LORD, the God of Israel, says: 'The jar of flour will not be used up and the jug of oil will not run dry until the day the LORD gives rain on the land.'"

She went away and did as Elijah had told her. So there was food every day for Elijah and for the woman and her family. For the jar of flour was not used up and the jug of oil did not run dry, in keeping with the word of the LORD spoken by Elijah.

Psalm 36:5–10   Your love, O LORD, reaches to the heavens,
               your faithfulness to the skies.

Your righteousness is like the mighty mountains,
  your justice like the great deep.
O LORD, you preserve both people and animals.
  How priceless is your unfailing love!
Both high and low among men
  find refuge in the shadow of your wings.
They feast in the abundance of your house;
  you give them drink from your river of delights.
For with you is the fountain of life;
  in your light we see light.

Continue your love to those who know you,
  your righteousness to the upright in heart.

1 Corinthians 1:18–31 The message of the cross is foolishness to those who
are perishing, but to us who are being saved it is the power of God. For it is
written:

"I will destroy the wisdom of the wise;
  the intelligence of the intelligent I will frustrate."

Where is the wise man? Where is the scholar? Where is the philosopher
of this age? Has not God made foolish the wisdom of the world? For since
in the wisdom of God the world through its wisdom did not know him, God
was pleased through the foolishness of what was preached to save those
who believe. Jews demand miraculous signs and Greeks look for wisdom,
but we preach Christ crucified: a stumbling-block to Jews and foolishness
to Gentiles, but to those whom God has called, both Jews and Greeks,
Christ the power of God and the wisdom of God. For the foolishness of God
is wiser than man's wisdom, and the weakness of God is stronger than
man's strength.

Brothers, think of what you were when you were called. Not many of
you were wise by human standards; not many were influential; not many
were of noble birth. But God chose the foolish things of the world to shame
the wise; God chose the weak things of the world to shame the strong. He
chose the lowly things of this world and the despised things – and the
things that are not – to nullify the things that are, so that no-one may boast
before him. It is because of him that you are in Christ Jesus, who has
become for us wisdom from God – that is, our righteousness, holiness and
redemption. Therefore, as it is written: "Let him who boasts boast in the
Lord."

John 2:1–11 On the third day a wedding took place at Cana in Galilee. Jesus'
mother was there, and Jesus and his disciples had also been invited to the
wedding. When the wine was gone, Jesus' mother said to him, "They have
no more wine."

"Dear woman, why do you involve me?" Jesus replied. "My time has not
yet come."

His mother said to the servants, "Do whatever he tells you."

Nearby stood six stone water jars, the kind used by the Jews for ceremonial washing, each holding from twenty to thirty gallons.

Jesus said to the servants, "Fill the jars with water"; so they filled them to the brim.

Then he told them, "Now draw some out and take it to the master of the banquet."

They did so, and the master of the banquet tasted the water that had been turned into wine. He did not realise where it had come from, though the servants who had drawn the water knew. Then he called the bridegroom aside and said, "Everyone brings out the choice wine first and then the cheaper wine after the guests have had too much to drink; but you have saved the best till now."

This, the first of his miraculous signs, Jesus performed at Cana in Galilee. He thus revealed his glory, and his disciples put their faith in him.

The Presentation of Christ in the Temple – 2 February

Candlemas

(Readings for Years A, B, C are the same)

Malachi 3:1–5   "See, I will send my messenger, who will prepare the way before me. Then suddenly the Lord you are seeking will come to his temple; the messenger of the covenant, whom you desire, will come," says the LORD Almighty.

But who can endure the day of his coming? Who can stand when he appears? For he will be like a refiner's fire or a launderer's soap. He will sit as a refiner and purifier of silver; he will purify the Levites and refine them like gold and silver. Then the LORD will have men who will bring offerings in righteousness, and the offerings of Judah and Jerusalem will be acceptable to the LORD, as in days gone by, as in former years.

"So I will come near to you for judgment. I will be quick to testify against sorcerers, adulterers and perjurers, against those who defraud labourers of their wages, who oppress the widows and the fatherless, and deprive aliens of justice, but do not fear me," says the LORD Almighty.

FIRST READING

Psalm 24:[1–6] 7–10   [The earth is the LORD's, and everything in it,
the world, and all who live in it;
for he founded it upon the seas
and established it upon the waters.

Who may ascend the hill of the LORD?
Who may stand in his holy place?
He who has clean hands and a pure heart,
who does not lift up his soul to an idol
or swear by what is false.

He will receive blessing from the LORD
and vindication from God his Saviour.
Such is the generation of those who seek him,
who seek your face, O God of Jacob.]

PSALM

Lift up your heads, O you gates;
>   be lifted up, you ancient doors,
>   that the King of glory may come in.
Who is this King of glory?
>   The LORD strong and mighty,
>   the LORD mighty in battle.
Lift up your heads, O you gates;
>   lift them up, you ancient doors,
>   that the King of glory may come in.
Who is he, this King of glory?
>   The LORD Almighty –
>   he is the King of glory.

Hebrews 2:14–18   Since the children brought to glory by God have flesh and blood, Jesus too shared in their humanity so that by his death he might destroy him who holds the power of death – that is, the devil – and free those who all their lives were held in slavery by their fear of death. For surely it is not angels he helps, but Abraham's descendants. For this reason he had to be made like his brothers in every way, in order that he might become a merciful and faithful high priest in service to God, and that he might make atonement for the sins of the people. Because he himself suffered when he was tempted, he is able to help those who are being tempted.

Luke 2:22–40   When the time of their purification according to the Law of Moses had been completed, Joseph and Mary took Jesus to Jerusalem to present him to the Lord (as it is written in the Law of the Lord, "Every first-born male is to be consecrated to the Lord"), and to offer a sacrifice in keeping with what is said in the Law of the Lord: "a pair of doves or two young pigeons".

Now there was a man in Jerusalem called Simeon, who was righteous and devout. He was waiting for the consolation of Israel, and the Holy Spirit was upon him. It had been revealed to him by the Holy Spirit that he would not die before he had seen the LORD's Christ. Moved by the Spirit, he went into the temple courts. When the parents brought in the child Jesus to do for him what the custom of the Law required, Simeon took him in his arms and praised God, saying:

"Sovereign Lord, as you have promised,
>   you now dismiss your servant in peace.
For my eyes have seen your salvation,
>   which you have prepared in the sight of all people,
a light for revelation to the Gentiles
>   and for glory to your people Israel."

The child's father and mother marvelled at what was said about him. Then Simeon blessed them and said to Mary, his mother: "This child is destined to cause the falling and rising of many in Israel, and to be a sign that will be spoken against, so that the thoughts of many hearts will be revealed. And a sword will pierce your own soul too."

There was also a prophet, Anna, the daughter of Phanuel, of the tribe of Asher. She was very old; she had lived with her husband seven years after her marriage, and then was a widow until she was eighty-four. She never left the temple but worshipped night and day, fasting and praying. Coming up to them at that very moment, she gave thanks to God and spoke about the child to all who were looking forward to the redemption of Jerusalem.

When Joseph and Mary had done everything required by the Law of the Lord, they returned to Galilee to their own town of Nazareth. And the child grew and became strong; he was filled with wisdom, and the grace of God was upon him.

ORDINARY TIME

Proper 1

Sunday between 3 and 9 February inclusive (if earlier than the Second Sunday before Lent)

Isaiah 58: 1–9a[b–12]

"Shout it aloud, do not hold back.
  Raise your voice like a trumpet.
Declare to my people their rebellion
  and to the house of Jacob their sins.
For day after day they seek me out;
  they seem eager to know my ways,
as if they were a nation that does what is right
  and has not forsaken the commands of its God.
They ask me for just decisions
  and seem eager for God to come near them.
'Why have we fasted,' they say,
  'and you have not seen it?
Why have we humbled ourselves,
  and you have not noticed?'

"Yet on the day of your fasting, you do as you please
  and exploit all your workers.
Your fasting ends in quarrelling and strife,
  and in striking each other with wicked fists.
You cannot fast as you do today
  and expect your voice to be heard on high.
Is this the kind of fast I have chosen,
  only a day for people to humble themselves?
Is it only for bowing one's head like a reed
  and for lying on sackcloth and ashes?
Is that what you call a fast,
  a day acceptable to the LORD?

"Is not this the kind of fasting I have chosen:
to loose the chains of injustice
  and untie the cords of the yoke,
to set the oppressed free
  and break every yoke?

FIRST READING (vertical marginal text)

Is it not to share your food with the hungry
    and to provide the poor wanderer with shelter –
when you see the naked, to clothe them,
        and not to turn away from your own flesh and
            blood?
Then your light will break forth like the dawn,
    and your healing will quickly appear;
then your righteousness will go before you,
    and the glory of the Lord will be your rear guard.
Then you will call, and the Lord will answer;
    you will cry for help, and he will say: Here am I.

["If you do away with the yoke of oppression,
    with the pointing finger and malicious talk,
and if you spend yourselves on behalf of the hungry
    and satisfy the needs of the oppressed,
then your light will rise in the darkness,
    and your night will become like the noonday.
The Lord will guide you always;
        he will satisfy your needs in a sun-scorched land
        and will strengthen your frame.
You will be like a well-watered garden,
    like a spring whose waters never fail.
Your people will rebuild the ancient ruins
    and will raise up the age-old foundations;
you will be called Repairer of Broken Walls,
    Restorer of Streets with Dwellings."]

Psalm 112:1–9 [10] Praise the Lord.

Blessed is the man who fears the Lord,
    who finds great delight in his commands.

His children will be mighty in the land;
    the generation of the upright will be blessed.
Wealth and riches are in his house,
    and his righteousness endures for ever.
Even in darkness light dawns for the upright,
        for the gracious and compassionate and
            righteous man.
Good will come to him who is generous and lends
        freely,
    who conducts his affairs with justice.
Surely he will never be shaken;
    the righteous will be remembered for ever.
He will have no fear of bad news;
    his heart is steadfast, trusting in the Lord.
His heart is secure, he will have no fear;
    in the end he will look in triumph on his foes.

P
S
A
L
M

He has scattered abroad his gifts to the poor,
   his righteousness endures for ever;
   his horn will be lifted high in honour.

[The wicked will see and be vexed,
   he will gnash his teeth and waste away;
   the longings of the wicked will come to nothing.]

1 Corinthians 2:1–12 [13–16]   When I came to you, brothers, I did not come
with eloquence or superior wisdom as I proclaimed to you the testimony
about God. For I resolved to know nothing while I was with you except
Jesus Christ and him crucified. I came to you in weakness and fear, and
with much trembling. My message and my preaching were not with wise
and persuasive words, but with a demonstration of the Spirit's power, so
that your faith might not rest on men's wisdom, but on God's power.

We do, however, speak a message of wisdom among the mature, but not
the wisdom of this age or of the rulers of this age, who are coming to nothing. No, we speak of God's secret wisdom, a wisdom that has been hidden
and that God destined for our glory before time began. None of the rulers
of this age understood it, for if they had, they would not have crucified the
Lord of glory. However, as it is written:

"No eye has seen,
   no ear has heard,
no mind has conceived
   what God has prepared for those who love him" –

but God has revealed it to us by his Spirit.

The Spirit searches all things, even the deep things of God. For who
among men knows the thoughts of a man except the man's spirit within
him? In the same way no-one knows the thoughts of God except the Spirit
of God. We have not received the spirit of the world but the Spirit who is
from God, that we may understand what God has freely given us. [This is
what we speak, not in words taught us by human wisdom but in words
taught by the Spirit, expressing spiritual truths in spiritual words. The
man without the Spirit does not accept the things that come from the Spirit
of God, for they are foolishness to him, and he cannot understand them,
because they are spiritually discerned. The spiritual man makes judgments about all things, but he himself is not subject to any man's judgment:

"For who has known the mind of the Lord
   that he may instruct him?"

But we have the mind of Christ.]

Matthew 5:13–20   Jesus said: "You are the salt of the earth. But if the salt
loses its saltiness, how can it be made salty again? It is no longer good for
anything, except to be thrown out and trampled by men.

"You are the light of the world. A city on a hill cannot be hidden. Neither
do people light a lamp and put it under a bowl. Instead they put it on its

stand, and it gives light to everyone in the house. In the same way, let your light shine before others, that they may see your good deeds and praise your Father in heaven.

"Do not think that I have come to abolish the Law or the Prophets; I have not come to abolish them but to fulfil them. I tell you the truth, until heaven and earth disappear, not the smallest letter, not the least stroke of a pen, will by any means disappear from the Law until everything is accomplished. Anyone who breaks one of the least of these commandments and teaches others to do the same will be called least in the kingdom of heaven, but whoever practises and teaches these commands will be called great in the kingdom of heaven. For I tell you that unless your righteousness surpasses that of the Pharisees and the teachers of the law, you will certainly not enter the kingdom of heaven."

Proper 2

Sunday between 10 and 16 February inclusive (if earlier than the Second Sunday before Lent)

Alternative first readings

Either **Deuteronomy 30:15–20**   Moses said: "See, I set before you today life and prosperity, death and destruction. For I command you today to love the LORD your God, to walk in his ways, and to keep his commands, decrees and laws; then you will live and increase, and the LORD your God will bless you in the land you are entering to possess.

But if your heart turns away and you are not obedient, and if you are drawn away to bow down to other gods and worship them, I declare to you this day that you will certainly be destroyed. You will not live long in the land you are crossing the Jordan to enter and possess.

This day I call heaven and earth as witnesses against you that I have set before you life and death, blessings and curses. Now choose life, so that you and your children may live and that you may love the LORD your God, listen to his voice, and hold fast to him. For the LORD is your life, and he will give you many years in the land he swore to give to your fathers, Abraham, Isaac and Jacob."

or **Ecclesiasticus 15: 15–20**

Psalm 119:1–8   Blessed are they whose ways are blameless,
who walk according to the law of the LORD.
Blessed are they who keep his statutes
and seek him with all their heart.
They do nothing wrong;
they walk in his ways.
You have laid down precepts
that are to be fully obeyed.
Oh, that my ways were steadfast
in obeying your decrees!
Then I would not be put to shame
when I consider all your commands.

I will praise you with an upright heart
    as I learn your righteous laws.
I will obey your decrees;
    do not utterly forsake me.

1 Corinthians 3:1–9   Brothers, I could not address you as spiritual but as worldly – mere infants in Christ. I gave you milk, not solid food, for you were not yet ready for it. Indeed, you are still not ready. You are still worldly. For since there is jealousy and quarrelling among you, are you not worldly? Are you not acting like mere men? For when one says, "I follow Paul," and another, "I follow Apollos," are you not mere men?

What, after all, is Apollos? And what is Paul? Only servants, through whom you came to believe – as the Lord has assigned to each his task. I planted the seed, Apollos watered it, but God made it grow. So neither he who plants nor he who waters is anything, but only God, who makes things grow. The man who plants and the man who waters have one purpose, and each will be rewarded according to his own labour. For we are God's fellow-workers; you are God's field, God's building.

Matthew 5:21–37   Jesus said: "You have heard that it was said to the people long ago, 'Do not murder, and anyone who murders will be subject to judgment.' But I tell you that anyone who is angry with a brother or sister will be subject to judgment. Again, anyone who says to a brother or sister, 'Raca,' is answerable to the Sanhedrin. But anyone who says, 'You fool!' will be in danger of the fire of hell.

"Therefore, if you are offering your gift at the altar and there remember that your brother has something against you, leave your gift there in front of the altar. First go and be reconciled to your brother; then come and offer your gift.

"Settle matters quickly with your adversary who is taking you to court. Do it while you are still together on the way, or he may hand you over to the judge, and the judge may hand you over to the officer, and you may be thrown into prison. I tell you the truth, you will not get out until you have paid the last penny.

"You have heard that it was said, 'Do not commit adultery.' But I tell you that anyone who looks at a woman lustfully has already committed adultery with her in his heart. If your right eye causes you to sin, gouge it out and throw it away. It is better for you to lose one part of your body than for your whole body to be thrown into hell. And if your right hand causes you to sin, cut it off and throw it away. It is better for you to lose one part of your body than for your whole body to go into hell.

"It has been said, 'Anyone who divorces his wife must give her a certificate of divorce.' But I tell you that anyone who divorces his wife, except for marital unfaithfulness, causes her to become an adulteress, and anyone who marries the divorced woman commits adultery.

"Again, you have heard that it was said to the people long ago, 'Do not break your oath, but keep the oaths you have made to the Lord.' But I tell you, Do not swear at all: either by heaven, for it is God's throne; or by the earth, for it is his footstool; or by Jerusalem, for it is the city of the Great King. And do not swear by your head, for you cannot make even one hair white or black. Simply let your 'Yes' be 'Yes', and your 'No', 'No'; anything beyond this comes from the evil one."

Proper 3

Sunday between 17 and 23 February inclusive (if earlier than the Second Sunday before Lent)

Leviticus 19:1–2, 9–18   The LORD said to Moses, "Speak to the entire assembly of Israel and say to them: 'Be holy because I, the LORD your God, am holy.

"'When you reap the harvest of your land, do not reap to the very edges of your field or gather the gleanings of your harvest. Do not go over your vineyard a second time or pick up the grapes that have fallen. Leave them for the poor and the alien. I am the LORD your God.

"'Do not steal.

"'Do not lie.

"'Do not deceive one another.

"'Do not swear falsely by my name and so profane the name of your God. I am the LORD.

"'Do not defraud your neighbour or rob him.

"'Do not hold back the wages of a hired man overnight.

"'Do not curse the deaf or put a stumbling-block in front of the blind, but fear your God. I am the LORD.

"'Do not pervert justice; do not show partiality to the poor or favouritism to the great, but judge your neighbour fairly.

"'Do not go about spreading slander among your people.

"'Do not do anything that endangers your neighbour's life. I am the LORD.

"'Do not hate your brother in your heart. Rebuke your neighbour frankly so that you will not share in his guilt.

"'Do not seek revenge or bear a grudge against one of your people, but love your neighbour as yourself. I am the LORD.'"

Psalm 119:33–40   Teach me, O LORD, to follow your decrees;
    then I will keep them to the end.
Give me understanding, and I will keep your law
    and obey it with all my heart.
Direct me in the path of your commands,
    for there I find delight.
Turn my heart towards your statutes
    and not towards selfish gain.
Turn my eyes away from worthless things;
    preserve my life according to your word.
Fulfil your promise to your servant,
    so that you may be feared.

FIRST READING

PSALM

> Take away the disgrace I dread,
>> for your laws are good.
> How I long for your precepts!
>> Preserve my life in your righteousness.

1 Corinthians 3:10–11, 16–23 By the grace God has given me, I laid a foundation as an expert builder, and someone else is building on it. But each one should be careful how he builds. For no-one can lay any foundation other than the one already laid, which is Jesus Christ.

Don't you know that you yourselves are God's temple and that God's Spirit lives in you? If anyone destroys God's temple, God will destroy him; for God's temple is sacred, and you are that temple.

Do not deceive yourselves. If any one of you thinks he is wise by the standards of this age, he should become a "fool" so that he may become wise. For the wisdom of this world is foolishness in God's sight. As it is written: "He catches the wise in their craftiness"; and again, "The LORD knows that the thoughts of the wise are futile." So then, no more boasting about men! All things are yours, whether Paul or Apollos or Cephas or the world or life or death or the present or the future – all are yours, and you are of Christ, and Christ is of God.

[margin: SECOND READING]

Matthew 5:38–48 Jesus said: "You have heard that it was said, 'Eye for eye, and tooth for tooth.' But I tell you, Do not resist an evil person. If someone strikes you on the right cheek, turn the other cheek also. And if someone wants to sue you and take your tunic, let him have your cloak as well. If someone forces you to go one mile, go with him two miles. Give to the one who asks you, and do not turn away from the one who wants to borrow from you.

"You have heard that it was said, 'Love your neighbour and hate your enemy.' But I tell you: Love your enemies and pray for those who persecute you, that you may be children of your Father in heaven. He causes his sun to rise on the evil and the good, and sends rain on the righteous and the unrighteous. If you love those who love you, what reward will you get? Are not even the tax collectors doing that? And if you greet only your own people, what are you doing more than others? Do not even pagans do that? Be perfect, therefore, as your heavenly Father is perfect."

[margin: GOSPEL]

Second Sunday Before Lent

Genesis 1:1 – 2:3 In the beginning God created the heavens and the earth. Now the earth was formless and empty, darkness was over the surface of the deep, and the Spirit of God was hovering over the waters.

And God said, "Let there be light," and there was light. God saw that the light was good, and he separated the light from the darkness. God called the light "day", and the darkness he called "night". And there was evening, and there was morning – the first day.

And God said, "Let there be an expanse between the waters to separate water from water." So God made the expanse and separated the water

[margin: FIRST READING]

under the expanse from the water above it. And it was so. God called the expanse "sky". And there was evening, and there was morning – the second day.

And God said, "Let the water under the sky be gathered to one place, and let dry ground appear." And it was so. God called the dry ground "land", and the gathered waters he called "seas". And God saw that it was good.

Then God said, "Let the land produce vegetation: seed-bearing plants and trees on the land that bear fruit with seed in it, according to their various kinds." And it was so. The land produced vegetation: plants bearing seed according to their kinds and trees bearing fruit with seed in it according to their kinds. And God saw that it was good. And there was evening, and there was morning – the third day.

And God said, "Let there be lights in the expanse of the sky to separate the day from the night, and let them serve as signs to mark seasons and days and years, and let them be lights in the expanse of the sky to give light on the earth." And it was so. God made two great lights – the greater light to govern the day and the lesser light to govern the night. He also made the stars. God set them in the expanse of the sky to give light on the earth, to govern the day and the night, and to separate light from darkness. And God saw that it was good. And there was evening, and there was morning – the fourth day.

And God said, "Let the water teem with living creatures, and let birds fly above the earth across the expanse of the sky." So God created the great creatures of the sea and every living and moving thing with which the water teems, according to their kinds, and every winged bird according to its kind. And God saw that it was good. God blessed them and said, "Be fruitful and increase in number and fill the water in the seas, and let the birds increase on the earth." And there was evening, and there was morning – the fifth day.

And God said, "Let the land produce living creatures according to their kinds: livestock, creatures that move along the ground, and wild animals, each according to its kind." And it was so. God made the wild animals according to their kinds, the livestock according to their kinds, and all the creatures that move along the ground according to their kinds. And God saw that it was good.

Then God said, "Let us make man in our image, in our likeness, and let them rule over the fish of the sea and the birds of the air, over the livestock, over all the earth, and over all the creatures that move along the ground."

So God created man
    in his own image,
in the image of God
    he created him;
male and female
    he created them.

God blessed them and said to them, "Be fruitful and increase in number; fill the earth and subdue it. Rule over the fish of the sea and the birds of the air and over every living creature that moves on the ground."

Then God said, "I give you every seed-bearing plant on the face of the whole earth and every tree that has fruit with seed in it. They will be yours for food. And to all the beasts of the earth and all the birds of the air and all the creatures that move on the ground – everything that has the breath of life in it – I give every green plant for food." And it was so.

God saw all that he had made, and it was very good. And there was evening, and there was morning – the sixth day.

Thus the heavens and the earth were completed in all their vast array.

By the seventh day God had finished the work he had been doing; so on the seventh day he rested from all his work. And God blessed the seventh day and made it holy, because on it he rested from all the work of creating that he had done.

Alternative Psalms

Either **Psalm 136** Give thanks to the LORD, for he is good. P
> *His love endures for ever.* S

Give thanks to the God of gods. A
> *His love endures for ever.* L

Give thanks to the Lord of lords: M
> *His love endures for ever.*

to him who alone does great wonders,
> *His love endures for ever.*

who by his understanding made the heavens,
> *His love endures for ever.*

who spread out the earth upon the waters,
> *His love endures for ever.*

who made the great lights –
> *His love endures for ever.*

the sun to govern the day,
> *His love endures for ever.*

the moon and stars to govern the night;
> *His love endures for ever.*

to him who struck down the firstborn of Egypt
> *His love endures for ever.*

and brought Israel out from among them
> *His love endures for ever.*

with a mighty hand and outstretched arm;
> *His love endures for ever.*

to him who divided the Red Sea asunder
> *His love endures for ever.*

and brought Israel through the midst of it,
> *His love endures for ever.*

but swept Pharaoh and his army into the Red Sea;
> *His love endures for ever.*

to him who led his people through the desert,
> *His love endures for ever.*

who struck down great kings,
> *His love endures for ever.*

and killed mighty kings –
> *His love endures for ever.*

Sihon king of the Amorites
> *His love endures for ever.*

and Og king of Bashan –
> *His love endures for ever.*

and gave their land as an inheritance,
> *His love endures for ever.*

an inheritance to his servant Israel;
> *His love endures for ever.*

to the One who remembered us in our low estate
> *His love endures for ever.*

and freed us from our enemies,
> *His love endures for ever.*

and who gives food to every creature.
> *His love endures for ever.*

Give thanks to the God of heaven.
> *His love endures for ever.*

or **Psalm 136:1–9, 23–26**

Give thanks to the Lord, for he is good.
> *His love endures for ever.*

Give thanks to the God of gods.
> *His love endures for ever.*

Give thanks to the Lord of lords:
> *His love endures for ever.*

to him who alone does great wonders,
> *His love endures for ever.*

who by his understanding made the heavens,
> *His love endures for ever.*

who spread out the earth upon the waters,
> *His love endures for ever.*

who made the great lights –
> *His love endures for ever.*

the sun to govern the day,
> *His love endures for ever.*

the moon and stars to govern the night;
> *His love endures for ever.*

to the One who remembered us in our low estate
> *His love endures for ever.*

P
S
A
L
M

and freed us from our enemies,
His love endures for ever.
and who gives food to every creature.
His love endures for ever.
Give thanks to the God of heaven.
His love endures for ever.

Romans 8:18–25   I consider that our present sufferings are not worth comparing with the glory that will be revealed in us. The creation waits in eager expectation for the sons of God to be revealed. For the creation was subjected to frustration, not by its own choice, but by the will of the one who subjected it, in hope that the creation itself will be liberated from its bondage to decay and brought into the glorious freedom of the children of God.

We know that the whole creation has been groaning as in the pains of childbirth right up to the present time. Not only so, but we ourselves, who have the firstfruits of the Spirit, groan inwardly as we wait eagerly for our adoption as sons, the redemption of our bodies. For in this hope we were saved. But hope that is seen is no hope at all. Who hopes for what he already has? But if we hope for what we do not yet have, we wait for it patiently.

[margin: SECOND READING]

Matthew 6:25–34   Jesus said: "I tell you, do not worry about your life, what you will eat or drink; or about your body, what you will wear. Is not life more important than food, and the body more important than clothes? Look at the birds of the air; they do not sow or reap or store away in barns, and yet your heavenly Father feeds them. Are you not much more valuable than they? Who of you by worrying can add a single hour to your life?

"And why do you worry about clothes? See how the lilies of the field grow. They do not labour or spin. Yet I tell you that not even Solomon in all his splendour was dressed like one of these. If that is how God clothes the grass of the field, which is here today and tomorrow is thrown into the fire, will he not much more clothe you, O you of little faith? So do not worry, saying, 'What shall we eat?' or 'What shall we drink?' or 'What shall we wear?' For the pagans run after all these things, and your heavenly Father knows that you need them. But seek first his kingdom and his righteousness, and all these things will be given to you as well. Therefore do not worry about tomorrow, for tomorrow will worry about itself. Each day has enough trouble of its own."

[margin: GOSPEL]

Sunday Next Before Lent

Exodus 24:12–18   The LORD said to Moses, "Come up to me on the mountain and stay here, and I will give you the tablets of stone, with the law and commands I have written for their instruction."

Then Moses set out with Joshua his assistant, and Moses went up on the mountain of God. He said to the elders, "Wait here for us until we come back to you. Aaron and Hur are with you, and anyone involved in a dispute can go to them."

[margin: FIRST READING]

When Moses went up on the mountain, the cloud covered it, and the glory of the LORD settled on Mount Sinai. For six days the cloud covered the mountain, and on the seventh day the LORD called to Moses from within the cloud. To the Israelites the glory of the LORD looked like a consuming fire on top of the mountain. Then Moses entered the cloud as he went on up the mountain. And he stayed on the mountain forty days and forty nights.

Alternative Psalms

Either **Psalm 2**

Why do the nations conspire
 and the peoples plot in vain?
The kings of the earth take their stand
 and the rulers gather together against the LORD
 and against his Anointed One.
"Let us break their chains," they say,
 "and throw off their fetters."

The One enthroned in heaven laughs;
 the LORD scoffs at them.
Then he rebukes them in his anger
 and terrifies them in his wrath, saying,
"I have installed my King
 on Zion, my holy hill."

I will proclaim the decree of the LORD:

He said to me, "You are my Son;
 today I have become your Father.
Ask of me,
 and I will make the nations your inheritance,
 the ends of the earth your possession.
You will rule them with an iron sceptre;
 you will dash them to pieces like pottery."

Therefore, you kings, be wise;
 be warned, you rulers of the earth.
Serve the LORD with fear
 and rejoice with trembling.
Kiss the Son, lest he be angry
 and you be destroyed in your way,
for his wrath can flare up in a moment.
 Blessed are all who take refuge in him.

or **Psalm 99**

The LORD reigns,
 let the nations tremble;
he sits enthroned between the cherubim,
 let the earth shake.
Great is the LORD in Zion;
 he is exalted over all the nations.
Let them praise your great and awesome name –
 he is holy.

The King is mighty, he loves justice –
you have established equity;
in Jacob you have done
what is just and right.
Exalt the LORD our God
and worship at his footstool;
he is holy.

Moses and Aaron were among his priests,
Samuel was among those who called on his name;
they called on the LORD
and he answered them.
He spoke to them from the pillar of cloud;
they kept his statutes and the decrees he gave them.

O LORD our God,
you answered them;
you were to Israel a forgiving God,
though you punished their misdeeds.
Exalt the LORD our God
and worship at his holy mountain,
for the LORD our God is holy.

2 Peter 1:16–21   We did not follow cleverly invented stories when we told you S R
about the power and coming of our Lord Jesus Christ, but we were eye- E E
witnesses of his majesty. For he received honour and glory from God the C A
Father when the voice came to him from the Majestic Glory, saying, "This O D
is my Son, whom I love; with him I am well pleased." We ourselves heard N I
this voice that came from heaven when we were with him on the sacred D N
mountain. G

And we have the word of the prophets made more certain, and you
will do well to pay attention to it, as to a light shining in a dark place, until
the day dawns and the morning star rises in your hearts. Above all, you
must understand that no prophecy of Scripture came about by the
prophet's own interpretation. For prophecy never had its origin in the will
of man, but men spoke from God as they were carried along by the Holy
Spirit.

Matthew 17:1–9   Jesus took with him Peter, James and John the brother of G
James, and led them up a high mountain by themselves. There he was O
transfigured before them. His face shone like the sun, and his clothes S
became as white as the light. Just then there appeared before them Moses P
and Elijah, talking with Jesus. E

Peter said to Jesus, "Lord, it is good for us to be here. If you wish, I will L
put up three shelters – one for you, one for Moses and one for Elijah."

While he was still speaking, a bright cloud enveloped them, and a voice
from the cloud said, "This is my Son, whom I love; with him I am well
pleased. Listen to him!"

When the disciples heard this, they fell face down to the ground, terrified. But Jesus came and touched them. "Get up," he said. "Don't be afraid." When they looked up, they saw no-one except Jesus.

As they were coming down the mountain, Jesus instructed them, "Don't tell anyone what you have seen, until the Son of Man has been raised from the dead."

LENT

Ash Wednesday

(Readings for Years A, B, C are the same)

Alternative first readings

Either **Joel 2:1–2, 12–17**

Blow the trumpet in Zion;   F
    sound the alarm on my holy hill.   I
Let all who live in the land tremble,   R
    for the day of the LORD is coming.   S
It is close at hand –   T
    a day of darkness and gloom,
    a day of clouds and blackness.   R
Like dawn spreading across the mountains   E
    a large and mighty army comes,   A
such as never was of old   D
    nor ever will be in ages to come.   I

"Even now," declares the LORD,   N
    "return to me with all your heart,   G
    with fasting and weeping and mourning."

Rend your heart
    and not your garments.
Return to the LORD your God,
    for he is gracious and compassionate,
slow to anger and abounding in love,
    and he relents from sending calamity.
Who knows? He may turn and have pity
    and leave behind a blessing –
grain offerings and drink offerings
    for the LORD your God.

Blow the trumpet in Zion,
    declare a holy fast,
    call a sacred assembly.
Gather the people,
    consecrate the assembly;
bring together the elders,
    gather the children,
    those nursing at the breast.

Let the bridegroom leave his room
   and the bride her chamber.
Let the priests, who minister before the Lord,
   weep between the temple porch and the altar.
Let them say, "Spare your people, O Lord.
   Do not make your inheritance an object of scorn,
   a byword among the nations.
Why should they say among the peoples,
   'Where is their God?'"

or **Isaiah 58:1–12**   "Shout it aloud, do not hold back.
   Raise your voice like a trumpet.
Declare to my people their rebellion
   and to the house of Jacob their sins.
For day after day they seek me out;
   they seem eager to know my ways,
as if they were a nation that does what is right
   and has not forsaken the commands of its God.
They ask me for just decisions
   and seem eager for God to come near them.
'Why have we fasted,' they say,
   'and you have not seen it?
Why have we humbled ourselves,
   and you have not noticed?'

"Yet on the day of your fasting, you do as you please
   and exploit all your workers.
Your fasting ends in quarrelling and strife,
   and in striking each other with wicked fists.
You cannot fast as you do today
   and expect your voice to be heard on high.
Is this the kind of fast I have chosen,
   only a day for a man to humble himself?
Is it only for bowing one's head like a reed
   and for lying on sackcloth and ashes?
Is that what you call a fast,
   a day acceptable to the Lord?

"Is not this the kind of fasting I have chosen:
to loose the chains of injustice
   and untie the cords of the yoke,
to set the oppressed free
   and break every yoke?
Is it not to share your food with the hungry
   and to provide the poor wanderer with shelter –
when you see the naked, to clothe them,
   and not to turn away from your own flesh and
      blood?

F
I
R
S
T

R
E
A
D
I
N
G

Then your light will break forth like the dawn,
    and your healing will quickly appear;
then your righteousness will go before you,
    and the glory of the LORD will be your rear guard.
Then you will call, and the LORD will answer;
    you will cry for help, and he will say: Here am I.

"If you do away with the yoke of oppression,
    with the pointing finger and malicious talk,
and if you spend yourselves on behalf of the hungry
    and satisfy the needs of the oppressed,
then your light will rise in the darkness,
    and your night will become like the noonday.
The LORD will guide you always;
    he will satisfy your needs in a sun-scorched land
    and will strengthen your frame.
You will be like a well-watered garden,
    like a spring whose waters never fail.
Your people will rebuild the ancient ruins
    and will raise up the age-old foundations;
you will be called Repairer of Broken Walls,
    Restorer of Streets with Dwellings."

Psalm 51:1–17 Have mercy on me, O God,
    according to your unfailing love;
according to your great compassion
    blot out my transgressions.
Wash away all my iniquity
    and cleanse me from my sin.

P
S
A
L
M

For I know my transgressions,
    and my sin is always before me.
Against you, you only, have I sinned
    and done what is evil in your sight,
so that you are proved right when you speak
    and justified when you judge.
Surely I was sinful at birth,
    sinful from the time my mother conceived me.
Surely you desire truth in the inner parts;
    you teach me wisdom in the inmost place.

Cleanse me with hyssop, and I shall be clean;
    wash me, and I shall be whiter than snow.
Let me hear joy and gladness;
    let the bones you have crushed rejoice.
Hide your face from my sins
    and blot out all my iniquity.
Create in me a pure heart, O God,
    and renew a steadfast spirit within me.

Do not cast me from your presence
or take your Holy Spirit from me.
Restore to me the joy of your salvation
and grant me a willing spirit, to sustain me.

Then I will teach transgressors your ways,
and sinners will turn back to you.
Save me from bloodguilt, O God,
the God who saves me,
and my tongue will sing of your righteousness.
O Lord, open my lips,
and my mouth will declare your praise.
You do not delight in sacrifice, or I would bring it;
you do not take pleasure in burnt offerings.
The sacrifices of God are a broken spirit;
a broken and contrite heart,
O God, you will not despise.

2 Corinthians 5:20b – 6:10   We implore you on Christ's behalf: Be reconciled to God. God made him who had no sin to be sin for us, so that in him we might become the righteousness of God.

As God's fellow-workers we urge you not to receive God's grace in vain. For he says,

"In the time of my favour I heard you,
and in the day of salvation I helped you."

I tell you, now is the time of God's favour, now is the day of salvation.

We put no stumbling-block in anyone's path, so that our ministry will not be discredited. Rather, as servants of God we commend ourselves in every way: in great endurance; in troubles, hardships and distresses; in beatings, imprisonments and riots; in hard work, sleepless nights and hunger; in purity, understanding, patience and kindness; in the Holy Spirit and in sincere love; in truthful speech and in the power of God; with weapons of righteousness in the right hand and in the left; through glory and dishonour, bad report and good report; genuine, yet regarded as impostors; known, yet regarded as unknown; dying, and yet we live on; beaten, and yet not killed; sorrowful, yet always rejoicing; poor, yet making many rich; having nothing, and yet possessing everything.

SECOND READING

Alternative Gospels

Either **Matthew 6:1–6, 16–21**   Jesus said: "Be careful not to do your 'acts of righteousness' before others, to be seen by them. If you do, you will have no reward from your Father in heaven.

"So when you give to the needy, do not announce it with trumpets, as the hypocrites do in the synagogues and on the streets, to be honoured by others. I tell you the truth, they have received their reward in full. But when you give to the needy, do not let your left hand know what your right hand

GOSPEL

is doing, so that your giving may be in secret. Then your Father, who sees what is done in secret, will reward you.

"And when you pray, do not be like the hypocrites, for they love to pray standing in the synagogues and on the street corners to be seen by others. I tell you the truth, they have received their reward in full. But when you pray, go into your room, close the door and pray to your Father, who is unseen. Then your Father, who sees what is done in secret, will reward you.

"When you fast, do not look sombre as the hypocrites do, for they disfigure their faces to show others they are fasting. I tell you the truth, they have received their reward in full. But when you fast, put oil on your head and wash your face, so that it will not be obvious to others that you are fasting, but only to your Father, who is unseen; and your Father, who sees what is done in secret, will reward you.

"Do not store up for yourselves treasures on earth, where moth and rust destroy, and where thieves break in and steal. But store up for yourselves treasures in heaven, where moth and rust do not destroy, and where thieves do not break in and steal. For where your treasure is, there your heart will be also."

or **John 8:1–11** Jesus went to the Mount of Olives. At dawn he appeared again in the temple courts, where all the people gathered round him, and he sat down to teach them. The teachers of the law and the Pharisees brought in a woman caught in adultery. They made her stand before the group and said to Jesus, "Teacher, this woman was caught in the act of adultery. In the Law Moses commanded us to stone such women. Now what do you say?" They were using this question as a trap, in order to have a basis for accusing him.

But Jesus bent down and started to write on the ground with his finger. When they kept on questioning him, he straightened up and said to them, "If any one of you is without sin, let him be the first to throw a stone at her." Again he stooped down and wrote on the ground.

At this, those who heard began to go away one at a time, the older ones first, until only Jesus was left, with the woman still standing there. Jesus straightened up and asked her, "Woman, where are they? Has no-one condemned you?"

"No-one, sir," she said.

"Then neither do I condemn you," Jesus declared. "Go now and leave your life of sin."

First Sunday of Lent

Genesis 2:15–17; 3:1–7 The Lord God took the man and put him in the Garden of Eden to work it and take care of it. And the Lord God commanded the man, "You are free to eat from any tree in the garden; but you must not eat from the tree of the knowledge of good and evil, for when you eat of it you will surely die."

Now the serpent was more crafty than any of the wild animals the Lord

God had made. He said to the woman, "Did God really say, 'You must not eat from any tree in the garden'?"

The woman said to the serpent, "We may eat fruit from the trees in the garden, but God did say, 'You must not eat fruit from the tree that is in the middle of the garden, and you must not touch it, or you will die.'"

"You will not surely die," the serpent said to the woman. "For God knows that when you eat of it your eyes will be opened, and you will be like God, knowing good and evil."

When the woman saw that the fruit of the tree was good for food and pleasing to the eye, and also desirable for gaining wisdom, she took some and ate it. She also gave some to her husband, who was with her, and he ate it. Then the eyes of both of them were opened, and they realised that they were naked; so they sewed fig leaves together and made coverings for themselves.

Psalm 32

> Blessed are those
>> whose transgressions are forgiven,
>> whose sins are covered.
> Blessed is the man
>> whose sin the Lord does not count against him
>> and in whose spirit is no deceit.
>
> When I kept silent,
>> my bones wasted away
>> through my groaning all day long.
> For day and night
>> your hand was heavy upon me;
> my strength was sapped
>> as in the heat of summer.
> Then I acknowledged my sin to you
>> and did not cover up my iniquity.
> I said, "I will confess
>> my transgressions to the Lord" –
> and you forgave
>> the guilt of my sin.
>
> Therefore let everyone who is godly pray to you
>> while you may be found;
> surely the rising of the mighty waters
>> will not reach them.
> You are my hiding-place;
>> you will protect me from trouble
>> and surround me with songs of deliverance.
>
> I will instruct you and teach you in the way you should go;
>> I will counsel you and watch over you.
> Do not be like the horse or the mule,
>> which have no understanding
> but must be controlled by bit and bridle

P
S
A
L
M

> or they will not come to you.
> Many are the woes of the wicked,
>> but the LORD's unfailing love
>> surrounds those who trust in him.
>
> Rejoice in the LORD and be glad, you righteous;
>> sing, all you who are upright in heart!

Romans 5:12–19 Just as sin entered the world through one man, and death
through sin, and in this way death came to all men, because all sinned –
for before the law was given, sin was in the world. But sin is not taken
into account when there is no law. Nevertheless, death reigned from
the time of Adam to the time of Moses, even over those who did not sin
by breaking a command, as did Adam, who was a pattern of the one to
come.

But the gift is not like the trespass. For if the many died by the trespass
of the one man, how much more did God's grace and the gift that came by
the grace of the one man, Jesus Christ, overflow to the many! Again, the
gift of God is not like the result of the one man's sin: The judgment followed one sin and brought condemnation, but the gift followed many
trespasses and brought justification. For if, by the trespass of the one man,
death reigned through that one man, how much more will those who
receive God's abundant provision of grace and of the gift of righteousness
reign in life through the one man, Jesus Christ.

Consequently, just as the result of one trespass was condemnation for
all men, so also the result of one act of righteousness was justification that
brings life for all men. For just as through the disobedience of the one man
the many were made sinners, so also through the obedience of the one man
the many will be made righteous.

SECOND READING

Matthew 4:1–11 Jesus was led by the Spirit into the desert to be tempted by
the devil. After fasting for forty days and forty nights, he was hungry. The
tempter came to him and said, "If you are the Son of God, tell these stones
to become bread."

Jesus answered, "It is written: 'Man does not live on bread alone, but on
every word that comes from the mouth of God.'"

Then the devil took him to the holy city and had him stand on the highest
point of the temple. "If you are the Son of God," he said, "throw yourself
down. For it is written:

> "'He will command his angels concerning you,
>> and they will lift you up in their hands,
> so that you will not strike your foot against a stone.'"

Jesus answered him, "It is also written: 'Do not put the Lord your God to
the test.'"

Again, the devil took him to a very high mountain and showed him all the
kingdoms of the world and their splendour. "All this I will give you," he
said, "if you will bow down and worship me."

GOSPEL

Jesus said to him, "Away from me, Satan! For it is written: 'Worship the LORD your God, and serve him only.'"

Then the devil left him, and angels came and attended him.

Second Sunday of Lent

Genesis 12:1–4a   The LORD had said to Abram, "Leave your country, your people and your father's household and go to the land I will show you.

> "I will make you into a great nation
>> and I will bless you;
> I will make your name great,
>> and you will be a blessing.
> I will bless those who bless you,
>> and whoever curses you I will curse;
> and all peoples on earth
>> will be blessed through you."

So Abram left, as the LORD had told him; and Lot went with him.

Psalm 121   I lift up my eyes to the hills –
>> where does my help come from?
> My help comes from the LORD,
>> the Maker of heaven and earth.

> He will not let your foot slip –
>> he who watches over you will not slumber;
> indeed, he who watches over Israel
>> will neither slumber nor sleep.

> The LORD watches over you –
>> the LORD is your shade at your right hand;
> the sun will not harm you by day,
>> nor the moon by night.

> The LORD will keep you from all harm –
>> he will watch over your life;
> the LORD will watch over your coming and going
>> both now and for evermore.

Romans 4:1–5, 13–17   What shall we say that Abraham, our forefather, discovered in this matter? If, in fact, Abraham was justified by works, he had something to boast about – but not before God. What does the Scripture say? "Abraham believed God, and it was credited to him as righteousness."

Now when a man works, his wages are not credited to him as a gift, but as an obligation. However, to the man who does not work but trusts God who justifies the wicked, his faith is credited as righteousness.

It was not through law that Abraham and his offspring received the promise that he would be heir of the world, but through the righteousness that comes by faith. For if those who live by law are heirs, faith has no value and the promise is worthless, because law brings wrath. And where there is no law there is no transgression.

Therefore, the promise comes by faith, so that it may be by grace and may be guaranteed to all Abraham's offspring – not only to those who are of the law but also to those who are of the faith of Abraham. He is the father of us all. As it is written: "I have made you a father of many nations." He is our father in the sight of God, in whom he believed – the God who gives life to the dead and calls things that are not as though they were.

John 3:1–17   There was a man of the Pharisees named Nicodemus, a member of the Jewish ruling council. He came to Jesus at night and said, "Rabbi, we know you are a teacher who has come from God. For no-one could perform the miraculous signs you are doing if God were not with him."

In reply Jesus declared, "I tell you the truth, no-one can see the kingdom of God unless he is born again."

"How can a man be born when he is old?" Nicodemus asked. "Surely he cannot enter a second time into his mother's womb to be born!"

Jesus answered, "I tell you the truth, no-one can enter the kingdom of God unless he is born of water and the Spirit. Flesh gives birth to flesh, but the Spirit gives birth to spirit. You should not be surprised at my saying, 'You must be born again.' The wind blows wherever it pleases. You hear its sound, but you cannot tell where it comes from or where it is going. So it is with everyone born of the Spirit."

"How can this be?" Nicodemus asked.

"You are Israel's teacher," said Jesus, "and do you not understand these things? I tell you the truth, we speak of what we know, and we testify to what we have seen, but still you people do not accept our testimony. I have spoken to you of earthly things and you do not believe; how then will you believe if I speak of heavenly things? No-one has ever gone into heaven except the one who came from heaven – the Son of Man. Just as Moses lifted up the snake in the desert, so the Son of Man must be lifted up, that everyone who believes in him may have eternal life.

"For God so loved the world that he gave his one and only Son, that whoever believes in him shall not perish but have eternal life. For God did not send his Son into the world to condemn the world, but to save the world through him."

Third Sunday of Lent

Exodus 17:1–7   The whole Israelite community set out from the Desert of Sin, travelling from place to place as the LORD commanded. They camped at Rephidim, but there was no water for the people to drink. So they quarrelled with Moses and said, "Give us water to drink."

Moses replied, "Why do you quarrel with me? Why do you put the LORD to the test?"

But the people were thirsty for water there, and they grumbled against Moses. They said, "Why did you bring us up out of Egypt to make us and our children and livestock die of thirst?"

Then Moses cried out to the LORD, "What am I to do with these people? They are almost ready to stone me."

The LORD answered Moses, "Walk on ahead of the people. Take with you some of the elders of Israel and take in your hand the staff with which you struck the Nile, and go. I will stand there before you by the rock at Horeb. Strike the rock, and water will come out of it for the people to drink." So Moses did this in the sight of the elders of Israel. And he called the place Massah and Meribah because the Israelites quarrelled and because they tested the LORD saying, "Is the LORD among us or not?"

Psalm 95   Come, let us sing for joy to the LORD;
  let us shout aloud to the Rock of our salvation.
Let us come before him with thanksgiving
  and extol him with music and song.

For the LORD is the great God,
  the great King above all gods.
In his hand are the depths of the earth,
  and the mountain peaks belong to him.
The sea is his, for he made it,
  and his hands formed the dry land.

Come, let us bow down in worship,
  let us kneel before the LORD our Maker;
for he is our God
  and we are the people of his pasture,
  the flock under his care.

Today, if you hear his voice,
  do not harden your hearts as you did at Meribah,
  as you did that day at Massah in the desert,
where your ancestors tested and tried me,
  though they had seen what I did.
For forty years I was angry with that generation;
  I said, "They are a people whose hearts go astray,
  and they have not known my ways."
So I declared on oath in my anger,
  "They shall never enter my rest."

P
S
A
L
M

Romans 5:1–11   Since we have been justified through faith, we have peace with God through our Lord Jesus Christ, through whom we have gained access by faith into this grace in which we now stand. And we rejoice in the hope of the glory of God. Not only so, but we also rejoice in our sufferings, because we know that suffering produces perseverance; perseverance, character; and character, hope. And hope does not disappoint us, because God has poured out his love into our hearts by the Holy Spirit, whom he has given us.

S R
E E
C A
O D
N I
D N
G

You see, at just the right time, when we were still powerless, Christ died for the ungodly. Very rarely will anyone die for a righteous man, though for a good man someone might possibly dare to die. But God demonstrates his own love for us in this: While we were still sinners, Christ died for us.

Since we have now been justified by his blood, how much more shall we be saved from God's wrath through him! For if, when we were God's enemies, we were reconciled to him through the death of his Son, how much more, having been reconciled, shall we be saved through his life! Not only is this so, but we also rejoice in God through our LORD Jesus Christ, through whom we have now received reconciliation.

John 4: 5–42   Jesus came to a town in Samaria called Sychar, near the plot of ground Jacob had given to his son Joseph. Jacob's well was there, and Jesus, tired as he was from the journey, sat down by the well. It was about the sixth hour.

When a Samaritan woman came to draw water, Jesus said to her, "Will you give me a drink?" (His disciples had gone into the town to buy food.)

The Samaritan woman said to him, "You are a Jew and I am a Samaritan woman. How can you ask me for a drink?" (For Jews do not associate with Samaritans.)

Jesus answered her, "If you knew the gift of God and who it is that asks you for a drink, you would have asked him and he would have given you living water."

"Sir," the woman said, "you have nothing to draw with and the well is deep. Where can you get this living water? Are you greater than our father Jacob, who gave us the well and drank from it himself, as did also his sons and his flocks and herds?"

Jesus answered, "Everyone who drinks this water will be thirsty again, but whoever drinks the water I give him will never thirst. Indeed, the water I give him will become in him a spring of water welling up to eternal life."

The woman said to him, "Sir, give me this water so that I won't get thirsty and have to keep coming here to draw water."

He told her, "Go, call your husband and come back."

"I have no husband," she replied.

Jesus said to her, "You are right when you say you have no husband. The fact is, you have had five husbands, and the man you now have is not your husband. What you have just said is quite true."

"Sir," the woman said, "I can see that you are a prophet. Our fathers worshipped on this mountain, but you Jews claim that the place where we must worship is in Jerusalem."

Jesus declared, "Believe me, woman, a time is coming when you will worship the Father neither on this mountain nor in Jerusalem. You Samaritans worship what you do not know; we worship what we do know, for salvation is from the Jews. Yet a time is coming and has now come when the true worshippers will worship the Father in spirit and truth, for they are the kind of worshippers the Father seeks. God is spirit, and his worshippers must worship in spirit and in truth."

The woman said, "I know that Messiah" (called Christ) "is coming. When he comes, he will explain everything to us."

Then Jesus declared, "I who speak to you am he."

Just then his disciples returned and were surprised to find him talking with a woman. But no-one asked, "What do you want?" or "Why are you talking with her?"

Then, leaving her water jar, the woman went back to the town and said to the people, "Come, see a man who told me everything I ever did. Could this be the Christ?" They came out of the town and made their way towards him.

Meanwhile his disciples urged him, "Rabbi, eat something."

But he said to them, "I have food to eat that you know nothing about."

Then his disciples said to each other, "Could someone have brought him food?"

"My food," said Jesus, "is to do the will of him who sent me and to finish his work. Do you not say, 'Four months more and then the harvest'? I tell you, open your eyes and look at the fields! They are ripe for harvest. Even now the reaper draws his wages, even now he harvests the crop for eternal life, so that the sower and the reaper may be glad together. Thus the saying 'One sows and another reaps' is true. I sent you to reap what you have not worked for. Others have done the hard work, and you have reaped the benefits of their labour."

Many of the Samaritans from that town believed in him because of the woman's testimony, "He told me everything I ever did." So when the Samaritans came to him, they urged him to stay with them, and he stayed two days. And because of his words many more became believers.

They said to the woman, "We no longer believe just because of what you said; now we have heard for ourselves, and we know that this man really is the Saviour of the world."

Fourth Sunday of Lent

Mothering Sunday may be celebrated in preference to the provision for the Fourth Sunday of Lent see pp 62–65

1 Samuel 16:1–13   The LORD said to Samuel, "How long will you mourn for Saul, since I have rejected him as king over Israel? Fill your horn with oil and be on your way; I am sending you to Jesse of Bethlehem. I have chosen one of his sons to be king."

But Samuel said, "How can I go? Saul will hear about it and kill me."

The LORD said, "Take a heifer with you and say, 'I have come to sacrifice to the LORD.' Invite Jesse to the sacrifice, and I will show you what to do. You are to anoint for me the one I indicate."

Samuel did what the LORD said. When he arrived at Bethlehem, the elders of the town trembled when they met him. They asked, "Do you come in peace?"

Samuel replied, "Yes, in peace; I have come to sacrifice to the LORD. Consecrate yourselves and come to the sacrifice with me." Then he consecrated Jesse and his sons and invited them to the sacrifice.

When they arrived, Samuel saw Eliab and thought, "Surely the LORD's anointed stands here before the LORD."

But the LORD said to Samuel, 'Do not consider his appearance or his height, for I have rejected him. The LORD does not look at the things man looks at. Man looks at the outward appearance, but the LORD looks at the heart."

Then Jesse called Abinadab and made him pass in front of Samuel. But Samuel said, "The LORD has not chosen this one either." Jesse then made Shammah pass by, but Samuel said, "Nor has the LORD chosen this one." Jesse made seven of his sons pass before Samuel, but Samuel said to him, "The LORD has not chosen these." So he asked Jesse, "Are these all the sons you have?"

"There is still the youngest," Jesse answered, "but he is tending the sheep."

Samuel said, "Send for him; we will not sit down until he arrives."

So he sent and had him brought in. He was ruddy, with a fine appearance and handsome features.

Then the LORD said, "Rise and anoint him; he is the one."

So Samuel took the horn of oil and anointed him in the presence of his brothers, and from that day on the Spirit of the LORD came upon David in power. Samuel then went to Ramah.

Psalm 23	The LORD is my shepherd, 　　I shall not be in want. 　　　　He makes me lie down in green pastures, 　　he leads me beside quiet waters, 　　　　he restores my soul. He guides me in paths of righteousness 　　for his name's sake. Even though I walk 　　through the valley of the shadow of death, I will fear no evil, 　　for you are with me; your rod and your staff, 　　they comfort me. You prepare a table before me 　　in the presence of my enemies. You anoint my head with oil; 　　my cup overflows. Surely goodness and love will follow me 　　all the days of my life, and I will dwell in the house of the LORD 　　for ever.	P S A L M

S R
E E

Ephesians 5:8–14　You were once darkness, but now you are light in the LORD. Live as children of light (for the fruit of the light consists in all goodness, righteousness and truth) and find out what pleases the LORD. Have nothing to do with the fruitless deeds of darkness, but rather expose them. For it is shameful even to mention what the disobedient do in secret. But every-

C A
O D
N I
D N
G

thing exposed by the light becomes visible, for it is light that makes everything visible. This is why it is said:

"Wake up, O sleeper,
    rise from the dead,
and Christ will shine on you."

John 9:1–41 As Jesus went along, he saw a man blind from birth. His disciples asked him, "Rabbi, who sinned, this man or his parents, that he was born blind?"

"Neither this man nor his parents sinned," said Jesus, "but this happened so that the work of God might be displayed in his life. As long as it is day, we must do the work of him who sent me. Night is coming, when no-one can work. While I am in the world, I am the light of the world."

Having said this, he spat on the ground, made some mud with the saliva, and put it on the man's eyes. "Go," he told him, "wash in the Pool of Siloam" (this word means Sent). So the man went and washed, and came home seeing.

His neighbours and those who had formerly seen him begging asked, "Isn't this the same man who used to sit and beg?" Some claimed that he was.

Others said, "No, he only looks like him."

But he himself insisted, "I am the man."

"How then were your eyes opened?" they demanded.

He replied, "The man they call Jesus made some mud and put it on my eyes. He told me to go to Siloam and wash. So I went and washed, and then I could see."

"Where is this man?" they asked him.

"I don't know," he said.

They brought to the Pharisees the man who had been blind. Now the day on which Jesus had made the mud and opened the man's eyes was a Sabbath. Therefore the Pharisees also asked him how he had received his sight. "He put mud on my eyes," the man replied, "and I washed, and now I see."

Some of the Pharisees said, "This man is not from God, for he does not keep the Sabbath."

But others asked, "How can a sinner do such miraculous signs?" So they were divided.

Finally they turned again to the blind man, "What have you to say about him? It was your eyes he opened."

The man replied, "He is a prophet."

The Jews still did not believe that he had been blind and had received his sight until they sent for the man's parents. "Is this your son?" they asked. "Is this the one you say was born blind? How is it that now he can see?" "

"We know he is our son," the parents answered, "and we know he was born blind. But how he can see now, or who opened his eyes, we don't know. Ask him. He is of age; he will speak for himself." His parents said this because they were afraid of the Jews, for already the Jews had decided that anyone who acknowledged that Jesus was the Christ would be put out of the synagogue. That was why his parents said, "He is of age; ask him."

A second time they summoned the man who had been blind. "Give glory to God," they said. "We know this man is a sinner."

He replied, "Whether he is a sinner or not, I don't know. One thing I do know. I was blind but now I see!"

Then they asked him, "What did he do to you? How did he open your eyes?"

He answered, "I have told you already and you did not listen. Why do you want to hear it again? Do you want to become his disciples, too?"

Then they hurled insults at him and said, "You are this fellow's disciple! We are disciples of Moses! We know that God spoke to Moses, but as for this fellow, we don't even know where he comes from."

The man answered, "Now that is remarkable! You don't know where he comes from, yet he opened my eyes. We know that God does not listen to sinners. He listens to the godly man who does his will. Nobody has ever heard of opening the eyes of a man born blind. If this man were not from God, he could do nothing."

To this they replied, "You were steeped in sin at birth; how dare you lecture us!" And they threw him out.

Jesus heard that they had thrown him out, and when he found him, he said, "Do you believe in the Son of Man?"

"Who is he, sir?" the man asked. "Tell me so that I may believe in him."

Jesus said, "You have now seen him; in fact, he is the one speaking with you."

Then the man said, "Lord, I believe," and he worshipped him.

Jesus said, "For judgment I have come into this world, so that the blind will see and those who see will become blind."

Some Pharisees who were with him heard him say this and asked, "What? Are we blind too?"

Jesus said, "If you were blind, you would not be guilty of sin; but now that you claim you can see, your guilt remains."

Mothering Sunday

Mothering Sunday may be celebrated in preference to the provision for the Fourth Sunday of Lent (Readings for Years A, B, C are the same)

Alternative first readings

Either **Exodus 2:1–10**   A man of the house of Levi married a Levite woman, and she became pregnant and gave birth to a son. When she saw that he was a fine child, she hid him for three months. But when she could hide him no longer, she got a papyrus basket for him and coated it with tar and pitch. Then she placed the child in it and put it among the reeds along the bank of the Nile. His sister stood at a distance to see what would happen to him.

Then Pharaoh's daughter went down to the Nile to bathe, and her attendants were walking along the river bank. She saw the basket among the

FIRST READING

reeds and sent her female slave to get it. She opened it and saw the baby. He was crying, and she felt sorry for him. "This is one of the Hebrew babies," she said.

Then his sister asked Pharaoh's daughter, "Shall I go and get one of the Hebrew women to nurse the baby for you?"

"Yes, go," she answered. And the girl went and got the baby's mother. Pharaoh's daughter said to her, "Take this baby and nurse him for me, and I will pay you." So the woman took the baby and nursed him. When the child grew older, she took him to Pharaoh's daughter and he became her son. She named him Moses, saying, "I drew him out of the water."

or **1 Samuel 1:20–28** In the course of time Hannah conceived and gave birth to a son. She named him Samuel, saying, "Because I asked the LORD for him."

When Elkanah went up with all his family to offer the annual sacrifice to the LORD and to fulfil his vow, Hannah did not go. She said to her husband, "After the boy is weaned, I will take him and present him before the LORD, and he will live there always."

"Do what seems best to you," Elkanah her husband told her. "Stay here until you have weaned him; only may the LORD make good his word." So the woman stayed at home and nursed her son until she had weaned him.

After he was weaned, she took the boy with her, young as he was, along with a three-year-old bull, an ephah of flour and a skin of wine, and brought him to the house of the LORD at Shiloh. When they had slaughtered the bull, they brought the boy to Eli, and she said to him, "As surely as you live, my LORD, I am the woman who stood here beside you praying to the LORD. I prayed for this child, and the LORD has granted me what I asked of him. So now I give him to the LORD. For his whole life he shall be given over to the LORD." And he worshipped the LORD there.

Alternative Psalms

Either **Psalm 34:11–20**

> Come, my children, listen to me;
> > I will teach you the fear of the LORD.
> Whoever among you loves life
> > and desires to see many good days,
> keep your tongue from evil
> > and your lips from speaking lies.
> Turn from evil and do good;
> > seek peace and pursue it.
>
> The eyes of the LORD are on the righteous
> > and his ears are attentive to their cry;
> the face of the LORD is against those who do evil,
> > to cut off the memory of them from the earth.
>
> The righteous cry out, and the LORD hears them;
> > he delivers them from all their troubles.
> The LORD is close to the broken-hearted
> > and saves those who are crushed in spirit.

The righteous may have many troubles,
but the LORD delivers them from them all;
he protects all their bones,
not one of them will be broken.

or **Psalm 127:1–4** Unless the LORD builds the house,
its builders labour in vain.
Unless the LORD watches over the city,
the watchmen stand watch in vain.
In vain you rise early
and stay up late,
toiling for food to eat –
for he grants sleep to those he loves.

Sons are a heritage from the LORD,
children a reward from him.
Like arrows in the hands of a warrior
are sons born in one's youth.

P
S
A
L
M

Alternative second readings

Either **2 Corinthians 1:3–7** Praise be to the God and Father of our Lord Jesus
Christ, the Father of compassion and the God of all comfort, who comforts
us in all our troubles, so that we can comfort those in any trouble with the
comfort we ourselves have received from God. For just as the sufferings of
Christ flow over into our lives, so also through Christ our comfort overflows. If we are distressed, it is for your comfort and salvation; if we are
comforted, it is for your comfort, which produces in you patient endurance
of the same sufferings we suffer. And our hope for you is firm, because we
know that just as you share in our sufferings, so also you share in our comfort.

S R
E E
C A
O D
N I
D N
  G

or **Colossians 3:12–17** As God's chosen people, holy and dearly loved, clothe
yourselves with compassion, kindness, humility, gentleness and patience.
Bear with each other and forgive whatever grievances you may have
against one another. Forgive as the LORD forgave you. And over all these
virtues put on love, which binds them all together in perfect unity.

Let the peace of Christ rule in your hearts, since as members of one
body you were called to peace. And be thankful. Let the word of Christ
dwell in you richly as you teach and admonish one another with all wisdom, and as you sing psalms, hymns and spiritual songs with gratitude in
your hearts to God. And whatever you do, whether in word or deed, do it all
in the name of the Lord Jesus, giving thanks to God the Father through
him.

S R
E E
C A
O D
N I
D N
  G

Alternative Gospels

G
O
S
P
E
L

Either **Luke 2:33–35** Jesus' father and mother marvelled at what Simeon
said about Jesus. Then Simeon blessed them and said to Mary, his mother:
"This child is destined to cause the falling and rising of many in Israel, and

to be a sign that will be spoken against, so that the thoughts of many hearts will be revealed. And a sword will pierce your own soul too.”

or **John 19:25–27** Near the cross of Jesus stood his mother, his mother's sis- G
ter, Mary the wife of Clopas, and Mary Magdalene. When Jesus saw his O
mother there, and the disciple whom he loved standing near by, he said to S
his mother, “Dear woman, here is your son,” and to the disciple, “Here is P
your mother.” From that time on, this disciple took her into his home. E

L

Fifth Sunday of Lent
Passiontide begins

Ezekiel 37:1–14 The hand of the Lord was upon me, and he brought me out F
by the Spirit of the Lord and set me in the middle of a valley; it was full of I
bones. He led me to and fro among them, and I saw a great many bones on R
the floor of the valley, bones that were very dry. He asked me, “Son of man, S
can these bones live?” T

I said, “O Sovereign Lord, you alone know.”

Then he said to me, “Prophesy to these bones and say to them, ‘Dry R
bones, hear the word of the Lord! This is what the Sovereign Lord says to E
these bones: I will make breath enter you, and you will come to life. I will A
attach tendons to you and make flesh come upon you and cover you with D
skin; I will put breath in you, and you will come to life. Then you will know I
that I am the Lord.’” N

So I prophesied as I was commanded. And as I was prophesying, there G
was a noise, a rattling sound, and the bones came together, bone to bone. I
looked, and tendons and flesh appeared on them and skin covered them, but
there was no breath in them.

Then he said to me, “Prophesy to the breath; prophesy, son of man, and
say to it, ‘This is what the Sovereign Lord says: Come from the four winds,
O breath, and breathe into these slain, that they may live.’” So I prophesied
as he commanded me, and breath entered them; they came to life and stood
up on their feet – a vast army.

Then he said to me: “Son of man, these bones are the whole house of
Israel. They say, ‘Our bones are dried up and our hope is gone; we are cut
off.’ Therefore prophesy and say to them: ‘This is what the Sovereign Lord
says: O my people, I am going to open your graves and bring you up from
them; I will bring you back to the land of Israel. Then you, my people, will
know that I am the Lord, when I open your graves and bring you up from
them. I will put my Spirit in you and you will live, and I will settle you in
your own land. Then you will know that I the Lord have spoken, and I have
done it, declares the Lord.’”

P

Psalm 130 Out of the depths I cry to you, O Lord; S
O Lord, hear my voice. A
Let your ears be attentive L
to my cry for mercy. M

If you, O LORD, kept a record of sins,
O LORD, who could stand?
But with you there is forgiveness;
therefore you are feared.

I wait for the LORD, my soul waits,
and in his word I put my hope.
My soul waits for the LORD
more than watchmen wait for the morning,
more than watchmen wait for the morning.

O Israel, put your hope in the LORD,
for with the LORD is unfailing love
and with him is full redemption.
He himself will redeem Israel
from all their sins.

Romans 8:6–11   The mind of sinful man is death, but the mind controlled by the Spirit is life and peace; the sinful mind is hostile to God. It does not submit to God's law, nor can it do so. Those controlled by the sinful nature cannot please God.

You, however, are controlled not by the sinful nature but by the Spirit, if the Spirit of God lives in you. And if anyone does not have the Spirit of Christ, he does not belong to Christ. But if Christ is in you, your body is dead because of sin, yet your spirit is alive because of righteousness. And if the Spirit of him who raised Jesus from the dead is living in you, he who raised Christ from the dead will also give life to your mortal bodies through his Spirit, who lives in you.

S E C O N D   R E A D I N G

John 11:1–45   A man named Lazarus was sick. He was from Bethany, the village of Mary and her sister Martha. This Mary, whose brother Lazarus now lay sick, was the same one who poured perfume on the Lord and wiped his feet with her hair. So the sisters sent word to Jesus, "Lord, the one you love is sick."

When he heard this, Jesus said, "This sickness will not end in death. No, it is for God's glory so that God's Son may be glorified through it." Jesus loved Martha and her sister and Lazarus. Yet when he heard that Lazarus was sick, he stayed where he was two more days.

Then he said to his disciples, "Let us go back to Judea."

"But Rabbi," they said, "a short while ago the Jews tried to stone you, and yet you are going back there?"

Jesus answered, "Are there not twelve hours of daylight? Those who walk by day will not stumble, for they see by this world's light. It is when they walk by night that they stumble, for they have no light."

After he had said this, he went on to tell them, "Our friend Lazarus has fallen asleep; but I am going there to wake him up."

His disciples replied, "Lord, if he sleeps, he will get better." Jesus had been speaking of his death, but his disciples thought he meant natural sleep.

G O S P E L

So then he told them plainly, "Lazarus is dead, and for your sake I am glad I was not there, so that you may believe. But let us go to him."

Then Thomas (called Didymus) said to the rest of the disciples, "Let us also go, that we may die with him."

On his arrival, Jesus found that Lazarus had already been in the tomb for four days. Bethany was less than two miles from Jerusalem, and many Jews had come to Martha and Mary to comfort them in the loss of their brother. When Martha heard that Jesus was coming, she went out to meet him, but Mary stayed at home.

"Lord," Martha said to Jesus, "if you had been here, my brother would not have died. But I know that even now God will give you whatever you ask."

Jesus said to her, "Your brother will rise again."

Martha answered, "I know he will rise again in the resurrection at the last day."

Jesus said to her, "I am the resurrection and the life. He who believes in me will live, even though he dies; and whoever lives and believes in me will never die. Do you believe this?"

"Yes, Lord," she told him, "I believe that you are the Christ, the Son of God, who was to come into the world."

And after she had said this, she went back and called her sister Mary aside. "The Teacher is here," she said, "and is asking for you." When Mary heard this, she got up quickly and went to him. Now Jesus had not yet entered the village, but was still at the place where Martha had met him. When the Jews who had been with Mary in the house, comforting her, noticed how quickly she got up and went out, they followed her, supposing she was going to the tomb to mourn there.

When Mary reached the place where Jesus was and saw him, she fell at his feet and said, "Lord, if you had been here, my brother would not have died."

When Jesus saw her weeping, and the Jews who had come along with her also weeping, he was deeply moved in spirit and troubled. "Where have you laid him?" he asked.

"Come and see, Lord," they replied.

Jesus wept.

Then the Jews said, "See how he loved him!"

But some of them said, "Could not he who opened the eyes of the blind man have kept this man from dying?"

Jesus, once more deeply moved, came to the tomb. It was a cave with a stone laid across the entrance. "Take away the stone," he said.

"But, Lord," said Martha, the sister of the dead man, "by this time there is a bad odour, for he has been there four days."

Then Jesus said, "Did I not tell you that if you believed, you would see the glory of God?"

So they took away the stone. Then Jesus looked up and said, "Father, I thank you that you have heard me. I knew that you always hear me, but I said this for the benefit of the people standing here, that they may believe that you sent me."

When he had said this, Jesus called in a loud voice, "Lazarus, come out!" The dead man came out, his hands and feet wrapped with strips of linen, and a cloth around his face.

Jesus said to them, "Take off the grave clothes and let him go."

Therefore many of the Jews who had come to visit Mary, and had seen what Jesus did, put their faith in him.

Palm Sunday

Liturgy of the Palms:

Matthew 21:1–11 As Jesus and his disciples approached Jerusalem and came to Bethphage on the Mount of Olives, Jesus sent two disciples, saying to them, "Go to the village ahead of you, and at once you will find a donkey tied there, with her colt by her. Untie them and bring them to me. If anyone says anything to you, say that the Lord needs them, and he will send them right away."

This took place to fulfil what was spoken through the prophet:

"Say to the Daughter of Zion,
  'See, your king comes to you,
gentle and riding on a donkey,
  on a colt, the foal of a donkey.'"

The disciples went and did as Jesus had instructed them. They brought the donkey and the colt, placed their cloaks on them, and Jesus sat on them. A very large crowd spread their cloaks on the road, while others cut branches from the trees and spread them on the road. The crowds that went ahead of him and those that followed shouted,

"Hosanna to the Son of David!"

"Blessed is he who comes in the name of the LORD!"

"Hosanna in the highest!"

When Jesus entered Jerusalem, the whole city was stirred and asked, "Who is this?"

The crowds answered, "This is Jesus, the prophet from Nazareth in Galilee."

Psalm 118:1–2, 19–29* Give thanks to the LORD, for he is good;
  his love endures for ever.

Let Israel say:
  "His love endures for ever."

Open for me the gates of righteousness;
  I will enter and give thanks to the LORD.
This is the gate of the LORD
  through which the righteous may enter.
I will give you thanks, for you answered me;
  you have become my salvation.

The stone the builders rejected
  has become the capstone;

the LORD has done this,
and it is marvellous in our eyes.
This is the day the LORD has made;
let us rejoice and be glad in it.

O LORD, save us;
O LORD, grant us success.
Blessed is he who comes in the name of the LORD.
From the house of the LORD we bless you.
The LORD is God,
and he has made his light shine upon us.
With boughs in hand, join in the festal procession
up to the horns of the altar.

You are my God, and I will give thanks;
you are my God, and I will exalt you.

Give thanks to the LORD, for he is good;
his love endures for ever.

Liturgy of the Passion:

Isaiah 50:4–9a
The Sovereign LORD has given me an instructed tongue,
to know the word that sustains the weary.
He wakens me morning by morning,
wakens my ear to listen like one being taught.
The Sovereign LORD has opened my ears,
and I have not been rebellious;
I have not drawn back.
I offered my back to those who beat me,
my cheeks to those who pulled out my beard;
I did not hide my face
from mocking and spitting.
Because the Sovereign LORD helps me,
I will not be disgraced.
Therefore have I set my face like flint,
and I know I will not be put to shame.
He who vindicates me is near.
Who then will bring charges against me?
Let us face each other!
Who are accusers?
Let them confront me!
It is the Sovereign LORD who helps me.

FIRST READING

Psalm 31:9–16*
Be merciful to me, O LORD, for I am in distress;
my eyes grow weak with sorrow,
my soul and my body with grief.
My life is consumed by anguish
and my years by groaning;
my strength fails because of my affliction,
and my bones grow weak.

PSALM

Because of all my enemies,
  I am the utter contempt of my neighbours;
I am a dread to my friends –
  those who see me on the street flee from me.
I am forgotten by them as though I were dead;
  I have become like broken pottery.
For I hear the slander of many;
  there is terror on every side;
they conspire against me
  and plot to take my life.

But I trust in you, O LORD;
  I say, "You are my God."
My times are in your hands;
  deliver me from my enemies
  and from those who pursue me.
Let your face shine on your servant;
  save me in your unfailing love.

Philippians 2:5–11 Your attitude should be the same as that of Christ Jesus:

Who, being in very nature God,
  did not consider equality with God something to be grasped,
but made himself nothing,
  taking the very nature of a servant,
  being made in human likeness.
And being found in appearance as a man,
  he humbled himself
  and became obedient to death – even death on a cross!
Therefore God exalted him to the highest place
  and gave him the name that is above every name,
that at the name of Jesus every knee should bow,
  in heaven and on earth and under the earth,
and every tongue confess that Jesus Christ is LORD,
  to the glory of God the Father.

SECOND READING

Alternative Gospels

Either **Matthew 26:14 – 27:66** One of the Twelve – the one called Judas Iscariot – went to the chief priests and asked, "What are you willing to give me if I hand Jesus over to you?" So they counted out for him thirty silver coins. From then on Judas watched for an opportunity to hand him over.

On the first day of the Feast of Unleavened Bread, the disciples came to Jesus and asked, "Where do you want us to make preparations for you to eat the Passover?"

He replied, "Go into the city to a certain man and tell him, 'The Teacher says: My appointed time is near. I am going to celebrate the Passover with my disciples at your house.'" So the disciples did as Jesus had directed them and prepared the Passover.

GOSPEL

When evening came, Jesus was reclining at the table with the Twelve. And while they were eating, he said, "I tell you the truth, one of you will betray me."

They were very sad and began to say to him one after the other, "Surely not I, Lord?"

Jesus replied, "The one who has dipped his hand into the bowl with me will betray me. The Son of Man will go just as it is written about him. But woe to that man who betrays the Son of Man! It would be better for him if he had not been born."

Then Judas, the one who would betray him, said, "Surely not I, Rabbi?" Jesus answered, "Yes, it is you."

While they were eating, Jesus took bread, gave thanks and broke it, and gave it to his disciples, saying, "Take and eat; this is my body."

Then he took the cup, gave thanks and offered it to them, saying, "Drink from it, all of you. This is my blood of the covenant, which is poured out for many for the forgiveness of sins. I tell you, I will not drink of this fruit of the vine from now on until that day when I drink it anew with you in my Father's kingdom."

When they had sung a hymn, they went out to the Mount of Olives.

Then Jesus told them, "This very night you will all fall away on account of me, for it is written:

"'I will strike the shepherd,
    and the sheep of the flock will be scattered.'

But after I have risen, I will go ahead of you into Galilee."

Peter replied, "Even if all fall away on account of you, I never will."

"I tell you the truth," Jesus answered, "this very night, before the cock crows, you will disown me three times."

But Peter declared, "Even if I have to die with you, I will never disown you." And all the other disciples said the same.

Then Jesus went with his disciples to a place called Gethsemane, and he said to them, "Sit here while I go over there and pray." He took Peter and the two sons of Zebedee along with him, and he began to be sorrowful and troubled. Then he said to them, "My soul is overwhelmed with sorrow to the point of death. Stay here and keep watch with me."

Going a little farther, he fell with his face to the ground and prayed, "My Father, if it is possible, may this cup be taken from me. Yet not as I will, but as you will."

Then he returned to his disciples and found them sleeping. "Could you men not keep watch with me for one hour?" he asked Peter. "Watch and pray so that you will not fall into temptation. The spirit is willing, but the body is weak."

He went away a second time and prayed, "My Father, if it is not possible for this cup to be taken away unless I drink it, may your will be done."

When he came back, he again found them sleeping, because their eyes were heavy. So he left them and went away once more and prayed the third time, saying the same thing.

Then he returned to the disciples and said to them, "Are you still sleeping and resting? Look, the hour is near, and the Son of Man is betrayed into the hands of sinners. Rise, let us go! Here comes my betrayer!"

While he was still speaking, Judas, one of the Twelve, arrived. With him was a large crowd armed with swords and clubs, sent from the chief priests and the elders of the people. Now the betrayer had arranged a signal with them: "The one I kiss is the man; arrest him." Going at once to Jesus, Judas said, "Greetings, Rabbi!" and kissed him.

Jesus replied, "Friend, do what you came for."

Then the men stepped forward, seized Jesus and arrested him. With that, one of Jesus' companions reached for his sword, drew it out and struck the servant of the high priest, cutting off his ear.

"Put your sword back in its place," Jesus said to him, "for all who draw the sword will die by the sword. Do you think I cannot call on my Father, and he will at once put at my disposal more than twelve legions of angels? But how then would the Scriptures be fulfilled that say it must happen in this way?"

At that time Jesus said to the crowd, "Am I leading a rebellion, that you have come out with swords and clubs to capture me? Every day I sat in the temple courts teaching, and you did not arrest me. But this has all taken place that the writings of the prophets might be fulfilled." Then all the disciples deserted him and fled.

Those who had arrested Jesus took him to Caiaphas, the high priest, where the teachers of the law and the elders had assembled. But Peter followed him at a distance, right up to the courtyard of the high priest. He entered and sat down with the guards to see the outcome.

The chief priests and the whole Sanhedrin were looking for false evidence against Jesus so that they could put him to death. But they did not find any, though many false witnesses came forward.

Finally two came forward and declared, "This fellow said, 'I am able to destroy the temple of God and rebuild it in three days.'"

Then the high priest stood up and said to Jesus, "Are you not going to answer? What is this testimony that these men are bringing against you?" But Jesus remained silent.

The high priest said to him, "I charge you under oath by the living God: Tell us if you are the Christ, the Son of God."

"Yes, it is as you say," Jesus replied. "But I say to all of you: In the future you will see the Son of Man sitting at the right hand of the Mighty One and coming on the clouds of heaven."

Then the high priest tore his clothes and said, "He has spoken blasphemy! Why do we need any more witnesses? Look, now you have heard the blasphemy. What do you think?"

"He is worthy of death," they answered.

Then they spat in his face and struck him with their fists. Others slapped him and said, "Prophesy to us, Christ. Who hit you?"

Now Peter was sitting out in the courtyard, and a female servant came to him. "You also were with Jesus of Galilee," she said.

But he denied it before them all. "I don't know what you're talking about," he said.

Then he went out to the gateway, where another girl saw him and said to the people there, "This fellow was with Jesus of Nazareth."

He denied it again, with an oath: "I don't know the man!"

After a little while, those standing there went up to Peter and said, "Surely you are one of them, for your accent gives you away."

Then he began to call down curses on himself and he swore to them, "I don't know the man!"

Immediately a cock crowed. Then Peter remembered the word Jesus had spoken: "Before the cock crows, you will disown me three times." And he went outside and wept bitterly.

Early in the morning, all the chief priests and the elders of the people came to the decision to put Jesus to death. They bound him, led him away and handed him over to Pilate, the governor.

When Judas, who had betrayed him, saw that Jesus was condemned, he was seized with remorse and returned the thirty silver coins to the chief priests and the elders. "I have sinned," he said, "for I have betrayed innocent blood."

"What is that to us?" they replied. "That's your responsibility."

So Judas threw the money into the temple and left. Then he went away and hanged himself.

The chief priests picked up the coins and said, "It is against the law to put this into the treasury, since it is blood money." So they decided to use the money to buy the potter's field as a burial place for foreigners. That is why it has been called the Field of Blood to this day. Then what was spoken by Jeremiah the prophet was fulfilled: "They took the thirty silver coins, the price set on him by the people of Israel, and they used them to buy the potter's field, as the Lord commanded me."

Meanwhile Jesus stood before the governor, and the governor asked him, "Are you the king of the Jews?"

"Yes, it is as you say," Jesus replied.

When he was accused by the chief priests and the elders, he gave no answer. Then Pilate asked him, "Don't you hear the testimony they are bringing against you?" But Jesus made no reply, not even to a single charge – to the great amazement of the governor.

Now it was the governor's custom at the Feast to release a prisoner chosen by the crowd. At that time they had a notorious prisoner, called Barabbas. So when the crowd had gathered, Pilate asked them, "Which one do you want me to release to you: Barabbas, or Jesus who is called Christ?" For he knew it was out of envy that they had handed Jesus over to him.

While Pilate was sitting on the judge's seat, his wife sent him this message: "Don't have anything to do with that innocent man, for I have suffered a great deal today in a dream because of him."

But the chief priests and the elders persuaded the crowd to ask for Barabbas and to have Jesus executed.

"Which of the two do you want me to release to you?" asked the governor.

"Barabbas," they answered.

"What shall I do, then, with Jesus who is called Christ?" Pilate asked.

They all answered, "Crucify him!"

"Why? What crime has he committed?" asked Pilate.

But they shouted all the louder, "Crucify him!"

When Pilate saw that he was getting nowhere, but that instead an uproar was starting, he took water and washed his hands in front of the crowd. "I am innocent of this man's blood," he said. "It is your responsibility!"

All the people answered, "Let his blood be on us and on our children!"

Then he released Barabbas to them. But he had Jesus flogged, and handed him over to be crucified.

Then the governor's soldiers took Jesus into the Praetorium and gathered the whole company of soldiers round him. They stripped him and put a scarlet robe on him, and then twisted together a crown of thorns and set it on his head. They put a staff in his right hand and knelt in front of him and mocked him. "Hail, king of the Jews!" they said. They spat on him, and took the staff and struck him on the head again and again. After they had mocked him, they took off the robe and put his own clothes on him. Then they led him away to crucify him.

As they were going out, they met a man from Cyrene, named Simon, and they forced him to carry the cross. They came to a place called Golgotha (which means The Place of the Skull). There they offered Jesus wine to drink, mixed with gall; but after tasting it, he refused to drink it. When they had crucified him, they divided up his clothes by casting lots. And sitting down, they kept watch over him there. Above his head they placed the written charge against him: THIS IS JESUS, THE KING OF THE JEWS. Two robbers were crucified with him, one on his right and one on his left. Those who passed by hurled insults at him, shaking their heads and saying, "You who are going to destroy the temple and build it in three days, save yourself! Come down from the cross, if you are the Son of God!"

In the same way the chief priests, the teachers of the law and the elders mocked him. "He saved others," they said, "but he can't save himself! He's the King of Israel! Let him come down now from the cross, and we will believe in him. He trusts in God. Let God rescue him now if he wants him, for he said, 'I am the Son of God.'" In the same way the robbers who were crucified with him also heaped insults on him.

From the sixth hour until the ninth hour darkness came over all the land. About the ninth hour Jesus cried out in a loud voice, "*Eloi, Eloi, lama sabachthani?*" – which means, "My God, my God, why have you forsaken me?"

When some of those standing there heard this, they said, "He's calling Elijah."

Immediately one of them ran and got a sponge. He filled it with wine vinegar, put it on a stick, and offered it to Jesus to drink. The rest said, "Now leave him alone. Let's see if Elijah comes to save him."

And when Jesus had cried out again in a loud voice, he gave up his spirit.

At that moment the curtain of the temple was torn in two from top to bottom. The earth shook and the rocks split. The tombs broke open and the bodies of many holy people who had died were raised to life. They came out of the tombs, and after Jesus' resurrection they went into the holy city and appeared to many people.

When the centurion and those with him who were guarding Jesus saw the earthquake and all that had happened, they were terrified, and exclaimed, "Surely he was the Son of God!"

Many women were there, watching from a distance. They had followed Jesus from Galilee to care for his needs. Among them were Mary Magdalene, Mary the mother of James and Joses, and the mother of Zebedee's sons.

As evening approached, there came a rich man from Arimathea, named Joseph, who had himself become a disciple of Jesus. Going to Pilate, he asked for Jesus' body, and Pilate ordered that it be given to him. Joseph took the body, wrapped it in a clean linen cloth, and placed it in his own new tomb that he had cut out of the rock. He rolled a big stone in front of the entrance to the tomb and went away. Mary Magdalene and the other Mary were sitting there opposite the tomb.

The next day, the one after Preparation Day, the chief priests and the Pharisees went to Pilate. "Sir," they said, "we remember that while he was still alive that deceiver said, 'After three days I will rise again.' So give the order for the tomb to be made secure until the third day. Otherwise, his disciples may come and steal the body and tell the people that he has been raised from the dead. This last deception will be worse than the first."

"Take a guard," Pilate answered. "Go, make the tomb as secure as you know how." So they went and made the tomb secure by putting a seal on the stone and posting the guard.

or **Matthew 27:11–54**   Jesus stood before Pilate, the governor, and Pilate asked him, "Are you the king of the Jews?"

"Yes, it is as you say," Jesus replied.

When he was accused by the chief priests and the elders, he gave no answer. Then Pilate asked him, "Don't you hear the testimony they are bringing against you?" But Jesus made no reply, not even to a single charge – to the great amazement of the governor.

Now it was the governor's custom at the Feast to release a prisoner chosen by the crowd. At that time they had a notorious prisoner, called Barabbas. So when the crowd had gathered, Pilate asked them, "Which one do you want me to release to you: Barabbas, or Jesus who is called Christ?" For he knew it was out of envy that they had handed Jesus over to him.

While Pilate was sitting on the judge's seat, his wife sent him this message: "Don't have anything to do with that innocent man, for I have suffered a great deal today in a dream because of him."

But the chief priests and the elders persuaded the crowd to ask for Barabbas and to have Jesus executed.

"Which of the two do you want me to release to you?" asked the governor.

"Barabbas," they answered.

"What shall I do, then, with Jesus who is called Christ?" Pilate asked.

They all answered, "Crucify him!"

"Why? What crime has he committed?" asked Pilate.

But they shouted all the louder, "Crucify him!"

When Pilate saw that he was getting nowhere, but that instead an uproar was starting, he took water and washed his hands in front of the crowd. "I am innocent of this man's blood," he said. "It is your responsibility!"

All the people answered, "Let his blood be on us and on our children!"

Then he released Barabbas to them. But he had Jesus flogged, and handed him over to be crucified.

Then the governor's soldiers took Jesus into the Praetorium and gathered the whole company of soldiers round him. They stripped him and put a scarlet robe on him, and then twisted together a crown of thorns and set it on his head. They put a staff in his right hand and knelt in front of him and mocked him. "Hail, king of the Jews!" they said. They spat on him, and took the staff and struck him on the head again and again. After they had mocked him, they took off the robe and put his own clothes on him. Then they led him away to crucify him.

As they were going out, they met a man from Cyrene, named Simon, and they forced him to carry the cross. They came to a place called Golgotha (which means The Place of the Skull). There they offered Jesus wine to drink, mixed with gall; but after tasting it, he refused to drink it. When they had crucified him, they divided up his clothes by casting lots. And sitting down, they kept watch over him there. Above his head they placed the written charge against him: THIS IS JESUS, THE KING OF THE JEWS. Two robbers were crucified with him, one on his right and one on his left. Those who passed by hurled insults at him, shaking their heads and saying, "You who are going to destroy the temple and build it in three days, save yourself! Come down from the cross, if you are the Son of God!"

In the same way the chief priests, the teachers of the law and the elders mocked him. "He saved others," they said, "but he can't save himself! He's the King of Israel! Let him come down now from the cross, and we will believe in him. He trusts in God. Let God rescue him now if he wants him, for he said, 'I am the Son of God.'" In the same way the robbers who were crucified with him also heaped insults on him.

From the sixth hour until the ninth hour darkness came over all the land. About the ninth hour Jesus cried out in a loud voice, "*Eloi, Eloi, lama sabachthani?*" – which means, "My God, my God, why have you forsaken me?"

When some of those standing there heard this, they said, "He's calling Elijah."

Immediately one of them ran and got a sponge. He filled it with wine vinegar, put it on a stick, and offered it to Jesus to drink. The rest said, "Now leave him alone. Let's see if Elijah comes to save him."

And when Jesus had cried out again in a loud voice, he gave up his spirit.

At that moment the curtain of the temple was torn in two from top to bottom. The earth shook and the rocks split. The tombs broke open and the bodies of many holy people who had died were raised to life. They came out of the tombs, and after Jesus' resurrection they went into the holy city and appeared to many people.

When the centurion and those with him who were guarding Jesus saw the earthquake and all that had happened, they were terrified, and exclaimed, "Surely he was the Son of God!"

Monday of Holy Week

(Readings for Years A, B, C are the same)

Isaiah 42:1–9 "Here is my servant, whom I uphold,
  my chosen one in whom I delight;
I will put my Spirit on him
  and he will bring justice to the nations.
He will not shout or cry out,
  or raise his voice in the streets.
A bruised reed he will not break,
  and a smouldering wick he will not snuff out.
In faithfulness he will bring forth justice;
  he will not falter or be discouraged
till he establishes justice on earth.
  In his law the islands will put their hope."

This is what God the LORD says –
he who created the heavens and stretched them out,
  who spread out the earth and all that comes out of it,
who gives breath to its people,
  and life to those who walk on it:
"I, the LORD, have called you in righteousness;
  I will take hold of your hand.
I will keep you and will make you
  to be a covenant for the people
  and a light for the Gentiles,
to open eyes that are blind,
  to free captives from prison
  and to release from the dungeon those who sit in darkness.

"I am the LORD; that is my name!
  I will not give my glory to another
  or my praise to idols.
See, the former things have taken place,
  and new things I declare;
 before they spring into being
  I announce them to you."

[Marginal text, vertical: FIRST READING]

Psalm 36:5–11   Your love, O LORD, reaches to the heavens,   P
        your faithfulness to the skies.   S
   Your righteousness is like the mighty mountains,   A
        your justice like the great deep.   L
   O LORD, you preserve both man and beast.   M
        How priceless is your unfailing love!
   Both high and low among men
        find refuge in the shadow of your wings.
   They feast in the abundance of your house;
        you give them drink from your river of delights.
   For with you is the fountain of life;
        in your light we see light.

   Continue your love to those who know you,
        your righteousness to the upright in heart.
   May the foot of the proud not come against me,
        nor the hand of the wicked drive me away.

Hebrews 9:11–15   When Christ came as high priest of the good things that S
are already here, he went through the greater and more perfect tabernacle E
that is not man-made, that is to say, not a part of this creation. He did not C
enter by means of the blood of goats and calves; but he entered the Most O
Holy Place once for all by his own blood, having obtained eternal redemp- N
tion. The blood of goats and bulls and the ashes of a heifer sprinkled on D
those who are ceremonially unclean sanctify them so that they are outwardly clean. How much more, then, will the blood of Christ, who through R
the eternal Spirit offered himself unblemished to God, cleanse our con- E
sciences from acts that lead to death, so that we may serve the living God! A

   For this reason Christ is the mediator of a new covenant, that those who D
are called may receive the promised eternal inheritance – now that he has I
died as a ransom to set them free from the sins committed under the first N
covenant.   G

John 12:1–11   Six days before the Passover, Jesus arrived at Bethany, where G
Lazarus lived, whom Jesus had raised from the dead. Here a dinner was O
given in Jesus' honour. Martha served, while Lazarus was among those S
reclining at the table with him. Then Mary took about a pint of pure nard, P
an expensive perfume; she poured it on Jesus' feet and wiped his feet with E
her hair. And the house was filled with the fragrance of the perfume.   L

   But one of his disciples, Judas Iscariot, who was later to betray him,
objected, "Why wasn't this perfume sold and the money given to the poor?
It was worth a year's wages." He did not say this because he cared about
the poor but because he was a thief; as keeper of the money bag, he used to
help himself to what was put into it.

   "Leave her alone," Jesus replied. "It was intended that she should save
this perfume for the day of my burial. You will always have the poor among
you, but you will not always have me."

Meanwhile a large crowd of Jews found out that Jesus was there and came, not only because of him but also to see Lazarus, whom he had raised from the dead. So the chief priests made plans to kill Lazarus as well, for on account of him many of the Jews were going over to Jesus and putting their faith in him.

Tuesday of Holy Week

(Readings for Years A, B, C are the same)

FIRST READING

Isaiah 49:1–7

Listen to me, you islands;
hear this, you distant nations:
Before I was born the LORD called me;
from my birth he has made mention of my name.
He made my mouth like a sharpened sword,
in the shadow of his hand he hid me;
he made me into a polished arrow
and concealed me in his quiver.
He said to me, "You are my servant,
Israel, in whom I will display my splendour."
But I said, "I have laboured to no purpose;
I have spent my strength in vain and for nothing.
Yet what is due to me is in the LORD's hand,
and my reward is with my God."

And now the LORD says –
he who formed me in the womb to be his servant
to bring Jacob back to him
and gather Israel to himself,
for I am honoured in the eyes of the LORD
and my God has been my strength –
he says:
"It is too small a thing for you to be my servant
to restore the tribes of Jacob
and bring back those of Israel I have kept.
I will also make you a light for the Gentiles,
that you may bring my salvation to the ends of the earth."

This is what the LORD says –
the Redeemer and Holy One of Israel –
to him who was despised and abhorred by the nation,
to the servant of rulers:
"Kings will see you and rise up,
princes will see and bow down,
because of the LORD, who is faithful,
the Holy One of Israel, who has chosen you."

PSALM

Psalm 71:1–14*

In you, O LORD, I have taken refuge;
let me never be put to shame.
Rescue me and deliver me in your righteousness;
turn your ear to me and save me.

Be my rock of refuge,
    to which I can always go;
give the command to save me,
    for you are my rock and my fortress.
Deliver me, O my God, from the hand of the wicked,
    from the grasp of evil and cruel men.

For you have been my hope, O Sovereign Lord,
    my confidence since my youth.
From my birth I have relied on you;
    you brought me forth from my mother's womb.
    I will ever praise you.
I have become like a portent to many,
    but you are my strong refuge.
My mouth is filled with your praise,
    declaring your splendour all day long.

Do not cast me away when I am old;
    do not forsake me when my strength is gone.
For my enemies speak against me;
    those who wait to kill me conspire together.
They say, "God has forsaken him;
    pursue him and seize him,
    for no-one will rescue him."
Be not far from me, O God;
    come quickly, O my God, to help me.
May my accusers perish in shame;
    may those who want to harm me
    be covered with scorn and disgrace.

But as for me, I shall always have hope;
    I will praise you more and more.

1 Corinthians 1:18–31   The message of the cross is foolishness to those who
are perishing, but to us who are being saved it is the power of God. For it is
written:

"I will destroy the wisdom of the wise;
    the intelligence of the intelligent I will frustrate."

Where is the wise man? Where is the scholar? Where is the philosopher
of this age? Has not God made foolish the wisdom of the world? For since
in the wisdom of God the world through its wisdom did not know him, God
was pleased through the foolishness of what was preached to save those
who believe. Jews demand miraculous signs and Greeks look for wisdom,
but we preach Christ crucified: a stumbling-block to Jews and foolishness
to Gentiles, but to those whom God has called, both Jews and Greeks,
Christ the power of God and the wisdom of God. For the foolishness of God
is wiser than man's wisdom, and the weakness of God is stronger than
man's strength.

SECOND READING

Brothers, think of what you were when you were called. Not many of you were wise by human standards; not many were influential; not many were of noble birth. But God chose the foolish things of the world to shame the wise; God chose the weak things of the world to shame the strong. He chose the lowly things of this world and the despised things – and the things that are not – to nullify the things that are, so that no-one may boast before him. It is because of him that you are in Christ Jesus, who has become for us wisdom from God – that is, our righteousness, holiness and redemption. Therefore, as it is written: "Let him who boasts boast in the Lord."

John 12:20–36   There were some Greeks among those who went up to Jerusalem to worship at the Feast of the Passover. They came to Philip, who was from Bethsaida in Galilee, with a request. "Sir," they said, "we would like to see Jesus." Philip went to tell Andrew; Andrew and Philip in turn told Jesus.

Jesus replied, "The hour has come for the Son of Man to be glorified. I tell you the truth, unless a grain of wheat falls to the ground and dies, it remains only a single seed. But if it dies, it produces many seeds. The man who loves his life will lose it, while the man who hates his life in this world will keep it for eternal life. Whoever serves me must follow me; and where I am, my servant also will be. My Father will honour the one who serves me.

"Now my heart is troubled, and what shall I say? 'Father, save me from this hour'? No, it was for this very reason I came to this hour. Father, glorify your name!"

Then a voice came from heaven, "I have glorified it, and will glorify it again." The crowd that was there and heard it said it had thundered; others said an angel had spoken to him.

Jesus said, "This voice was for your benefit, not mine. Now is the time for judgment on this world; now the prince of this world will be driven out. But I, when I am lifted up from the earth, will draw all people to myself." He said this to show the kind of death he was going to die.

The crowd spoke up, "We have heard from the Law that the Christ will remain for ever, so how can you say, 'The Son of Man must be lifted up'? Who is this 'Son of Man'?"

Then Jesus told them, "You are going to have the light just a little while longer. Walk while you have the light, before darkness overtakes you. Those who walk in the dark do not know where they are going. Put your trust in the light while you have it, so that you may become children of light." When he had finished speaking, Jesus left and hid himself from them.

Wednesday of Holy Week

(Readings for Years A, B, C are the same)

Isaiah 50:4–9a   The Sovereign Lord has given me an instructed tongue, to know the word that sustains the weary.

He wakens me morning by morning,
    wakens my ear to listen like one being taught.
The Sovereign Lord has opened my ears,
    and I have not been rebellious;
    I have not drawn back.
I offered my back to those who beat me,
    my cheeks to those who pulled out my beard;
I did not hide my face
    from mocking and spitting.
Because the Sovereign Lord helps me,
    I will not be disgraced.
Therefore have I set my face like flint,
    and I know I will not be put to shame.
He who vindicates me is near.
    Who then will bring charges against me?
    Let us face each other!
Who are accusers?
    Let them confront me!
It is the Sovereign Lord who helps me.

Psalm 70

Hasten, O God, to save me;
    O Lord, come quickly to help me.
May those who seek my life
    be put to shame and confusion;
may all who desire my ruin
    be turned back in disgrace.
May those who say to me, "Aha! Aha!"
    turn back because of their shame.
But may all who seek you
    rejoice and be glad in you;
may those who love your salvation always say,
    "Let God be exalted!"

Yet I am poor and needy;
    come quickly to me, O God.
You are my help and my deliverer;
    O Lord, do not delay.

Hebrews 12:1–3 Since we are surrounded by such a great cloud of witnesses, let us throw off everything that hinders and the sin that so easily entangles, and let us run with perseverance the race marked out for us. Let us fix our eyes on Jesus, the author and perfecter of our faith, who for the joy set before him endured the cross, scorning its shame, and sat down at the right hand of the throne of God. Consider him who endured such opposition from sinful men, so that you will not grow weary and lose heart.

John 13:21–32 Jesus was troubled in spirit and testified, "I tell you the truth, one of you is going to betray me."

His disciples stared at one another, at a loss to know which of them he
meant. One of them, the disciple whom Jesus loved, was reclining next to
him. Simon Peter motioned to this disciple and said, "Ask him which one he
means."

Leaning back against Jesus, he asked him, "Lord, who is it?"

Jesus answered, "It is the one to whom I will give this piece of bread
when I have dipped it in the dish." Then, dipping the piece of bread, he gave
it to Judas Iscariot, son of Simon. As soon as Judas took the bread, Satan
entered into him.

"What you are about to do, do quickly," Jesus told him, but no-one at the
meal understood why Jesus said this to him. Since Judas had charge of the
money, some thought Jesus was telling him to buy what was needed for the
Feast, or to give something to the poor. As soon as Judas had taken the
bread, he went out. And it was night.

When he was gone, Jesus said, "Now is the Son of Man glorified and God
is glorified in him. If God is glorified in him, God will glorify the Son in himself, and will glorify him at once."

GOSPEL

Maundy Thursday

(Readings for Years A, B, C are the same)

Exodus 12:1–4 [5–10] 11–14   The LORD said to Moses and Aaron in Egypt,
"This month is to be for you the first month, the first month of your year.
Tell the whole community of Israel that on the tenth day of this month each
man is to take a lamb for his family, one for each household. If any household is too small for a whole lamb, they must share one with their nearest
neighbour, having taken into account the number of people there are. You
are to determine the amount of lamb needed in accordance with what each
person will eat. [The animals you choose must be year–old males without
defect, and you may take them from the sheep or the goats. Take care of
them until the fourteenth day of the month, when all the people of the community of Israel must slaughter them at twilight. Then they are to take
some of the blood and put it on the sides and tops of the door-frames of the
houses where they eat the lambs. That same night they are to eat the meat
roasted over the fire, along with bitter herbs, and bread made without
yeast. Do not eat the meat raw or cooked in water, but roast it over the fire
– head, legs and inner parts. Do not leave any of it till morning; if some is
left till morning, you must burn it.] This is how you are to eat it: with your
cloak tucked into your belt, your sandals on your feet and your staff in your
hand. Eat it in haste; it is the LORD's Passover.

"On that same night I will pass through Egypt and strike down every
firstborn – both people and animals – and I will bring judgment on all the
gods of Egypt. I am the LORD. The blood will be a sign for you on the houses
where you are; and when I see the blood, I will pass over you. No destructive plague will touch you when I strike Egypt.

"This is a day you are to commemorate; for the generations to come you
shall celebrate it as a festival to the LORD – a lasting ordinance."

FIRST READING

Psalm 116:1–2, 12–19*   I love the Lord, for he heard my voice;
  he heard my cry for mercy.
Because he turned his ear to me,
  I will call on him as long as I live.

How can I repay the Lord
  for all his goodness to me?
I will lift up the cup of salvation
  and call on the name of the Lord.
I will fulfil my vows to the Lord
  in the presence of all his people.

Precious in the sight of the Lord
  is the death of his saints.
O Lord, truly I am your servant;
  I am your servant, the son of your maidservant;
  you have freed me from my chains.

I will sacrifice a thank-offering to you
  and call on the name of the Lord.
I will fulfil my vows to the Lord
  in the presence of all his people,
in the courts of the house of the Lord –
  in your midst, O Jerusalem.

Praise the Lord.

(margin: PSALM)

1 Corinthians 11:23–26   I received from the Lord what I also passed on to you: The Lord Jesus, on the night he was betrayed, took bread, and when he had given thanks, he broke it and said, "This is my body, which is for you; do this in remembrance of me." In the same way, after supper he took the cup, saying, "This cup is the new covenant in my blood; do this, whenever you drink it, in remembrance of me." For whenever you eat this bread and drink this cup, you proclaim the Lord's death until he comes.

(margin: SECOND READING)

John 13:1–17, 31b–35   It was just before the Passover Feast. Jesus knew that the time had come for him to leave this world and go to the Father. Having loved his own who were in the world, he now showed them the full extent of his love.

 The evening meal was being served, and the devil had already prompted Judas Iscariot, son of Simon, to betray Jesus. Jesus knew that the Father had put all things under his power, and that he had come from God and was returning to God; so he got up from the meal, took off his outer clothing, and wrapped a towel round his waist. After that, he poured water into a basin and began to wash his disciples' feet, drying them with the towel that was wrapped round him.

 He came to Simon Peter, who said to him, "Lord, are you going to wash my feet?"

 Jesus replied, "You do not realise now what I am doing, but later you will understand."

(margin: GOSPEL)

"No," said Peter, "you shall never wash my feet."

Jesus answered, "Unless I wash you, you have no part with me."

"Then, Lord," Simon Peter replied, "not just my feet but my hands and my head as well!"

Jesus answered, "A person who has had a bath needs only to wash his feet; his whole body is clean. And you are clean, though not every one of you." For he knew who was going to betray him, and that was why he said not every one was clean.

When he had finished washing their feet, he put on his clothes and returned to his place. "Do you understand what I have done for you?" he asked them. "You call me 'Teacher' and 'Lord', and rightly so, for that is what I am. Now that I, your Lord and Teacher, have washed your feet, you also should wash one another's feet. I have set you an example that you should do as I have done for you. I tell you the truth, no servant is greater than his master, nor is a messenger greater than the one who sent him. Now that you know these things, you will be blessed if you do them.

"Now is the Son of Man glorified and God is glorified in him. If God is glorified in him, God will glorify the Son in himself, and will glorify him at once.

"My children, I will be with you only a little longer. You will look for me, and just as I told the Jews, so I tell you now: Where I am going, you cannot come.

"A new command I give you: Love one another. As I have loved you, so you must love one another. By this all men will know that you are my disciples, if you love one another."

Good Friday

(Readings for Years A, B, C are the same)

Isaiah 52:13 – 53:12

> See, my servant will act wisely;
> > he will be raised and lifted up and highly exalted.
> Just as there were many who were appalled at him –
> > his appearance was so disfigured beyond that of any man
> > and his form marred beyond human likeness –
> so will he sprinkle many nations,
> > and kings will shut their mouths because of him.
> For what they were not told, they will see,
> > and what they have not heard, they will understand.
>
> Who has believed our message
> > and to whom has the arm of the LORD been revealed?
> He grew up before him like a tender shoot,
> > and like a root out of dry ground.
> He had no beauty or majesty to attract us to him,
> > nothing in his appearance that we should desire him.

FIRST READING

He was despised and rejected by men,
a man of sorrows, and familiar with suffering.
Like one from whom men hide their faces
he was despised, and we esteemed him not.

Surely he took up our infirmities
and carried our sorrows,
yet we considered him stricken by God,
smitten by him, and afflicted.
But he was pierced for our transgressions,
he was crushed for our iniquities;
the punishment that brought us peace was upon him,
and by his wounds we are healed.
We all, like sheep, have gone astray,
each of us has turned to our own way;
and the LORD has laid on him
the iniquity of us all.

He was oppressed and afflicted,
yet he did not open his mouth;
he was led like a lamb to the slaughter,
and as a sheep before her shearers is silent,
so he did not open his mouth.
By oppression and judgment he was taken away.
And who can speak of his descendants?
For he was cut off from the land of the living;
for the transgression of my people he was stricken.
He was assigned a grave with the wicked,
and with the rich in his death,
though he had done no violence,
nor was any deceit in his mouth.

Yet it was the LORD's will to crush him and cause him
to suffer,
and though the LORD makes his life a guilt offering,
he will see his offspring and prolong his days,
and the will of the LORD will prosper in his hand.
After the suffering of his soul,
he will see the light of life and be satisfied;
by his knowledge my righteous servant will justify
many,
and he will bear their iniquities.
Therefore I will give him a portion among the great,
and he will divide the spoils with the strong,
because he poured out his life unto death,
and was numbered with the transgressors.
For he bore the sin of many,
and made intercession for the transgressors.

Psalm 22*   My God, my God, why have you forsaken me?

    Why are you so far from saving me,
        so far from the words of my groaning?
    O my God, I cry out by day, but you do not answer,
        by night, and am not silent.

    Yet you are enthroned as the Holy One;
        you are the praise of Israel.
    In you our fathers put their trust;
        they trusted and you delivered them.
    They cried to you and were saved;
        in you they trusted and were not disappointed.

    But I am a worm and not a man,
        scorned by men and despised by the people.
    All who see me mock me;
        they hurl insults, shaking their heads:
    "He trusts in the LORD;
        let the LORD rescue him.
    Let him deliver him,
        since he delights in him."

    Yet you brought me out of the womb;
        you made me trust in you
        even at my mother's breast.
    From birth I was cast upon you;
        from my mother's womb you have been my God.
    Do not be far from me,
        for trouble is near
        and there is no-one to help.

    Many bulls surround me;
        strong bulls of Bashan encircle me.
    Roaring lions tearing their prey
        open their mouths wide against me.
    I am poured out like water,
        and all my bones are out of joint.
    My heart has turned to wax;
        it has melted away within me.
    My strength is dried up like a potsherd,
        and my tongue sticks to the roof of my mouth;
        you lay me in the dust of death.
    Dogs have surrounded me;
        a band of evil men has encircled me,
        they have pierced my hands and my feet.
    I can count all my bones;
        people stare and gloat over me.
    They divide my garments among them
        and cast lots for my clothing.

But you, O LORD, be not far off;
  O my Strength, come quickly to help me.
Deliver my life from the sword,
  my precious life from the power of the dogs.
Rescue me from the mouth of the lions;
  save me from the horns of the wild oxen.

I will declare your name to my brothers;
  in the congregation I will praise you.
You who fear the LORD, praise him!
  All you descendants of Jacob, honour him!
  Revere him, all you descendants of Israel!
For he has not despised or disdained
  the suffering of the afflicted one;
he has not hidden his face from him
  but has listened to his cry for help.

From you comes the theme of my praise in the great assembly;
  before those who fear you will I fulfil my vows.
The poor will eat and be satisfied;
  they who seek the LORD will praise him –
  may your hearts live for ever!
All the ends of the earth
  will remember and turn to the LORD,
and all the families of the nations
  will bow down before him,
for dominion belongs to the LORD
  and he rules over the nations.

All the rich of the earth will feast and worship;
  all who go down to the dust will kneel before him –
  those who cannot keep themselves alive.
Posterity will serve him;
  future generations will be told about the LORD.
They will proclaim his righteousness
  to a people yet unborn –
  for he has done it.

Alternative second readings

Either **Hebrews 10:16–25**   The Holy Spirit says:

"This is the covenant I will make with them
  after that time, says the Lord.
I will put my laws in their hearts,
  and I will write them on their minds."

Then he adds:

"Their sins and lawless acts
  I will remember no more."

And where these have been forgiven, there is no longer any sacrifice for sin.

SECOND READING

Therefore, brothers, since we have confidence to enter the Most Holy Place by the blood of Jesus, by a new and living way opened for us through the curtain, that is, his body, and since we have a great priest over the house of God, let us draw near to God with a sincere heart in full assurance of faith, having our hearts sprinkled to cleanse us from a guilty conscience and having our bodies washed with pure water. Let us hold unswervingly to the hope we profess, for he who promised is faithful. And let us consider how we may spur one another on towards love and good deeds. Let us not give up meeting together, as some are in the habit of doing, but let us encourage one another – and all the more as you see the Day approaching.

or **Hebrews 4:14–16; 5:7–9** Since we have a great high priest who has gone S R through the heavens, Jesus the Son of God, let us hold firmly to the faith we E E profess. For we do not have a high priest who is unable to sympathise with C A our weaknesses, but we have one who has been tempted in every way, just O D as we are – yet was without sin. Let us then approach the throne of grace N I with confidence, so that we may receive mercy and find grace to help us in D N our time of need.   G

During the days of Jesus' life on earth, he offered up prayers and petitions with loud cries and tears to the one who could save him from death, and he was heard because of his reverent submission. Although he was a son, he learned obedience from what he suffered and, once made perfect, he became the source of eternal salvation for all who obey him.

John 18:1 – 19:42 When Jesus had finished praying, he left with his disciples G and crossed the Kidron Valley. On the other side there was an olive grove, O and he and his disciples went into it.   S

Now Judas, who betrayed him, knew the place, because Jesus had often P met there with his disciples. So Judas came to the grove, guiding a detach- E ment of soldiers and some officials from the chief priests and Pharisees. L They were carrying torches, lanterns and weapons.

Jesus, knowing all that was going to happen to him, went out and asked them, "Who is it you want?"

"Jesus of Nazareth," they replied.

"I am he," Jesus said. (And Judas the traitor was standing there with them.) When Jesus said, "I am he," they drew back and fell to the ground.

Again he asked them, "Who is it you want?"

And they said, "Jesus of Nazareth."

"I told you that I am he," Jesus answered. "If you are looking for me, then let these men go." This happened so that the words he had spoken would be fulfilled: "I have not lost one of those you gave me."

Then Simon Peter, who had a sword, drew it and struck the high priest's servant, cutting off his right ear. (The servant's name was Malchus.)

Jesus commanded Peter, "Put your sword away! Shall I not drink the cup the Father has given me?"

Then the detachment of soldiers with its commander and the Jewish officials arrested Jesus. They bound him and brought him first to Annas, who was the father-in-law of Caiaphas, the high priest that year. Caiaphas was the one who had advised the Jews that it would be good if one man died for the people.

Simon Peter and another disciple were following Jesus. Because this disciple was known to the high priest, he went with Jesus into the high priest's courtyard, but Peter had to wait outside at the door. The other disciple, who was known to the high priest, came back, spoke to the girl on duty there and brought Peter in.

"You are not one of his disciples, are you?" the girl at the door asked Peter.

He replied, "I am not."

It was cold, and the servants and officials stood round a fire they had made to keep warm. Peter also was standing with them, warming himself.

Meanwhile, the high priest questioned Jesus about his disciples and his teaching.

"I have spoken openly to the world," Jesus replied. "I always taught in synagogues or at the temple, where all the Jews come together. I said nothing in secret. Why question me? Ask those who heard me. Surely they know what I said."

When Jesus said this, one of the officials near by struck him in the face. "Is this the way you answer the high priest?" he demanded.

"If I said something wrong," Jesus replied, "testify as to what is wrong. But if I spoke the truth, why did you strike me?" Then Annas sent him, still bound, to Caiaphas the high priest.

As Simon Peter stood warming himself, he was asked, "You are not one of his disciples, are you?"

He denied it, saying, "I am not."

One of the high priest's servants, a relative of the man whose ear Peter had cut off, challenged him, "Didn't I see you with him in the olive grove?" Again Peter denied it, and at that moment a cock began to crow.

Then the Jews led Jesus from Caiaphas to the palace of the Roman governor. By now it was early morning, and to avoid ceremonial uncleanness the Jews did not enter the palace; they wanted to be able to eat the Passover. So Pilate came out to them and asked, "What charges are you bringing against this man?"

"If he were not a criminal," they replied, "we would not have handed him over to you."

Pilate said, "Take him yourselves and judge him by your own law."

"But we have no right to execute anyone," the Jews objected. This happened so that the words Jesus had spoken indicating the kind of death he was going to die would be fulfilled.

Pilate then went back inside the palace, summoned Jesus and asked him, "Are you the king of the Jews?"

"Is that your own idea," Jesus asked, "or did others talk to you about me?"

"Am I a Jew?" Pilate replied. "It was your people and your chief priests who handed you over to me. What is it you have done?"

Jesus said, "My kingdom is not of this world. If it were, my servants would fight to prevent my arrest by the Jews. But now my kingdom is from another place."

"You are a king, then!" said Pilate.

Jesus answered, "You are right in saying I am a king. In fact, for this reason I was born, and for this I came into the world, to testify to the truth. Everyone on the side of truth listens to me."

"What is truth?" Pilate asked. With this he went out again to the Jews and said, "I find no basis for a charge against him. But it is your custom for me to release to you one prisoner at the time of the Passover. Do you want me to release 'the king of the Jews'?"

They shouted back, "No, not him! Give us Barabbas!" Now Barabbas had taken part in a rebellion.

Then Pilate took Jesus and had him flogged. The soldiers twisted together a crown of thorns and put it on his head. They clothed him in a purple robe and went up to him again and again, saying, "Hail, king of the Jews!" And they struck him in the face.

Once more Pilate came out and said to the Jews, "Look, I am bringing him out to you to let you know that I find no basis for a charge against him." When Jesus came out wearing the crown of thorns and the purple robe, Pilate said to them, "Here is the man!"

As soon as the chief priests and their officials saw him, they shouted, "Crucify! Crucify!"

But Pilate answered, "You take him and crucify him. As for me, I find no basis for a charge against him."

The Jews insisted, "We have a law, and according to that law he must die, because he claimed to be the Son of God."

When Pilate heard this, he was even more afraid, and he went back inside the palace. "Where do you come from?" he asked Jesus, but Jesus gave him no answer. "Do you refuse to speak to me?" Pilate said. "Don't you realise I have power either to free you or to crucify you?"

Jesus answered, "You would have no power over me if it were not given to you from above. Therefore the one who handed me over to you is guilty of a greater sin."

From then on, Pilate tried to set Jesus free, but the Jews kept shouting, "If you let this man go, you are no friend of Caesar. Anyone who claims to be a king opposes Caesar."

When Pilate heard this, he brought Jesus out and sat down on the judge's seat at a place known as the Stone Pavement (which in Aramaic is Gabbatha). It was the day of Preparation of Passover Week, about the sixth hour.

"Here is your king," Pilate said to the Jews.

But they shouted, "Take him away! Take him away! Crucify him!"

"Shall I crucify your king?" Pilate asked.

"We have no king but Caesar," the chief priests answered.

Finally Pilate handed him over to them to be crucified.

So the soldiers took charge of Jesus. Carrying his own cross, he went out to the place of the Skull (which in Aramaic is called Golgotha). Here they crucified him, and with him two others – one on each side and Jesus in the middle.

Pilate had a notice prepared and fastened to the cross. It read: JESUS OF NAZARETH, THE KING OF THE JEWS. Many of the Jews read this sign, for the place where Jesus was crucified was near the city, and the sign was written in Aramaic, Latin and Greek. The chief priests of the Jews protested to Pilate, "Do not write 'The King of the Jews', but that this man claimed to be king of the Jews."

Pilate answered, "What I have written, I have written."

When the soldiers crucified Jesus, they took his clothes, dividing them into four shares, one for each of them, with the undergarment remaining. This garment was seamless, woven in one piece from top to bottom.

"Let's not tear it," they said to one another. "Let's decide by lot who will get it."

This happened that the scripture might be fulfilled which said,

"They divided my garments among them
and cast lots for my clothing."

So this is what the soldiers did.

Near the cross of Jesus stood his mother, his mother's sister, Mary the wife of Clopas, and Mary Magdalene. When Jesus saw his mother there, and the disciple whom he loved standing near by, he said to his mother, "Dear woman, here is your son," and to the disciple, "Here is your mother." From that time on, this disciple took her into his home.

Later, knowing that all was now completed, and so that the Scripture would be fulfilled, Jesus said, "I am thirsty." A jar of wine vinegar was there, so they soaked a sponge in it, put the sponge on a stalk of the hyssop plant, and lifted it to Jesus' lips. When he had received the drink, Jesus said, "It is finished." With that, he bowed his head and gave up his spirit.

Now it was the day of Preparation, and the next day was to be a special Sabbath. Because the Jews did not want the bodies left on the crosses during the Sabbath, they asked Pilate to have the legs broken and the bodies taken down. The soldiers therefore came and broke the legs of the first man who had been crucified with Jesus, and then those of the other. But when they came to Jesus and found that he was already dead, they did not break his legs. Instead, one of the soldiers pierced Jesus' side with a spear, bringing a sudden flow of blood and water. The man who saw it has given testimony, and his testimony is true. He knows that he tells the truth, and he testifies so that you also may believe. These things happened so that the scripture would be fulfilled: "Not one of his bones will be broken," and, as another scripture says, "They will look on the one they have pierced."

Later, Joseph of Arimathea asked Pilate for the body of Jesus. Now Joseph was a disciple of Jesus, but secretly because he feared the Jews. With Pilate's permission, he came and took the body away. He was accompanied by Nicodemus, the man who earlier had visited Jesus at night.

Nicodemus brought a mixture of myrrh and aloes, about seventy-five pounds. Taking Jesus' body, the two of them wrapped it, with the spices, in strips of linen. This was in accordance with Jewish burial customs. At the place where Jesus was crucified, there was a garden, and in the garden a new tomb, in which no-one had ever been laid. Because it was the Jewish day of Preparation and since the tomb was near by, they laid Jesus there.

Easter Eve

(Readings for Years A, B, C are the same and are for use at services other than the Easter Vigil)

Alternative first readings

Either **Job 14:1–14** "Man born of woman   F
 is of few days and full of trouble.   I
He springs up like a flower and withers away;   R
 like a fleeting shadow, he does not endure.   S
Do you fix your eye on such a one?   T
 Will you bring him before you for judgment?
Who can bring what is pure from the impure?   R
 No-one!   E
Man's days are determined;   A
 you have decreed the number of his months   D
 and have set limits he cannot exceed.   I
So look away from him and let him alone,   N
 till he has put in his time like a hired man.   G

"At least there is hope for a tree:
 If it is cut down, it will sprout again,
 and its new shoots will not fail.
Its roots may grow old in the ground
 and its stump die in the soil,
yet at the scent of water it will bud
 and put forth shoots like a plant.
But man dies and is laid low;
 he breathes his last and is no more.
As water disappears from the sea
 or a river bed becomes parched and dry,
so man lies down and does not rise;
 till the heavens are no more, men will not awake
 or be roused from their sleep.

"If only you would hide me in the grave
 and conceal me till your anger has passed!
If only you would set me a time
 and then remember me!
If a man dies, will he live again?
 All the days of my hard service
 I will wait for my renewal to come."

or Lamentations 3:1–9, 19–24

I am the man who has seen affliction
  by the rod of his wrath.
He has driven me away and made me walk
  in darkness rather than light;
indeed, he has turned his hand against me
  again and again, all day long.

He has made my skin and my flesh grow old
  and has broken my bones.
He has besieged me and surrounded me
  with bitterness and hardship.
He has made me dwell in darkness
  like those long dead.

He has walled me in so that I cannot escape;
  he has weighed me down with chains.
Even when I call out or cry for help,
  he shuts out my prayer.
He has barred my way with blocks of stone;
  he has made my paths crooked.

I remember my affliction and my wandering,
  the bitterness and the gall.
I well remember them,
  and my soul is downcast within me.
Yet this I call to mind
  and therefore I have hope:

Because of the LORD's great love we are not consumed,
  for his compassions never fail.
They are new every morning;
  great is your faithfulness.
I say to myself, "The LORD is my portion;
  therefore I will wait for him."

FIRST READING

Psalm 31:1–4, 15–16*

In you, O LORD, I have taken refuge;
  let me never be put to shame;
  deliver me in your righteousness.
Turn your ear to me,
  come quickly to my rescue;
be my rock of refuge,
  a strong fortress to save me.
Since you are my rock and my fortress,
  for the sake of your name lead and guide me.
Free me from the trap that is set for me,
  for you are my refuge.

My times are in your hands;
  deliver me from my enemies
  and from those who pursue me.

PSALM

Let your face shine on your servant;
save me in your unfailing love.

1 Peter 4:1–8   Since Christ suffered in his body, arm yourselves also with the S
same attitude, because he who has suffered in his body is done with sin. As E
a result, he does not live the rest of his earthly life for evil human desires, C
but rather for the will of God. For you have spent enough time in the past O
doing what pagans choose to do – living in debauchery, lust, drunkenness, N
orgies, carousing and detestable idolatry. They think it strange that you do D
not plunge with them into the same flood of dissipation, and they heap
abuse on you. But they will have to give account to him who is ready to R
judge the living and the dead. For this is the reason the gospel was E
preached even to those who are now dead, so that they might be judged A
according to men in regard to the body, but live according to God in regard D
to the spirit.   I

The end of all things is near. Therefore be clear minded and self-con- N
trolled so that you can pray. Above all, love each other deeply, because love G
covers over a multitude of sins.

Alternative Gospels

Either **Matthew 27:57–66**   As evening approached, there came a rich man G
from Arimathea, named Joseph, who had himself become a disciple of O
Jesus. Going to Pilate, he asked for Jesus' body, and Pilate ordered that it S
be given to him. Joseph took the body, wrapped it in a clean linen cloth, and P
placed it in his own new tomb that he had cut out of the rock. He rolled a big E
stone in front of the entrance to the tomb and went away. Mary Magdalene L
and the other Mary were sitting there opposite the tomb.

The next day, the one after Preparation Day, the chief priests and the
Pharisees went to Pilate. "Sir," they said, "we remember that while he was
still alive that deceiver said, 'After three days I will rise again.' So give the
order for the tomb to be made secure until the third day. Otherwise, his disciples may come and steal the body and tell the people that he has been
raised from the dead. This last deception will be worse than the first."

"Take a guard," Pilate answered. "Go, make the tomb as secure as you
know how." So they went and made the tomb secure by putting a seal on the
stone and posting the guard.

or **John 19:38–42**   Joseph of Arimathea asked Pilate for the body of Jesus. G
Now Joseph was a disciple of Jesus, but secretly because he feared the Jews. O
With Pilate's permission, he came and took the body away. He was accom- S
panied by Nicodemus, the man who earlier had visited Jesus at night. P
Nicodemus brought a mixture of myrrh and aloes, about seventy-five E
pounds. Taking Jesus' body, the two of them wrapped it, with the spices, in L
strips of linen. This was in accordance with Jewish burial customs. At the
place where Jesus was crucified, there was a garden, and in the garden a
new tomb, in which no-one had ever been laid. Because it was the Jewish
day of Preparation and since the tomb was near by, they laid Jesus there.

EASTER

Easter Vigil

A selection of Old Testament readings and a reading from Romans for Years A, B, C appear here, as well as the Gospel for Year A (p 112). A minimum of three Old Testament readings (including Exodus 14) must be used, together with the Romans reading and the Gospel which is different for each year. Years B and C have their own Gospel.

Genesis 1:1 – 2.4a   In the beginning God created the heavens and the earth. Now the earth was formless and empty, darkness was over the surface of the deep, and the Spirit of God was hovering over the waters.

And God said, "Let there be light," and there was light. God saw that the light was good, and he separated the light from the darkness. God called the light "day", and the darkness he called "night". And there was evening, and there was morning – the first day.

And God said, "Let there be an expanse between the waters to separate water from water." So God made the expanse and separated the water under the expanse from the water above it. And it was so. God called the expanse "sky". And there was evening, and there was morning – the second day.

And God said, "Let the water under the sky be gathered to one place, and let dry ground appear." And it was so. God called the dry ground "land", and the gathered waters he called "seas". And God saw that it was good.

Then God said, "Let the land produce vegetation: seed-bearing plants and trees on the land that bear fruit with seed in it, according to their various kinds." And it was so. The land produced vegetation: plants bearing seed according to their kinds and trees bearing fruit with seed in it according to their kinds. And God saw that it was good. And there was evening, and there was morning – the third day.

And God said, "Let there be lights in the expanse of the sky to separate the day from the night, and let them serve as signs to mark seasons and days and years, and let them be lights in the expanse of the sky to give light on the earth." And it was so. God made two great lights – the greater light to govern the day and the lesser light to govern the night. He also made the stars. God set them in the expanse of the sky to give light on the earth, to govern the day and the night, and to separate light from darkness. And God saw that it was good. And there was evening, and there was morning – the fourth day.

And God said, "Let the water teem with living creatures, and let birds fly above the earth across the expanse of the sky." So God created the great creatures of the sea and every living and moving thing with which the water teems, according to their kinds, and every winged bird according to its kind. And God saw that it was good. God blessed them and said, "Be fruitful and increase in number and fill the water in the seas, and let the birds increase on the earth." And there was evening, and there was morning – the fifth day.

And God said, "Let the land produce living creatures according to their kinds: livestock, creatures that move along the ground, and wild animals, each according to its kind." And it was so. God made the wild animals according to their kinds, the livestock according to their kinds, and all the creatures that move along the ground according to their kinds. And God saw that it was good.

Then God said, "Let us make man in our image, in our likeness, and let them rule over the fish of the sea and the birds of the air, over the livestock, over all the earth, and over all the creatures that move along the ground."

So God created man
   in his own image,
in the image of God
   he created him;
male and female
   he created them.

God blessed them and said to them, "Be fruitful and increase in number; fill the earth and subdue it. Rule over the fish of the sea and the birds of the air and over every living creature that moves on the ground."

Then God said, "I give you every seed-bearing plant on the face of the whole earth and every tree that has fruit with seed in it. They will be yours for food. And to all the beasts of the earth and all the birds of the air and all the creatures that move on the ground – everything that has the breath of life in it – I give every green plant for food." And it was so.

God saw all that he had made, and it was very good. And there was evening, and there was morning – the sixth day.

Thus the heavens and the earth were completed in all their vast array. By the seventh day God had finished the work he had been doing; so on the seventh day he rested from all his work. And God blessed the seventh day and made it holy, because on it he rested from all the work of creating that he had done.

This is the account of the heavens and the earth when they were created.

Psalm 136:1–9, 23–26   Give thanks to the LORD, for he is good.
     His love endures for ever.
   Give thanks to the God of gods.
     His love endures for ever.
   Give thanks to the Lord of lords:
     His love endures for ever.
   to him who alone does great wonders,
     His love endures for ever.
   who by his understanding made the heavens,
     His love endures for ever.
   who spread out the earth upon the waters,
     His love endures for ever.
   who made the great lights –
     His love endures for ever.

the sun to govern the day,
> *His love endures for ever.*

the moon and stars to govern the night;
> *His love endures for ever.*

to the One who remembered us in our low estate
> *His love endures for ever.*

and freed us from our enemies,
> *His love endures for ever.*

and who gives food to every creature.
> *His love endures for ever.*

Give thanks to the God of heaven.
> *His love endures for ever.*

Genesis 7:1–5, 11–18; 8:6–18; 9:8–13   The Lord said to Noah, "Go into the ark, you and your whole family, because I have found you righteous in this generation. Take with you seven of every kind of clean animal, a male and its mate, and two of every kind of unclean animal, a male and its mate, and also seven of every kind of bird, male and female, to keep their various kinds alive throughout the earth. Seven days from now I will send rain on the earth for forty days and forty nights, and I will wipe from the face of the earth every living creature I have made."

And Noah did all that the Lord commanded him.

In the six hundredth year of Noah's life, on the seventeenth day of the second month – on that day all the springs of the great deep burst forth, and the floodgates of the heavens were opened. And rain fell on the earth for forty days and forty nights.

On that very day Noah and his sons, Shem, Ham and Japheth, together with his wife and the wives of his three sons, entered the ark. They had with them every wild animal according to its kind, all livestock according to their kinds, every creature that moves along the ground according to its kind and every bird according to its kind, everything with wings. Pairs of all creatures that have the breath of life in them came to Noah and entered the ark. The animals going in were male and female of every living thing, as God had commanded Noah. Then the Lord shut him in.

For forty days the flood kept coming on the earth, and as the waters increased they lifted the ark high above the earth. The waters rose and increased greatly on the earth, and the ark floated on the surface of the water.

After forty days Noah opened the window he had made in the ark and sent out a raven, and it kept flying back and forth until the water had dried up from the earth. Then he sent out a dove to see if the water had receded from the surface of the ground. But the dove could find no place to set its feet because there was water over all the surface of the earth; so it returned to Noah in the ark. He reached out his hand and took the dove and brought it back to himself in the ark. He waited seven more days and again sent out the dove from the ark. When the dove returned to him in the evening, there in its beak was a freshly plucked olive leaf! Then Noah knew that the water had receded from the earth. He waited seven more days and sent the dove out again, but this time it did not return to him.

By the first day of the first month of Noah's six hundred and first year, the water had dried up from the earth. Noah then removed the covering from the ark and saw that the surface of the ground was dry. By the twenty-seventh day of the second month the earth was completely dry.

Then God said to Noah, "Come out of the ark, you and your wife and your sons and their wives. Bring out every kind of living creature that is with you – the birds, the animals, and all the creatures that move along the ground – so they can multiply on the earth and be fruitful and increase in number upon it."

So Noah came out, together with his sons and his wife and his sons' wives.

Then God said to Noah and to his sons with him: "I now establish my covenant with you and with your descendants after you and with every living creature that was with you – the birds, the livestock and all the wild animals, all those that came out of the ark with you – every living creature on earth. I establish my covenant with you: Never again will all life be cut off by the waters of a flood; never again will there be a flood to destroy the earth."

And God said, "This is the sign of the covenant I am making between me and you and every living creature with you, a covenant for all generations to come: I have set my rainbow in the clouds, and it will be the sign of the covenant between me and the earth."

Psalm 46 God is our refuge and strength,
> an ever–present help in trouble.
Therefore we will not fear, though the earth give way
> and the mountains fall into the heart of the sea,
though its waters roar and foam
> and the mountains quake with their surging.

There is a river whose streams make glad the city of God,
> the holy place where the Most High dwells.
God is within her, she will not fall;
> God will help her at break of day.
Nations are in uproar, kingdoms fall;
> he lifts his voice, the earth melts.

The Lord Almighty is with us;
> the God of Jacob is our fortress.

Come and see the works of the Lord,
> the desolations he has brought on the earth.
He makes wars cease to the ends of the earth;
> he breaks the bow and shatters the spear,
> he burns the shields with fire.
"Be still, and know that I am God;
> I will be exalted among the nations,
> I will be exalted in the earth."

The LORD Almighty is with us;
the God of Jacob is our fortress.

Genesis 22:1–18 God tested Abraham. He said to him, "Abraham!"

"Here I am," he replied.

Then God said, "Take your son, your only son, Isaac, whom you love, and go to the region of Moriah. Sacrifice him there as a burnt offering on one of the mountains I will tell you about."

Early the next morning Abraham got up and saddled his donkey. He took with him two of his servants and his son Isaac. When he had cut enough wood for the burnt offering, he set out for the place God had told him about. On the third day Abraham looked up and saw the place in the distance. He said to his servants, "Stay here with the donkey while I and the boy go over there. We will worship and then we will come back to you."

Abraham took the wood for the burnt offering and placed it on his son Isaac, and he himself carried the fire and the knife. As the two of them went on together, Isaac spoke up and said to his father Abraham, "Father?"

"Yes, my son?" Abraham replied.

"The fire and wood are here," Isaac said, "but where is the lamb for the burnt offering?"

Abraham answered, "God himself will provide the lamb for the burnt offering, my son." And the two of them went on together.

When they reached the place God had told him about, Abraham built an altar there and arranged the wood on it. He bound his son Isaac and laid him on the altar, on top of the wood. Then he reached out his hand and took the knife to slay his son. But the angel of the LORD called out to him from heaven, "Abraham! Abraham!"

"Here I am," he replied.

"Do not lay a hand on the boy," he said. "Do not do anything to him. Now I know that you fear God, because you have not withheld from me your son, your only son."

Abraham looked up and there in a thicket he saw a ram caught by its horns. He went over and took the ram and sacrificed it as a burnt offering instead of his son. So Abraham called that place The LORD Will Provide. And to this day it is said, "On the mountain of the LORD it will be provided."

The angel of the LORD called to Abraham from heaven a second time and said, "I swear by myself, declares the LORD, that because you have done this and have not withheld your son, your only son, I will surely bless you and make your descendants as numerous as the stars in the sky and as the sand on the seashore. Your descendants will take possession of the cities of their enemies, and through your offspring all nations on earth will be blessed, because you have obeyed me."

Psalm 16 Keep me safe, O God,
for in you I take refuge.

I said to the LORD, "You are my LORD;

apart from you I have no good thing."
As for the saints who are in the land,
    they are the glorious ones in whom is all my delight.
The sorrows of those will increase
    who run after other gods.
I will not pour out their libations of blood
    or take up their names on my lips.

Lord, you have assigned me my portion and my cup;
    you have made my lot secure.
The boundary lines have fallen for me in pleasant places;
    surely I have a delightful inheritance.

I will praise the Lord, who counsels me;
    even at night my heart instructs me.
I have set the Lord always before me.
    Because he is at my right hand,
    I shall not be shaken.

Therefore my heart is glad and my tongue rejoices;
    my body also will rest secure,
because you will not abandon me to the grave,
    nor will you let your Holy One see decay.
You have made known to me the path of life;
    you will fill me with joy in your presence,
    with eternal pleasures at your right hand.

Exodus 14:10–31; 15:20–21   As Pharaoh approached the Israelites by the sea, the Israelites looked up, and there were the Egyptians, marching after them. They were terrified and cried out to the Lord. They said to Moses, "Was it because there were no graves in Egypt that you brought us to the desert to die? What have you done to us by bringing us out of Egypt? Didn't we say to you in Egypt, 'Leave us alone; let us serve the Egyptians'? It would have been better for us to serve the Egyptians than to die in the desert!"

Moses answered the people, "Do not be afraid. Stand firm and you will see the deliverance the Lord will bring you today. The Egyptians you see today you will never see again. The Lord will fight for you; you need only to be still."

Then the Lord said to Moses, "Why are you crying out to me? Tell the Israelites to move on. Raise your staff and stretch out your hand over the sea to divide the water so that the Israelites can go through the sea on dry ground. I will harden the hearts of the Egyptians so that they will go in after them. And I will gain glory through Pharaoh and all his army, through his chariots and his horsemen. The Egyptians will know that I am the Lord when I gain glory through Pharaoh, his chariots and his horsemen."

Then the angel of God, who had been travelling in front of Israel's army, withdrew and went behind them. The pillar of cloud also moved from in front and stood behind them, coming between the armies of Egypt and

Israel. Throughout the night the cloud brought darkness to the one side and light to the other; so neither went near the other all night long.

Then Moses stretched out his hand over the sea, and all that night the LORD drove the sea back with a strong east wind and turned it into dry land. The waters were divided, and the Israelites went through the sea on dry ground, with a wall of water on their right and on their left.

The Egyptians pursued them, and all Pharaoh's horses and chariots and horsemen followed them into the sea. During the last watch of the night the LORD looked down from the pillar of fire and cloud at the Egyptian army and threw it into confusion. He made the wheels of their chariots come off so that they had difficulty driving. And the Egyptians said, "Let's get away from the Israelites! The LORD is fighting for them against Egypt."

Then the LORD said to Moses, "Stretch out your hand over the sea so that the waters may flow back over the Egyptians and their chariots and horsemen." Moses stretched out his hand over the sea, and at daybreak the sea went back to its place. The Egyptians were fleeing towards it, and the LORD swept them into the sea. The water flowed back and covered the chariots and horsemen – the entire army of Pharaoh that had followed the Israelites into the sea. Not one of them survived.

But the Israelites went through the sea on dry ground, with a wall of water on their right and on their left. That day the LORD saved Israel from the hands of the Egyptians, and Israel saw the Egyptians lying dead on the shore. And when the Israelites saw the great power the LORD displayed against the Egyptians, the people feared the LORD and put their trust in him and in Moses his servant.

Then Miriam the prophetess, Aaron's sister, took a tambourine in her hand, and all the women followed her, with tambourines and dancing. Miriam sang to them:

"Sing to the LORD,
   for he is highly exalted.
The horse and its rider
   he has hurled into the sea."

Canticle:

Exodus 15:1b–13, 17–18   "I will sing to the LORD,
        for he is highly exalted.
     The horse and its rider
        he has hurled into the sea.
     The LORD is my strength and my song;
        he has become my salvation.
     He is my God, and I will praise him,
        my father's God, and I will exalt him.
     The LORD is a warrior;
        the LORD is his name.
     Pharaoh's chariots and his army
        he has hurled into the sea.

The best of Pharaoh's officers
  are drowned in the Red Sea.
The deep waters have covered them;
  they sank to the depths like a stone.

"Your right hand, O Lord,
  was majestic in power.
Your right hand, O Lord,
  shattered the enemy.
In the greatness of your majesty
  you threw down those who opposed you.
You unleashed your burning anger;
  it consumed them like stubble.
By the blast of your nostrils
  the waters piled up.
The surging waters stood firm like a wall;
  the deep waters congealed in the heart of the
    sea.

"The enemy boasted,
  'I will pursue, I will overtake them.
I will divide the spoils;
  I will gorge myself on them.
I will draw my sword
  and my hand will destroy them.'
But you blew with your breath,
  and the sea covered them.
They sank like lead
  in the mighty waters.

"Who among the gods is like you, O Lord?
  Who is like you –
    majestic in holiness,
    awesome in glory,
    working wonders?
You stretched out your right hand
  and the earth swallowed them.

"In your unfailing love you will lead
  the people you have redeemed.
In your strength you will guide them
  to your holy dwelling.
You will bring them in and plant them
  on the mountain of your inheritance –
the place, O Lord, you made for your dwelling,
  the sanctuary, O Lord, your hands established.
The Lord will reign
  for ever and ever."

Isaiah 55:1–11   "Come, all you who are thirsty,
    come to the waters;
and you who have no money,
    come, buy and eat!
Come, buy wine and milk
    without money and without cost.
Why spend money on what is not bread,
    and your labour on what does not satisfy?
Listen, listen to me, and eat what is good,
    and your soul will delight in the richest of fare.
Give ear and come to me;
    hear me, that your soul may live.
I will make an everlasting covenant with you,
    my faithful love promised to David.
See, I have made him a witness to the peoples,
    a leader and commander of the peoples.
Surely you will summon nations you know not,
    and nations that do not know you will hasten to you,
because of the LORD your God,
    the Holy One of Israel,
    for he has endowed you with splendour."

Seek the LORD while he may be found;
    call on him while he is near.
Let the wicked forsake his way
    and the evil man his thoughts.
Let him turn to the LORD, and he will have mercy on him,
    and to our God, for he will freely pardon.

"For my thoughts are not your thoughts,
    neither are your ways my ways,"
                                    declares the LORD.
"As the heavens are higher than the earth,
    so are my ways higher than your ways
    and my thoughts than your thoughts.
As the rain and the snow
    come down from heaven,
and do not return to it
    without watering the earth
and making it bud and flourish,
    so that it yields seed for the sower and bread for the
        eater,
so is my word that goes out from my mouth:
    It will not return to me empty,
but will accomplish what I desire
    and achieve the purpose for which I sent it."

Canticle:

Isaiah 12:2–6

"Surely God is my salvation;
    I will trust and not be afraid.
The LORD, the LORD, is my strength and my song;
    he has become my salvation."
With joy you will draw water
    from the wells of salvation.

In that day you will say:

"Give thanks to the LORD, call on his name;
    make known among the nations what he has
        done,
    and proclaim that his name is exalted.
Sing to the LORD, for he has done glorious things;
    let this be known to all the world.
Shout aloud and sing for joy, people of Zion,
    for great is the Holy One of Israel among you."

Either **Baruch 3:9–15, 32 – 4:4**

or **Proverbs 8:1–8, 19–21; 9:4b–6**

Does not wisdom call out?
    Does not understanding raise her voice?
On the heights along the way,
    where the paths meet, she takes her stand;
beside the gates leading into the city,
    at the entrances, she cries aloud:
"To you, O men, I call out;
    I raise my voice to all mankind.
You who are simple, gain prudence;
    you who are foolish, gain understanding.
Listen, for I have worthy things to say;
    I open my lips to speak what is right.
My mouth speaks what is true,
    for my lips detest wickedness.
All the words of my mouth are just;
    none of them is crooked or perverse.

"My fruit is better than fine gold;
    what I yield surpasses choice silver.
I walk in the way of righteousness,
    along the paths of justice,
bestowing wealth on those who love me
    and making their treasuries full."

She says to those who lack judgment,
"Come, eat my food
    and drink the wine I have mixed.
Leave your simple ways and you will live;
    walk in the way of understanding."

Psalm 19   The heavens declare the glory of God;
　　　　　the skies proclaim the work of his hands.
Day after day they pour forth speech;
　　　　　night after night they display knowledge.
There is no speech or language
　　　　　where their voice is not heard.
Their voice goes out into all the earth,
　　　　　their words to the ends of the world.

In the heavens he has pitched a tent for the sun,
　　　　　which is like a bridegroom coming forth from his pavilion,
　　　　　like a champion rejoicing to run his course.
It rises at one end of the heavens
　　　　　and makes its circuit to the other;
　　　　　nothing is hidden from its heat.

The law of the LORD is perfect,
　　　　　reviving the soul.
The statutes of the LORD are trustworthy,
　　　　　making wise the simple.
The precepts of the LORD are right,
　　　　　giving joy to the heart.
The commands of the LORD are radiant,
　　　　　giving light to the eyes.
The fear of the LORD is pure,
　　　　　enduring for ever.
The ordinances of the LORD are sure
　　　　　and altogether righteous.
They are more precious than gold,
　　　　　than much pure gold;
they are sweeter than honey,
　　　　　than honey from the comb.
By them is your servant warned;
　　　　　in keeping them there is great reward.

Who can discern their errors?
　　　　　Forgive my hidden faults.
Keep your servant also from wilful sins;
　　　　　may they not rule over me.
Then will I be blameless,
　　　　　innocent of great transgression.

May the words of my mouth and the meditation of my heart
　　　　　be pleasing in your sight,
　　　　　O LORD, my Rock and my Redeemer.

Ezekiel 36:24–28   This is what the Sovereign LORD says: 'I will take you out of
the nations; I will gather you from all the countries and bring you back into
your own land. I will sprinkle clean water on you, and you will be clean; I

will cleanse you from all your impurities and from all your idols. I will give you a new heart and put a new spirit in you; I will remove from you your heart of stone and give you a heart of flesh. And I will put my Spirit in you and move you to follow my decrees and be careful to keep my laws. You will live in the land I gave your forefathers; you will be my people, and I will be your God.'

Psalms 42, 43   As the deer pants for streams of water,
    so my soul pants for you, O God.
My soul thirsts for God, for the living God.
    When can I go and meet with God?
My tears have been my food
    day and night,
while men say to me all day long,
    "Where is your God?"
These things I remember
    as I pour out my soul:
how I used to go with the multitude,
    leading the procession to the house of God,
with shouts of joy and thanksgiving
    among the festive throng.

Why are you downcast, O my soul?
    Why so disturbed within me?
Put your hope in God,
    for I will yet praise him,
    my Saviour and my God.

My soul is downcast within me;
    therefore I will remember you
from the land of the Jordan,
    the heights of Hermon – from Mount Mizar.
Deep calls to deep
    in the roar of your waterfalls;
all your waves and breakers
    have swept over me.

By day the LORD directs his love,
    at night his song is with me –
    a prayer to the God of my life.
I say to God my Rock,
    "Why have you forgotten me?
Why must I go about mourning,
    oppressed by the enemy?"
My bones suffer mortal agony
    as my foes taunt me,
saying to me all day long,
    "Where is your God?"

Why are you downcast, O my soul?
　　Why so disturbed within me?
Put your hope in God,
　　for I will yet praise him,
　　my Saviour and my God.

Vindicate me, O God,
　　and plead my cause against an ungodly nation;
　　rescue me from deceitful and wicked men.
You are God my stronghold.
　　Why have you rejected me?
Why must I go about mourning,
　　oppressed by the enemy?
Send forth your light and your truth,
　　let them guide me;
let them bring me to your holy mountain,
　　to the place where you dwell.
Then will I go to the altar of God,
　　to God, my joy and my delight.
I will praise you with the harp,
　　O God, my God.

Why are you downcast, O my soul?
　　Why so disturbed within me?
Put your hope in God,
　　for I will yet praise him,
　　my Saviour and my God.

Ezekiel 37:1–14　　The hand of the Lord was upon me, and he brought me out by the Spirit of the Lord and set me in the middle of a valley; it was full of bones. He led me to and fro among them, and I saw a great many bones on the floor of the valley, bones that were very dry. He asked me, "Son of man, can these bones live?"

I said, "O Sovereign Lord, you alone know."

Then he said to me, "Prophesy to these bones and say to them, 'Dry bones, hear the word of the Lord! This is what the Sovereign Lord says to these bones: I will make breath enter you, and you will come to life. I will attach tendons to you and make flesh come upon you and cover you with skin; I will put breath in you, and you will come to life. Then you will know that I am the Lord.'"

So I prophesied as I was commanded. And as I was prophesying, there was a noise, a rattling sound, and the bones came together, bone to bone. I looked, and tendons and flesh appeared on them and skin covered them, but there was no breath in them.

Then he said to me, "Prophesy to the breath; prophesy, son of man, and say to it, 'This is what the Sovereign Lord says: Come from the four winds, O breath, and breathe into these slain, that they may live.'" So I prophesied as he commanded me, and breath entered them; they came to life and stood up on their feet – a vast army.

Then he said to me: "Son of man, these bones are the whole house of Israel. They say, 'Our bones are dried up and our hope is gone; we are cut off.' Therefore prophesy and say to them: 'This is what the Sovereign LORD says: O my people, I am going to open your graves and bring you up from them; I will bring you back to the land of Israel. Then you, my people, will know that I am the LORD, when I open your graves and bring you up from them. I will put my Spirit in you and you will live, and I will settle you in your own land. Then you will know that I the LORD have spoken, and I have done it, declares the LORD.'"

Psalm 143 O LORD, hear my prayer,
  listen to my cry for mercy;
 in your faithfulness and righteousness
  come to my relief.
Do not bring your servant into judgment,
 for no-one living is righteous before you.

The enemy pursues me,
 he crushes me to the ground;
he makes me dwell in darkness
 like those long dead.
So my spirit grows faint within me;
 my heart within me is dismayed.

I remember the days of long ago;
 I meditate on all your works
 and consider what your hands have done.
I spread out my hands to you;
 my soul thirsts for you like a parched land.

Answer me quickly, O LORD;
 my spirit fails.
Do not hide your face from me
 or I will be like those who go down to the pit.
Let the morning bring me word of your unfailing love,
 for I have put my trust in you.
Show me the way I should go,
 for to you I lift up my soul.
Rescue me from my enemies, O LORD,
 for I hide myself in you.
Teach me to do your will,
 for you are my God;
may your good Spirit
 lead me on level ground.

For your name's sake, O LORD, preserve my life;
 in your righteousness, bring me out of trouble.

In your unfailing love, silence my enemies;
    destroy all my foes,
      for I am your servant.

Zephaniah 3:14–20   Sing, O Daughter of Zion;
    shout aloud, O Israel!
Be glad and rejoice with all your heart,
    O Daughter of Jerusalem!
The LORD has taken away your punishment,
    he has turned back your enemy.
The LORD, the King of Israel, is with you;
    never again will you fear any harm.
On that day they will say to Jerusalem,
    "Do not fear, O Zion;
    do not let your hands hang limp.
The LORD your God is with you,
    he is mighty to save.
He will take great delight in you,
    he will quiet you with his love,
    he will rejoice over you with singing."

"The sorrows for the appointed feasts
    I will remove from you;
    they are a burden and a reproach to you.
At that time I will deal
    with all who oppressed you;
I will rescue the lame
    and gather those who have been scattered.
I will give them praise and honour
    in every land where they were put to shame.
At that time I will gather you;
    at that time I will bring you home.
I will give you honour and praise
    among all the peoples of the earth
when I restore your fortunes
    before your very eyes,"
                    says the LORD.

Psalm 98   Sing to the LORD a new song,
    for he has done marvellous things;
his right hand and his holy arm
    have worked salvation for him.
The LORD has made his salvation known
    and revealed his righteousness to the nations.
He has remembered his love
    and his faithfulness to the house of Israel;
all the ends of the earth have seen
    the salvation of our God.

Shout for joy to the Lord, all the earth,
   burst into jubilant song with music;
make music to the Lord with the harp,
   with the harp and the sound of singing,
with trumpets and the blast of the ram's horn –
   shout for joy before the Lord, the King.

Let the sea resound, and everything in it,
   the world, and all who live in it.
Let the rivers clap their hands,
   let the mountains sing together for joy;
let them sing before the Lord,
   for he comes to judge the earth.
He will judge the world in righteousness
   and the peoples with equity.

Romans 6:3–11   Don't you know that all of us who were baptised into Christ Jesus were baptised into his death? We were therefore buried with him through baptism into death in order that, just as Christ was raised from the dead through the glory of the Father, we too may live a new life.

If we have been united with him like this in his death, we will certainly also be united with him in his resurrection. For we know that our old self was crucified with him so that the body of sin might be done away with, that we should no longer be slaves to sin – because anyone who has died has been freed from sin.

Now if we died with Christ, we believe that we will also live with him. For we know that since Christ was raised from the dead, he cannot die again; death no longer has mastery over him. The death he died, he died to sin once for all; but the life he lives, he lives to God.

In the same way, count yourselves dead to sin but alive to God in Christ Jesus.

Psalm 114   When Israel came out of Egypt,
         the house of Jacob from a people of foreign tongue,
      Judah became God's sanctuary,
         Israel his dominion.

      The sea looked and fled,
         the Jordan turned back;
      the mountains skipped like rams,
         the hills like lambs.

      Why was it, O sea, that you fled,
         O Jordan, that you turned back,
      you mountains, that you skipped like rams,
         you hills, like lambs?

      Tremble, O earth, at the presence of the Lord,
         at the presence of the God of Jacob,
      who turned the rock into a pool,
         the hard rock into springs of water.

Years B and C have their own Gospel see p 279 and p 437 respectively

Matthew 28:1–10 After the Sabbath, at dawn on the first day of the week, G
Mary Magdalene and the other Mary went to look at the tomb.   O

There was a violent earthquake, for an angel of the Lord came down S
from heaven and, going to the tomb, rolled back the stone and sat on it. His P
appearance was like lightning, and his clothes were white as snow. The E
guards were so afraid of him that they shook and became like dead men.   L

The angel said to the women, "Do not be afraid, for I know that you are
looking for Jesus, who was crucified. He is not here; he has risen, just as he Y
said. Come and see the place where he lay. Then go quickly and tell his dis- E
ciples: 'He has risen from the dead and is going ahead of you into Galilee. A
There you will see him.' Now I have told you."   R

So the women hurried away from the tomb, afraid yet filled with joy, and
ran to tell his disciples. Suddenly Jesus met them. "Greetings," he said. A
They came to him, clasped his feet and worshipped him. Then Jesus said to
them, "Do not be afraid. Go and tell my brothers to go to Galilee; there they
will see me."

Easter Day

Acts 10:34–43 should be read as either the first or second reading

Alternative first readings

Either **Acts 10:34–43** Peter began to speak: "I now realise how true it is that F
God does not show favouritism but accepts men from every nation who I
fear him and do what is right. You know the message God sent to the peo- R
ple of Israel, telling the good news of peace through Jesus Christ, who is S
Lord of all. You know what has happened throughout Judea, beginning in T
Galilee after the baptism that John preached – how God anointed Jesus of
Nazareth with the Holy Spirit and power, and how he went around doing R
good and healing all who were under the power of the devil, because God E
was with him.   A

"We are witnesses of everything he did in the country of the Jews and in D
Jerusalem. They killed him by hanging him on a tree, but God raised him I
from the dead on the third day and caused him to be seen. He was not seen N
by all the people, but by witnesses whom God had already chosen – by us G
who ate and drank with him after he rose from the dead. He commanded us
to preach to the people and to testify that he is the one whom God appointed
as judge of the living and the dead. All the prophets testify about him that
everyone who believes in him receives forgiveness of sins through his
name."

         F R

or **Jeremiah 31:1–6** "At that time," declares the LORD, "I will be the God of all I E
the clans of Israel, and they will be my people."   R A
This is what the LORD says: S D

> "The people who survive the sword   T I
> will find favour in the desert;   N
> I will come to give rest to Israel."   G

The LORD appeared to us in the past, saying:

> "I have loved you with an everlasting love;
> I have drawn you with loving-kindness.
> I will build you up again
> and you will be rebuilt, O Virgin Israel.
> Again you will take up your tambourines
> and go out to dance with the joyful.
> Again you will plant vineyards
> on the hills of Samaria;
> the farmers will plant them
> and enjoy their fruit.
> There will be a day when watchmen cry out
> on the hills of Ephraim,
> 'Come, let us go up to Zion,
> to the LORD our God.'"

Psalm 118:1–2,
14–24★

Give thanks to the LORD, for he is good;
his love endures for ever.

Let Israel say:
"His love endures for ever."

The LORD is my strength and my song;
he has become my salvation.

Shouts of joy and victory
resound in the tents of the righteous:
"The LORD's right hand has done mighty things!
The LORD's right hand is lifted high;
the LORD's right hand has done mighty things!"

I will not die but live,
and will proclaim what the LORD has done.
The LORD has chastened me severely,
but he has not given me over to death.

Open for me the gates of righteousness;
I will enter and give thanks to the LORD.
This is the gate of the LORD
through which the righteous may enter.
I will give you thanks, for you answered me;
you have become my salvation.

The stone the builders rejected
has become the capstone;
the LORD has done this,
and it is marvellous in our eyes.
This is the day the LORD has made;
let us rejoice and be glad in it.

Alternative second readings

Either **Colossians 3:1–4** Since you have been raised with Christ, set your hearts on things above, where Christ is seated at the right hand of God. Set your minds on things above, not on earthly things. For you died, and your life is now hidden with Christ in God. When Christ, who is your life, appears, then you also will appear with him in glory.

or **Acts 10:34–43** Peter began to speak: "I now realise how true it is that God does not show favouritism but accepts men from every nation who fear him and do what is right. You know the message God sent to the people of Israel, telling the good news of peace through Jesus Christ, who is Lord of all. You know what has happened throughout Judea, beginning in Galilee after the baptism that John preached – how God anointed Jesus of Nazareth with the Holy Spirit and power, and how he went around doing good and healing all who were under the power of the devil, because God was with him.

"We are witnesses of everything he did in the country of the Jews and in Jerusalem. They killed him by hanging him on a tree, but God raised him from the dead on the third day and caused him to be seen. He was not seen by all the people, but by witnesses whom God had already chosen – by us who ate and drank with him after he rose from the dead. He commanded us to preach to the people and to testify that he is the one whom God appointed as judge of the living and the dead. All the prophets testify about him that everyone who believes in him receives forgiveness of sins through his name."

Alternative Gospels

Either **John 20:1–18** Early on the first day of the week, while it was still dark, Mary Magdalene went to the tomb and saw that the stone had been removed from the entrance. So she came running to Simon Peter and the other disciple, the one Jesus loved, and said, "They have taken the Lord out of the tomb, and we don't know where they have put him!"

So Peter and the other disciple started for the tomb. Both were running, but the other disciple outran Peter and reached the tomb first. He bent over and looked in at the strips of linen lying there but did not go in. Then Simon Peter, who was behind him, arrived and went into the tomb. He saw the strips of linen lying there, as well as the burial cloth that had been around Jesus' head. The cloth was folded up by itself, separate from the linen. Finally the other disciple, who had reached the tomb first, also went inside. He saw and believed. (They still did not understand from Scripture that Jesus had to rise from the dead.)

Then the disciples went back to their homes, but Mary stood outside the tomb crying. As she wept, she bent over to look into the tomb and saw two angels in white, seated where Jesus' body had been, one at the head and the other at the foot.

They asked her, "Woman, why are you crying?"

"They have taken my Lord away," she said, "and I don't know where they have put him." At this, she turned round and saw Jesus standing there, but she did not realise that it was Jesus.

"Woman," he said, "why are you crying? Who is it you are looking for?"

Thinking he was the gardener, she said, "Sir, if you have carried him away, tell me where you have put him, and I will get him."

Jesus said to her, "Mary."

She turned towards him and cried out in Aramaic, "Rabboni!" (which means Teacher).

Jesus said, "Do not hold on to me, for I have not yet returned to the Father. Go instead to my brothers and tell them, 'I am returning to my Father and your Father, to my God and your God.'"

Mary Magdalene went to the disciples with the news: "I have seen the Lord!" And she told them that he had said these things to her.

or **Matthew 28:1–10**   After the Sabbath, at dawn on the first day of the week, Mary Magdalene and the other Mary went to look at the tomb.

There was a violent earthquake, for an angel of the Lord came down from heaven and, going to the tomb, rolled back the stone and sat on it. His appearance was like lightning, and his clothes were white as snow. The guards were so afraid of him that they shook and became like dead men.

The angel said to the women, "Do not be afraid, for I know that you are looking for Jesus, who was crucified. He is not here; he has risen, just as he said. Come and see the place where he lay. Then go quickly and tell his disciples: 'He has risen from the dead and is going ahead of you into Galilee. There you will see him.' Now I have told you."

So the women hurried away from the tomb, afraid yet filled with joy, and ran to tell his disciples. Suddenly Jesus met them. "Greetings," he said. They came to him, clasped his feet and worshipped him. Then Jesus said to them, "Do not be afraid. Go and tell my brothers to go to Galilee; there they will see me."

Old Testament Readings for Sundays in Eastertide

*For those who require an Old Testament reading on the Sundays in Easter-
tide, provision is made as following. If used, the reading from Acts must be
used as the second reading.*

Easter 2

Exodus 14:10–31; 15:20–21   As Pharaoh approached the Israelites by the sea,
the Israelites looked up, and there were the Egyptians, marching after
them. They were terrified and cried out to the LORD. They said to Moses,
"Was it because there were no graves in Egypt that you brought us to the
desert to die? What have you done to us by bringing us out of Egypt? Didn't
we say to you in Egypt, 'Leave us alone; let us serve the Egyptians'? It
would have been better for us to serve the Egyptians than to die in the
desert!"

Moses answered the people, "Do not be afraid. Stand firm and you will
see the deliverance the LORD will bring you today. The Egyptians you see
today you will never see again. The LORD will fight for you; you need only to
be still."

Then the LORD said to Moses, "Why are you crying out to me? Tell
the Israelites to move on. Raise your staff and stretch out your hand
over the sea to divide the water so that the Israelites can go through the
sea on dry ground. I will harden the hearts of the Egyptians so that they
will go in after them. And I will gain glory through Pharaoh and all his
army, through his chariots and his horsemen. The Egyptians will know that
I am the LORD when I gain glory through Pharaoh, his chariots and his
horsemen."

Then the angel of God, who had been travelling in front of Israel's army,
withdrew and went behind them. The pillar of cloud also moved from in
front and stood behind them, coming between the armies of Egypt and
Israel. Throughout the night the cloud brought darkness to the one side and
light to the other; so neither went near the other all night long.

Then Moses stretched out his hand over the sea, and all that night the
LORD drove the sea back with a strong east wind and turned it into dry land.
The waters were divided, and the Israelites went through the sea on dry
ground, with a wall of water on their right and on their left.

The Egyptians pursued them, and all Pharaoh's horses and chariots and
horsemen followed them into the sea. During the last watch of the night the
LORD looked down from the pillar of fire and cloud at the Egyptian army
and threw it into confusion. He made the wheels of their chariots come off
so that they had difficulty driving. And the Egyptians said, "Let's get away
from the Israelites! The LORD is fighting for them against Egypt."

Then the LORD said to Moses, "Stretch out your hand over the sea so that
the waters may flow back over the Egyptians and their chariots and horsemen." Moses stretched out his hand over the sea, and at daybreak the sea
went back to its place. The Egyptians were fleeing towards it, and the LORD

swept them into the sea. The water flowed back and covered the chariots and horsemen – the entire army of Pharaoh that had followed the Israelites into the sea. Not one of them survived.

But the Israelites went through the sea on dry ground, with a wall of water on their right and on their left. That day the LORD saved Israel from the hands of the Egyptians, and Israel saw the Egyptians lying dead on the shore. And when the Israelites saw the great power the LORD displayed against the Egyptians, the people feared the LORD and put their trust in him and in Moses his servant.

Then Miriam the prophetess, Aaron's sister, took a tambourine in her hand, and all the women followed her, with tambourines and dancing. Miriam sang to them:

> "Sing to the LORD,
>> for he is highly exalted.
> The horse and its rider
>> he has hurled into the sea."

Easter 3

Zephaniah 3:14–20

> Sing, O Daughter of Zion;
>> shout aloud, O Israel!
> Be glad and rejoice with all your heart,
>> O Daughter of Jerusalem!
> The LORD has taken away your punishment,
>> he has turned back your enemy.
> The LORD, the King of Israel, is with you;
>> never again will you fear any harm.
> On that day they will say to Jerusalem,
>> "Do not fear, O Zion;
>> do not let your hands hang limp.
> The LORD your God is with you,
>> he is mighty to save.
> He will take great delight in you,
>> he will quiet you with his love,
>> he will rejoice over you with singing."

> "The sorrows for the appointed feasts
>> I will remove from you;
>> they are a burden and a reproach to you.
> At that time I will deal
>> with all who oppressed you;
> I will rescue the lame
>> and gather those who have been scattered.
> I will give them praise and honour
>> in every land where they were put to shame.
> At that time I will gather you;
>> at that time I will bring you home.

I will give you honour and praise
    among all the peoples of the earth
when I restore your fortunes
    before your very eyes,"
                    says the LORD.

Easter 4

Genesis 7 The LORD said to Noah, "Go into the ark, you and your whole family, because I have found you righteous in this generation. Take with you seven of every kind of clean animal, a male and its mate, and two of every kind of unclean animal, a male and its mate, and also seven of every kind of bird, male and female, to keep their various kinds alive throughout the earth. Seven days from now I will send rain on the earth for forty days and forty nights, and I will wipe from the face of the earth every living creature I have made."

And Noah did all that the LORD commanded him.

Noah was six hundred years old when the floodwaters came on the earth. And Noah and his sons and his wife and his sons' wives entered the ark to escape the waters of the flood. Pairs of clean and unclean animals, of birds and of all creatures that move along the ground, male and female, came to Noah and entered the ark, as God had commanded Noah. And after the seven days the floodwaters came on the earth.

In the six hundredth year of Noah's life, on the seventeenth day of the second month – on that day all the springs of the great deep burst forth, and the floodgates of the heavens were opened. And rain fell on the earth for forty days and forty nights.

On that very day Noah and his sons, Shem, Ham and Japheth, together with his wife and the wives of his three sons, entered the ark. They had with them every wild animal according to its kind, all livestock according to their kinds, every creature that moves along the ground according to its kind and every bird according to its kind, everything with wings. Pairs of all creatures that have the breath of life in them came to Noah and entered the ark. The animals going in were male and female of every living thing, as God had commanded Noah. Then the LORD shut him in.

For forty days the flood kept coming on the earth, and as the waters increased they lifted the ark high above the earth. The waters rose and increased greatly on the earth, and the ark floated on the surface of the water. They rose greatly on the earth, and all the high mountains under the entire heavens were covered. The waters rose and covered the mountains to a depth of more than twenty feet. Every living thing that moved on the earth perished – birds, livestock, wild animals, all the creatures that swarm over the earth, and all mankind. Everything on dry land that had the breath of life in its nostrils died. Every living thing on the face of the earth was wiped out; men and animals and the creatures that move along the ground and the birds of the air were wiped from the earth. Only Noah was left, and those with him in the ark.

The waters flooded the earth for a hundred and fifty days.

Easter 5

Genesis 8: 1–19   God remembered Noah and all the wild animals and the live-stock that were with him in the ark, and he sent a wind over the earth, and the waters receded. Now the springs of the deep and the floodgates of the heavens had been closed, and the rain had stopped falling from the sky. The water receded steadily from the earth. At the end of the hundred and fifty days the water had gone down, and on the seventeenth day of the seventh month the ark came to rest on the mountains of Ararat. The waters continued to recede until the tenth month, and on the first day of the tenth month the tops of the mountains became visible.

After forty days Noah opened the window he had made in the ark and sent out a raven, and it kept flying back and forth until the water had dried up from the earth. Then he sent out a dove to see if the water had receded from the surface of the ground. But the dove could find no place to set its feet because there was water over all the surface of the earth; so it returned to Noah in the ark. He reached out his hand and took the dove and brought it back to himself in the ark. He waited seven more days and again sent out the dove from the ark. When the dove returned to him in the evening, there in its beak was a freshly plucked olive leaf! Then Noah knew that the water had receded from the earth. He waited seven more days and sent the dove out again, but this time it did not return to him.

By the first day of the first month of Noah's six hundred and first year, the water had dried up from the earth. Noah then removed the covering from the ark and saw that the surface of the ground was dry. By the twenty-seventh day of the second month the earth was completely dry.

Then God said to Noah, "Come out of the ark, you and your wife and your sons and their wives. Bring out every kind of living creature that is with you – the birds, the animals, and all the creatures that move along the ground – so they can multiply on the earth and be fruitful and increase in number upon it."

So Noah came out, together with his sons and his wife and his sons' wives. All the animals and all the creatures that move along the ground and all the birds – everything that moves on the earth – came out of the ark, one kind after another.

Easter 6

Genesis 8:20–9:17   Noah built an altar to the LORD and, taking some of all the clean animals and clean birds, he sacrificed burnt offerings on it. The LORD smelled the pleasing aroma and said in his heart: "Never again will I curse the ground because of man, even though every inclination of his heart is evil from childhood. And never again will I destroy all living creatures, as I have done.

> "As long as the earth endures,
>> seedtime and harvest,
>> cold and heat,
>> summer and winter,

day and night
will never cease."

Then God blessed Noah and his sons, saying to them, "Be fruitful and increase in number and fill the earth. The fear and dread of you will fall upon all the beasts of the earth and all the birds of the air, upon every creature that moves along the ground, and upon all the fish of the sea; they are given into your hands. Everything that lives and moves will be food for you. Just as I gave you the green plants, I now give you everything.

"But you must not eat meat that has its lifeblood still in it. And for your lifeblood I will surely demand an accounting. I will demand an accounting from every animal. And from each man, too, I will demand an accounting for the life of his fellow man.

"Whoever sheds the blood of man,
   by men shall his blood be shed;
for in the image of God
   has God made man.

As for you, be fruitful and increase in number; multiply on the earth and increase upon it."

Then God said to Noah and to his sons with him: "I now establish my covenant with you and with your descendants after you and with every living creature that was with you – the birds, the livestock and all the wild animals, all those that came out of the ark with you – every living creature on earth. I establish my covenant with you: Never again will all life be cut off by the waters of a flood; never again will there be a flood to destroy the earth."

And God said, "This is the sign of the covenant I am making between me and you and every living creature with you, a covenant for all generations to come: I have set my rainbow in the clouds, and it will be the sign of the covenant between me and the earth. Whenever I bring clouds over the earth and the rainbow appears in the clouds, I will remember my covenant between me and you and all living creatures of every kind. Never again will the waters become a flood to destroy all life. Whenever the rainbow appears in the clouds, I will see it and remember the everlasting covenant between God and all living creatures of every kind on the earth."

So God said to Noah, "This is the sign of the covenant I have established between me and all life on the earth."

Easter 7

Ezekiel 36:24–28   This is what the Sovereign LORD says: "I will take you out of the nations; I will gather you from all the countries and bring you back into your own land. I will sprinkle clean water on you, and you will be clean; I will cleanse you from all your impurities and from all your idols. I will give you a new heart and put a new spirit in you; I will remove from you your heart of stone and give you a heart of flesh. And I will put my Spirit in you and move you to follow my decrees and be careful to keep my laws. You will live in the land I gave your forefathers; you will be my people, and I will be your God."

Second Sunday of Easter

Acts 2:14a, 22–32   Peter stood up with the Eleven, raised his voice and F
addressed the crowd: I

"Men of Israel, listen to this: Jesus of Nazareth was a man accredited by R
God to you by miracles, wonders and signs, which God did among you S
through him, as you yourselves know. This man was handed over to you by T
God's set purpose and foreknowledge; and you, with the help of wicked
men, put him to death by nailing him to the cross. But God raised him from R
the dead, freeing him from the agony of death, because it was impossible E
for death to keep its hold on him. David said about him: A

"'I saw the Lord always before me.   D
Because he is at my right hand,   I
I will not be shaken.   N
Therefore my heart is glad and my tongue rejoices;   G
my body also will live in hope,
because you will not abandon me to the grave,
nor will you let your Holy One see decay.
You have made known to me the paths of life;
you will fill me with joy in your presence.'

"Brothers, I can tell you confidently that the patriarch David died and
was buried, and his tomb is here to this day. But he was a prophet and knew
that God had promised him on oath that he would place one of his descendants on his throne. Seeing what was ahead, he spoke of the resurrection of
the Christ, that he was not abandoned to the grave, nor did his body see decay. God has raised this Jesus to life, and we are all witnesses of the fact."

Psalm 16   Keep me safe, O God,   P
for in you I take refuge.   S

I said to the LORD, "You are my LORD;   A
apart from you I have no good thing."   L
As for the saints who are in the land,   M
they are the glorious ones in whom is all my delight.
The sorrows of those will increase
who run after other gods.
I will not pour out their libations of blood
or take up their names on my lips.

LORD, you have assigned me my portion and my cup;
you have made my lot secure.
The boundary lines have fallen for me in pleasant places;
surely I have a delightful inheritance.

I will praise the LORD, who counsels me;
even at night my heart instructs me.
I have set the LORD always before me.
Because he is at my right hand,
I shall not be shaken.

Therefore my heart is glad and my tongue rejoices;
    my body also will rest secure,
because you will not abandon me to the grave,
    nor will you let your Holy One see decay.
You have made known to me the path of life;
    you will fill me with joy in your presence,
    with eternal pleasures at your right hand.

1 Peter 1:3–9 Praise be to the God and Father of our Lord Jesus Christ! In his great mercy he has given us new birth into a living hope through the resurrection of Jesus Christ from the dead, and into an inheritance that can never perish, spoil or fade – kept in heaven for you, who through faith are shielded by God's power until the coming of the salvation that is ready to be revealed in the last time. In this you greatly rejoice, though now for a little while you may have had to suffer grief in all kinds of trials. These have come so that your faith – of greater worth than gold, which perishes even though refined by fire – may be proved genuine and may result in praise, glory and honour when Jesus Christ is revealed. Though you have not seen him, you love him; and even though you do not see him now, you believe in him and are filled with an inexpressible and glorious joy, for you are receiving the goal of your faith, the salvation of your souls.

SECOND READING

John 20:19–31 On the evening of that first day of the week, when the disciples were together, with the doors locked for fear of the Jews, Jesus came and stood among them and said, "Peace be with you!" After he said this, he showed them his hands and side. The disciples were overjoyed when they saw the Lord.

Again Jesus said, "Peace be with you! As the Father has sent me, I am sending you." And with that he breathed on them and said, "Receive the Holy Spirit. If you forgive anyone his sins, they are forgiven; if you do not forgive them, they are not forgiven."

Now Thomas (called Didymus), one of the Twelve, was not with the disciples when Jesus came. So the other disciples told him, "We have seen the Lord!"

But he said to them, "Unless I see the nail marks in his hands and put my finger where the nails were, and put my hand into his side, I will not believe it."

A week later his disciples were in the house again, and Thomas was with them. Though the doors were locked, Jesus came and stood among them and said, "Peace be with you!" Then he said to Thomas, "Put your finger here; see my hands. Reach out your hand and put it into my side. Stop doubting and believe."

Thomas said to him, "My Lord and my God!"

Then Jesus told him, "Because you have seen me, you have believed; blessed are those who have not seen and yet have believed."

Jesus did many other miraculous signs in the presence of his disciples, which are not recorded in this book. But these are written that you may

GOSPEL

believe that Jesus is the Christ, the Son of God, and that by believing you may have life in his name.

Third Sunday of Easter

Acts 2:14a, 36–41   Peter stood up with the Eleven, raised his voice and addressed the crowd:

"Let all Israel be assured of this: God has made this Jesus, whom you crucified, both Lord and Christ."

When the people heard this, they were cut to the heart and said to Peter and the other apostles, "Brothers, what shall we do?"

Peter replied, "Repent and be baptised, every one of you, in the name of Jesus Christ for the forgiveness of your sins. And you will receive the gift of the Holy Spirit. The promise is for you and your children and for all who are far off – for all whom the Lord our God will call."

With many other words he warned them; and he pleaded with them, "Save yourselves from this corrupt generation." Those who accepted his message were baptised, and about three thousand were added to their number that day.

Psalm 116:1–4, 12–19*

I love the LORD, for he heard my voice;
    he heard my cry for mercy.
Because he turned his ear to me,
    I will call on him as long as I live.

The cords of death entangled me,
    the anguish of the grave came upon me;
    I was overcome by trouble and sorrow.
Then I called on the name of the LORD:
    "O LORD, save me!"

How can I repay the LORD
    for all his goodness to me?
I will lift up the cup of salvation
    and call on the name of the LORD.
I will fulfil my vows to the LORD
    in the presence of all his people.

Precious in the sight of the LORD
    is the death of his saints.
O LORD, truly I am your servant;
    I am your servant, the son of your maidservant;
    you have freed me from my chains.

I will sacrifice a thank-offering to you
    and call on the name of the LORD.
I will fulfil my vows to the LORD
    in the presence of all his people,
in the courts of the house of the LORD –
    in your midst, O Jerusalem.

Praise the LORD.

1 Peter 1:17–23 Since you call on a Father who judges each man's work S R impartially, live your lives as strangers here in reverent fear. For you E E know that it was not with perishable things such as silver or gold that you C A were redeemed from the empty way of life handed down to you from your O D forefathers, but with the precious blood of Christ, a lamb without blemish N I or defect. He was chosen before the creation of the world, but was D N revealed in these last times for your sake. Through him you believe in God, G who raised him from the dead and glorified him, and so your faith and hope are in God.

Now that you have purified yourselves by obeying the truth so that you have sincere love for your brothers, love one another deeply, from the heart. For you have been born again, not of perishable seed, but of imperishable, through the living and enduring word of God.

Luke 24:13–35 That same day two of the disciples were going to a village G called Emmaus, about seven miles from Jerusalem. They were talking O with each other about everything that had happened. As they talked and S discussed these things with each other, Jesus himself came up and walked P along with them; but they were kept from recognising him. E

He asked them, "What are you discussing together as you walk along?" L

They stood still, their faces downcast. One of them, named Cleopas, asked him, "Are you only a visitor to Jerusalem and do not know the things that have happened there in these days?"

"What things?" he asked.

"About Jesus of Nazareth," they replied. "He was a prophet, powerful in word and deed before God and all the people. The chief priests and our rulers handed him over to be sentenced to death, and they crucified him; but we had hoped that he was the one who was going to redeem Israel. And what is more, it is the third day since all this took place. In addition, some of our women amazed us. They went to the tomb early this morning but didn't find his body. They came and told us that they had seen a vision of angels, who said he was alive. Then some of our companions went to the tomb and found it just as the women had said, but him they did not see."

He said to them, "How foolish you are, and how slow of heart to believe all that the prophets have spoken! Did not the Christ have to suffer these things and then enter his glory?" And beginning with Moses and all the Prophets, he explained to them what was said in all the Scriptures concerning himself. As they approached the village to which they were going, Jesus acted as if he were going further. But they urged him strongly, "Stay with us, for it is nearly evening; the day is almost over." So he went in to stay with them.

When he was at the table with them, he took bread, gave thanks, broke it and began to give it to them. Then their eyes were opened and they recognised him, and he disappeared from their sight. They asked each other, "Were not our hearts burning within us while he talked with us on the road and opened the Scriptures to us?"

They got up and returned at once to Jerusalem. There they found the Eleven and those with them, assembled together and saying, "It is true! The Lord has risen and has appeared to Simon." Then the two told what had happened on the way, and how Jesus was recognised by them when he broke the bread.

Fourth Sunday of Easter

Acts 2:42–47   The believers devoted themselves to the apostles' teaching and to the fellowship, to the breaking of bread and to prayer. Everyone was filled with awe, and many wonders and miraculous signs were done by the apostles. All the believers were together and had everything in common. Selling their possessions and goods, they gave to anyone as he had need. Every day they continued to meet together in the temple courts. They broke bread in their homes and ate together with glad and sincere hearts, praising God and enjoying the favour of all the people. And the Lord added to their number daily those who were being saved.

F R
I E
R A
S D
T I
N
G

Psalm 23   The LORD is my shepherd, I shall not be in want.
    He makes me lie down in green pastures,
he leads me beside quiet waters,
    he restores my soul.
He guides me in paths of righteousness
    for his name's sake.
Even though I walk
    through the valley of the shadow of death,
I will fear no evil,
    for you are with me;
your rod and your staff,
    they comfort me.

You prepare a table before me
    in the presence of my enemies.
You anoint my head with oil;
    my cup overflows.
Surely goodness and love will follow me
    all the days of my life,
and I will dwell in the house of the LORD
    for ever.

P
S
A
L
M

1 Peter 2:19–25   It is commendable if a man bears up under the pain of unjust suffering because he is conscious of God. But how is it to your credit if you receive a beating for doing wrong and endure it? But if you suffer for doing good and you endure it, this is commendable before God. To this you were called, because Christ suffered for you, leaving you an example, that you should follow in his steps.

    "He committed no sin,
      and no deceit was found in his mouth."

S R
E E
C A
O D
N I
D N
G

When they hurled their insults at him, he did not retaliate; when he suffered, he made no threats. Instead, he entrusted himself to him who judges justly. He himself bore our sins in his body on the tree, so that we might die to sins and live for righteousness; by his wounds you have been healed. For you were like sheep going astray, but now you have returned to the Shepherd and Overseer of your souls.

John 10:1–10 Jesus said: "I tell you the truth, the man who does not enter the sheep pen by the gate, but climbs in by some other way, is a thief and a robber. The man who enters by the gate is the shepherd of his sheep. The watchman opens the gate for him, and the sheep listen to his voice. He calls his own sheep by name and leads them out. When he has brought out all his own, he goes on ahead of them, and his sheep follow him because they know his voice. But they will never follow a stranger; in fact, they will run away from him because they do not recognise a stranger's voice." Jesus used this figure of speech, but they did not understand what he was telling them.

Therefore Jesus said again, "I tell you the truth, I am the gate for the sheep. All who ever came before me were thieves and robbers, but the sheep did not listen to them. I am the gate; whoever enters through me will be saved. He will come in and go out, and find pasture. The thief comes only to steal and kill and destroy; I have come that they may have life, and have it to the full."

Fifth Sunday of Easter

Acts 7:55–60 Stephen, full of the Holy Spirit, looked up to heaven and saw the glory of God, and Jesus standing at the right hand of God. "Look," he said, "I see heaven open and the Son of Man standing at the right hand of God."

At this they covered their ears and, yelling at the top of their voices, they all rushed at him, dragged him out of the city and began to stone him. Meanwhile, the witnesses laid their clothes at the feet of a young man named Saul.

While they were stoning him, Stephen prayed, "Lord Jesus, receive my spirit." Then he fell on his knees and cried out, "Lord, do not hold this sin against them." When he had said this, he fell asleep.

Psalm 31:1–5, 15–16* In you, O LORD, I have taken refuge;
  let me never be put to shame;
    deliver me in your righteousness.
  Turn your ear to me,
    come quickly to my rescue;
  be my rock of refuge,
    a strong fortress to save me.
  Since you are my rock and my fortress,
    for the sake of your name lead and guide me.

Free me from the trap that is set for me,
for you are my refuge.
Into your hands I commit my spirit;
redeem me, O LORD, the God of truth.

My times are in your hands;
deliver me from my enemies
and from those who pursue me.
Let your face shine on your servant;
save me in your unfailing love.

1 Peter 2:2–10 Like newborn babies, crave pure spiritual milk, so that by it
you may grow up in your salvation, now that you have tasted that the Lord
is good.

As you come to him, the living Stone – rejected by men but chosen by
God and precious to him – you also, like living stones, are being built into a
spiritual house to be a holy priesthood, offering spiritual sacrifices acceptable to God through Jesus Christ. For in Scripture it says:

"See, I lay a stone in Zion,
a chosen and precious cornerstone,
and the one who trusts in him
will never be put to shame."

Now to you who believe, this stone is precious. But to those who do not
believe,

"The stone the builders rejected
has become the capstone,"

and,

"A stone that causes men to stumble
and a rock that makes them fall."

They stumble because they disobey the message – which is also what they
were destined for.

But you are a chosen people, a royal priesthood, a holy nation, a people
belonging to God, that you may declare the praises of him who called you
out of darkness into his wonderful light. Once you were not a people, but
now you are the people of God; once you had not received mercy, but now
you have received mercy.

John 14:1–14 Jesus said: "Do not let your hearts be troubled. Trust in God;
trust also in me. In my Father's house are many rooms; if it were not so, I
would have told you. I am going there to prepare a place for you. And if I go
and prepare a place for you, I will come back and take you to be with me
that you also may be where I am. You know the way to the place where I am
going."

Thomas said to him, "Lord, we don't know where you are going, so how
can we know the way?"

Jesus answered, "I am the way and the truth and the life. No-one comes to the Father except through me. If you really knew me, you would know my Father as well. From now on, you do know him and have seen him."

Philip said, "Lord, show us the Father and that will be enough for us."

Jesus answered: "Don't you know me, Philip, even after I have been among you such a long time? Anyone who has seen me has seen the Father. How can you say, 'Show us the Father'? Don't you believe that I am in the Father, and that the Father is in me? The words I say to you are not just my own. Rather, it is the Father, living in me, who is doing his work. Believe me when I say that I am in the Father and the Father is in me; or at least believe on the evidence of the miracles themselves. I tell you the truth, anyone who has faith in me will do what I have been doing. He will do even greater things than these, because I am going to the Father. And I will do whatever you ask in my name, so that the Son may bring glory to the Father. You may ask me for anything in my name, and I will do it."

Sixth Sunday of Easter

Acts 17:22–31   Paul stood up in the meeting of the Areopagus and said: "Men of Athens! I see that in every way you are very religious. For as I walked around and looked carefully at your objects of worship, I even found an altar with this inscription: TO AN UNKNOWN GOD. Now what you worship as something unknown I am going to proclaim to you.

"The God who made the world and everything in it is the Lord of heaven and earth and does not live in temples built by hands. And he is not served by human hands, as if he needed anything, because he himself gives all men life and breath and everything else. From one man he made every nation of men, that they should inhabit the whole earth; and he determined the times set for them and the exact places where they should live. God did this so that men would seek him and perhaps reach out for him and find him, though he is not far from each one of us. 'For in him we live and move and have our being.' As some of your own poets have said, 'We are his offspring.'

"Therefore since we are God's offspring, we should not think that the divine being is like gold or silver or stone – an image made by man's design and skill. In the past God overlooked such ignorance, but now he commands all people everywhere to repent. For he has set a day when he will judge the world with justice by the man he has appointed. He has given proof of this to all men by raising him from the dead."

Psalm 66:8–20   Praise our God, O peoples,
      let the sound of his praise be heard;
he has preserved our lives
      and kept our feet from slipping.
For you, O God, tested us;
      you refined us like silver.
You brought us into prison
      and laid burdens on our backs.

You let men ride over our heads;
  we went through fire and water,
  but you brought us to a place of abundance.

I will come to your temple with burnt offerings
  and fulfil my vows to you –
vows my lips promised and my mouth spoke
  when I was in trouble.
I will sacrifice fat animals to you
  and an offering of rams;
  I will offer bulls and goats.

Come and listen, all you who fear God;
  let me tell you what he has done for me.
I cried out to him with my mouth;
  his praise was on my tongue.
If I had cherished sin in my heart,
  the Lord would not have listened;
but God has surely listened
  and heard my voice in prayer.
Praise be to God,
  who has not rejected my prayer
  or withheld his love from me!

1 Peter 3:13–22   Who is going to harm you if you are eager to do good? But S
even if you should suffer for what is right, you are blessed. "Do not fear E
what they fear; do not be frightened." But in your hearts set apart Christ as C
Lord. Always be prepared to give an answer to everyone who asks you to O
give the reason for the hope that you have. But do this with gentleness and N
respect, keeping a clear conscience, so that those who speak maliciously D
against your good behaviour in Christ may be ashamed of their slander. It
is better, if it is God's will, to suffer for doing good than for doing evil. For R
Christ died for sins once for all, the righteous for the unrighteous, to bring E
you to God. He was put to death in the body but made alive by the Spirit, A
through whom also he went and preached to the spirits in prison who dis- D
obeyed long ago when God waited patiently in the days of Noah while the I
ark was being built. In it only a few people, eight in all, were saved through N
water, and this water symbolises baptism that now saves you also – not the G
removal of dirt from the body but the pledge of a good conscience towards
God. It saves you by the resurrection of Jesus Christ, who has gone into
heaven and is at God's right hand – with angels, authorities and powers in
submission to him.

John 14:15–21   Jesus said: "If you love me, you will obey what I command. G
And I will ask the Father, and he will give you another Counsellor to be with O
you for ever – the Spirit of truth. The world cannot accept him, because it S
neither sees him nor knows him. But you know him, for he lives with you P
and will be in you. I will not leave you as orphans; I will come to you. Before E
long, the world will not see me any more, but you will see me. Because I L

live, you also will live. On that day you will realise that I am in my Father, and you are in me, and I am in you. Whoever has my commands and obeys them, he is the one who loves me. He who loves me will be loved by my Father, and I too will love him and show myself to him."

Ascension Day

(Readings for Years A, B, C are the same and the reading from Acts must be used as either the first or second reading.)

Alternative first readings

Either **Acts 1:1–11** In my former book, Theophilus, I wrote about all that Jesus began to do and to teach until the day he was taken up to heaven, after giving instructions through the Holy Spirit to the apostles he had chosen. After his suffering, he showed himself to these men and gave many convincing proofs that he was alive. He appeared to them over a period of forty days and spoke about the kingdom of God. On one occasion, while he was eating with them, he gave them this command: "Do not leave Jerusalem, but wait for the gift my Father promised, which you have heard me speak about. For John baptised with water, but in a few days you will be baptised with the Holy Spirit."

So when they met together, they asked him, "Lord, are you at this time going to restore the kingdom to Israel?"

He said to them: "It is not for you to know the times or dates the Father has set by his own authority. But you will receive power when the Holy Spirit comes on you; and you will be my witnesses in Jerusalem, and in all Judea and Samaria, and to the ends of the earth."

After he said this, he was taken up before their very eyes, and a cloud hid him from their sight.

They were looking intently up into the sky as he was going, when suddenly two men dressed in white stood beside them. "Men of Galilee," they said, "why do you stand here looking into the sky? This same Jesus, who has been taken from you into heaven, will come back in the same way you have seen him go into heaven."

or **Daniel 7:9–14** Daniel said: "As I looked,

thrones were set in place,
  and the Ancient of Days took his seat.
His clothing was as white as snow;
  the hair of his head was white like wool.
His throne was flaming with fire,
  and its wheels were all ablaze.
A river of fire was flowing,
  coming out from before him.
Thousands upon thousands attended him;
  ten thousand times ten thousand stood before him.
The court was seated,
  and the books were opened.

"Then I continued to watch because of the boastful words the horn was speaking. I kept looking until the beast was slain and its body destroyed and thrown into the blazing fire. (The other beasts had been stripped of their authority, but were allowed to live for a period of time.)

"In my vision at night I looked, and there before me was one like a son of man, coming with the clouds of heaven. He approached the Ancient of Days and was led into his presence. He was given authority, glory and sovereign power; all peoples, nations and men of every language worshipped him. His dominion is an everlasting dominion that will not pass away, and his kingdom is one that will never be destroyed."

Alternative Psalms

Either **Psalm 47**
Clap your hands, all you nations;
    shout to God with cries of joy.
How awesome is the LORD Most High,
    the great King over all the earth!
He subdued nations under us,
    peoples under our feet.
He chose our inheritance for us,
    the pride of Jacob, whom he loved.

God has ascended amid shouts of joy,
    the LORD amid the sounding of trumpets.
Sing praises to God, sing praises;
    sing praises to our King, sing praises.

For God is the King of all the earth;
    sing to him a psalm of praise.
God reigns over the nations;
    God is seated on his holy throne.
The nobles of the nations assemble
    as the people of the God of Abraham,
for the kings of the earth belong to God;
    he is greatly exalted.

P
S
A
L
M

or **Psalm 93**
The LORD reigns, he is robed in majesty;
    the LORD is robed in majesty
    and is armed with strength.
The world is firmly established;
    it cannot be moved.
Your throne was established long ago;
    you are from all eternity.

The seas have lifted up, O LORD,
    the seas have lifted up their voice;
    the seas have lifted up their pounding waves.
Mightier than the thunder of the great waters,
    mightier than the breakers of the sea –
    the LORD on high is mighty.

P
S
A
L
M

> Your statutes stand firm;
> holiness adorns your house
> for endless days, O LORD.

Alternative second readings

Either **Ephesians 1:15–23**   Ever since I heard about your faith in the Lord s Jesus and your love for all the saints, I have not stopped giving thanks E for you, remembering you in my prayers. I keep asking that the God C of our Lord Jesus Christ, the glorious Father, may give you the Spirit O of wisdom and revelation, so that you may know him better. I pray also N that the eyes of your heart may be enlightened in order that you may D know the hope to which he has called you, the riches of his glorious inheritance in the saints, and his incomparably great power for us R who believe. That power is like the working of his mighty strength, E which he exerted in Christ when he raised him from the dead and seated A him at his right hand in the heavenly realms, far above all rule and D authority, power and dominion, and every title that can be given, not only I in the present age but also in the one to come. And God placed all things N under his feet and appointed him to be head over everything for the G church, which is his body, the fulness of him who fills everything in every way.

or **Acts 1:1–11**   In my former book, Theophilus, I wrote about all that Jesus s began to do and to teach until the day he was taken up to heaven, after giv- E ing instructions through the Holy Spirit to the apostles he had chosen. C After his suffering, he showed himself to these men and gave many con- O vincing proofs that he was alive. He appeared to them over a period of N forty days and spoke about the kingdom of God. On one occasion, while he D was eating with them, he gave them this command: "Do not leave Jerusalem, but wait for the gift my Father promised, which you have heard R me speak about. For John baptised with water, but in a few days you will be E baptised with the Holy Spirit."   A

So when they met together, they asked him, "Lord, are you at this time D going to restore the kingdom to Israel?"   I

He said to them: "It is not for you to know the times or dates the Father N has set by his own authority. But you will receive power when the Holy G Spirit comes on you; and you will be my witnesses in Jerusalem, and in all Judea and Samaria, and to the ends of the earth."

After he said this, he was taken up before their very eyes, and a cloud hid him from their sight.

They were looking intently up into the sky as he was going, when suddenly two men dressed in white stood beside them. "Men of Galilee," they said, "why do you stand here looking into the sky? This same Jesus, who has been taken from you into heaven, will come back in the same way you have seen him go into heaven."

Luke 24:44–53 Jesus said to the disciples, "This is what I told you while I was still with you: Everything must be fulfilled that is written about me in the Law of Moses, the Prophets and the Psalms." G O S

Then he opened their minds so they could understand the Scriptures. He told them, "This is what is written: The Christ will suffer and rise from the dead on the third day, and repentance and forgiveness of sins will be preached in his name to all nations, beginning at Jerusalem. You are witnesses of these things. I am going to send you what my Father has promised; but stay in the city until you have been clothed with power from on high." P E L

When he had led them out to the vicinity of Bethany, he lifted up his hands and blessed them. While he was blessing them, he left them and was taken up into heaven. Then they worshipped him and returned to Jerusalem with great joy. And they stayed continually at the temple, praising God.

Seventh Sunday of Easter

Sunday after Ascension Day

Acts 1:6–14 When the apostles met together, they asked Jesus, "Lord, are you at this time going to restore the kingdom to Israel?" F I

He said to them: "It is not for you to know the times or dates the Father has set by his own authority. But you will receive power when the Holy Spirit comes on you; and you will be my witnesses in Jerusalem, and in all Judea and Samaria, and to the ends of the earth." R S T

After he said this, he was taken up before their very eyes, and a cloud hid him from their sight. R E

They were looking intently up into the sky as he was going, when suddenly two men dressed in white stood beside them. "Men of Galilee," they said, "why do you stand here looking into the sky? This same Jesus, who has been taken from you into heaven, will come back in the same way you have seen him go into heaven." A D I N G

Then they returned to Jerusalem from the hill called the Mount of Olives, a Sabbath day's walk from the city. When they arrived, they went upstairs to the room where they were staying. Those present were Peter, John, James and Andrew; Philip and Thomas, Bartholomew and Matthew; James son of Alphaeus and Simon the Zealot, and Judas son of James. They all joined together constantly in prayer, along with the women and Mary the mother of Jesus, and with his brothers.

Psalm 68:1–10, 32–35*

May God arise, may his enemies be scattered; P
   may his foes flee before him. S
As smoke is blown away by the wind, A
   may you blow them away; L
as wax melts before the fire, M
   may the wicked perish before God.

But may the righteous be glad
and rejoice before God;
may they be happy and joyful.

Sing to God, sing praise to his name,
extol him who rides on the clouds –
his name is the LORD –
and rejoice before him.
A father to the fatherless, a defender of widows,
is God in his holy dwelling.
God sets the lonely in families,
he leads forth the prisoners with singing;
but the rebellious live in a sun-scorched land.

When you went out before your people, O God,
when you marched through the wasteland,
the earth shook,
the heavens poured down rain,
before God, the One of Sinai,
before God, the God of Israel.
You gave abundant showers, O God;
you refreshed your weary inheritance.
Your people settled in it,
and from your bounty, O God, you
provided for the poor.

Sing to God, O kingdoms of the earth,
sing praise to the LORD,
to him who rides the ancient skies above,
who thunders with mighty voice.
Proclaim the power of God,
whose majesty is over Israel,
whose power is in the skies.
You are awesome, O God, in your sanctuary;
the God of Israel gives power and
strength to his people.

Praise be to God!

1 Peter 4:12–14; 5:6–11   Dear friends, do not be surprised at the painful trial S R
you are suffering, as though something strange were happening to you. E E
But rejoice that you participate in the sufferings of Christ, so that you may C A
be overjoyed when his glory is revealed. If you are insulted because of the O D
name of Christ, you are blessed, for the Spirit of glory and of God rests on N I
you.   D N

Humble yourselves, therefore, under God's mighty hand, that he may G
lift you up in due time. Cast all your anxiety on him because he cares for
you.

Be self-controlled and alert. Your enemy the devil prowls around like a
roaring lion looking for someone to devour. Resist him, standing firm in the

faith, because you know that your brothers throughout the world are undergoing the same kind of sufferings.

And the God of all grace, who called you to his eternal glory in Christ, after you have suffered a little while, will himself restore you and make you strong, firm and steadfast. To him be the power for ever and ever. Amen.

John 17: 1–11   Jesus looked towards heaven and prayed:

"Father, the time has come. Glorify your Son, that your Son may glorify you. For you granted him authority over all people that he might give eternal life to all those you have given him. Now this is eternal life: that they may know you, the only true God, and Jesus Christ, whom you have sent. I have brought you glory on earth by completing the work you gave me to do. And now, Father, glorify me in your presence with the glory I had with you before the world began.

"I have revealed you to those whom you gave me out of the world. They were yours; you gave them to me and they have obeyed your word. Now they know that everything you have given me comes from you. For I gave them the words you gave me and they accepted them. They knew with certainty that I came from you, and they believed that you sent me. I pray for them. I am not praying for the world, but for those you have given me, for they are yours. All I have is yours, and all you have is mine. And glory has come to me through them. I will remain in the world no longer, but they are still in the world, and I am coming to you. Holy Father, protect them by the power of your name – the name you gave me – so that they may be one as we are one."

Pentecost – Whit Sunday

The reading from Acts must be used as either the first or second reading.

Alternative first reading

Either **Acts 2:1–21**   When the day of Pentecost came, the disciples were all together in one place. Suddenly a sound like the blowing of a violent wind came from heaven and filled the whole house where they were sitting. They saw what seemed to be tongues of fire that separated and came to rest on each of them. All of them were filled with the Holy Spirit and began to speak in other tongues as the Spirit enabled them.

Now there were staying in Jerusalem God-fearing Jews from every nation under heaven. When they heard this sound, a crowd came together in bewilderment, because each one heard them speaking in his own language. Utterly amazed, they asked: "Are not all these men who are speaking Galileans? Then how is it that each of us hears them in his own native language? Parthians, Medes and Elamites; residents of Mesopotamia, Judea and Cappadocia, Pontus and Asia, Phrygia and Pamphylia, Egypt and the parts of Libya near Cyrene; visitors from Rome (both

Jews and converts to Judaism); Cretans and Arabs – we hear them declaring the wonders of God in our own tongues!" Amazed and perplexed, they asked one another, "What does this mean?"

Some, however, made fun of them and said, "They have had too much wine."

Then Peter stood up with the Eleven, raised his voice and addressed the crowd: "Fellow Jews and all of you who live in Jerusalem, let me explain this to you; listen carefully to what I say. These men are not drunk, as you suppose. It's only nine in the morning! No, this is what was spoken by the prophet Joel:

> "'In the last days, God says,
>   I will pour out my Spirit on all people.
> Your sons and daughters will prophesy,
>   your young men will see visions,
>   your old men will dream dreams.
> Even on my servants, both men and women,
>   I will pour out my Spirit in those days,
>   and they will prophesy.
> I will show wonders in the heaven above
>   and signs on the earth below,
>   blood and fire and billows of smoke.
> The sun will be turned to darkness
>   and the moon to blood
>   before the coming of the great and glorious day of the Lord.
> And everyone who calls
>   on the name of the Lord will be saved.'"

or **Numbers 11:24–30**   Moses went out and told the people what the Lord had said. He brought together seventy of their elders and made them stand round the Tent. Then the Lord came down in the cloud and spoke with him, and he took of the Spirit that was on him and put the Spirit on the seventy elders. When the Spirit rested on them, they prophesied, but they did not do so again.

However, two men, whose names were Eldad and Medad, had remained in the camp. They were listed among the elders, but did not go out to the Tent. Yet the Spirit also rested on them, and they prophesied in the camp. A young man ran and told Moses, "Eldad and Medad are prophesying in the camp."

Joshua son of Nun, who had been Moses' assistant since youth, spoke up and said, "Moses, my lord, stop them!"

But Moses replied, "Are you jealous for my sake? I wish that all the Lord's people were prophets and that the Lord would put his Spirit on them!" Then Moses and the elders of Israel returned to the camp.

Psalm 104:24–34, 35b*   How many are your works, O Lord!
                             In wisdom you made them all;
                             the earth is full of your creatures.

There is the sea, vast and spacious,
    teeming with creatures beyond number –
    living things both large and small.
There the ships go to and fro,
    and the leviathan, which you formed to
      frolic there.

These all look to you
    to give them their food at the proper time.
When you give it to them,
    they gather it up;
when you open your hand,
    they are satisfied with good things.
When you hide your face,
    they are terrified;
when you take away their breath,
    they die and return to the dust.
When you send your Spirit,
    they are created,
    and you renew the face of the earth.

May the glory of the LORD endure for ever;
    may the LORD rejoice in his works –
he who looks at the earth, and it trembles,
    who touches the mountains, and they smoke.

I will sing to the LORD all my life;
    I will sing praise to my God as long as I live.
May my meditation be pleasing to him,
    as I rejoice in the LORD.

Praise the LORD, O my soul.

Praise the LORD.

Alternative second readings

Either **1 Corinthians 12:3b–13**   No-one can say, "Jesus is Lord," except by the
Holy Spirit.

    There are different kinds of gifts, but the same Spirit. There are differ-
ent kinds of service, but the same Lord. There are different kinds of
working, but the same God works all of them in all men.

    Now to each one the manifestation of the Spirit is given for the com-
mon good. To one there is given through the Spirit the message of wisdom,
to another the message of knowledge by means of the same Spirit, to
another faith by the same Spirit, to another gifts of healing by that one
Spirit, to another miraculous powers, to another prophecy, to another dis-
tinguishing between spirits, to another speaking in different kinds of
tongues, and to still another the interpretation of tongues. All these are the
work of one and the same Spirit, and he gives them to each one, just as he
determines.

The body is a unit, though it is made up of many parts; and though all its parts are many, they form one body. So it is with Christ. For we were all baptised by one Spirit into one body – whether Jews or Greeks, slave or free – and we were all given the one Spirit to drink.

or **Acts 2:1–21** When the day of Pentecost came, the disciples were all together in one place. Suddenly a sound like the blowing of a violent wind came from heaven and filled the whole house where they were sitting. They saw what seemed to be tongues of fire that separated and came to rest on each of them. All of them were filled with the Holy Spirit and began to speak in other tongues as the Spirit enabled them.

Now there were staying in Jerusalem God-fearing Jews from every nation under heaven. When they heard this sound, a crowd came together in bewilderment, because each one heard them speaking in his own language. Utterly amazed, they asked: "Are not all these men who are speaking Galileans? Then how is it that each of us hears them in his own native language? Parthians, Medes and Elamites; residents of Mesopotamia, Judea and Cappadocia, Pontus and Asia, Phrygia and Pamphylia, Egypt and the parts of Libya near Cyrene; visitors from Rome (both Jews and converts to Judaism); Cretans and Arabs – we hear them declaring the wonders of God in our own tongues!" Amazed and perplexed, they asked one another, "What does this mean?"

Some, however, made fun of them and said, "They have had too much wine."

Then Peter stood up with the Eleven, raised his voice and addressed the crowd: "Fellow Jews and all of you who live in Jerusalem, let me explain this to you; listen carefully to what I say. These men are not drunk, as you suppose. It's only nine in the morning! No, this is what was spoken by the prophet Joel:

"'In the last days, God says,
    I will pour out my Spirit on all people.
Your sons and daughters will prophesy,
    your young men will see visions,
    your old men will dream dreams.
Even on my servants, both men and women,
    I will pour out my Spirit in those days,
    and they will prophesy.
I will show wonders in the heaven above
    and signs on the earth below,
    blood and fire and billows of smoke.
The sun will be turned to darkness
    and the moon to blood
    before the coming of the great and glorious day of the Lord.
And everyone who calls
    on the name of the Lord will be saved.'"

Alternative Gospels

Either **John 20:19–23**   On the evening of the first day of the week, when the disciples were together, with the doors locked for fear of the Jews, Jesus came and stood among them and said, "Peace be with you!" After he said this, he showed them his hands and side. The disciples were overjoyed when they saw the Lord.

Again Jesus said, "Peace be with you! As the Father has sent me, I am sending you." And with that he breathed on them and said, "Receive the Holy Spirit. If you forgive anyone his sins, they are forgiven; if you do not forgive them, they are not forgiven."

or **John 7:37–39**   On the last and greatest day of the Feast, Jesus stood and said in a loud voice, "If anyone is thirsty, let him come to me and drink. Whoever believes in me, as the Scripture has said, streams of living water will flow from within him." By this he meant the Spirit, whom those who believed in him were later to receive. Up to that time the Spirit had not been given, since Jesus had not yet been glorified.

ORDINARY TIME

Trinity Sunday

Isaiah 40:12–17, 27–31

Who has measured the waters in the hollow of his hand,
> or with the breadth of his hand marked off the heavens?
Who has held the dust of the earth in a basket,
> or weighed the mountains on the scales
> and the hills in a balance?
Who has understood the mind of the LORD,
> or instructed him as his counsellor?
Whom did the LORD consult to enlighten him,
and who taught him the right way?
Who was it that taught him knowledge
> or showed him the path of understanding?

Surely the nations are like a drop in a bucket;
> they are regarded as dust on the scales;
> he weighs the islands as though they were fine dust.
Lebanon is not sufficient for altar fires,
> nor its animals enough for burnt offerings.
Before him all the nations are as nothing;
> they are regarded by him as worthless
> and less than nothing.

Why do you say, O Jacob,
> and complain, O Israel,
"My way is hidden from the LORD;
> my cause is disregarded by my God"?
Do you not know?
> Have you not heard?

The LORD is the everlasting God,
>the Creator of the ends of the earth.

He will not grow tired or weary,
>and his understanding no-one can fathom.

He gives strength to the weary
>and increases the power of the weak.

Even youths grow tired and weary,
>and young men stumble and fall;

but those who hope in the LORD
>will renew their strength.

They will soar on wings like eagles;
>they will run and not grow weary,
>they will walk and not be faint.

Psalm 8   O LORD, our LORD,
>how majestic is your name in all the earth!

You have set your glory
>above the heavens.

From the lips of children and infants
>you have ordained praise

because of your enemies,
>to silence the foe and the avenger.

When I consider your heavens,
>the work of your fingers,

the moon and the stars,
>which you have set in place,

what is man that you are mindful of him,
>the son of man that you care for him?

You made him a little lower than the heavenly beings
>and crowned him with glory and honour.

You made him ruler over the works of your hands;
>you put everything under his feet:

all flocks and herds,
>and the beasts of the field,

the birds of the air,
>and the fish of the sea,
>all that swim the paths of the seas.

O LORD, our LORD,
>how majestic is your name in all the earth!

2 Corinthians 13:11–13   Finally, brothers, good-bye. Aim for perfection, listen to my appeal, be of one mind, live in peace. And the God of love and peace will be with you.

>Greet one another with a holy kiss. All the saints send their greetings.

Matthew 28:16–20 The eleven disciples went to Galilee, to the mountain G
where Jesus had told them to go. When they saw him, they worshipped him; O
but some doubted. Then Jesus came to them and said, "All authority in S
heaven and on earth has been given to me. Therefore go and make disci- P
ples of all nations, baptising them in the name of the Father and of the E
Son and of the Holy Spirit, and teaching them to obey everything I have L
commanded you. And surely I am with you always, to the very end of the
age."

If the Sunday between 24 and 28 May inclusive follows Trinity Sunday, Proper 3 (p 40) is used.

Thanksgiving for Holy Communion
Thursday after Trinity Sunday (Corpus Christi)

(Readings for Years A, B, C are the same)

Genesis 14:18–20 Melchizedek king of Salem brought out bread and wine. F R
He was priest of God Most High, and he blessed Abram, saying, I E

> "Blessed be Abram by God Most High, R A
>> Creator of heaven and earth. S D
> And blessed be God Most High, T I
>> who delivered your enemies into your hand." N
>
> Then Abram gave him a tenth of everything. G

Psalm 116:12–19 How can I repay the LORD P
>> for all his goodness to me? S
> I will lift up the cup of salvation A
>> and call on the name of the LORD. L
> I will fulfil my vows to the LORD M
>> in the presence of all his people.
>
> Precious in the sight of the LORD
>> is the death of his saints.
> O LORD, truly I am your servant;
>> I am your servant, the son of your maidservant;
>> you have freed me from my chains.
>
> I will sacrifice a thank-offering to you
>> and call on the name of the LORD.
> I will fulfil my vows to the LORD
>> in the presence of all his people,
> in the courts of the house of the LORD –
>> in your midst, O Jerusalem. S R
>
> Praise the LORD. E E

C A
1 Corinthians 11:23–26 I received from the LORD what I also passed on to O D
you: The LORD Jesus, on the night he was betrayed, took bread, and when he N I
had given thanks, he broke it and said, "This is my body, which is for you; D N
do this in remembrance of me." In the same way, after supper he took the G

cup, saying, "This cup is the new covenant in my blood; do this, whenever you drink it, in remembrance of me." For whenever you eat this bread and drink this cup, you proclaim the LORD's death until he comes.

John 6:51–58   Jesus said: "I am the living bread that came down from heaven. Whoever eats of this bread will live for ever. This bread is my flesh, which I will give for the life of the world."

Then the Jews began to argue sharply among themselves, "How can this man give us his flesh to eat?"

Jesus said to them, "I tell you the truth, unless you eat the flesh of the Son of Man and drink his blood, you have no life in you. Those who eat my flesh and drink my blood have eternal life, and I will raise them up at the last day. For my flesh is real food and my blood is real drink. Those who eat my flesh and drink my blood remains in me, and I in them. Just as the living Father sent me and I live because of the Father, so the one who feeds on me will live because of me. This is the bread that came down from heaven. Your ancestors ate manna and died, but whoever feeds on this bread will live for ever."

Proper 4

Sunday between 29 May and 4 June inclusive (if after Trinity Sunday)
On the Sundays after Trinity, alternative Old Testament readings and Psalms are provided. The first pair of readings headed 'continuous' offer semi-continuous reading of Old Testament texts but allow the Old Testament reading and its complementary Psalm to stand independently of the other readings. The second pair of readings headed 'related' relate the Old Testament reading and the Psalm to the Gospel reading.

It is unhelpful to move from one type of pair to another from week to week. Either 'continuous' or 'related' readings should be followed for the whole sequence of Sundays after Trinity.

CONTINUOUS

Genesis 6:9–22; 7:24 – 8:1, 14–19   This is the account of Noah.

Noah was a righteous man, blameless among the people of his time, and he walked with God. Noah had three sons: Shem, Ham and Japheth.

Now the earth was corrupt in God's sight and was full of violence. God saw how corrupt the earth had become, for all the people on earth had corrupted their ways. So God said to Noah, "I am going to put an end to all people, for the earth is filled with violence because of them. I am surely going to destroy both them and the earth. So make yourself an ark of cypress wood; make rooms in it and coat it with pitch inside and out. This is how you are to build it: The ark is to be 450 feet long, 75 feet wide and 45 feet high. Make a roof for it and finish the ark to within 18 inches of the top. Put a door in the side of the ark and make lower, middle and upper decks. I am going to bring floodwaters on the earth to destroy all life under the heavens, every creature that has the breath of life in it. Everything on earth will perish. But I will establish my covenant with you, and you will enter the ark – you and your sons and your wife and your sons' wives with you. You are to bring into the ark two of all living creatures, male and female, to keep them alive with you. Two of every kind of bird, of every kind of animal and of every kind of creature that moves along the ground will come to you to be kept alive. You are to take every kind of food that is to be eaten and store it away as food for you and for them."

Noah did everything just as God commanded him.

The waters flooded the earth for a hundred and fifty days. But God remembered Noah and all the wild animals and the livestock that were with him in the ark, and he sent a wind over the earth, and the waters receded.

By the twenty-seventh day of the second month the earth was completely dry.

Then God said to Noah, "Come out of the ark, you and your wife and your sons and their wives. Bring out every kind of living creature that is with you – the birds, the animals, and all the creatures that move along the ground – so they can multiply on the earth and be fruitful and increase in number upon it."

So Noah came out, together with his sons and his wife and his sons' wives. All the animals and all the creatures that move along the ground and all the birds – everything that moves on the earth – came out of the ark, one kind after another.

and **Psalm 46**   God is our refuge and strength,   P
            an ever-present help in trouble.   S
        Therefore we will not fear, though the earth give way   A
            and the mountains fall into the heart of the sea,   L
        though its waters roar and foam   M
            and the mountains quake with their surging.

There is a river whose streams make glad the city of God,
    the holy place where the Most High dwells.
God is within her, she will not fall;
    God will help her at break of day.
Nations are in uproar, kingdoms fall;
    he lifts his voice, the earth melts.

The Lord Almighty is with us;
    the God of Jacob is our fortress.

Come and see the works of the Lord,
    the desolations he has brought on the earth.
He makes wars cease to the ends of the earth;
    he breaks the bow and shatters the spear,
    he burns the shields with fire.
"Be still, and know that I am God;
    I will be exalted among the nations,
    I will be exalted in the earth."

The Lord Almighty is with us;
    the God of Jacob is our fortress.

Or **RELATED**

Deuteronomy 11:18-21, 26–28   Moses summoned all Israel and said: "Fix these words of mine in your hearts and minds; tie them as symbols on your hands and bind them on your foreheads. Teach them to your children, talking about them when you sit at home and when you walk along the road, when you lie down and when you get up. Write them on the door-frames of your houses and on your gates, so that your days and the days of your children may be many in the land that the LORD swore to give your forefathers, as many as the days that the heavens are above the earth.

"See, I am setting before you today a blessing and a curse – the blessing if you obey the commands of the LORD your God that I am giving you today; the curse if you disobey the commands of the LORD your God and turn from the way that I command you today by following other gods, which you have not known."

FIRST READING

and **Psalm 31:1–5, 19–24***

In you, O LORD, I have taken refuge;
  let me never be put to shame;
  deliver me in your righteousness.
Turn your ear to me,
  come quickly to my rescue;
be my rock of refuge,
  a strong fortress to save me.
Since you are my rock and my fortress,
  for the sake of your name lead and guide me.
Free me from the trap that is set for me,
  for you are my refuge.
Into your hands I commit my spirit;
  redeem me, O LORD, the God of truth.

How great is your goodness,
  which you have stored up for those who fear you,
which you bestow in the sight of men
  on those who take refuge in you.
In the shelter of your presence you hide them
  from the intrigues of men;
in your dwelling you keep them safe
  from accusing tongues.

Praise be to the LORD,
  for he showed his wonderful love to me
  when I was in a besieged city.
In my alarm I said,
  "I am cut off from your sight!"
Yet you heard my cry for mercy
  when I called to you for help.

PSALM

> Love the Lord, all his saints!
> The Lord preserves the faithful,
> but the proud he pays back in full.
> Be strong and take heart,
> all you who hope in the Lord.

Romans 1:16–17; 3:22b–28 [29–31]   I am not ashamed of the gospel, because s it is the power of God for the salvation of everyone who believes: first for E the Jew, then for the Gentile. For in the gospel a righteousness from God is c revealed, a righteousness that is by faith from first to last, just as it is writ- o ten: "The righteous will live by faith."   N

There is no difference, for all have sinned and fall short of the glory of D God, and are justified freely by his grace through the redemption that came by Christ Jesus. God presented him as a sacrifice of atonement, R through faith in his blood. He did this to demonstrate his justice, because E in his forbearance he had left the sins committed beforehand unpunished A – he did it to demonstrate his justice at the present time, so as to be just and D the one who justifies those who have faith in Jesus.   I

Where, then, is boasting? It is excluded. On what principle? On that of N observing the law? No, but on that of faith. For we maintain that a man is G justified by faith apart from observing the law. [Is God the God of Jews only? Is he not the God of Gentiles too? Yes, of Gentiles too, since there is only one God, who will justify the circumcised by faith and the uncircum-cised through that same faith. Do we, then, nullify the law by this faith? Not at all! Rather, we uphold the law.]

Matthew 7:21–29   Jesus said: "Not everyone who says to me, 'Lord, Lord,' G will enter the kingdom of heaven, but only he who does the will of my o Father who is in heaven. Many will say to me on that day, 'Lord, Lord, did s we not prophesy in your name, and in your name drive out demons and per- P form many miracles?' Then I will tell them plainly, 'I never knew you. E Away from me, you evildoers!'   L

"Therefore everyone who hears these words of mine and puts them into practice is like a wise man who built his house on the rock. The rain came down, the streams rose, and the winds blew and beat against that house; yet it did not fall, because it had its foundation on the rock. But everyone who hears these words of mine and does not put them into practice is like a fool-ish man who built his house on sand. The rain came down, the streams rose, and the winds blew and beat against that house, and it fell with a great crash."

When Jesus had finished saying these things, the crowds were amazed at his teaching, because he taught as one who had authority, and not as their teachers of the law.

Proper 5

Sunday between 5 and 11 June inclusive (if after Trinity Sunday)
Choose either 'continuous' or 'related' Old Testament and Psalm readings.

CONTINUOUS

Genesis 12:1–9   The LORD had said to Abram, "Leave your country, your people and your father's household and go to the land I will show you.

> "I will make you into a great nation
>> and I will bless you;
> I will make your name great,
>> and you will be a blessing.
> I will bless those who bless you,
>> and whoever curses you I will curse;
> and all peoples on earth
>> will be blessed through you."

So Abram left, as the LORD had told him; and Lot went with him. Abram was seventy-five years old when he set out from Haran. He took his wife Sarai, his nephew Lot, all the possessions they had accumulated and the people they had acquired in Haran, and they set out for the land of Canaan, and they arrived there.

Abram travelled through the land as far as the site of the great tree of Moreh at Shechem. At that time the Canaanites were in the land. The LORD appeared to Abram and said, "To your offspring I will give this land." So he built an altar there to the LORD, who had appeared to him.

From there he went on towards the hills east of Bethel and pitched his tent, with Bethel on the west and Ai on the east. There he built an altar to the LORD and called on the name of the LORD. Then Abram set out and continued towards the Negev.

and **Psalm 33:1–12**   Sing joyfully to the LORD, you righteous;
> it is fitting for the upright to praise him.
Praise the LORD with the harp;
> make music to him on the ten-stringed lyre.
Sing to him a new song;
> play skilfully, and shout for joy.

For the word of the LORD is right and true;
> he is faithful in all he does.
The LORD loves righteousness and justice;
> the earth is full of his unfailing love.

By the word of the LORD were the heavens made,
> their starry host by the breath of his mouth.
He gathers the waters of the sea into jars;
> he puts the deep into storehouses.
Let all the earth fear the LORD;
> let all the people of the world revere him.

For he spoke, and it came to be;
　　he commanded, and it stood firm.
The LORD foils the plans of the nations;
　　he thwarts the purposes of the peoples.
But the plans of the LORD stand firm for ever,
　　the purposes of his heart through all generations.

Blessed is the nation whose God is the LORD,
　　the people he chose for his inheritance.

Or **RELATED**

Hosea 5:15 – 6:6　　Hear the word of the LORD:　　　　　　　F

"I will go back to my place　　　　　　　　　　　　　I
　　until Israel admits their guilt.　　　　　　　　R
And they will seek my face;　　　　　　　　　　　S
　　in their misery they will earnestly seek me."　　T

"Come, let us return to the LORD.　　　　　　　　R
He has torn us to pieces　　　　　　　　　　　　E
　　but he will heal us;　　　　　　　　　　　　A
he has injured us　　　　　　　　　　　　　　D
　　but he will bind up our wounds.　　　　　　　I
After two days he will revive us;　　　　　　　　N
　　on the third day he will restore us,　　　　　　G
　　that we may live in his presence.
Let us acknowledge the LORD;
　　let us press on to acknowledge him.
As surely as the sun rises,
　　he will appear;
he will come to us like the winter rains,
　　like the spring rains that water the earth."

"What can I do with you, Ephraim?
　　What can I do with you, Judah?
Your love is like the morning mist,
　　like the early dew that disappears.
Therefore I cut you in pieces with my prophets,
　　I killed you with the words of my mouth;
　　my judgments flashed like lightning upon you.
For I desire mercy, not sacrifice,
　　and acknowledgment of God rather than
　　　　burnt offerings."

and **Psalm 50:7–15**　　"Hear, O my people, and I will speak,　　　P
　　O Israel, and I will testify against you:　　　S
　　I am God, your God.　　　　　　　　　A
I do not rebuke you for your sacrifices　　　L
　　or your burnt offerings, which are ever before me.　M

I have no need of a bull from your stall
   or of goats from your pens,
for every animal of the forest is mine,
   and the cattle on a thousand hills.
I know every bird in the mountains,
   and the creatures of the field are mine.
If I were hungry I would not tell you,
   for the world is mine, and all that is in it.
Do I eat the flesh of bulls
   or drink the blood of goats?
Sacrifice thank-offerings to God,
   fulfil your vows to the Most High,
and call upon me in the day of trouble;
   I will deliver you and you will honour me."

Romans 4:13–25 It was not through law that Abraham and his offspring
received the promise that he would be heir of the world, but through the
righteousness that comes by faith. For if those who live by law are heirs,
faith has no value and the promise is worthless, because law brings wrath.
And where there is no law there is no transgression.

Therefore, the promise comes by faith, so that it may be by grace and
may be guaranteed to all Abraham's offspring – not only to those who are
of the law but also to those who are of the faith of Abraham. He is the father
of us all. As it is written: "I have made you a father of many nations." He is
our father in the sight of God, in whom he believed – the God who gives life
to the dead and calls things that are not as though they were.

Against all hope, Abraham in hope believed and so became the father of
many nations, just as it had been said to him, "So shall your offspring be."
Without weakening in his faith, he faced the fact that his body was as good
as dead – since he was about a hundred years old – and that Sarah's womb
was also dead. Yet he did not waver through unbelief regarding the
promise of God, but was strengthened in his faith and gave glory to God,
being fully persuaded that God had power to do what he had promised.
This is why "it was credited to him as righteousness." The words "it was
credited to him" were written not for him alone, but also for us, to whom
God will credit righteousness – for us who believe in him who raised Jesus
our Lord from the dead. He was delivered over to death for our sins and
was raised to life for our justification.

Matthew 9:9–13, 18–26 Jesus saw a man named Matthew sitting at the tax
collector's booth. "Follow me," he told him, and Matthew got up and followed him.

While Jesus was having dinner at Matthew's house, many tax collectors
and "sinners" came and ate with him and his disciples. When the Pharisees
saw this, they asked his disciples, "Why does your teacher eat with tax collectors and 'sinners'?"

On hearing this, Jesus said, "It is not the healthy who need a doctor, but the sick. But go and learn what this means: 'I desire mercy, not sacrifice.' For I have not come to call the righteous, but sinners."

While he was speaking, a ruler came and knelt before him and said, "My daughter has just died. But come and put your hand on her, and she will live." Jesus got up and went with him, and so did his disciples.

Just then a woman who had been subject to bleeding for twelve years came up behind him and touched the edge of his cloak. She said to herself, "If I only touch his cloak, I will be healed."

Jesus turned and saw her. "Take heart, daughter," he said, "your faith has healed you." And the woman was healed from that moment.

When Jesus entered the ruler's house and saw the flute players and the noisy crowd, he said, "Go away. The girl is not dead but asleep." But they laughed at him. After the crowd had been put outside, he went in and took the girl by the hand, and she got up. News of this spread through all that region.

Proper 6

Sunday between 12 and 18 June inclusive (if after Trinity Sunday)
Choose either 'continuous' or 'related' Old Testament and Psalm readings.

CONTINUOUS

Genesis 18:1–15 [21:1–7] The LORD appeared to Abraham near the great trees of Mamre while he was sitting at the entrance to his tent in the heat of the day. Abraham looked up and saw three men standing nearby. When he saw them, he hurried from the entrance of his tent to meet them and bowed low to the ground.

He said, "If I have found favour in your eyes, my lord, do not pass your servant by. Let a little water be brought, and then you may all wash your feet and rest under this tree. Let me get you something to eat, so you can be refreshed and then go on your way – now that you have come to your servant."

"Very well," they answered, "do as you say."

So Abraham hurried into the tent to Sarah. "Quick," he said, "get three seahs of fine flour and knead it and bake some bread."

Then he ran to the herd and selected a choice, tender calf and gave it to a servant, who hurried to prepare it. He then brought some curds and milk and the calf that had been prepared, and set these before them. While they ate, he stood near them under a tree.

"Where is your wife Sarah?" they asked him.

"There, in the tent," he said.

Then the LORD said, "I will surely return to you about this time next year, and Sarah your wife will have a son."

Now Sarah was listening at the entrance to the tent, which was behind him. Abraham and Sarah were already old and well advanced in years, and Sarah was past the age of childbearing. So Sarah laughed to herself as she thought, "After I am worn out and my master is old, will I now have this pleasure?"

FIRST READING

Then the Lord said to Abraham, "Why did Sarah laugh and say, 'Will I really have a child, now that I am old?' Is anything too hard for the Lord? I will return to you at the appointed time next year and Sarah will have a son."

Sarah was afraid, so she lied and said, "I did not laugh."

But he said, "Yes, you did laugh."

[The Lord was gracious to Sarah as he had said, and the Lord did for Sarah what he had promised. Sarah became pregnant and bore a son to Abraham in his old age, at the very time God had promised him. Abraham gave the name Isaac to the son Sarah bore him. When his son Isaac was eight days old, Abraham circumcised him, as God commanded him. Abraham was a hundred years old when his son Isaac was born to him.

Sarah said, "God has brought me laughter, and everyone who hears about this will laugh with me." And she added, "Who would have said to Abraham that Sarah would nurse children? Yet I have borne him a son in his old age."]

and **Psalm 116:1–2, 12–19***

I love the Lord, for he heard my voice;
    he heard my cry for mercy.
Because he turned his ear to me,
    I will call on him as long as I live.

How can I repay the Lord
    for all his goodness to me?
I will lift up the cup of salvation
    and call on the name of the Lord.
I will fulfil my vows to the Lord
    in the presence of all his people.

Precious in the sight of the Lord
    is the death of his saints.
O Lord, truly I am your servant;
    I am your servant, the son of your
        maidservant;
    you have freed me from my chains.

I will sacrifice a thank-offering to you
    and call on the name of the Lord.
I will fulfil my vows to the Lord
    in the presence of all his people,
in the courts of the house of the Lord –
    in your midst, O Jerusalem.

Praise the Lord.

PSALM

FRIERAND SDTING

Or **RELATED**

Exodus 19:2–8a After the Israelites set out from Rephidim, they entered the Desert of Sinai, and they camped there in the desert in front of the mountain.

Then Moses went up to God, and the Lord called to him from the mountain and said, "This is what you are to say to the house of Jacob and what you are to tell the people of Israel: 'You yourselves have seen what I did to Egypt, and how I carried you on eagles' wings and brought you to myself. Now if you obey me fully and keep my covenant, then out of all nations you will be my treasured possession. Although the whole earth is mine, you will be for me a kingdom of priests and a holy nation.' These are the words you are to speak to the Israelites."

So Moses went back and summoned the elders of the people and set before them all the words the LORD had commanded him to speak. The people all responded together, "We will do everything the LORD has said."

and **Psalm 100**

Shout for joy to the LORD, all the earth. P
Worship the LORD with gladness; S
  come before him with joyful songs. A
Know that the LORD is God. L
  It is he who made us, and we are his; M
  we are his people, the sheep of his pasture.

Enter his gates with thanksgiving
  and his courts with praise;
  give thanks to him and praise his name.
For the LORD is good and his love endures for ever;
  his faithfulness continues through all generations.

Romans 5:1–8 Since we have been justified through faith, we have peace S R with God through our LORD Jesus Christ, through whom we have gained E E access by faith into this grace in which we now stand. And we rejoice in the C A hope of the glory of God. Not only so, but we also rejoice in our sufferings, O D because we know that suffering produces perseverance; perseverance, N I character; and character, hope. And hope does not disappoint us, because D N God has poured out his love into our hearts by the Holy Spirit, whom he has G given us.

You see, at just the right time, when we were still powerless, Christ died for the ungodly. Very rarely will anyone die for a righteous man, though for a good man someone might possibly dare to die. But God demonstrates his own love for us in this: While we were still sinners, Christ died for us.

Matthew 9:35–10:8 [9–23] Jesus went through all the towns and villages, G teaching in their synagogues, preaching the good news of the kingdom and O healing every disease and sickness. When he saw the crowds, he had com- S passion on them, because they were harassed and helpless, like sheep P without a shepherd. Then he said to his disciples, "The harvest is plentiful E but the workers are few. Ask the Lord of the harvest, therefore, to send out L workers into his harvest field."

He called his twelve disciples to him and gave them authority to drive out evil spirits and to heal every disease and sickness.

These are the names of the twelve apostles: first, Simon (who is called Peter) and his brother Andrew; James son of Zebedee, and his brother

John; Philip and Bartholomew; Thomas and Matthew the tax collector; James son of Alphaeus, and Thaddaeus; Simon the Zealot and Judas Iscariot, who betrayed him.

These twelve Jesus sent out with the following instructions: "Do not go among the Gentiles or enter any town of the Samaritans. Go rather to the lost sheep of Israel. As you go, preach this message: 'The kingdom of heaven is near.' Heal the sick, raise the dead, cleanse those who have leprosy, drive out demons. Freely you have received, freely give." ["Do not take along any gold or silver or copper in your belts; take no bag for the journey, or extra tunic, or sandals or a staff; for the worker is worth his keep.

"Whatever town or village you enter, search for some worthy person there and stay at his house until you leave. As you enter the home, give it your greeting. If the home is deserving, let your peace rest on it; if it is not, let your peace return to you. If anyone will not welcome you or listen to your words, shake the dust off your feet when you leave that home or town. I tell you the truth, it will be more bearable for Sodom and Gomorrah on the day of judgment than for that town. I am sending you out like sheep among wolves. Therefore be as shrewd as snakes and as innocent as doves.

"Be on your guard against men; they will hand you over to the local councils and flog you in their synagogues. On my account you will be brought before governors and kings as witnesses to them and to the Gentiles. But when they arrest you, do not worry about what to say or how to say it. At that time you will be given what to say, for it will not be you speaking, but the Spirit of your Father speaking through you.

"Brother will betray brother to death, and a father his child; children will rebel against their parents and have them put to death. All men will hate you because of me, but he who stands firm to the end will be saved. When you are persecuted in one place, flee to another. I tell you the truth, you will not finish going through the cities of Israel before the Son of Man comes."]

Proper 7

Sunday between 19 and 25 June inclusive (if after Trinity Sunday)
Choose either 'continuous' or 'related' Old Testament and Psalm readings.

CONTINUOUS

Genesis 21:8–21   Isaac grew and was weaned, and on the day he was weaned Abraham held a great feast. But Sarah saw that the son whom Hagar the Egyptian had borne to Abraham was mocking, and she said to Abraham, "Get rid of that slave woman and her son, for that slave woman's son will never share in the inheritance with my son Isaac."

The matter distressed Abraham greatly because it concerned his son. But God said to him, "Do not be so distressed about the boy and your maidservant. Listen to whatever Sarah tells you, because it is through Isaac that your offspring will be reckoned. I will make the son of the maidservant into a nation also, because he is your offspring."

Early the next morning Abraham took some food and a skin of water and gave them to Hagar. He set them on her shoulders and then sent her off with the boy. She went on her way and wandered in the desert of Beersheba.

When the water in the skin was gone, she put the boy under one of the bushes. Then she went off and sat down nearby, about a bow-shot away, for she thought, "I cannot watch the boy die." And as she sat there nearby, she began to sob.

God heard the boy crying, and the angel of God called to Hagar from heaven and said to her, "What is the matter, Hagar? Do not be afraid; God has heard the boy crying as he lies there. Lift the boy up and take him by the hand, for I will make him into a great nation."

Then God opened her eyes and she saw a well of water. So she went and filled the skin with water and gave the boy a drink.

God was with the boy as he grew up. He lived in the desert and became an archer. While he was living in the Desert of Paran, his mother got a wife for him from Egypt.

and **Psalm 86:1–10, 16–17***   Hear, O LORD, and answer me,

> for I am poor and needy.
> Guard my life, for I am devoted to you.
>> You are my God; save your servant
>> who trusts in you.
> Have mercy on me, O Lord,
>> for I call to you all day long.
> Bring joy to your servant,
>> for to you, O Lord,
>> I lift up my soul.

> You are forgiving and good, O Lord,
>> abounding in love to all who call to you.
> Hear my prayer, O LORD;
>> listen to my cry for mercy.
> In the day of my trouble I will call to you,
>> for you will answer me.

> Among the gods there is none like you, O Lord;
>> no deeds can compare with yours.
> All the nations you have made
>> will come and worship before you, O Lord;
>> they will bring glory to your name.
> For you are great and do marvellous deeds;
>> you alone are God.

> Turn to me and have mercy on me;
>> grant your strength to your servant
>> and save the son of your maidservant.
> Give me a sign of your goodness,
>> that my enemies may see it and be put to shame,
>> for you, O LORD, have helped me and comforted me.

PSALM

Or **RELATED**

Jeremiah 20:7–13

O Lord, you deceived me, and I was deceived;
    you overpowered me and prevailed.
I am ridiculed all day long;
    everyone mocks me.
Whenever I speak, I cry out
    proclaiming violence and destruction.
So the word of the Lord has brought me
    insult and reproach all day long.
But if I say, "I will not mention him
    or speak any more in his name,"
his word is in my heart like a fire,
    a fire shut up in my bones.
I am weary of holding it in;
    indeed, I cannot.
I hear many whispering,
    "Terror on every side!
    Report him! Let's report him!"
All my friends
    are waiting for me to slip, saying,
"Perhaps he will be deceived;
    then we will prevail over him
    and take our revenge on him."

But the Lord is with me like a mighty
    warrior;
    so my persecutors will stumble and not
    prevail.
They will fail and be thoroughly disgraced;
    their dishonour will never be forgotten.
O Lord Almighty, you who examine the
    righteous
    and probe the heart and mind,
let me see your vengeance upon them,
    for to you I have committed my cause.

Sing to the Lord!
    Give praise to the Lord!
He rescues the life of the needy
    from the hands of the wicked.

FIRST READING

and **Psalm 69:7–10 [11–15]
16–18***

I endure scorn for your sake,
    and shame covers my face.
I am a stranger to my brothers,
    an alien to my own mother's sons;
    for zeal for your house consumes me,
    and the insults of those who insult you
    fall on me.

PSALM

When I weep and fast,
 I must endure scorn.
[When I put on sackcloth,
 people make sport of me.
Those who sit at the gate mock me,
 and I am the song of the drunkards.

But I pray to you, O Lord,
 in the time of your favour;
in your great love, O God,
 answer me with your sure salvation.
Rescue me from the mire,
 do not let me sink;
deliver me from those who hate me,
 from the deep waters.
Do not let the floodwaters engulf me
 or the depths swallow me up
 or the pit close its mouth over me.]

Answer me, O Lord, out of the goodness
 of your love;
 in your great mercy turn to me.
Do not hide your face from your servant;
 answer me quickly, for I am in trouble.
Come near and rescue me;
 redeem me because of my foes.

Romans 6:1b–11 Shall we go on sinning, so that grace may increase? By no
means! We died to sin; how can we live in it any longer? Or don't you know
that all of us who were baptised into Christ Jesus were baptised into his
death? We were therefore buried with him through baptism into death in
order that, just as Christ was raised from the dead through the glory of the
Father, we too may live a new life.

SECOND READING

If we have been united with him like this in his death, we will certainly
also be united with him in his resurrection. For we know that our old self
was crucified with him so that the body of sin might be done away with, that
we should no longer be slaves to sin – because anyone who has died has
been freed from sin.

Now if we died with Christ, we believe that we will also live with him.
For we know that since Christ was raised from the dead, he cannot die
again; death no longer has mastery over him. The death he died, he died to
sin once for all; but the life he lives, he lives to God.

In the same way, count yourselves dead to sin but alive to God in Christ
Jesus.

Matthew 10:24–39 Jesus said: "A student is not above his teacher, nor a servant above his master. It is enough for the student to be like his teacher,
and the servant like his master. If the head of the house has been called
Beelzebub, how much more the members of his household!

GOSPEL

"So do not be afraid of them. There is nothing concealed that will not be disclosed, or hidden that will not be made known. What I tell you in the dark, speak in the daylight; what is whispered in your ear, proclaim from the roofs. Do not be afraid of those who kill the body but cannot kill the soul. Rather, be afraid of the One who can destroy both soul and body in hell. Are not two sparrows sold for a penny? Yet not one of them will fall to the ground apart from the will of your Father. And even the very hairs of your head are all numbered. So don't be afraid; you are worth more than many sparrows.

"Whoever acknowledges me before men, I will also acknowledge him before my Father in heaven. But whoever disowns me before men, I will disown him before my Father in heaven.

"Do not suppose that I have come to bring peace to the earth. I did not come to bring peace, but a sword. For I have come to turn

"'a man against his father,
    a daughter against her mother,
a daughter-in-law against her mother-in-law –
    a man's enemies will be the members of his own household.'

"Anyone who loves his father or mother more than me is not worthy of me; anyone who loves his son or daughter more than me is not worthy of me; and anyone who does not take his cross and follow me is not worthy of me. Whoever finds his life will lose it, and whoever loses his life for my sake will find it."

Proper 8

Sunday between 26 June and 2 July inclusive (if after Trinity Sunday)
Choose either 'continuous' or 'related' Old Testament and Psalm readings.

CONTINUOUS

Genesis 22:1–14   God tested Abraham. He said to him, "Abraham!"

"Here I am," he replied.

Then God said, "Take your son, your only son, Isaac, whom you love, and go to the region of Moriah. Sacrifice him there as a burnt offering on one of the mountains I will tell you about."

Early the next morning Abraham got up and saddled his donkey. He took with him two of his servants and his son Isaac. When he had cut enough wood for the burnt offering, he set out for the place God had told him about. On the third day Abraham looked up and saw the place in the distance. He said to his servants, "Stay here with the donkey while I and the boy go over there. We will worship and then we will come back to you."

Abraham took the wood for the burnt offering and placed it on his son Isaac, and he himself carried the fire and the knife. As the two of them went on together, Isaac spoke up and said to his father Abraham, "Father?"

"Yes, my son?" Abraham replied.

"The fire and wood are here," Isaac said, "but where is the lamb for the burnt offering?"

Abraham answered, "God himself will provide the lamb for the burnt offering, my son." And the two of them went on together.

When they reached the place God had told him about, Abraham built an altar there and arranged the wood on it. He bound his son Isaac and laid him on the altar, on top of the wood. Then he reached out his hand and took the knife to slay his son. But the angel of the LORD called out to him from heaven, "Abraham! Abraham!"

"Here I am," he replied.

"Do not lay a hand on the boy," he said. "Do not do anything to him. Now I know that you fear God, because you have not withheld from me your son, your only son."

Abraham looked up and there in a thicket he saw a ram caught by its horns. He went over and took the ram and sacrificed it as a burnt offering instead of his son. So Abraham called that place The LORD Will Provide. And to this day it is said, "On the mountain of the LORD it will be provided."

and **Psalm 13**	How long, O LORD? Will you forget me for ever?	P
	How long will you hide your face from me?	S
	How long must I wrestle with my thoughts	A
	and every day have sorrow in my heart?	L
	How long will my enemy triumph over me?	M

Look on me and answer, O LORD my God.
    Give light to my eyes, or I will sleep in death;
my enemy will say, "I have overcome him,"
    and my foes will rejoice when I fall.

But I trust in your unfailing love;
    my heart rejoices in your salvation.
I will sing to the LORD,
    for he has been good to me.

Or **RELATED**

Jeremiah 28:5–9   The prophet Jeremiah replied to the prophet Hananiah F R before the priests and all the people who were standing in the house of the I E LORD. He said, "Amen! May the LORD do so! May the LORD fulfil the words R A you have prophesied by bringing the articles of the LORD's house and all the S D exiles back to this place from Babylon. Nevertheless, listen to what I have T I to say in your hearing and in the hearing of all the people: From early times N the prophets who preceded you and me have prophesied war, disaster and G plague against many countries and great kingdoms. But the prophet who prophesies peace will be recognised as one truly sent by the LORD only if his prediction comes true."

		P
		S
and **Psalm 89: 1–4,**	I will sing of the LORD's great love for ever;	A
15–18*	with my mouth I will make your faithfulness	L
	known through all generations.	M

I will declare that your love stands firm for ever,
that you established your faithfulness
in heaven itself.

You said, "I have made a covenant with my
chosen one,
I have sworn to David my servant,
'I will establish your line for ever
and make your throne firm through all
generations.'"

Blessed are those who have learned to acclaim you,
who walk in the light of your presence, O LORD.
They rejoice in your name all day long;
they exult in your righteousness.
For you are their glory and strength,
and by your favour you exalt our horn.
Indeed, our shield belongs to the LORD,
our king to the Holy One of Israel.

Romans 6:12–23   Do not let sin reign in your mortal body so that you obey its
evil desires. Do not offer the parts of your body to sin, as instruments of
wickedness, but rather offer yourselves to God, as those who have been
brought from death to life; and offer the parts of your body to him as
instruments of righteousness. For sin shall not be your master, because
you are not under law, but under grace.

What then? Shall we sin because we are not under law but under grace?
By no means! Don't you know that when you offer yourselves to someone
to obey him as slaves, you are slaves to the one whom you obey – whether
you are slaves to sin, which leads to death, or to obedience, which leads to
righteousness? But thanks be to God that, though you used to be slaves to
sin, you wholeheartedly obeyed the form of teaching to which you were
entrusted. You have been set free from sin and have become slaves to
righteousness.

I put this in human terms because you are weak in your natural selves.
Just as you used to offer the parts of your body in slavery to impurity and
to ever-increasing wickedness, so now offer them in slavery to righteousness leading to holiness. When you were slaves to sin, you were free from
the control of righteousness. What benefit did you reap at that time from
the things you are now ashamed of? Those things result in death! But now
that you have been set free from sin and have become slaves to God, the
benefit you reap leads to holiness, and the result is eternal life. For the
wages of sin is death, but the gift of God is eternal life in Christ Jesus our
Lord.

Matthew 10:40–42   Jesus said: "He who receives you receives me, and he
who receives me receives the one who sent me. Anyone who receives a
prophet because he is a prophet will receive a prophet's reward, and anyone who receives a righteous man because he is a righteous man will

receive a righteous man's reward. And if anyone gives even a cup of cold water to one of these little ones because he is my disciple, I tell you the truth, he will certainly not lose his reward."

Proper 9

Sunday between 3 and 9 July inclusive (if after Trinity Sunday)
Choose either 'continuous' or 'related' Old Testament and Psalm readings.

CONTINUOUS

Genesis 24:34–38, 42–49, 58–67   The man said to Laban, "I am Abraham's servant. The LORD has blessed my master abundantly, and he has become wealthy. He has given him sheep and cattle, silver and gold, menservants and maidservants, and camels and donkeys. My master's wife Sarah has borne him a son in her old age, and he has given him everything he owns. And my master made me swear an oath, and said, 'You must not get a wife for my son from the daughters of the Canaanites, in whose land I live, but go to my father's family and to my own clan, and get a wife for my son.'

"When I came to the spring today, I said, 'O LORD, God of my master Abraham, if you will, please grant success to the journey on which I have come. See, I am standing beside this spring; if a maiden comes out to draw water and I say to her, "Please let me drink a little water from your jar," and if she says to me, "Drink, and I'll draw water for your camels too," let her be the one the LORD has chosen for my master's son.'

"Before I finished praying in my heart, Rebekah came out, with her jar on her shoulder. She went down to the spring and drew water, and I said to her, 'Please give me a drink.'

"She quickly lowered her jar from her shoulder and said, 'Drink, and I'll water your camels too.' So I drank, and she watered the camels also.

"I asked her, 'Whose daughter are you?'

"She said, 'The daughter of Bethuel son of Nahor, whom Milcah bore to him.'

"Then I put the ring in her nose and the bracelets on her arms, and I bowed down and worshipped the LORD. I praised the LORD, the God of my master Abraham, who had led me on the right road to get the granddaughter of my master's brother for his son. Now if you will show kindness and faithfulness to my master, tell me; and if not, tell me, so I may know which way to turn."

So they called Rebekah and asked her, "Will you go with this man?"

"I will go," she said.

So they sent their sister Rebekah on her way, along with her nurse and Abraham's servant and his men. And they blessed Rebekah and said to her,

"Our sister, may you increase
    to thousands upon thousands;
may your offspring possess
    the gates of their enemies."

Then Rebekah and her maids got ready and mounted their camels and went back with the man. So the servant took Rebekah and left.

Now Isaac had come from Beer Lahai Roi, for he was living in the Negev. He went out to the field one evening to meditate, and as he looked up, he saw camels approaching. Rebekah also looked up and saw Isaac. She got down from her camel and asked the servant, "Who is that man in the field coming to meet us?"

"He is my master," the servant answered. So she took her veil and covered herself.

Then the servant told Isaac all he had done. Isaac brought her into the tent of his mother Sarah, and he married Rebekah. So she became his wife, and he loved her; and Isaac was comforted after his mother's death.

and **Psalm 45: 10–17**	Listen, O daughter, consider and give ear:	P
	Forget your people and your father's house.	S
	The king is enthralled by your beauty;	A
	honour him, for he is your lord.	L
	The Daughter of Tyre will come with a gift,	M
	people of wealth will seek your favour.	

All glorious is the princess within [her chamber];
  her gown is interwoven with gold.
In embroidered garments she is led to the king;
  her virgin companions follow her
    and are brought to you.
They are led in with joy and gladness;
  they enter the palace of the king.

Your sons will take the place of your fathers;
  you will make them princes throughout the land.
I will perpetuate your memory through all
    generations;
  therefore the nations will praise you for ever
    and ever.

or Canticle:

Song of Solomon **2: 8–13**	Listen! My lover!	C
	Look! Here he comes,	A
	leaping across the mountains,	N
	bounding over the hills.	T
	My lover is like a gazelle or a young stag.	I
	Look! There he stands behind our wall,	C
	gazing through the windows,	L
	peering through the lattice.	E

My lover spoke and said to me,
  "Arise, my darling,
    my beautiful one, and come with me.
See! the winter is past;
  the rains are over and gone.
Flowers appear on the earth;
  the season of singing has come,

the cooing of doves
  is heard in our land.
The fig-tree forms its early fruit;
  the blossoming vines spread their fragrance.
Arise, come, my darling;
  my beautiful one, come with me."

Or **RELATED**

FIRST READING

Zechariah 9:9–12 Rejoice greatly, O Daughter of Zion!
  Shout, Daughter of Jerusalem!
See, your king comes to you,
  righteous and having salvation,
  gentle and riding on a donkey,
  on a colt, the foal of a donkey.
I will take away the chariots from Ephraim
  and the war-horses from Jerusalem,
  and the battle-bow will be broken.
He will proclaim peace to the nations.
  His rule will extend from sea to sea
  and from the River to the ends of the earth.
As for you, because of the blood of my
    covenant with you,
I will free your prisoners from the waterless pit.
Return to your fortress, O prisoners of hope;
  even now I announce that I will restore
    twice as much to you.

PSALM

and **Psalm 145:8–14** The LORD is gracious and compassionate,
  slow to anger and rich in love.
The LORD is good to all;
  he has compassion on all he has made.
All you have made will praise you, O LORD;
  your saints will extol you.
They will tell of the glory of your kingdom
  and speak of your might,
so that all men may know of your mighty acts
  and the glorious splendour of your kingdom.
Your kingdom is an everlasting kingdom,
  and your dominion endures through all generations.

The LORD is faithful to all his promises
  and loving towards all he has made.
The LORD upholds all those who fall
  and lifts up all who are bowed down.

SECOND

Romans 7:15–25a I do not understand what I do. For what I want to do I do not do, but what I hate I do. And if I do what I do not want to do, I agree that the law is good. As it is, it is no longer I myself who do it, but it is sin living in me. I know that nothing good lives in me, that is, in my sinful nature. For I have the desire to do what is good, but I cannot carry it out. For what I do is not the good I want to do; no, the evil I do not want to do – this I keep on doing. Now if I do what I do not want to do, it is no longer I who do it, but it is sin living in me that does it.

So I find this law at work: When I want to do good, evil is right there with me. For in my inner being I delight in God's law; but I see another law at work in the members of my body, waging war against the law of my mind and making me a prisoner of the law of sin at work within my members. What a wretched man I am! Who will rescue me from this body of death? Thanks be to God – through Jesus Christ our LORD!

Matthew 11:16–19, 25–30   Jesus asked: "To what can I compare this genera- tion? They are like children sitting in the market-places and calling out to others:

> "'We played the flute for you,
>   and you did not dance;
> we sang a dirge,
>   and you did not mourn.'

For John came neither eating nor drinking, and they say, 'He has a demon.' The Son of Man came eating and drinking, and they say, 'Here is a glutton and a drunkard, a friend of tax collectors and "sinners".' But wisdom is proved right by her actions."

And Jesus went on to say, "I praise you, Father, Lord of heaven and earth, because you have hidden these things from the wise and learned, and revealed them to little children. Yes, Father, for this was your good pleasure.

"All things have been committed to me by my Father. No-one knows the Son except the Father, and no-one knows the Father except the Son and those to whom the Son chooses to reveal him.

"Come to me, all you who are weary and burdened, and I will give you rest. Take my yoke upon you and learn from me, for I am gentle and humble in heart, and you will find rest for your souls. For my yoke is easy and my burden is light."

Proper 10

Sunday between 10 and 16 July inclusive (if after Trinity Sunday)
Choose either 'continuous' or 'related' Old Testament and Psalm readings.

CONTINUOUS

Genesis 25:19–34   This is the account of Abraham's son Isaac.

Abraham became the father of Isaac, and Isaac was forty years old when he married Rebekah daughter of Bethuel the Aramean from Paddan Aram and sister of Laban the Aramean.

Isaac prayed to the LORD on behalf of his wife, because she was barren. The LORD answered his prayer, and his wife Rebekah became pregnant.

The babies jostled each other within her, and she said, "Why is this happening to me?" So she went to enquire of the LORD.

The LORD said to her,

"Two nations are in your womb,
    and two peoples from within you will be separated;
one people will be stronger than the other,
    and the older will serve the younger."

When the time came for her to give birth, there were twin boys in her womb. The first to come out was red, and his whole body was like a hairy garment; so they named him Esau. After this, his brother came out, with his hand grasping Esau's heel; so he was named Jacob. Isaac was sixty years old when Rebekah gave birth to them.

The boys grew up, and Esau became a skilful hunter, a man of the open country, while Jacob was a quiet man, staying among the tents. Isaac, who had a taste for wild game, loved Esau, but Rebekah loved Jacob.

Once when Jacob was cooking some stew, Esau came in from the open country, famished. He said to Jacob, "Quick, let me have some of that red stew! I'm famished!" (That is why he was also called Edom.)

Jacob replied, "First sell me your birthright."

"Look, I am about to die," Esau said. "What good is the birthright to me?"

But Jacob said, "Swear to me first." So he swore an oath to him, selling his birthright to Jacob.

Then Jacob gave Esau some bread and some lentil stew. He ate and drank, and then got up and left.

So Esau despised his birthright.

and **Psalm 119:105–112**

Your word is a lamp to my feet
    and a light for my path.
I have taken an oath and confirmed it,
    that I will follow your righteous laws.
I have suffered much;
    preserve my life, O LORD, according to your word.
Accept, O LORD, the willing praise of my mouth,
    and teach me your laws.
Though I constantly take my life in my hands,
    I will not forget your law.
The wicked have set a snare for me,
    but I have not strayed from your precepts.
Your statutes are my heritage for ever;
    they are the joy of my heart.
My heart is set on keeping your decrees
    to the very end.

Or **RELATED**

Isaiah 55:10–13

"As the rain and the snow
    come down from heaven,

P
S
A
L
M

F
I
R
S
T

and do not return to it   R
   without watering the earth   E
and making it bud and flourish,   A
   so that it yields seed for the sower   D
     and bread for the eater,   I
so is my word that goes out from my mouth: N
   It will not return to me empty,   G
but will accomplish what I desire
   and achieve the purpose for which I sent it.
You will go out in joy
   and be led forth in peace;
the mountains and hills
   will burst into song before you,
and all the trees of the field
   will clap their hands.
Instead of the thornbush will grow the pine tree,
   and instead of briers the myrtle will grow.
This will be for the LORD's renown,
   for an everlasting sign,
   which will not be destroyed."

and **Psalm 65:[1–8] 9–13***   [Praise awaits you, O God, in Zion;   P
   to you our vows will be fulfilled.   S
O you who hear prayer,   A
   to you all people will come.   L
When we were overwhelmed by sins,   M
   you forgave our transgressions.
Blessed are those you choose
   and bring near to live in your courts!
We are filled with the good things of your house,
   of your holy temple.

You answer us with awesome deeds of
     righteousness,
   O God our Saviour,
the hope of all the ends of the earth
   and of the farthest seas,
who formed the mountains by your power,
   having armed yourself with strength,
who stilled the roaring of the seas,
   the roaring of their waves,
   and the turmoil of the nations.
Those living far away fear your wonders;
   where morning dawns and evening fades
   you call forth songs of joy.]

You care for the land and water it;
   you enrich it abundantly.

The streams of God are filled with water
    to provide the people with corn,
    for so you have ordained it.
You drench its furrows
    and level its ridges;
you soften it with showers
    and bless its crops.
You crown the year with your bounty,
    and your carts overflow with abundance.
The grasslands of the desert overflow;
    the hills are clothed with gladness.
The meadows are covered with flocks
    and the valleys are mantled with corn;
    they shout for joy and sing.

Romans 8:1–11 There is now no condemnation for those who are in Christ Jesus, because through Christ Jesus the law of the Spirit of life set me free from the law of sin and death. For what the law was powerless to do in that it was weakened by the sinful nature, God did by sending his own Son in the likeness of sinful man to be a sin offering. And so he condemned sin in sinful man, in order that the righteous requirements of the law might be fully met in us, who do not live according to the sinful nature but according to the Spirit.

Those who live according to the sinful nature have their minds set on what that nature desires; but those who live in accordance with the Spirit have their minds set on what the Spirit desires. The mind of sinful man is death, but the mind controlled by the Spirit is life and peace; the sinful mind is hostile to God. It does not submit to God's law, nor can it do so. Those controlled by the sinful nature cannot please God.

You, however, are controlled not by the sinful nature but by the Spirit, if the Spirit of God lives in you. And if anyone does not have the Spirit of Christ, he does not belong to Christ. But if Christ is in you, your body is dead because of sin, yet your spirit is alive because of righteousness. And if the Spirit of him who raised Jesus from the dead is living in you, he who raised Christ from the dead will also give life to your mortal bodies through his Spirit, who lives in you.

Matthew 13:1–9, 18–23 Jesus went out of the house and sat by the lake. Such large crowds gathered round him that he got into a boat and sat in it, while all the people stood on the shore. Then he told them many things in parables, saying: "A farmer went out to sow his seed. As he was scattering the seed, some fell along the path, and the birds came and ate it up. Some fell on rocky places, where it did not have much soil. It sprang up quickly, because the soil was shallow. But when the sun came up, the plants were scorched, and they withered because they had no root. Other seed fell among thorns, which grew up and choked the plants. Still other seed fell on good soil, where it produced a crop – a hundred, sixty or thirty times what was sown. Those who have ears, let him hear."

"Listen then to what the parable of the sower means: When anyone hears the message about the kingdom and does not understand it, the evil one comes and snatches away what was sown in his heart. This is the seed sown along the path. The one who received the seed that fell on rocky places is the man who hears the word and at once receives it with joy. But since he has no root, he lasts only a short time. When trouble or persecution comes because of the word, he quickly falls away. The one who received the seed that fell among the thorns is the man who hears the word, but the worries of this life and the deceitfulness of wealth choke it, making it unfruitful. But the one who received the seed that fell on good soil is the man who hears the word and understands it. He produces a crop, yielding a hundred, sixty or thirty times what was sown."

Proper 11

Sunday between 17 and 23 July inclusive (if after Trinity Sunday)
Choose either 'continuous' or 'related' Old Testament and Psalm readings.

CONTINUOUS

Genesis 28:10–19a   Jacob left Beersheba and set out for Haran. When he F reached a certain place, he stopped for the night because the sun had set. I Taking one of the stones there, he put it under his head and lay down to R sleep. He had a dream in which he saw a stairway resting on the earth, with S its top reaching to heaven, and the angels of God were ascending and T descending on it. There above it stood the Lord, and he said: "I am the Lord, the God of your father Abraham and the God of Isaac. I will give you R and your descendants the land on which you are lying. Your descendants E will be like the dust of the earth, and you will spread out to the west and to A the east, to the north and to the south. All peoples on earth will be blessed D through you and your offspring. I am with you and will watch over you I wherever you go, and I will bring you back to this land. I will not leave you N until I have done what I have promised you." G

When Jacob awoke from his sleep, he thought, "Surely the Lord is in this place, and I was not aware of it." He was afraid and said, "How awesome is this place! This is none other than the house of God; this is the gate of heaven."

Early the next morning Jacob took the stone he had placed under his head and set it up as a pillar and poured oil on top of it. He called that place Bethel.

and **Psalm 139: 1–12, 23–24***	O Lord, you have searched me and you know me.	P
		S
	You know when I sit and when I rise;	A
	you perceive my thoughts from afar.	L
	You discern my going out and my lying down;	M
	you are familiar with all my ways.	

Before a word is on my tongue
　　you know it completely, O Lord.

You hem me in – behind and before;
　　you have laid your hand upon me.
Such knowledge is too wonderful for me,
　　too lofty for me to attain.

Where can I go from your Spirit?
　　Where can I flee from your presence?
If I go up to the heavens, you are there;
　　if I make my bed in the depths, you are there.
If I rise on the wings of the dawn,
　　if I settle on the far side of the sea,
even there your hand will guide me,
　　your right hand will hold me fast.

If I say, "Surely the darkness will hide me
　　and the light become night around me,"
even the darkness will not be dark to you;
　　the night will shine like the day,
　　for darkness is as light to you.

Search me, O God, and know my heart;
　　test me and know my anxious thoughts.
See if there is any offensive way in me,
　　and lead me in the way everlasting.

Or **RELATED**
Wisdom of Solomon 12:13, 16–19

Or **Isaiah 44:6–8**　　"This is what the Lord says –　　F R
　　　　Israel's King and Redeemer, the Lord Almighty:　　I E
I am the first and I am the last;　　R A
　　apart from me there is no God.　　S D
Who then is like me? Let him proclaim it.　　T I
　　Let him declare and lay out before me　　N
what has happened since I established my ancient　　G
　　　　people,
　　and what is yet to come –
　　yes, let them foretell what will come.
Do not tremble, do not be afraid.
　　Did I not proclaim this and foretell it long ago?
You are my witnesses. Is there any God besides me?
　　No, there is no other Rock; I know not one."

　　　　　　　　　　　　　　　　　　　　　　P
and **Psalm 86:11–17**　　Teach me your way, O Lord,　　S
　　and I will walk in your truth;　　A
give me an undivided heart,　　L
　　that I may fear your name.　　M

I will praise you, O Lord my God, with all my heart;
　　I will glorify your name for ever.
For great is your love towards me;
　　you have delivered me from the depths of the grave.

The arrogant are attacking me, O God;
　　a band of ruthless men seeks my life –
　　men without regard for you.
But you, O Lord, are a compassionate and gracious God,
　　slow to anger, abounding in love and faithfulness.
Turn to me and have mercy on me;
　　grant your strength to your servant
　　and save the son of your maidservant.
Give me a sign of your goodness,
　　that my enemies may see it and be put to shame,
　　for you, O Lord, have helped me and comforted me.

Romans 8:12–25　Brothers, we have an obligation – but it is not to the sinful nature, to live according to it. For if you live according to the sinful nature, you will die; but if by the Spirit you put to death the misdeeds of the body, you will live, because those who are led by the Spirit of God are sons of God. For you did not receive a spirit that makes you a slave again to fear, but you received the Spirit of adoption. And by him we cry, "*Abba*, Father." The Spirit himself testifies with our spirit that we are God's children. Now if we are children, then we are heirs – heirs of God and co-heirs with Christ, if indeed we share in his sufferings in order that we may also share in his glory.

I consider that our present sufferings are not worth comparing with the glory that will be revealed in us. The creation waits in eager expectation for the children of God to be revealed. For the creation was subjected to frustration, not by its own choice, but by the will of the one who subjected it, in hope that the creation itself will be liberated from its bondage to decay and brought into the glorious freedom of the children of God.

We know that the whole creation has been groaning as in the pains of childbirth right up to the present time. Not only so, but we ourselves, who have the firstfruits of the Spirit, groan inwardly as we wait eagerly for our adoption as sons, the redemption of our bodies. For in this hope we were saved. But hope that is seen is no hope at all. Who hopes for what he already has? But if we hope for what we do not yet have, we wait for it patiently.

Matthew 13:24–30, 36–43　Jesus told a parable to the crowd: "The kingdom of heaven is like a man who sowed good seed in his field. But while everyone was sleeping, his enemy came and sowed weeds among the wheat, and went away. When the wheat sprouted and formed ears, then the weeds also appeared.

"The owner's servants came to him and said, 'Sir, didn't you sow good seed in your field? Where then did the weeds come from?'

"'An enemy did this,' he replied.

"The servants asked him, 'Do you want us to go and pull them up?' "'No,' he answered, 'because while you are pulling the weeds, you may root up the wheat with them. Let both grow together until the harvest. At that time I will tell the harvesters: First collect the weeds and tie them in bundles to be burned; then gather the wheat and bring it into my barn.'"

Then Jesus left the crowd and went into the house. His disciples came to him and said, "Explain to us the parable of the weeds in the field."

He answered, "The one who sowed the good seed is the Son of Man. The field is the world, and the good seed stands for the sons of the kingdom. The weeds are the sons of the evil one, and the enemy who sows them is the devil. The harvest is the end of the age, and the harvesters are angels.

"As the weeds are pulled up and burned in the fire, so it will be at the end of the age. The Son of Man will send out his angels, and they will weed out of his kingdom everything that causes sin and all who do evil. They will throw them into the fiery furnace, where there will be weeping and gnashing of teeth. Then the righteous will shine like the sun in the kingdom of their Father. He who has ears, let him hear."

Proper 12

Sunday between 24 and 30 July inclusive (if after Trinity Sunday)
Choose either 'continuous' or 'related' Old Testament and Psalm readings.

CONTINUOUS

Genesis 29:15–28   Laban said to Jacob, "Just because you are a relative of mine, should you work for me for nothing? Tell me what your wages should be."

Now Laban had two daughters; the name of the older was Leah, and the name of the younger was Rachel. Leah had weak eyes, but Rachel was lovely in form, and beautiful. Jacob was in love with Rachel and said, "I'll work for you seven years in return for your younger daughter Rachel."

Laban said, "It's better that I give her to you than to some other man. Stay here with me." So Jacob served seven years to get Rachel, but they seemed like only a few days to him because of his love for her.

Then Jacob said to Laban, "Give me my wife. My time is completed, and I want to lie with her."

So Laban brought together all the people of the place and gave a feast. But when evening came, he took his daughter Leah and gave her to Jacob, and Jacob lay with her. And Laban gave his servant Zilpah to his daughter as her maidservant.

When morning came, there was Leah! So Jacob said to Laban, "What is this you have done to me? I served you for Rachel, didn't I? Why have you deceived me?"

Laban replied, "It is not our custom here to give the younger daughter in marriage before the older one. Finish this daughter's bridal week; then we will give you the younger one also, in return for another seven years of work."

FIRST READING

And Jacob did so. He finished the week with Leah, and then Laban gave him his daughter Rachel to be his wife.

and **Psalm 105:1–11, 45b**	Give thanks to the Lord, call on his name;	P
	make known among the nations what he has	S
	done.	A
	Sing to him, sing praise to him;	L
	tell of all his wonderful acts.	M

Glory in his holy name;
    let the hearts of those who seek the Lord rejoice.
Look to the Lord and his strength;
    seek his face always.

Remember the wonders he has done,
    his miracles, and the judgments he
        pronounced,
O descendants of Abraham his servant,
    O children of Jacob, his chosen ones.
He is the Lord our God;
    his judgments are in all the earth.

He remembers his covenant for ever,
    the word he commanded, for a thousand
        generations,
the covenant he made with Abraham,
    the oath he swore to Isaac.
He confirmed it to Jacob as a decree,
    to Israel as an everlasting covenant:
"To you I will give the land of Canaan
    as the portion you will inherit."

Praise the Lord.

or **Psalm 128**	Blessed are all who fear the Lord,	P
	who walk in his ways.	S
	You will eat the fruit of your labour;	A
	blessings and prosperity will be yours.	L
	Your wife will be like a fruitful vine	M

    within your house;
your sons will be like olive shoots
    round your table.
Thus is the man blessed
    who fears the Lord.

May the Lord bless you from Zion
    all the days of your life;
may you see the prosperity of Jerusalem,
    and may you live to see your children's
        children.

Peace be upon Israel.

Or **RELATED**

1 Kings 3:5–12   At Gibeon the LORD appeared to Solomon during the night in
a dream, and God said, "Ask for whatever you want me to give you."

Solomon answered, "You have shown great kindness to your servant,
my father David, because he was faithful to you and righteous and upright
in heart. You have continued this great kindness to him and have given him
a son to sit on his throne this very day.

"Now, O LORD my God, you have made your servant king in place of my
father David. But I am only a little child and do not know how to carry out
my duties. Your servant is here among the people you have chosen, a great
people, too numerous to count or number. So give your servant a discerning heart to govern your people and to distinguish between right and
wrong. For who is able to govern this great people of yours?"

The Lord was pleased that Solomon had asked for this. So God said to
him, "Since you have asked for this and not for long life or wealth for yourself, nor have asked for the death of your enemies but for discernment in
administering justice, I will do what you have asked. I will give you a wise
and discerning heart, so that there will never have been anyone like you,
nor will there ever be."

and **Psalm 119:129–136**

Your statutes are wonderful;
  therefore I obey them.
The unfolding of your words gives light;
  it gives understanding to the simple.
I open my mouth and pant,
  longing for your commands.
Turn to me and have mercy on me,
  as you always do to those who love your name.
Direct my footsteps according to your word;
  let no sin rule over me.
Redeem me from the oppression of men,
  that I may obey your precepts.
Make your face shine upon your servant
  and teach me your decrees.
Streams of tears flow from my eyes,
  for your law is not obeyed.

Romans 8:26–39   The Spirit helps us in our weakness. We do not know what
we ought to pray for, but the Spirit himself intercedes for us with groans
that words cannot express. And he who searches our hearts knows the
mind of the Spirit, because the Spirit intercedes for the saints in accordance with God's will.

And we know that in all things God works for the good of those who love
him, who have been called according to his purpose. For those God foreknew
he also predestined to be conformed to the likeness of his Son, that he might

be the firstborn among many brothers. And those he predestined, he also called; those he called, he also justified; those he justified, he also glorified.

What, then, shall we say in response to this? If God is for us, who can be against us? He who did not spare his own Son, but gave him up for us all – how will he not also, along with him, graciously give us all things? Who will bring any charge against those whom God has chosen? It is God who justifies. Who is he that condemns? Christ Jesus, who died – more than that, who was raised to life – is at the right hand of God and is also interceding for us. Who shall separate us from the love of Christ? Shall trouble or hardship or persecution or famine or nakedness or danger or sword? As it is written:

"For your sake we face death all day long;
    we are considered as sheep to be slaughtered."

No, in all these things we are more than conquerors through him who loved us. For I am convinced that neither death nor life, neither angels nor demons, neither the present nor the future, nor any powers, neither height nor depth, nor anything else in all creation, will be able to separate us from the love of God that is in Christ Jesus our Lord.

Matthew 13:31–33, 44–52 Jesus told the crowd a parable: "The kingdom of heaven is like a mustard seed, which a man took and planted in his field. Though it is the smallest of all your seeds, yet when it grows, it is the largest of garden plants and becomes a tree, so that the birds of the air come and perch in its branches."

He told them another parable: "The kingdom of heaven is like yeast that a woman took and mixed into a large amount of flour until it worked all through the dough."

"The kingdom of heaven is like treasure hidden in a field. When a man found it, he hid it again, and then in his joy went and sold all he had and bought that field.

"Again, the kingdom of heaven is like a merchant looking for fine pearls. When he found one of great value, he went away and sold everything he had and bought it.

"Once again, the kingdom of heaven is like a net that was let down into the lake and caught all kinds of fish. When it was full, the fishermen pulled it up on the shore. Then they sat down and collected the good fish in baskets, but threw the bad away. This is how it will be at the end of the age. The angels will come and separate the wicked from the righteous and throw them into the fiery furnace, where there will be weeping and gnashing of teeth.

"Have you understood all these things?" Jesus asked.

"Yes," they replied.

He said to them, "Therefore every teacher of the law who has been instructed about the kingdom of heaven is like the owner of a house who brings out of the storeroom new treasures as well as old."

Proper 13

Sunday between 31 July and 6 August inclusive (if after Trinity Sunday)
Choose either 'continuous' or 'related' Old Testament and Psalm readings.

CONTINUOUS

Genesis 32:22–31   At night Jacob got up and took his two wives, his two maid- F
servants and his eleven sons and crossed the ford of the Jabbok. After he I
had sent them across the stream, he sent over all his possessions. So Jacob R
was left alone, and a man wrestled with him till daybreak. When the man S
saw that he could not overpower him, he touched the socket of Jacob's hip T
so that his hip was wrenched as he wrestled with the man. Then the man
said, "Let me go, for it is daybreak."   R

But Jacob replied, "I will not let you go unless you bless me."   E
The man asked him, "What is your name?"   A
"Jacob," he answered.   D
Then the man said, "Your name will no longer be Jacob, but Israel, be- I
cause you have struggled with both God and with men and have overcome." N
Jacob said, "Please tell me your name."   G
But he replied, "Why do you ask my name?" Then he blessed him there.
So Jacob called the place Peniel, saying, "It is because I saw God face to
face, and yet my life was spared."

The sun rose above him as he passed Peniel, and he was limping because
of his hip.

and **Psalm 17:1–7, 15***   Hear, O LORD, my righteous plea;   P
       listen to my cry.   S
Give ear to my prayer –   A
       it does not rise from deceitful lips.   L
May my vindication come from you;   M
       may your eyes see what is right.
Though you probe my heart and examine me at night,
       though you test me, you will find nothing;
       I have resolved that my mouth will not sin.
As for the deeds of men –
       by the word of your lips
I have kept myself
       from the ways of the violent.
My steps have held to your paths;
       my feet have not slipped.

I call on you, O God, for you will answer me;
       give ear to me and hear my prayer.
Show the wonder of your great love,
       you who save by your right hand
       those who take refuge in you from their foes.

And I – in righteousness I shall see your face;
       when I awake, I shall be satisfied with seeing
         your likeness.

Or **RELATED**

Isaiah 55:1–5

"Come, all you who are thirsty,
come to the waters;
and you who have no money,
come, buy and eat!
Come, buy wine and milk
without money and without cost.
Why spend money on what is not bread,
and your labour on what does not satisfy?
Listen, listen to me, and eat what is good,
and your soul will delight in the richest of fare.
Give ear and come to me;
hear me, that your soul may live.
I will make an everlasting covenant with you,
my faithful love promised to David.
See, I have made him a witness to the peoples,
a leader and commander of the peoples.
Surely you will summon nations you know not,
and nations that do not know you will hasten to
you,
because of the LORD your God,
the Holy One of Israel,
for he has endowed you with splendour."

F
I
R
S
T

R
E
A
D
I
N
G

and **Psalm 145:8–9,
14–21***

The LORD is gracious and compassionate,
slow to anger and rich in love.
The LORD is good to all;
he has compassion on all he has made.

The LORD upholds all those who fall
and lifts up all who are bowed down.
The eyes of all look to you,
and you give them their food at the proper
time.
You open your hand
and satisfy the desires of every living thing.

The LORD is righteous in all his ways
and loving towards all he has made.
The LORD is near to all who call on him,
to all who call on him in truth.
He fulfils the desires of those who fear him;
he hears their cry and saves them.
The LORD watches over all who love him,
but all the wicked he will destroy.

My mouth will speak in praise of the LORD.
Let every creature praise his holy name
for ever and ever.

P
S
A
L
M

Romans 9:1–5   I speak the truth in Christ – I am not lying, my conscience
confirms it in the Holy Spirit – I have great sorrow and unceasing anguish
in my heart. For I could wish that I myself were cursed and cut off from
Christ for the sake of my brothers, those of my own race, the people of
Israel. Theirs is the adoption as sons; theirs the divine glory, the covenants,
the receiving of the law, the temple worship and the promises. Theirs are
the patriarchs, and from them is traced the human ancestry of Christ, who
is God over all, for ever praised! Amen.

S R
E E
C A
O D
N I
D N
G

Matthew 14:13–21   When Jesus heard about the death of John the Baptist, he
withdrew by boat privately to a solitary place. Hearing of this, the crowds
followed him on foot from the towns. When Jesus landed and saw a large
crowd, he had compassion on them and healed their sick.

As evening approached, the disciples came to him and said, "This is a
remote place, and it's already getting late. Send the crowds away, so that
they can go to the villages and buy themselves some food."

Jesus replied, "They do not need to go away. You give them something to
eat."

"We have here only five loaves of bread and two fish," they answered.

"Bring them here to me," he said. And he directed the people to sit down
on the grass. Taking the five loaves and the two fish and looking up to
heaven, he gave thanks and broke the loaves. Then he gave them to the disciples, and the disciples gave them to the people. They all ate and were
satisfied, and the disciples picked up twelve basketfuls of broken pieces
that were left over. The number of those who ate was about five thousand
men, besides women and children.

G
O
S
P
E
L

Proper 14

Sunday between 7 and 13 August inclusive (if after Trinity Sunday)
Choose either 'continuous' or 'related' Old Testament and Psalm readings.

CONTINUOUS

Genesis 37:1–4, 12–28   Jacob lived in the land where his father had stayed,
the land of Canaan.

This is the account of Jacob.

Joseph, a young man of seventeen, was tending the flocks with his brothers, the sons of Bilhah and the sons of Zilpah, his father's wives, and he
brought their father a bad report about them.

Now Israel loved Joseph more than any of his other sons, because he had
been born to him in his old age; and he made a richly ornamented robe for
him. When his brothers saw that their father loved him more than any of
them, they hated him and could not speak a kind word to him.

Now his brothers had gone to graze their father's flocks near Shechem,
and Israel said to Joseph, "As you know, your brothers are grazing the
flocks near Shechem. Come, I am going to send you to them."

"Very well," he replied.

F
I
R
S
T

R
E
A
D
I
N
G

So he said to him, "Go and see if all is well with your brothers and with the flocks, and bring word back to me." Then he sent him off from the Valley of Hebron.

When Joseph arrived at Shechem, a man found him wandering around in the fields and asked him, "What are you looking for?"

He replied, "I'm looking for my brothers. Can you tell me where they are grazing their flocks?"

"They have moved on from here," the man answered. "I heard them say, 'Let's go to Dothan.'"

So Joseph went after his brothers and found them near Dothan. But they saw him in the distance, and before he reached them, they plotted to kill him.

"Here comes that dreamer!" they said to each other. "Come now, let's kill him and throw him into one of these cisterns and say that a ferocious animal devoured him. Then we'll see what comes of his dreams."

When Reuben heard this, he tried to rescue him from their hands. "Let's not take his life," he said. "Don't shed any blood. Throw him into this cistern here in the desert, but don't lay a hand on him." Reuben said this to rescue him from them and take him back to his father.

So when Joseph came to his brothers, they stripped him of his robe – the richly ornamented robe he was wearing – and they took him and threw him into the cistern. Now the cistern was empty; there was no water in it.

As they sat down to eat their meal, they looked up and saw a caravan of Ishmaelites coming from Gilead. Their camels were loaded with spices, balm and myrrh, and they were on their way to take them down to Egypt.

Judah said to his brothers, "What will we gain if we kill our brother and cover up his blood? Come, let's sell him to the Ishmaelites and not lay our hands on him; after all, he is our brother, our own flesh and blood." His brothers agreed.

So when the Midianite merchants came by, his brothers pulled Joseph up out of the cistern and sold him for twenty shekels of silver to the Ishmaelites, who took him to Egypt.

and **Psalm 105:1–6, 16–22, 45b***	Give thanks to the Lord, call on his name;	P
	make known among the nations what he has done.	S
	Sing to him, sing praise to him;	A
	tell of all his wonderful acts.	L
	Glory in his holy name;	M
	let the hearts of those who seek the Lord rejoice.	

Look to the Lord and his strength;
seek his face always.

Remember the wonders he has done,
his miracles, and the judgments he pronounced,
O descendants of Abraham his servant,
O children of Jacob, his chosen ones.

He called down famine on the land
and destroyed all their supplies of food;

and he sent a man before them –
    Joseph, sold as a slave.
They bruised his feet with shackles,
    his neck was put in irons,
till what he foretold came to pass,
    till the word of the LORD proved him true.
The king sent and released him,
    the ruler of peoples set him free.
He made him master of his household,
    ruler over all he possessed,
to instruct his princes as he pleased
    and teach his elders wisdom.

    Praise the LORD.

Or **RELATED**

1 Kings 19:9–18   Elijah went into a cave at Horeb and spent the night there. F

    And the word of the LORD came to him: "What are you doing here, Eli- I
jah?"

    He replied, "I have been very zealous for the LORD God Almighty. The S
Israelites have rejected your covenant, broken down your altars, and put T
your prophets to death with the sword. I am the only one left, and now they
are trying to kill me too." R

    The LORD said, "Go out and stand on the mountain in the presence of the E
LORD, for the LORD is about to pass by." A

    Then a great and powerful wind tore the mountains apart and shattered D
the rocks before the LORD, but the LORD was not in the wind. After the wind I
there was an earthquake, but the LORD was not in the earthquake. After the N
earthquake came a fire, but the LORD was not in the fire. And after the fire G
came a gentle whisper. When Elijah heard it, he pulled his cloak over his
face and went out and stood at the mouth of the cave.

    Then a voice said to him, "What are you doing here, Elijah?"

    He replied, "I have been very zealous for the LORD God Almighty. The
Israelites have rejected your covenant, broken down your altars, and put
your prophets to death with the sword. I am the only one left, and now they
are trying to kill me too."

    The LORD said to him, "Go back the way you came, and go to the Desert
of Damascus. When you get there, anoint Hazael king over Aram. Also,
anoint Jehu son of Nimshi king over Israel, and anoint Elisha son of
Shaphat from Abel Meholah to succeed you as prophet. Jehu will put to
death any who escape the sword of Hazael, and Elisha will put to death any
who escape the sword of Jehu. Yet I reserve seven thousand in Israel – all
whose knees have not bowed down to Baal and all whose mouths have not
kissed him." P

S

and **Psalm 85:8–13**   I will listen to what God the LORD will say; A
    he promises peace to his people, his saints – L
    but let them not return to folly. M

Surely his salvation is near those who fear him,
　　that his glory may dwell in our land.

Love and faithfulness meet together;
　　righteousness and peace kiss each other.
Faithfulness springs forth from the earth,
　　and righteousness looks down from heaven.
The LORD will indeed give what is good,
　　and our land will yield its harvest.
Righteousness goes before him
　　and prepares the way for his steps.

Romans 10:5–15   Moses describes in this way the righteousness that is by S
the law: "The man who does these things will live by them." But the right- E
eousness that is by faith says: "Do not say in your heart, 'Who will ascend C
into heaven?'" (that is, to bring Christ down) "or 'Who will descend into the O
deep?'" (that is, to bring Christ up from the dead). But what does it say? N
"The word is near you; it is in your mouth and in your heart," that is, the D
word of faith we are proclaiming: That if you confess with your mouth,
"Jesus is Lord," and believe in your heart that God raised him from the R
dead, you will be saved. For it is with your heart that you believe and are E
justified, and it is with your mouth that you confess and are saved. As the A
Scripture says, "Anyone who trusts in him will never be put to shame." For D
there is no difference between Jew and Gentile – the same Lord is Lord of I
all and richly blesses all who call on him, for, "Everyone who calls on the N
name of the Lord will be saved."　　　　　　　　　　　　　　　　　G

How, then, can they call on the one they have not believed in? And how
can they believe in the one of whom they have not heard? And how can they
hear without someone preaching to them? And how can they preach unless
they are sent? As it is written, "How beautiful are the feet of those who
bring good news!"

Matthew 14:22–33   Jesus made the disciples get into the boat and go on ahead G
of him to the other side of the lake, while he dismissed the crowd. After he O
had dismissed them, he went up on a mountainside by himself to pray. S
When evening came, he was there alone, but the boat was already a con- P
siderable distance from land, buffeted by the waves because the wind was E
against it.　　　　　　　　　　　　　　　　　　　　　　　　　　L

During the fourth watch of the night Jesus went out to them, walking on
the lake. When the disciples saw him walking on the lake, they were terrified. "It's a ghost," they said, and cried out in fear.

But Jesus immediately said to them: "Take courage! It is I. Don't be
afraid."

"Lord, if it's you," Peter replied, "tell me to come to you on the water."

"Come," he said.

Then Peter got down out of the boat, walked on the water and came
towards Jesus. But when he saw the wind, he was afraid and, beginning to
sink, cried out, "Lord, save me!"

Immediately Jesus reached out his hand and caught him. "You of little faith," he said, "why did you doubt?"

And when they climbed into the boat, the wind died down. Then those who were in the boat worshipped him, saying, "Truly you are the Son of God."

Proper 15

Sunday between 14 and 20 August inclusive (if after Trinity Sunday)
Choose either 'continuous' or 'related' Old Testament and Psalm readings.

CONTINUOUS

Genesis 45:1–15 Joseph could no longer control himself before all his attendants, and he cried out, "Make everyone leave my presence!" So there was no-one with Joseph when he made himself known to his brothers. And he wept so loudly that the Egyptians heard him, and Pharaoh's household heard about it.

Joseph said to his brothers, "I am Joseph! Is my father still living?" But his brothers were not able to answer him, because they were terrified at his presence.

Then Joseph said to his brothers, "Come close to me." When they had done so, he said, "I am your brother Joseph, the one you sold into Egypt! And now, do not be distressed and do not be angry with yourselves for selling me here, because it was to save lives that God sent me ahead of you. For two years now there has been famine in the land, and for the next five years there will not be ploughing and reaping. But God sent me ahead of you to preserve for you a remnant on earth and to save your lives by a great deliverance.

"So then, it was not you who sent me here, but God. He made me father to Pharaoh, lord of his entire household and ruler of all Egypt. Now hurry back to my father and say to him, 'This is what your son Joseph says: God has made me lord of all Egypt. Come down to me; don't delay. You shall live in the region of Goshen and be near me – you, your children and grandchildren, your flocks and herds, and all you have. I will provide for you there, because five years of famine are still to come. Otherwise you and your household and all who belong to you will become destitute.'

"You can see for yourselves, and so can my brother Benjamin, that it is really I who am speaking to you. Tell my father about all the honour accorded me in Egypt and about everything you have seen. And bring my father down here quickly."

Then he threw his arms around his brother Benjamin and wept, and Benjamin embraced him, weeping. And he kissed all his brothers and wept over them. Afterwards his brothers talked with him.

and **Psalm 133** How good and pleasant it is
　　　　　　　when brothers live together in unity!
　　　　　It is like precious oil poured on the head,
　　　　　　　running down on the beard,

running down on Aaron's beard,
> down upon the collar of his robes.
It is as if the dew of Hermon
> were falling on Mount Zion.
For there the L<small>ORD</small> bestows his blessing,
> even life for evermore.

Or **RELATED**

Isaiah 56:1, 6–8   This is what the L<small>ORD</small> says:

> "Maintain justice
>> and do what is right,
> for my salvation is close at hand
>> and my righteousness will soon be revealed.

> "And foreigners who bind themselves to the L<small>ORD</small>
>> to serve him,
> to love the name of the L<small>ORD</small>,
>> and to worship him,
> all who keep the Sabbath without desecrating it
>> and who hold fast to my covenant –
> these I will bring to my holy mountain
>> and give them joy in my house of prayer.
> Their burnt offerings and sacrifices
>> will be accepted on my altar;
> for my house will be called
>> a house of prayer for all nations."
> The Sovereign L<small>ORD</small> declares –
>> he who gathers the exiles of Israel:
> "I will gather still others to them
>> besides those already gathered."

and **Psalm 67**   May God be gracious to us and bless us
> and make his face shine upon us,
> that your ways may be known on earth,
>> your salvation among all nations.

> May the peoples praise you, O God;
>> may all the peoples praise you.
> May the nations be glad and sing for joy,
>> for you rule the peoples justly
>> and guide the nations of the earth.
> May the peoples praise you, O God;
>> may all the peoples praise you.

> Then the land will yield its harvest,
>> and God, our God, will bless us.
> God will bless us,
>> and all the ends of the earth will fear him.

Romans 11:1–2a, 29–32   I ask: Did God reject his people? By no means! I am an Israelite myself, a descendant of Abraham, from the tribe of Benjamin. God did not reject his people, whom he foreknew, for God's gifts and his call are irrevocable. Just as you who were at one time disobedient to God have now received mercy as a result of their disobedience, so they too have now become disobedient in order that they too may now receive mercy as a result of God's mercy to you. For God has bound all men over to disobe- dience so that he may have mercy on them all.

Matthew 15: [10–20] 21–28   [Jesus called the crowd to him and said, "Listen and understand. What goes into a man's mouth does not make him 'unclean', but what comes out of his mouth, that is what makes him 'unclean'."

Then the disciples came to him and asked, "Do you know that the Phar- isees were offended when they heard this?"

He replied, "Every plant that my heavenly Father has not planted will be pulled up by the roots. Leave them; they are blind guides. If a blind man leads a blind man, both will fall into a pit."

Peter said, "Explain the parable to us."

"Are you still so dull?" Jesus asked them. "Don't you see that whatever enters the mouth goes into the stomach and then out of the body? But the things that come out of the mouth come from the heart, and these make a man 'unclean'. For out of the heart come evil thoughts, murder, adultery, sexual immorality, theft, false testimony, slander. These are what make a man 'unclean'; but eating with unwashed hands does not make him 'unclean'."]

Jesus withdrew to the region of Tyre and Sidon. A Canaanite woman from that vicinity came to him, crying out, "Lord, Son of David, have mercy on me! My daughter is suffering terribly from demon-possession."

Jesus did not answer a word. So his disciples came to him and urged him, "Send her away, for she keeps crying out after us."

He answered, "I was sent only to the lost sheep of Israel."

The woman came and knelt before him. "Lord, help me!" she said.

He replied, "It is not right to take the children's bread and toss it to their dogs."

"Yes, Lord," she said, "but even the dogs eat the crumbs that fall from their masters' table."

Then Jesus answered, "Woman, you have great faith! Your request is granted." And her daughter was healed from that very hour.

Proper 16

Sunday between 21 and 27 August inclusive (if after Trinity Sunday)
Choose either 'continuous' or 'related' Old Testament and Psalm readings.

CONTINUOUS

Exodus 1:8 – 2:10   A new king, who did not know about Joseph, came to power in Egypt. "Look," he said to his people, "the Israelites have become much too numerous for us. Come, we must deal shrewdly with them or they will become even more numerous and, if war breaks out, will join our enemies, fight against us and leave the country."

So they put slave masters over them to oppress them with forced labour, and they built Pithom and Rameses as store cities for Pharaoh. But the more they were oppressed, the more they multiplied and spread; so the Egyptians came to dread the Israelites and worked them ruthlessly. They made their lives bitter with hard labour in brick and mortar and with all kinds of work in the fields; in all their hard labour the Egyptians used them ruthlessly.

The king of Egypt said to the Hebrew midwives, whose names were Shiphrah and Puah, "When you help the Hebrew women in childbirth and observe them on the delivery stool, if it is a boy, kill him; but if it is a girl, let her live." The midwives, however, feared God and did not do what the king of Egypt had told them to do; they let the boys live. Then the king of Egypt summoned the midwives and asked them, "Why have you done this? Why have you let the boys live?"

The midwives answered Pharaoh, "Hebrew women are not like Egyptian women; they are vigorous and give birth before the midwives arrive."

So God was kind to the midwives and the people increased and became even more numerous. And because the midwives feared God, he gave them families of their own.

Then Pharaoh gave this order to all his people: "Every boy that is born you must throw into the Nile, but let every girl live."

Now a man of the house of Levi married a Levite woman, and she became pregnant and gave birth to a son. When she saw that he was a fine child, she hid him for three months. But when she could hide him no longer, she got a papyrus basket for him and coated it with tar and pitch. Then she placed the child in it and put it among the reeds along the bank of the Nile. His sister stood at a distance to see what would happen to him.

Then Pharaoh's daughter went down to the Nile to bathe, and her attendants were walking along the river bank. She saw the basket among the reeds and sent her slave girl to get it. She opened it and saw the baby. He was crying, and she felt sorry for him. "This is one of the Hebrew babies," she said.

Then his sister asked Pharaoh's daughter, "Shall I go and get one of the Hebrew women to nurse the baby for you?"

"Yes, go," she answered. And the girl went and got the baby's mother. Pharaoh's daughter said to her, "Take this baby and nurse him for me, and I will pay you." So the woman took the baby and nursed him. When the child grew older, she took him to Pharaoh's daughter and he became her son. She named him Moses, saying, "I drew him out of the water."

and **Psalm 124**   If the LORD had not been on our side –
                 let Israel say –
          if the LORD had not been on our side
             when people attacked us,

when their anger flared against us,
> they would have swallowed us alive;
the flood would have engulfed us,
> the torrent would have swept over us,
the raging waters
> would have swept us away.

Praise be to the LORD,
> who has not let us be torn by their teeth.
We have escaped like a bird
> out of the fowler's snare;
the snare has been broken,
> and we have escaped.
Our help is in the name of the LORD,
> the Maker of heaven and earth.

Or **RELATED**

Isaiah 51:1–6   "Listen to me, you who pursue righteousness   F
> and who seek the LORD: I
Look to the rock from which you were cut   R
> and to the quarry from which you were hewn;   S
look to Abraham, your father,   T
> and to Sarah, who gave you birth.
When I called him he was but one,   R
> and I blessed him and made him many.   E
The LORD will surely comfort Zion   A
> and will look with compassion on all her ruins; D
he will make her deserts like Eden,   I
> her wastelands like the garden of the LORD.   N
Joy and gladness will be found in her,   G
> thanksgiving and the sound of singing.

"Listen to me, my people;
> hear me, my nation:
The law will go out from me;
> my justice will become a light to the nations.
My righteousness draws near speedily,
> my salvation is on the way,
> and my arm will bring justice to the nations.
The islands will look to me
> and wait in hope for my arm.
Lift up your eyes to the heavens,
> look at the earth beneath;
the heavens will vanish like smoke,
> the earth will wear out like a garment
> and its inhabitants die like flies.
But my salvation will last for ever,
> my righteousness will never fail."

and **Psalm 138**   I will praise you, O Lord, with all my heart;   P
before the "gods" I will sing your praise.   S

I will bow down towards your holy temple   A
and will praise your name   L
for your love and your faithfulness,   M
for you have exalted above all things
your name and your word.
When I called, you answered me;
you made me bold and stout-hearted.

May all the kings of the earth praise you, O Lord,
when they hear the words of your mouth.
May they sing of the ways of the Lord,
for the glory of the Lord is great.

Though the Lord is on high, he looks upon the lowly,
but the proud he knows from afar.
Though I walk in the midst of trouble,
you preserve my life;
you stretch out your hand against the anger of my foes,
with your right hand you save me.
The Lord will fulfil his purpose for me;
your love, O Lord, endures for ever –
do not abandon the works of your hands.

Romans 12:1–8   I urge you, brothers, in view of God's mercy, to offer your S
bodies as living sacrifices, holy and pleasing to God – this is your spiritual E
act of worship. Do not conform any longer to the pattern of this world, but C
be transformed by the renewing of your mind. Then you will be able to test O
and approve what God's will is – his good, pleasing and perfect will.   N

For by the grace given me I say to every one of you: Do not think of your- D
self more highly than you ought, but rather think of yourself with sober
judgment, in accordance with the measure of faith God has given you. Just R
as each of us has one body with many members, and these members do not E
all have the same function, so in Christ we who are many form one body, A
and each member belongs to all the others. We have different gifts, accord- D
ing to the grace given us. If a man's gift is prophesying, then let him use it I
in proportion to his faith. If it is serving, let him serve; if it is teaching, let N
him teach; if it is encouraging, let him encourage; if it is contributing to the G
needs of others, let him give generously; if it is leadership, let him govern
diligently; if it is showing mercy, let him do it cheerfully.

Matthew 16:13–20   When Jesus came to the region of Caesarea Philippi, he G
asked his disciples, "Who do people say the Son of Man is?"   O

They replied, "Some say John the Baptist; others say Elijah; and still S
others, Jeremiah or one of the prophets."   P

"But what about you?" he asked. "Who do you say I am?"   E
Simon Peter answered, "You are the Christ, the Son of the living God." L

Jesus replied, "Blessed are you, Simon son of Jonah, for this was not revealed to you by man, but by my Father in heaven. And I tell you that you are Peter, and on this rock I will build my church, and the gates of Hades will not overcome it. I will give you the keys of the kingdom of heaven; whatever you bind on earth will be bound in heaven, and whatever you loose on earth will be loosed in heaven." Then he warned his disciples not to tell anyone that he was the Christ.

Proper 17

Sunday between 28 August and 3 September inclusive (if after Trinity Sunday)
Choose either 'continuous' or 'related' Old Testament and Psalm readings.

CONTINUOUS

Exodus 3:1–15 Moses was tending the flock of Jethro his father-in-law, the priest of Midian, and he led the flock to the far side of the desert and came to Horeb, the mountain of God. There the angel of the LORD appeared to him in flames of fire from within a bush. Moses saw that though the bush was on fire it did not burn up. So Moses thought, "I will go over and see this strange sight – why the bush does not burn up."

When the LORD saw that he had gone over to look, God called to him from within the bush, "Moses! Moses!"

And Moses said, "Here I am."

"Do not come any closer," God said. "Take off your sandals, for the place where you are standing is holy ground." Then he said, "I am the God of your father, the God of Abraham, the God of Isaac and the God of Jacob." At this, Moses hid his face, because he was afraid to look at God.

The LORD said, "I have indeed seen the misery of my people in Egypt. I have heard them crying out because of their slave drivers, and I am concerned about their suffering. So I have come down to rescue them from the hand of the Egyptians and to bring them up out of that land into a good and spacious land, a land flowing with milk and honey – the home of the Canaanites, Hittites, Amorites, Perizzites, Hivites and Jebusites. And now the cry of the Israelites has reached me, and I have seen the way the Egyptians are oppressing them. So now, go. I am sending you to Pharaoh to bring my people the Israelites out of Egypt."

But Moses said to God, "Who am I, that I should go to Pharaoh and bring the Israelites out of Egypt?"

And God said, "I will be with you. And this will be the sign to you that it is I who have sent you: When you have brought the people out of Egypt, you will worship God on this mountain."

Moses said to God, "Suppose I go to the Israelites and say to them, 'The God of your fathers has sent me to you,' and they ask me, 'What is his name?' Then what shall I tell them?"

God said to Moses, "I AM WHO I AM. This is what you are to say to the Israelites: 'I AM has sent me to you.'"

God also said to Moses, "Say to the Israelites, 'The LORD, the God of your fathers – the God of Abraham, the God of Isaac and the God of Jacob – has sent me to you.' This is my name for ever, the name by which I am to be remembered from generation to generation."

and **Psalm 105:1–6, 23–26, 45c***	Give thanks to the Lᴏʀᴅ, call on his name;	P
	make known among the nations what he has done.	S
	Sing to him, sing praise to him;	A
	tell of all his wonderful acts.	L
	Glory in his holy name;	M
	let the hearts of those who seek the Lᴏʀᴅ rejoice.	

Look to the Lᴏʀᴅ and his strength;
  seek his face always.

Remember the wonders he has done,
  his miracles, and the judgments he pronounced,
O descendants of Abraham his servant,
  O children of Jacob, his chosen ones.

Then Israel entered Egypt;
  Jacob lived as an alien in the land of Ham.
The Lᴏʀᴅ made his people very fruitful;
  he made them too numerous for their foes,
whose hearts he turned to hate his people,
  to conspire against his servants.
He sent Moses his servant,
  and Aaron, whom he had chosen.

Praise the Lᴏʀᴅ.

Or **RELATED**

Jeremiah 15:15–21	You understand, O Lᴏʀᴅ;	F
	remember me and care for me.	I
	Avenge me on my persecutors.	R
	You are long-suffering – do not take me away;	S
	think of how I suffer reproach for your sake.	T
	When your words came, I ate them;	
	they were my joy and my heart's delight,	R
	for I bear your name,	E
	O Lᴏʀᴅ God Almighty.	A
	I never sat in the company of revellers,	D
	never made merry with them;	I
	I sat alone because your hand was on me	N
	and you had filled me with indignation.	G

Why is my pain unending
  and my wound grievous and incurable?
Will you be to me like a deceptive brook,
  like a spring that fails?

Therefore this is what the Lᴏʀᴅ says:

  "If you repent, I will restore you
    that you may serve me;

if you utter worthy, not worthless, words,
you will be my spokesman.
Let this people turn to you,
but you must not turn to them.
I will make you a wall to this people,
a fortified wall of bronze;
they will fight against you
but will not overcome you,
for I am with you
to rescue and save you,"
declares the LORD.
"I will save you from the hands of the wicked
and redeem you from the grasp of the cruel."

and **Psalm 26:1–8**
Vindicate me, O LORD,
for I have led a blameless life;
I have trusted in the LORD
without wavering.
Test me, O LORD, and try me,
examine my heart and my mind;
for your love is ever before me,
and I walk continually in your truth.
I do not sit with the deceitful,
nor do I consort with hypocrites;
I abhor the assembly of evildoers
and refuse to sit with the wicked.
I wash my hands in innocence,
and go about your altar, O LORD,
proclaiming aloud your praise
and telling of all your wonderful deeds.
I love the house where you live, O LORD,
the place where your glory dwells.

PSALM

Romans 12:9–21   Love must be sincere. Hate what is evil; cling to what is good. Be devoted to one another in brotherly love. Honour one another above yourselves. Never be lacking in zeal, but keep your spiritual fervour, serving the LORD. Be joyful in hope, patient in affliction, faithful in prayer. Share with God's people who are in need. Practise hospitality.

SECOND READING

Bless those who persecute you; bless and do not curse. Rejoice with those who rejoice; mourn with those who mourn. Live in harmony with one another. Do not be proud, but be willing to associate with people of low position. Do not be conceited.

Do not repay anyone evil for evil. Be careful to do what is right in the eyes of everybody. If it is possible, as far as it depends on you, live at peace with everyone. Do not take revenge, my friends, but leave room for God's wrath, for it is written: "It is mine to avenge; I will repay," says the LORD. On the contrary:

"If your enemy is hungry, feed him;
   if he is thirsty, give him something to drink.
In doing this, you will heap burning coals on his head."
Do not be overcome by evil, but overcome evil with good.

Matthew 16:21–28   Jesus began to explain to his disciples that he must go to G
Jerusalem and suffer many things at the hands of the elders, chief priests O
and teachers of the law, and that he must be killed and on the third day be S
raised to life.   P

Peter took him aside and began to rebuke him. "Never, Lord!" he said. E
"This shall never happen to you!"   L

Jesus turned and said to Peter, "Get behind me, Satan! You are a stumbling-block to me; you do not have in mind the things of God, but the things
of men."

Then Jesus said to his disciples, "If anyone would come after me, he
must deny himself and take up his cross and follow me. For whoever wants
to save his life will lose it, but whoever loses his life for me will find it. What
good will it be for a man if he gains the whole world, yet forfeits his soul?
Or what can a man give in exchange for his soul? For the Son of Man is
going to come in his Father's glory with his angels, and then he will reward
each person according to what he has done. I tell you the truth, some who
are standing here will not taste death before they see the Son of Man coming in his kingdom."

Proper 18

Sunday between 4 and 10 September inclusive (if after Trinity Sunday)
Choose either 'continuous' or 'related' Old Testament and Psalm readings.

CONTINUOUS

Exodus 12:1–14   The LORD said to Moses and Aaron in Egypt, "This month is F
to be for you the first month, the first month of your year. Tell the whole I
community of Israel that on the tenth day of this month each man is to take R
a lamb for his family, one for each household. If any household is too small S
for a whole lamb, they must share one with their nearest neighbour, having T
taken into account the number of people there are. You are to determine
the amount of lamb needed in accordance with what each person will eat. R
The animals you choose must be year-old males without defect, and you E
may take them from the sheep or the goats. Take care of them until the A
fourteenth day of the month, when all the people of the community of D
Israel must slaughter them at twilight. Then they are to take some of the I
blood and put it on the sides and tops of the door-frames of the houses N
where they eat the lambs. That same night they are to eat the meat roasted G
over the fire, along with bitter herbs, and bread made without yeast. Do not
eat the meat raw or cooked in water, but roast it over the fire – head, legs
and inner parts. Do not leave any of it till morning; if some is left till morning, you must burn it. This is how you are to eat it: with your cloak tucked

into your belt, your sandals on your feet and your staff in your hand. Eat it in haste; it is the LORD's Passover.

"On that same night I will pass through Egypt and strike down every firstborn – both men and animals – and I will bring judgment on all the gods of Egypt. I am the LORD. The blood will be a sign for you on the houses where you are; and when I see the blood, I will pass over you. No destructive plague will touch you when I strike Egypt.

"This is a day you are to commemorate; for the generations to come you shall celebrate it as a festival to the LORD – a lasting ordinance."

and **Psalm 149**   Praise the LORD.

> Sing to the LORD a new song,
> > his praise in the assembly of the saints.
>
> Let Israel rejoice in their Maker;
> > let the people of Zion be glad in their King.
> Let them praise his name with dancing
> > and make music to him with tambourine and harp.
> For the LORD takes delight in his people;
> > he crowns the humble with salvation.
> Let the saints rejoice in this honour
> > and sing for joy on their beds.
>
> May the praise of God be in their mouths
> > and a double-edged sword in their hands,
> to inflict vengeance on the nations
> > and punishment on the peoples,
> to bind their kings with fetters,
> > their nobles with shackles of iron,
> to carry out the sentence written against them.
> > This is the glory of all his saints.
>
> Praise the LORD.

Or **RELATED**

Ezekiel 33:7–11   The word of the LORD came to Ezekiel: "Son of man, I have made you a watchman for the house of Israel; so hear the word I speak and give them warning from me. When I say to the wicked, 'O wicked man, you will surely die,' and you do not speak out to dissuade him from his ways, that wicked man will die for his sins, and I will hold you accountable for his blood. But if you do warn the wicked man to turn from his ways and he does not do so, he will die for his sins, but you will be saved yourself.

"Son of man, say to the house of Israel, 'This is what you are saying: "Our offences and sins weigh us down, and we are wasting away because of them. How then can we live?"' Say to them, 'As surely as I live, declares the Sovereign LORD, I take no pleasure in the death of the wicked, but rather that they turn from their ways and live. Turn! Turn from your evil ways! Why will you die, O house of Israel?'"

and **Psalm 119:33–40**

Teach me, O LORD, to follow your decrees;
> then I will keep them to the end.

Give me understanding, and I will keep your law
> and obey it with all my heart.

Direct me in the path of your commands,
> for there I find delight.

Turn my heart towards your statutes
> and not towards selfish gain.

Turn my eyes away from worthless things;
> preserve my life according to your word.

Fulfil your promise to your servant,
> so that you may be feared.

Take away the disgrace I dread,
> for your laws are good.

How I long for your precepts!
> Preserve my life in your righteousness.

P
S
A
L
M

Romans 13:8–14   Let no debt remain outstanding, except the continuing debt to love one another, for he who loves his fellow-man has fulfilled the law. The commandments, "Do not commit adultery," "Do not murder," "Do not steal," "Do not covet," and whatever other commandment there may be, are summed up in this one rule: "Love your neighbour as yourself." Love does no harm to its neighbour. Therefore love is the fulfilment of the law.

S E C O N D R E A D I N G

And do this, understanding the present time. The hour has come for you to wake up from your slumber, because our salvation is nearer now than when we first believed. The night is nearly over; the day is almost here. So let us put aside the deeds of darkness and put on the armour of light. Let us behave decently, as in the daytime, not in orgies and drunkenness, not in sexual immorality and debauchery, not in dissension and jealousy. Rather, clothe yourselves with the Lord Jesus Christ, and do not think about how to gratify the desires of the sinful nature.

Matthew 18:15–20   Jesus said: "If your brother sins against you, go and show him his fault, just between the two of you. If he listens to you, you have won your brother over. But if he will not listen, take one or two others along, so that 'every matter may be established by the testimony of two or three witnesses.' If he refuses to listen to them, tell it to the church; and if he refuses to listen even to the church, treat him as you would a pagan or a tax collector.

G O S P E L

"I tell you the truth, whatever you bind on earth will be bound in heaven, and whatever you loose on earth will be loosed in heaven.

"Again, I tell you that if two of you on earth agree about anything you ask for, it will be done for you by my Father in heaven. For where two or three come together in my name, there am I with them."

Proper 19

Sunday between 11 and 17 September inclusive (if after Trinity Sunday)
Choose either 'continuous' or 'related' Old Testament and Psalm readings.

CONTINUOUS

Exodus 14:19–31 The angel of God, who had been travelling in front of
Israel's army, withdrew and went behind them. The pillar of cloud also
moved from in front and stood behind them, coming between the armies of
Egypt and Israel. Throughout the night the cloud brought darkness to the
one side and light to the other; so neither went near the other all night long.

Then Moses stretched out his hand over the sea, and all that night the
Lord drove the sea back with a strong east wind and turned it into dry land.
The waters were divided, and the Israelites went through the sea on dry
ground, with a wall of water on their right and on their left.

The Egyptians pursued them, and all Pharaoh's horses and chariots
and horsemen followed them into the sea. During the last watch of the
night the Lord looked down from the pillar of fire and cloud at the Egyptian army and threw it into confusion. He made the wheels of their chariots
come off so that they had difficulty driving. And the Egyptians said,
"Let's get away from the Israelites! The Lord is fighting for them against
Egypt."

Then the Lord said to Moses, "Stretch out your hand over the sea so that
the waters may flow back over the Egyptians and their chariots and horsemen." Moses stretched out his hand over the sea, and at daybreak the sea
went back to its place. The Egyptians were fleeing towards it, and the Lord
swept them into the sea. The water flowed back and covered the chariots
and horsemen – the entire army of Pharaoh that had followed the Israelites
into the sea. Not one of them survived.

But the Israelites went through the sea on dry ground, with a wall of
water on their right and on their left. That day the Lord saved Israel from
the hands of the Egyptians, and Israel saw the Egyptians lying dead on the
shore. And when the Israelites saw the great power the Lord displayed
against the Egyptians, the people feared the Lord and put their trust in him
and in Moses his servant.

and **Psalm 114**   When Israel came out of Egypt,
     the house of Jacob from a people of foreign tongue,
Judah became God's sanctuary,
     Israel his dominion.

The sea looked and fled,
     the Jordan turned back;
the mountains skipped like rams,
     the hills like lambs.

Why was it, O sea, that you fled,
     O Jordan, that you turned back,
you mountains, that you skipped like rams,
     you hills, like lambs?

Tremble, O earth, at the presence of the Lord,
 at the presence of the God of Jacob,
who turned the rock into a pool,
 the hard rock into springs of water.

or Canticle:

Exodus 15:1b–11,
20–21

"I will sing to the LORD,
 for he is highly exalted.
The horse and its rider
 he has hurled into the sea.
The LORD is my strength and my song;
 he has become my salvation.
He is my God, and I will praise him,
 my father's God, and I will exalt him.
The LORD is a warrior;
 the LORD is his name.
Pharaoh's chariots and his army
 he has hurled into the sea.
The best of Pharaoh's officers
 are drowned in the Red Sea.
The deep waters have covered them;
 they sank to the depths like a stone.

"Your right hand, O LORD,
 was majestic in power.
Your right hand, O LORD,
 shattered the enemy.
In the greatness of your majesty
 you threw down those who opposed you.
You unleashed your burning anger;
 it consumed them like stubble.
By the blast of your nostrils
 the waters piled up.
The surging waters stood firm like a wall;
 the deep waters congealed
  in the heart of the sea.

"The enemy boasted,
 'I will pursue, I will overtake them.
I will divide the spoils;
 I will gorge myself on them.
I will draw my sword
 and my hand will destroy them.'
But you blew with your breath,
 and the sea covered them.
They sank like lead
 in the mighty waters.

C
A
N
T
I
L
E

"Who among the gods is like you, O Lord?
　　Who is like you –
　　　　majestic in holiness,
　　　　awesome in glory,
　　　　working wonders?"

Then Miriam the prophetess, Aaron's sister, took a tambourine in her hand, and all the women followed her, with tambourines and dancing. Miriam sang to them:

"Sing to the Lord,
　　for he is highly exalted.
The horse and its rider
　　he has hurled into the sea."

Or **RELATED**

Genesis 50:15–21　　When Joseph's brothers saw that their father was dead, they said, "What if Joseph holds a grudge against us and pays us back for all the wrongs we did to him?" So they sent word to Joseph, saying, "Your father left these instructions before he died: 'This is what you are to say to Joseph: I ask you to forgive your brothers the sins and the wrongs they committed in treating you so badly.' Now please forgive the sins of the servants of the God of your father." When their message came to him, Joseph wept.

His brothers then came and threw themselves down before him. "We are your slaves," they said.

But Joseph said to them, "Don't be afraid. Am I in the place of God? You intended to harm me, but God intended it for good to accomplish what is now being done, the saving of many lives. So then, don't be afraid. I will provide for you and your children." And he reassured them and spoke kindly to them.

and **Psalm 103:[1–7] 8–13***　　[Praise the Lord, O my soul;
　　all my inmost being, praise his holy name.
Praise the Lord, O my soul,
　　and forget not all his benefits –
who forgives all your sins
and heals all your diseases,
who redeems your life from the pit
　　and crowns you with love and compassion,
who satisfies your desires with good things
　　so that your youth is renewed like the eagle's.

The Lord works righteousness
　　and justice for all the oppressed.

He made known his ways to Moses,
　　his deeds to the people of Israel:
The Lord is compassionate and gracious,
　　slow to anger, abounding in love.]

The LORD will not always accuse,
  nor will he harbour his anger for ever;
he does not treat us as our sins deserve
  or repay us according to our iniquities.
For as high as the heavens are above the earth,
  so great is his love for those who fear him;
as far as the east is from the west,
  so far has he removed our transgressions
    from us.
As a father has compassion on his children,
  so the LORD has compassion on those who
    fear him.

Romans 14:1–12 Accept him whose faith is weak, without passing judgment on
disputable matters. One man's faith allows him to eat everything, but another
man, whose faith is weak, eats only vegetables. The man who eats everything
must not look down on him who does not, and the man who does not eat everything must not condemn the man who does, for God has accepted him. Who
are you to judge someone else's servant? To his own master he stands or falls.
And he will stand, for the Lord is able to make him stand.

One man considers one day more sacred than another; another man considers every day alike. Each one should be fully convinced in his own mind.
He who regards one day as special, does so to the Lord. He who eats meat,
eats to the Lord, for he gives thanks to God; and he who abstains, does so to
the Lord and gives thanks to God. For none of us lives to himself alone and
none of us dies to himself alone. If we live, we live to the Lord; and if we die,
we die to the Lord. So, whether we live or die, we belong to the Lord.

For this very reason, Christ died and returned to life so that he might be
the LORD of both the dead and the living. You, then, why do you judge your
brother? Or why do you look down on your brother? For we will all stand
before God's judgment seat. It is written:

"'As surely as I live,' says the Lord,
  'Every knee will bow before me;
every tongue will confess to God.'"

So then, each of us will give an account of himself to God.

Matthew 18:21–35 Peter came to Jesus and asked, "Lord, how many times
shall I forgive someone who sins against me? Up to seven times?"

Jesus answered, "I tell you, not seven times, but seventy-seven times.

"Therefore, the kingdom of heaven is like a king who wanted to settle
accounts with his servants. As he began the settlement, a man who owed
him ten thousand talents was brought to him. Since he was not able to pay,
the master ordered that he and his wife and his children and all that he had
be sold to repay the debt.

"The servant fell on his knees before him. 'Be patient with me,' he
begged, 'and I will pay back everything.' The servant's master took pity on
him, cancelled the debt and let him go.

"But when that servant went out, he found one of his fellow-servants who owed him a hundred denarii. He grabbed him and began to choke him. 'Pay back what you owe me!' he demanded.

"His fellow-servant fell to his knees and begged him, 'Be patient with me, and I will pay you back.'

"But he refused. Instead, he went off and had the man thrown into prison until he could pay the debt. When the other servants saw what had happened, they were greatly distressed and went and told their master everything that had happened.

"Then the master called the servant in. 'You wicked servant,' he said, 'I cancelled all that debt of yours because you begged me to. Shouldn't you have had mercy on your fellow-servant just as I had on you?' In anger his master turned him over to the jailers to be tortured, until he should pay back all he owed.

"This is how my heavenly Father will treat each of you unless you forgive one another from your heart."

Proper 20

Sunday between 18 and 24 September inclusive (if after Trinity Sunday)
Choose either 'continuous' or 'related' Old Testament and Psalm readings.

CONTINUOUS

Exodus 16:2–15 In the desert the whole Israelite community grumbled against Moses and Aaron. The Israelites said to them, "If only we had died by the LORD's hand in Egypt! There we sat round pots of meat and ate all the food we wanted, but you have brought us out into this desert to starve this entire assembly to death."

Then the LORD said to Moses, "I will rain down bread from heaven for you. The people are to go out each day and gather enough for that day. In this way I will test them and see whether they will follow my instructions. On the sixth day they are to prepare what they bring in, and that is to be twice as much as they gather on the other days."

So Moses and Aaron said to all the Israelites, "In the evening you will know that it was the LORD who brought you out of Egypt, and in the morning you will see the glory of the LORD, because he has heard your grumbling against him. Who are we, that you should grumble against us?" Moses also said, "You will know that it was the LORD when he gives you meat to eat in the evening and all the bread you want in the morning, because he has heard your grumbling against him. Who are we? You are not grumbling against us, but against the LORD."

Then Moses told Aaron, "Say to the entire Israelite community, 'Come before the LORD, for he has heard your grumbling.'"

While Aaron was speaking to the whole Israelite community, they looked towards the desert, and there was the glory of the LORD appearing in the cloud.

The LORD said to Moses, "I have heard the grumbling of the Israelites.

Tell them, 'At twilight you will eat meat, and in the morning you will be filled with bread. Then you will know that I am the LORD your God.'"

That evening quail came and covered the camp, and in the morning there was a layer of dew around the camp. When the dew was gone, thin flakes like frost on the ground appeared on the desert floor. When the Israelites saw it, they said to each other, "What is it?" For they did not know what it was.

Moses said to them, "It is the bread the LORD has given you to eat."

and **Psalm 105:1–6, 37–45***

Give thanks to the LORD, call on his name;
   make known among the nations what he has done.
Sing to him, sing praise to him;
   tell of all his wonderful acts.
Glory in his holy name;
   let the hearts of those who seek the LORD rejoice.
Look to the LORD and his strength;
   seek his face always.

Remember the wonders he has done,
   his miracles, and the judgments he pronounced,
O descendants of Abraham his servant,
   O sons of Jacob, his chosen ones.

He brought out Israel, laden with silver and gold,
   and from among their tribes no-one faltered.
Egypt was glad when they left,
   because dread of Israel had fallen on them.
He spread out a cloud as a covering,
   and a fire to give light at night.
They asked, and he brought them quail
   and satisfied them with the bread of heaven.
He opened the rock, and water gushed out;
   like a river it flowed in the desert.

For he remembered his holy promise
   given to his servant Abraham.
He brought out his people with rejoicing,
   his chosen ones with shouts of joy;
he gave them the lands of the nations,
   and they fell heir to what others had toiled for –
that they might keep his precepts
   and observe his laws.

Praise the LORD.

Or **RELATED**

Jonah 3:10 – 4:11   When God saw what the people of Nineveh did and how they turned from their evil ways, he had compassion and did not bring upon them the destruction he had threatened.

But Jonah was greatly displeased and became angry. He prayed to the LORD, "O LORD, is this not what I said when I was still at home? That is why I was so quick to flee to Tarshish. I knew that you are a gracious and compassionate God, slow to anger and abounding in love, a God who relents from sending calamity. Now, O LORD, take away my life, for it is better for me to die than to live."

But the LORD replied, "Have you any right to be angry?"

Jonah went out and sat down at a place east of the city. There he made himself a shelter, sat in its shade and waited to see what would happen to the city. Then the LORD God provided a vine and made it grow up over Jonah to give shade for his head to ease his discomfort, and Jonah was very happy about the vine. But at dawn the next day God provided a worm, which chewed the vine so that it withered. When the sun rose, God provided a scorching east wind, and the sun blazed on Jonah's head so that he grew faint. He wanted to die, and said, "It would be better for me to die than to live."

But God said to Jonah, "Do you have a right to be angry about the vine?"

"I do," he said. "I am angry enough to die."

But the LORD said, "You have been concerned about this vine, though you did not tend it or make it grow. It sprang up overnight and died overnight. But Nineveh has more than a hundred and twenty thousand people who cannot tell their right hand from their left, and many cattle as well. Should I not be concerned about that great city?"

and **Psalm 145:1–8**

I will exalt you, my God the King;
    I will praise your name for ever and ever.
Every day I will praise you
    and extol your name for ever and ever.

Great is the LORD and most worthy of praise;
    his greatness no-one can fathom.
One generation will commend your works to another;
    they will tell of your mighty acts.
They will speak of the glorious splendour of your
      majesty,
    and I will meditate on your wonderful works.
They will tell of the power of your awesome works,
    and I will proclaim your great deeds.
They will celebrate your abundant goodness
    and joyfully sing of your righteousness.
The LORD is gracious and compassionate,
    slow to anger and rich in love.

P S A L M

Philippians 1: 21–30 For me, to live is Christ and to die is gain. If I am to go on living in the body, this will mean fruitful labour for me. Yet what shall I choose? I do not know! I am torn between the two: I desire to depart and be with Christ, which is better by far; but it is more necessary for you that I remain in the body. Convinced of this, I know that I will remain, and I will

S E C O N D R E A D I N G

continue with all of you for your progress and joy in the faith, so that through my being with you again your joy in Christ Jesus will overflow on account of me.

Whatever happens, conduct yourselves in a manner worthy of the gospel of Christ. Then, whether I come and see you or only hear about you in my absence, I will know that you stand firm in one spirit, contending as one man for the faith of the gospel without being frightened in any way by those who oppose you. This is a sign to them that they will be destroyed, but that you will be saved – and that by God. For it has been granted to you on behalf of Christ not only to believe on him, but also to suffer for him, since you are going through the same struggle you saw I had, and now hear that I still have.

Matthew 20:1–16   Jesus said: "The kingdom of heaven is like a landowner who went out early in the morning to hire men to work in his vineyard. He agreed to pay them a denarius for the day and sent them into his vineyard.

"About the third hour he went out and saw others standing in the market-place doing nothing. He told them, 'You also go and work in my vineyard, and I will pay you whatever is right.' So they went.

"He went out again about the sixth hour and the ninth hour and did the same thing. About the eleventh hour he went out and found still others standing around. He asked them, 'Why have you been standing here all day long doing nothing?'

"'Because no-one has hired us,' they answered.

"He said to them, 'You also go and work in my vineyard.'

"When evening came, the owner of the vineyard said to his foreman, 'Call the workers and pay them their wages, beginning with the last ones hired and going on to the first.'

"The workers who were hired about the eleventh hour came and each received a denarius. So when those came who were hired first, they expected to receive more. But each one of them also received a denarius. When they received it, they began to grumble against the landowner. 'These men who were hired last worked only one hour,' they said, 'and you have made them equal to us who have borne the burden of the work and the heat of the day.'

"But he answered one of them, 'Friend, I am not being unfair to you. Didn't you agree to work for a denarius? Take your pay and go. I want to give the man who was hired last the same as I gave you. Don't I have the right to do what I want with my own money? Or are you envious because I am generous?'

"So the last will be first, and the first will be last."

(marginal text alongside the Matthew reading: G O S P E L)

Proper 21

Sunday between 25 September and 1 October inclusive (if after Trinity Sunday)
Choose either 'continuous' or 'related' Old Testament and Psalm readings.

CONTINUOUS

Exodus 17:1–7   The whole Israelite community set out from the Desert of Sin, travelling from place to place as the Lord commanded. They camped

(marginal text alongside Proper 21 section: F R I E R A S D T I N G)

at Rephidim, but there was no water for the people to drink. So they quarrelled with Moses and said, "Give us water to drink."

Moses replied, "Why do you quarrel with me? Why do you put the LORD to the test?"

But the people were thirsty for water there, and they grumbled against Moses. They said, "Why did you bring us up out of Egypt to make us and our children and livestock die of thirst?"

Then Moses cried out to the LORD, "What am I to do with these people? They are almost ready to stone me."

The LORD answered Moses, "Walk on ahead of the people. Take with you some of the elders of Israel and take in your hand the staff with which you struck the Nile, and go. I will stand there before you by the rock at Horeb. Strike the rock, and water will come out of it for the people to drink." So Moses did this in the sight of the elders of Israel. And he called the place Massah and Meribah because the Israelites quarrelled and because they tested the LORD saying, "Is the LORD among us or not?"

and **Psalm 78: 1–4, 12–16***

O my people, hear my teaching;
    listen to the words of my mouth.
I will open my mouth in parables,
    I will utter hidden things, things from of old –
what we have heard and known,
    what our ancestors have told us.
We will not hide them from their children;
    we will tell the next generation
the praiseworthy deeds of the LORD,
    his power, and the wonders he has done.

He did miracles in the sight of their fathers
    in the land of Egypt, in the region of Zoan.
He divided the sea and led them through;
    he made the water stand firm like a wall.
He guided them with the cloud by day
    and with light from the fire all night.
He split the rocks in the desert
    and gave them water as abundant as the seas;
he brought streams out of a rocky crag
    and made water flow down like rivers.

PSALM

Or **RELATED**

Ezekiel 18:1–4, 25–32 The word of the LORD came to me: "What do you people mean by quoting this proverb about the land of Israel:

"'The parents eat sour grapes,
    and the children's teeth are set on edge'?

"As surely as I live, declares the Sovereign LORD, you will no longer quote this proverb in Israel. For every living soul belongs to me, the father as well as the son – both alike belong to me. The soul who sins is the one who will die.

FRIDAY READING

"Yet you say, 'The way of the LORD is not just.' Hear, O house of Israel: Is my way unjust? Is it not your ways that are unjust? If a righteous man turns from his righteousness and commits sin, he will die for it; because of the sin he has committed he will die. But if a wicked man turns away from the wickedness he has committed and does what is just and right, he will save his life. Because he considers all the offences he has committed and turns away from them, he will surely live; he will not die. Yet the house of Israel says, 'The way of the LORD is not just.' Are my ways unjust, O house of Israel? Is it not your ways that are unjust?

"Therefore, O house of Israel, I will judge you, each one according to his ways, declares the Sovereign LORD. Repent! Turn away from all your offences; then sin will not be your downfall. Rid yourselves of all the offences you have committed, and get a new heart and a new spirit. Why will you die, O house of Israel? For I take no pleasure in the death of any-one, declares the Sovereign LORD. Repent and live!"

and **Psalm 25: 1–9**

To you, O LORD, I lift up my soul;
  in you I trust, O my God.
Do not let me be put to shame,
  nor let my enemies triumph over me.
No-one whose hope is in you
  will ever be put to shame,
but they will be put to shame
  who are treacherous without excuse.

Show me your ways, O LORD,
  teach me your paths;
guide me in your truth and teach me,
  for you are God my Saviour,
  and my hope is in you all day long.
Remember, O LORD, your great mercy and love,
  for they are from of old.
Remember not the sins of my youth
  and my rebellious ways;
according to your love remember me,
  for you are good, O LORD.

Good and upright is the LORD;
  therefore he instructs sinners in his ways.
He guides the humble in what is right
  and teaches them his way.

Philippians 2:1–13   If you have any encouragement from being united with Christ, if any comfort from his love, if any fellowship with the Spirit, if any tenderness and compassion, then make my joy complete by being like-minded, having the same love, being one in spirit and purpose. Do nothing out of selfish ambition or vain conceit, but in humility consider others bet-ter than yourselves. Each of you should look not only to your own interests, but also to the interests of others.

Your attitude should be the same as that of Christ Jesus:

Who, being in very nature God,
   did not consider equality with God something to be grasped,
but made himself nothing,
   taking the very nature of a servant,
   being made in human likeness.
And being found in appearance as a man,
   he humbled himself
   and became obedient to death – even death on a cross!
Therefore God exalted him to the highest place
   and gave him the name that is above every name,
that at the name of Jesus every knee should bow,
   in heaven and on earth and under the earth,
and every tongue confess that Jesus Christ is Lord,
   to the glory of God the Father.

Therefore, my dear friends, as you have always obeyed – not only in my presence, but now much more in my absence – continue to work out your salvation with fear and trembling, for it is God who works in you to will and to act according to his good purpose.

Matthew 21:23–32   Jesus entered the temple courts, and, while he was teaching, the chief priests and the elders of the people came to him. "By what authority are you doing these things?" they asked. "And who gave you this authority?"

Jesus replied, "I will also ask you one question. If you answer me, I will tell you by what authority I am doing these things. John's baptism – where did it come from? Was it from heaven, or from men?"

They discussed it among themselves and said, "If we say, 'From heaven', he will ask, 'Then why didn't you believe him?' But if we say, 'From men' – we are afraid of the people, for they all hold that John was a prophet."

So they answered Jesus, "We don't know."

Then he said, "Neither will I tell you by what authority I am doing these things.

"What do you think? There was a man who had two sons. He went to the first and said, 'Son, go and work today in the vineyard.'

"'I will not,' he answered, but later he changed his mind and went.

"Then the father went to the other son and said the same thing. He answered, 'I will, sir,' but he did not go.

"Which of the two did what his father wanted?"

"The first," they answered.

Jesus said to them, "I tell you the truth, the tax collectors and the prostitutes are entering the kingdom of God ahead of you. For John came to you to show you the way of righteousness, and you did not believe him, but the tax collectors and the prostitutes did. And even after you saw this, you did not repent and believe him."

Proper 22

Sunday between 2 and 8 Ocobter inclusive (if after Trinity Sunday)
Choose either 'continuous' or 'related' Old Testament and Psalm readings.

CONTINUOUS

Exodus 20:1–4, 7–9, 12–20   God spoke these words: F

"I am the LORD your God, who brought you out of Egypt, out of the land   I
of slavery.   R

"You shall have no other gods before me.   S

"You shall not make for yourself an idol in the form of anything in   T
heaven above or on the earth beneath or in the waters below.

"You shall not misuse the name of the LORD your God, for the LORD will   R
not hold anyone guiltless who misuses his name.   E

"Remember the Sabbath day by keeping it holy. Six days you shall   A
labour and do all your work.   D

"Honour your father and your mother, so that you may live long in the   I
land the LORD your God is giving you.   N

"You shall not murder.   G

"You shall not commit adultery.

"You shall not steal.

"You shall not give false testimony against your neighbour.

"You shall not covet your neighbour's house. You shall not covet your
neighbour's wife, or his manservant or maidservant, his ox or donkey, or
anything that belongs to your neighbour."

When the people saw the thunder and lightning and heard the trumpet
and saw the mountain in smoke, they trembled with fear. They stayed at a
distance and said to Moses, "Speak to us yourself and we will listen. But do
not have God speak to us or we will die."

Moses said to the people, "Do not be afraid. God has come to test you, so
that the fear of God will be with you to keep you from sinning."

and **Psalm 19***   The heavens declare the glory of God;   P
the skies proclaim the work of his hands.   S

Day after day they pour forth speech;   A
night after night they display knowledge.   L

There is no speech or language   M
where their voice is not heard.

Their voice goes out into all the earth,
their words to the ends of the world.

In the heavens he has pitched a tent for the sun,
which is like a bridegroom coming forth from his
pavilion,
like a champion rejoicing to run his course.

It rises at one end of the heavens
and makes its circuit to the other;
nothing is hidden from its heat.

The law of the LORD is perfect,
  reviving the soul.
The statutes of the LORD are trustworthy,
  making wise the simple.
The precepts of the LORD are right,
  giving joy to the heart.
The commands of the LORD are radiant,
  giving light to the eyes.
The fear of the LORD is pure,
  enduring for ever.
The ordinances of the LORD are sure
  and altogether righteous.
They are more precious than gold,
  than much pure gold;
they are sweeter than honey,
  than honey from the comb.
By them is your servant warned;
  in keeping them there is great reward.

Who can discern his errors?
  Forgive my hidden faults.
Keep your servant also from wilful sins;
  may they not rule over me.
Then will I be blameless,
  innocent of great transgression.

May the words of my mouth and the meditation of my
    heart
  be pleasing in your sight,
  O LORD, my Rock and my Redeemer.

Or RELATED

Isaiah 5:1–7   I will sing for the one I love
  a song about his vineyard:
My loved one had a vineyard
  on a fertile hillside.
He dug it up and cleared it of stones
  and planted it with the choicest vines.
He built a watchtower in it
  and cut out a winepress as well.
Then he looked for a crop of good grapes,
  but it yielded only bad fruit.

"Now you dwellers in Jerusalem and men of Judah,
  judge between me and my vineyard.
What more could have been done for my vineyard
  than I have done for it?
When I looked for good grapes,
  why did it yield only bad?

FIRST READING

Now I will tell you
what I am going to do to my vineyard:
I will take away its hedge,
and it will be destroyed;
I will break down its wall,
and it will be trampled.
I will make it a wasteland,
neither pruned nor cultivated,
and briers and thorns will grow there.
I will command the clouds
not to rain on it."

The vineyard of the LORD Almighty
is the house of Israel,
and the men of Judah
are the garden of his delight.
And he looked for justice, but saw bloodshed;
for righteousness, but heard cries of distress.

and **Psalm 80:7–15**   Restore us, O God Almighty;
make your face shine upon us,
that we may be saved.

You brought a vine out of Egypt;
you drove out the nations and planted it.
You cleared the ground for it,
and it took root and filled the land.
The mountains were covered with its shade,
the mighty cedars with its branches.
It sent out its boughs to the Sea,
its shoots as far as the River.

Why have you broken down its walls
so that all who pass by pick its grapes?
Boars from the forest ravage it
and the creatures of the field feed on it.
Return to us, O God Almighty!
Look down from heaven and see!
Watch over this vine,
the root your right hand has planted,
the son you have raised up for yourself.

Philippians 3:4b–14   If anyone else thinks he has reasons to put confidence in
the flesh, I have more: circumcised on the eighth day, of the people of
Israel, of the tribe of Benjamin, a Hebrew of Hebrews; in regard to the law,
a Pharisee; as for zeal, persecuting the church; as for legalistic righteousness, faultless.

But whatever was to my profit I now consider loss for the sake of Christ.

What is more, I consider everything a loss compared to the surpassing greatness of knowing Christ Jesus my Lord, for whose sake I have lost all things. I consider them rubbish, that I may gain Christ and be found in him, not having a righteousness of my own that comes from the law, but that which is through faith in Christ – the righteousness that comes from God and is by faith. I want to know Christ and the power of his resurrection and the fellowship of sharing in his sufferings, becoming like him in his death, and so, somehow, to attain to the resurrection from the dead.

Not that I have already obtained all this, or have already been made perfect, but I press on to take hold of that for which Christ Jesus took hold of me. Brothers, I do not consider myself yet to have taken hold of it. But one thing I do: Forgetting what is behind and straining towards what is ahead, I press on towards the goal to win the prize for which God has called me heavenwards in Christ Jesus.

Matthew 21:33–46 Jesus told a parable: "There was a landowner who planted a vineyard. He put a wall around it, dug a winepress in it and built a watchtower. Then he rented the vineyard to some farmers and went away on a journey. When the harvest time approached, he sent his servants to the tenants to collect his fruit.

"The tenants seized his servants; they beat one, killed another, and stoned a third. Then he sent other servants to them, more than the first time, and the tenants treated them in the same way. Last of all, he sent his son to them. 'They will respect my son,' he said.

"But when the tenants saw the son, they said to each other, 'This is the heir. Come, let's kill him and take his inheritance.' So they took him and threw him out of the vineyard and killed him.

"Therefore, when the owner of the vineyard comes, what will he do to those tenants?"

"He will bring those wretches to a wretched end," they replied, "and he will rent the vineyard to other tenants, who will give him his share of the crop at harvest time."

Jesus said to them, "Have you never read in the Scriptures:

"'The stone the builders rejected
    has become the capstone;
the Lord has done this,
    and it is marvellous in our eyes'?

"Therefore I tell you that the kingdom of God will be taken away from you and given to a people who will produce its fruit. He who falls on this stone will be broken to pieces, but he on whom it falls will be crushed."

When the chief priests and the Pharisees heard Jesus' parables, they knew he was talking about them. They looked for a way to arrest him, but they were afraid of the crowd because the people held that he was a prophet.

Proper 23

Sunday between 9 and 15 October inclusive (if after Trinity Sunday)
Choose either 'continuous' or 'related' Old Testament and Psalm readings.

CONTINUOUS

Exodus 32:1–14   When the Israelites saw that Moses was so long in coming down from the mountain, they gathered round Aaron and said, "Come, make us gods who will go before us. As for this fellow Moses who brought us up out of Egypt, we don't know what has happened to him."

Aaron answered them, "Take off the gold ear-rings that your wives, your sons and your daughters are wearing, and bring them to me." So all the people took off their ear-rings and brought them to Aaron. He took what they handed him and made it into an idol cast in the shape of a calf, fashioning it with a tool. Then they said, "These are your gods, O Israel, who brought you up out of Egypt."

When Aaron saw this, he built an altar in front of the calf and announced, "Tomorrow there will be a festival to the LORD." So the next day the people rose early and sacrificed burnt offerings and presented fellow-ship offerings. Afterwards they sat down to eat and drink and got up to indulge in revelry.

Then the LORD said to Moses, "Go down, because your people, whom you brought up out of Egypt, have become corrupt. They have been quick to turn away from what I commanded them and have made themselves an idol cast in the shape of a calf. They have bowed down to it and sacrificed to it and have said, 'These are your gods, O Israel, who brought you up out of Egypt.'

"I have seen these people," the LORD said to Moses, "and they are a stiff-necked people. Now leave me alone so that my anger may burn against them and that I may destroy them. Then I will make you into a great nation."

But Moses sought the favour of the LORD his God. "O LORD," he said, "why should your anger burn against your people, whom you brought out of Egypt with great power and a mighty hand? Why should the Egyptians say, 'It was with evil intent that he brought them out, to kill them in the mountains and to wipe them off the face of the earth'? Turn from your fierce anger; relent and do not bring disaster on your people. Remember your servants Abraham, Isaac and Israel, to whom you swore by your own self: 'I will make your descendants as numerous as the stars in the sky and I will give your descendants all this land I promised them, and it will be their inheritance for ever.'" Then the LORD relented and did not bring on his people the disaster he had threatened.

and **Psalm 106: 1–6,**   Praise the LORD.

      19–23*   Give thanks to the LORD, for he is good;
                   his love endures for ever.
            Who can proclaim the mighty acts of the LORD
                   or fully declare his praise?

Blessed are those who maintain justice,
    who constantly do what is right.
Remember me, O L<small>ORD</small>, when you show favour
     to your people,
    come to my aid when you save them,
that I may enjoy the prosperity of your chosen ones,
    that I may share in the joy of your nation
    and join your inheritance in giving praise.

We have sinned, even as our ancestors did;
    we have done wrong and acted wickedly.
At Horeb they made a calf
    and worshipped an idol cast from metal.
They exchanged their Glory
    for an image of a bull, which eats grass.
They forgot the God who saved them,
    who had done great things in Egypt,
miracles in the land of Ham
    and awesome deeds by the Red Sea.
So he said he would destroy them –
    had not Moses, his chosen one,
stood in the breach before him
    to keep his wrath from destroying them.

Or **RELATED**

Isaiah 25:1–9

O L<small>ORD</small>, you are my God;
    I will exalt you and praise your name,
for in perfect faithfulness
    you have done marvellous things,
    things planned long ago.
You have made the city a heap of rubble,
    the fortified town a ruin,
the foreigners' stronghold a city no more;
    it will never be rebuilt.
Therefore strong peoples will honour you;
    cities of ruthless nations will revere you.
You have been a refuge for the poor,
    a refuge for the needy in their distress,
a shelter from the storm
    and a shade from the heat.
For the breath of the ruthless
    is like a storm driving against a wall
    and like the heat of the desert.
You silence the uproar of foreigners;
    as heat is reduced by the shadow of a cloud,
    so the song of the ruthless is stilled.

FIRST READING

On this mountain the LORD Almighty will prepare
  a feast of rich food for all peoples,
a banquet of aged wine –
  the best of meats and the finest of wines.
On this mountain he will destroy
  the shroud that enfolds all peoples,
the sheet that covers all nations;
  he will swallow up death for ever.
The Sovereign LORD will wipe away the tears
  from all faces;
he will remove the disgrace of his people
  from all the earth.
                                        The LORD has spoken.

In that day they will say,

"Surely this is our God;
  we trusted in him, and he saved us.
This is the LORD, we trusted in him;
  let us rejoice and be glad in his salvation."

and **Psalm 23** The LORD is my shepherd, I shall not be in want.
  He makes me lie down in green pastures,
he leads me beside quiet waters,
  he restores my soul.
He guides me in paths of righteousness
  for his name's sake.
Even though I walk
  through the valley of the shadow of death,
I will fear no evil,
  for you are with me;
your rod and your staff,
  they comfort me.

You prepare a table before me
  in the presence of my enemies.
You anoint my head with oil;
  my cup overflows.
Surely goodness and love will follow me
  all the days of my life,
and I will dwell in the house of the LORD
  for ever.

Philippians 4:1–9 My brothers, you whom I love and long for, my joy and
crown, stand firm in the LORD, dear friends!
  I plead with Euodia and I plead with Syntyche to agree with each other
in the LORD. Yes, and I ask you, loyal yoke-fellow, help these women who
have contended at my side in the cause of the gospel, along with Clement
and the rest of my fellow-workers, whose names are in the book of life.

Rejoice in the Lord always. I will say it again: Rejoice! Let your gentleness be evident to all. The Lord is near. Do not be anxious about anything, but in everything, by prayer and petition, with thanksgiving, present your requests to God. And the peace of God, which transcends all understanding, will guard your hearts and your minds in Christ Jesus.

Finally, brothers, whatever is true, whatever is noble, whatever is right, whatever is pure, whatever is lovely, whatever is admirable – if anything is excellent or praiseworthy – think about such things. Whatever you have learned or received or heard from me, or seen in me – put it into practice. And the God of peace will be with you.

Matthew 22:1–14   Jesus spoke in parables, saying: "The kingdom of heaven G is like a king who prepared a wedding banquet for his son. He sent his ser- O vants to those who had been invited to the banquet to tell them to come, but S they refused to come. P

"Then he sent some more servants and said, 'Tell those who have been E invited that I have prepared my dinner: My oxen and fattened cattle have L been slaughtered, and everything is ready. Come to the wedding banquet.'

"But they paid no attention and went off – one to his field, another to his business. The rest seized his servants, ill-treated them and killed them. The king was enraged. He sent his army and destroyed those murderers and burned their city.

"Then he said to his servants, 'The wedding banquet is ready, but those I invited did not deserve to come. Go to the street corners and invite to the banquet anyone you find.' So the servants went out into the streets and gathered all the people they could find, both good and bad, and the wedding hall was filled with guests.

"But when the king came in to see the guests, he noticed someone there who was not wearing wedding clothes. 'Friend,' he asked, 'how did you get in here without wedding clothes?' The man was speechless.

"Then the king told the attendants, 'Tie him hand and foot, and throw him outside, into the darkness, where there will be weeping and gnashing of teeth.'

"For many are invited, but few are chosen."

Proper 24

Sunday between 16 and 22 October inclusive (if after Trinity Sunday)
Choose either 'continuous' or 'related' Old Testament and Psalm readings.

CONTINUOUS

Exodus 33:12–23   Moses said to the LORD, "You have been telling me, 'Lead F R these people,' but you have not let me know whom you will send with me. I E You have said, 'I know you by name and you have found favour with me.' If R A you are pleased with me, teach me your ways so I may know you and con- S D tinue to find favour with you. Remember that this nation is your people." T I

The LORD replied, "My Presence will go with you, and I will give you N rest." G

Then Moses said to him, "If your Presence does not go with us, do not send us up from here. How will anyone know that you are pleased with me and with your people unless you go with us? What else will distinguish me and your people from all the other people on the face of the earth?"

And the LORD said to Moses, "I will do the very thing you have asked, because I am pleased with you and I know you by name."

Then Moses said, "Now show me your glory."

And the LORD said, "I will cause all my goodness to pass in front of you, and I will proclaim my name, the LORD, in your presence. I will have mercy on whom I will have mercy, and I will have compassion on whom I will have compassion. But," he said, "you cannot see my face, for no-one may see me and live."

Then the LORD said, "There is a place near me where you may stand on a rock. When my glory passes by, I will put you in a cleft in the rock and cover you with my hand until I have passed by. Then I will remove my hand and you will see my back; but my face must not be seen."

and **Psalm 99*** The LORD reigns,
    let the nations tremble;
he sits enthroned between the cherubim,
    let the earth shake.
Great is the LORD in Zion;
    he is exalted over all the nations.
Let them praise your great and awesome name –
    he is holy.

The King is mighty, he loves justice –
    you have established equity;
in Jacob you have done
    what is just and right.
Exalt the LORD our God
    and worship at his footstool;
    he is holy.

Moses and Aaron were among his priests,
    Samuel was among those who called on his name;
they called on the LORD
    and he answered them.
He spoke to them from the pillar of cloud;
    they kept his statutes and the decrees he gave them.

O LORD our God,
    you answered them;
you were to Israel a forgiving God,
    though you punished their misdeeds.
Exalt the LORD our God
    and worship at his holy mountain,
    for the LORD our God is holy.

Isaiah 45:1–7

"This is what the Lord says to his anointed,
  to Cyrus, whose right hand I take hold of
to subdue nations before him
  and to strip kings of their armour,
to open doors before him
  so that gates will not be shut:
I will go before you
  and will level the mountains;
I will break down gates of bronze
  and cut through bars of iron.
I will give you the treasures of darkness,
  riches stored in secret places,
so that you may know that I am the Lord,
  the God of Israel, who summons you by name.
For the sake of Jacob my servant,
  of Israel my chosen,
I summon you by name
  and bestow on you a title of honour,
  though you do not acknowledge me.
I am the Lord, and there is no other;
  apart from me there is no God.
I will strengthen you,
  though you have not acknowledged me,
so that from the rising of the sun
  to the place of its setting
people may know there is none besides me.
  I am the Lord, and there is no other.
I form the light and create darkness,
  I bring prosperity and create disaster;
  I, the Lord, do all these things."

FIRST READING

and **Psalm 96:1–9**
[10–13]

Sing to the Lord a new song;
  sing to the Lord, all the earth.
Sing to the Lord, praise his name;
  proclaim his salvation day after day.
Declare his glory among the nations,
  his marvellous deeds among all peoples.

For great is the Lord and most worthy of praise;
  he is to be feared above all gods.
For all the gods of the nations are idols,
  but the Lord made the heavens.
Splendour and majesty are before him;
  strength and glory are in his sanctuary.

Ascribe to the Lord, O families of nations,
  ascribe to the Lord glory and strength.

PSALM

Ascribe to the LORD the glory due to his name;
bring an offering and come into his courts.
Worship the LORD in the splendour of his holiness;
tremble before him, all the earth.

[Say among the nations, "The LORD reigns."
The world is firmly established, it cannot be
moved;
he will judge the peoples with equity.
Let the heavens rejoice, let the earth be glad;
let the sea resound, and all that is in it;
let the fields be jubilant, and everything in them.
Then all the trees of the forest will sing for joy;
they will sing before the LORD, for he comes,
he comes to judge the earth.
He will judge the world in righteousness
and the peoples in his truth.]

1 Thessalonians 1:1–10   Paul, Silas and Timothy,

To the church of the Thessalonians in God the Father and the LORD Jesus
Christ:

Grace and peace to you.

We always thank God for all of you, mentioning you in our prayers. We
continually remember before our God and Father your work produced by
faith, your labour prompted by love, and your endurance inspired by hope
in our LORD Jesus Christ.

For we know, brothers loved by God, that he has chosen you, because
our gospel came to you not simply with words, but also with power, with the
Holy Spirit and with deep conviction. You know how we lived among you
for your sake. You became imitators of us and of the Lord; in spite of
severe suffering, you welcomed the message with the joy given by the
Holy Spirit. And so you became a model to all the believers in Macedonia
and Achaia. The Lord's message rang out from you not only in Macedonia
and Achaia – your faith in God has become known everywhere. Therefore
we do not need to say anything about it, for they themselves report what
kind of reception you gave us. They tell how you turned to God from idols
to serve the living and true God, and to wait for his Son from heaven, whom
he raised from the dead – Jesus, who rescues us from the coming wrath.

Matthew 22:15–22   The Pharisees went out and laid plans to trap Jesus in his
words. They sent their disciples to him along with the Herodians.
"Teacher," they said, "we know you are a man of integrity and that you
teach the way of God in accordance with the truth. You aren't swayed by
men, because you pay no attention to who they are. Tell us then, what is
your opinion? Is it right to pay taxes to Caesar or not?"

But Jesus, knowing their evil intent, said, "You hypocrites, why are you
trying to trap me? Show me the coin used for paying the tax." They brought

him a denarius, and he asked them, "Whose portrait is this? And whose inscription?"

"Caesar's," they replied.

Then he said to them, "Give to Caesar what is Caesar's, and to God what is God's."

When they heard this, they were amazed. So they left him and went away.

Proper 25

Sunday between 23 and 29 October inclusive (if after Trinity Sunday)
Choose either 'continuous' or 'related' Old Testament and Psalm readings.
Bible Sunday may be celebrated in preference to the provision for the Last Sunday after Trinity.

CONTINUOUS

Deuteronomy 34:1–12 Moses climbed Mount Nebo from the plains of Moab to the top of Pisgah, across from Jericho. There the LORD showed him the whole land – from Gilead to Dan, all of Naphtali, the territory of Ephraim and Manasseh, all the land of Judah as far as the western sea, the Negev and the whole region from the Valley of Jericho, the City of Palms, as far as Zoar. Then the LORD said to him, "This is the land I promised on oath to Abraham, Isaac and Jacob when I said, 'I will give it to your descendants.' I have let you see it with your eyes, but you will not cross over into it."

And Moses the servant of the LORD died there in Moab, as the LORD had said. He buried him in Moab, in the valley opposite Beth Peor, but to this day no-one knows where his grave is. Moses was a hundred and twenty years old when he died, yet his eyes were not weak nor his strength gone. The Israelites grieved for Moses in the plains of Moab thirty days, until the time of weeping and mourning was over.

Now Joshua son of Nun was filled with the spirit of wisdom because Moses had laid his hands on him. So the Israelites listened to him and did what the LORD had commanded Moses.

Since then, no prophet has risen in Israel like Moses, whom the LORD knew face to face, who did all those miraculous signs and wonders the LORD sent him to do in Egypt – to Pharaoh and to all his officials and to his whole land. For no-one has ever shown the mighty power or performed the awesome deeds that Moses did in the sight of all Israel.

Psalm 90: 1–6, 13–17*

LORD, you have been our dwelling-place
    throughout all generations.
Before the mountains were born
    or you brought forth the earth and the world,
    from everlasting to everlasting you are God.
You turn people back to dust,
    saying, "Return to dust, O sons of men."
For a thousand years in your sight
    are like a day that has just gone by,
    or like a watch in the night.

You sweep men away in the sleep of death;
　　they are like the new grass of the morning –
though in the morning it springs up new,
　　by evening it is dry and withered.

Relent, O Lord! How long will it be?
　　Have compassion on your servants.
Satisfy us in the morning with your unfailing love,
　　that we may sing for joy and be glad all our days.
Make us glad for as many days as you have
　　　　afflicted us,
　　for as many years as we have seen trouble.
May your deeds be shown to your servants,
　　your splendour to their children.
May the favour of the Lord our God rest upon us;
　　establish the work of our hands for us –
　　yes, establish the work of our hands.

Or **RELATED**

Leviticus 19:1–2, 15–18　The Lord said to Moses, "Speak to the entire assembly of Israel and say to them: 'Be holy because I, the Lord your God, am holy.

　"'Do not pervert justice; do not show partiality to the poor or favouritism to the great, but judge your neighbour fairly.

　"'Do not go about spreading slander among your people.

　"'Do not do anything that endangers your neighbour's life. I am the Lord.

　"'Do not hate your brother in your heart. Rebuke your neighbour frankly so that you will not share in his guilt.

　"'Do not seek revenge or bear a grudge against one of your people, but love your neighbour as yourself. I am the Lord.'"

Psalm 1　Blessed is the man
　　who does not walk in the counsel of the wicked
or stand in the way of sinners
　　or sit in the seat of mockers.
But his delight is in the law of the Lord,
　　and on his law he meditates day and night.
He is like a tree planted by streams of water,
　　who yields its fruit in season
and whose leaf does not wither.
　　Whatever he does prospers.

Not so the wicked!
　　They are like chaff
　　that the wind blows away.
Therefore the wicked will not stand in the judgment,
　　nor sinners in the assembly of the righteous.

F R
I E
R A
S D
T I
　N
　G

P
S
A
L
M

For the LORD watches over the way of the righteous,
but the way of the wicked will perish.

1 Thessalonians 2:1–8 You know, brothers, that our visit to you was not a fail-
ure. We had previously suffered and been insulted in Philippi, as you know,
but with the help of our God we dared to tell you his gospel in spite of
strong opposition. For the appeal we make does not spring from error or
impure motives, nor are we trying to trick you. On the contrary, we speak
as men approved by God to be entrusted with the gospel. We are not trying
to please men but God, who tests our hearts. You know we never used flat-
tery, nor did we put on a mask to cover up greed – God is our witness. We
were not looking for praise from men, not from you or anyone else.

As apostles of Christ we could have been a burden to you, but we were
gentle among you, like a mother caring for her little children. We loved you
so much that we were delighted to share with you not only the gospel of
God but our lives as well, because you had become so dear to us.

Matthew 22:34–46 Hearing that Jesus had silenced the Sadducees, the Pharisees got together. One of them, an expert in the law, tested him with this
question: "Teacher, which is the greatest commandment in the Law?"

Jesus replied: "'Love the Lord your God with all your heart and with all
your soul and with all your mind.' This is the first and greatest commandment. And the second is like it: 'Love your neighbour as yourself.' All the
Law and the Prophets hang on these two commandments."

While the Pharisees were gathered together, Jesus asked them, "What
do you think about the Christ? Whose son is he?"

"The son of David," they replied.

He said to them, "How is it then that David, speaking by the Spirit, calls
him 'Lord'? For he says,

"'The Lord said to my Lord:
"Sit at my right hand
until I put your enemies
under your feet."'

If then David calls him 'Lord', how can he be his son?" No-one could say
a word in reply, and from that day on no-one dared to ask him any more
questions.

Bible Sunday

Bible Sunday may be celebrated in preference to the provision for the Last Sunday after Trinity

Nehemiah 8:1–4a, [5–6] 8–12 All the Israelite people assembled as one man
in the square before the Water Gate. They told Ezra the scribe to bring out
the Book of the Law of Moses, which the LORD had commanded for Israel.

So on the first day of the seventh month, Ezra the priest brought the Law
before the assembly, which was made up of men and women and all who
were able to understand. He read it aloud from daybreak till noon as he

faced the square before the Water Gate in the presence of the men, women and others who could understand. And all the people listened attentively to the Book of the Law.

Ezra the scribe stood on a high wooden platform built for the occasion.

[Ezra opened the book. All the people could see him because he was standing above them; and as he opened it, the people all stood up. Ezra praised the LORD, the great God; and all the people lifted their hands and responded, "Amen! Amen!" Then they bowed down and worshipped the LORD with their faces to the ground.]

The Levites also read from the Book of the Law of God, making it clear and giving the meaning so that the people could understand what was being read.

Then Nehemiah the governor, Ezra the priest and scribe, and the Levites who were instructing the people said to them all, "This day is sacred to the LORD your God. Do not mourn or weep." For all the people had been weeping as they listened to the words of the Law.

Nehemiah said, "Go and enjoy choice food and sweet drinks, and send some to those who have nothing prepared. This day is sacred to our Lord. Do not grieve, for the joy of the LORD is your strength."

The Levites calmed all the people, saying, "Be still, for this is a sacred day. Do not grieve."

Then all the people went away to eat and drink, to send portions of food and to celebrate with great joy, because they now understood the words that had been made known to them.

Psalm 119:9–16 How can the young keep their way pure?   P
   By living according to your word.   S
I seek you with all my heart;   A
   do not let me stray from your commands.   L
I have hidden your word in my heart   M
   that I might not sin against you.
Praise be to you, O LORD;
   teach me your decrees.
With my lips I recount
   all the laws that come from your mouth.
I rejoice in following your statutes
   as one rejoices in great riches.
I meditate on your precepts
   and consider your ways.
I delight in your decrees;
   I will not neglect your word.   S
    E

Colossians 3:12–17 As God's chosen people, holy and dearly loved, clothe C
yourselves with compassion, kindness, humility, gentleness and patience. O
Bear with each other and forgive whatever grievances you may have N
against one another. Forgive as the Lord forgave you. And over all these D
virtues put on love, which binds them all together in perfect unity. C

Let the peace of Christ rule in your hearts, since as members of one body you were called to peace. And be thankful. Let the word of Christ dwell in you richly as you teach and admonish one another with all wisdom, and as you sing psalms, hymns and spiritual songs with gratitude in your hearts to God. And whatever you do, whether in word or deed, do it all in the name of the Lord Jesus, giving thanks to God the Father through him.

Matthew 24:30–35   Jesus said: "The sign of the Son of Man will appear in the G sky, and all the nations of the earth will mourn. They will see the Son of O Man coming on the clouds of the sky, with power and great glory. And he S will send his angels with a loud trumpet call, and they will gather his elect P from the four winds, from one end of the heavens to the other.   E

"Now learn this lesson from the fig-tree: As soon as its twigs get tender L and its leaves come out, you know that summer is near. Even so, when you see all these things, you know that it is near, right at the door. I tell you the truth, this generation will certainly not pass away until all these things have happened. Heaven and earth will pass away, but my words will never pass away."

Dedication Festival

The First Sunday in October or Last Sunday after Trinity

Alternative first readings

Either **1 Kings 8:22–30**   Solomon stood before the altar of the LORD in front of F the whole assembly of Israel, spread out his hands towards heaven and I said: R

"O LORD, God of Israel, there is no God like you in heaven above or on S earth below – you who keep your covenant of love with your servants who T continue wholeheartedly in your way. You have kept your promise to your servant David my father; with your mouth you have promised and with R your hand you have fulfilled it – as it is today.   E

"Now LORD, God of Israel, keep for your servant David my father the A promises you made to him when you said, 'You shall never fail to have a D man to sit before me on the throne of Israel, if only your sons are careful in I all they do to walk before me as you have done.' And now, O God of Israel, N let your word that you promised your servant David my father come true. G

"But will God really dwell on earth? The heavens, even the highest heaven, cannot contain you. How much less this temple I have built! Yet give attention to your servant's prayer and his plea for mercy, O LORD my God. Hear the cry and the prayer that your servant is praying in your presence this day. May your eyes be open towards this temple night and day, this place of which you said, 'My Name shall be there,' so that you will hear the prayer your servant prays towards this place. Hear the supplication of your servant and of your people Israel when they pray towards this place. Hear from heaven, your dwelling-place, and when you hear, forgive."

or **Revelation 21:9–14**   One of the seven angels who had the seven bowls full of the seven last plagues came and said to me, "Come, I will show you the bride, the wife of the Lamb." And he carried me away in the Spirit to a mountain great and high, and showed me the Holy City, Jerusalem, coming down out of heaven from God. It shone with the glory of God, and its brilliance was like that of a very precious jewel, like a jasper, clear as crystal. It had a great, high wall with twelve gates, and with twelve angels at the gates. On the gates were written the names of the twelve tribes of Israel. There were three gates on the east, three on the north, three on the south and three on the west. The wall of the city had twelve foundations, and on them were the names of the twelve apostles of the Lamb.

Psalm 122   I rejoiced with those who said to me,
    "Let us go to the house of the LORD."
  Our feet are standing
    in your gates, O Jerusalem.

  Jerusalem is built like a city
    that is closely compacted together.
  That is where the tribes go up,
    the tribes of the LORD,
  to praise the name of the LORD
    according to the statute given to Israel.
  There the thrones for judgment stand,
    the thrones of the house of David.

  Pray for the peace of Jerusalem:
    "May those who love you be secure.
  May there be peace within your walls
    and security within your citadels."
  For the sake of my brothers and friends,
    I will say, "Peace be within you."
  For the sake of the house of the LORD our God,
    I will seek your prosperity.

Hebrews 12:18–24   You have not come to a mountain that can be touched and that is burning with fire; to darkness, gloom and storm; to a trumpet blast or to such a voice speaking words that those who heard it begged that no further word be spoken to them, because they could not bear what was commanded: "If even an animal touches the mountain, it must be stoned." The sight was so terrifying that Moses said, "I am trembling with fear."

    But you have come to Mount Zion, to the heavenly Jerusalem, the city of the living God. You have come to thousands upon thousands of angels in joyful assembly, to the church of the firstborn, whose names are written in heaven. You have come to God, the judge of all men, to the spirits of righteous men made perfect, to Jesus the mediator of a new covenant, and to the sprinkled blood that speaks a better word than the blood of Abel.

Matthew 21:12–16   Jesus entered the temple area and drove out all who were buying and selling there. He overturned the tables of the money-changers and the benches of those selling doves. "It is written," he said to them, "'My house will be called a house of prayer,' but you are making it a 'den of robbers'."

The blind and the lame came to him at the temple, and he healed them. But when the chief priests and the teachers of the law saw the wonderful things he did and the children shouting in the temple area, "Hosanna to the Son of David," they were indignant.

"Do you hear what these children are saying?" they asked him.

"Yes," replied Jesus, "have you never read,

"'From the lips of children and infants
    you have ordained praise'?"

All Saints Day

Sunday between 30 October and 5 November or, if this is not kept as All Saint's Sunday, on 1 November itself

Revelation 7:9–17   I looked and there before me was a great multitude that no-one could count, from every nation, tribe, people and language, standing before the throne and in front of the Lamb. They were wearing white robes and were holding palm branches in their hands. And they cried out in a loud voice:

"Salvation belongs to our God,
    who sits on the throne,
    and to the Lamb."

All the angels were standing round the throne and around the elders and the four living creatures. They fell down on their faces before the throne and worshipped God, saying:

"Amen!
Praise and glory
and wisdom and thanks and honour
and power and strength
be to our God for ever and ever.
Amen!"

Then one of the elders asked me, "These in white robes – who are they, and where did they come from?"

I answered, "Sir, you know."

And he said, "These are they who have come out of the great tribulation; they have washed their robes and made them white in the blood of the Lamb. Therefore,

"they are before the throne of God
    and serve him day and night in his temple;
and he who sits on the throne will spread his tent over them.

Never again will they hunger;
　　never again will they thirst.
The sun will not beat upon them,
　　nor any scorching heat.
For the Lamb at the centre of the throne will be their shepherd;
　　he will lead them to springs of living water.
And God will wipe away every tear from their eyes."

Psalm 34:1–10　　I will extol the Lord at all times;　　　　　　　P
　　　　　　　his praise will always be on my lips.　　　　　　　S
　　　　　　My soul will boast in the Lord;　　　　　　　　　　A
　　　　　　　let the afflicted hear and rejoice.　　　　　　　L
　　　　　　Glorify the Lord with me:　　　　　　　　　　　M
　　　　　　　let us exalt his name together.

　　　　　　I sought the Lord, and he answered me;
　　　　　　　he delivered me from all my fears.
　　　　　　Those who look to him are radiant;
　　　　　　　their faces are never covered with shame.
　　　　　　This poor man called, and the Lord heard him;
　　　　　　　he saved him out of all his troubles.
　　　　　　The angel of the Lord encamps around those who fear him,
　　　　　　　and he delivers them.

　　　　　　Taste and see that the Lord is good;
　　　　　　　blessed are those who take refuge in him.
　　　　　　Fear the Lord, you his saints,
　　　　　　　for those who fear him lack nothing.
　　　　　　The lions may grow weak and hungry,
　　　　　　　but those who seek the Lord lack no good thing.

1 John 3:1–3　　How great is the love the Father has lavished on us, that we　S R
should be called children of God! And that is what we are! The reason the　E E
world does not know us is that it did not know him. Dear friends, now we　C A
are children of God, and what we will be has not yet been made known. But　O D
we know that when he appears, we shall be like him, for we shall see him as　N I
he is. Everyone who has this hope in him purifies himself, just as he is pure.　D N
　　　　　　　　　　　　　　　　　　　　　　　　　　　　　G

Matthew 5:1–12　　When Jesus saw the crowds, he went up on a mountainside　G
and sat down. His disciples came to him, and he began to teach them, say-　O
ing:　　　　　　　　　　　　　　　　　　　　　　　　　　S
　　　　　　　　　　　　　　　　　　　　　　　　　　　　P
　　"Blessed are the poor in spirit,　　　　　　　　　　　　E
　　　for theirs is the kingdom of heaven.　　　　　　　　　L
　　Blessed are those who mourn,
　　　for they will be comforted.
　　Blessed are the meek,
　　　for they will inherit the earth.

Blessed are those who hunger and thirst for righteousness,
    for they will be filled.
Blessed are the merciful,
    for they will be shown mercy.
Blessed are the pure in heart,
    for they will see God.
Blessed are the peacemakers,
    for they will be called children of God.
Blessed are those who are persecuted because of righteousness,
    for theirs is the kingdom of heaven.

"Blessed are you when people insult you, persecute you and falsely say all kinds of evil against you because of me. Rejoice and be glad, because great is your reward in heaven, for in the same way they persecuted the prophets who were before you."

For use on 1 November if the material for All Saints' Day is used on the Sunday

(Readings for Years A, B, C are the same)

Alternative first readings

Either **Isaiah 56:3–8**   Let no foreigners who have bound themselves
                to the Lord say,
            "The Lord will surely exclude me from his people."
        And let not any eunuch complain,
            "I am only a dry tree."

        For this is what the Lord says:

        "To the eunuchs who keep my Sabbaths,
            who choose what pleases me
            and hold fast to my covenant –
        to them I will give within my temple and its walls
            a memorial and a name
            better than sons and daughters;
        I will give them an everlasting name
            that will not be cut off.
        And foreigners who bind themselves to the Lord
            to serve him,
        to love the name of the Lord,
            and to worship him,
        all who keep the Sabbath without desecrating it
            and who hold fast to my covenant –
        these I will bring to my holy mountain
            and give them joy in my house of prayer.
        Their burnt offerings and sacrifices
            will be accepted on my altar;

(margin: F I R S T   R E A D I N G)

for my house will be called
    a house of prayer for all nations."
The Sovereign Lord declares –
    he who gathers the exiles of Israel:
"I will gather still others to them
    besides those already gathered."

or **2 Esdras 2:42–48**

Psalm 33:1–5   Sing joyfully to the Lord, you righteous;
    it is fitting for the upright to praise him.
Praise the Lord with the harp;
    make music to him on the ten-stringed lyre.
Sing to him a new song;
    play skilfully, and shout for joy.

For the word of the Lord is right and true;
    he is faithful in all he does.
The Lord loves righteousness and justice;
    the earth is full of his unfailing love.

Hebrews 12:18–24   You have not come to a mountain that can be touched and that is burning with fire; to darkness, gloom and storm; to a trumpet blast or to such a voice speaking words that those who heard it begged that no further word be spoken to them, because they could not bear what was commanded: "If even an animal touches the mountain, it must be stoned." The sight was so terrifying that Moses said, "I am trembling with fear."

But you have come to Mount Zion, to the heavenly Jerusalem, the city of the living God. You have come to thousands upon thousands of angels in joyful assembly, to the church of the firstborn, whose names are written in heaven. You have come to God, the judge of all men, to the spirits of righteous men made perfect, to Jesus the mediator of a new covenant, and to the sprinkled blood that speaks a better word than the blood of Abel.

Matthew 5:1–12   When Jesus saw the crowds, he went up on a mountainside and sat down. His disciples came to him, and he began to teach them, saying:

"Blessed are the poor in spirit,
    for theirs is the kingdom of heaven.
Blessed are those who mourn,
    for they will be comforted.
Blessed are the meek,
    for they will inherit the earth.
Blessed are those who hunger and thirst for righteousness,
    for they will be filled.
Blessed are the merciful,
    for they will be shown mercy.

Blessed are the pure in heart,
  for they will see God.
Blessed are the peacemakers,
  for they will be called children of God.
Blessed are those who are persecuted because of righteousness,
  for theirs is the kingdom of heaven.

"Blessed are you when people insult you, persecute you and falsely say all kinds of evil against you because of me. Rejoice and be glad, because great is your reward in heaven, for in the same way they persecuted the prophets who were before you."

Fourth Sunday Before Advent

Sunday between 30 October and 5 November inclusive
For use if the Feast of All Saints was celebrated on 1 November and alternative propers are needed

Micah 3:5–12 This is what the LORD says:

"As for the prophets
  who lead my people astray,
if one feeds them,
  they proclaim 'peace';
if he does not,
  they prepare to wage war against him.
Therefore night will come over you, without visions,
  and darkness, without divination.
The sun will set for the prophets,
  and the day will go dark for them.
The seers will be ashamed
  and the diviners disgraced.
They will all cover their faces
  because there is no answer from God."

But as for me, I am filled with power,
  with the Spirit of the LORD,
  and with justice and might,
to declare to Jacob his transgression,
  to Israel his sin.
Hear this, you leaders of the house of Jacob,
  you rulers of the house of Israel,
who despise justice
  and distort all that is right;
who build Zion with bloodshed,
  and Jerusalem with wickedness.
Her leaders judge for a bribe,
  her priests teach for a price,
  and her prophets tell fortunes for money.
Yet they lean upon the LORD and say,
  "Is not the LORD among us?
  No disaster will come upon us."

FIRST READING

Therefore because of you,
    Zion will be ploughed like a field,
Jerusalem will become a heap of rubble,
    the temple hill a mound overgrown with thickets.

Psalm 43*   Vindicate me, O God,
        and plead my cause against an ungodly nation;
        rescue me from deceitful and wicked men.
    You are God my stronghold.
        Why have you rejected me?
    Why must I go about mourning,
        oppressed by the enemy?
    Send forth your light and your truth,
        let them guide me;
    let them bring me to your holy mountain,
        to the place where you dwell.
    Then will I go to the altar of God,
        to God, my joy and my delight.
    I will praise you with the harp,
        O God, my God.

    Why are you downcast, O my soul?
        Why so disturbed within me?
    Put your hope in God,
        for I will yet praise him,
        my Saviour and my God.

(margin: P S A L M)

1 Thessalonians 2:9–13   Surely you remember, brothers, our toil and hardship; we worked night and day in order not to be a burden to anyone while we preached the gospel of God to you.

You are witnesses, and so is God, of how holy, righteous and blameless we were among you who believed. For you know that we dealt with each of you as a father deals with his own children, encouraging, comforting and urging you to live lives worthy of God, who calls you into his kingdom and glory.

And we also thank God continually because, when you received the word of God, which you heard from us, you accepted it not as the word of men, but as it actually is, the word of God, which is at work in you who believe.

(margin: S E C O N D)

Matthew 24:1–14   Jesus left the temple and was walking away when his disciples came up to him to call his attention to its buildings. "Do you see all these things?" he asked. "I tell you the truth, not one stone here will be left on another; every one will be thrown down."

As Jesus was sitting on the Mount of Olives, the disciples came to him privately. "Tell us," they said, "when will this happen, and what will be the sign of your coming and of the end of the age?"

(margin: G O S P E L)

Jesus answered: "Watch out that no-one deceives you. For many will come in my name, claiming, 'I am the Christ,' and will deceive many. You will hear of wars and rumours of wars, but see to it that you are not alarmed. Such things must happen, but the end is still to come. Nation will rise against nation, and kingdom against kingdom. There will be famines and earthquakes in various places. All these are the beginning of birth-pains.

"Then you will be handed over to be persecuted and put to death, and you will be hated by all nations because of me. At that time many will turn away from the faith and will betray and hate each other, and many false prophets will appear and deceive many people. Because of the increase of wickedness, the love of most will grow cold, but he who who stands firm to the end will be saved. And this gospel of the kingdom will be preached in the whole world as a testimony to all nations, and then the end will come."

Third Sunday Before Advent

Sunday between 6 and 12 November inclusive

Alternatives provided for the first reading and its complementary Psalm or Canticle

Either **Wisdom of Solomon 6:12–16**

and Canticle: **Wisdom of Solomon 6:17–20**

Or **Amos 5:18–24**

Woe to you who long	F
for the day of the LORD!	I
Why do you long for the day of the LORD?	R
That day will be darkness, not light.	S
It will be as though a man fled from a lion	T
only to meet a bear,	
as though he entered his house	R
and rested his hand on the wall	E
only to have a snake bite him.	A
Will not the day of the LORD be darkness, not light –	D
pitch-dark, without a ray of brightness?	I
"I hate, I despise your religious feasts;	N
I cannot stand your assemblies.	G

Even though you bring me burnt offerings and
    grain offerings,
    I will not accept them.
Though you bring choice fellowship offerings,
    I will have no regard for them.
Away with the noise of your songs!
    I will not listen to the music of your harps.
But let justice roll on like a river,
    righteousness like a never-failing stream!

and **Psalm 70**   Hasten, O God, to save me;   P
                      O Lᴏʀᴅ, come quickly to help me.   S

                      May those who seek my life   A
                          be put to shame and confusion;   L
                      may all who desire my ruin   M
                          be turned back in disgrace.
                      May those who say to me, "Aha! Aha!"
                          turn back because of their shame.
                      But may all who seek you
                          rejoice and be glad in you;
                      may those who love your salvation always say,
                          "Let God be exalted!"

                      Yet I am poor and needy;
                          come quickly to me, O God.
                      You are my help and my deliverer;
                          O Lᴏʀᴅ, do not delay.

1 Thessalonians 4:13–18   Brothers, we do not want you to be ignorant about   S R
those who fall asleep, or to grieve like the rest of men, who have no hope.   E E
We believe that Jesus died and rose again and so we believe that God will   C A
bring with Jesus those who have fallen asleep in him. According to the   O D
Lord's own word, we tell you that we who are still alive, who are left till the   N I
coming of the Lord, will certainly not precede those who have fallen   D N
asleep. For the Lord himself will come down from heaven, with a loud com-   G
mand, with the voice of the archangel and with the trumpet call of God, and
the dead in Christ will rise first. After that, we who are still alive and are
left will be caught up together with them in the clouds to meet the Lord in
the air. And so we will be with the Lord for ever. Therefore encourage each
other with these words.

Matthew 25:1–13   Jesus said: "The kingdom of heaven will be like ten virgins   G
who took their lamps and went out to meet the bridegroom. Five of them   O
were foolish and five were wise. The foolish ones took their lamps but did   S
not take any oil with them. The wise, however, took oil in jars along with   P
their lamps. The bridegroom was a long time in coming, and they all   E
became drowsy and fell asleep.   L

   "At midnight the cry rang out: 'Here's the bridegroom! Come out to
meet him!'

   "Then all the virgins woke up and trimmed their lamps. The foolish ones
said to the wise, 'Give us some of your oil; our lamps are going out.'

   "'No,' they replied, 'there may not be enough for both us and you.
Instead, go to those who sell oil and buy some for yourselves.'

   "But while they were on their way to buy the oil, the bridegroom
arrived. The virgins who were ready went in with him to the wedding banquet. And the door was shut.

   "Later the others also came. 'Sir! Sir!' they said. 'Open the door for
us!'

"But he replied, 'I tell you the truth, I don't know you.'
"Therefore keep watch, because you do not know the day or the hour."

Second Sunday Before Advent

Sunday between 13 and 19 November inclusive

Zephaniah 1:7, 12–18

"Be silent before the Sovereign LORD,
    for the day of the LORD is near.
The LORD has prepared a sacrifice;
    he has consecrated those he has invited.

"At that time I will search Jerusalem with lamps
    and punish those who are complacent,
    who are like wine left on its dregs,
who think, 'The LORD will do nothing,
    either good or bad.'
Their wealth will be plundered,
    their houses demolished.
They will build houses
    but not live in them;
they will plant vineyards
    but not drink the wine.

"The great day of the LORD is near –
    near and coming quickly.
Listen! The cry on the day of the LORD will be bitter,
    the shouting of the warrior there.
That day will be a day of wrath,
    a day of distress and anguish,
a day of trouble and ruin,
    a day of darkness and gloom,
    a day of clouds and blackness,
a day of trumpet and battle cry
    against the fortified cities
    and against the corner towers.
I will bring distress on the people
    and they will walk like blind men,
    because they have sinned against the LORD.
Their blood will be poured out like dust
    and their entrails like filth.
Neither their silver nor their gold
    will be able to save them
    on the day of the LORD's wrath.
In the fire of his jealousy
    the whole world will be consumed,
for he will make a sudden end
    of all who live in the earth."

FIRST READING

Psalm 90:1–8
[9–11] 12*

LORD, you have been our dwelling–place
    throughout all generations.
Before the mountains were born
    or you brought forth the earth and the world,
    from everlasting to everlasting you are God.
You turn men back to dust,
    saying, "Return to dust,O sons of men."
For a thousand years in your sight
    are like a day that has just gone by,
    or like a watch in the night.
You sweep men away in the sleep of death;
    they are like the new grass of the morning –
though in the morning it springs up new,
    by evening it is dry and withered.

We are consumed by your anger
    and terrified by your indignation.
You have set our iniquities before you,
    our secret sins in the light of your presence.
[All our days pass away under your wrath;
    we finish our years with a moan.
The length of our days is seventy years –
    or eighty, if we have the strength;
yet their span is but trouble and sorrow,
    for they quickly pass, and we fly away.

Who knows the power of your anger?
    For your wrath is as great as the fear that is due to you.]
Teach us to number our days aright,
    that we may gain a heart of wisdom.

1 Thessalonians 5:1–11   About times and dates we do not need to write to you, S
for you know very well that the day of the Lord will come like a thief in the E
night. While people are saying, "Peace and safety", destruction will come C
on them suddenly, as labour pains on a pregnant woman, and they will not O
escape.   N
    But you, brothers, are not in darkness so that this day should surprise D
you like a thief. You are all sons of the light and sons of the day. We do not
belong to the night or to the darkness. So then, let us not be like others, who R
are asleep, but let us be alert and self-controlled. For those who sleep, E
sleep at night, and those who get drunk, get drunk at night. But since we A
belong to the day, let us be self-controlled, putting on faith and love as a D
breastplate, and the hope of salvation as a helmet. For God did not appoint I
us to suffer wrath but to receive salvation through our Lord Jesus Christ. N
He died for us so that, whether we are awake or asleep, we may live G
together with him. Therefore encourage one another and build each other
up, just as in fact you are doing.

Matthew 25:14–30 Jesus said: "The kingdom of heaven will be like a man G going on a journey, who called his servants and entrusted his property to O them. To one he gave five talents of money, to another two talents, and to S another one talent, each according to his ability. Then he went on his jour- P ney. The man who had received the five talents went at once and put his E money to work and gained five more. So also, the one with the two talents L gained two more. But the man who had received the one talent went off, dug a hole in the ground and hid his master's money.

"After a long time the master of those servants returned and settled accounts with them. The man who had received the five talents brought the other five. 'Master,' he said, 'you entrusted me with five talents. See, I have gained five more.'

"His master replied, 'Well done, good and faithful servant! You have been faithful with a few things; I will put you in charge of many things. Come and share your master's happiness!'

"The man with the two talents also came. 'Master,' he said, 'you entrusted me with two talents; see, I have gained two more.'

"His master replied, 'Well done, good and faithful servant! You have been faithful with a few things; I will put you in charge of many things. Come and share your master's happiness!'

"Then the man who had received the one talent came. 'Master,' he said, 'I knew that you are a hard man, harvesting where you have not sown and gathering where you have not scattered seed. So I was afraid and went out and hid your talent in the ground. See, here is what belongs to you.'

"His master replied, 'You wicked, lazy servant! So you knew that I harvest where I have not sown and gather where I have not scattered seed? Well then, you should have put my money on deposit with the bankers, so that when I returned I would have received it back with interest.

"'Take the talent from him and give it to the one who has the ten talents. For everyone who has will be given more, and he will have an abundance. Whoever does not have, even what he has will be taken from him. And throw that worthless servant outside, into the darkness, where there will be weeping and gnashing of teeth.'"

Christist the King

Sunday between 20 and 26 November inclusive

Ezekiel 34:11–16, 20–24 This is what the Sovereign LORD says: I myself will F R search for my sheep and look after them. As a shepherd looks after his I E scattered flocks when he is with them, so will I look after my sheep. I will R A rescue them from all the places where they were scattered on a day of S D clouds and darkness. I will bring them out from the nations and gather T I them from the countries, and I will bring them into their own land. I will N pasture them on the mountains of Israel, in the ravines and in all the set- G tlements in the land. I will tend them in a good pasture, and the mountain heights of Israel will be their grazing land. There they will lie down in good grazing land, and there they will feed in a rich pasture on the mountains of

Israel. I myself will tend my sheep and make them lie down, declares the Sovereign LORD. I will search for the lost and bring back the strays. I will bind up the injured and strengthen the weak, but the sleek and the strong I will destroy. I will shepherd the flock with justice.

Therefore this is what the Sovereign LORD says to them: See, I myself will judge between the fat sheep and the lean sheep. Because you shove with flank and shoulder, butting all the weak sheep with your horns until you have driven them away, I will save my flock, and they will no longer be plundered. I will judge between one sheep and another. I will place over them one shepherd, my servant David, and he will tend them; he will tend them and be their shepherd. I the LORD will be their God, and my servant David will be prince among them. I the LORD have spoken.

Psalm 95:1–7a*
Come, let us sing for joy to the LORD;
  let us shout aloud to the Rock of our salvation.
Let us come before him with thanksgiving
  and extol him with music and song.

For the LORD is the great God,
  the great King above all gods.
In his hand are the depths of the earth,
  and the mountain peaks belong to him.
The sea is his, for he made it,
  and his hands formed the dry land.

Come, let us bow down in worship,
  let us kneel before the LORD our Maker;
for he is our God
  and we are the people of his pasture,
  the flock under his care.

Ephesians 1:15–23 Ever since I heard about your faith in the Lord Jesus and your love for all the saints, I have not stopped giving thanks for you, remembering you in my prayers. I keep asking that the God of our Lord Jesus Christ, the glorious Father, may give you the Spirit of wisdom and revelation, so that you may know him better. I pray also that the eyes of your heart may be enlightened in order that you may know the hope to which he has called you, the riches of his glorious inheritance in the saints, and his incomparably great power for us who believe. That power is like the working of his mighty strength, which he exerted in Christ when he raised him from the dead and seated him at his right hand in the heavenly realms, far above all rule and authority, power and dominion, and every title that can be given, not only in the present age but also in the one to come. And God placed all things under his feet and appointed him to be head over everything for the church, which is his body, the fulness of him who fills everything in every way.

Matthew 25:31–46   Jesus said: "When the Son of Man comes in his glory, and
all the angels with him, he will sit on his throne in heavenly glory. All the
nations will be gathered before him, and he will separate the people one
from another as a shepherd separates the sheep from the goats. He will put
the sheep on his right and the goats on his left.

GOSPEL

"Then the King will say to those on his right, 'Come, you who are blessed
by my Father; take your inheritance, the kingdom prepared for you since
the creation of the world. For I was hungry and you gave me something to
eat, I was thirsty and you gave me something to drink, I was a stranger and
you invited me in, I needed clothes and you clothed me, I was sick and you
looked after me, I was in prison and you came to visit me.'

"Then the righteous will answer him, 'Lord, when did we see you hungry
and feed you, or thirsty and give you something to drink? When did we see
you a stranger and invite you in, or needing clothes and clothe you? When
did we see you sick or in prison and go to visit you?'

"The King will reply, 'I tell you the truth, whatever you did for one of the
least of these brothers of mine, you did for me.'

"Then he will say to those on his left, 'Depart from me, you who are
cursed, into the eternal fire prepared for the devil and his angels. For I was
hungry and you gave me nothing to eat, I was thirsty and you gave me nothing to drink, I was a stranger and you did not invite me in, I needed clothes
and you did not clothe me, I was sick and in prison and you did not look
after me.'

"They also will answer, 'Lord, when did we see you hungry or thirsty or
a stranger or needing clothes or sick or in prison, and did not help you?'

"He will reply, 'I tell you the truth, whatever you did not do for one of the
least of these, you did not do for me.'

"Then they will go away to eternal punishment, but the righteous to
eternal life."

CHURCH OF ENGLAND
LECTIONARY FOR THE PRINCIPAL
SUNDAY SERVICE (RCL AMENDED)

Year B

THE SEASONS: ADVENT

First Sunday of Advent

Isaiah 64:1–9 Oh, that you would rend the heavens and come down,
> that the mountains would tremble before you!
> As when fire sets twigs ablaze
> > and causes water to boil,
> come down to make your name known to your enemies
> > and cause the nations to quake before you!
> For when you did awesome things that we did not expect,
> > you came down, and the mountains trembled before you.
> Since ancient times no-one has heard,
> > no ear has perceived,
> no eye has seen any God besides you,
> > who acts on behalf of those who wait for him.
> You come to the help of those who gladly do right,
> > who remember your ways.
> But when we continued to sin against them,
> > you were angry.
> > How then can we be saved?
> All of us have become like one who is unclean,
> > and all our righteous acts are like filthy rags;
> we all shrivel up like a leaf,
> > and like the wind our sins sweep us away.
> No-one calls on your name
> > or strives to lay hold of you;
> for you have hidden your face from us
> > and made us waste away because of our sins.
>
> Yet, O LORD, you are our Father.
> > We are the clay, you are the potter;
> > we are all the work of your hand.
> Do not be angry beyond measure, O LORD;
> > do not remember our sins for ever.
> Oh, look upon us we pray,
> > for we are all your people.

FIRST READING

Psalm 80:1–7, 17–19 Hear us, O Shepherd of Israel,
you who lead Joseph like a flock;
you who sit enthroned between the cherubim,
shine forth
before Ephraim, Benjamin and Manasseh.
Awaken your might;
come and save us.

Restore us, O God;
make your face shine upon us,
that we may be saved.

O LORD God Almighty,
how long will your anger smoulder
against the prayers of your people?
You have fed them with the bread of tears;
you have made them drink tears by the bowlful.
You have made us a source of contention to
our neighbours,
and our enemies mock us.

Restore us, O God Almighty;
make your face shine upon us,
that we may be saved.

Let your hand rest on the man at your right hand,
the son of man you have raised up for yourself.
Then we will not turn away from you;
revive us, and we will call on your name.

Restore us, O LORD God Almighty;
make your face shine upon us,
that we may be saved.

1 Corinthians 1:3–9 Grace and peace to you from God our Father and the
Lord Jesus Christ.

I always thank God for you because of his grace given you in Christ
Jesus. For in him you have been enriched in every way – in all your speaking and in all your knowledge – because our testimony about Christ was
confirmed in you. Therefore you do not lack any spiritual gift as you
eagerly wait for our Lord Jesus Christ to be revealed. He will keep you
strong to the end, so that you will be blameless on the day of our Lord Jesus
Christ. God, who has called you into fellowship with his Son Jesus Christ
our Lord, is faithful.

Mark 13:24–37 Jesus said: "'In those days,
the sun will be darkened,
and the moon will not give its light;
the stars will fall from the sky,
and the heavenly bodies will be shaken.'

"At that time people will see the Son of Man coming in clouds with great power and glory. And he will send his angels and gather his elect from the four winds, from the ends of the earth to the ends of the heavens.

"Now learn this lesson from the fig-tree: As soon as its twigs get tender and its leaves come out, you know that summer is near. Even so, when you see these things happening, you know that it is near, right at the door. I tell you the truth, this generation will certainly not pass away until all these things have happened. Heaven and earth will pass away, but my words will never pass away.

"No-one knows about that day or hour, not even the angels in heaven, nor the Son, but only the Father. Be on guard! Be alert! You do not know when that time will come. It's like a man going away: He leaves his house and puts his servants in charge, each with his assigned task, and tells the one at the door to keep watch.

"Therefore keep watch because you do not know when the owner of the house will come back – whether in the evening, or at midnight, or when the cock crows, or at dawn. If he comes suddenly, do not let him find you sleeping. What I say to you, I say to everyone: 'Watch!'"

Second Sunday of Advent

Isaiah 40:1–11

Comfort, comfort my people,
    says your God.
Speak tenderly to Jerusalem,
    and proclaim to her
that her hard service has been completed,
    that her sin has been paid for,
that she has received from the LORD's hand
    double for all her sins.

A voice of one calling:
"In the desert prepare
    the way for the LORD;
make straight in the wilderness
    a highway for our God.
Every valley shall be raised up,
    every mountain and hill made low;
the rough ground shall become level,
    the rugged places a plain.
And the glory of the LORD will be revealed,
    and all mankind together will see it.
        For the mouth of the LORD has spoken."

A voice says, "Cry out."
    And I said, "What shall I cry?"

"All people are like grass,
    and all their glory is like the flowers of the field.

FIRST READING

The grass withers and the flowers fall,
>because the breath of the LORD blows on them.
>Surely the people are grass.
The grass withers and the flowers fall,
>but the word of our God stands for ever."

You who bring good tidings to Zion,
>go up on a high mountain.
You who bring good tidings to Jerusalem,
>lift up your voice with a shout,
lift it up, do not be afraid;
>say to the towns of Judah,
>"Here is your God!"
See, the Sovereign LORD comes with power,
>and his arm rules for him.
See, his reward is with him,
>and his recompense accompanies him.
He tends his flock like a shepherd:
>He gathers the lambs in his arms
and carries them close to his heart;
>he gently leads those that have young.

Psalm 85:1–2, 8–13* You showed favour to your land, O LORD;
>you restored the fortunes of Jacob.
You forgave the iniquity of your people
>and covered all their sins.

I will listen to what God the LORD will say;
>he promises peace to his people, his saints –
>but let them not return to folly.
Surely his salvation is near those who fear him,
>that his glory may dwell in our land.

Love and faithfulness meet together;
>righteousness and peace kiss each other.
Faithfulness springs forth from the earth,
>and righteousness looks down from heaven.
The LORD will indeed give what is good,
>and our land will yield its harvest.
Righteousness goes before him
>and prepares the way for his steps.

P S A L M

S R E E C A O D N I D N G

2 Peter 3:8–15a Do not forget this one thing, dear friends: With the Lord a day is like a thousand years, and a thousand years are like a day. The Lord is not slow in keeping his promise, as some understand slowness. He is patient with you, not wanting anyone to perish, but everyone to come to repentance.

But the day of the Lord will come like a thief. The heavens will disappear with a roar; the elements will be destroyed by fire, and the earth and everything in it will be laid bare.

Since everything will be destroyed in this way, what kind of people ought you to be? You ought to live holy and godly lives as you look forward to the day of God and speed its coming. That day will bring about the destruction of the heavens by fire, and the elements will melt in the heat. But in keeping with his promise we are looking forward to a new heaven and a new earth, the home of righteousness.

So then, dear friends, since you are looking forward to this, make every effort to be found spotless, blameless and at peace with him. Bear in mind that our Lord's patience means salvation.

Mark 1:1–8   The beginning of the gospel about Jesus Christ, the Son of God.

It is written in Isaiah the prophet:

"I will send my messenger ahead of you,
   who will prepare your way" –
"a voice of one calling in the desert,
'Prepare the way for the Lord,
   make straight paths for him.'"

And so John came, baptising in the desert region and preaching a baptism of repentance for the forgiveness of sins. The whole Judean countryside and all the people of Jerusalem went out to him. Confessing their sins, they were baptised by him in the Jordan River. John wore clothing made of camel's hair, with a leather belt round his waist, and he ate locusts and wild honey. And this was his message: "After me will come one more powerful than I, the thongs of whose sandals I am not worthy to stoop down and untie. I baptise you with water, but he will baptise you with the Holy Spirit."

Third Sunday of Advent

Isaiah 61:1–4, 8–11   The Spirit of the Sovereign Lord is on me,
            because the Lord has anointed me
            to preach good news to the poor.
         He has sent me to bind up the broken-hearted,
            to proclaim freedom for the captives
            and release from darkness for the prisoners,
         to proclaim the year of the Lord's favour
            and the day of vengeance of our God,
         to comfort all who mourn,
            and provide for those who grieve in Zion –
         to bestow on them a crown of beauty
            instead of ashes,
         the oil of gladness
            instead of mourning,

and a garment of praise
    instead of a spirit of despair.
They will be called oaks of righteousness,
    a planting of the LORD
    for the display of his splendour.
They will rebuild the ancient ruins
    and restore the places long devastated;
they will renew the ruined cities
    that have been devastated for generations.

"For I, the LORD, love justice;
    I hate robbery and iniquity.
In my faithfulness I will reward them
    and make an everlasting covenant with them.
Their descendants will be known among the nations
    and their offspring among the peoples.
All who see them will acknowledge
    that they are a people the LORD has blessed."

I delight greatly in the LORD;
    my soul rejoices in my God.
For he has clothed me with garments of salvation
    and arrayed me in a robe of righteousness,
as a bridegroom adorns his head like a priest,
    and as a bride adorns herself with her jewels.
For as the soil makes the young plant come up
    and a garden causes seeds to grow,
so the Sovereign LORD will make righteousness
      and praise
    spring up before all nations.

Alternative Psalm or Canticle

Either Psalm 126   When the LORD brought back the captives to Zion,   P
    we were like men who dreamed.   S
Our mouths were filled with laughter,   A
    our tongues with songs of joy.   L
Then it was said among the nations,   M
    "The LORD has done great things for them."
The LORD has done great things for us,
    and we are filled with joy.
Restore our fortunes, O LORD,
    like streams in the Negev.
Those who sow in tears
    will reap with songs of joy.
Those who go out weeping,
    carrying seed to sow,
will return with songs of joy,
    carrying sheaves with them.

or Canticle: **Magnificat**

Luke 1:46b–55 Mary said:

> "My soul glorifies the Lord
>> and my spirit rejoices in God my Saviour,
> for he has been mindful
>> of the humble state of his servant.
> From now on all generations will call me blessed,
>> for the Mighty One has done great things for me –
>> holy is his name.
> His mercy extends to those who fear him,
>> from generation to generation.
> He has performed mighty deeds with his arm;
>> he has scattered those who are proud in their inmost
>>> thoughts.
> He has brought down rulers from their thrones
>> but has lifted up the humble.
> He has filled the hungry with good things
>> but has sent the rich away empty.
> He has helped his servant Israel,
>> remembering to be merciful
> to Abraham and his descendants for ever,
>> even as he said to our fathers."

1 Thessalonians 5:16–24 Be joyful always; pray continually; give thanks in
all circumstances, for this is God's will for you in Christ Jesus.

Do not put out the Spirit's fire; do not treat prophecies with contempt.
Test everything. Hold on to the good. Avoid every kind of evil.

May God himself, the God of peace, sanctify you through and through.
May your whole spirit, soul and body be kept blameless at the coming of
our Lord Jesus Christ. The one who calls you is faithful and he will do it.

John 1:6–8, 19–28 There came a man who was sent from God; his name was
John. He came as a witness to testify concerning that light, so that through
him all men might believe. He himself was not the light; he came only as a
witness to the light.

Now this was John's testimony when the Jews of Jerusalem sent priests
and Levites to ask him who he was. He did not fail to confess, but confessed
freely, "I am not the Christ."

They asked him, "Then who are you? Are you Elijah?"

He said, "I am not."

"Are you the Prophet?"

He answered, "No."

Finally they said, "Who are you? Give us an answer to take back to those
who sent us. What do you say about yourself?"

John replied in the words of Isaiah the prophet, "I am the voice of one
calling in the desert, 'Make straight the way for the Lord.'"

Now some Pharisees who had been sent questioned him, "Why then do you baptise if you are not the Christ, nor Elijah, nor the Prophet?"

"I baptise with water," John replied, "but among you stands one you do not know. He is the one who comes after me, the thongs of whose sandals I am not worthy to untie."

This all happened at Bethany on the other side of the Jordan, where John was baptising.

Fourth Sunday of Advent

2 Samuel 7:1–11, 16   After King David was settled in his palace and the LORD had given him rest from all his enemies around him, he said to Nathan the prophet, "Here I am, living in a palace of cedar, while the ark of God remains in a tent."

Nathan replied to the king, "Whatever you have in mind, go ahead and do it, for the LORD is with you."

That night the word of the LORD came to Nathan, saying:

"Go and tell my servant David, 'This is what the LORD says: Are you the one to build me a house to dwell in? I have not dwelt in a house from the day I brought the Israelites up out of Egypt to this day. I have been moving from place to place with a tent as my dwelling. Wherever I have moved with all the Israelites, did I ever say to any of their rulers whom I commanded to shepherd my people Israel, "Why have you not built me a house of cedar?"'

"Now then, tell my servant David, 'This is what the LORD Almighty says: I took you from the pasture and from following the flock to be ruler over my people Israel. I have been with you wherever you have gone, and I have cut off all your enemies from before you. Now I will make your name great, like the names of the greatest men of the earth. And I will provide a place for my people Israel and will plant them so that they can have a home of their own and no longer be disturbed. Wicked people shall not oppress them any more, as they did at the beginning and have done ever since the time I appointed leaders over my people Israel. I will also give you rest from all your enemies.

"'The LORD declares to you that the LORD himself will establish a house for you: your house and your kingdom shall endure for ever before me; your throne shall be established for ever.'"

Alternative Canticle or Psalm

Canticle: **Magnificat**

Luke 1:46b–55   Mary said:

> "My soul glorifies the Lord
>   and my spirit rejoices in God my Saviour,
> for he has been mindful
>   of the humble state of his servant.

From now on all generations will call me blessed,
　for the Mighty One has done great things for me –
　holy is his name.
His mercy extends to those who fear him,
　from generation to generation.
He has performed mighty deeds with his arm;
　he has scattered those who are proud in their inmost
　　thoughts.
He has brought down rulers from their thrones
　but has lifted up the humble.
He has filled the hungry with good things
　but has sent the rich away empty.
He has helped his servant Israel,
　remembering to be merciful
to Abraham and his descendants for ever,
　even as he said to our fathers."

or **Psalm 89:1–4,**
19–26*

I will sing of the Lord's great love for ever;
　with my mouth I will make your faithfulness
　　known through all generations.
I will declare that your love stands firm for ever,
　that you established your faithfulness
　　in heaven itself.

You said, "I have made a covenant with my
　　chosen one,
　I have sworn to David my servant,
'I will establish your line for ever
　and make your throne firm through all
　　generations.'"

Once you spoke in a vision,
　to your faithful people you said:
"I have bestowed strength on a warrior;
　I have exalted a young man from among the
　　people.
I have found David my servant;
　with my sacred oil I have anointed him.
My hand will sustain him;
　surely my arm will strengthen him.
No enemy will subject him to tribute;
　no wicked person will oppress him.
I will crush his foes before him
　and strike down his adversaries.
My faithful love will be with him,
　and through my name his horn will be exalted.
I will set his hand over the sea,
　his right hand over the rivers.

P
S
A
L
M

He will call out to me, 'You are my Father,
my God, the Rock my Saviour.'"

Romans 16:25–27   Now to him who is able to establish you by my gospel and
the proclamation of Jesus Christ, according to the revelation of the mystery hidden for long ages past, but now revealed and made known through
the prophetic writings by the command of the eternal God, so that all
nations might believe and obey him – to the only wise God be glory for ever
through Jesus Christ! Amen.

S R
E E
C A
O D
N I
D N
G

Luke 1:26–38   In the sixth month, God sent the angel Gabriel to Nazareth, a
town in Galilee, to a virgin pledged to be married to a man named Joseph,
a descendant of David. The virgin's name was Mary. The angel went to her
and said, "Greetings, you who are highly favoured! The Lord is with you."

G
O
S
P
E
L

Mary was greatly troubled at his words and wondered what kind of
greeting this might be. But the angel said to her, "Do not be afraid, Mary,
you have found favour with God. You will be with child and give birth to a
son, and you are to give him the name Jesus. He will be great and will be
called the Son of the Most High. The Lord God will give him the throne of
his father David, and he will reign over the house of Jacob for ever; his
kingdom will never end."

"How will this be," Mary asked the angel, "since I am a virgin?"

The angel answered, "The Holy Spirit will come upon you, and the
power of the Most High will overshadow you. So the holy one to be born will
be called the Son of God. Even Elizabeth your relative is going to have a
child in her old age, and she who was said to be barren is in her sixth month.
For nothing is impossible with God."

"I am the Lord's servant," Mary answered. "May it be to me as you have
said." Then the angel left her.

CHRISTMAS

Christmas Eve
For text of readings for Years A, B, C see pp 9–11

Christmas Day – 25 December
*Any of the sets of readings on pp 11–18 may be used on the evening of Christmas
Eve and on Christmas Day. Set III should be used at some service during the
celebration.*

CHRISTMAS, SET I, YEARS A, B, C
see pp 11–13

CHRISTMAS, SET II, YEARS A, B, C
see pp 13–15

CHRISTMAS, SET III, YEARS A, B, C
see pp 15–18

First Sunday of Christmas

Isaiah 61:10 – 62:3 I delight greatly in the Lord;
 my soul rejoices in my God.
For he has clothed me with garments of salvation
 and arrayed me in a robe of righteousness,
as a bridegroom adorns his head like a priest,
 and as a bride adorns herself with her jewels.
For as the soil makes the young plant come up
 and a garden causes seeds to grow,
so the Sovereign Lord will make
  righteousness and praise
 spring up before all nations.

For Zion's sake I will not keep silent,
 for Jerusalem's sake I will not remain quiet,
till her righteousness shines out like the dawn,
 her salvation like a blazing torch.
The nations will see your righteousness,
 and all kings your glory;
you will be called by a new name
 that the mouth of the Lord will bestow.
You will be a crown of splendour in the Lord's hand,
 a royal diadem in the hand of your God.

Psalm 148* Praise the Lord.

Praise the Lord from the heavens,
 praise him in the heights above.
Praise him, all his angels,
 praise him, all his heavenly hosts.
Praise him, sun and moon,
 praise him, all you shining stars.
Praise him, you highest heavens
 and you waters above the skies.
Let them praise the name of the Lord,
 for he commanded and they were created.
He set them in place for ever and ever;
 he gave a decree that will never pass away.

Praise the Lord from the earth,
 you great sea creatures and all ocean depths,
lightning and hail, snow and clouds,
 stormy winds that do his bidding,
you mountains and all hills,
 fruit trees and all cedars,
wild animals and all cattle,
 small creatures and flying birds,
kings of the earth and all nations,
 you princes and all rulers on earth,

> young men and maidens,
> > old men and children.
>
> Let them praise the name of the Lord,
> > for his name alone is exalted;
> > his splendour is above the earth and the heavens.
> He has raised up for his people a horn,
> > the praise of all his saints,
> > of Israel, the people close to his heart.
>
> Praise the Lord.

Galatians 4:4–7   When the time had fully come, God sent his Son, born of a woman, born under law, to redeem those under law, that we might receive the full rights of sons. Because you are sons, God sent the Spirit of his Son into our hearts, the Spirit who calls out, "*Abba*, Father." So you are no longer a slave, but a son; and since you are a son, God has made you also an heir.

Luke 2:15–21   When the angels had left the shepherds and gone into heaven, the shepherds said to one another, "Let's go to Bethlehem and see this thing that has happened, which the Lord has told us about."

So they hurried off and found Mary and Joseph, and the baby, who was lying in the manger. When they had seen him, they spread the word concerning what had been told them about this child, and all who heard it were amazed at what the shepherds said to them. But Mary treasured up all these things and pondered them in her heart. The shepherds returned, glorifying and praising God for all the things they had heard and seen, which were just as they had been told.

On the eighth day, when it was time to circumcise him, he was named Jesus, the name the angel had given him before he had been conceived.

Second Sunday of Christmas

For text of readings for Years A, B, C see pp 20–22.

EPIPHANY

The Epiphany – 6 January

For text of readings for Years A, B, C see pp 22–24.

The Baptism of Christ

The First Sunday of Epiphany

Genesis 1:1–5   In the beginning God created the heavens and the earth. Now the earth was formless and empty, darkness was over the surface of the deep, and the Spirit of God was hovering over the waters.

And God said, "Let there be light," and there was light. God saw that the light was good, and he separated the light from the darkness. God called the light "day", and the darkness he called "night". And there was evening, and there was morning – the first day.

Psalm 29 Ascribe to the Lord, O mighty ones,
        ascribe to the Lord glory and strength.
    Ascribe to the Lord the glory due to his name;
        worship the Lord in the splendour of his holiness.

    The voice of the Lord is over the waters;
        the God of glory thunders,
        the Lord thunders over the mighty waters.
    The voice of the Lord is powerful;
        the voice of the Lord is majestic.
    The voice of the Lord breaks the cedars;
        the Lord breaks in pieces the cedars of Lebanon.
    He makes Lebanon skip like a calf,
        Sirion like a young wild ox.
    The voice of the Lord strikes
        with flashes of lightning.
    The voice of the Lord shakes the desert;
        the Lord shakes the Desert of Kadesh.
    The voice of the Lord twists the oaks
        and strips the forests bare.
    And in his temple all cry, "Glory!"

    The Lord sits enthroned over the flood;
        the Lord is enthroned as King for ever.
    The Lord gives strength to his people;
        the Lord blesses his people with peace.

P
S
A
L
M

Acts 19:1–7 While Apollos was at Corinth, Paul took the road through the interior and arrived at Ephesus. There he found some disciples and asked them, "Did you receive the Holy Spirit when you believed?"
    They answered, "No, we have not even heard that there is a Holy Spirit."
    So Paul asked, "Then what baptism did you receive?"
    "John's baptism," they replied.
    Paul said, "John's baptism was a baptism of repentance. He told the people to believe in the one coming after him, that is, in Jesus." On hearing this, they were baptised into the name of the Lord Jesus. When Paul placed his hands on them, the Holy Spirit came on them, and they spoke in tongues and prophesied. There were about twelve men in all.

S R
E E
C A
O D
N I
D N
G

Mark 1:4–11 John came, baptising in the desert region and preaching a baptism of repentance for the forgiveness of sins. The whole Judean countryside and all the people of Jerusalem went out to him. Confessing their sins, they were baptised by him in the Jordan River. John wore clothing made of camel's hair, with a leather belt round his waist, and he ate locusts and wild honey. And this was his message: "After me will come one more powerful than I, the thongs of whose sandals I am not worthy to stoop down and untie. I baptise you with water, but he will baptise you with the Holy Spirit."

G
O
S
P
E
L

At that time Jesus came from Nazareth in Galilee and was baptised by John in the Jordan. As Jesus was coming up out of the water, he saw heaven being torn open and the Spirit descending on him like a dove. And a voice came from heaven: "You are my Son, whom I love; with you I am well pleased."

Second Sunday of Epiphany

I Samuel 3:1–10 [11–20]   The boy Samuel ministered before the LORD under Eli. In those days the word of the LORD was rare; there were not many visions.

One night Eli, whose eyes were becoming so weak that he could barely see, was lying down in his usual place. The lamp of God had not yet gone out, and Samuel was lying down in the temple of the LORD, where the ark of God was. Then the LORD called Samuel.

Samuel answered, "Here I am." And he ran to Eli and said, "Here I am; you called me."

But Eli said, "I did not call; go back and lie down." So he went and lay down.

Again the LORD called, "Samuel!" And Samuel got up and went to Eli and said, "Here I am; you called me."

"My son," Eli said, "I did not call; go back and lie down."

Now Samuel did not yet know the LORD: The word of the LORD had not yet been revealed to him.

The LORD called Samuel a third time, and Samuel got up and went to Eli and said, "Here I am; you called me."

Then Eli realised that the LORD was calling the boy. So Eli told Samuel, "Go and lie down, and if he calls you, say, 'Speak, LORD, for your servant is listening.'" So Samuel went and lay down in his place.

The LORD came and stood there, calling as at the other times, "Samuel! Samuel!"

Then Samuel said, "Speak, for your servant is listening."

[And the LORD said to Samuel: "See, I am about to do something in Israel that will make the ears of everyone who hears of it tingle. At that time I will carry out against Eli everything I spoke against his family – from beginning to end. For I told him that I would judge his family for ever because of the sin he knew about; his sons made themselves contemptible, and he failed to restrain them. Therefore, I swore to the house of Eli, 'The guilt of Eli's house will never be atoned for by sacrifice or offering.'"

Samuel lay down until morning and then opened the doors of the house of the LORD. He was afraid to tell Eli the vision, but Eli called him and said, "Samuel, my son."

Samuel answered, "Here I am."

"What was it he said to you?" Eli asked. "Do not hide it from me. May God deal with you, be it ever so severely, if you hide from me anything he told you." So Samuel told him everything, hiding nothing from him. Then Eli said, "He is the LORD; let him do what is good in his eyes."

The LORD was with Samuel as he grew up, and he let none of his words fall to the ground. And all Israel from Dan to Beersheba recognised that Samuel was attested as a prophet of the LORD.]

Psalm 139:1–6, 13–18*

O LORD, you have searched me
    and you know me.
You know when I sit and when I rise;
    you perceive my thoughts from afar.
You discern my going out and my lying down;
    you are familiar with all my ways.
Before a word is on my tongue
    you know it completely, O LORD.

You hem me in – behind and before;
    you have laid your hand upon me.
Such knowledge is too wonderful for me,
    too lofty for me to attain.

For you created my inmost being;
    you knit me together in my mother's womb.
I praise you because I am fearfully and wonderfully
        made;
    your works are wonderful,
    I know that full well.
My frame was not hidden from you
    when I was made in the secret place.
When I was woven together in the depths of the earth,
    your eyes saw my unformed body.
All the days ordained for me
    were written in your book
    before one of them came to be.

How precious to me are your thoughts, O God!
    How vast is the sum of them!
Were I to count them,
    they would outnumber the grains of sand.
When I awake,
    I am still with you.

Revelation 5:1–10 I saw in the right hand of him who sat on the throne a scroll with writing on both sides and sealed with seven seals. And I saw a mighty angel proclaiming in a loud voice, "Who is worthy to break the seals and open the scroll?" But no–one in heaven or on earth or under the earth could open the scroll or even look inside it. I wept and wept because no-one was found who was worthy to open the scroll or look inside. Then one of the elders said to me, "Do not weep! See, the Lion of the tribe of Judah, the Root of David, has triumphed. He is able to open the scroll and its seven seals."

Then I saw a Lamb, looking as if it had been slain, standing in the centre of the throne, encircled by the four living creatures and the elders. He had seven horns and seven eyes, which are the seven spirits of God sent out into all the earth. He came and took the scroll from the right hand of him who sat on the throne. And when he had taken it, the four living creatures and the twenty-four elders fell down before the Lamb. Each one had a harp and they were holding golden bowls full of incense, which are the prayers of the saints. And they sang a new song:

"You are worthy to take the scroll
   and to open its seals,
because you were slain,
   and with your blood you purchased men for God
   from every tribe and language and people and nation.
You have made them to be a kingdom and priests to serve our God,
   and they will reign on the earth."

John 1:43–51 Jesus decided to leave for Galilee. Finding Philip, he said to him, "Follow me."

Philip, like Andrew and Peter, was from the town of Bethsaida. Philip found Nathanael and told him, "We have found the one Moses wrote about in the Law, and about whom the prophets also wrote – Jesus of Nazareth, the son of Joseph."

"Nazareth! Can anything good come from there?" Nathanael asked.

"Come and see," said Philip.

When Jesus saw Nathanael approaching, he said of him, "Here is a true Israelite, in whom there is nothing false."

"How do you know me?" Nathanael asked.

Jesus answered, "I saw you while you were still under the fig-tree before Philip called you."

Then Nathanael declared, "Rabbi, you are the Son of God; you are the King of Israel."

Jesus said, "You believe because I told you I saw you under the fig-tree. You shall see greater things than that." He then added, "I tell you the truth, you shall see heaven open, and the angels of God ascending and descending on the Son of Man."

Third Sunday of Epiphany

Genesis 14:17–20 After Abram returned from defeating Kedorlaomer and the kings allied with him, the king of Sodom came out to meet him in the Valley of Shaveh (that is, the King's Valley).

Then Melchizedek king of Salem brought out bread and wine. He was priest of God Most High, and he blessed Abram, saying,

"Blessed be Abram by God Most High,
   Creator of heaven and earth.
And blessed be God Most High,
   who delivered your enemies into your hand."

Then Abram gave him a tenth of everything.

Psalm 128   Blessed are all who fear the LORD,
                        who walk in his ways.
                  You will eat the fruit of your labour;
                        blessings and prosperity will be yours.
                  Your wife will be like a fruitful vine
                        within your house;
                  your children will be like olive shoots
                        round your table.
                  Thus are those blessed
                        who fear the LORD.

                  May the LORD bless you from Zion
                        all the days of your life;
                  may you see the prosperity of Jerusalem,
                        and may you live to see your children's children.

                  Peace be upon Israel.

Revelation 19:6–10   I heard what sounded like a great multitude, like the
roar of rushing waters and like loud peals of thunder, shouting:

"Hallelujah!
For our LORD God Almighty reigns.
Let us rejoice and be glad
and give him glory!
For the wedding of the Lamb has come,
and his bride has made herself ready.
Fine linen, bright and clean,
was given her to wear."
(Fine linen stands for the righteous acts of the saints.)

Then the angel said to me, "Write: 'Blessed are those who are invited to
the wedding supper of the Lamb!'" And he added, "These are the true
words of God."

At this I fell at his feet to worship him. But he said to me, "Do not do it!
I am a fellow-servant with you and with your brothers who hold to the testimony of Jesus. Worship God! For the testimony of Jesus is the spirit of
prophecy."

John 2:1–11   On the third day a wedding took place at Cana in Galilee. Jesus'
mother was there, and Jesus and his disciples had also been invited to the
wedding. When the wine was gone, Jesus' mother said to him, "They have
no more wine."

"Dear woman, why do you involve me?" Jesus replied. "My time has not
yet come."

His mother said to the servants, "Do whatever he tells you."

Nearby stood six stone water jars, the kind used by the Jews for ceremonial washing, each holding from twenty to thirty gallons.

Jesus said to the servants, "Fill the jars with water"; so they filled them
to the brim.

Then he told them, "Now draw some out and take it to the master of the banquet."

They did so, and the master of the banquet tasted the water that had been turned into wine. He did not realise where it had come from, though the servants who had drawn the water knew. Then he called the bridegroom aside and said, "Everyone brings out the choice wine first and then the cheaper wine after the guests have had too much to drink; but you have saved the best till now."

This, the first of his miraculous signs, Jesus performed at Cana in Galilee. He thus revealed his glory, and his disciples put their faith in him.

Fourth Sunday of Epiphany

Deuteronomy 18:15–20 Moses said: The LORD your God will raise up for you a prophet like me from among your own brothers. You must listen to him. For this is what you asked of the LORD your God at Horeb on the day of the assembly when you said, "Let us not hear the voice of the LORD our God nor see this great fire any more, or we will die." *FIRST READING*

The LORD said to me: "What they say is good. I will raise up for them a prophet like you from among their brothers, and I will put my words in his mouth, and he will tell them everything I command. If anyone does not listen to my words that the prophet speaks in my name, I myself will call him to account. But a prophet who presumes to speak in my name anything I have not commanded him to say, or a prophet who speaks in the name of other gods, must be put to death."

Psalm 111 Praise the LORD. *PSALM*

> I will extol the LORD with all my heart
> > in the council of the upright and in the assembly.
>
> Great are the works of the LORD;
> > they are pondered by all who delight in them.
> Glorious and majestic are his deeds,
> > and his righteousness endures for ever.
> He has caused his wonders to be remembered;
> > the LORD is gracious and compassionate.
> He provides food for those who fear him;
> > he remembers his covenant for ever.
> He has shown his people the power of his works,
> > giving them the lands of other nations.
> The works of his hands are faithful and just;
> > all his precepts are trustworthy.
> They are steadfast for ever and ever,
> > done in faithfulness and uprightness.
> He provided redemption for his people;
> > he ordained his covenant for ever –
> > > holy and awesome is his name.

The fear of the LORD is the beginning of wisdom;
    all who follow his precepts have good understanding.
    To him belongs eternal praise.

Revelation 12:1–5a   A great and wondrous sign appeared in heaven: a woman S R
clothed with the sun, with the moon under her feet and a crown of twelve E E
stars on her head. She was pregnant and cried out in pain as she was about C A
to give birth. Then another sign appeared in heaven: an enormous red O D
dragon with seven heads and ten horns and seven crowns on his heads. His N I
tail swept a third of the stars out of the sky and flung them to the earth. The D N
dragon stood in front of the woman who was about to give birth, so that he G
might devour her child the moment it was born. She gave birth to a son, a
male child, who will rule all the nations with an iron sceptre.

Mark 1:21–28   Jesus and his disciples went to Capernaum, and when the Sab- G
bath came, Jesus went into the synagogue and began to teach. The people O
were amazed at his teaching, because he taught them as one who had S
authority, not as the teachers of the law. Just then a man in their synagogue P
who was possessed by an evil spirit cried out, "What do you want with us, E
Jesus of Nazareth? Have you come to destroy us? I know who you are – the L
Holy One of God!"

"Be quiet!" said Jesus sternly. "Come out of him!" The evil spirit shook
the man violently and came out of him with a shriek.

The people were all so amazed that they asked each other, "What is this?
A new teaching – and with authority! He even gives orders to evil spirits
and they obey him." News about him spread quickly over the whole region
of Galilee.

The Presentation of Christ in the Temple – 2 February

Candlemas

For text of readings for Years A, B, C see pp 33–35.

ORDINARY TIME

Proper 1

Sunday between 3 and 9 February inclusive (if earlier than the Second Sunday before Lent)

Isaiah 40:21–31   Do you not know?   F R
            Have you not heard?   I E
    Has it not been told you from the beginning?   R A
            Have you not understood since the earth was founded?   S D
    He sits enthroned above the circle of the earth,   T I
            and its people are like grasshoppers.   N
    He stretches out the heavens like a canopy,   G
            and spreads them out like a tent to live in.
        He brings princes to naught
            and reduces the rulers of this world to nothing.

No sooner are they planted,
　　no sooner are they sown,
　　no sooner do they take root in the ground,
than he blows on them and they wither,
　　and a whirlwind sweeps them away like chaff.

"To whom will you compare me?
　　Or who is my equal?" says the Holy One.
Lift your eyes and look to the heavens:
　　Who created all these?
He who brings out the starry host one by one,
　　and calls them each by name.
Because of his great power and mighty strength,
　　not one of them is missing.

Why do you say, O Jacob,
　　and complain, O Israel,
"My way is hidden from the Lord;
　　my cause is disregarded by my God"?
Do you not know?
　　Have you not heard?
The Lord is the everlasting God,
　　the Creator of the ends of the earth.
He will not grow tired or weary,
　　and his understanding no-one can fathom.
He gives strength to the weary
　　and increases the power of the weak.
Even youths grow tired and weary,
　　and young men stumble and fall;
but those who hope in the Lord
　　will renew their strength.
They will soar on wings like eagles;
　　they will run and not grow weary,
　　they will walk and not be faint.

Psalm 147:1–11,
20c*　Praise the Lord.

How good it is to sing praises to our God,
　　how pleasant and fitting to praise him!

The Lord builds up Jerusalem;
　　he gathers the exiles of Israel.
He heals the broken-hearted
　　and binds up their wounds.

He determines the number of the stars
　　and calls them each by name.
Great is our Lord and mighty in power;
　　his understanding has no limit.
　　The Lord sustains the humble
　　　　but casts the wicked to the ground.

PSALM

Sing to the LORD with thanksgiving;
> make music to our God on the harp.

He covers the sky with clouds;
> he supplies the earth with rain
> and makes grass grow on the hills.

He provides food for the cattle
> and for the young ravens when they call.

His pleasure is not in the strength of the horse,
> nor his delight in the legs of a man;

the LORD delights in those who fear him,
> who put their hope in his unfailing love.

Praise the LORD.

1 Corinthians 9:16–23   When I preach the gospel, I cannot boast, for I am
compelled to preach. Woe to me if I do not preach the gospel! If I preach
voluntarily, I have a reward; if not voluntarily, I am simply discharging the
trust committed to me. What then is my reward? Just this: that in preaching the gospel I may offer it free of charge, and so not make use of my
rights in preaching it.

Though I am free and belong to no man, I make myself a slave to everyone, to win as many as possible. To the Jews I became like a Jew, to win
the Jews. To those under the law I became like one under the law (though
I myself am not under the law), so as to win those under the law. To those
not having the law I became like one not having the law (though I am
not free from God's law but am under Christ's law), so as to win those
not having the law. To the weak I became weak, to win the weak. I have
become all things to all men so that by all possible means I might save
some. I do all this for the sake of the gospel, that I may share in its
blessings.

Mark 1:29–39   Jesus left the synagogue, and went with James and John to the
home of Simon and Andrew. Simon's mother-in-law was in bed with a fever,
and they told Jesus about her. So he went to her, took her hand and helped
her up. The fever left her and she began to wait on them.

That evening after sunset the people brought to Jesus all the sick and
demon-possessed. The whole town gathered at the door, and Jesus healed
many who had various diseases. He also drove out many demons, but he
would not let the demons speak because they knew who he was.

Very early in the morning, while it was still dark, Jesus got up, left the
house and went off to a solitary place, where he prayed. Simon and his companions went to look for him, and when they found him, they exclaimed:
"Everyone is looking for you!"

Jesus replied, "Let us go somewhere else – to the nearby villages – so
that I can preach there also. That is why I have come." So he travelled
throughout Galilee, preaching in their synagogues and driving out
demons.

Proper 2

Sunday between 10 and 16 February inclusive (if earlier than the Second Sunday before Lent)

2 Kings 5:1–14   Naaman was commander of the army of the king of Aram. He F
was a great man in the sight of his master and highly regarded, because I
through him the LORD had given victory to Aram. He was a valiant soldier, R
but he had leprosy.   S

Now bands from Aram had gone out and had taken captive a young girl T
from Israel, and she served Naaman's wife. She said to her mistress, "If
only my master would see the prophet who is in Samaria! He would cure R
him of his leprosy."   E

Naaman went to his master and told him what the girl from Israel had A
said. "By all means, go," the king of Aram replied. "I will send a letter to the D
king of Israel." So Naaman left, taking with him ten talents of silver, six I
thousand shekels of gold and ten sets of clothing. The letter that he took to N
the king of Israel read: "With this letter I am sending my servant Naaman G
to you so that you may cure him of his leprosy."

As soon as the king of Israel read the letter, he tore his robes and said,
"Am I God? Can I kill and bring back to life? Why does this fellow send
someone to me to be cured of his leprosy? See how he is trying to pick a
quarrel with me!"

When Elisha the man of God heard that the king of Israel had torn his
robes, he sent him this message: "Why have you torn your robes? Make the
man come to me and he will know that there is a prophet in Israel." So Naaman went with his horses and chariots and stopped at the door of Elisha's
house. Elisha sent a messenger to say to him, "Go, wash yourself seven
times in the Jordan, and your flesh will be restored and you will be
cleansed."

But Naaman went away angry and said, "I thought that he would surely
come out to me and stand and call on the name of the LORD his God, wave
his hand over the spot and cure me of my leprosy. Are not Abana and
Pharpar, the rivers of Damascus, better than any of the waters of Israel?
Couldn't I wash in them and be cleansed?" So he turned and went off in a
rage.

Naaman's servants went to him and said, "My father, if the prophet
had told you to do some great thing, would you not have done it? How much
more, then, when he tells you, 'Wash and be cleansed'?" So he went down
and dipped himself in the Jordan seven times, as the man of God had told
him, and his flesh was restored and became clean like that of a young boy.

Psalm 30   I will exalt you, O LORD,   P
     for you lifted me out of the depths   S
          and did not let my enemies gloat over me.   A
O LORD my God, I called to you for help   L
     and you healed me.   M
O LORD, you brought me up from the grave;
     you spared me from going down into the pit.

Sing to the LORD, you saints of his;
   praise his holy name.
For his anger lasts only a moment,
   but his favour lasts a lifetime;
weeping may remain for a night,
   but rejoicing comes in the morning.

When I felt secure, I said,
   "I shall never be shaken."
O LORD, when you favoured me,
   you made my mountain stand firm;
but when you hid your face,
   I was dismayed.

To you, O LORD, I called;
   to the LORD I cried for mercy:
"What gain is there in my destruction,
   in my going down into the pit?
Will the dust praise you?
   Will it proclaim your faithfulness?
Hear, O LORD, and be merciful to me;
   O LORD, be my help."

You turned my wailing into dancing;
   you removed my sackcloth and clothed me with joy,
that my heart may sing to you and not be silent.
   O LORD my God, I will give you thanks for ever.

1 Corinthians 9:24–27   Do you not know that in a race all the runners run, but
only one gets the prize? Run in such a way as to get the prize. Everyone who
competes in the games goes into strict training. They do it to get a crown
that will not last; but we do it to get a crown that will last for ever. Therefore I do not run like a man running aimlessly; I do not fight like a man
beating the air. No, I beat my body and make it my slave so that after I have
preached to others, I myself will not be disqualified for the prize.

SECOND
READING

Mark 1:40–45   A man with leprosy came to Jesus and begged him on his
knees, "If you are willing, you can make me clean."

   Filled with compassion, Jesus reached out his hand and touched the
man. "I am willing," he said. "Be clean!" Immediately the leprosy left him
and he was cured.

   Jesus sent him away at once with a strong warning: "See that you
don't tell this to anyone. But go, show yourself to the priest and offer
the sacrifices that Moses commanded for your cleansing, as a testimony to
them." Instead he went out and began to talk freely, spreading the news. As
a result, Jesus could no longer enter a town openly but stayed outside in
lonely places. Yet the people still came to him from everywhere.

GOSPEL

Proper 3

Sunday between 17 and 23 February inclusive (if earlier than the Second Sunday before Lent)

Isaiah 43:18–25

"Forget the former things;
　do not dwell on the past.
See, I am doing a new thing!
　Now it springs up; do you not perceive it?
I am making a way in the desert
　and streams in the wasteland.
The wild animals honour me,
　the jackals and the owls,
because I provide water in the desert
　and streams in the wasteland,
to give drink to my people, my chosen,
　the people I formed for myself
　that they may proclaim my praise.

"Yet you have not called upon me, O Jacob,
　you have not wearied yourselves for me, O Israel.
You have not brought me sheep for burnt offerings,
　nor honoured me with your sacrifices.
I have not burdened you with grain offerings
　nor wearied you with demands for incense.
You have not bought any fragrant calamus for me,
　or lavished on me the fat of your sacrifices.
But you have burdened me with your sins
　and wearied me with your offences.

"I, even I, am he who blots out
　your transgressions, for my own sake,
　and remembers your sins no more."

Psalm 41

Blessed are those who have regard for the weak;
　the LORD delivers him in times of trouble.
The LORD will protect him and preserve his life;
　he will bless him in the land
　and not surrender him to the desire of his foes.
The LORD will sustain him on his sick-bed
　and restore him from his bed of illness.

I said, "O LORD, have mercy on me;
　heal me, for I have sinned against you."
My enemies say of me in malice,
　"When will he die and his name perish?"
Whenever one comes to see me,
　he speaks falsely, while his heart gathers slander;
　then he goes out and spreads it abroad.

All my enemies whisper together against me;
　they imagine the worst for me, saying,

"A vile disease has beset him;
    he will never get up from the place where he lies."
Even my close friend, whom I trusted,
    he who shared my bread,
        has lifted up his heel against me.

But you, O Lord, have mercy on me;
    raise me up, that I may repay them.
I know that you are pleased with me,
    for my enemy does not triumph over me.
In my integrity you uphold me
    and set me in your presence for ever.

Praise be to the Lord, the God of Israel,
    from everlasting to everlasting.
                              Amen and Amen.

2 Corinthians 1:18–22   As surely as God is faithful, our message to you is not S R
"Yes" and "No". For the Son of God, Jesus Christ, who was preached among E E
you by me and Silas and Timothy, was not "Yes" and "No", but in him it has C A
always been "Yes". For no matter how many promises God has made, they O D
are "Yes" in Christ. And so through him the "Amen" is spoken by us to the N I
glory of God. Now it is God who makes both us and you stand firm in Christ. D N
He anointed us, set his seal of ownership on us, and put his Spirit in our   G
hearts as a deposit, guaranteeing what is to come.

Mark 2:1–12   A few days later, when Jesus again entered Capernaum, the G
people heard that he had come home. So many gathered that there was no O
room left, not even outside the door, and he preached the word to them. S
Some men came, bringing to him a paralytic, carried by four of them. Since P
they could not get him to Jesus because of the crowd, they made an open- E
ing in the roof above Jesus and, after digging through it, lowered the mat L
the paralysed man was lying on. When Jesus saw their faith, he said to the
paralytic, "Son, your sins are forgiven."

Now some teachers of the law were sitting there, thinking to themselves, "Why does this fellow talk like that? He's blaspheming! Who can
forgive sins but God alone?"

Immediately Jesus knew in his spirit that this was what they were thinking in their hearts, and he said to them, "Why are you thinking these
things? Which is easier: to say to the paralytic, 'Your sins are forgiven,' or
to say, 'Get up, take your mat and walk'? But that you may know that the
Son of Man has authority on earth to forgive sins . . ." He said to the paralytic, "I tell you, get up, take your mat and go home." He got up, took his
mat and walked out in full view of them all. This amazed everyone and they
praised God, saying, "We have never seen anything like this!"

Second Sunday Before Lent

Proverbs 8:1, 22–31   Does not wisdom call out?   F

Does not understanding raise her voice?   I

She cries aloud: R

"The Lord brought me forth as the first of his works,   S

before his deeds of old;   T

I was appointed from eternity,

from the beginning, before the world began.   R

When there were no oceans, I was given birth,   E

when there were no springs abounding with water;   A

before the mountains were settled in place,   D

before the hills, I was given birth,   I

before he made the earth or its fields   N

or any of the dust of the world.   G

I was there when he set the heavens in place,

when he marked out the horizon on the face

of the deep,

when he established the clouds above

and fixed securely the fountains of the deep,

when he gave the sea its boundary

so that the waters would not overstep his command,

and when he marked out the foundations of the earth.

Then I was the craftsman at his side.

I was filled with delight day after day,

rejoicing always in his presence,

rejoicing in his whole world

and delighting in mankind."

Psalm 104:24–35   How many are your works, O Lord!   P

In wisdom you made them all;   S

the earth is full of your creatures.   A

There is the sea, vast and spacious,   L

teeming with creatures beyond number –   M

living things both large and small.

There the ships go to and fro,

and the leviathan, which you formed to frolic there.

These all look to you

to give them their food at the proper time.

When you give it to them,

they gather it up;

when you open your hand,

they are satisfied with good things.

When you hide your face,

they are terrified;

when you take away their breath,

they die and return to the dust.

When you send your Spirit,
    they are created,
        and you renew the face of the earth.

May the glory of the Lord endure for ever;
    may the Lord rejoice in his works –
he who looks at the earth, and it trembles,
    who touches the mountains, and they smoke.

I will sing to the Lord all my life;
    I will sing praise to my God as long as I live.
May my meditation be pleasing to him,
    as I rejoice in the Lord.
But may sinners vanish from the earth
    and the wicked be no more.

Praise the Lord, O my soul.

Praise the Lord.

Colossians 1:15–20   Christ Jesus is the image of the invisible God, the first-born over all creation. For by him all things were created: things in heaven and on earth, visible and invisible, whether thrones or powers or rulers or authorities; all things were created by him and for him. He is before all things, and in him all things hold together. And he is the head of the body, the church; he is the beginning and the firstborn from among the dead, so that in everything he might have the supremacy. For God was pleased to have all his fulness dwell in him, and through him to reconcile to himself all things, whether things on earth or things in heaven, by making peace through his blood, shed on the cross.

SECOND READING

John 1:1–14   In the beginning was the Word, and the Word was with God, and the Word was God. He was with God in the beginning.

Through him all things were made; without him nothing was made that has been made. In him was life, and that life was the light of men. The light shines in the darkness, but the darkness has not understood it.

GOSPEL

There came a man who was sent from God; his name was John. He came as a witness to testify concerning that light, so that through him all men might believe. He himself was not the light; he came only as a witness to the light. The true light that gives light to everyone was coming into the world.

He was in the world, and though the world was made through him, the world did not recognise him. He came to that which was his own, but his own did not receive him. Yet to all who received him, to those who believed in his name, he gave the right to become children of God – children born not of natural descent, nor of human decision or a husband's will, but born of God.

The Word became flesh and made his dwelling among us. We have seen his glory, the glory of the One and Only, who came from the Father, full of grace and truth.

2 Kings 2:1–12 When the LORD was about to take Elijah up to heaven in a F whirlwind, Elijah and Elisha were on their way from Gilgal. Elijah said to I Elisha, "Stay here; the LORD has sent me to Bethel." R

But Elisha said, "As surely as the LORD lives and as you live, I will not S leave you." So they went down to Bethel. T

The company of the prophets at Bethel came out to Elisha and asked, "Do you know that the LORD is going to take your master from you today?" R

"Yes, I know," Elisha replied, "but do not speak of it." E

Then Elijah said to him, "Stay here, Elisha; the LORD has sent me to Jeri- A cho." D

And he replied, "As surely as the LORD lives and as you live, I will not I leave you." So they went to Jericho. N

The company of the prophets at Jericho went up to Elisha and asked G him, "Do you know that the LORD is going to take your master from you today?"

"Yes, I know," he replied, "but do not speak of it."

Then Elijah said to him, "Stay here; the LORD has sent me to the Jordan."

And he replied, "As surely as the LORD lives and as you live, I will not leave you." So the two of them walked on.

Fifty men of the company of the prophets went and stood at a distance, facing the place where Elijah and Elisha had stopped at the Jordan. Elijah took his cloak, rolled it up and struck the water with it. The water divided to the right and to the left, and the two of them crossed over on dry ground.

When they had crossed, Elijah said to Elisha, "Tell me, what can I do for you before I am taken from you?"

"Let me inherit a double portion of your spirit," Elisha replied.

"You have asked a difficult thing," Elijah said, "yet if you see me when I am taken from you, it will be yours – otherwise not."

As they were walking along and talking together, suddenly a chariot of fire and horses of fire appeared and separated the two of them, and Elijah went up to heaven in a whirlwind. Elisha saw this and cried out, "My father! My father! The chariots and horsemen of Israel!" And Elisha saw him no more. Then he took hold of his own clothes and tore them apart.

Psalm 50:1–6   The Mighty One, God, the LORD, P
    speaks and summons the earth S
    from the rising of the sun to the place where it sets. A
From Zion, perfect in beauty, L
    God shines forth. M
Our God comes and will not be silent;
    a fire devours before him,
    and around him a tempest rages.
He summons the heavens above,
    and the earth, that he may judge his people:
"Gather to me my consecrated ones,
    who made a covenant with me by sacrifice."

And the heavens proclaim his righteousness,
for God himself is judge.

2 Corinthians 4:3–6   If our gospel is veiled, it is veiled to those who are per- S R
ishing. The god of this age has blinded the minds of unbelievers, so that E E
they cannot see the light of the gospel of the glory of Christ, who is the C A
image of God. For we do not preach ourselves, but Jesus Christ as Lord, O D
and ourselves as your servants for Jesus' sake. For God, who said, "Let N I
light shine out of darkness," made his light shine in our hearts to give us D N
the light of the knowledge of the glory of God in the face of Christ.   G

Mark 9:2–9   Jesus took Peter, James and John with him and led them up a G
high mountain, where they were all alone. There he was transfigured O
before them. His clothes became dazzling white, whiter than anyone in the S
world could bleach them. And there appeared before them Elijah and P
Moses, who were talking with Jesus.   E

Peter said to Jesus, "Rabbi, it is good for us to be here. Let us put up L
three shelters – one for you, one for Moses and one for Elijah." (He did not
know what to say, they were so frightened.)

Then a cloud appeared and enveloped them, and a voice came from the
cloud: "This is my Son, whom I love. Listen to him!"

Suddenly, when they looked round, they no longer saw anyone with them
except Jesus.

As they were coming down the mountain, Jesus gave them orders not to
tell anyone what they had seen until the Son of Man had risen from the
dead.

LENT

Ash Wednesday

For text of readings for years A, B, C see pp 48–52.

First Sunday of Lent

Genesis 9:8–17   God said to Noah and to his sons with him: "I now establish F
my covenant with you and with your descendants after you and with every I
living creature that was with you – the birds, the livestock and all the wild R
animals, all those that came out of the ark with you – every living creature S
on earth. I establish my covenant with you: Never again will all life be cut T
off by the waters of a flood; never again will there be a flood to destroy the
earth."   R

And God said, "This is the sign of the covenant I am making between me E
and you and every living creature with you, a covenant for all generations A
to come: I have set my rainbow in the clouds, and it will be the sign of the D
covenant between me and the earth. Whenever I bring clouds over the I
earth and the rainbow appears in the clouds, I will remember my covenant N
between me and you and all living creatures of every kind. Never again G

will the waters become a flood to destroy all life. Whenever the rainbow appears in the clouds, I will see it and remember the everlasting covenant between God and all living creatures of every kind on the earth."

So God said to Noah, "This is the sign of the covenant I have established between me and all life on the earth."

Psalm 25:1–10
To you, O LORD, I lift up my soul;
    in you I trust, O my God.
Do not let me be put to shame,
    nor let my enemies triumph over me.
No-one whose hope is in you
    will ever be put to shame,
but they will be put to shame
    who are treacherous without excuse.

Show me your ways, O LORD,
    teach me your paths;
guide me in your truth and teach me,
    for you are God my Saviour,
    and my hope is in you all day long.
Remember, O LORD, your great mercy and love,
    for they are from of old.
Remember not the sins of my youth
    and my rebellious ways;
according to your love remember me,
    for you are good, O LORD.

Good and upright is the LORD;
    therefore he instructs sinners in his ways.
He guides the humble in what is right
    and teaches them his way.
All the ways of the LORD are loving and faithful
    for those who keep the demands of his covenant.

PSALM

1 Peter 3:18–22 Christ died for sins once for all, the righteous for the unrighteous, to bring you to God. He was put to death in the body but made alive by the Spirit, through whom also he went and preached to the spirits in prison who disobeyed long ago when God waited patiently in the days of Noah while the ark was being built. In it only a few people, eight in all, were saved through water, and this water symbolises baptism that now saves you also – not the removal of dirt from the body but the pledge of a good conscience towards God. It saves you by the resurrection of Jesus Christ, who has gone into heaven and is at God's right hand – with angels, authorities and powers in submission to him.

SECOND READING

Mark 1:9–15 Jesus came from Nazareth in Galilee and was baptised by John in the Jordan. As Jesus was coming up out of the water, he saw heaven being torn open and the Spirit descending on him like a dove. And a voice

GOSPEL

came from heaven: "You are my Son, whom I love; with you I am well pleased."

At once the Spirit sent him out into the desert, and he was in the desert for forty days, being tempted by Satan. He was with the wild animals, and angels attended him.

After John was put in prison, Jesus went into Galilee, proclaiming the good news of God. "The time has come," he said. "The kingdom of God is near. Repent and believe the good news!"

Second Sunday of Lent

Genesis 17:1–7, 15–16 When Abram was ninety-nine years old, the LORD appeared to him and said, "I am God Almighty; walk before me and be blameless. I will confirm my covenant between me and you and will greatly increase your numbers."

Abram fell face down, and God said to him, "As for me, this is my covenant with you: You will be the father of many nations. No longer will you be called Abram; your name will be Abraham, for I have made you a father of many nations. I will make you very fruitful; I will make nations of you, and kings will come from you. I will establish my covenant as an everlasting covenant between me and you and your descendants after you for the generations to come, to be your God and the God of your descendants after you.

God also said to Abraham, "As for Sarai your wife, you are no longer to call her Sarai; her name will be Sarah. I will bless her and will surely give you a son by her. I will bless her so that she will be the mother of nations; kings of peoples will come from her."

Psalm 22:23–31 You who fear the LORD, praise him!
All you descendants of Jacob, honour him!
Revere him, all you descendants of Israel!
For he has not despised or disdained
the suffering of the afflicted one;
he has not hidden his face from him
but has listened to his cry for help.

From you comes the theme of my praise
in the great assembly;
before those who fear you will I fulfil my vows.
The poor will eat and be satisfied;
they who seek the LORD will praise him –
may your hearts live for ever!
All the ends of the earth
will remember and turn to the LORD,
and all the families of the nations
will bow down before him,
for dominion belongs to the LORD
and he rules over the nations.

All the rich of the earth will feast and worship;
> all who go down to the dust will kneel before him –
> those who cannot keep themselves alive.
Posterity will serve him;
> future generations will be told about the LORD.
They will proclaim his righteousness
> to a people yet unborn –
> for he has done it.

Romans 4:13–25 It was not through law that Abraham and his offspring received the promise that he would be heir of the world, but through the righteousness that comes by faith. For if those who live by law are heirs, faith has no value and the promise is worthless, because law brings wrath. And where there is no law there is no transgression.

Therefore, the promise comes by faith, so that it may be by grace and may be guaranteed to all Abraham's offspring – not only to those who are of the law but also to those who are of the faith of Abraham. He is the father of us all. As it is written: "I have made you a father of many nations." He is our father in the sight of God, in whom he believed – the God who gives life to the dead and calls things that are not as though they were.

Against all hope, Abraham in hope believed and so became the father of many nations, just as it had been said to him, "So shall your offspring be." Without weakening in his faith, he faced the fact that his body was as good as dead – since he was about a hundred years old – and that Sarah's womb was also dead. Yet he did not waver through unbelief regarding the promise of God, but was strengthened in his faith and gave glory to God, being fully persuaded that God had power to do what he had promised. This is why "it was credited to him as righteousness." The words "it was credited to him" were written not for him alone, but also for us, to whom God will credit righteousness – for us who believe in him who raised Jesus our Lord from the dead. He was delivered over to death for our sins and was raised to life for our justification.

Mark 8:31–38 Jesus began to teach his disciples that the Son of Man must suffer many things and be rejected by the elders, chief priests and teachers of the law, and that he must be killed and after three days rise again. He spoke plainly about this, and Peter took him aside and began to rebuke him.

But when Jesus turned and looked at his disciples, he rebuked Peter. "Get behind me, Satan!" he said. "You do not have in mind the things of God, but the things of men."

Then he called the crowd to him along with his disciples and said: "If anyone would come after me, he must deny himself and take up his cross and follow me. For whoever wants to save his life will lose it, but whoever loses his life for me and for the gospel will save it. What good is it for a man to gain the whole world, yet forfeit his soul? Or what can a man give in exchange for his soul? If anyone is ashamed of me and my words in this adulterous and sinful generation, the Son of Man will be ashamed of him when he comes in his Father's glory with the holy angels."

Third Sunday of Lent

Exodus 20:1–17   God spoke all these words:

"I am the LORD your God, who brought you out of Egypt, out of the land of slavery.

"You shall have no other gods before me.

"You shall not make for yourself an idol in the form of anything in heaven above or on the earth beneath or in the waters below. You shall not bow down to them or worship them; for I, the LORD your God, am a jealous God, punishing the children for the sin of the parents to the third and fourth generation of those who hate me, but showing love to a thousand generations of those who love me and keep my commandments.

"You shall not misuse the name of the LORD your God, for the LORD will not hold anyone guiltless who misuses his name.

"Remember the Sabbath day by keeping it holy. Six days you shall labour and do all your work, but the seventh day is a Sabbath to the LORD your God. On it you shall not do any work, neither you, nor your son or daughter, nor your manservant or maidservant, nor your animals, nor the alien within your gates. For in six days the LORD made the heavens and the earth, the sea, and all that is in them, but he rested on the seventh day. Therefore the LORD blessed the Sabbath day and made it holy.

"Honour your father and your mother, so that you may live long in the land the LORD your God is giving you.

"You shall not murder.

"You shall not commit adultery.

"You shall not steal.

"You shall not give false testimony against your neighbour.

"You shall not covet your neighbour's house. You shall not covet your neighbour's wife, or his manservant or maidservant, his ox or donkey, or anything that belongs to your neighbour."

Psalm 19*   The heavens declare the glory of God;
> the skies proclaim the work of his hands.

Day after day they pour forth speech;
> night after night they display knowledge.

There is no speech or language
> where their voice is not heard.

Their voice goes out into all the earth,
> their words to the ends of the world.

In the heavens he has pitched a tent for the sun,
> which is like a bridegroom coming forth from his pavilion,
> like a champion rejoicing to run his course.

It rises at one end of the heavens
    and makes its circuit to the other;
    nothing is hidden from its heat.

The law of the LORD is perfect,
    reviving the soul.
The statutes of the LORD are trustworthy,
    making wise the simple.
The precepts of the LORD are right,
    giving joy to the heart.
The commands of the LORD are radiant,
    giving light to the eyes.
The fear of the LORD is pure,
    enduring for ever.
The ordinances of the LORD are sure
    and altogether righteous.

They are more precious than gold,
    than much pure gold;
they are sweeter than honey,
    than honey from the comb.
By them is your servant warned;
    in keeping them there is great reward.

Who can discern their errors?
    Forgive my hidden faults.
Keep your servant also from wilful sins;
    may they not rule over me.
Then will I be blameless,
    innocent of great transgression.

May the words of my mouth and the meditation of my heart
    be pleasing in your sight,
    O LORD, my Rock and my Redeemer.

1 Corinthians 1:18–25 The message of the cross is foolishness to those who SECOND READING are perishing, but to us who are being saved it is the power of God. For it is written:

> "I will destroy the wisdom of the wise;
> the intelligence of the intelligent I will frustrate."

Where is the wise man? Where is the scholar? Where is the philosopher of this age? Has not God made foolish the wisdom of the world? For since in the wisdom of God the world through its wisdom did not know him, God was pleased through the foolishness of what was preached to save those who believe. Jews demand miraculous signs and Greeks look for wisdom, but we preach Christ crucified: a stumbling-block to Jews and foolishness to Gentiles, but to those whom God has called, both Jews and Greeks, Christ the power of God and the wisdom of God. For the foolishness of God is wiser than man's wisdom, and the weakness of God is stronger than man's strength.

John 2:13–22   When it was almost time for the Jewish Passover, Jesus went G up to Jerusalem. In the temple courts he found men selling cattle, sheep O and doves, and others sitting at tables exchanging money. So he made a S whip out of cords, and drove all from the temple area, both sheep and P cattle; he scattered the coins of the money-changers and overturned E their tables. To those who sold doves he said, "Get these out of here! How L dare you turn my Father's house into a market!"

His disciples remembered that it is written: "Zeal for your house will consume me."

Then the Jews demanded of him, "What miraculous sign can you show us to prove your authority to do all this?"

Jesus answered them, "Destroy this temple, and I will raise it again in three days."

The Jews replied, "It has taken forty-six years to build this temple, and you are going to raise it in three days?" But the temple he had spoken of was his body. After he was raised from the dead, his disciples recalled what he had said. Then they believed the Scripture and the words that Jesus had spoken.

Fourth Sunday of Lent

Mothering Sunday may be celebrated in preference to the provision for the Fourth Sunday of Lent see pp 62–65.

Numbers 21:4–9   The Israelites travelled from Mount Hor along the route to F R the Red Sea, to go round Edom. But the people grew impatient on the way; I E they spoke against God and against Moses, and said, "Why have you R A brought us up out of Egypt to die in the desert? There is no bread! There is S D no water! And we detest this miserable food!"   T I

Then the LORD sent venomous snakes among them; they bit the people N and many Israelites died. The people came to Moses and said, "We sinned G when we spoke against the LORD and against you. Pray that the LORD will take the snakes away from us." So Moses prayed for the people.

The LORD said to Moses, "Make a snake and put it up on a pole; anyone who is bitten can look at it and live." So Moses made a bronze snake and put it up on a pole. Then when anyone was bitten by a snake and looked at the bronze snake, that person lived.

Psalm 107:1–3,   Give thanks to the LORD, for he is good;   P
17–22*   his love endures for ever.   S
                Let the redeemed of the LORD say this –   A
                    those he redeemed from the hand of the foe,   L
                those he gathered from the lands,   M
                    from east and west, from north and south.

                Some became fools through their rebellious ways
                    and suffered affliction because of their iniquities.

They loathed all food
and drew near the gates of death.
Then they cried to the LORD in their trouble,
and he saved them from their distress.
He sent forth his word and healed them;
he rescued them from the grave.
Let them give thanks to the LORD for his unfailing love
and his wonderful deeds for men.
Let them sacrifice thank-offerings
and tell of his works with songs of joy.

Ephesians 2:1–10   You were dead in your transgressions and sins, in which S
you used to live when you followed the ways of this world and of the ruler E
of the kingdom of the air, the spirit who is now at work in those who are dis- C
obedient. All of us also lived among them at one time, gratifying the O
cravings of our sinful nature and following its desires and thoughts. Like N
the rest, we were by nature objects of wrath. But because of his great love D
for us, God, who is rich in mercy, made us alive with Christ even when we
were dead in transgressions – it is by grace you have been saved. And God R
raised us up with Christ and seated us with him in the heavenly realms in E
Christ Jesus, in order that in the coming ages he might show the incom- A
parable riches of his grace, expressed in his kindness to us in Christ Jesus. D
For it is by grace you have been saved, through faith – and this not from I
yourselves, it is the gift of God – not by works, so that no-one can boast. For N
we are God's workmanship, created in Christ Jesus to do good works, G
which God prepared in advance for us to do.

John 3:14–21   Jesus said: "Just as Moses lifted up the snake in the desert, so G
the Son of Man must be lifted up, that everyone who believes in him may O
have eternal life. S

"For God so loved the world that he gave his one and only Son, that who- P
ever believes in him shall not perish but have eternal life. For God did not E
send his Son into the world to condemn the world, but to save the world L
through him. Whoever believes in him is not condemned, but whoever does
not believe stands condemned already because he has not believed in the
name of God's one and only Son. This is the verdict: Light has come into the
world, but men loved darkness instead of light because their deeds were
evil. Everyone who does evil hates the light, and will not come into the light
for fear that his deeds will be exposed. But whoever lives by the truth
comes into the light, so that it may be seen plainly that what he has done has
been done through God."

Mothering Sunday

*Mothering Sunday may be celebrated in preference to the provision for the Fourth Sunday of Lent
or text of readings for Years A, B, C see pp 62–65.*

Fifth Sunday of Lent

Passiontide begins

Jeremiah 31:31–34

"The time is coming," declares the LORD,
   "when I will make a new covenant
with the house of Israel
   and with the house of Judah.
It will not be like the covenant
   I made with their forefathers
when I took them by the hand
   to lead them out of Egypt,
because they broke my covenant,
   though I was a husband to them,"
               declares the LORD.
"This is the covenant that I will make with the
    house of Israel
after that time," declares the LORD.
"I will put my law in their minds
   and write it on their hearts.
I will be their God,
   and they will be my people.
No longer will a man teach his neighbour,
   or a man his brother, saying, 'Know the LORD,'
because they will all know me,
   from the least of them to the greatest,"
               declares the LORD.
"For I will forgive their wickedness
   and will remember their sins no more."

FIRST READING

Alterative Psalms

Either **Psalm 51:1–12**

Have mercy on me, O God,
   according to your unfailing love;
according to your great compassion
   blot out my transgressions.
Wash away all my iniquity
   and cleanse me from my sin.

For I know my transgressions,
   and my sin is always before me.
Against you, you only, have I sinned
   and done what is evil in your sight,
so that you are proved right when you speak
   and justified when you judge.
Surely I was sinful at birth,
   sinful from the time my mother conceived me.
Surely you desire truth in the inner parts;
   you teach me wisdom in the inmost place.

PSALM

Cleanse me with hyssop, and I shall be clean;
    wash me, and I shall be whiter than snow.
Let me hear joy and gladness;
    let the bones you have crushed rejoice.
Hide your face from my sins
    and blot out all my iniquity.

Create in me a pure heart, O God,
    and renew a steadfast spirit within me.
Do not cast me from your presence
    or take your Holy Spirit from me.
Restore to me the joy of your salvation
    and grant me a willing spirit, to sustain me.

or **Psalm 119:9–16**

How can a young man keep his way pure?
    By living according to your word.
I seek you with all my heart;
    do not let me stray from your commands.
I have hidden your word in my heart
    that I might not sin against you.
Praise be to you, O LORD;
    teach me your decrees.
With my lips I recount
    all the laws that come from your mouth.
I rejoice in following your statutes
    as one rejoices in great riches.
I meditate on your precepts
    and consider your ways.
I delight in your decrees;
    I will not neglect your word.

PSALM

Hebrews 5:5–10 Christ did not take upon himself the glory of becoming a
high priest. But God said to him,

SECOND READING

"You are my Son;
    today I have become your Father."

And he says in another place,

"You are a priest for ever,
    in the order of Melchizedek."

During the days of Jesus' life on earth, he offered up prayers and petitions with loud cries and tears to the one who could save him from death, and he was heard because of his reverent submission. Although he was a son, he learned obedience from what he suffered and, once made perfect, he became the source of eternal salvation for all who obey him and was designated by God to be high priest in the order of Melchizedek.

GOSPEL

John 12:20–33 There were some Greeks among those who went up to
Jerusalem to worship at the Feast of the Passover. They came to Philip,

who was from Bethsaida in Galilee, with a request. "Sir," they said, "we would like to see Jesus." Philip went to tell Andrew; Andrew and Philip in turn told Jesus.

Jesus replied, "The hour has come for the Son of Man to be glorified. I tell you the truth, unless a grain of wheat falls to the ground and dies, it remains only a single seed. But if it dies, it produces many seeds. The man who loves his life will lose it, while the man who hates his life in this world will keep it for eternal life. Whoever serves me must follow me; and where I am, my servant also will be. My Father will honour the one who serves me.

"Now my heart is troubled, and what shall I say? 'Father, save me from this hour'? No, it was for this very reason I came to this hour. Father, glorify your name!"

Then a voice came from heaven, "I have glorified it, and will glorify it again." The crowd that was there and heard it said it had thundered; others said an angel had spoken to him.

Jesus said, "This voice was for your benefit, not mine. Now is the time for judgment on this world; now the prince of this world will be driven out. But I, when I am lifted up from the earth, will draw all men to myself." He said this to show the kind of death he was going to die.

Palm Sunday

Liturgy of the Palms

Alternative Gospels

Either **Mark 11:1–11** As Jesus and his disciples approached Jerusalem and came to Bethphage and Bethany at the Mount of Olives, Jesus sent two of his disciples, saying to them, "Go to the village ahead of you, and just as you enter it, you will find a colt tied there, which no-one has ever ridden. Untie it and bring it here. If anyone asks you, 'Why are you doing this?' tell him, 'The Lord needs it and will send it back here shortly.'"

They went and found a colt outside in the street, tied at a doorway. As they untied it, some people standing there asked, "What are you doing, untying that colt?" They answered as Jesus had told them to, and the people let them go. When they brought the colt to Jesus and threw their cloaks over it, he sat on it. Many people spread their cloaks on the road, while others spread branches they had cut in the fields. Those who went ahead and those who followed shouted,

"Hosanna!"

"Blessed is he who comes in the name of the Lord!"

"Blessed is the coming kingdom of our father David!"

"Hosanna in the highest!"

Jesus entered Jerusalem and went to the temple. He looked around at everything, but since it was already late, he went out to Bethany with the Twelve.

or **John 12:12–16**   The great crowd that had come for the Feast of the
Passover heard that Jesus was on his way to Jerusalem. They took palm
branches and went out to meet him, shouting,

> "Hosanna!"
> "Blessed is he who comes in the name of the Lord!"
> "Blessed is the King of Israel!"

Jesus found a young donkey and sat upon it, as it is written,

> "Do not be afraid, O Daughter of Zion;
>> see, your king is coming,
>> seated on a donkey's colt."

At first his disciples did not understand all this. Only after Jesus was
glorified did they realise that these things had been written about him and
that they had done these things to him.

G
O
S
P
E
L

Psalm 118:1–2,   Give thanks to the LORD, for he is good;
19–24*   his love endures for ever.

> Let Israel say:
>> "His love endures for ever."

> Open for me the gates of righteousness;
>> I will enter and give thanks to the LORD.
> This is the gate of the LORD
>> through which the righteous may enter.
> I will give you thanks, for you answered me;
>> you have become my salvation.

> The stone the builders rejected
>> has become the capstone;
> the LORD has done this,
>> and it is marvellous in our eyes.
> This is the day the LORD has made;
>> let us rejoice and be glad in it.

P
S
A
L
M

Liturgy of the Passion

Isaiah 50:4–9a   The Sovereign LORD has given me an instructed tongue,
> to know the word that sustains the weary.
He wakens me morning by morning,
> wakens my ear to listen like one being taught.
The Sovereign LORD has opened my ears,
> and I have not been rebellious;
> I have not drawn back.
I offered my back to those who beat me,
> my cheeks to those who pulled out my beard;
I did not hide my face
> from mocking and spitting.
Because the Sovereign LORD helps me,
> I will not be disgraced.

F
I
R
S
T

R
E
A
D
I
N
G

Therefore have I set my face like flint,
and I know I will not be put to shame.
He who vindicates me is near.
Who then will bring charges against me?
Let us face each other!
Who are accusers?
Let them confront me!
It is the Sovereign LORD who helps me.

Psalm 31:9–16* Be merciful to me, O LORD, for I am in distress;
my eyes grow weak with sorrow,
my soul and my body with grief.
My life is consumed by anguish
and my years by groaning;
my strength fails because of my affliction,
and my bones grow weak.
Because of all my enemies,
I am the utter contempt of my neighbours;
I am a dread to my friends –
those who see me on the street flee from me.
I am forgotten by them as though I were dead;
I have become like broken pottery.
For I hear the slander of many;
there is terror on every side;
they conspire against me
and plot to take my life.

But I trust in you, O LORD;
I say, "You are my God."
My times are in your hands;
deliver me from my enemies
and from those who pursue me.
Let your face shine on your servant;
save me in your unfailing love.

Philippians 2:5–11 Your attitude should be the same as that of Christ
Jesus:

Who, being in very nature God,
did not consider equality with God something to be grasped,
but made himself nothing,
taking the very nature of a servant,
being made in human likeness.
And being found in appearance as a man,
he humbled himself
and became obedient to death – even death on a cross!
Therefore God exalted him to the highest place
and gave him the name that is above every name,

that at the name of Jesus every knee should bow,
   in heaven and on earth and under the earth,
and every tongue confess that Jesus Christ is LORD,
   to the glory of God the Father.

Alternative Gospels

Either **Mark 14:1 – 15:47** The Passover and the Feast of Unleavened Bread
were only two days away, and the chief priests and the teachers of the law
were looking for some sly way to arrest Jesus and kill him. "But not during
the Feast," they said, "or the people may riot."

While he was in Bethany, reclining at the table in the home of a man
known as Simon the Leper, a woman came with an alabaster jar of very
expensive perfume, made of pure nard. She broke the jar and poured the
perfume on his head.

Some of those present were saying indignantly to one another, "Why this
waste of perfume? It could have been sold for more than a year's wages
and the money given to the poor." And they rebuked her harshly.

"Leave her alone," said Jesus. "Why are you bothering her? She has
done a beautiful thing to me. The poor you will always have with you, and
you can help them any time you want. But you will not always have me. She
did what she could. She poured perfume on my body beforehand to prepare
for my burial. I tell you the truth, wherever the gospel is preached
throughout the world, what she has done will also be told, in memory of
her."

Then Judas Iscariot, one of the Twelve, went to the chief priests to
betray Jesus to them. They were delighted to hear this and promised to
give him money. So he watched for an opportunity to hand him over.

On the first day of the Feast of Unleavened Bread, when it was cus-
tomary to sacrifice the Passover lamb, Jesus' disciples asked him,
"Where do you want us to go and make preparations for you to eat the
Passover?"

So he sent two of his disciples, telling them, "Go into the city, and a man
carrying a jar of water will meet you. Follow him. Say to the owner of the
house he enters, 'The Teacher asks: Where is my guest room, where I may
eat the Passover with my disciples?' He will show you a large upper room,
furnished and ready. Make preparations for us there."

The disciples left, went into the city and found things just as Jesus had
told them. So they prepared the Passover.

When evening came, Jesus arrived with the Twelve. While they were
reclining at the table eating, he said, "I tell you the truth, one of you will
betray me – one who is eating with me."

They were saddened, and one by one they said to him, "Surely not I?"

"It is one of the Twelve," he replied, "one who dips bread into the bowl
with me. The Son of Man will go just as it is written about him. But woe to
that man who betrays the Son of Man! It would be better for him if he had
not been born."

While they were eating, Jesus took bread, gave thanks and broke it, and gave it to his disciples, saying, "Take it; this is my body."

Then he took the cup, gave thanks and offered it to them, and they all drank from it.

"This is my blood of the covenant, which is poured out for many," he said to them. "I tell you the truth, I will not drink again of the fruit of the vine until that day when I drink it anew in the kingdom of God."

When they had sung a hymn, they went out to the Mount of Olives.

"You will all fall away," Jesus told them, "for it is written:

"'I will strike the shepherd,
    and the sheep will be scattered.'

But after I have risen, I will go ahead of you into Galilee."

Peter declared, "Even if all fall away, I will not."

"I tell you the truth," Jesus answered, "today – yes, tonight – before the cock crows twice you yourself will disown me three times."

But Peter insisted emphatically, "Even if I have to die with you, I will never disown you." And all the others said the same.

They went to a place called Gethsemane, and Jesus said to his disciples, "Sit here while I pray." He took Peter, James and John along with him, and he began to be deeply distressed and troubled. "My soul is overwhelmed with sorrow to the point of death," he said to them. "Stay here and keep watch."

Going a little farther, he fell to the ground and prayed that if possible the hour might pass from him. "*Abba*, Father," he said, "everything is possible for you. Take this cup from me. Yet not what I will, but what you will."

Then he returned to his disciples and found them sleeping. "Simon," he said to Peter, "are you asleep? Could you not keep watch for one hour? Watch and pray so that you will not fall into temptation. The spirit is willing, but the body is weak."

Once more he went away and prayed the same thing. When he came back, he again found them sleeping, because their eyes were heavy. They did not know what to say to him.

Returning the third time, he said to them, "Are you still sleeping and resting? Enough! The hour has come. Look, the Son of Man is betrayed into the hands of sinners. Rise! Let us go! Here comes my betrayer!"

Just as he was speaking, Judas, one of the Twelve, appeared. With him was a crowd armed with swords and clubs, sent from the chief priests, the teachers of the law, and the elders.

Now the betrayer had arranged a signal with them: "The one I kiss is the man; arrest him and lead him away under guard." Going at once to Jesus, Judas said, "Rabbi!" and kissed him. The men seized Jesus and arrested him. Then one of those standing near drew his sword and struck the servant of the high priest, cutting off his ear.

"Am I leading a rebellion," said Jesus, "that you have come out with swords and clubs to capture me? Every day I was with you, teaching in the temple courts, and you did not arrest me. But the Scriptures must be fulfilled." Then everyone deserted him and fled.

A young man, wearing nothing but a linen garment, was following Jesus. When they seized him, he fled naked, leaving his garment behind.

They took Jesus to the high priest, and all the chief priests, elders and teachers of the law came together. Peter followed him at a distance, right into the courtyard of the high priest. There he sat with the guards and warmed himself at the fire.

The chief priests and the whole Sanhedrin were looking for evidence against Jesus so that they could put him to death, but they did not find any. Many testified falsely against him, but their statements did not agree.

Then some stood up and gave this false testimony against him: "We heard him say, 'I will destroy this manmade temple and in three days will build another, not made by man.'" Yet even then their testimony did not agree.

Then the high priest stood up before them and asked Jesus, "Are you not going to answer? What is this testimony that these men are bringing against you?" But Jesus remained silent and gave no answer.

Again the high priest asked him, "Are you the Christ, the Son of the Blessed One?"

"I am," said Jesus. "And you will see the Son of Man sitting at the right hand of the Mighty One and coming on the clouds of heaven."

The high priest tore his clothes. "Why do we need any more witnesses?" he asked. "You have heard the blasphemy. What do you think?"

They all condemned him as worthy of death. Then some began to spit at him; they blindfolded him, struck him with their fists, and said, "Prophesy!" And the guards took him and beat him.

While Peter was below in the courtyard, one of the servant girls of the high priest came by. When she saw Peter warming himself, she looked closely at him.

"You also were with that Nazarene, Jesus," she said.

But he denied it. "I don't know or understand what you're talking about," he said, and went out into the entrance.

When the servant girl saw him there, she said again to those standing around, "This fellow is one of them." Again he denied it.

After a little while, those standing near said to Peter, "Surely you are one of them, for you are a Galilean."

He began to call down curses on himself, and he swore to them, "I don't know this man you're talking about."

Immediately the cock crowed the second time. Then Peter remembered the word Jesus had spoken to him: "Before the cock crows twice you will disown me three times." And he broke down and wept.

Very early in the morning, the chief priests, with the elders, the teachers of the law and the whole Sanhedrin, reached a decision. They bound Jesus, led him away and turned him over to Pilate.

"Are you the king of the Jews?" asked Pilate.

"Yes, it is as you say," Jesus replied.

The chief priests accused him of many things. So again Pilate asked him, "Aren't you going to answer? See how many things they are accusing you of."

But Jesus still made no reply, and Pilate was amazed.

Now it was the custom at the Feast to release a prisoner whom the people requested. A man called Barabbas was in prison with the insurrectionists who had committed murder in the uprising. The crowd came up and asked Pilate to do for them what he usually did.

"Do you want me to release to you the king of the Jews?" asked Pilate, knowing it was out of envy that the chief priests had handed Jesus over to him. But the chief priests stirred up the crowd to have Pilate release Barabbas instead.

"What shall I do, then, with the one you call the king of the Jews?" Pilate asked them.

"Crucify him!" they shouted.

"Why? What crime has he committed?" asked Pilate.

But they shouted all the louder, "Crucify him!"

Wanting to satisfy the crowd, Pilate released Barabbas to them. He had Jesus flogged, and handed him over to be crucified.

The soldiers led Jesus away into the palace (that is, the Praetorium) and called together the whole company of soldiers. They put a purple robe on him, then twisted together a crown of thorns and set it on him. And they began to call out to him, "Hail, king of the Jews!" Again and again they struck him on the head with a staff and spat on him. Falling on their knees, they paid homage to him. And when they had mocked him, they took off the purple robe and put his own clothes on him. Then they led him out to crucify him.

A certain man from Cyrene, Simon, the father of Alexander and Rufus, was passing by on his way in from the country, and they forced him to carry the cross. They brought Jesus to the place called Golgotha (which means The Place of the Skull). Then they offered him wine mixed with myrrh, but he did not take it. And they crucified him. Dividing up his clothes, they cast lots to see what each would get.

It was the third hour when they crucified him. The written notice of the charge against him read: THE KING OF THE JEWS. They crucified two robbers with him, one on his right and one on his left. Those who passed by hurled insults at him, shaking their heads and saying, "So! You who are going to destroy the temple and build it in three days, come down from the cross and save yourself!"

In the same way the chief priests and the teachers of the law mocked him among themselves. "He saved others," they said, "but he can't save himself! Let this Christ, this King of Israel, come down now from the cross, that we may see and believe." Those crucified with him also heaped insults on him.

At the sixth hour darkness came over the whole land until the ninth hour. And at the ninth hour Jesus cried out in a loud voice, "*Eloi, Eloi, lama sabachthani?*" – which means, "My God, my God, why have you forsaken me?"

When some of those standing near heard this, they said, "Listen, he's calling Elijah."

A man ran, filled a sponge with wine vinegar, put it on a stick, and offered it to Jesus to drink. "Now leave him alone. Let's see if Elijah comes to take him down," he said.

With a loud cry, Jesus breathed his last.

The curtain of the temple was torn in two from top to bottom. And when the centurion, who stood there in front of Jesus, heard his cry and saw how he died, he said, "Surely this man was the Son of God!"

Some women were watching from a distance. Among them were Mary Magdalene, Mary the mother of James the younger and of Joses, and Salome. In Galilee these women had followed him and cared for his needs. Many other women who had come up with him to Jerusalem were also there.

It was Preparation Day (that is, the day before the Sabbath). So as evening approached, Joseph of Arimathea, a prominent member of the Council, who was himself waiting for the kingdom of God, went boldly to Pilate and asked for Jesus' body. Pilate was surprised to hear that he was already dead. Summoning the centurion, he asked him if Jesus had already died. When he learned from the centurion that it was so, he gave the body to Joseph. So Joseph bought some linen cloth, took down the body, wrapped it in the linen, and placed it in a tomb cut out of rock. Then he rolled a stone against the entrance of the tomb. Mary Magdalene and Mary the mother of Joses saw where he was laid.

or **Mark 15:1–39 [40–47]**   Very early in the morning, the chief priests, with the elders, the teachers of the law and the whole Sanhedrin, reached a decision. They bound Jesus, led him away and turned him over to Pilate. **G O S P E L**

"Are you the king of the Jews?" asked Pilate.

"Yes, it is as you say," Jesus replied.

The chief priests accused him of many things. So again Pilate asked him, "Aren't you going to answer? See how many things they are accusing you of."

But Jesus still made no reply, and Pilate was amazed.

Now it was the custom at the Feast to release a prisoner whom the people requested. A man called Barabbas was in prison with the insurrectionists who had committed murder in the uprising. The crowd came up and asked Pilate to do for them what he usually did.

"Do you want me to release to you the king of the Jews?" asked Pilate, knowing it was out of envy that the chief priests had handed Jesus over to him. But the chief priests stirred up the crowd to have Pilate release Barabbas instead.

"What shall I do, then, with the one you call the king of the Jews?" Pilate asked them.

"Crucify him!" they shouted.

"Why? What crime has he committed?" asked Pilate.

But they shouted all the louder, "Crucify him!"

Wanting to satisfy the crowd, Pilate released Barabbas to them. He had Jesus flogged, and handed him over to be crucified.

The soldiers led Jesus away into the palace (that is, the Praetorium) and called together the whole company of soldiers. They put a purple robe on him, then twisted together a crown of thorns and set it on him. And they began to call out to him, "Hail, king of the Jews!" Again and again they struck him on the head with a staff and spat on him. Falling on their knees, they paid homage to him. And when they had mocked him, they took off the purple robe and put his own clothes on him. Then they led him out to crucify him.

A certain man from Cyrene, Simon, the father of Alexander and Rufus, was passing by on his way in from the country, and they forced him to carry the cross. They brought Jesus to the place called Golgotha (which means The Place of the Skull). Then they offered him wine mixed with myrrh, but he did not take it. And they crucified him. Dividing up his clothes, they cast lots to see what each would get.

It was the third hour when they crucified him. The written notice of the charge against him read: THE KING OF THE JEWS. They crucified two robbers with him, one on his right and one on his left. Those who passed by hurled insults at him, shaking their heads and saying, "So! You who are going to destroy the temple and build it in three days, come down from the cross and save yourself!"

In the same way the chief priests and the teachers of the law mocked him among themselves. "He saved others," they said, "but he can't save himself! Let this Christ, this King of Israel, come down now from the cross, that we may see and believe." Those crucified with him also heaped insults on him.

At the sixth hour darkness came over the whole land until the ninth hour. And at the ninth hour Jesus cried out in a loud voice, "*Eloi, Eloi, lama sabachthani?*" – which means, "My God, my God, why have you forsaken me?"

When some of those standing near heard this, they said, "Listen, he's calling Elijah."

A man ran, filled a sponge with wine vinegar, put it on a stick, and offered it to Jesus to drink. "Now leave him alone. Let's see if Elijah comes to take him down," he said.

With a loud cry, Jesus breathed his last.

The curtain of the temple was torn in two from top to bottom. And when the centurion, who stood there in front of Jesus, heard his cry and saw how he died, he said, "Surely this man was the Son of God!"

[Some women were watching from a distance. Among them were Mary Magdalene, Mary the mother of James the younger and of Joses, and Salome. In Galilee these women had followed him and cared for his needs. Many other women who had come up with him to Jerusalem were also there.

It was Preparation Day (that is, the day before the Sabbath). So as evening approached, Joseph of Arimathea, a prominent member of the Council, who was himself waiting for the kingdom of God, went boldly to Pilate and asked for Jesus' body. Pilate was surprised to hear that he was already dead. Summoning the centurion, he asked him if Jesus had already died. When he learned from the centurion that it was so, he gave the body to Joseph. So Joseph bought some linen cloth, took down the body, wrapped it in the linen, and placed it in a tomb cut out of rock. Then he rolled a stone against the entrance of the tomb. Mary Magdalene and Mary the mother of Joses saw where he was laid.]

Monday of Holy Week

For text of readings for Years A, B, C see pp 77–79.

Tuesday of Holy Week

For text of readings for Years A, B, C see pp 79–81.

Wednesday of Holy Week

For text of readings for Years A, B, C see pp 81–83.

Maundy Thursday

For text of readings for Years A, B, C see pp 83–85.

Good Friday

For text of readings for Years A, B, C see pp 85–93.

Easter Eve

For text of readings for Years A, B, C see pp 93–95.

EASTER

Easter Vigil

A selection of Old Testament readings and a reading from Romans for Years A, B, C is given on pp 96–112. A minimum of three Old Testament readings (including Exodus 14) must be used, together with the Romans reading and the Gospel which is different for each year. Only the Gospel for Year B appears here as Years A and C have their own Gospel.

Mark 16:1–8 When the Sabbath was over, Mary Magdalene, Mary the G Y mother of James, and Salome bought spices so that they might go to anoint O E Jesus' body. Very early on the first day of the week, just after sunrise, they S A were on their way to the tomb and they asked each other, "Who will roll the P R stone away from the entrance of the tomb?"   E

But when they looked up, they saw that the stone, which was very large, L B had been rolled away. As they entered the tomb, they saw a young man dressed in a white robe sitting on the right side, and they were alarmed.

"Don't be alarmed," he said. "You are looking for Jesus the Nazarene, who was crucified. He has risen! He is not here. See the place where they laid him. But go, tell his disciples and Peter, 'He is going ahead of you into Galilee. There you will see him, just as he told you.'"

Trembling and bewildered, the women went out and fled from the tomb. They said nothing to anyone, because they were afraid.

Easter Day

Acts 10: 34–43 should be read as either the first or second reading.

Alternative first readings

Either **Acts 10:34-43**   Peter began to speak: "I now realise how true it is that God does not show favouritism but accepts men from every nation who fear him and do what is right. You know the message God sent to the people of Israel, telling the good news of peace through Jesus Christ, who is Lord of all. You know what has happened throughout Judea, beginning in Galilee after the baptism that John preached – how God anointed Jesus of Nazareth with the Holy Spirit and power, and how he went around doing good and healing all who were under the power of the devil, because God was with him.

"We are witnesses of everything he did in the country of the Jews and in Jerusalem. They killed him by hanging him on a tree, but God raised him from the dead on the third day and caused him to be seen. He was not seen by all the people, but by witnesses whom God had already chosen – by us who ate and drank with him after he rose from the dead. He commanded us to preach to the people and to testify that he is the one whom God appointed as judge of the living and the dead. All the prophets testify about him that everyone who believes in him receives forgiveness of sins through his name."

or **Isaiah 25:6–9**   On this mountain the Lord Almighty will prepare
    a feast of rich food for all peoples,
a banquet of aged wine –
    the best of meats and the finest of wines.
On this mountain he will destroy
    the shroud that enfolds all peoples,
the sheet that covers all nations;
    he will swallow up death for ever.
The Sovereign Lord will wipe away the tears
    from all faces;
he will remove the disgrace of his people
    from all the earth.
                The Lord has spoken.

In that day they will say,

"Surely this is our God;
    we trusted in him, and he saved us.

This is the Lord, we trusted in him;
  let us rejoice and be glad in his salvation."

Psalm 118:1–2,   Give thanks to the Lord, for he is good;   P
14–24*   his love endures for ever.   S

Let Israel say: A
  "His love endures for ever."   L

                                          M
The Lord is my strength and my song;
  he has become my salvation.

Shouts of joy and victory
  resound in the tents of the righteous:
"The Lord's right hand has done mighty things!
  The Lord's right hand is lifted high;
the Lord's right hand has done mighty things!"

I will not die but live,
  and will proclaim what the Lord has done.
The Lord has chastened me severely,
  but he has not given me over to death.

Open for me the gates of righteousness;
  I will enter and give thanks to the Lord.
This is the gate of the Lord
  through which the righteous may enter.
I will give you thanks, for you answered me;
  you have become my salvation.

The stone the builders rejected
  has become the capstone;
the Lord has done this,
  and it is marvellous in our eyes.
This is the day the Lord has made;
  let us rejoice and be glad in it.

Alternative second readings

Either **1 Corinthians 15:1–11**   Brothers, I want to remind you of the gospel I   S R
preached to you, which you received and on which you have taken your   E E
stand. By this gospel you are saved, if you hold firmly to the word I   C A
preached to you. Otherwise, you have believed in vain.   O D

For what I received I passed on to you as of first importance: that Christ   N I
died for our sins according to the Scriptures, that he was buried, that he   D N
was raised on the third day according to the Scriptures, and that he   G
appeared to Peter, and then to the Twelve. After that, he appeared to more
than five hundred of the brothers at the same time, most of whom are still
living, though some have fallen asleep. Then he appeared to James, then to
all the apostles, and last of all he appeared to me also, as to one abnormally
born.

For I am the least of the apostles and do not even deserve to be called an apostle, because I persecuted the church of God. But by the grace of God I am what I am, and his grace to me was not without effect. No, I worked harder than all of them – yet not I, but the grace of God that was with me. Whether, then, it was I or they, this is what we preach, and this is what you believed.

Acts 10:34–43 Peter began to speak: "I now realise how true it is that God does not show favouritism but accepts men from every nation who fear him and do what is right. You know the message God sent to the people of Israel, telling the good news of peace through Jesus Christ, who is Lord of all. You know what has happened throughout Judea, beginning in Galilee after the baptism that John preached – how God anointed Jesus of Nazareth with the Holy Spirit and power, and how he went around doing good and healing all who were under the power of the devil, because God was with him.

"We are witnesses of everything he did in the country of the Jews and in Jerusalem. They killed him by hanging him on a tree, but God raised him from the dead on the third day and caused him to be seen. He was not seen by all the people, but by witnesses whom God had already chosen – by us who ate and drank with him after he rose from the dead. He commanded us to preach to the people and to testify that he is the one whom God appointed as judge of the living and the dead. All the prophets testify about him that everyone who believes in him receives forgiveness of sins through his name."

(margin: SECOND READING)

Alternative Gospels

Either **John 20:1–18** Early on the first day of the week, while it was still dark, Mary Magdalene went to the tomb and saw that the stone had been removed from the entrance. So she came running to Simon Peter and the other disciple, the one Jesus loved, and said, "They have taken the Lord out of the tomb, and we don't know where they have put him!"

So Peter and the other disciple started for the tomb. Both were running, but the other disciple outran Peter and reached the tomb first. He bent over and looked in at the strips of linen lying there but did not go in. Then Simon Peter, who was behind him, arrived and went into the tomb. He saw the strips of linen lying there, as well as the burial cloth that had been around Jesus' head. The cloth was folded up by itself, separate from the linen. Finally the other disciple, who had reached the tomb first, also went inside. He saw and believed. (They still did not understand from Scripture that Jesus had to rise from the dead.)

Then the disciples went back to their homes, but Mary stood outside the tomb crying. As she wept, she bent over to look into the tomb and saw two angels in white, seated where Jesus' body had been, one at the head and the other at the foot.

They asked her, "Woman, why are you crying?"

(margin: GOSPEL)

"They have taken my Lord away," she said, "and I don't know where they have put him." At this, she turned round and saw Jesus standing there, but she did not realise that it was Jesus.

"Woman," he said, "why are you crying? Who is it you are looking for?"

Thinking he was the gardener, she said, "Sir, if you have carried him away, tell me where you have put him, and I will get him."

Jesus said to her, "Mary."

She turned towards him and cried out in Aramaic, "Rabboni!" (which means Teacher).

Jesus said, "Do not hold on to me, for I have not yet returned to the Father. Go instead to my brothers and tell them, 'I am returning to my Father and your Father, to my God and your God.'"

Mary Magdalene went to the disciples with the news: "I have seen the Lord!" And she told them that he had said these things to her.

or **Mark 16:1–8**   When the Sabbath was over, Mary Magdalene, Mary the G mother of James, and Salome bought spices so that they might go to anoint O Jesus' body. Very early on the first day of the week, just after sunrise, they S were on their way to the tomb and they asked each other, "Who will roll the P stone away from the entrance of the tomb?"   E

But when they looked up, they saw that the stone, which was very large, L had been rolled away. As they entered the tomb, they saw a young man dressed in a white robe sitting on the right side, and they were alarmed.

"Don't be alarmed," he said. "You are looking for Jesus the Nazarene, who was crucified. He has risen! He is not here. See the place where they laid him. But go, tell his disciples and Peter, 'He is going ahead of you into Galilee. There you will see him, just as he told you.'"

Trembling and bewildered, the women went out and fled from the tomb. They said nothing to anyone, because they were afraid.

Old Testament Readings for Sundays in Eastertide

For those who require an Old Testament reading on the Sundays in Easter-tide, provision is made as following. If used, the reading from Acts must be used as the second reading.

Easter 2

Exodus 14:10–31; 15:20–21   As Pharaoh approached the Israelites by the sea, the Israelites looked up, and there were the Egyptians, marching after them. They were terrified and cried out to the LORD. They said to Moses, "Was it because there were no graves in Egypt that you brought us to the desert to die? What have you done to us by bringing us out of Egypt? Didn't we say to you in Egypt, 'Leave us alone; let us serve the Egyptians'? It would have been better for us to serve the Egyptians than to die in the desert!"

Moses answered the people, "Do not be afraid. Stand firm and you will see the deliverance the LORD will bring you today. The Egyptians you see today you will never see again. The LORD will fight for you; you need only to be still."

Then the LORD said to Moses, "Why are you crying out to me? Tell the Israelites to move on. Raise your staff and stretch out your hand over the sea to divide the water so that the Israelites can go through the sea on dry ground. I will harden the hearts of the Egyptians so that they will go in after them. And I will gain glory through Pharaoh and all his army, through his chariots and his horsemen. The Egyptians will know that I am the LORD when I gain glory through Pharaoh, his chariots and his horsemen."

Then the angel of God, who had been travelling in front of Israel's army, withdrew and went behind them. The pillar of cloud also moved from in front and stood behind them, coming between the armies of Egypt and Israel. Throughout the night the cloud brought darkness to the one side and light to the other; so neither went near the other all night long.

Then Moses stretched out his hand over the sea, and all that night the LORD drove the sea back with a strong east wind and turned it into dry land. The waters were divided, and the Israelites went through the sea on dry ground, with a wall of water on their right and on their left.

The Egyptians pursued them, and all Pharaoh's horses and chariots and horsemen followed them into the sea. During the last watch of the night the LORD looked down from the pillar of fire and cloud at the Egyptian army and threw it into confusion. He made the wheels of their chariots come off so that they had difficulty driving. And the Egyptians said, "Let's get away from the Israelites! The LORD is fighting for them against Egypt."

Then the LORD said to Moses, "Stretch out your hand over the sea so that the waters may flow back over the Egyptians and their chariots and horse-men." Moses stretched out his hand over the sea, and at daybreak the sea went back to its place. The Egyptians were fleeing towards it, and the LORD swept them into the sea. The water flowed back and covered the chariots and horsemen – the entire army of Pharaoh that had followed the Israelites into the sea. Not one of them survived.

But the Israelites went through the sea on dry ground, with a wall of water on their right and on their left. That day the LORD saved Israel from the hands of the Egyptians, and Israel saw the Egyptians lying dead on the shore. And when the Israelites saw the great power the LORD displayed against the Egyptians, the people feared the LORD and put their trust in him and in Moses his servant.

Then Miriam the prophetess, Aaron's sister, took a tambourine in her hand, and all the women followed her, with tambourines and dancing. Miriam sang to them:

"Sing to the LORD,
　for he is highly exalted.
The horse and its rider
　he has hurled into the sea."

Easter 3

Zephaniah 3:14–20　Sing, O Daughter of Zion;
　　　　shout aloud, O Israel!
Be glad and rejoice with all your heart,
　　O Daughter of Jerusalem!
The LORD has taken away your punishment,
　　he has turned back your enemy.
The LORD, the King of Israel, is with you;
　　never again will you fear any harm.
On that day they will say to Jerusalem,
　　"Do not fear, O Zion;
　　do not let your hands hang limp.
The LORD your God is with you,
　　he is mighty to save.
He will take great delight in you,
　　he will quiet you with his love,
　　he will rejoice over you with singing."

"The sorrows for the appointed feasts
　　I will remove from you;
　　they are a burden and a reproach to you.
At that time I will deal
　　with all who oppressed you;
I will rescue the lame
　　and gather those who have been scattered.
I will give them praise and honour
　　in every land where they were put to shame.
At that time I will gather you;
　　at that time I will bring you home.
I will give you honour and praise
　　among all the peoples of the earth

> when I restore your fortunes
> before your very eyes,"
>
> says the LORD.

Easter 4

Genesis 7:1–5, 11–18; 8: 6–18; 9:8–13   The LORD said to Noah, "Go into the ark, you and your whole family, because I have found you righteous in this generation. Take with you seven of every kind of clean animal, a male and its mate, and two of every kind of unclean animal, a male and its mate, and also seven of every kind of bird, male and female, to keep their various kinds alive throughout the earth. Seven days from now I will send rain on the earth for forty days and forty nights, and I will wipe from the face of the earth every living creature I have made."

And Noah did all that the LORD commanded him.

In the six hundredth year of Noah's life, on the seventeenth day of the second month – on that day all the springs of the great deep burst forth, and the floodgates of the heavens were opened. And rain fell on the earth for forty days and forty nights.

On that very day Noah and his sons, Shem, Ham and Japheth, together with his wife and the wives of his three sons, entered the ark. They had with them every wild animal according to its kind, all livestock according to their kinds, every creature that moves along the ground according to its kind and every bird according to its kind, everything with wings. Pairs of all creatures that have the breath of life in them came to Noah and entered the ark. The animals going in were male and female of every living thing, as God had commanded Noah. Then the LORD shut him in.

For forty days the flood kept coming on the earth, and as the waters increased they lifted the ark high above the earth. The waters rose and increased greatly on the earth, and the ark floated on the surface of the water.

After forty days Noah opened the window he had made in the ark and sent out a raven, and it kept flying back and forth until the water had dried up from the earth. Then he sent out a dove to see if the water had receded from the surface of the ground. But the dove could find no place to set its feet because there was water over all the surface of the earth; so it returned to Noah in the ark. He reached out his hand and took the dove and brought it back to himself in the ark. He waited seven more days and again sent out the dove from the ark. When the dove returned to him in the evening, there in its beak was a freshly plucked olive leaf! Then Noah knew that the water had receded from the earth. He waited seven more days and sent the dove out again, but this time it did not return to him.

By the first day of the first month of Noah's six hundred and first year, the water had dried up from the earth. Noah then removed the covering from the ark and saw that the surface of the ground was dry. By the twenty–seventh day of the second month the earth was completely dry.

Then God said to Noah, "Come out of the ark, you and your wife and your sons and their wives. Bring out every kind of living creature that is with you – the birds, the animals, and all the creatures that move along the ground – so they can multiply on the earth and be fruitful and increase in number upon it."

So Noah came out, together with his sons and his wife and his sons' wives.

Then God said to Noah and to his sons with him: "I now establish my covenant with you and with your descendants after you and with every living creature that was with you – the birds, the livestock and all the wild animals, all those that came out of the ark with you – every living creature on earth. I establish my covenant with you: Never again will all life be cut off by the waters of a flood; never again will there be a flood to destroy the earth."

And God said, "This is the sign of the covenant I am making between me and you and every living creature with you, a covenant for all generations to come: I have set my rainbow in the clouds, and it will be the sign of the covenant between me and the earth."

Easter 5

Either Baruch 3:9–15, 32 – 4:4

or Genesis 22:1–18   God tested Abraham. He said to him, "Abraham!"

"Here I am," he replied.

Then God said, "Take your son, your only son, Isaac, whom you love, and go to the region of Moriah. Sacrifice him there as a burnt offering on one of the mountains I will tell you about."

Early the next morning Abraham got up and saddled his donkey. He took with him two of his servants and his son Isaac. When he had cut enough wood for the burnt offering, he set out for the place God had told him about. On the third day Abraham looked up and saw the place in the distance. He said to his servants, "Stay here with the donkey while I and the boy go over there. We will worship and then we will come back to you."

Abraham took the wood for the burnt offering and placed it on his son Isaac, and he himself carried the fire and the knife. As the two of them went on together, Isaac spoke up and said to his father Abraham, "Father?"

"Yes, my son?" Abraham replied.

"The fire and wood are here," Isaac said, "but where is the lamb for the burnt offering?"

Abraham answered, "God himself will provide the lamb for the burnt offering, my son." And the two of them went on together.

When they reached the place God had told him about, Abraham built an altar there and arranged the wood on it. He bound his son Isaac and laid him on the altar, on top of the wood. Then he reached out his hand and took the knife to slay his son. But the angel of the LORD called out to him from heaven, "Abraham! Abraham!"

"Here I am," he replied.

"Do not lay a hand on the boy," he said. "Do not do anything to him. Now I know that you fear God, because you have not withheld from me your son, your only son."

Abraham looked up and there in a thicket he saw a ram caught by its horns. He went over and took the ram and sacrificed it as a burnt offering instead of his son. So Abraham called that place The Lord Will Provide. And to this day it is said, "On the mountain of the Lord it will be provided."

The angel of the Lord called to Abraham from heaven a second time and said, "I swear by myself, declares the Lord, that because you have done this and have not withheld your son, your only son, I will surely bless you and make your descendants as numerous as the stars in the sky and as the sand on the seashore. Your descendants will take possession of the cities of their enemies, and through your offspring all nations on earth will be blessed, because you have obeyed me."

Easter 6

Isaiah 55:1–11   "Come, all you who are thirsty,
come to the waters;
and you who have no money,
come, buy and eat!
Come, buy wine and milk
without money and without cost.
Why spend money on what is not bread,
and your labour on what does not satisfy?
Listen, listen to me, and eat what is good,
and your soul will delight in the richest of fare.
Give ear and come to me;
hear me, that your soul may live.
I will make an everlasting covenant with you,
my faithful love promised to David.
See, I have made him a witness to the peoples,
a leader and commander of the peoples.
Surely you will summon nations you know not,
and nations that do not know you will hasten to you,
because of the Lord your God,
the Holy One of Israel,
for he has endowed you with splendour."

Seek the Lord while he may be found;
call on him while he is near.
Let the wicked forsake his way
and the evil man his thought.
Let him turn to the Lord, and he will have mercy on him,
and to our God, for he will freely pardon.
"For my thoughts are not your thoughts,
neither are your ways my ways,"
declares the Lord.

"As the heavens are higher than the earth,
    so are my ways higher than your ways
    and my thoughts than your thoughts.
As the rain and the snow
    come down from heaven,
and do not return to it
    without watering the earth
and making it bud and flourish,
    so that it yields seed for the sower and bread for the eater,
so is my word that goes out from my mouth:
    It will not return to me empty,
but will accomplish what I desire
    and achieve the purpose for which I sent it."

Easter 7

Ezekiel 36:24–28   This is what the Sovereign LORD says: "I will take you out of the nations; I will gather you from all the countries and bring you back into your own land. I will sprinkle clean water on you, and you will be clean; I will cleanse you from all your impurities and from all your idols. I will give you a new heart and put a new spirit in you; I will remove from you your heart of stone and give you a heart of flesh. And I will put my Spirit in you and move you to follow my decrees and be careful to keep my laws. You will live in the land I gave your forefathers; you will be my people, and I will be your God."

Second Sunday of Easter

Acts 4:32–35   All the believers were one in heart and mind. No-one claimed F R
that any of his possessions was his own, but they shared everything they I E
had. With great power the apostles continued to testify to the resurrection R A
of the Lord Jesus, and much grace was upon them all. There were no needy S D
persons among them. For from time to time those who owned lands T I
or houses sold them, brought the money from the sales and put it at the   N
apostles' feet, and it was distributed to anyone as he had need.   G

Psalm 133   How good and pleasant it is   P
    when brothers live together in unity!   S
It is like precious oil poured on the head,   A
    running down on the beard,   L
running down on Aaron's beard,   M
    down upon the collar of his robes.
It is as if the dew of Hermon
    were falling on Mount Zion.
For there the LORD bestows his blessing,
    even life for evermore.

1 John 1:1 – 2:2   That which was from the beginning, which we have heard, S
which we have seen with our eyes, which we have looked at and our hands E
have touched – this we proclaim concerning the Word of life. The life C
appeared; we have seen it and testify to it, and we proclaim to you the eter- O
nal life, which was with the Father and has appeared to us. We proclaim to N
you what we have seen and heard, so that you also may have fellowship D
with us. And our fellowship is with the Father and with his Son, Jesus
Christ. We write this to make our joy complete.   R

    This is the message we have heard from him and declare to you: God is E
light; in him there is no darkness at all. If we claim to have fellowship with A
him yet walk in the darkness, we lie and do not live by the truth. But if we D
walk in the light, as he is in the light, we have fellowship with one another, I
and the blood of Jesus, his Son, purifies us from all sin.   N

    If we claim to be without sin, we deceive ourselves and the truth is not G
in us. If we confess our sins, he is faithful and just and will forgive us our
sins and purify us from all unrighteousness. If we claim we have not
sinned, we make him out to be a liar and his word has no place in our lives.

    My dear children, I write this to you so that you will not sin. But if any-
body does sin, we have one who speaks to the Father in our defence – Jesus
Christ, the Righteous One. He is the atoning sacrifice for our sins, and not
only for ours but also for the sins of the whole world.

    G

John 20:19–31   On the evening of that first day of the week, when the disci- O
ples were together, with the doors locked for fear of the Jews, Jesus came S
and stood among them and said, "Peace be with you!" After he said this, he P
showed them his hands and side. The disciples were overjoyed when they E
saw the Lord.   L

Again Jesus said, "Peace be with you! As the Father has sent me, I am sending you." And with that he breathed on them and said, "Receive the Holy Spirit. If you forgive anyone his sins, they are forgiven; if you do not forgive them, they are not forgiven."

Now Thomas (called Didymus), one of the Twelve, was not with the disciples when Jesus came. So the other disciples told him, "We have seen the Lord!"

But he said to them, "Unless I see the nail marks in his hands and put my finger where the nails were, and put my hand into his side, I will not believe it."

A week later his disciples were in the house again, and Thomas was with them. Though the doors were locked, Jesus came and stood among them and said, "Peace be with you!" Then he said to Thomas, "Put your finger here; see my hands. Reach out your hand and put it into my side. Stop doubting and believe."

Thomas said to him, "My Lord and my God!"

Then Jesus told him, "Because you have seen me, you have believed; blessed are those who have not seen and yet have believed."

Jesus did many other miraculous signs in the presence of his disciples, which are not recorded in this book. But these are written that you may believe that Jesus is the Christ, the Son of God, and that by believing you may have life in his name.

Third Sunday of Easter

Acts 3:12–19 Peter said: "Men of Israel, why does this surprise you? Why do you stare at us as if by our own power or godliness we had made this man walk? The God of Abraham, Isaac and Jacob, the God of our fathers, has glorified his servant Jesus. You handed him over to be killed, and you disowned him before Pilate, though he had decided to let him go. You disowned the Holy and Righteous One and asked that a murderer be released to you. You killed the author of life, but God raised him from the dead. We are witnesses of this. By faith in the name of Jesus, this man whom you see and know was made strong. It is Jesus' name and the faith that comes through him that has given this complete healing to him, as you can all see.

"Now, brothers, I know that you acted in ignorance, as did your leaders. But this is how God fulfilled what he had foretold through all the prophets, saying that his Christ would suffer. Repent, then, and turn to God, so that your sins may be wiped out, that times of refreshing may come from the Lord.

Psalm 4 Answer me when I call to you,
　　O my righteous God.
Give me relief from my distress;
　　be merciful to me and hear my prayer.

How long, O men, will you turn my glory into shame?
　　How long will you love delusions and seek false gods?

Know that the LORD has set apart the godly for himself;
the LORD will hear when I call to him.

In your anger do not sin;
when you are on your beds,
search your hearts and be silent.
Offer right sacrifices
and trust in the LORD.

Many are asking, "Who can show us any good?"
Let the light of your face shine upon us, O LORD.
You have filled my heart with greater joy
than when their grain and new wine abound.
I will lie down and sleep in peace,
for you alone, O LORD,
make me dwell in safety.

1 John 3:1–7 How great is the love the Father has lavished on us, that we
should be called children of God! And that is what we are! The reason the
world does not know us is that it did not know him. Dear friends, now we
are children of God, and what we will be has not yet been made known. But
we know that when he appears, we shall be like him, for we shall see him
as he is. Everyone who has this hope in him purifies himself, just as he is
pure.

Everyone who sins breaks the law; in fact, sin is lawlessness. But you
know that he appeared so that he might take away our sins. And in him is no
sin. No-one who lives in him keeps on sinning. No-one who continues to sin
has either seen him or known him.

Dear children, do not let anyone lead you astray. He who does what is
right is righteous, just as he is righteous.

Luke 24:36b–48 Jesus stood among the disciples and said to them, "Peace be
with you."

They were startled and frightened, thinking they saw a ghost. He said to
them, "Why are you troubled, and why do doubts rise in your minds? Look
at my hands and my feet. It is I myself! Touch me and see; a ghost does not
have flesh and bones, as you see I have."

When he had said this, he showed them his hands and feet. And while
they still did not believe it because of joy and amazement, he asked them,
"Do you have anything here to eat?" They gave him a piece of broiled fish,
and he took it and ate it in their presence.

He said to them, "This is what I told you while I was still with you:
Everything must be fulfilled that is written about me in the Law of Moses,
the Prophets and the Psalms."

Then he opened their minds so they could understand the Scriptures. He
told them, "This is what is written: The Christ will suffer and rise from the
dead on the third day, and repentance and forgiveness of sins will be
preached in his name to all nations, beginning at Jerusalem. You are witnesses of these things.

Fourth Sunday of Easter

Acts 4:5–12 The rulers, elders and teachers of the law met in Jerusalem. F
Annas the high priest was there, and so were Caiaphas, John, Alexander I
and the other men of the high priest's family. They had Peter and John R
brought before them and began to question them: "By what power or what S
name did you do this?" T

Then Peter, filled with the Holy Spirit, said to them: "Rulers and elders
of the people! If we are being called to account today for an act of kindness R
shown to a cripple and are asked how he was healed, then know this, you E
and all the people of Israel: It is by the name of Jesus Christ of Nazareth, A
whom you crucified but whom God raised from the dead, that this man D
stands before you healed. He is I

"'the stone you builders rejected, N
which has become the capstone.' G

Salvation is found in no-one else, for there is no other name under
heaven given to men by which we must be saved."

Psalm 23 The LORD is my shepherd, I shall not be in want. P
He makes me lie down in green pastures, S
he leads me beside quiet waters, A
he restores my soul. L
He guides me in paths of righteousness M
for his name's sake.
Even though I walk
through the valley of the shadow of death,
I will fear no evil,
for you are with me;
your rod and your staff,
they comfort me.

You prepare a table before me
in the presence of my enemies.
You anoint my head with oil;
my cup overflows.
Surely goodness and love will follow me
all the days of my life,
and I will dwell in the house of the LORD for ever.

1 John 3:16–24 This is how we know what love is: Jesus Christ laid down his S R
life for us. And we ought to lay down our lives for our brothers. If anyone E E
has material possessions and sees his brother in need but has no pity on C A
him, how can the love of God be in him? Dear children, let us not love with O D
words or tongue but with actions and in truth. This then is how we know N I
that we belong to the truth, and how we set our hearts at rest in his pres- D N
ence whenever our hearts condemn us. For God is greater than our hearts, G
and he knows everything.

Dear friends, if our hearts do not condemn us, we have confidence before God and receive from him anything we ask, because we obey his commands and do what pleases him. And this is his command: to believe in the name of his Son, Jesus Christ, and to love one another as he commanded us. Those who obey his commands live in him, and he in them. And this is how we know that he lives in us: We know it by the Spirit he gave us.

John 10:11–18 Jesus said: "I am the good shepherd. The good shepherd lays down his life for the sheep. The hired hand is not the shepherd who owns the sheep. So when he sees the wolf coming, he abandons the sheep and runs away. Then the wolf attacks the flock and scatters it. The man runs away because he is a hired hand and cares nothing for the sheep.

"I am the good shepherd; I know my sheep and my sheep know me – just as the Father knows me and I know the Father – and I lay down my life for the sheep. I have other sheep that are not of this sheep pen. I must bring them also. They too will listen to my voice, and there shall be one flock and one shepherd. The reason my Father loves me is that I lay down my life – only to take it up again. No-one takes it from me, but I lay it down of my own accord. I have authority to lay it down and authority to take it up again. This command I received from my Father."

GOSPEL

Fifth Sunday of Easter

Acts 8:26–40 An angel of the Lord said to Philip, "Go south to the road – the desert road – that goes down from Jerusalem to Gaza." So he started out, and on his way he met an Ethiopian eunuch, an important official in charge of all the treasury of Candace, queen of the Ethiopians. This man had gone to Jerusalem to worship, and on his way home was sitting in his chariot reading the book of Isaiah the prophet. The Spirit told Philip, "Go to that chariot and stay near it."

Then Philip ran up to the chariot and heard the man reading Isaiah the prophet. "Do you understand what you are reading?" Philip asked.

"How can I," he said, "unless someone explains it to me?" So he invited Philip to come up and sit with him.

The eunuch was reading this passage of Scripture:

FIRST READING

"He was led like a sheep to the slaughter,
and as a lamb before the shearer is silent,
so he did not open his mouth.
In his humiliation he was deprived of justice.
Who can speak of his descendants?
For his life was taken from the earth."

The eunuch asked Philip, "Tell me, please, who is the prophet talking about, himself or someone else?" Then Philip began with that very passage of Scripture and told him the good news about Jesus.

As they travelled along the road, they came to some water and the eunuch said, "Look, here is water. Why shouldn't I be baptised?" And he gave orders to stop the chariot. Then both Philip and the eunuch went down into the water and Philip baptised him. When they came up out of the water, the Spirit of the Lord suddenly took Philip away, and the eunuch did not see him again, but went on his way rejoicing. Philip, however, appeared at Azotus and travelled about, preaching the gospel in all the towns until he reached Caesarea.

Psalm 22:25–31   From you comes the theme of my praise   P
                            in the great assembly;   S
                          before those who fear you will I fulfil my vows.   A
                       The poor will eat and be satisfied;   L
                            they who seek the Lord will praise him –   M
                          may your hearts live for ever!
                       All the ends of the earth
                            will remember and turn to the Lord,
                       and all the families of the nations
                            will bow down before him,
                       for dominion belongs to the Lord
                            and he rules over the nations.

                       All the rich of the earth will feast and worship;
                            all who go down to the dust will kneel before him –
                            those who cannot keep themselves alive.
                       Posterity will serve him;
                            future generations will be told about the Lord.
                       They will proclaim his righteousness
                            to a people yet unborn –
                            for he has done it.

1 John 4:7–21   Dear friends, let us love one another, for love comes from   S
God. Everyone who loves has been born of God and knows God. Whoever   E
does not love does not know God, because God is love. This is how God   C
showed his love among us: He sent his one and only Son into the world that   O
we might live through him. This is love: not that we loved God, but that he   N
loved us and sent his Son as an atoning sacrifice for our sins. Dear friends,   D
since God so loved us, we also ought to love one another. No-one has ever
seen God; but if we love one another, God lives in us and his love is made   R
complete in us.   E

   We know that we live in him and he in us, because he has given us of his   A
Spirit. And we have seen and testify that the Father has sent his Son to be   D
the Saviour of the world. If anyone acknowledges that Jesus is the Son of   I
God, God lives in him and he in God. And so we know and rely on the love   N
God has for us.   G

   God is love. Whoever lives in love lives in God, and God in him. In this
way, love is made complete among us so that we will have confidence on the
day of judgment, because in this world we are like him. There is no fear in
love. But perfect love drives out fear, because fear has to do with punishment. The one who fears is not made perfect in love.

   We love because he first loved us. If anyone says, "I love God," yet hates his brother, he is a liar. For anyone who does not love his brother, whom he has seen, cannot love God, whom he has not seen. And he has given us this command: Whoever loves God must also love his brother.

John 15:1–8 Jesus said: "I am the true vine, and my Father is the gardener. He cuts off every branch in me that bears no fruit, while every branch that does bear fruit he prunes so that it will be even more fruitful. You are already clean because of the word I have spoken to you. Remain in me, and I will remain in you. No branch can bear fruit by itself; it must remain in the vine. Neither can you bear fruit unless you remain in me.

"I am the vine; you are the branches. If a man remains in me and I in him, he will bear much fruit; apart from me you can do nothing. If anyone does not remain in me, he is like a branch that is thrown away and withers; such branches are picked up, thrown into the fire and burned. If you remain in me and my words remain in you, ask whatever you wish, and it will be given you. This is to my Father's glory, that you bear much fruit, showing yourselves to be my disciples."

Sixth Sunday of Easter

Acts 10:44–48 While Peter was speaking, the Holy Spirit came on all who heard the message. The circumcised believers who had come with Peter were astonished that the gift of the Holy Spirit had been poured out even on the Gentiles. For they heard them speaking in tongues and praising God.

Then Peter said, "Can anyone keep these people from being baptised with water? They have received the Holy Spirit just as we have." So he ordered that they be baptised in the name of Jesus Christ. Then they asked Peter to stay with them for a few days.

Psalm 98 Sing to the LORD a new song,
  for he has done marvellous things;
his right hand and his holy arm
  have worked salvation for him.
The LORD has made his salvation known
  and revealed his righteousness to the nations.
He has remembered his love
  and his faithfulness to the house of Israel;
all the ends of the earth have seen
  the salvation of our God.

Shout for joy to the LORD, all the earth,
  burst into jubilant song with music;
make music to the LORD with the harp,
  with the harp and the sound of singing,
with trumpets and the blast of the ram's horn –
  shout for joy before the LORD, the King.

Let the sea resound, and everything in it,
  the world, and all who live in it.

Let the rivers clap their hands,
  let the mountains sing together for joy;
let them sing before the LORD,
  for he comes to judge the earth.
He will judge the world in righteousness
  and the peoples with equity.

1 John 5:1–6   Everyone who believes that Jesus is the Christ is born of God, and everyone who loves the father loves his child as well. This is how we know that we love the children of God: by loving God and carrying out his commands. This is love for God: to obey his commands. And his commands are not burdensome, for everyone born of God overcomes the world. This is the victory that has overcome the world, even our faith. Who is it that overcomes the world? Only he who believes that Jesus is the Son of God.

> This is the one who came by water and blood – Jesus Christ. He did not come by water only, but by water and blood. And it is the Spirit who testifies, because the Spirit is the truth.

SECOND READING

John 15:9–17   Jesus said: "As the Father has loved me, so have I loved you. Now remain in my love. If you obey my commands, you will remain in my love, just as I have obeyed my Father's commands and remain in his love. I have told you this so that my joy may be in you and that your joy may be complete. My command is this: Love each other as I have loved you. Greater love has no-one than this, that he lay down his life for his friends. You are my friends if you do what I command. I no longer call you servants, because a servant does not know his master's business. Instead, I have called you friends, for everything that I learned from my Father I have made known to you. You did not choose me, but I chose you and appointed you to go and bear fruit – fruit that will last. Then the Father will give you whatever you ask in my name. This is my command: Love each other."

GOSPEL

Ascension Day

For text of readings for Years A, B, C see pp 130–133.

Seventh Sunday of Easter

Acts 1:15–17, 21–26   Peter stood up among the believers (a group numbering about a hundred and twenty) and said, "Brothers, the Scripture had to be fulfilled which the Holy Spirit spoke long ago through the mouth of David concerning Judas, who served as guide for those who arrested Jesus – he was one of our number and shared in this ministry.

> Therefore it is necessary to choose one of the men who have been with us the whole time the Lord Jesus went in and out among us, beginning from John's baptism to the time when Jesus was taken up from us. For one of these must become a witness with us of his resurrection."

FIRST READING

So they proposed two men: Joseph called Barsabbas (also known as Justus) and Matthias. Then they prayed, "Lord, you know everyone's heart.

Show us which of these two you have chosen to take over this apostolic ministry, which Judas left to go where he belongs." Then they cast lots, and the lot fell to Matthias; so he was added to the eleven apostles.

Psalm 1 Blessed is the man
  who does not walk in the counsel of the wicked
or stand in the way of sinners
  or sit in the seat of mockers.
But his delight is in the law of the LORD,
  and on his law he meditates day and night.
He is like a tree planted by streams of water,
  which yields its fruit in season
and whose leaf does not wither.
  Whatever he does prospers.

Not so the wicked!
  They are like chaff
  that the wind blows away.
Therefore the wicked will not stand in the judgment,
  nor sinners in the assembly of the righteous.

For the LORD watches over the way of the righteous,
  but the way of the wicked will perish.

1 John 5:9–13 We accept man's testimony, but God's testimony is greater because it is the testimony of God, which he has given about his Son. Anyone who believes in the Son of God has this testimony in his heart. Anyone who does not believe God has made him out to be a liar, because he has not believed the testimony God has given about his Son. And this is the testimony: God has given us eternal life, and this life is in his Son. He who has the Son has life; he who does not have the Son of God does not have life.

I write these things to you who believe in the name of the Son of God so that you may know that you have eternal life.

John 17:6–19 Jesus looked towards heaven and prayed: "Father, I have revealed you to those whom you gave me out of the world. They were yours; you gave them to me and they have obeyed your word. Now they know that everything you have given me comes from you. For I gave them the words you gave me and they accepted them. They knew with certainty that I came from you, and they believed that you sent me. I pray for them. I am not praying for the world, but for those you have given me, for they are yours. All I have is yours, and all you have is mine. And glory has come to me through them. I will remain in the world no longer, but they are still in the world, and I am coming to you. Holy Father, protect them by the power of your name – the name you gave me – so that they may be one as we are one. While I was with them, I protected them and kept them safe by that name you gave me. None has been lost except the one doomed to destruction so that Scripture would be fulfilled.

"I am coming to you now, but I say these things while I am still in the world, so that they may have the full measure of my joy within them. I have given them your word and the world has hated them, for they are not of the world any more than I am of the world. My prayer is not that you take them out of the world but that you protect them from the evil one. They are not of the world, even as I am not of it. Sanctify them by the truth; your word is truth. As you sent me into the world, I have sent them into the world. For them I sanctify myself, that they too may be truly sanctified."

Pentecost – Whit Sunday

(The reading from Acts must be used as either the first or second reading.)

Alternative first readings

Either **Acts 2:1–21** When the day of Pentecost came, the disciples were all together in one place. Suddenly a sound like the blowing of a violent wind came from heaven and filled the whole house where they were sitting. They saw what seemed to be tongues of fire that separated and came to rest on each of them. All of them were filled with the Holy Spirit and began to speak in other tongues as the Spirit enabled them.

Now there were staying in Jerusalem God-fearing Jews from every nation under heaven. When they heard this sound, a crowd came together in bewilderment, because each one heard them speaking in his own language. Utterly amazed, they asked: "Are not all these men who are speaking Galileans? Then how is it that each of us hears them in his own native language? Parthians, Medes and Elamites; residents of Mesopotamia, Judea and Cappadocia, Pontus and Asia, Phrygia and Pamphylia, Egypt and the parts of Libya near Cyrene; visitors from Rome (both Jews and converts to Judaism); Cretans and Arabs – we hear them declaring the wonders of God in our own tongues!" Amazed and perplexed, they asked one another, "What does this mean?"

Some, however, made fun of them and said, "They have had too much wine."

Then Peter stood up with the Eleven, raised his voice and addressed the crowd: "Fellow Jews and all of you who live in Jerusalem, let me explain this to you; listen carefully to what I say. These men are not drunk, as you suppose. It's only nine in the morning! No, this is what was spoken by the prophet Joel:

"'In the last days, God says,
I will pour out my Spirit on all people.
Your sons and daughters will prophesy,
your young men will see visions,
your old men will dream dreams.

Even on my servants, both men and women,
    I will pour out my Spirit in those days,
      and they will prophesy.
I will show wonders in the heaven above
    and signs on the earth below,
      blood and fire and billows of smoke.
The sun will be turned to darkness
    and the moon to blood
      before the coming of the great and glorious day of the Lord.
And everyone who calls
    on the name of the Lord will be saved.'"

or **Ezekiel 37:1–14**   The hand of the Lord was upon me, and he brought me out by the Spirit of the Lord and set me in the middle of a valley; it was full of bones. He led me to and fro among them, and I saw a great many bones on the floor of the valley, bones that were very dry. He asked me, "Son of man, can these bones live?"

I said, "O Sovereign Lord, you alone know."

Then he said to me, "Prophesy to these bones and say to them, 'Dry bones, hear the word of the Lord! This is what the Sovereign Lord says to these bones: I will make breath enter you, and you will come to life. I will attach tendons to you and make flesh come upon you and cover you with skin; I will put breath in you, and you will come to life. Then you will know that I am the Lord.'"

So I prophesied as I was commanded. And as I was prophesying, there was a noise, a rattling sound, and the bones came together, bone to bone. I looked, and tendons and flesh appeared on them and skin covered them, but there was no breath in them.

Then he said to me, "Prophesy to the breath; prophesy, son of man, and say to it, 'This is what the Sovereign Lord says: Come from the four winds, O breath, and breathe into these slain, that they may live.'" So I prophesied as he commanded me, and breath entered them; they came to life and stood up on their feet – a vast army.

Then he said to me: "Son of man, these bones are the whole house of Israel. They say, 'Our bones are dried up and our hope is gone; we are cut off.' Therefore prophesy and say to them: 'This is what the Sovereign Lord says: O my people, I am going to open your graves and bring you up from them; I will bring you back to the land of Israel. Then you, my people, will know that I am the Lord, when I open your graves and bring you up from them. I will put my Spirit in you and you will live, and I will settle you in your own land. Then you will know that I the Lord have spoken, and I have done it, declares the Lord.'"

Psalm 104:24–34, 35b*   How many are your works, O Lord!
        In wisdom you made them all;
        the earth is full of your creatures.

There is the sea, vast and spacious,
>> teeming with creatures beyond number –
>> living things both large and small.
There the ships go to and fro,
>> and the leviathan, which you formed to
>>> frolic there.

These all look to you
>> to give them their food at the proper time.
When you give it to them,
>> they gather it up;
when you open your hand,
>> they are satisfied with good things.
When you hide your face,
>> they are terrified;
when you take away their breath,
>> they die and return to the dust.
When you send your Spirit,
>> they are created,
>> and you renew the face of the earth.

May the glory of the LORD endure for ever;
>> may the LORD rejoice in his works –
he who looks at the earth, and it trembles,
>> who touches the mountains, and they smoke.

I will sing to the LORD all my life;
>> I will sing praise to my God as long as I live.
May my meditation be pleasing to him,
>> as I rejoice in the LORD.

Praise the LORD, O my soul.

Praise the LORD.

Alternative second readings

Either **Romans 8:22–27** We know that the whole creation has been groaning as in the pains of childbirth right up to the present time. Not only so, but we ourselves, who have the firstfruits of the Spirit, groan inwardly as we wait eagerly for our adoption as sons, the redemption of our bodies. For in this hope we were saved. But hope that is seen is no hope at all. Who hopes for what he already has? But if we hope for what we do not yet have, we wait for it patiently.

In the same way, the Spirit helps us in our weakness. We do not know what we ought to pray for, but the Spirit himself intercedes for us with groans that words cannot express. And he who searches our hearts knows the mind of the Spirit, because the Spirit intercedes for the saints in accordance with God's will.

or **Acts 2:1–21** When the day of Pentecost came, the disciples were all together in one place. Suddenly a sound like the blowing of a violent wind came from heaven and filled the whole house where they were sitting. They saw what seemed to be tongues of fire that separated and came to rest on each of them. All of them were filled with the Holy Spirit and began to speak in other tongues as the Spirit enabled them.

Now there were staying in Jerusalem God-fearing Jews from every nation under heaven. When they heard this sound, a crowd came together in bewilderment, because each one heard them speaking in his own language. Utterly amazed, they asked: "Are not all these men who are speaking Galileans? Then how is it that each of us hears them in his own native language? Parthians, Medes and Elamites; residents of Mesopotamia, Judea and Cappadocia, Pontus and Asia, Phrygia and Pamphylia, Egypt and the parts of Libya near Cyrene; visitors from Rome (both Jews and converts to Judaism); Cretans and Arabs – we hear them declaring the wonders of God in our own tongues!" Amazed and perplexed, they asked one another, "What does this mean?"

Some, however, made fun of them and said, "They have had too much wine."

Then Peter stood up with the Eleven, raised his voice and addressed the crowd: "Fellow Jews and all of you who live in Jerusalem, let me explain this to you; listen carefully to what I say. These men are not drunk, as you suppose. It's only nine in the morning! No, this is what was spoken by the prophet Joel:

"'In the last days, God says,
  I will pour out my Spirit on all people.
Your sons and daughters will prophesy,
  your young men will see visions,
  your old men will dream dreams.
Even on my servants, both men and women,
  I will pour out my Spirit in those days,
  and they will prophesy.
I will show wonders in the heaven above
  and signs on the earth below,
  blood and fire and billows of smoke.
The sun will be turned to darkness
  and the moon to blood
  before the coming of the great and glorious day of the Lord.
And everyone who calls
  on the name of the LORD will be saved.'"

John 15:26–27; 16:4b–15 Jesus said: "When the Counsellor comes, whom I will send to you from the Father, the Spirit of truth who goes out from the Father, he will testify about me. And you also must testify, for you have been with me from the beginning.

"I did not tell you this at first because I was with you.

"Now I am going to him who sent me, yet none of you asks me, 'Where are you going?' Because I have said these things, you are filled with grief.

But I tell you the truth: It is for your good that I am going away. Unless I go away, the Counsellor will not come to you; but if I go, I will send him to you. When he comes, he will convict the world of guilt in regard to sin and righteousness and judgment: in regard to sin, because men do not believe in me; in regard to righteousness, because I am going to the Father, where you can see me no longer; and in regard to judgment, because the prince of this world now stands condemned.

"I have much more to say to you, more than you can now bear. But when he, the Spirit of truth, comes, he will guide you into all truth. He will not speak on his own; he will speak only what he hears, and he will tell you what is yet to come. He will bring glory to me by taking from what is mine and making it known to you. All that belongs to the Father is mine. That is why I said the Spirit will take from what is mine and make it known to you."

ORDINARY TIME

Trinity Sunday

Isaiah 6:1–8 In the year that King Uzziah died, I saw the Lord seated on a throne, high and exalted, and the train of his robe filled the temple. Above him were seraphs, each with six wings: With two wings they covered their faces, with two they covered their feet, and with two they were flying. And they were calling to one another:

> "Holy, holy, holy is the LORD Almighty;
>> the whole earth is full of his glory."

At the sound of their voices the doorposts and thresholds shook and the temple was filled with smoke.

"Woe to me!" I cried. "I am ruined! For I am a man of unclean lips, and I live among a people of unclean lips, and my eyes have seen the King, the LORD Almighty."

Then one of the seraphs flew to me with a live coal in his hand, which he had taken with tongs from the altar. With it he touched my mouth and said, "See, this has touched your lips; your guilt is taken away and your sin atoned for."

Then I heard the voice of the Lord saying, "Whom shall I send? And who will go for us?"

And I said, "Here am I. Send me!"

Psalm 29
> Ascribe to the LORD, O mighty ones,
>> ascribe to the LORD glory and strength.
> Ascribe to the LORD the glory due to his name;
>> worship the LORD in the splendour of his holiness.
>
> The voice of the LORD is over the waters;
>> the God of glory thunders,
>> the LORD thunders over the mighty waters.
> The voice of the LORD is powerful;
>> the voice of the LORD is majestic.

FIRST READING

PSALM

The voice of the LORD breaks the cedars;
the LORD breaks in pieces the cedars of Lebanon.
He makes Lebanon skip like a calf,
Sirion like a young wild ox.
The voice of the LORD strikes
with flashes of lightning.
The voice of the LORD shakes the desert;
the LORD shakes the Desert of Kadesh.
The voice of the LORD twists the oaks
and strips the forests bare.
And in his temple all cry, "Glory!"

The LORD sits enthroned over the flood;
the LORD is enthroned as King for ever.
The LORD gives strength to his people;
the LORD blesses his people with peace.

Romans 8:12–17 Brothers, we have an obligation – but it is not to the sinful
nature, to live according to it. For if you live according to the sinful nature,
you will die; but if by the Spirit you put to death the misdeeds of the body,
you will live, because those who are led by the Spirit of God are sons of
God. For you did not receive a spirit that makes you a slave again to fear,
but you received the Spirit of sonship. And by him we cry, "*Abba*, Father."
The Spirit himself testifies with our spirit that we are God's children. Now
if we are children, then we are heirs – heirs of God and co-heirs with Christ,
if indeed we share in his sufferings in order that we may also share in his
glory.

John 3:1–17 There was a man of the Pharisees named Nicodemus, a member of the Jewish ruling council. He came to Jesus at night and said,
"Rabbi, we know you are a teacher who has come from God. For no-one
could perform the miraculous signs you are doing if God were not with
him."

In reply Jesus declared, "I tell you the truth, no-one can see the kingdom
of God unless he is born again."

"How can a man be born when he is old?" Nicodemus asked. "Surely he
cannot enter a second time into his mother's womb to be born!"

Jesus answered, "I tell you the truth, no-one can enter the kingdom of
God unless he is born of water and the Spirit. Flesh gives birth to flesh, but
the Spirit gives birth to spirit. You should not be surprised at my saying,
'You must be born again.' The wind blows wherever it pleases. You hear its
sound, but you cannot tell where it comes from or where it is going. So it is
with everyone born of the Spirit."

"How can this be?" Nicodemus asked.

"You are Israel's teacher," said Jesus, "and do you not understand these
things? I tell you the truth, we speak of what we know, and we testify to
what we have seen, but still you people do not accept our testimony. I have

spoken to you of earthly things and you do not believe; how then will you believe if I speak of heavenly things? No-one has ever gone into heaven except the one who came from heaven – the Son of Man. Just as Moses lifted up the snake in the desert, so the Son of Man must be lifted up, that everyone who believes in him may have eternal life.

"For God so loved the world that he gave his one and only Son, that whoever believes in him shall not perish but have eternal life. For God did not send his Son into the world to condemn the world, but to save the world through him."

If the Sunday between 24 and 28 May inclusive follows Trinity Sunday, Proper 3 (p 255) is used.

Thanksgiving for Holy Communion
Thursday after Trinity Sunday (Corpus Christi)

For text of readings for Years A, B, C see pp 141–142.

Proper 4

Sunday between 29 May and 4 June inclusive (if after Trinity Sunday)
On the Sundays after Trinity, alternative Old Testament readings and Psalms are provided. The first pair of readings headed 'continuous' offer semi-continuous reading of Old Testament texts but allow the Old Testament reading and its complementary Psalm to stand independently of the other readings. The second pair of readings headed 'related' relate the Old Testament reading and the Psalm to the Gospel reading.

It is unhelpful to move from one type of pair to another from week to week. Either 'continuous' or 'related' readings should be followed for the whole sequence of Sundays after Trinity.

CONTINUOUS

1 Samuel 3:1–10 [11–20]   The boy Samuel ministered before the LORD under Eli. In those days the word of the LORD was rare; there were not many visions.

One night Eli, whose eyes were becoming so weak that he could barely see, was lying down in his usual place. The lamp of God had not yet gone out, and Samuel was lying down in the temple of the LORD, where the ark of God was. Then the LORD called Samuel.

Samuel answered, "Here I am." And he ran to Eli and said, "Here I am; you called me."

But Eli said, "I did not call; go back and lie down." So he went and lay down.

Again the LORD called, "Samuel!" And Samuel got up and went to Eli and said, "Here I am; you called me."

"My son," Eli said, "I did not call; go back and lie down."

Now Samuel did not yet know the LORD: The word of the LORD had not yet been revealed to him.

The LORD called Samuel a third time, and Samuel got up and went to Eli and said, "Here I am; you called me."

Then Eli realised that the LORD was calling the boy. So Eli told Samuel,

"Go and lie down, and if he calls you, say, 'Speak, Lord, for your servant is listening.'" So Samuel went and lay down in his place.

The Lord came and stood there, calling as at the other times, "Samuel! Samuel!"

Then Samuel said, "Speak, for your servant is listening."

[And the Lord said to Samuel: "See, I am about to do something in Israel that will make the ears of everyone who hears of it tingle. At that time I will carry out against Eli everything I spoke against his family – from beginning to end. For I told him that I would judge his family for ever because of the sin he knew about; his sons made themselves contemptible, and he failed to restrain them. Therefore, I swore to the house of Eli, 'The guilt of Eli's house will never be atoned for by sacrifice or offering.'"

Samuel lay down until morning and then opened the doors of the house of the Lord. He was afraid to tell Eli the vision, but Eli called him and said, "Samuel, my son."

Samuel answered, "Here I am."

"What was it he said to you?" Eli asked. "Do not hide it from me. May God deal with you, be it ever so severely, if you hide from me anything he told you." So Samuel told him everything, hiding nothing from him. Then Eli said, "He is the Lord; let him do what is good in his eyes."

The Lord was with Samuel as he grew up, and he let none of his words fall to the ground. And all Israel from Dan to Beersheba recognised that Samuel was attested as a prophet of the Lord.]

and **Psalm 139:**	O Lord, you have searched me	P
1–6, 13–18	and you know me.	S
	You know when I sit and when I rise;	A
	you perceive my thoughts from afar.	L
	You discern my going out and my lying down;	M
	you are familiar with all my ways.	

Before a word is on my tongue
    you know it completely, O Lord.

You hem me in – behind and before;
    you have laid your hand upon me.
Such knowledge is too wonderful for me,
    too lofty for me to attain.

For you created my inmost being;
    you knit me together in my mother's womb.
I praise you because I am fearfully and wonderfully made;
    your works are wonderful,
    I know that full well.
My frame was not hidden from you
    when I was made in the secret place.
When I was woven together in the depths of the earth,
    your eyes saw my unformed body.

All the days ordained for me
were written in your book
before one of them came to be.

How precious to me are your thoughts, O God!
How vast is the sum of them!
Were I to count them,
they would outnumber the grains of sand.
When I awake,
I am still with you.

Or **RELATED**

Deuteronomy 5:12–15 "Observe the Sabbath day by keeping it holy, as the F R
LORD your God has commanded you. Six days you shall labour and do all I E
your work, but the seventh day is a Sabbath to the LORD your God. On it you R A
shall not do any work, neither you, nor your son or daughter, nor your S D
manservant or maidservant, nor your ox, your donkey or any of your ani- T I
mals, nor the alien within your gates, so that your manservant and N
maidservant may rest, as you do. Remember that you were slaves in Egypt G
and that the LORD your God brought you out of there with a mighty hand
and an outstretched arm. Therefore the LORD your God has commanded
you to observe the Sabbath day."

and **Psalm 81:1–10** Sing for joy to God our strength;   P
shout aloud to the God of Jacob!   S
Begin the music, strike the tambourine,   A
play the melodious harp and lyre.   L

Sound the ram's horn at the New Moon,   M
and when the moon is full, on the day of our Feast;
this is a decree for Israel,
an ordinance of the God of Jacob.
He established it as a statute for Joseph
when he went out against Egypt,
where we heard a language we did not understand.

He says, "I removed the burden from their shoulders;
their hands were set free from the basket.
In your distress you called and I rescued you,
I answered you out of a thundercloud;
I tested you at the waters of Meribah.

"Hear, O my people, and I will warn you –
if you would but listen to me, O Israel!
You shall have no foreign god among you;
you shall not bow down to an alien god.
I am the LORD your God,
who brought you up out of Egypt.
Open wide your mouth and I will fill it."

2 Corinthians 4:5–12 We do not preach ourselves, but Jesus Christ as Lord, and ourselves as your servants for Jesus' sake. For God, who said, "Let light shine out of darkness," made his light shine in our hearts to give us the light of the knowledge of the glory of God in the face of Christ.

But we have this treasure in jars of clay to show that this all-surpassing power is from God and not from us. We are hard pressed on every side, but not crushed; perplexed, but not in despair; persecuted, but not abandoned; struck down, but not destroyed. We always carry around in our body the death of Jesus, so that the life of Jesus may also be revealed in our body. For we who are alive are always being given over to death for Jesus' sake, so that his life may be revealed in our mortal body. So then, death is at work in us, but life is at work in you.

Mark 2:23 – 3:6 One Sabbath Jesus was going through the cornfields, and as his disciples walked along, they began to pick some ears of corn. The Pharisees said to him, "Look, why are they doing what is unlawful on the Sabbath?"

He answered, "Have you never read what David did when he and his companions were hungry and in need? In the days of Abiathar the high priest, he entered the house of God and ate the consecrated bread, which is lawful only for priests to eat. And he also gave some to his companions."

Then he said to them, "The Sabbath was made for man, not man for the Sabbath. So the Son of Man is Lord even of the Sabbath."

Another time he went into the synagogue, and a man with a shrivelled hand was there. Some of them were looking for a reason to accuse Jesus, so they watched him closely to see if he would heal him on the Sabbath. Jesus said to the man with the shrivelled hand, "Stand up in front of everyone."

Then Jesus asked them, "Which is lawful on the Sabbath: to do good or to do evil, to save life or to kill?" But they remained silent.

He looked round at them in anger and, deeply distressed at their stubborn hearts, said to the man, "Stretch out your hand." He stretched it out, and his hand was completely restored. Then the Pharisees went out and began to plot with the Herodians how they might kill Jesus.

Proper 5

Sunday between 5 and 11 June inclusive (if after Trinity Sunday)
Choose either 'continuous' or 'related' Old Testament and Psalm readings.

CONTINUOUS

1 Samuel 8:4–11 [12–15] 16–20 [11:14–15] All the elders of Israel gathered together and came to Samuel at Ramah. They said to him, "You are old, and your sons do not walk in your ways; now appoint a king to lead us, such as all the other nations have."

But when they said, "Give us a king to lead us," this displeased Samuel; so he prayed to the LORD. And the LORD told him: "Listen to all that the people are saying to you; it is not you they have rejected, but they have rejected me as their king. As they have done from the day I brought them up out of Egypt until this day, forsaking me and serving other gods, so they are doing to you. Now listen to them; but warn them solemnly and let them know what the king who will reign over them will do."

Samuel told all the words of the LORD to the people who were asking him for a king. He said, "This is what the king who will reign over you will do: He will take your sons and make them serve with his chariots and horses, and they will run in front of his chariots. [Some he will assign to be commanders of thousands and commanders of fifties, and others to plough his ground and reap his harvest, and still others to make weapons of war and equipment for his chariots. He will take your daughters to be perfumers and cooks and bakers. He will take the best of your fields and vineyards and olive groves and give them to his attendants. He will take a tenth of your grain and of your vintage and give it to his officials and attendants.] Your menservants and maidservants and the best of your cattle and donkeys he will take for his own use. He will take a tenth of your flocks, and you yourselves will become his slaves. When that day comes, you will cry out for relief from the king you have chosen, and the LORD will not answer you in that day."

But the people refused to listen to Samuel. "No!" they said. "We want a king over us. Then we shall be like all the other nations, with a king to lead us and to go out before us and fight our battles."

[Then Samuel said to the people, "Come, let us go to Gilgal and there reaffirm the kingship." So all the people went to Gilgal and confirmed Saul as king in the presence of the LORD. There they sacrificed fellowship offerings before the LORD, and Saul and all the Israelites held a great celebration.]

and **Psalm 138**

I will praise you, O LORD, with all my heart;
    before the "gods" I will sing your praise.
I will bow down towards your holy temple
    and will praise your name
    for your love and your faithfulness,
for you have exalted above all things
    your name and your word.
When I called, you answered me;
    you made me bold and stout-hearted.

May all the kings of the earth praise you, O LORD,
    when they hear the words of your mouth.
May they sing of the ways of the LORD,
    for the glory of the LORD is great.

Though the LORD is on high, he looks upon the lowly,
    but the proud he knows from afar.
Though I walk in the midst of trouble,
    you preserve my life;
you stretch out your hand against the anger of my foes,
    with your right hand you save me.

P
S
A
L
M

The LORD will fulfil his purpose for me;
>your love, O LORD, endures for ever –
>do not abandon the works of your hands.

Or **RELATED**

Genesis 3:8–15   The man and his wife heard the sound of the LORD God as he F
was walking in the garden in the cool of the day, and they hid from the LORD I
God among the trees of the garden. But the LORD God called to the man, R
"Where are you?" S

He answered, "I heard you in the garden, and I was afraid because I was T
naked; so I hid."

And he said, "Who told you that you were naked? Have you eaten from R
the tree from which I commanded you not to eat?" E

The man said, "The woman you put here with me – she gave me some A
fruit from the tree, and I ate it." D

Then the LORD God said to the woman, "What is this you have done?" I

The woman said, "The serpent deceived me, and I ate." N

So the LORD God said to the serpent, "Because you have done this, G

"Cursed are you above all the livestock
>and all the wild animals!
You will crawl on your belly
>and you will eat dust
>all the days of your life.
And I will put enmity
>between you and the woman,
>and between your offspring and hers;
he will crush your head,
>and you will strike his heel."

and **Psalm 130**   Out of the depths I cry to you, O LORD; P
>O LORD, hear my voice. S
>Let your ears be attentive A
>>to my cry for mercy. L

M
>If you, O LORD, kept a record of sins,
>O LORD, who could stand?
>But with you there is forgiveness;
>>therefore you are feared.

>I wait for the LORD, my soul waits,
>>and in his word I put my hope.
>My soul waits for the LORD
>>more than watchmen wait for the morning,
>>more than watchmen wait for the morning.

>O Israel, put your hope in the LORD,
>>for with the LORD is unfailing love
>>and with him is full redemption.

He himself will redeem Israel
from all their sins.

2 Corinthians 4:13 – 5:1 It is written: "I believed; therefore I have spoken." S
With that same spirit of faith we also believe and therefore speak, because E
we know that the one who raised the Lord Jesus from the dead will also C
raise us with Jesus and present us with you in his presence. All this is for O
your benefit, so that the grace that is reaching more and more people may N
cause thanksgiving to overflow to the glory of God. D

Therefore we do not lose heart. Though outwardly we are wasting away,
yet inwardly we are being renewed day by day. For our light and momen- R
tary troubles are achieving for us an eternal glory that far outweighs them E
all. So we fix our eyes not on what is seen, but on what is unseen. For what A
is seen is temporary, but what is unseen is eternal. D

Now we know that if the earthly tent we live in is destroyed, we have I
a building from God, an eternal house in heaven, not built by human N
hands. G

Mark 3:20-35 Jesus entered a house, and again a crowd gathered, so that he G
and his disciples were not even able to eat. When his family heard about O
this, they went to take charge of him, for they said, "He is out of his mind." S

And the teachers of the law who came down from Jerusalem said, "He is P
possessed by Beelzebub! By the prince of demons he is driving out E
demons." L

So Jesus called them and spoke to them in parables: "How can Satan
drive out Satan? If a kingdom is divided against itself, that kingdom cannot
stand. If a house is divided against itself, that house cannot stand. And if
Satan opposes himself and is divided, he cannot stand; his end has come. In
fact, no-one can enter a strong man's house and carry off his possessions
unless he first ties up the strong man. Then he can rob his house. I tell
you the truth, all the sins and blasphemies of men will be forgiven. But
whoever blasphemes against the Holy Spirit will never be forgiven but is
guilty of an eternal sin."

He said this because they were saying, "He has an evil spirit."

Then Jesus' mother and brothers arrived. Standing outside, they sent
someone in to call him. A crowd was sitting around him, and they told him,
"Your mother and brothers are outside looking for you."

"Who are my mother and my brothers?" he asked.

Then he looked at those seated in a circle around him and said, "Here
are my mother and my brothers! Whoever does God's will is my brother
and sister and mother."

Proper 6

Sunday between 12 and 18 June inclusive (if after Trinity Sunday)
Choose either 'continuous' or 'related' Old Testament and Psalm readings.

CONTINUOUS

1 Samuel 15:34 – 16:13   Samuel left for Ramah, but Saul went up to his home F
in Gibeah of Saul. Until the day Samuel died, he did not go to see Saul again, I
though Samuel mourned for him. And the LORD was grieved that he had R
made Saul king over Israel. S

The LORD said to Samuel, "How long will you mourn for Saul, since I T
have rejected him as king over Israel? Fill your horn with oil and be on
your way; I am sending you to Jesse of Bethlehem. I have chosen one of his R
sons to be king." E

But Samuel said, "How can I go? Saul will hear about it and kill A
me." D

The LORD said, "Take a heifer with you and say, 'I have come to sacrifice I
to the LORD.' Invite Jesse to the sacrifice, and I will show you what to do. N
You are to anoint for me the one I indicate." G

Samuel did what the LORD said. When he arrived at Bethlehem, the
elders of the town trembled when they met him. They asked, "Do you come
in peace?"

Samuel replied, "Yes, in peace; I have come to sacrifice to the LORD. Consecrate yourselves and come to the sacrifice with me." Then he
consecrated Jesse and his sons and invited them to the sacrifice.

When they arrived, Samuel saw Eliab and thought, "Surely the LORD's
anointed stands here before the LORD."

But the LORD said to Samuel, 'Do not consider his appearance or his
height, for I have rejected him. The LORD does not look at the things people
look at. Human beings look at the outward appearance, but the LORD looks
at the heart."

Then Jesse called Abinadab and made him pass in front of Samuel. But
Samuel said, "The LORD has not chosen this one either." Jesse then made
Shammah pass by, but Samuel said, "Nor has the LORD chosen this one."
Jesse made seven of his sons pass before Samuel, but Samuel said to him,
"The LORD has not chosen these." So he asked Jesse, "Are these all the sons
you have?" "There is still the youngest," Jesse answered, "but he is tending
the sheep."

Samuel said, "Send for him; we will not sit down until he arrives."

So he sent and had him brought in. He was ruddy, with a fine appearance
and handsome features.

Then the LORD said, "Rise and anoint him; he is the one."

So Samuel took the horn of oil and anointed him in the presence of his
brothers, and from that day on the Spirit of the LORD came upon David in
power. Samuel then went to Ramah.

and **Psalm 20**

May the LORD answer you when you are in distress;   P
    may the name of the God of Jacob protect you.   S
May he send you help from the sanctuary   A
    and grant you support from Zion.   L
May he remember all your sacrifices   M
    and accept your burnt offerings.

May he give you the desire of your heart
    and make all your plans succeed.
We will shout for joy when you are victorious
    and will lift up our banners in the name of our God.
May the LORD grant all your requests.

Now I know that the LORD saves his anointed;
    he answers him from his holy heaven
    with the saving power of his right hand.
Some trust in chariots and some in horses,
    but we trust in the name of the LORD our God.
They are brought to their knees and fall,
    but we rise up and stand firm.

O LORD, save the king!
    Answer us when we call!

Or RELATED

Ezekiel 17:22–24 "This is what the Sovereign LORD says: I myself will take a F R
shoot from the very top of a cedar and plant it; I will break off a tender I E
sprig from its topmost shoots and plant it on a high and lofty mountain. On R A
the mountain heights of Israel I will plant it; it will produce branches and S D
bear fruit and become a splendid cedar. Birds of every kind will nest in it; T I
they will find shelter in the shade of its branches. All the trees of the field N
will know that I the LORD bring down the tall tree and make the low tree G
grow tall. I dry up the green tree and make the dry tree flourish.
  "I the LORD have spoken, and I will do it."

and **Psalm 92:1–4,** It is good to praise the LORD   P
12–15*   and make music to your name, O Most High,   S
to proclaim your love in the morning   A
    and your faithfulness at night,   L
to the music of the ten-stringed lyre   M
    and the melody of the harp.

For you make me glad by your deeds, O LORD;
    I sing for joy at the work of your hands.

The righteous will flourish like a palm tree,
    they will grow like a cedar of Lebanon;
planted in the house of the LORD,
    they will flourish in the courts of our God.
They will still bear fruit in old age,
    they will stay fresh and green,

proclaiming, "The LORD is upright;
he is my Rock, and there is no wickedness in him."

2 Corinthians 5:6–10 [11–13] 14–17   We are always confident and know that as S long as we are at home in the body we are away from the Lord. We live by faith, not by sight. We are confident, I say, and would prefer to be away from the body and at home with the Lord. So we make it our goal to please him, whether we are at home in the body or away from it. For we must all appear before the judgment seat of Christ, that each one may receive what is due to him for the things done while in the body, whether good or bad.

[Since, then, we know what it is to fear the LORD, we try to persuade men. What we are is plain to God, and I hope it is also plain to your conscience. We are not trying to commend ourselves to you again, but are giving you an opportunity to take pride in us, so that you can answer those who take pride in what is seen rather than in what is in the heart. If we are out of our mind, it is for the sake of God; if we are in our right mind, it is for you.] For Christ's love compels us, because we are convinced that one died for all, and therefore all died. And he died for all, that those who live should no longer live for themselves but for him who died for them and was raised again.

So from now on we regard no-one from a worldly point of view. Though we once regarded Christ in this way, we do so no longer. Therefore, if anyone is in Christ, he is a new creation; the old has gone, the new has come!

Mark 4:26–34   Jesus said, "This is what the kingdom of God is like. A man scatters seed on the ground. Night and day, whether he sleeps or gets up, the seed sprouts and grows, though he does not know how. All by itself the soil produces corn – first the stalk, then the ear, then the full grain in the ear. As soon as the grain is ripe, he puts the sickle to it, because the harvest has come."

Again he said, "What shall we say the kingdom of God is like, or what parable shall we use to describe it? It is like a mustard seed, which is the smallest seed you plant in the ground. Yet when planted, it grows and becomes the largest of all garden plants, with such big branches that the birds of the air can perch in its shade."

With many similar parables Jesus spoke the word to them, as much as they could understand. He did not say anything to them without using a parable. But when he was alone with his own disciples, he explained everything.

Proper 7

Sunday between 19 and 25 June inclusive (if after Trinity Sunday)
Choose either 'continuous' or 'related' Old Testament and Psalm readings.

CONTINUOUS

1 Samuel 17:[1a, 4–11, 17, 19–23] 32–49   [The Philistines gathered their forces for war and assembled at Socoh in Judah.

A champion named Goliath, who was from Gath, came out of the Philistine camp. He was over nine feet tall. He had a bronze helmet on his head and wore a coat of scale armour of bronze weighing five thousand shekels; on his legs he wore bronze greaves, and a bronze javelin was slung on his back. His spear shaft was like a weaver's rod, and its iron point weighed six hundred shekels. His shield-bearer went ahead of him.

Goliath stood and shouted to the ranks of Israel, "Why do you come out and line up for battle? Am I not a Philistine, and are you not the servants of Saul? Choose a man and have him come down to me. If he is able to fight and kill me, we will become your subjects; but if I overcome him and kill him, you will become our subjects and serve us." Then the Philistine said, "This day I defy the ranks of Israel! Give me a man and let us fight each other." On hearing the Philistine's words, Saul and all the Israelites were dismayed and terrified.

Now Jesse said to his son David, "Take this ephah of roasted grain and these ten loaves of bread for your brothers and hurry to the camp. "They are with Saul and all the men of Israel in the Valley of Elah, fighting against the Philistines."

Early in the morning David left the flock with a shepherd, loaded up and set out, as Jesse had directed. He reached the camp as the army was going out to its battle positions, shouting the war cry. Israel and the Philistines were drawing up their lines facing each other. David left his things with the keeper of supplies, ran to the battle lines and greeted his brothers. As he was talking with them, Goliath, the Philistine champion from Gath, stepped out from his lines and shouted his usual defiance, and David heard it.]

David said to Saul, "Let no-one lose heart on account of this Philistine; your servant will go and fight him."

Saul replied, "You are not able to go out against this Philistine and fight him; you are only a boy, and he has been a fighting man from his youth."

But David said to Saul, "Your servant has been keeping his father's sheep. When a lion or a bear came and carried off a sheep from the flock, I went after it, struck it and rescued the sheep from its mouth. When it turned on me, I seized it by its hair, struck it and killed it. Your servant has killed both the lion and the bear; this uncircumcised Philistine will be like one of them, because he has defied the armies of the living God. The LORD who delivered me from the paw of the lion and the paw of the bear will deliver me from the hand of this Philistine."

Saul said to David, "Go, and the LORD be with you."

Then Saul dressed David in his own tunic. He put a coat of armour on him and a bronze helmet on his head. David fastened on his sword over the tunic and tried walking around, because he was not used to them.

"I cannot go in these," he said to Saul, "because I am not used to them." So he took them off. Then he took his staff in his hand, chose five smooth stones from the stream, put them in the pouch of his shepherd's bag and, with his sling in his hand, approached the Philistine.

Meanwhile, the Philistine, with his shield-bearer in front of him, kept coming closer to David. He looked David over and saw that he was only a boy, ruddy and handsome, and he despised him. He said to David, "Am I a dog, that you come at me with sticks?" And the Philistine cursed David by his gods. "Come here," he said, "and I'll give your flesh to the birds of the air and the beasts of the field!"

David said to the Philistine, "You come against me with sword and spear and javelin, but I come against you in the name of the LORD Almighty, the God of the armies of Israel, whom you have defied. This day the LORD will hand you over to me, and I'll strike you down and cut off your head. Today I will give the carcasses of the Philistine army to the birds of the air and the beasts of the earth, and the whole world will know that there is a God in Israel. All those gathered here will know that it is not by sword or spear that the LORD saves; for the battle is the LORD's, and he will give all of you into our hands."

As the Philistine moved closer to attack him, David ran quickly towards the battle line to meet him. Reaching into his bag and taking out a stone, he slung it and struck the Philistine on the forehead. The stone sank into his forehead, and he fell face down on the ground.

and **Psalm 9:9–20** The LORD is a refuge for the oppressed,
a stronghold in times of trouble.
Those who know your name will trust in you,
for you, LORD, have never forsaken those who seek you.

Sing praises to the LORD, enthroned in Zion;
proclaim among the nations what he has done.
For he who avenges blood remembers;
he does not ignore the cry of the afflicted.

O LORD, see how my enemies persecute me!
Have mercy and lift me up from the gates of death,
that I may declare your praises
in the gates of the Daughter of Zion
and there rejoice in your salvation.
The nations have fallen into the pit they have dug;
their feet are caught in the net they have hidden.
The LORD is known by his justice;
the wicked are ensnared by the work of their hands.

The wicked return to the grave,
all the nations that forget God.
But the needy will not always be forgotten,
nor the hope of the afflicted ever perish.

Arise, O LORD, let not mortals triumph;
let the nations be judged in your presence.
Strike them with terror, O LORD;
let the nations know they are but men.

Or **CONTINUOUS**

1 Samuel 17:57 – 18:5, 10–16 As soon as David returned from killing the Philistine, Abner took him and brought him before Saul, with David still holding the Philistine's head.

"Whose son are you, young man?" Saul asked him.

David said, "I am the son of your servant Jesse of Bethlehem."

After David had finished talking with Saul, Jonathan became one in spirit with David, and he loved him as himself. From that day Saul kept David with him and did not let him return to his father's house. And Jonathan made a covenant with David because he loved him as himself. Jonathan took off the robe he was wearing and gave it to David, along with his tunic, and even his sword, his bow and his belt.

Whatever Saul sent him to do, David did it so successfully that Saul gave him a high rank in the army. This pleased all the people, and Saul's officers as well.

The next day an evil spirit from God came forcefully upon Saul. He was prophesying in his house, while David was playing the harp, as he usually did. Saul had a spear in his hand and he hurled it, saying to himself, "I'll pin David to the wall." But David eluded him twice.

Saul was afraid of David, because the LORD was with David but had left Saul. So he sent David away from him and gave him command over a thousand men, and David led the troops in their campaigns. In everything he did he had great success, because the LORD was with him. When Saul saw how successful he was, he was afraid of him. But all Israel and Judah loved David, because he led them in their campaigns.

and **Psalm 133**

How good and pleasant it is
 when brothers live together in unity!
It is like precious oil poured on the head,
 running down on the beard,
running down on Aaron's beard,
 down upon the collar of his robes.
It is as if the dew of Hermon
 were falling on Mount Zion.
For there the LORD bestows his blessing,
 even life for evermore.

P S A L M

Or **RELATED**

Job 38:1–11

The LORD answered Job out of the storm. He said:

"Who is this that darkens my counsel
 with words without knowledge?
Brace yourself like a man;
 I will question you,
 and you shall answer me.

"Where were you when I laid the earth's foundation?
 Tell me, if you understand.
Who marked off its dimensions? Surely you know!
 Who stretched a measuring line across it?
On what were its footings set,
 or who laid its cornerstone –

F I R S T   R E A D I N G

while the morning stars sang together
and all the angels shouted for joy?

"Who shut up the sea behind doors
when it burst forth from the womb,
when I made the clouds its garment
and wrapped it in thick darkness,
when I fixed limits for it
and set its doors and bars in place,
when I said, 'This far you may come and no farther;
here is where your proud waves halt'?"

and **Psalm 107:1–3, 23–32***

P
S
A
L
M

Give thanks to the LORD, for he is good;
his love endures for ever.
Let the redeemed of the LORD say this –
those he redeemed from the hand of the foe,
those he gathered from the lands,
from east and west, from north and south.

Others went out on the sea in ships;
they were merchants on the mighty waters.
They saw the works of the LORD,
his wonderful deeds in the deep.
For he spoke and stirred up a tempest
that lifted high the waves.
They mounted up to the heavens and went down
to the depths;
in their peril their courage melted away.
They reeled and staggered like drunken men;
they were at their wits' end.
Then they cried out to the LORD in their trouble,
and he brought them out of their distress.
He stilled the storm to a whisper;
the waves of the sea were hushed.
They were glad when it grew calm,
and he guided them to their desired haven.
Let them give thanks to the LORD for his unfailing love
and his wonderful deeds for men.
Let them exalt him in the assembly of the people
and praise him in the council of the elders.

2 Corinthians 6:1–13   As God's fellow-workers we urge you not to receive
God's grace in vain. For he says,

S R
E E
C A
O D
N I
D N
G

"In the time of my favour I heard you,
and in the day of salvation I helped you."

I tell you, now is the time of God's favour, now is the day of salvation.
We put no stumbling-block in anyone's path, so that our ministry will not
be discredited. Rather, as servants of God we commend ourselves in every

way: in great endurance; in troubles, hardships and distresses; in beatings, imprisonments and riots; in hard work, sleepless nights and hunger; in purity, understanding, patience and kindness; in the Holy Spirit and in sincere love; in truthful speech and in the power of God; with weapons of righteousness in the right hand and in the left; through glory and dishonour, bad report and good report; genuine, yet regarded as impostors; known, yet regarded as unknown; dying, and yet we live on; beaten, and yet not killed; sorrowful, yet always rejoicing; poor, yet making many rich; having nothing, and yet possessing everything.

We have spoken freely to you, Corinthians, and opened wide our hearts to you. We are not withholding our affection from you, but you are withholding yours from us. As a fair exchange – I speak as to my children – open wide your hearts also.

Mark 4:35-41 When evening came, Jesus said to his disciples, "Let us go over to the other side." Leaving the crowd behind, they took him along, just as he was, in the boat. There were also other boats with him. A furious squall came up, and the waves broke over the boat, so that it was nearly swamped. Jesus was in the stern, sleeping on a cushion. The disciples woke him and said to him, "Teacher, don't you care if we drown?"

He got up, rebuked the wind and said to the waves, "Quiet! Be still!" Then the wind died down and it was completely calm.

He said to his disciples, "Why are you so afraid? Do you still have no faith?"

They were terrified and asked each other, "Who is this? Even the wind and the waves obey him!"

G O S P E L

Proper 8

Sunday between 26 June and 2 July inclusive (if after Trinity Sunday)
Choose either 'continuous' or 'related' Old Testament and Psalm readings.

2 Samuel 1:1, 17–27 After the death of Saul, David returned from defeating the Amalekites and stayed in Ziklag two days.

David took up this lament concerning Saul and his son Jonathan, and ordered that the men of Judah be taught this lament of the bow (it is written in the Book of Jashar):

"Your glory, O Israel, lies slain on your heights.
 How the mighty have fallen!

"Tell it not in Gath,
 proclaim it not in the streets of Ashkelon,
lest the daughters of the Philistines be glad,
 lest the daughters of the uncircumcised rejoice.

"O mountains of Gilboa,
 may you have neither dew nor rain,
 nor fields that yield offerings of grain.
For there the shield of the mighty was defiled,
 the shield of Saul – no longer rubbed with oil.

F I R S T R E A D I N G

From the blood of the slain,
   from the flesh of the mighty,
the bow of Jonathan did not turn back,
   the sword of Saul did not return unsatisfied.

"Saul and Jonathan –
   in life they were loved and gracious,
   and in death they were not parted.
They were swifter than eagles,
   they were stronger than lions.

"O daughters of Israel,
   weep for Saul,
who clothed you in scarlet and finery,
   who adorned your garments with ornaments of gold.

"How the mighty have fallen in battle!
   Jonathan lies slain on your heights.
I grieve for you, Jonathan my brother;
   you were very dear to me.
Your love for me was wonderful,
   more wonderful than that of women.

"How the mighty have fallen!
   The weapons of war have perished!"

Psalm 130   Out of the depths I cry to you, O LORD;
   O LORD, hear my voice.
Let your ears be attentive
   to my cry for mercy.

If you, O LORD, kept a record of sins,
   O LORD, who could stand?
But with you there is forgiveness;
   therefore you are feared.

I wait for the LORD, my soul waits,
   and in his word I put my hope.
My soul waits for the LORD
   more than watchmen wait for the morning,
   more than watchmen wait for the morning.

O Israel, put your hope in the LORD,
   for with the LORD is unfailing love
   and with him is full redemption.
He himself will redeem Israel
   from all their sins.

Or **RELATED**

Wisdom of Solomon 1:13–15; 2:23–24

(Which may be replaced by Lamentations 3:23–33 as the first reading)

and choice of Canticle or Psalm:

Either Lamentations 3:23–33

The LORD's compassions are new every morning;
  great is your faithfulness.
I say to myself, "The LORD is my portion;
  therefore I will wait for him."

The LORD is good to those whose hope is in him;
  to the one who seeks him;
it is good to wait quietly
  for the salvation of the LORD.
It is good for a man to bear the yoke
  while he is young.

Let him sit alone in silence,
  for the LORD has laid it on him.
Let him bury his face in the dust –
  there may yet be hope.
Let him offer his cheek to one who would strike him,
  and let him be filled with disgrace.

For people are not cast off
  by the Lord for ever.
Though he brings grief, he will show compassion,
  so great is his unfailing love.
For he does not willingly bring affliction
  or grief to the children of men.

C A N T I C L E

or Psalm 30

I will exalt you, O LORD,
  for you lifted me out of the depths
  and did not let my enemies gloat over me.
O LORD my God, I called to you for help
  and you healed me.
O LORD, you brought me up from the grave;
  you spared me from going down into the pit.

Sing to the LORD, you saints of his;
  praise his holy name.
For his anger lasts only a moment,
  but his favour lasts a lifetime;
weeping may remain for a night,
  but rejoicing comes in the morning.

When I felt secure, I said,
  "I shall never be shaken."
O LORD, when you favoured me,
  you made my mountain stand firm;
but when you hid your face,
  I was dismayed.

To you, O LORD, I called;
  to the LORD I cried for mercy:

P S A L M

"What gain is there in my destruction,
  in my going down into the pit?
Will the dust praise you?
  Will it proclaim your faithfulness?
Hear, O LORD, and be merciful to me;
  O LORD, be my help."

You turned my wailing into dancing;
  you removed my sackcloth and clothed me with joy,
that my heart may sing to you and not be silent.
  O LORD my God, I will give you thanks for ever.

2 Corinthians 8:7–15   Just as you excel in everything – in faith, in speech, in
knowledge, in complete earnestness and in your love for us – see that you
also excel in this grace of giving.

I am not commanding you, but I want to test the sincerity of your love by
comparing it with the earnestness of others. For you know the grace of our
Lord Jesus Christ, that though he was rich, yet for your sakes he became
poor, so that you through his poverty might become rich.

And here is my advice about what is best for you in this matter: Last
year you were the first not only to give but also to have the desire to do so.
Now finish the work, so that your eager willingness to do it may be matched
by your completion of it, according to your means. For if the willingness is
there, the gift is acceptable according to what one has, not according to
what he does not have.

Our desire is not that others might be relieved while you are hard
pressed, but that there might be equality. At the present time your plenty
will supply what they need, so that in turn their plenty will supply what
you need. Then there will be equality, as it is written: "He who gathered
much did not have too much, and he who gathered little did not have too
little."

Mark 5:21–43   When Jesus had crossed over by boat to the other side of the
lake, a large crowd gathered round him while he was by the lake. Then one
of the synagogue rulers, named Jairus, came there. Seeing Jesus, he fell at
his feet and pleaded earnestly with him, "My little daughter is dying.
Please come and put your hands on her so that she will be healed and live."
So Jesus went with him.

A large crowd followed and pressed around him. And a woman was
there who had been subject to bleeding for twelve years. She had suffered
a great deal under the care of many doctors and had spent all she had, yet
instead of getting better she grew worse. When she heard about Jesus, she
came up behind him in the crowd and touched his cloak, because she
thought, "If I just touch his clothes, I will be healed." Immediately
her bleeding stopped and she felt in her body that she was freed from her
suffering.

At once Jesus realised that power had gone out from him. He turned around in the crowd and asked, "Who touched my clothes?"

"You see the people crowding against you," his disciples answered, "and yet you can ask, 'Who touched me?'"

But Jesus kept looking around to see who had done it. Then the woman, knowing what had happened to her, came and fell at his feet and, trembling with fear, told him the whole truth. He said to her, "Daughter, your faith has healed you. Go in peace and be freed from your suffering."

While Jesus was still speaking, some men came from the house of Jairus, the synagogue ruler. "Your daughter is dead," they said. "Why bother the teacher any more?"

Ignoring what they said, Jesus told the synagogue ruler, "Don't be afraid; just believe."

He did not let anyone follow him except Peter, James and John the brother of James. When they came to the home of the synagogue ruler, Jesus saw a commotion, with people crying and wailing loudly. He went in and said to them, "Why all this commotion and wailing? The child is not dead but asleep." But they laughed at him.

After he put them all out, he took the child's father and mother and the disciples who were with him, and went in where the child was. He took her by the hand and said to her, *"Talitha koum!"* (which means, "Little girl, I say to you, get up!"). Immediately the girl stood up and walked around (she was twelve years old). At this they were completely astonished. He gave strict orders not to let anyone know about this, and told them to give her something to eat.

Proper 9

Sunday between 3 and 9 July inclusive (if after Trinity Sunday)
Choose either 'continuous' or 'related' Old Testament and Psalm readings.

CONTINUOUS

2 Samuel 5:1–5, 9–10   All the tribes of Israel came to David at Hebron and said, "We are your own flesh and blood. In the past, while Saul was king over us, you were the one who led Israel on their military campaigns. And the LORD said to you, 'You shall shepherd my people Israel, and you shall become their ruler.'"

When all the elders of Israel had come to King David at Hebron, the king made a compact with them at Hebron before the LORD, and they anointed David king over Israel.

David was thirty years old when he became king, and he reigned for forty years. In Hebron he reigned over Judah for seven years and six months, and in Jerusalem he reigned over all Israel and Judah for thirty-three years.

David then took up residence in the fortress and called it the City of David. He built up the area around it, from the supporting terraces inward. And he became more and more powerful, because the LORD God Almighty was with him.

FIRST READING

and **Psalm 48**   Great is the Lord, and most worthy of praise,   P
   in the city of our God, his holy mountain.   S
  It is beautiful in its loftiness,   A
   the joy of the whole earth.   L
  Like the utmost heights of Zaphon is Mount Zion,   M
   the city of the Great King.
  God is in her citadels;
   he has shown himself to be her fortress.

  When the kings joined forces,
   when they advanced together,
  they saw her and were astounded;
   they fled in terror.
  Trembling seized them there,
   pain like that of a woman in labour.
  You destroyed them like ships of Tarshish
   shattered by an east wind.

  As we have heard,
   so have we seen
  in the city of the Lord Almighty,
   in the city of our God:
   God makes her secure for ever.

  Within your temple, O God,
   we meditate on your unfailing love.
  Like your name, O God,
   your praise reaches to the ends of the earth;
   your right hand is filled with righteousness.
  Mount Zion rejoices,
   the villages of Judah are glad
   because of your judgments.

  Walk about Zion, go round her,
   count her towers,
  consider well her ramparts,
   view her citadels,
   that you may tell of them to the next generation.
  For this God is our God for ever and ever;
   he will be our guide even to the end.

Or **RELATED**

Ezekiel 2:1–5   The Lord to me, "Son of man, stand up on your feet and I will   F R
speak to you." As he spoke, the Spirit came into me and raised me to my   I E
feet, and I heard him speaking to me.   R A
  He said: "Son of man, I am sending you to the Israelites, to a rebellious   S D
nation that has rebelled against me; they and their forefathers have been   T I
in revolt against me to this very day. The people to whom I am sending you   N
are obstinate and stubborn. Say to them, 'This is what the Sovereign Lord   G

says.' And whether they listen or fail to listen – for they are a rebellious house – they will know that a prophet has been among them."

and **Psalm 123**   I lift up my eyes to you, P
  to you whose throne is in heaven. S

As the eyes of slaves look to the hand of their master, A
  as the eyes of a maid look to the hand of L
    her mistress, M
so our eyes look to the LORD our God,
  till he shows us his mercy.

Have mercy on us, O LORD, have mercy on us,
  for we have endured much contempt.
We have endured much ridicule from the proud,
  much contempt from the arrogant.

2 Corinthians 12:2–10   I know a man in Christ who fourteen years ago was S caught up to the third heaven. Whether it was in the body or out of the E body I do not know – God knows. And I know that this man – whether in the C body or apart from the body I do not know, but God knows – was caught O up to paradise. He heard inexpressible things, things that man is not N permitted to tell. I will boast about a man like that, but I will not boast D about myself, except about my weaknesses. Even if I should choose to boast, I would not be a fool, because I would be speaking the truth. But I R refrain, so no-one will think more of me than is warranted by what I do E or say. A

To keep me from becoming conceited because of these surpassingly D great revelations, there was given me a thorn in my flesh, a messenger of I Satan, to torment me. Three times I pleaded with the LORD to take it away N from me. But he said to me, "My grace is sufficient for you, for my power G is made perfect in weakness." Therefore I will boast all the more gladly about my weaknesses, so that Christ's power may rest on me. That is why, for Christ's sake, I delight in weaknesses, in insults, in hardships, in persecutions, in difficulties. For when I am weak, then I am strong.

Mark 6:1–13   Jesus went to his home town, accompanied by his disciples. G When the Sabbath came, he began to teach in the synagogue, and many who O heard him were amazed. S

"Where did this man get these things?" they asked. "What's this wis- P dom that has been given him, that he even does miracles! Isn't this the E carpenter? Isn't this Mary's son and the brother of James, Joseph, Judas L and Simon? Aren't his sisters here with us?" And they took offence at him.

Jesus said to them, "Only in his home town, among his relatives and in his own house is a prophet without honour." He could not do any miracles there, except lay his hands on a few sick people and heal them. And he was amazed at their lack of faith.

Then Jesus went round teaching from village to village. Calling the Twelve to him, he sent them out two by two and gave them authority over evil spirits.

These were his instructions: "Take nothing for the journey except a staff – no bread, no bag, no money in your belts. Wear sandals but not an extra tunic. Whenever you enter a house, stay there until you leave that town. And if any place will not welcome you or listen to you, shake the dust off your feet when you leave, as a testimony against them."

They went out and preached that people should repent. They drove out many demons and anointed many sick people with oil and healed them.

Proper 10

Sunday between 10 and 16 July inclusive (if after Trinity Sunday)
Choose either 'continuous' or 'related' Old Testament and Psalm readings.

CONTINUOUS

2 Samuel 6:1–5, 12b–19   David brought together out of Israel chosen men, thirty thousand in all. He and all his men set out from Baalah of Judah to bring up from there the ark of God, which is called by the Name, the name of the LORD Almighty, who is enthroned between the cherubim that are on the ark. They set the ark of God on a new cart and brought it from the house of Abinadab, which was on the hill. Uzzah and Ahio, sons of Abinadab, were guiding the new cart with the ark of God on it, and Ahio was walking in front of it. David and the whole house of Israel were celebrating with all their might before the LORD, with songs and with harps, lyres, tambourines, sistrums and cymbals.

So David went down and brought up the ark of God from the house of Obed-Edom to the City of David with rejoicing. When those who were carrying the ark of the LORD had taken six steps, he sacrificed a bull and a fattened calf. David, wearing a linen ephod, danced before the LORD with all his might, while he and the entire house of Israel brought up the ark of the LORD with shouts and the sound of trumpets.

As the ark of the LORD was entering the City of David, Michal daughter of Saul watched from a window. And when she saw King David leaping and dancing before the LORD, she despised him in her heart.

They brought the ark of the LORD and set it in its place inside the tent that David had pitched for it, and David sacrificed burnt offerings and fellowship offerings before the LORD. After he had finished sacrificing the burnt offerings and fellowship offerings, he blessed the people in the name of the LORD Almighty. Then he gave a loaf of bread, a cake of dates and a cake of raisins to each person in the whole crowd of Israelites, both men and women. And all the people went to their homes.

and **Psalm 24**   The earth is the LORD's, and everything in it,
　　　　　　　　the world, and all who live in it;
　　　　　　　for he founded it upon the seas
　　　　　　　　and established it upon the waters.

Who may ascend the hill of the LORD?
  Who may stand in his holy place?
He who has clean hands and a pure heart,
  who does not lift up his soul to an idol
  or swear by what is false.
He will receive blessing from the LORD
  and vindication from God his Saviour.
Such is the generation of those who seek him,
  who seek your face, O God of Jacob.

Lift up your heads, O you gates;
  be lifted up, you ancient doors,
  that the King of glory may come in.
Who is this King of glory?
  The LORD strong and mighty,
  the LORD mighty in battle.
Lift up your heads, O you gates;
  lift them up, you ancient doors,
  that the King of glory may come in.
Who is he, this King of glory?
  The LORD Almighty –
  he is the King of glory.

Or RELATED

Amos 7:7–15 This is what the Sovereign LORD showed me: the LORD was
standing by a wall that had been built true to plumb, with a plumb-line in
his hand. And the LORD asked me, "What do you see, Amos?"

"A plumb-line," I replied.

Then the LORD said, "Look, I am setting a plumb-line among my people
Israel; I will spare them no longer.

"The high places of Isaac will be destroyed
  and the sanctuaries of Israel will be ruined;
  with my sword I will rise against the house of Jeroboam."

Then Amaziah the priest of Bethel sent a message to Jeroboam king of
Israel: "Amos is raising a conspiracy against you in the very heart of
Israel. The land cannot bear all his words. For this is what Amos is saying:

"'Jeroboam will die by the sword,
  and Israel will surely go into exile,
  away from their native land.'"

Then Amaziah said to Amos, "Get out, you seer! Go back to the land of
Judah. Earn your bread there and do your prophesying there. Don't prophesy any more at Bethel, because this is the king's sanctuary and the temple
of the kingdom."

Amos answered Amaziah, "I was neither a prophet nor a prophet's son,
but I was a shepherd, and I also took care of sycamore-fig trees. But the
LORD took me from tending the flock and said to me, 'Go, prophesy to my
people Israel.'"

and **Psalm 85:8–13**   I will listen to what God the LORD will say; P
he promises peace to his people, his saints – S
but let them not return to folly. A
Surely his salvation is near those who fear him, L
that his glory may dwell in our land. M

Love and faithfulness meet together;
righteousness and peace kiss each other.
Faithfulness springs forth from the earth,
and righteousness looks down from heaven.
The LORD will indeed give what is good,
and our land will yield its harvest.
Righteousness goes before him
and prepares the way for his steps.

Ephesians 1:3–14   Praise be to the God and Father of our Lord Jesus Christ, S
who has blessed us in the heavenly realms with every spiritual blessing in E
Christ. For he chose us in him before the creation of the world to be holy C
and blameless in his sight. In love he predestined us to be adopted as his O
sons through Jesus Christ, in accordance with his pleasure and will – to the N
praise of his glorious grace, which he has freely given us in the One he D
loves. In him we have redemption through his blood, the forgiveness of
sins, in accordance with the riches of God's grace that he lavished on us R
with all wisdom and understanding. And he made known to us the mystery E
of his will according to his good pleasure, which he purposed in Christ, to A
be put into effect when the times will have reached their fulfilment – to D
bring all things in heaven and on earth together under one head, even I
Christ. N

In him we were also chosen, having been predestined according to the G
plan of him who works out everything in conformity with the purpose of
his will, in order that we, who were the first to hope in Christ, might be for
the praise of his glory. And you also were included in Christ when you
heard the word of truth, the gospel of your salvation. Having believed, you
were marked in him with a seal, the promised Holy Spirit, who is a deposit
guaranteeing our inheritance until the redemption of those who are God's
possession – to the praise of his glory.

Mark 6:14–29   King Herod heard about Jesus, for Jesus' name had become G
well known. Some were saying, "John the Baptist has been raised from the O
dead, and that is why miraculous powers are at work in him." S

Others said, "He is Elijah." P

And still others claimed, "He is a prophet, like one of the prophets of E
long ago." L

But when Herod heard this, he said, "John, whom I beheaded, has been
raised from the dead!"

For Herod himself had given orders to have John arrested, and he had
him bound and put in prison. He did this because of Herodias, his brother

Philip's wife, whom he had married. For John had been saying to Herod, "It is not lawful for you to have your brother's wife." So Herodias nursed a grudge against John and wanted to kill him. But she was not able to, because Herod feared John and protected him, knowing him to be a righteous and holy man. When Herod heard John, he was greatly puzzled; yet he liked to listen to him.

Finally the opportune time came. On his birthday Herod gave a banquet for his high officials and military commanders and the leading men of Galilee. When the daughter of Herodias came in and danced, she pleased Herod and his dinner guests.

The king said to the girl, "Ask me for anything you want, and I'll give it to you." And he promised her with an oath, "Whatever you ask I will give you, up to half my kingdom."

She went out and said to her mother, "What shall I ask for?"

"The head of John the Baptist," she answered.

At once the girl hurried in to the king with the request: "I want you to give me right now the head of John the Baptist on a platter."

The king was greatly distressed, but because of his oaths and his dinner guests, he did not want to refuse her. So he immediately sent an executioner with orders to bring John's head. The man went, beheaded John in the prison, and brought back his head on a platter. He presented it to the girl, and she gave it to her mother. On hearing of this, John's disciples came and took his body and laid it in a tomb.

Proper 11

Sunday between 17 and 23 July inclusive (if after Trinity Sunday)
Choose either 'continuous' or 'related' Old Testament and Psalm readings.

CONTINUOUS

2 Samuel 7:1–14a   After King David was settled in his palace and the LORD had given him rest from all his enemies around him, he said to Nathan the prophet, "Here I am, living in a palace of cedar, while the ark of God remains in a tent."

Nathan replied to the king, "Whatever you have in mind, go ahead and do it, for the LORD is with you."

That night the word of the LORD came to Nathan, saying:

"Go and tell my servant David, 'This is what the LORD says: Are you the one to build me a house to dwell in? I have not dwelt in a house from the day I brought the Israelites up out of Egypt to this day. I have been moving from place to place with a tent as my dwelling. Wherever I have moved with all the Israelites, did I ever say to any of their rulers whom I commanded to shepherd my people Israel, "Why have you not built me a house of cedar?"'

"Now then, tell my servant David, 'This is what the LORD Almighty says: I took you from the pasture and from following the flock to be ruler over my people Israel. I have been with you wherever you have gone, and I have cut off all your enemies from before you. Now I will make your name great, like the names of the greatest men of the earth. And I will provide a place for my people Israel and will plant them so that they can have a home of their own and no longer be disturbed. Wicked people shall not oppress them any more, as they did at the beginning and have done ever since the time I appointed leaders over my people Israel. I will also give you rest from all your enemies.

"'The LORD declares to you that the LORD himself will establish a house for you: When your days are over and you rest with your fathers, I will raise up your offspring to succeed you, who will come from your own body, and I will establish his kingdom. He is the one who will build a house for my Name, and I will establish the throne of his kingdom for ever. I will be his father, and he shall be my son.'"

and **Psalm 89:20–37**
> I have found David my servant;
>> with my sacred oil I have anointed him.
> My hand will sustain him;
>> surely my arm will strengthen him.
> No enemy will subject him to tribute;
>> no wicked person will oppress him.
> I will crush his foes before him
>> and strike down his adversaries.
> My faithful love will be with him,
>> and through my name his horn will be exalted.
> I will set his hand over the sea,
>> his right hand over the rivers.
> He will call out to me, 'You are my Father,
>> my God, the Rock my Saviour.'
> I will also appoint him my firstborn,
>> the most exalted of the kings of the earth.
> I will maintain my love to him for ever,
>> and my covenant with him will never fail.
> I will establish his line for ever,
>> his throne as long as the heavens endure.
>
> "If his sons forsake my law
>> and do not follow my statutes,
> if they violate my decrees
>> and fail to keep my commands,
> I will punish their sin with the rod,
>> their iniquity with flogging;
> but I will not take my love from him,
>> nor will I ever betray my faithfulness.
> I will not violate my covenant
>> or alter what my lips have uttered.
> Once for all, I have sworn by my holiness –
>> and I will not lie to David –
> that his line will continue for ever
>> and his throne endure before me like the sun;

> it will be established for ever like the moon,
>> the faithful witness in the sky."

Or **RELATED**

Jeremiah 23:1–6 "Woe to the shepherds who are destroying and scattering the sheep of my pasture!" declares the LORD. Therefore this is what the LORD, the God of Israel, says to the shepherds who tend my people: "Because you have scattered my flock and driven them away and have not bestowed care on them, I will bestow punishment on you for the evil you have done," declares the LORD. "I myself will gather the remnant of my flock out of all the countries where I have driven them and will bring them back to their pasture, where they will be fruitful and increase in number. I will place shepherds over them who will tend them, and they will no longer be afraid or terrified, nor will any be missing," declares the LORD.

> "The days are coming," declares the LORD,
>> "when I will raise up to David a righteous Branch,
> a King who will reign wisely
>> and do what is just and right in the land.
> In his days Judah will be saved
>> and Israel will live in safety.
> This is the name by which he will be called:
>> The LORD Our Righteousness."

and Psalm 23 The LORD is my shepherd, I shall not be in want.
>> He makes me lie down in green pastures,
> he leads me beside quiet waters,
>> he restores my soul.
> He guides me in paths of righteousness
>> for his name's sake.
> Even though I walk
>> through the valley of the shadow of death,
> I will fear no evil,
>> for you are with me;
> your rod and your staff,
>> they comfort me.

> You prepare a table before me
>> in the presence of my enemies.
> You anoint my head with oil;
>> my cup overflows.
> Surely goodness and love will follow me
>> all the days of my life,
> and I will dwell in the house of the LORD
>> for ever.

Ephesians 2:11–22 Remember that formerly you who are Gentiles by birth and called "uncircumcised" by those who call themselves "the circumcision" (that done in the body by the hands of men) – remember that at that time you were separate from Christ, excluded from citizenship in Israel and foreigners to the covenants of the promise, without hope and without God in the world. But now in Christ Jesus you who once were far away have been brought near through the blood of Christ.

For he himself is our peace, who has made the two one and has destroyed the barrier, the dividing wall of hostility, by abolishing in his flesh the law with its commandments and regulations. His purpose was to create in himself one new man out of the two, thus making peace, and in this one body to reconcile both of them to God through the cross, by which he put to death their hostility. He came and preached peace to you who were far away and peace to those who were near. For through him we both have access to the Father by one Spirit.

Consequently, you are no longer foreigners and aliens, but fellow-citizens with God's people and members of God's household, built on the foundation of the apostles and prophets, with Christ Jesus himself as the chief cornerstone. In him the whole building is joined together and rises to become a holy temple in the Lord. And in him you too are being built together to become a dwelling in which God lives by his Spirit.

Mark 6:30–34, 53–56 The apostles gathered round Jesus and reported to him all they had done and taught. Then, because so many people were coming and going that they did not even have a chance to eat, he said to them, "Come with me by yourselves to a quiet place and get some rest."

So they went away by themselves in a boat to a solitary place. But many who saw them leaving recognised them and ran on foot from all the towns and got there ahead of them. When Jesus landed and saw a large crowd, he had compassion on them, because they were like sheep without a shepherd. So he began teaching them many things.

Later, when Jesus and his disciples had crossed over the lake again, they landed at Gennesaret and anchored there. As soon as they got out of the boat, people recognised Jesus. They ran throughout that whole region and carried the sick on mats to wherever they heard he was. And wherever he went – into villages, towns or countryside – they placed the sick in the market-places. They begged him to let them touch even the edge of his cloak, and all who touched him were healed.

Proper 12

Sunday between 24 and 30 July inclusive (if after Trinity Sunday)
Choose either 'continuous' or 'related' Old Testament and Psalm readings.

CONTINUOUS

2 Samuel 11:1–15 In the spring, at the time when kings go off to war, David sent Joab out with the king's men and the whole Israelite army. They destroyed the Ammonites and besieged Rabbah. But David remained in Jerusalem. One evening David got up from his bed and walked around on the roof of the palace. From the roof he saw a woman bathing. The woman was very beautiful, and David sent someone to find out about her. The man said, "Isn't this Bathsheba, the daughter of Eliam and the wife of Uriah the Hittite?" Then David sent messengers to get her. She came to him, and he slept with her. (She had purified herself from her uncleanness.) Then she went back home. The woman conceived and sent word to David, saying, "I am pregnant."

So David sent this word to Joab: "Send me Uriah the Hittite." And Joab sent him to David. When Uriah came to him, David asked him how Joab was, how the soldiers were and how the war was going. Then David said to Uriah, "Go down to your house and wash your feet." So Uriah left the palace, and a gift from the king was sent after him. But Uriah slept at the entrance to the palace with all his master's servants and did not go down to his house.

When David was told, "Uriah did not go home," he asked him, "Haven't you just come from a distance? Why didn't you go home?"

Uriah said to David, "The ark and Israel and Judah are staying in tents, and my master Joab and my lord's men are camped in the open fields. How could I go to my house to eat and drink and lie with my wife? As surely as you live, I will not do such a thing!"

Then David said to him, "Stay here one more day, and tomorrow I will send you back." So Uriah remained in Jerusalem that day and the next. At David's invitation, he ate and drank with him, and David made him drunk. But in the evening Uriah went out to sleep on his mat among his master's servants; he did not go home.

In the morning David wrote a letter to Joab and sent it with Uriah. In it he wrote, "Put Uriah in the front line where the fighting is fiercest. Then withdraw from him so that he will be struck down and die."

and **Psalm 14**

P
S
A
L
M

The fool says in his heart,
    "There is no God."
They are corrupt, their deeds are vile;
    there is no-one who does good.

The LORD looks down from heaven
    on the sons of men
to see if there are any who understand,
    any who seek God.
All have turned aside,
    they have together become corrupt;
there is no-one who does good,
    not even one.

Will evildoers never learn –
    those who devour my people as if eating bread
    and who do not call on the LORD?
There they are, overwhelmed with dread,
    for God is present in the company of the righteous.
You evildoers frustrate the plans of the poor,
    but the LORD is their refuge.

Oh, that salvation for Israel would come out of Zion!
    When the LORD restores the fortunes of his people,
    let Jacob rejoice and Israel be glad!

2 Kings 4:42–44   A man came from Baal Shalishah, bringing Elisha, the man F R
of God, twenty loaves of barley bread baked from the first ripe corn, along I E
with some ears of new corn. "Give it to the people to eat," Elisha said. R A

"How can I set this before a hundred men?" his servant asked. S D

But Elisha answered, "Give it to the people to eat. For this is what the T I
Lord says: 'They will eat and have some left over.'" Then he set it before N
them, and they ate and had some left over, according to the word of the Lord. G

and **Psalm 145:**   All you have made will praise you, O Lord; P
10–18   your saints will extol you. S

They will tell of the glory of your kingdom A
    and speak of your might, L
so that all people may know of your mighty acts M
    and the glorious splendour of your kingdom.
Your kingdom is an everlasting kingdom,
    and your dominion endures through all generations.

The Lord is faithful to all his promises
    and loving towards all he has made.
The Lord upholds all those who fall
    and lifts up all who are bowed down.
The eyes of all look to you,
    and you give them their food at the proper time.
You open your hand
    and satisfy the desires of every living thing.

The Lord is righteous in all his ways
    and loving towards all he has made.
The Lord is near to all who call on him,
    to all who call on him in truth.

Ephesians 3:14–21   I kneel before the Father, from whom his whole family in S R
heaven and on earth derives its name. I pray that out of his glorious riches E E
he may strengthen you with power through his Spirit in your inner being, C A
so that Christ may dwell in your hearts through faith. And I pray that you, O D
being rooted and established in love, may have power, together with all the N I
saints, to grasp how wide and long and high and deep is the love of Christ, D N
and to know this love that surpasses knowledge – that you may be filled to G
the measure of all the fulness of God.

Now to him who is able to do immeasurably more than all we ask or
imagine, according to his power that is at work within us, to him be glory in
the church and in Christ Jesus throughout all generations, for ever and
ever! Amen.

G
O
S

John 6:1–21   Jesus crossed to the far shore of the Sea of Galilee (that is, the P
Sea of Tiberias), and a great crowd of people followed him because they E
L

saw the miraculous signs he had performed on the sick. Then Jesus went up on a mountainside and sat down with his disciples. The Jewish Passover Feast was near.

When Jesus looked up and saw a great crowd coming towards him, he said to Philip, "Where shall we buy bread for these people to eat?" He asked this only to test him, for he already had in mind what he was going to do.

Philip answered him, "Eight months' wages would not buy enough bread for each one to have a bite!"

Another of his disciples, Andrew, Simon Peter's brother, spoke up, "Here is a boy with five small barley loaves and two small fish, but how far will they go among so many?"

Jesus said, "Make the people sit down." There was plenty of grass in that place, and the men sat down, about five thousand of them. Jesus then took the loaves, gave thanks, and distributed to those who were seated as much as they wanted. He did the same with the fish.

When they had all had enough to eat, he said to his disciples, "Gather the pieces that are left over. Let nothing be wasted." So they gathered them and filled twelve baskets with the pieces of the five barley loaves left over by those who had eaten.

After the people saw the miraculous sign that Jesus did, they began to say, "Surely this is the Prophet who is to come into the world." Jesus, knowing that they intended to come and make him king by force, withdrew again to a mountain by himself.

When evening came, his disciples went down to the lake, where they got into a boat and set off across the lake for Capernaum. By now it was dark, and Jesus had not yet joined them. A strong wind was blowing and the waters grew rough. When they had rowed three or three and a half miles, they saw Jesus approaching the boat, walking on the water; and they were terrified. But he said to them, "It is I; don't be afraid." Then they were willing to take him into the boat, and immediately the boat reached the shore where they were heading.

Proper 13

Sunday between 31 July and 6 August inclusive (if after Trinity Sunday)
Choose either 'continuous' or 'related' Old Testament and Psalm readings.

CONTINUOUS

2 Samuel 11:26 – 12:13a   When Uriah's wife, Bathsheba, heard that her husband was dead, she mourned for him. After the time of mourning was over, David had her brought to his house, and she became his wife and bore him a son. But the thing David had done displeased the LORD.

The LORD sent Nathan to David. When he came to him, he said, "There were two men in a certain town, one rich and the other poor. The rich man had a very large number of sheep and cattle, but the poor man had nothing except one little ewe lamb that he had bought. He raised it, and it grew up with him and his children. It shared his food, drank from his cup and even slept in his arms. It was like a daughter to him.

"Now a traveller came to the rich man, but the rich man refrained from taking one of his own sheep or cattle to prepare a meal for the traveller who had come to him. Instead, he took the ewe lamb that belonged to the poor man and prepared it for the one who had come to him."

David burned with anger against the man and said to Nathan, "As surely as the LORD lives, the one who did this deserves to die! He must pay for that lamb four times over, because he did such a thing and had no pity."

Then Nathan said to David, "You are the man! This is what the LORD, the God of Israel, says: 'I anointed you king over Israel, and I delivered you from the hand of Saul. I gave your master's house to you, and your master's wives into your arms. I gave you the house of Israel and Judah. And if all this had been too little, I would have given you even more. Why did you despise the word of the LORD by doing what is evil in his eyes? You struck down Uriah the Hittite with the sword and took his wife to be your own. You killed him with the sword of the Ammonites. Now, therefore, the sword shall never depart from your house, because you despised me and took the wife of Uriah the Hittite to be your own.'

"This is what the LORD says: 'Out of your own household I am going to bring calamity upon you. Before your very eyes I will take your wives and give them to one who is close to you, and he will lie with your wives in broad daylight. You did it in secret, but I will do this thing in broad daylight before all Israel.'"

Then David said to Nathan, "I have sinned against the LORD."

and **Psalm 51:1–12**

Have mercy on me, O God,
    according to your unfailing love;
according to your great compassion
    blot out my transgressions.
Wash away all my iniquity
    and cleanse me from my sin.

For I know my transgressions,
    and my sin is always before me.
Against you, you only, have I sinned
    and done what is evil in your sight,
so that you are proved right when you speak
    and justified when you judge.
Surely I was sinful at birth,
    sinful from the time my mother conceived me.
Surely you desire truth in the inner parts;
    you teach me wisdom in the inmost place.

Cleanse me with hyssop, and I shall be clean;
    wash me, and I shall be whiter than snow.
Let me hear joy and gladness;
    let the bones you have crushed rejoice.
Hide your face from my sins
    and blot out all my iniquity.

PSALM

Create in me a pure heart, O God,
 and renew a steadfast spirit within me.
Do not cast me from your presence
 or take your Holy Spirit from me.
Restore to me the joy of your salvation
 and grant me a willing spirit, to sustain me.

Or **RELATED**

Exodus 16:2–4, 9–15 In the desert the whole Israelite community grumbled F against Moses and Aaron. The Israelites said to them, "If only we had died I by the LORD's hand in Egypt! There we sat round pots of meat and ate all the R food we wanted, but you have brought us out into this desert to starve this S entire assembly to death."   T

 Then the LORD said to Moses, "I will rain down bread from heaven for you. The people are to go out each day and gather enough for that day. In R this way I will test them and see whether they will follow my instructions." E

 Then Moses told Aaron, "Say to the entire Israelite community, 'Come A before the LORD, for he has heard your grumbling.'" D

 While Aaron was speaking to the whole Israelite community, they I looked towards the desert, and there was the glory of the LORD appearing N in the cloud. G

 The LORD said to Moses, "I have heard the grumbling of the Israelites. Tell them, 'At twilight you will eat meat, and in the morning you will be filled with bread. Then you will know that I am the LORD your God.'"

 That evening quail came and covered the camp, and in the morning there was a layer of dew around the camp. When the dew was gone, thin flakes like frost on the ground appeared on the desert floor. When the Israelites saw it, they said to each other, "What is it?" For they did not know what it was.

 Moses said to them, "It is the bread the LORD has given you to eat."

and **Psalm 78:23–29** The LORD gave a command to the skies above P
  and opened the doors of the heavens; S
he rained down manna for the people to eat, A
  he gave them the grain of heaven. L
Men ate the bread of angels; M
  he sent them all the food they could eat.
He let loose the east wind from the heavens
  and led forth the south wind by his power.
He rained meat down on them like dust,
  flying birds like sand on the seashore.
He made them come down inside their camp,
  all around their tents.
They ate till they had more than enough,
  for he had given them what they craved.

Ephesians 4:1–16   As a prisoner for the Lord, I urge you to live a life worthy of the calling you have received. Be completely humble and gentle; be patient, bearing with one another in love. Make every effort to keep the unity of the Spirit through the bond of peace. There is one body and one Spirit – just as you were called to one hope when you were called – one Lord, one faith, one baptism; one God and Father of all, who is over all and through all and in all.

But to each one of us grace has been given as Christ apportioned it. This is why it says:

"When he ascended on high,
  he led captives in his train
  and gave gifts to men."

(What does "he ascended" mean except that he also descended to the lower, earthly regions? He who descended is the very one who ascended higher than all the heavens, in order to fill the whole universe.) It was he who gave some to be apostles, some to be prophets, some to be evangelists, and some to be pastors and teachers, to prepare God's people for works of service, so that the body of Christ may be built up until we all reach unity in the faith and in the knowledge of the Son of God and become mature, attaining to the whole measure of the fulness of Christ.

Then we will no longer be infants, tossed back and forth by the waves, and blown here and there by every wind of teaching and by the cunning and craftiness of men in their deceitful scheming. Instead, speaking the truth in love, we will in all things grow up into him who is the Head, that is, Christ. From him the whole body, joined and held together by every supporting ligament, grows and builds itself up in love, as each part does its work.

John 6:24–35   Once the crowd realised that neither Jesus nor his disciples were at the place where the people had eaten the bread after the Lord had given thanks, they got into the boats and went to Capernaum in search of Jesus.

When they found him on the other side of the lake, they asked him, "Rabbi, when did you get here?"

Jesus answered, "I tell you the truth, you are looking for me, not because you saw miraculous signs but because you ate the loaves and had your fill. Do not work for food that spoils, but for food that endures to eternal life, which the Son of Man will give you. On him God the Father has placed his seal of approval."

Then they asked him, "What must we do to do the works God requires?"

Jesus answered, "The work of God is this: to believe in the one he has sent."

So they asked him, "What miraculous sign then will you give that we may see it and believe you? What will you do? Our forefathers ate the manna in the desert; as it is written: 'He gave them bread from heaven to eat.'"

Jesus said to them, "I tell you the truth, it is not Moses who has given you the bread from heaven, but it is my Father who gives you the true bread from heaven. For the bread of God is he who comes down from heaven and gives life to the world."

"Sir," they said, "from now on give us this bread."

Then Jesus declared, "I am the bread of life. He who comes to me will never go hungry, and he who believes in me will never be thirsty."

Proper 14

Sunday between 7 and 13 August inclusive (if after Trinity Sunday)
Choose either 'continuous' or 'related' Old Testament and Psalm readings.

CONTINUOUS

2 Samuel 18:5–9, 15, 31–33 King David commanded Joab, Abishai and Ittai, "Be gentle with the young man Absalom for my sake." And all the troops heard the king giving orders concerning Absalom to each of the commanders.

The army marched into the field to fight Israel, and the battle took place in the forest of Ephraim. There the army of Israel was defeated by David's men, and the casualties that day were great – twenty thousand men. The battle spread out over the whole countryside, and the forest claimed more lives that day than the sword.

Now Absalom happened to meet David's men. He was riding his mule, and as the mule went under the thick branches of a large oak, Absalom's head got caught in the tree. He was left hanging in mid-air, while the mule he was riding kept on going.

And ten of Joab's armour-bearers surrounded Absalom, struck him and killed him.

Then Joab said to a Cushite, "Go, tell the king what you have seen." The Cushite arrived and said, "My lord the king, hear the good news! The LORD has delivered you today from all who rose up against you."

The king asked the Cushite, "Is the young man Absalom safe?"

The Cushite replied, "May the enemies of my lord the king and all who rise up to harm you be like that young man."

The king was shaken. He went up to the room over the gateway and wept. As he went, he said: "O my son Absalom! My son, my son Absalom! If only I had died instead of you – O Absalom, my son, my son!"

and **Psalm 130** Out of the depths I cry to you, O LORD;
　　　　O LORD, hear my voice.
Let your ears be attentive
　　　　to my cry for mercy.

If you, O LORD, kept a record of sins,
　　　　O LORD, who could stand?
But with you there is forgiveness;
　　　　therefore you are feared.

I wait for the LORD, my soul waits,
　　　　and in his word I put my hope.

My soul waits for the LORD
more than watchmen wait for the morning,
more than watchmen wait for the morning.

O Israel, put your hope in the LORD,
for with the LORD is unfailing love
and with him is full redemption.
He himself will redeem Israel
from all their sins.

Or RELATED

1 Kings 19:4–8   Elijah went a day's journey into the desert. He came to a broom tree, sat down under it and prayed that he might die. "I have had enough, LORD," he said. "Take my life; I am no better than my ancestors." Then he lay down under the tree and fell asleep.

All at once an angel touched him and said, "Get up and eat." He looked around, and there by his head was a cake of bread baked over hot coals, and a jar of water. He ate and drank and then lay down again.

The angel of the LORD came back a second time and touched him and said, "Get up and eat, for the journey is too much for you." So he got up and ate and drank. Strengthened by that food, he travelled for forty days and forty nights until he reached Horeb, the mountain of God.

and **Psalm 34:1–8**   I will extol the LORD at all times;
his praise will always be on my lips.
My soul will boast in the LORD;
let the afflicted hear and rejoice.
Glorify the LORD with me:
let us exalt his name together.

I sought the LORD, and he answered me;
he delivered me from all my fears.
Those who look to him are radiant;
their faces are never covered with shame.
This poor man called, and the LORD heard him;
he saved him out of all his troubles.
The angel of the LORD encamps around those who fear
him,
and he delivers them.

Taste and see that the LORD is good;
blessed are those who take refuge in him.

Ephesians 4:25 – 5:2   Each of you must put off falsehood and speak truthfully to his neighbour, for we are all members of one body. "In your anger do not sin": Do not let the sun go down while you are still angry, and do not give the devil a foothold. He who has been stealing must steal no longer, but must work, doing something useful with his own hands, that he may have something to share with those in need.

Do not let any unwholesome talk come out of your mouths, but only what is helpful for building others up according to their needs, that it may benefit those who listen. And do not grieve the Holy Spirit of God, with whom you were sealed for the day of redemption. Get rid of all bitterness, rage and anger, brawling and slander, along with every form of malice. Be kind and compassionate to one another, forgiving each other, just as in Christ God forgave you.

Be imitators of God, therefore, as dearly loved children and live a life of love, just as Christ loved us and gave himself up for us as a fragrant offering and sacrifice to God.

John 6:35, 41–51 Jesus declared, "I am the bread of life. He who comes to me will never go hungry, and he who believes in me will never be thirsty."

At this the Jews began to grumble about him because he said, "I am the bread that came down from heaven." They said, "Is this not Jesus, the son of Joseph, whose father and mother we know? How can he now say, 'I came down from heaven'?"

"Stop grumbling among yourselves," Jesus answered. "No-one can come to me unless the Father who sent me draws him, and I will raise him up at the last day. It is written in the Prophets: 'They will all be taught by God.' Everyone who listens to the Father and learns from him comes to me. No-one has seen the Father except the one who is from God; only he has seen the Father. I tell you the truth, he who believes has everlasting life. I am the bread of life. Your forefathers ate the manna in the desert, yet they died. But here is the bread that comes down from heaven, which a man may eat and not die. I am the living bread that came down from heaven. If anyone eats of this bread, he will live for ever. This bread is my flesh, which I will give for the life of the world."

Proper 15

Sunday between 14 and 20 August inclusive (if after Trinity Sunday)
Choose either 'continuous' or 'related' Old Testament and Psalm readings.

CONTINUOUS

1 Kings 2:10–12; 3:3–14 David rested with his fathers and was buried in the City of David. He had reigned for forty years over Israel – seven years in Hebron and thirty-three in Jerusalem. So Solomon sat on the throne of his father David, and his rule was firmly established.

Solomon showed his love for the LORD by walking according to the statutes of his father David, except that he offered sacrifices and burned incense on the high places.

The king went to Gibeon to offer sacrifices, for that was the most important high place, and Solomon offered a thousand burnt offerings on that altar. At Gibeon the LORD appeared to Solomon during the night in a dream, and God said, "Ask for whatever you want me to give you."

Solomon answered, "You have shown great kindness to your servant, my father David, because he was faithful to you and righteous and upright in heart. You have continued this great kindness to him and have given him a son to sit on his throne this very day.

"Now, O LORD my God, you have made your servant king in place of my father David. But I am only a little child and do not know how to carry out my duties. Your servant is here among the people you have chosen, a great people, too numerous to count or number. So give your servant a discerning heart to govern your people and to distinguish between right and wrong. For who is able to govern this great people of yours?"

The LORD was pleased that Solomon had asked for this. So God said to him, "Since you have asked for this and not for long life or wealth for yourself, nor have asked for the death of your enemies but for discernment in administering justice, I will do what you have asked. I will give you a wise and discerning heart, so that there will never have been anyone like you, nor will there ever be. Moreover, I will give you what you have not asked for – both riches and honour – so that in your lifetime you will have no equal among kings. And if you walk in my ways and obey my statutes and commands as David your father did, I will give you a long life."

and **Psalm 111**	Praise the LORD.

I will extol the LORD with all my heart
    in the council of the upright and in the assembly.

Great are the works of the LORD;
    they are pondered by all who delight in them.
Glorious and majestic are his deeds,
    and his righteousness endures for ever.
He has caused his wonders to be remembered;
    the LORD is gracious and compassionate.
He provides food for those who fear him;
    he remembers his covenant for ever.
He has shown his people the power of his works,
    giving them the lands of other nations.
The works of his hands are faithful and just;
    all his precepts are trustworthy.
They are steadfast for ever and ever,
    done in faithfulness and uprightness.
He provided redemption for his people;
    he ordained his covenant for ever –
    holy and awesome is his name.

The fear of the LORD is the beginning of wisdom;
    all who follow his precepts have good understanding.
    To him belongs eternal praise.

Or **RELATED**

Proverbs 9:1–6   Wisdom has built her house;
    she has hewn out its seven pillars.
She has prepared her meat and mixed her wine;
    she has also set her table.

She has sent out her servants, and she calls
   from the highest point of the city.
"Let all who are simple come in here!"
   she says to those who lack judgment.
"Come, eat my food
   and drink the wine I have mixed.
Leave your simple ways and you will live;
   walk in the way of understanding."

and **Psalm 34:9–14**   Fear the Lord, you his saints,
   for those who fear him lack nothing.
The lions may grow weak and hungry,
   but those who seek the Lord lack no good thing.

Come, my children, listen to me;
   I will teach you the fear of the Lord.
Whoever among you loves life
   and desires to see many good days,
keep your tongue from evil
   and your lips from speaking lies.
Turn from evil and do good;
   seek peace and pursue it.

P S A L M

Ephesians 5:15–20   Be very careful how you live – not as unwise but as wise, making the most of every opportunity, because the days are evil. Therefore do not be foolish, but understand what the Lord's will is. Do not get drunk on wine, which leads to debauchery. Instead, be filled with the Spirit. Speak to one another with psalms, hymns and spiritual songs. Sing and make music in your heart to the Lord, always giving thanks to God the Father for everything, in the name of our Lord Jesus Christ.

R E A D I N G

John 6:51–58   Jesus said: "I am the living bread that came down from heaven. If anyone eats of this bread, he will live for ever. This bread is my flesh, which I will give for the life of the world."

Then the Jews began to argue sharply among themselves, "How can this man give us his flesh to eat?"

Jesus said to them, "I tell you the truth, unless you can eat the flesh of the Son of Man and drink his blood, you have no life in you. Whoever eats my flesh and drinks my blood has eternal life, and I will raise him up at the last day. For my flesh is real food and my blood is real drink. Whoever eats my flesh and drinks my blood remains in me, and I in him. Just as the living Father sent me and I live because of the Father, so the one who feeds on me will live because of me. This is the bread that came down from heaven. Your forefathers ate manna and died, but he who feeds on this bread will live for ever."

G O S P E L

Proper 16

Sunday between 21 and 27 August inclusive (if after Trinity Sunday)
Choose either 'continuous' or 'related' Old Testament and Psalm readings.

CONTINUOUS

1 Kings 8:[1, 6, 10–11] 22–30, 41–43   [King Solomon summoned into his pres- F
ence at Jerusalem the elders of Israel, all the heads of the tribes and the I
chiefs of the Israelite families, to bring up the ark of the LORD's covenant R
from Zion, the City of David. S

The priests then brought the ark of the LORD's covenant to its place in T
the inner sanctuary of the temple, the Most Holy Place, and put it beneath
the wings of the cherubim. R

When the priests withdrew from the Holy Place, the cloud filled the tem- E
ple of the LORD. And the priests could not perform their service because of A
the cloud, for the glory of the LORD filled his temple.] D

Then Solomon stood before the altar of the LORD in front of the whole I
assembly of Israel, spread out his hands towards heaven and said: N

"O LORD, God of Israel, there is no God like you in heaven above or on G
earth below – you who keep your covenant of love with your servants who
continue wholeheartedly in your way. You have kept your promise to your
servant David my father; with your mouth you have promised and with
your hand you have fulfilled it – as it is today.

"Now LORD, God of Israel, keep for your servant David my father the
promises you made to him when you said, 'You shall never fail to have a
man to sit before me on the throne of Israel, if only your sons are careful in
all they do to walk before me as you have done.' And now, O God of Israel,
let your word that you promised your servant David my father come true.

"But will God really dwell on earth? The heavens, even the highest
heaven, cannot contain you. How much less this temple I have built! Yet
give attention to your servant's prayer and his plea for mercy, O LORD my
God. Hear the cry and the prayer that your servant is praying in your presence this day. May your eyes be open towards this temple night and day,
this place of which you said, 'My Name shall be there,' so that you will hear
the prayer your servant prays towards this place. Hear the supplication of
your servant and of your people Israel when they pray towards this place.
Hear from heaven, your dwelling-place, and when you hear, forgive.

"As for the foreigner who does not belong to your people Israel but has
come from a distant land because of your name – for men will hear of your
great name and your mighty hand and your outstretched arm – when he
comes and prays towards this temple, then hear from heaven, your
dwelling-place, and do whatever the foreigner asks of you, so that all the
peoples of the earth may know your name and fear you, as do your own
people Israel, and may know that this house I have built bears your Name." P

and **Psalm 84**   How lovely is your dwelling-place, S
O LORD Almighty! A
My soul yearns, even faints, L
for the courts of the LORD; M

my heart and my flesh cry out
    for the living God.

Even the sparrow has found a home,
    and the swallow a nest for herself,
    where she may have her young –
a place near your altar,
    O LORD Almighty, my King and my God.
Blessed are those who dwell in your house;
    they are ever praising you.

Blessed are those whose strength is in you,
    who have set their hearts on pilgrimage.
As they pass through the Valley of Baca,
    they make it a place of springs;
    the autumn rains also cover it with pools.
They go from strength to strength,
    till each appears before God in Zion.

Hear my prayer, O LORD God Almighty;
    listen to me, O God of Jacob.
Look upon our shield, O God;
    look with favour on your anointed one.

Better is one day in your courts
    than a thousand elsewhere;
I would rather be a doorkeeper in the house of my God
    than dwell in the tents of the wicked.
For the LORD God is a sun and shield;
    the LORD bestows favour and honour;
no good thing does he withhold
    from those whose walk is blameless.

O LORD Almighty,
    blessed is the man who trusts in you.

or RELATED

Joshua 24:1–2a, 14–18   Joshua assembled all the tribes of Israel at Shechem. He summoned the elders, leaders, judges and officials of Israel, and they presented themselves before God.

Joshua said to all the people,

"Fear the LORD and serve him with all faithfulness. Throw away the gods your forefathers worshipped beyond the River and in Egypt, and serve the LORD. But if serving the LORD seems undesirable to you, then choose for yourselves this day whom you will serve, whether the gods your forefathers served beyond the River, or the gods of the Amorites, in whose land you are living. But as for me and my household, we will serve the LORD."

Then the people answered, "Far be it from us to forsake the LORD to serve other gods! It was the LORD our God himself who brought us and our fathers up out of Egypt, from that land of slavery, and performed those great signs before our eyes. He protected us on our entire journey and among all the nations through which we travelled. And the LORD drove out before us all the nations, including the Amorites, who lived in the land. We too will serve the LORD, because he is our God."

and **Psalm 34:**
15–22

The eyes of the LORD are on the righteous
    and his ears are attentive to their cry;
the face of the LORD is against those who do evil,
    to cut off the memory of them from the earth.

The righteous cry out, and the LORD hears them;
    he delivers them from all their troubles.
The LORD is close to the broken-hearted
    and saves those who are crushed in spirit.

The righteous may have many troubles,
    but the LORD delivers them from them all;
he protects all their bones,
    not one of them will be broken.

Evil will slay the wicked;
    the foes of the righteous will be condemned.
The LORD redeems his servants;
    no-one will be condemned who takes refuge in him.

Ephesians 6:10–20 Be strong in the Lord and in his mighty power. Put on the full armour of God so that you can take your stand against the devil's schemes. For our struggle is not against flesh and blood, but against the rulers, against the authorities, against the powers of this dark world and against the spiritual forces of evil in the heavenly realms. Therefore put on the full armour of God, so that when the day of evil comes, you may be able to stand your ground, and after you have done everything, to stand. Stand firm then, with the belt of truth buckled round your waist, with the breast-plate of righteousness in place, and with your feet fitted with the readiness that comes from the gospel of peace. In addition to all this, take up the shield of faith, with which you can extinguish all the flaming arrows of the evil one. Take the helmet of salvation and the sword of the Spirit, which is the word of God. And pray in the Spirit on all occasions with all kinds of prayers and requests. With this in mind, be alert and always keep on pray-ing for all the saints.

Pray also for me, that whenever I open my mouth, words may be given me so that I will fearlessly make known the mystery of the gospel, for which I am an ambassador in chains. Pray that I may declare it fearlessly, as I should.

John 6:56–69 Jesus said to the Jews: "Whoever eats my flesh and drinks my blood remains in me, and I in him. Just as the living Father sent me and I live because of the Father, so the one who feeds on me will live because of me. This is the bread that came down from heaven. Your forefathers ate manna and died, but he who feeds on this bread will live for ever." He said this while teaching in the synagogue in Capernaum.

On hearing it, many of his disciples said, "This is a hard teaching. Who can accept it?"

Aware that his disciples were grumbling about this, Jesus said to them, "Does this offend you? What if you see the Son of Man ascend to where he was before! The Spirit gives life; the flesh counts for nothing. The words I have spoken to you are spirit and they are life. Yet there are some of you who do not believe." For Jesus had known from the beginning which of them did not believe and who would betray him. He went on to say, "This is why I told you that no-one can come to me unless the Father has enabled him."

From this time many of his disciples turned back and no longer followed him.

"You do not want to leave too, do you?" Jesus asked the Twelve.

Simon Peter answered him, "Lord, to whom shall we go? You have the words of eternal life. We believe and know that you are the Holy One of God."

Proper 17

Sunday between 28 August and 3 September inclusive (if after Trinity Sunday)
Choose either 'continuous' or 'related' Old Testament and Psalm readings.

CONTINUOUS

Song of Solomon 2:8–13

Listen! My lover!
> Look! Here he comes,
leaping across the mountains,
> bounding over the hills.
My lover is like a gazelle or a young stag.
> Look! There he stands behind our wall,
gazing through the windows,
> peering through the lattice.
My lover spoke and said to me,
> "Arise, my darling,
> my beautiful one, and come with me.
See! The winter is past;
> the rains are over and gone.
Flowers appear on the earth;
> the season of singing has come,
the cooing of doves
> is heard in our land.
The fig-tree forms its early fruit;
> the blossoming vines spread their fragrance.
Arise, come, my darling;
> my beautiful one, come with me."

FIRST READING

and **Psalm 45:1–2, 6–9***

My heart is stirred by a noble theme
    as I recite my verses for the king;
        my tongue is the pen of a skilful writer.

You are the most excellent of men
    and your lips have been anointed with grace,
        since God has blessed you for ever.

Your throne, O God, will last for ever and ever;
    a sceptre of justice will be the sceptre of
        your kingdom.
You love righteousness and hate wickedness;
    therefore God, your God, has set you above
        your companions
    by anointing you with the oil of joy.
All your robes are fragrant with myrrh and aloes
        and cassia;
    from palaces adorned with ivory
    the music of the strings makes you glad.
Daughters of kings are among your honoured
        women;
    at your right hand is the royal bride in gold of
        Ophir.

Or **RELATED**

Deuteronomy 4:1–2, 6–9 Moses said: Hear now, O Israel, the decrees and laws I am about to teach you. Follow them so that you may live and may go in and take possession of the land that the LORD, the God of your fathers, is giving you. Do not add to what I command you and do not subtract from it, but keep the commands of the LORD your God that I give you.

Observe them carefully, for this will show your wisdom and understanding to the nations, who will hear about all these decrees and say, "Surely this great nation is a wise and understanding people." What other nation is so great as to have their gods near them the way the LORD our God is near us whenever we pray to him? And what other nation is so great as to have such righteous decrees and laws as this body of laws I am setting before you today? Only be careful, and watch yourselves closely so that you do not forget the things your eyes have seen or let them slip from your heart as long as you live. Teach them to your children and to their children after them.

and **Psalm 15** LORD, who may dwell in your sanctuary?
    Who may live on your holy hill?

He whose walk is blameless
    and who does what is righteous,
who speaks the truth from his heart
    and has no slander on his tongue,

who does his neighbour no wrong
    and casts no slur on his fellow-man,
who despises a vile man
    but honours those who fear the LORD,
who keeps his oath
    even when it hurts,
who lends his money without usury
    and does not accept a bribe against the innocent.

He who does these things
    will never be shaken.

James 1:17–27 Every good and perfect gift is from above, coming down from the Father of the heavenly lights, who does not change like shifting shadows. He chose to give us birth through the word of truth, that we might be a kind of firstfruits of all he created.

My dear brothers, take note of this: Everyone should be quick to listen, slow to speak and slow to become angry, for man's anger does not bring about the righteous life that God desires. Therefore, get rid of all moral filth and the evil that is so prevalent, and humbly accept the word planted in you, which can save you.

Do not merely listen to the word, and so deceive yourselves. Do what it says. Anyone who listens to the word but does not do what it says is like a man who looks at his face in a mirror and, after looking at himself, goes away and immediately forgets what he looks like. But the man who looks intently into the perfect law that gives freedom, and continues to do this, not forgetting what he has heard, but doing it – he will be blessed in what he does.

If anyone considers himself religious and yet does not keep a tight rein on his tongue, he deceives himself and his religion is worthless. Religion that God our Father accepts as pure and faultless is this: to look after orphans and widows in their distress and to keep oneself from being polluted by the world.

Mark 7:1–8, 14–15, 21–23 The Pharisees and some of the teachers of the law who had come from Jerusalem gathered round Jesus and saw some of his disciples eating food with hands that were "unclean", that is, unwashed. (The Pharisees and all the Jews do not eat unless they give their hands a ceremonial washing, holding to the tradition of the elders. When they come from the market-place they do not eat unless they wash. And they observe many other traditions, such as the washing of cups, pitchers and kettles.)

So the Pharisees and teachers of the law asked Jesus, "Why don't your disciples live according to the tradition of the elders instead of eating their food with 'unclean' hands?"

He replied, "Isaiah was right when he prophesied about you hypocrites; as it is written:

"'These people honour me with their lips,
  but their hearts are far from me.
They worship me in vain;
  their teachings are but rules taught by men.'
You have let go of the commands of God and are holding on to the traditions of men."

Jesus called the crowd to him and said, "Listen to me, everyone, and understand this. Nothing outside a man can make him 'unclean' by going into him. Rather, it is what comes out of a man that makes him 'unclean'.

For from within, out of men's hearts, come evil thoughts, sexual immorality, theft, murder, adultery, greed, malice, deceit, lewdness, envy, slander, arrogance and folly. All these evils come from inside and make a man 'unclean'."

Proper 18

Sunday between 4 and 10 September inclusive (if after Trinity Sunday)
Choose either 'continuous' or 'related' Old Testament and Psalm readings.

CONTINUOUS

Proverbs 22:1–2,
8–9, 22–23

A good name is more desirable than great riches;
  to be esteemed is better than silver or gold.
Rich and poor have this in common:
  The LORD is the Maker of them all.

He who sows wickedness reaps trouble,
  and the rod of his fury will be destroyed.

A generous man will himself be blessed,
  for he shares his food with the poor.

Do not exploit the poor because they are poor
  and do not crush the needy in court,
for the LORD will take up their case
  and will plunder those who plunder them.

and **Psalm 125**

Those who trust in the LORD are like Mount Zion,
  which cannot be shaken but endures for ever.
As the mountains surround Jerusalem,
  so the LORD surrounds his people
  both now and for evermore.

The sceptre of the wicked will not remain
  over the land allotted to the righteous,
for then the righteous might use
  their hands to do evil.

Do good, O LORD, to those who are good,
  to those who are upright in heart.
But those who turn to crooked ways
  the LORD will banish with the evildoers.

Peace be upon Israel.

Or RELATED

Isaiah 35:4–7a   Say to those with fearful hearts,
    "Be strong, do not fear;
your God will come,
    he will come with vengeance;
with divine retribution
he will come to save you."

Then will the eyes of the blind be opened
    and the ears of the deaf unstopped.
Then will the lame leap like a deer,
    and the mute tongue shout for joy.
Water will gush forth in the wilderness
    and streams in the desert.
The burning sand will become a pool,
    the thirsty ground bubbling springs.

and **Psalm 146**   Praise the LORD.

Praise the LORD, O my soul.
    I will praise the LORD all my life;
    I will sing praise to my God as long as I live.

Do not put your trust in princes,
    in mortal men, who cannot save.
When their spirit departs, they return to the ground;
    on that very day their plans come to nothing.

Blessed is he whose help is the God of Jacob,
    whose hope is in the LORD their God,
the Maker of heaven and earth,
    the sea, and everything in them –
    the LORD, who remains faithful for ever.
He upholds the cause of the oppressed
    and gives food to the hungry.
The LORD sets prisoners free,
    the LORD gives sight to the blind,
the LORD lifts up those who are bowed down,
    the LORD loves the righteous.
The LORD watches over the alien
    and sustains the fatherless and the widow,
    but he frustrates the ways of the wicked.

The LORD reigns for ever,
    your God, O Zion, for all generations.
Praise the LORD.

James 2:1–10 [11–13] 14–17   My brothers, as believers in our glorious Lord Jesus Christ, don't show favouritism. Suppose a man comes into your meeting wearing a gold ring and fine clothes, and a poor man in shabby clothes also comes in. If you show special attention to the man wearing fine clothes and say, "Here's a good seat for you," but say to the poor man, "You stand there" or "Sit on the floor by my feet," have you not discriminated among yourselves and become judges with evil thoughts?

Listen, my dear brothers: Has not God chosen those who are poor in the eyes of the world to be rich in faith and to inherit the kingdom he promised those who love him? But you have insulted the poor. Is it not the rich who are exploiting you? Are they not the ones who are dragging you into court? Are they not the ones who are slandering the noble name of him to whom you belong?

If you really keep the royal law found in Scripture, "Love your neighbour as yourself," you are doing right. But if you show favouritism, you sin and are convicted by the law as law-breakers. For whoever keeps the whole law and yet stumbles at just one point is guilty of breaking all of it. [For he who said, "Do not commit adultery," also said, "Do not murder." If you do not commit adultery but do commit murder, you have become a law-breaker.

Speak and act as those who are going to be judged by the law that gives freedom, because judgment without mercy will be shown to anyone who has not been merciful. Mercy triumphs over judgment!]

What good is it, my brothers, if a man claims to have faith but has no deeds? Can such faith save him? Suppose a brother or sister is without clothes and daily food. If one of you says to him, "Go, I wish you well; keep warm and well fed," but does nothing about his physical needs, what good is it? In the same way, faith by itself, if it is not accompanied by action, is dead.

Mark 7:24–37 Jesus went to the vicinity of Tyre. He entered a house and did not want anyone to know it; yet he could not keep his presence secret. In fact, as soon as she heard about him, a woman whose little daughter was possessed by an evil spirit came and fell at his feet. The woman was a Greek, born in Syrian Phoenicia. She begged Jesus to drive the demon out of her daughter.

"First let the children eat all they want," he told her, "for it is not right to take the children's bread and toss it to their dogs."

"Yes, Lord," she replied, "but even the dogs under the table eat the children's crumbs."

Then he told her, "For such a reply, you may go; the demon has left your daughter."

She went home and found her child lying on the bed, and the demon gone.

Then Jesus left the vicinity of Tyre and went through Sidon, down to the Sea of Galilee and into the region of the Decapolis. There some people brought to him a man who was deaf and could hardly talk, and they begged him to place his hand on the man.

After he took him aside, away from the crowd, Jesus put his fingers into the man's ears. Then he spat and touched the man's tongue. He looked up to heaven and with a deep sigh said to him, *"Ephphatha!"* (which means, "Be opened!"). At this, the man's ears were opened, his tongue was loosened and he began to speak plainly.

Jesus commanded them not to tell anyone. But the more he did so, the more they kept talking about it. People were overwhelmed with amazement. "He has done everything well," they said. "He even makes the deaf hear and the mute speak."

Proper 19

Sunday between 11 and 17 September inclusive (if after Trinity Sunday)
Choose either 'continuous' or 'related' Old Testament and Psalm readings.

CONTINUOUS

Proverbs 1: 20–33

Wisdom calls aloud in the street,
  she raises her voice in the public squares;
at the head of the noisy streets she cries out,
  in the gateways of the city she makes her speech:

"How long will you simple ones love your simple ways?
  How long will mockers delight in mockery
  and fools hate knowledge?
If you had responded to my rebuke,
  I would have poured out my heart to you
  and made my thoughts known to you.
But since you rejected me when I called
  and no-one gave heed when I stretched out my hand,
since you ignored all my advice
  and would not accept my rebuke,
I in turn will laugh at your disaster;
  I will mock when calamity overtakes you –
when calamity overtakes you like a storm,
  when disaster sweeps over you like a whirlwind,
  when distress and trouble overwhelm you.

"Then they will call to me but I will not answer;
  they will look for me but will not find me.
Since they hated knowledge
  and did not choose to fear the LORD,
since they would not accept my advice
  and spurned my rebuke,
they will eat the fruit of their ways
  and be filled with the fruit of their schemes.
For the waywardness of the simple will kill them,
  and the complacency of fools will destroy them;
but whoever listens to me will live in safety
  and be at ease, without fear of harm."

FIRST READING

and Psalm 19*

The heavens declare the glory of God;
  the skies proclaim the work of his hands.

PSALM

Day after day they pour forth speech;
  night after night they display knowledge.
There is no speech or language
  where their voice is not heard.
Their voice goes out into all the earth,
  their words to the ends of the world.

In the heavens he has pitched a tent for the sun,
  which is like a bridegroom coming forth from his
    pavilion,
  like a champion rejoicing to run his course.
It rises at one end of the heavens
  and makes its circuit to the other;
  nothing is hidden from its heat.

The law of the LORD is perfect,
  reviving the soul.
The statutes of the LORD are trustworthy,
  making wise the simple.
The precepts of the LORD are right,
  giving joy to the heart.
The commands of the LORD are radiant,
  giving light to the eyes.
The fear of the LORD is pure,
  enduring for ever.
The ordinances of the LORD are sure
  and altogether righteous.
They are more precious than gold,
  than much pure gold;
they are sweeter than honey,
  than honey from the comb.
By them is your servant warned;
  in keeping them there is great reward.

Who can discern his errors?
  Forgive my hidden faults.
Keep your servant also from wilful sins;
  may they not rule over me.
Then will I be blameless,
  innocent of great transgression.

May the words of my mouth and the meditation of my heart
  be pleasing in your sight,
  O LORD, my Rock and my Redeemer.

or Canticle: **Wisdom of Solomon 7:26 – 8:1**

Or **RELATED**

Isaiah 50:4–9a   The Sovereign LORD has given me an instructed tongue,
       to know the word that sustains the weary.

He wakens me morning by morning,
wakens my ear to listen like one being taught.
The Sovereign LORD has opened my ears,
and I have not been rebellious;
I have not drawn back.
I offered my back to those who beat me,
my cheeks to those who pulled out my beard;
I did not hide my face
from mocking and spitting.
Because the Sovereign LORD helps me,
I will not be disgraced.
Therefore have I set my face like flint,
and I know I will not be put to shame.
He who vindicates me is near.
Who then will bring charges against me?
Let us face each other!
Who are accusers?
Let them confront me!
It is the Sovereign LORD who helps me.

and **Psalm 116:1–9** I love the LORD, for he heard my voice;
he heard my cry for mercy.
Because he turned his ear to me,
I will call on him as long as I live.

The cords of death entangled me,
the anguish of the grave came upon me;
I was overcome by trouble and sorrow.
Then I called on the name of the LORD:
"O LORD, save me!"

The LORD is gracious and righteous;
our God is full of compassion.
The LORD protects the simple-hearted;
when I was in great need, he saved me.

Be at rest once more, O my soul,
for the LORD has been good to you.

For you, O LORD, have delivered my soul from
death,
my eyes from tears,
my feet from stumbling,
that I may walk before the LORD
in the land of the living.

James 3:1–12 Not many of you should presume to be teachers, my brothers,
because you know that we who teach will be judged more strictly. We all
stumble in many ways. If anyone is never at fault in what he says, he is a
perfect man, able to keep his whole body in check.

PSALM

SRE ECA OD NI DN G

When we put bits into the mouths of horses to make them obey us, we can turn the whole animal. Or take ships as an example. Although they are so large and are driven by strong winds, they are steered by a very small rudder wherever the pilot wants to go. Likewise the tongue is a small part of the body, but it makes great boasts. Consider what a great forest is set on fire by a small spark. The tongue also is a fire, a world of evil among the parts of the body. It corrupts the whole person, sets the whole course of his life on fire, and is itself set on fire by hell.

All kinds of animals, birds, reptiles and creatures of the sea are being tamed and have been tamed by man, but no man can tame the tongue. It is a restless evil, full of deadly poison.

With the tongue we praise our Lord and Father, and with it we curse men, who have been made in God's likeness. Out of the same mouth come praise and cursing. My brothers, this should not be. Can both fresh water and salt water flow from the same spring? My brothers, can a fig-tree bear olives, or a grapevine bear figs? Neither can a salt spring produce fresh water.

Mark 8:27–38 Jesus and his disciples went on to the villages around Caesarea Philippi. On the way he asked them, "Who do people say I am?"

They replied, "Some say John the Baptist; others say Elijah; and still others, one of the prophets."

"But what about you?" he asked. "Who do you say I am?"

Peter answered, "You are the Christ."

Jesus warned them not to tell anyone about him.

He then began to teach them that the Son of Man must suffer many things and be rejected by the elders, chief priests and teachers of the law, and that he must be killed and after three days rise again. He spoke plainly about this, and Peter took him aside and began to rebuke him.

But when Jesus turned and looked at his disciples, he rebuked Peter. "Get behind me, Satan!" he said. "You do not have in mind the things of God, but things of men."

Then he called the crowd to him along with his disciples and said: "If anyone would come after me, he must deny himself and take up his cross and follow me. For whoever wants to save his life will lose it, but whoever loses his life for me and for the gospel will save it. What good is it for a man to gain the whole world, yet forfeit his soul? Or what can a man give in exchange for his soul? If anyone is ashamed of me and my words in this adulterous and sinful generation, the Son of Man will be ashamed of him when he comes in his Father's glory with the holy angels."

Proper 20

Sunday between 18 and 24 September inclusive (if after Trinity Sunday)
Choose either 'continuous' or 'related' Old Testament and Psalm readings.

CONTINUOUS

Proverbs 31:10–31 A wife of noble character who can find?
She is worth far more than rubies.

Her husband has full confidence in her
　　and lacks nothing of value.
She brings him good, not harm,
　　all the days of her life.
She selects wool and flax
　　and works with eager hands.
She is like the merchant ships,
　　bringing her food from afar.
She gets up while it is still dark;
　　she provides food for her family
　　and portions for her servant girls.
She considers a field and buys it;
　　out of her earnings she plants a vineyard.
She sets about her work vigorously;
　　her arms are strong for her tasks.
She sees that her trading is profitable,
　　and her lamp does not go out at night.
In her hand she holds the distaff
　　and grasps the spindle with her fingers.
She opens her arms to the poor
　　and extends her hands to the needy.
When it snows, she has no fear for her household;
　　for all of them are clothed in scarlet.
She makes coverings for her bed;
　　she is clothed in fine linen and purple.
Her husband is respected at the city gate,
　　where he takes his seat among the elders of the land.
She makes linen garments and sells them,
　　and supplies the merchants with sashes.
She is clothed with strength and dignity;
　　she can laugh at the days to come.
She speaks with wisdom,
　　and faithful instruction is on her tongue.
She watches over the affairs of her household
　　and does not eat the bread of idleness.
Her children arise and call her blessed;
　　her husband also, and he praises her:
"Many women do noble things,
　　but you surpass them all."
Charm is deceptive, and beauty is fleeting;
　　but a woman who fears the LORD is to be praised.
Give her the reward she has earned,
　　and let her works bring her praise at the city gate.

nd **Psalm 1**　Blessed is the man
　　who does not walk in the counsel of the wicked

or stand in the way of sinners
>   or sit in the seat of mockers.
But his delight is in the law of the LORD,
>   and on his law he meditates day and night.
He is like a tree planted by streams of water,
>   which yields its fruit in season
and whose leaf does not wither.
>   Whatever he does prospers.

Not so the wicked!
>   They are like chaff
>   that the wind blows away.
Therefore the wicked will not stand in the judgment,
>   nor sinners in the assembly of the righteous.

For the LORD watches over the way of the righteous,
>   but the way of the wicked will perish.

Or **RELATED**

Wisdom of Solomon 1:16 – 2:1, 12–22

or **Jeremiah 11:18–20**   Because the LORD revealed their plot to me, I knew it, for at that time he showed me what they were doing. I had been like a gentle lamb led to the slaughter; I did not realise that they had plotted against me, saying,

>   "Let us destroy the tree and its fruit;
>   >   let us cut him off from the land of the living,
>   >   that his name be remembered no more."
>   But, O LORD Almighty, you who judge righteously
>   >   and test the heart and mind,
>   let me see your vengeance upon them,
>   >   for to you I have committed my cause."

and **Psalm 54**   Save me, O God, by your name;
>   vindicate me by your might.
Hear my prayer, O God;
>   listen to the words of my mouth.

Strangers are attacking me;
>   ruthless men seek my life –
>   people without regard for God.

Surely God is my help;
>   the Lord is the one who sustains me.

Let evil recoil on those who slander me;
>   in your faithfulness destroy them.

I will sacrifice a freewill offering to you;
>   I will praise your name, O LORD,
>   for it is good.

For he has delivered me from all my troubles,
and my eyes have looked in triumph on my foes.

James 3:13 – 4:3, 7–8a Who is wise and understanding among you? Let him show it by his good life, by deeds done in the humility that comes from wisdom. But if you harbour bitter envy and selfish ambition in your hearts, do not boast about it or deny the truth. Such "wisdom" does not come down from heaven but is earthly, unspiritual, of the devil. For where you have envy and selfish ambition, there you find disorder and every evil practice.

But the wisdom that comes from heaven is first of all pure; then peace-loving, considerate, submissive, full of mercy and good fruit, impartial and sincere. Peacemakers who sow in peace raise a harvest of righteousness.

What causes fights and quarrels among you? Don't they come from your desires that battle within you? You want something but don't get it. You kill and covet, but you cannot have what you want. You quarrel and fight. You do not have, because you do not ask God. When you ask, you do not receive, because you ask with wrong motives, that you may spend what you get on your pleasures.

Submit yourselves, then, to God. Resist the devil, and he will flee from you. Come near to God and he will come near to you.

Mark 9:30–37 Jesus and his disciples passed through Galilee. Jesus did not want anyone to know where they were, because he was teaching his disciples. He said to them, "The Son of Man is going to be betrayed into the hands of men. They will kill him, and after three days he will rise." But they did not understand what he meant and were afraid to ask him about it. They came to Capernaum. When he was in the house, he asked them, "What were you arguing about on the road?" But they kept quiet because on the way they had argued about who was the greatest.

Sitting down, Jesus called the Twelve and said "If anyone wants to be first, he must be the very last, and the servant of all."

He took a little child and had him stand among them. Taking the child in his arms, he said to them, "Whoever welcomes one of these little children in my name welcomes me; and whoever welcomes me does not welcome me but the one who sent me."

Proper 21

Sunday between 25 September and 1 October inclusive (if after Trinity Sunday)
Choose either 'continuous' or 'related' Old Testament and Psalm readings.

CONTINUOUS

Esther 7:1–6, 9–10; 9:20–22 King Xerxes and Haman went to dine with Queen Esther, and as they were drinking wine on that second day, the king again asked, "Queen Esther, what is your petition? It will be given you. What is your request? Even up to half the kingdom, it will be granted."

Then Queen Esther answered, "If I have found favour with you, O king, and if it pleases your majesty, grant me my life – this is my petition. And spare my people – this is my request. For I and my people have been sold for destruction and slaughter and annihilation. If we had merely been sold as male and female slaves, I would have kept quiet, because no such distress would justify disturbing the king."

King Xerxes asked Queen Esther, "Who is he? Where is the man who has dared to do such a thing?"

Esther said, "The adversary and enemy is this vile Haman."

Then Haman was terrified before the king and queen.

Then Harbona, one of the eunuchs attending the king, said, "A gallows seventy-five feet high stands by Haman's house. He had it made for Mordecai, who spoke up to help the king."

The king said, "Hang him on it!" So they hanged Haman on the gallows he had prepared for Mordecai. Then the king's fury subsided.

Mordecai recorded these events, and he sent letters to all the Jews throughout the provinces of King Xerxes, near and far, to have them celebrate annually the fourteenth and fifteenth days of the month of Adar as the time when the Jews got relief from their enemies, and as the month when their sorrow was turned into joy and their mourning into a day of celebration. He wrote to them to observe the days as days of feasting and joy and giving presents of food to one another and gifts to the poor.

and **Psalm 124**   If the LORD had not been on our side –
>>> let Israel say –
>> if the LORD had not been on our side
>>> when men attacked us,
>> when their anger flared against us,
>>> they would have swallowed us alive;
>> the flood would have engulfed us,
>>> the torrent would have swept over us,
>> the raging waters
>>> would have swept us away.

>> Praise be to the LORD,
>>> who has not let us be torn by their teeth.
>> We have escaped like a bird
>>> out of the fowler's snare;
>> the snare has been broken,
>>> and we have escaped.
>> Our help is in the name of the LORD,
>>> the Maker of heaven and earth.

Or **RELATED**

Numbers 11:4–6, 10–16, 24–29   The rabble began to crave other food, and again the Israelites started wailing and said, "If only we had meat to eat! We remember the fish we ate in Egypt at no cost – also the cucumbers, melons, leeks, onions and garlic. But now we have lost our appetite; we never see anything but this manna!"

Moses heard the people of every family wailing, each at the entrance to his tent. The LORD became exceedingly angry, and Moses was troubled. He asked the LORD, "Why have you brought this trouble on your servant? What have I done to displease you that you put the burden of all these people on me? Did I conceive all these people? Did I give them birth? Why do you tell me to carry them in my arms, as a nurse carries an infant, to the land you promised on oath to their forefathers? Where can I get meat for all these people? They keep wailing to me, 'Give us meat to eat!' I cannot carry all these people by myself; the burden is too heavy for me. If this is how you are going to treat me, put me to death right now – if I have found favour in your eyes – and do not let me face my own ruin."

The LORD said to Moses: "Bring me seventy of Israel's elders who are known to you as leaders and officials among the people. Make them come to the Tent of Meeting, that they may stand there with you."

So Moses went out and told the people what the LORD had said. He brought together seventy of their elders and made them stand round the Tent. Then the LORD came down in the cloud and spoke with him, and he took of the Spirit that was on him and put the Spirit on the seventy elders. When the Spirit rested on them, they prophesied, but they did not do so again.

However, two men, whose names were Eldad and Medad, had remained in the camp. They were listed among the elders, but did not go out to the Tent. Yet the Spirit also rested on them, and they prophesied in the camp. A young man ran and told Moses, "Eldad and Medad are prophesying in the camp."

Joshua son of Nun, who had been Moses' assistant since youth, spoke up and said, "Moses, my lord, stop them!"

But Moses replied, "Are you jealous for my sake? I wish that all the LORD's people were prophets and that the LORD would put his Spirit on them!"

nd **Psalm 19:7–14**

> The law of the LORD is perfect,
> > reviving the soul.
> The statutes of the LORD are trustworthy,
> > making wise the simple.
> The precepts of the LORD are right,
> > giving joy to the heart.
> The commands of the LORD are radiant,
> > giving light to the eyes.
> The fear of the LORD is pure,
> > enduring for ever.
> The ordinances of the LORD are sure
> > and altogether righteous.
> They are more precious than gold,
> > than much pure gold;
> they are sweeter than honey,
> > than honey from the comb.

P
S
A
L
M

By them is your servant warned;
    in keeping them there is great reward.
Who can discern their errors?
    Forgive my hidden faults.
Keep your servant also from wilful sins;
    may they not rule over me.
Then will I be blameless,
    innocent of great transgression.

May the words of my mouth and the meditation of my heart
    be pleasing in your sight,
      O LORD, my Rock and my Redeemer.

James 5:13–20 Is any one of you in trouble? He should pray. Is anyone happy? Let him sing songs of praise. Is any one of you sick? He should call the elders of the church to pray over him and anoint him with oil in the name of the Lord. And the prayer offered in faith will make the sick person well; the Lord will raise him up. If he has sinned, he will be forgiven. Therefore confess your sins to each other and pray for each other so that you may be healed. The prayer of a righteous man is powerful and effective.

Elijah was a man just like us. He prayed earnestly that it would not rain, and it did not rain on the land for three and a half years. Again he prayed, and the heavens gave rain, and the earth produced its crops.

My brothers, if one of you should wander from the truth and someone should bring him back, remember this: Whoever turns a sinner from the error of his way will save him from death and cover over a multitude of sins.

Mark 9:38–50 "Teacher," said John, "we saw someone driving out demons in your name and we told him to stop, because he was not one of us."

"Do not stop him," Jesus said. "No-one who does a miracle in my name can in the next moment say anything bad about me, for whoever is not against us is for us. I tell you the truth, anyone who gives you a cup of water in my name because you belong to Christ will certainly not lose his reward.

"If anyone causes one of these little ones who believe in me to sin, it would be better for him to be thrown into the sea with a large millstone tied around his neck. If your hand causes you to sin, cut it off. It is better for you to enter life maimed than with two hands to go into hell, where the fire never goes out. And if your foot causes you to sin, cut it off. It is better for you to enter life crippled than to have two feet and be thrown into hell. And if your eye causes you to sin, pluck it out. It is better for you to enter the kingdom of God with one eye than to have two eyes and be thrown into hell, where

    "'their worm does not die,
      and the fire is not quenched.'

Everyone will be salted with fire.

"Salt is good, but if it loses its saltiness, how can you make it salty again? Have salt in yourselves, and be at peace with each other."

Proper 22

Sunday between 2 and 8 October inclusive (if after Trinity Sunday)
Choose either 'continuous' or 'related' Old Testament and Psalm readings.

CONTINUOUS

Job 1:1; 2:1–10 In the land of Uz there lived a man whose name was Job. This F man was blameless and upright; he feared God and shunned evil.   I

One day the angels came to present themselves before the LORD, and R Satan also came with them to present himself before him. And the LORD S said to Satan, "Where have you come from?"   T

Satan answered the LORD, "From roaming through the earth and going to and fro in it."   R

Then the LORD said to Satan, "Have you considered my servant Job? E There is no-one on earth like him; he is blameless and upright, a man who A fears God and shuns evil. And he still maintains his integrity, though you D incited me against him to ruin him without any reason."   I

"Skin for skin!" Satan replied. "A man will give all he has for his own N life. But stretch out your hand and strike his flesh and bones, and he will G surely curse you to your face."

The LORD said to Satan, "Very well, then, he is in your hands; but you must spare his life."

So Satan went out from the presence of the LORD and afflicted Job with painful sores from the soles of his feet to the top of his head. Then Job took a piece of broken pottery and scraped himself with it as he sat among the ashes.

His wife said to him, "Are you still holding on to your integrity? Curse God and die!"

He replied, "You are talking like a foolish woman. Shall we accept good from God, and not trouble?"

In all this, Job did not sin in what he said.

and **Psalm 26**   Vindicate me, O LORD,   P
   for I have led a blameless life;   S
  I have trusted in the LORD   A
   without wavering.   L
  Test me, O LORD, and try me,   M
   examine my heart and my mind;
  for your love is ever before me,
   and I walk continually in your truth.
  I do not sit with deceitful men,
   nor do I consort with hypocrites;
  I abhor the assembly of evildoers
   and refuse to sit with the wicked.

I wash my hands in innocence,
> and go about your altar, O Lord,
proclaiming aloud your praise
> and telling of all your wonderful deeds.
I love the house where you live, O Lord,
> the place where your glory dwells.

Do not take away my soul along with sinners,
> my life with bloodthirsty men,
in whose hands are wicked schemes,
> whose right hands are full of bribes.
But I lead a blameless life;
> redeem me and be merciful to me.

My feet stand on level ground;
> in the great assembly I will praise the Lord.

Or RELATED

Genesis 2:18–24   The Lord God said, "It is not good for the man to be alone. I will make a helper suitable for him."

Now the Lord God had formed out of the ground all the beasts of the field and all the birds of the air. He brought them to the man to see what he would name them; and whatever the man called each living creature, that was its name. So the man gave names to all the livestock, the birds of the air and all the beasts of the field.

But for Adam no suitable helper was found. So the Lord God caused the man to fall into a deep sleep; and while he was sleeping, he took one of the man's ribs and closed up the place with flesh. Then the Lord God made a woman from the rib he had taken out of the man, and he brought her to the man.

The man said,

> "This is now bone of my bones
> > and flesh of my flesh;
> she shall be called 'woman',
> > for she was taken out of man."

For this reason a man will leave his father and mother and be united to his wife, and they will become one flesh.

and **Psalm 8**   O Lord, our Lord,
> how majestic is your name in all the earth!

You have set your glory
> above the heavens.
From the lips of children and infants
> you have ordained praise
because of your enemies,
> to silence the foe and the avenger.

When I consider your heavens,
> the work of your fingers,

the moon and the stars,
  which you have set in place,
what is man that you are mindful of him,
  the son of man that you care for him?
You made him a little lower than the heavenly
    beings
  and crowned him with glory and honour.

You made him ruler over the works of your hands;
  you put everything under his feet:
all flocks and herds,
  and the beasts of the field,
the birds of the air,
  and the fish of the sea,
  all that swim the paths of the seas.
O LORD, our Lord,
  how majestic is your name in all the earth!

Hebrews 1:1–4; 2:5–12   In the past God spoke to our forefathers through
the prophets at many times and in various ways, but in these last days
he has spoken to us by his Son, whom he appointed heir of all things,
and through whom he made the universe. The Son is the radiance of
God's glory and the exact representation of his being, sustaining all
things by his powerful word. After he had provided purification for sins,
he sat down at the right hand of the Majesty in heaven. So he became as
much superior to the angels as the name he has inherited is superior to
theirs.

It is not to angels that he has subjected the world to come, about which
we are speaking. But there is a place where someone has testified:

"What is man that you are mindful of him,
  the son of man that you care for him?
You made him a little lower than the angels;
  you crowned him with glory and honour
and put everything under his feet."

In putting everything under him, God left nothing that is not subject to
him. Yet at present we do not see everything subject to him. But we see
Jesus, who was made a little lower than the angels, now crowned with glory
and honour because he suffered death, so that by the grace of God he might
taste death for everyone.

In bringing many sons to glory, it was fitting that God, for whom and
through whom everything exists, should make the author of their salvation
perfect through suffering. Both the one who makes men holy and those
who are made holy are of the same family. So Jesus is not ashamed to call
them brothers. He says,

"I will declare your name to my brothers;
  in the presence of the congregation I will sing your praises."

Mark 10:2–16 Some Pharisees came and tested Jesus by asking, "Is it lawful for a man to divorce his wife?"

"What did Moses command you?" he replied.

They said, "Moses permitted a man to write a certificate of divorce and send her away."

"It was because your hearts were hard that Moses wrote you this law," Jesus replied. "But at the beginning of creation God 'made them male and female'. 'For this reason a man will leave his father and mother and be united to his wife, and the two will become one flesh.' So they are no longer two, but one. Therefore what God has joined together, let man not separate."

When they were in the house again, the disciples asked Jesus about this. He answered, "Anyone who divorces his wife and marries another woman commits adultery against her. And if she divorces her husband and marries another man, she commits adultery."

People were bringing little children to Jesus to have him touch them, but the disciples rebuked them. When Jesus saw this, he was indignant. He said to them, "Let the little children come to me, and do not hinder them, for the kingdom of God belongs to such as these. I tell you the truth, anyone who will not receive the kingdom of God like a little child will never enter it." And he took the children in his arms, put his hands on them and blessed them.

GOSPEL

Proper 23

Sunday between 9 and 15 October inclusive (if after Trinity Sunday)
Choose either 'continuous' or 'related' Old Testament and Psalm readings.

CONTINUOUS

Job 23:1–9, Job replied to Eliphaz:

16–17 "Even today my complaint is bitter;

"Even today my complaint is bitter;
>   his hand is heavy in spite of my groaning.
If only I knew where to find God;
>   if only I could go to his dwelling!
I would state my case before him
>   and fill my mouth with arguments.
I would find out what he would answer me,
>   and consider what he would say.
Would he oppose me with great power?
>   No, he would not press charges against me.
There the upright could present their case before him,
>   and there I would be delivered for ever from my judge.

"But if I go to the east, he is not there;
>   if I go to the west, I do not find him.
When he is at work in the north, I do not see him;
>   when he turns to the south, I catch no glimpse of him.

"God has made my heart faint;
>   the Almighty has terrified me.

FIRST READING

Yet I am not silenced by the darkness,
by the thick darkness that covers my face."

and **Psalm 22:1–15**   My God, my God, why have you forsaken me?
Why are you so far from saving me,
so far from the words of my groaning?
O my God, I cry out by day, but you do not answer,
by night, and am not silent.

Yet you are enthroned as the Holy One;
you are the praise of Israel.
In you our fathers put their trust;
they trusted and you delivered them.
They cried to you and were saved;
in you they trusted and were not disappointed.

But I am a worm and not a man,
scorned by men and despised by the people.
All who see me mock me;
they hurl insults, shaking their heads:
"He trusts in the LORD;
let the LORD rescue him.
Let him deliver him,
since he delights in him."

Yet you brought me out of the womb;
you made me trust in you
even at my mother's breast.
From birth I was cast upon you;
from my mother's womb you have been my God.
Do not be far from me,
for trouble is near
and there is no-one to help.

Many bulls surround me;
strong bulls of Bashan encircle me.
Roaring lions tearing their prey
open their mouths wide against me.
I am poured out like water,
and all my bones are out of joint.
My heart has turned to wax;
it has melted away within me.
My strength is dried up like a potsherd,
and my tongue sticks to the roof of my mouth;
you lay me in the dust of death.

Or **RELATED**

Amos 5:6–7, 10–15   Seek the LORD and live,
or he will sweep through the house of Joseph like
a fire;

it will devour,
 and Bethel will have no-one to quench it.

You who turn justice into bitterness
 and cast righteousness to the ground,
you hate the one who reproves in court
 and despise him who tells the truth.

You trample on the poor
 and force him to give you grain.
Therefore, though you have built stone mansions,
 you will not live in them;
though you have planted lush vineyards,
 you will not drink their wine.
For I know how many are your offences
 and how great your sins.

You oppress the righteous and take bribes
 and you deprive the poor of justice in the courts.
Therefore the prudent man keeps quiet in such
  times,
 for the times are evil.

Seek good, not evil,
 that you may live.
Then the Lord God Almighty will be with you,
 just as you say he is.
Hate evil, love good;
 maintain justice in the courts.
Perhaps the Lord God Almighty will have mercy
 on the remnant of Joseph.

and **Psalm 90:12–17** Teach us to number our days aright,
 that we may gain a heart of wisdom.

Relent, O Lord! How long will it be?
 Have compassion on your servants.
Satisfy us in the morning with your unfailing love,
 that we may sing for joy and be glad all our days.
Make us glad for as many days as you have afflicted us,
 for as many years as we have seen trouble.
May your deeds be shown to your servants,
 your splendour to their children.
May the favour of the Lord our God rest upon us;
 establish the work of our hands for us –
 yes, establish the work of our hands.

Hebrews 4:12–16 The word of God is living and active. Sharper than any
double-edged sword, it penetrates even to dividing soul and spirit, joints
and marrow; it judges the thoughts and attitudes of the heart. Nothing in

all creation is hidden from God's sight. Everything is uncovered and laid bare before the eyes of him to whom we must give account.

Therefore, since we have a great high priest who has gone through the heavens, Jesus the Son of God, let us hold firmly to the faith we profess. For we do not have a high priest who is unable to sympathise with our weaknesses, but we have one who has been tempted in every way, just as we are – yet was without sin. Let us then approach the throne of grace with confidence, so that we may receive mercy and find grace to help us in our time of need.

Mark 10:17–31   As Jesus started on his way, someone ran up to him and fell on his knees before him. "Good teacher," he asked, "what must I do to inherit eternal life?"

"Why do you call me good?" Jesus answered. "No-one is good – except God alone. You know the commandments: 'Do not murder, do not commit adultery, do not steal, do not give false testimony, do not defraud, honour your father and mother.'"

"Teacher," he declared, "all these I have kept since I was a boy."

Jesus looked at him and loved him. "One thing you lack," he said. "Go, sell everything you have and give to the poor, and you will have treasure in heaven. Then come, follow me."

At this the man's face fell. He went away sad, because he had great wealth.

Jesus looked around and said to his disciples, "How hard it is for the rich to enter the kingdom of God!"

The disciples were amazed at his words. But Jesus said again, "Children, how hard it is to enter the kingdom of God! It is easier for a camel to go through the eye of a needle than for the rich to enter the kingdom of God."

The disciples were even more amazed, and said to each other, "Who then can be saved?"

Jesus looked at them and said, "Humanly, this is impossible, but not with God; all things are possible with God."

Peter said to him, "We have left everything to follow you!"

"I tell you the truth," Jesus replied, "no-one who has left home or brothers or sisters or mother or father or children or fields for me and the gospel will fail to receive a hundred times as much in this present age (homes, brothers, sisters, mothers, children and fields – and with them, persecutions) and in the age to come, eternal life. But many who are first will be last, and the last first."

GOSPEL

roper 24

nday between 16 and 22 October inclusive (if after Trinity Sunday)
100se either 'continuous' or 'related' Old Testament and Psalm readings.

FIRST READING

ONTINUOUS

b 38:1–7 [34–41]   The LORD answered Job out of the storm. He said:

"Who is this that darkens my counsel
    with words without knowledge?

Brace yourself like a man;
   I will question you,
   and you shall answer me.

"Where were you when I laid the earth's foundation?
   Tell me, if you understand.
Who marked off its dimensions? Surely you know!
   Who stretched a measuring line across it?
On what were its footings set,
   or who laid its cornerstone –
while the morning stars sang together
   and all the angels shouted for joy?

["Can you raise your voice to the clouds
   and cover yourself with a flood of water?
Do you send the lightning bolts on their way?
   Do they report to you, 'Here we are'?
Who endowed the heart with wisdom
   or gave understanding to the mind?
Who has the wisdom to count the clouds?
   Who can tip over the water jars of the heavens
when the dust becomes hard
   and the clods of earth stick together?

"Do you hunt the prey for the lioness
   and satisfy the hunger of the lions
when they crouch in their dens
   or lie in wait in a thicket?
Who provides food for the raven
   when its young cry out to God
   and wander about for lack of food?"]

and **Psalm 104:1–9,**   Praise the LORD, O my soul.
24, 35c*
O LORD my God, you are very great;
   you are clothed with splendour and majesty.
He wraps himself in light as with a garment;
   he stretches out the heavens like a tent
   and lays the beams of his upper chambers on their
      waters.
He makes the clouds his chariot
   and rides on the wings of the wind.
He makes winds his messengers,
   flames of fire his servants.

He set the earth on its foundations;
   it can never be moved.
You covered it with the deep as with a garment;
   the waters stood above the mountains.
But at your rebuke the waters fled,
   at the sound of your thunder they took to flight;

they flowed over the mountains,
　　they went down into the valleys,
　　to the place you assigned for them.
You set a boundary they cannot cross;
　　never again will they cover the earth.

How many are your works, O LORD!
　　In wisdom you made them all;
　　the earth is full of your creatures.

Praise the LORD.

Or **RELATED**

Isaiah 53:4–12　Surely he took up our infirmities
　　　　and carried our sorrows,
　　yet we considered him stricken by God,
　　　　smitten by him, and afflicted.
　But he was pierced for our transgressions,
　　　he was crushed for our iniquities;
　the punishment that brought us peace was upon him,
　　　and by his wounds we are healed.
　We all, like sheep, have gone astray,
　　　each of us has turned to his own way;
　and the LORD has laid on him
　　　the iniquity of us all.

He was oppressed and afflicted,
　　yet he did not open his mouth;
he was led like a lamb to the slaughter,
　　　and as a sheep before her shearers is silent,
　　　so he did not open his mouth.
By oppression and judgment he was taken away.
　　And who can speak of his descendants?
For he was cut off from the land of the living;
　　　for the transgression of my people he was stricken.
He was assigned a grave with the wicked,
　　and with the rich in his death,
though he had done no violence,
　　nor was any deceit in his mouth.

Yet it was the LORD's will to crush him and
　　　cause him to suffer,
　and though the LORD makes his life a guilt offering,
he will see his offspring and prolong his days,
　　and the will of the LORD will prosper in his hand.
After the suffering of his soul,
　　he will see the light of life and be satisfied;
by his knowledge my righteous servant will justify many,
　　and he will bear their iniquities.

FIRST

READING

Therefore I will give him a portion among the great,
    and he will divide the spoils with the strong,
because he poured out his life unto death,
    and was numbered with the transgressors.
For he bore the sin of many,
    and made intercession for the transgressors.

and **Psalm 91:9–16**   If you make the Most High your dwelling –
    even the LORD, who is my refuge –
then no harm will befall you,
    no disaster will come near your tent.
For he will command his angels concerning you
    to guard you in all your ways;
they will lift you up in their hands,
    so that you will not strike your foot against a stone.
You will tread upon the lion and the cobra;
    you will trample the great lion and the serpent.

"Because he loves me," says the LORD, "I will rescue him;
    I will protect him, for he acknowledges my name.
He will call upon me, and I will answer him;
    I will be with him in trouble,
    I will deliver him and honour him.
With long life will I satisfy him
    and show him my salvation."

Hebrews 5:1–10   Every high priest is selected from among men and is appointed to represent them in matters related to God, to offer gifts and sacrifices for sins. He is able to deal gently with those who are ignorant and are going astray, since he himself is subject to weakness. This is why he has to offer sacrifices for his own sins, as well as for the sins of the people.

No-one takes this honour upon himself; he must be called by God, just as Aaron was. So Christ also did not take upon himself the glory of becoming a high priest. But God said to him,

"You are my Son;
    today I have become your Father."

And he says in another place,

"You are a priest for ever,
    in the order of Melchizedek."

During the days of Jesus' life on earth, he offered up prayers and petitions with loud cries and tears to the one who could save him from death, and he was heard because of his reverent submission. Although he was a son, he learned obedience from what he suffered and, once made perfect, he became the source of eternal salvation for all who obey him and was designated by God to be high priest in the order of Melchizedek.

Mark 10:35–45   James and John, the sons of Zebedee, came to Jesus. "Teacher," they said, "we want you to do for us whatever we ask."

"What do you want me to do for you?" he asked.

They replied, "Let one of us sit at your right and the other at your left in your glory."

"You don't know what you are asking," Jesus said. "Can you drink the cup I drink or be baptised with the baptism I am baptised with?"

"We can," they answered.

Jesus said to them, "You will drink the cup I drink and be baptised with the baptism I am baptised with, but to sit at my right or left is not for me to grant. These places belong to those for whom they have been prepared."

When the ten heard about this, they became indignant with James and John. Jesus called them together and said, "You know that those who are regarded as rulers of the Gentiles lord it over them, and their high officials exercise authority over them. Not so with you. Instead, whoever wants to become great among you must be your servant, and whoever wants to be first must be slave of all. For even the Son of Man did not come to be served, but to serve, and to give his life as a ransom for many."

Proper 25

Sunday between 23 and 29 October inclusive (if after Trinity Sunday)
Choose either 'continuous' or 'related' Old Testament and Psalm readings.
Bible Sunday may be celebrated in preference to the provision for the Last Sunday after Trinity.

CONTINUOUS

Job 42:1–6, 10–17   Job replied to the LORD:

"I know that you can do all things;	F
no plan of yours can be thwarted.	I
	R
You asked, 'Who is this that obscures my counsel without knowledge?'	S
Surely I spoke of things I did not understand,	T
things too wonderful for me to know.	
"You said, 'Listen now, and I will speak;	R
I will question you,	E
and you shall answer me.'	A
My ears had heard of you	D
but now my eyes have seen you.	I
Therefore I despise myself	N
and repent in dust and ashes."	G

After Job had prayed for his friends, the LORD made him prosperous again and gave him twice as much as he had before. All his brothers an sisters and everyone who had known him before came and ate with him in his house. They comforted and consoled him over all the trouble the LORD had brought upon him, and each one gave him a piece of silver and a gold ring.

The LORD blessed the latter part of Job's life more than the first. He had fourteen thousand sheep, six thousand camels, a thousand yoke of oxen and a thousand donkeys. And he also had seven sons and three daughters. The first daughter he named Jemimah, the second Keziah and the third Keren-Happuch. Nowhere in all the land were there found women as beautiful as Job's daughters, and their father granted them an inheritance along with their brothers.

After this, Job lived a hundred and forty years; he saw his children and their children to the fourth generation. And so he died, old and full of years.

and **Psalm 34:1–8, 19–22***

I will extol the Lord at all times;
    his praise will always be on my lips.
My soul will boast in the Lord;
    let the afflicted hear and rejoice.
Glorify the Lord with me:
    let us exalt his name together.

I sought the Lord, and he answered me;
    he delivered me from all my fears.
Those who look to him are radiant;
    their faces are never covered with shame.
This poor man called, and the Lord heard him;
    he saved him out of all his troubles.
The angel of the Lord encamps around those
      who fear him,
    and he delivers them.

Taste and see that the Lord is good;
    blessed are those who take refuge in him.

A righteous man may have many troubles,
    but the Lord delivers him from them all;
he protects all his bones,
    not one of them will be broken.

Evil will slay the wicked;
    the foes of the righteous will be condemned.
The Lord redeems his servants;
    no-one will be condemned who takes refuge in him.

Or **RELATED**

Jeremiah 31:7–9

This is what the Lord says:

"Sing with joy for Jacob;
    shout for the foremost of the nations.
Make your praises heard, and say,
    'O Lord, save your people,
    the remnant of Israel.'
See, I will bring them from the land of the north
    and gather them from the ends of the earth.
Among them will be the blind and the lame,
    expectant mothers and women in labour;
    a great throng will return.
They will come with weeping;
    they will pray as I bring them back.

I will lead them beside streams of water
    on a level path where they will not stumble,
because I am Israel's father,
    and Ephraim is my firstborn son."

and **Psalm 126**

When the LORD brought back the captives to Zion,
    we were like men who dreamed.
Our mouths were filled with laughter,
    our tongues with songs of joy.
Then it was said among the nations,
    "The LORD has done great things for them."
The LORD has done great things for us,
    and we are filled with joy.
Restore our fortunes, O LORD,
    like streams in the Negev.
Those who sow in tears
    will reap with songs of joy.
Those who go out weeping,
    carrying seed to sow,
will return with songs of joy,
    carrying sheaves with them.

Hebrews 7:23–28

There have been many Levitical priests, since death prevented them from continuing in office; but because Jesus lives for ever, he has a permanent priesthood. Therefore he is able to save completely those who come to God through him, because he always lives to intercede for them.

Such a high priest meets our need – one who is holy, blameless, pure, set apart from sinners, exalted above the heavens. Unlike the other high priests, he does not need to offer sacrifices day after day, first for his own sins, and then for the sins of the people. He sacrificed for their sins once for all when he offered himself. For the law appoints as high priests men who are weak; but the oath, which came after the law, appointed the Son, who has been made perfect for ever.

Mark 10:46–52

Jesus and his disciples came to Jericho. As they, together with a large crowd, were leaving the city, a blind man, Bartimaeus (that is, the Son of Timaeus), was sitting by the roadside begging. When he heard that it was Jesus of Nazareth, he began to shout, "Jesus, Son of David, have mercy on me!"

Many rebuked him and told him to be quiet, but he shouted all the more, "Son of David, have mercy on me!"

Jesus stopped and said, "Call him."

So they called to the blind man, "Cheer up! On your feet! He's calling you." Throwing his cloak aside, he jumped to his feet and came to Jesus.

"What do you want me to do for you?" Jesus asked him.

The blind man said, "Rabbi, I want to see."

"Go," said Jesus, "your faith has healed you." Immediately he received his sight and followed Jesus along the road.

Bible Sunday

Bible Sunday may be celebrated in preference to the provision for the Last Sunday after Trinity.

Isaiah 55:1–11   "Come, all you who are thirsty,
come to the waters;
and you who have no money,
come, buy and eat!
Come, buy wine and milk
without money and without cost.
Why spend money on what is not bread,
and your labour on what does not satisfy?
Listen, listen to me, and eat what is good,
and your soul will delight in the richest of fare.
Give ear and come to me;
hear me, that your soul may live.
I will make an everlasting covenant with you,
my faithful love promised to David.
See, I have made him a witness to the peoples,
a leader and commander of the peoples.
Surely you will summon nations you know not,
and nations that do not know you will hasten to you,
because of the Lord your God,
the Holy One of Israel,
for he has endowed you with splendour."

Seek the Lord while he may be found;
call on him while he is near.
Let the wicked forsake their ways
and the evil man his thoughts.
Let him turn to the Lord, and he will have mercy on him,
and to our God, for he will freely pardon.

"For my thoughts are not your thoughts,
neither are your ways my ways,"
declares the Lord.

"As the heavens are higher than the earth,
so are my ways higher than your ways
and my thoughts than your thoughts.
As the rain and the snow
come down from heaven,
and do not return to it
without watering the earth
and making it bud and flourish,
so that it yields seed for the sower and bread for the eater,

FIRST READING

so is my word that goes out from my mouth:
It will not return to me empty,
but will accomplish what I desire
and achieve the purpose for which I sent it."

Psalm 19:7–14 The law of the LORD is perfect,

reviving the soul.
The statutes of the LORD are trustworthy,
making wise the simple.
The precepts of the LORD are right,
giving joy to the heart.
The commands of the LORD are radiant,
giving light to the eyes.
The fear of the LORD is pure,
enduring for ever.
The ordinances of the LORD are sure
and altogether righteous.
They are more precious than gold,
than much pure gold;
they are sweeter than honey,
than honey from the comb.
By them is your servant warned;
in keeping them there is great reward.

Who can discern their errors?
Forgive my hidden faults.
Keep your servant also from wilful sins;
may they not rule over me.
Then will I be blameless,
innocent of great transgression.

May the words of my mouth and the meditation of my heart
be pleasing in your sight,
O LORD, my Rock and my Redeemer.

Timothy 3:14 – 4:5 Continue in what you have learned and have become

convinced of, because you know those from whom you learned it, and how
from infancy you have known the holy Scriptures, which are able to make
you wise for salvation through faith in Christ Jesus. All Scripture is God-
breathed and is useful for teaching, rebuking, correcting and training in
righteousness, so that the man of God may be thoroughly equipped for
every good work.

In the presence of God and of Christ Jesus, who will judge the living and
the dead, and in view of his appearing and his kingdom, I give you this
charge: Preach the Word; be prepared in season and out of season; correct,
rebuke and encourage – with great patience and careful instruction. For
the time will come when men will not put up with sound doctrine. Instead,
to suit their own desires, they will gather around them a great number of

teachers to say what their itching ears want to hear. They will turn their ears away from the truth and turn aside to myths. But you, keep your head in all situations, endure hardship, do the work of an evangelist, discharge all the duties of your ministry.

John 5:36b–47   Jesus said: "The very work that the Father has given me to finish, and which I am doing, testifies that the Father has sent me. And the Father who sent me has himself testified concerning me. You have never heard his voice nor seen his form, nor does his word dwell in you, for you do not believe the one he sent. You diligently study the Scriptures because you think that by them you possess eternal life. These are the Scriptures that testify about me, yet you refuse to come to me to have life.

"I do not accept praise from men, but I know you. I know that you do not have the love of God in your hearts. I have come in my Father's name, and you do not accept me; but if someone else comes in his own name, you will accept him. How can you believe if you accept praise from one another, yet make no effort to obtain the praise that comes from the only God?

"But do not think I will accuse you before the Father. Your accuser is Moses, on whom your hopes are set. If you believed Moses, you would believe me, for he wrote about me. But since you do not believe what he wrote, how are you going to believe what I say?"

Dedication Festival

The First Sunday in October or Last Sunday after Trinity

Alternative first readings

Either **Genesis 28:11–18**   When Jacob reached a certain place, he stopped for the night because the sun had set. Taking one of the stones there, he put it under his head and lay down to sleep. He had a dream in which he saw a stairway resting on the earth, with its top reaching to heaven, and the angels of God were ascending and descending on it. There above it stood the LORD, and he said: "I am the LORD, the God of your father Abraham and the God of Isaac. I will give you and your descendants the land on which you are lying. Your descendants will be like the dust of the earth, and you will spread out to the west and to the east, to the north and to the south. All peoples on earth will be blessed through you and your offspring. I am with you and will watch over you wherever you go, and I will bring you back to this land. I will not leave you until I have done what I have promised you."

When Jacob awoke from his sleep, he thought, "Surely the LORD is in this place, and I was not aware of it." He was afraid and said, "How awesome is this place! This is none other than the house of God; this is the gate of heaven."

Early the next morning Jacob took the stone he had placed under his head and set it up as a pillar and poured oil on top of it.

or Revelation 21:9–14   One of the seven angels who had the seven bowls full of the seven last plagues came and said to me, "Come, I will show you the bride, the wife of the Lamb." And he carried me away in the Spirit to a mountain great and high, and showed me the Holy City, Jerusalem, coming down out of heaven from God. It shone with the glory of God, and its bril- liance was like that of a very precious jewel, like a jasper, clear as crystal. It had a great, high wall with twelve gates, and with twelve angels at the gates. On the gates were written the names of the twelve tribes of Israel. There were three gates on the east, three on the north, three on the south and three on the west. The wall of the city had twelve foundations, and on them were the names of the twelve apostles of the Lamb.

Psalm 122   I rejoiced with those who said to me,
    "Let us go to the house of the LORD."
Our feet are standing
    in your gates, O Jerusalem.

Jerusalem is built like a city
    that is closely compacted together.
That is where the tribes go up,
    the tribes of the LORD,
to praise the name of the LORD
    according to the statute given to Israel.
There the thrones for judgment stand,
    the thrones of the house of David.

Pray for the peace of Jerusalem:
    "May those who love you be secure.
May there be peace within your walls
    and security within your citadels."
For the sake of my relatives and friends,
    I will say, "Peace be within you."
For the sake of the house of the LORD our God,
    I will seek your prosperity.

Peter 2:1–10   Rid yourselves of all malice and all deceit, hypocrisy, envy, and slander of every kind. Like newborn babies, crave pure spiritual milk, so that by it you may grow up in your salvation, now that you have tasted that the LORD is good.

As you come to him, the living Stone – rejected by men but chosen by God and precious to him – you also, like living stones, are being built into a spiritual house to be a holy priesthood, offering spiritual sacrifices accept- able to God through Jesus Christ. For in Scripture it says:

"See, I lay a stone in Zion,
    a chosen and precious cornerstone,
and the one who trusts in him
    will never be put to shame."

Now to you who believe, this stone is precious. But to those who do not believe,

> "The stone the builders rejected
> has become the capstone,"

and,

> "A stone that causes men to stumble
> and a rock that makes them fall."

They stumble because they disobey the message – which is also what they were destined for.

But you are a chosen people, a royal priesthood, a holy nation, a people belonging to God, that you may declare the praises of him who called you out of darkness into his wonderful light. Once you were not a people, but now you are the people of God; once you had not received mercy, but now you have received mercy.

John 10:22–29   The time came for the Feast of Dedication at Jerusalem. It was winter, and Jesus was in the temple area walking in Solomon's Colonnade. The Jews gathered round him, saying, "How long will you keep us in suspense? If you are the Christ, tell us plainly."

Jesus answered, "I did tell you, but you do not believe. The miracles I do in my Father's name speak for me, but you do not believe because you are not my sheep. My sheep listen to my voice; I know them, and they follow me. I give them eternal life, and they shall never perish; no-one can snatch them out of my hand. My Father, who has given them to me, is greater than all; no-one can snatch them out of my Father's hand."

G O S P E L

All Saints' Day

Sunday between 30 October and 5 November or, if this is not kept as All Saint's Sunday, on 1 November itself

Alternative first readings

Either **Wisdom 3:1–9**

or **Isaiah 25:6–9**   On this mountain the LORD Almighty will prepare
> a feast of rich food for all peoples,
> a banquet of aged wine –
> the best of meats and the finest of wines.
> On this mountain he will destroy
> the shroud that enfolds all peoples,
> the sheet that covers all nations;
> he will swallow up death for ever.
> The Sovereign LORD will wipe away the tears
> from all faces;
> he will remove the disgrace of his people
> from all the earth.
> The LORD has spoken.

FIRST READING

In that day they will say,

"Surely this is our God;
    we trusted in him, and he saved us.
This is the LORD, we trusted in him;
    let us rejoice and be glad in his salvation."

Psalm 24:1–6   The earth is the LORD's, and everything in it,
    the world, and all who live in it;
for he founded it upon the seas
    and established it upon the waters.

Who may ascend the hill of the LORD?
    Who may stand in his holy place?
He who has clean hands and a pure heart,
    who does not lift up his soul to an idol
    or swear by what is false.
He will receive blessing from the LORD
    and vindication from God their Saviour.
Such is the generation of those who seek him,
    who seek your face, O God of Jacob.

P S A L M

Revelation 21:1–6a   I saw a new heaven and a new earth, for the first heaven and the first earth had passed away, and there was no longer any sea. I saw the Holy City, the new Jerusalem, coming down out of heaven from God, prepared as a bride beautifully dressed for her husband. And I heard a loud voice from the throne saying, "Now the dwelling of God is with men, and he will live with them. They will be his people, and God himself will be with them and be their God. He will wipe every tear from their eyes. There will be no more death or mourning or crying or pain, for the old order of things has passed away."

He who was seated on the throne said, "I am making everything new!" Then he said, "Write this down, for these words are trustworthy and true."

He said to me: "It is done. I am the Alpha and the Omega, the Beginning and the End."

S E C O N D
R E A D I N G

John 11:32–44   When Mary reached the place where Jesus was and saw him, she fell at his feet and said, "Lord, if you had been here, my brother would not have died."

When Jesus saw her weeping, and the Jews who had come along with her also weeping, he was deeply moved in spirit and troubled. "Where have you laid him?" he asked.

"Come and see, Lord," they replied.

Jesus wept.

Then the Jews said, "See how he loved him!"

But some of them said, "Could not he who opened the eyes of the blind man have kept this man from dying?"

Jesus, once more deeply moved, came to the tomb. It was a cave with a stone laid across the entrance. "Take away the stone," he said.

G O S P E L

"But, Lord," said Martha, the sister of the dead man, "by this time there is a bad odour, for he has been there four days."

Then Jesus said, "Did I not tell you that if you believed, you would see the glory of God?"

So they took away the stone. Then Jesus looked up and said, "Father, I thank you that you have heard me. I knew that you always hear me, but I said this for the benefit of the people standing here, that they may believe that you sent me."

When he had said this, Jesus called in a loud voice, "Lazarus, come out!" The dead man came out, his hands and feet wrapped with strips of linen, and a cloth around his face.

Jesus said to them, "Take off the grave clothes and let him go."

On 1 November if the material for All Saint's Day is used on the Sunday, use text of readings for Years A, B, C on pp 221–223.

Fourth Sunday Before Advent

Sunday between 30 October and 5 November inclusive
For use if the Feast of All Saints was celebrated on 1 November and alternative propers are needed.

Deuteronomy 6:1–9 Moses said: These are the commands, decrees and laws F
the LORD your God directed me to teach you to observe in the land that you I
are crossing the Jordan to possess, so that you, your children and their R
children after them may fear the LORD your God as long as you live by S
keeping all his decrees and commands that I give you, and so that you may T
enjoy long life. Hear, O Israel, and be careful to obey so that it may go well
with you and that you may increase greatly in a land flowing with milk and R
honey, just as the LORD, the God of your fathers, promised you.   E

Hear, O Israel: The LORD our God, the LORD is one. Love the LORD your A
God with all your heart and with all your soul and with all your strength. D
These commandments that I give you today are to be upon your hearts. I
Impress them on your children. Talk about them when you sit at home and N
when you walk along the road, when you lie down and when you get up. Tie G
them as symbols on your hands and bind them on your foreheads. Write
them on the door-frames of your houses and on your gates.

Psalm 119:1–8 Blessed are they whose ways are blameless,   P
    who walk according to the law of the LORD.   S
Blessed are they who keep his statutes   A
    and seek him with all their heart.   L
They do nothing wrong;   M
    they walk in his ways.
You have laid down precepts
    that are to be fully obeyed.
Oh, that my ways were steadfast
    in obeying your decrees!
Then I would not be put to shame
    when I consider all your commands.

I will praise you with an upright heart
    as I learn your righteous laws.
I will obey your decrees;
    do not utterly forsake me.

Hebrews 9:11–14 When Christ came as high priest of the good things that are already here, he went through the greater and more perfect tabernacle that is not man-made, that is to say, not a part of this creation. He did not enter by means of the blood of goats and calves; but he entered the Most Holy Place once for all by his own blood, having obtained eternal redemption. The blood of goats and bulls and the ashes of a heifer sprinkled on those who are ceremonially unclean sanctify them so that they are outwardly clean. How much more, then, will the blood of Christ, who through the eternal Spirit offered himself unblemished to God, cleanse our consciences from acts that lead to death, so that we may serve the living God!

SECOND READING

Mark 12:28–34 One of the teachers of the law came and heard the Sadducees debating with Jesus. Noticing that Jesus had given them a good answer, he asked him, "Of all the commandments, which is the most important?"

"The most important one," answered Jesus, "is this: 'Hear, O Israel, the Lord our God, the Lord is one. Love the Lord your God with all your heart and with all your soul and with all your mind and with all your strength.' The second is this: 'Love your neighbour as yourself.' There is no commandment greater than these."

"Well said, teacher," the man replied. "You are right in saying that God is one and there is no other but him. To love him with all your heart, with all your understanding and with all your strength, and to love your neighbour as yourself is more important than all burnt offerings and sacrifices."

When Jesus saw that he had answered wisely, he said to him, "You are not far from the kingdom of God." And from then on no-one dared ask him any more questions.

GOSPEL

Third Sunday Before Advent

Sunday between 6 and 12 November inclusive

Jonah 3:1–5, 10 The word of the LORD came to Jonah a second time: "Go to the great city of Nineveh and proclaim to it the message I give you."

Jonah obeyed the word of the LORD and went to Nineveh. Now Nineveh was a very important city – a visit required three days. On the first day, Jonah started into the city. He proclaimed: "Forty more days and Nineveh will be overturned." The Ninevites believed God. They declared a fast, and all of them, from the greatest to the least, put on sackcloth.

When God saw what they did and how they turned from their evil ways, he had compassion and did not bring upon them the destruction he had threatened.

FIRST READING

Psalm 62:5–12   Find rest, O my soul, in God alone;
my hope comes from him.
He alone is my rock and my salvation;
he is my fortress, I shall not be shaken.
My salvation and my honour depend on God;
he is my mighty rock, my refuge.
Trust in him at all times, O people;
pour out your hearts to him,
for God is our refuge.

Lowborn men are but a breath,
the highborn are but a lie;
if weighed on a balance, they are nothing;
together they are only a breath.
Do not trust in extortion
or take pride in stolen goods;
though your riches increase,
do not set your heart on them.

One thing God has spoken,
two things have I heard:
that you, O God, are strong,
and that you, O Lord, are loving.
Surely you will reward each person
according to what he has done.

P S A L M

Hebrews 9:24–28   Christ did not enter a man-made sanctuary that was only a copy of the true one; he entered heaven itself, now to appear for us in God's presence. Nor did he enter heaven to offer himself again and again, the way the high priest enters the Most Holy Place every year with blood that is not his own. Then Christ would have had to suffer many times since the creation of the world. But now he has appeared once for all at the end of the ages to do away with sin by the sacrifice of himself. Just as man is destined to die once, and after that to face judgment, so Christ was sacrificed once to take away the sins of many people; and he will appear a second time, not to bear sin, but to bring salvation to those who are waiting for him.

S E C O N D R E A D I N G

Mark 1:14–20   After John was put in prison, Jesus went into Galilee, proclaiming the good news of God. "The time has come," he said. "The kingdom of God is near. Repent and believe the good news!"

As Jesus walked beside the Sea of Galilee, he saw Simon and his brother Andrew casting a net into the lake, for they were fishermen. "Come, follow me," Jesus said, "and I will make you fishers of men." At once they left their nets and followed him.

When he had gone a little farther, he saw James son of Zebedee and his brother John in a boat, preparing their nets. Without delay he called them, and they left their father Zebedee in the boat with the hired men and followed him.

G O S P E L

Second Sunday Before Advent

Sunday between 13 and 19 November inclusive

Daniel 12:1–3 "At that time Michael, the great prince who protects your peo- F R
ple, will arise. There will be a time of distress such as has not happened I E
from the beginning of nations until then. But at that time your people – R A
everyone whose name is found written in the book – will be delivered. Mul- S D
titudes who sleep in the dust of the earth will awake: some to everlasting T I
life, others to shame and everlasting contempt. Those who are wise will N
shine like the brightness of the heavens, and those who lead many to right- G
eousness, like the stars for ever and ever."

Psalm 16 Keep me safe, O God, P
for in you I take refuge. S

I said to the Lord, "You are my Lord; A
apart from you I have no good thing." L

As for the saints who are in the land, M
they are the glorious ones in whom is all my delight.
The sorrows of those will increase
who run after other gods.
I will not pour out their libations of blood
or take up their names on my lips.

Lord, you have assigned me my portion and my cup;
you have made my lot secure.
The boundary lines have fallen for me in pleasant places;
surely I have a delightful inheritance.

I will praise the Lord, who counsels me;
even at night my heart instructs me.
I have set the Lord always before me.
Because he is at my right hand,
I shall not be shaken.

Therefore my heart is glad and my tongue rejoices;
my body also will rest secure,
because you will not abandon me to the grave,
nor will you let your Holy One see decay.
You have made known to me the path of life;
you will fill me with joy in your presence,
with eternal pleasures at your right hand.

Hebrews 10:11–14 [15–18] 19–25 Day after day every priest stands and per- S R
forms his religious duties; again and again he offers the same sacrifices, E E
which can never take away sins. But when this priest had offered for all C A
time one sacrifice for sins, he sat down at the right hand of God. Since O D
that time he waits for his enemies to be made his footstool, because by N I
one sacrifice he has made perfect for ever those who are being made D N
holy. G

[The Holy Spirit also testifies to us about this. First he says:

"This is the covenant I will make with them
after that time, says the LORD.
I will put my laws in their hearts,
and I will write them on their minds."

Then he adds:

"Their sins and lawless acts
I will remember no more."

And where these have been forgiven, there is no longer any sacrifice for sin.]

Therefore, brothers, since we have confidence to enter the Most Holy Place by the blood of Jesus, by a new and living way opened for us through the curtain, that is, his body, and since we have a great priest over the house of God, let us draw near to God with a sincere heart in full assurance of faith, having our hearts sprinkled to cleanse us from a guilty conscience and having our bodies washed with pure water. Let us hold unswervingly to the hope we profess, for he who promised is faithful. And let us consider how we may spur one another on towards love and good deeds. Let us not give up meeting together, as some are in the habit of doing, but let us encourage one another – and all the more as you see the Day approaching.

Mark 13:1–8 As Jesus was leaving the temple, one of his disciples said to him, "Look, Teacher! What massive stones! What magnificent buildings!"

"Do you see all these great buildings?" replied Jesus. "Not one stone here will be left on another; every one will be thrown down."

As Jesus was sitting on the Mount of Olives opposite the temple, Peter, James, John and Andrew asked him privately, "Tell us, when will these things happen? And what will be the sign that they are all about to be fulfilled?"

Jesus said to them: "Watch out that no-one deceives you. Many will come in my name, claiming, 'I am he,' and will deceive many. When you hear of wars and rumours of wars, do not be alarmed. Such things must happen, but the end is still to come. Nation will rise against nation, and kingdom against kingdom. There will be earthquakes in various places, and famines. These are the beginning of birth-pains."

GOSPEL

Christ The King

Sunday between 20 and 26 November inclusive

Daniel 7:9–10, 13–14 Daniel said: "As I looked,

"thrones were set in place,
and the Ancient of Days took his seat.
His clothing was as white as snow;
the hair of his head was white like wool.

FIRST READING

His throne was flaming with fire,
  and its wheels were all ablaze.
A river of fire was flowing,
  coming out from before him.
Thousands upon thousands attended him;
  ten thousand times ten thousand stood before him.
The court was seated,
  and the books were opened.

"In my vision at night I looked, and there before me was one like a son of man, coming with the clouds of heaven. He approached the Ancient of Days and was led into his presence. He was given authority, glory and sovereign power; all peoples, nations and men of every language worshipped him. His dominion is an everlasting dominion that will not pass away, and his kingdom is one that will never be destroyed."

Psalm 93   The LORD reigns, he is robed in majesty;   P
  the LORD is robed in majesty   S
  and is armed with strength.   A
The world is firmly established;   L
  it cannot be moved.   M
Your throne was established long ago;
  you are from all eternity.

The seas have lifted up, O LORD,
  the seas have lifted up their voice;
  the seas have lifted up their pounding waves.
Mightier than the thunder of the great waters,
  mightier than the breakers of the sea –
  the LORD on high is mighty.

Your statutes stand firm;
  holiness adorns your house
  for endless days, O LORD.

Revelation 1:4b–8   Grace and peace to you from him who is, and who was,   S R
and who is to come, and from the seven spirits before his throne, and from   E E
Jesus Christ, who is the faithful witness, the firstborn from the dead, and   C A
the ruler of the kings of the earth.   O D
  To him who loves us and has freed us from our sins by his blood, and has   N I
made us to be a kingdom and priests to serve his God and Father – to him   D N
be glory and power for ever and ever! Amen.   G

Look, he is coming with the clouds,
  and every eye will see him,
even those who pierced him;
  and all the peoples of the earth will mourn because of him.
                    So shall it be! Amen.

"I am the Alpha and the Omega," says the LORD God, "who is, and who was, and who is to come, the Almighty."

John 18:33–37   Pilate went back inside the palace, summoned Jesus and asked him, "Are you the king of the Jews?"

"Is that your own idea," Jesus asked, "or did others talk to you about me?"

"Am I a Jew?" Pilate replied. "It was your people and your chief priests who handed you over to me. What is it you have done?"

Jesus said, "My kingdom is not of this world. If it were, my servants would fight to prevent my arrest by the Jews. But now my kingdom is from another place."

"You are a king, then!" said Pilate.

Jesus answered, "You are right in saying I am a king. In fact, for this reason I was born, and for this I came into the world, to testify to the truth. Everyone on the side of truth listens to me."

GOSPEL

CHURCH OF ENGLAND LECTIONARY FOR THE PRINCIPAL SUNDAY SERVICE (RCL AMENDED)

Year C

THE SEASONS: ADVENT

First Sunday of Advent

Jeremiah 33:14–16   "'The days are coming,' declares the LORD, 'when I will
fulfil the gracious promise I made to the house of Israel and to the house of
Judah.

> "'In those days and at that time
>> I will make a righteous Branch sprout from David's line;
>> he will do what is just and right in the land.
> In those days Judah will be saved
>> and Jerusalem will live in safety.
> This is the name by which it will be called:
>> The LORD Our Righteousness.'"

F R
I E
R A
S D
T I
N
G

Psalm 25:1–10
> To you, O LORD, I lift up my soul;
>> in you I trust, O my God.
> Do not let me be put to shame,
>> nor let my enemies triumph over me.
> No-one whose hope is in you
>> will ever be put to shame,
> but they will be put to shame
>> who are treacherous without excuse.
>
> Show me your ways, O LORD,
>> teach me your paths;
> guide me in your truth and teach me,
>> for you are God my Saviour,
>> and my hope is in you all day long.
> Remember, O LORD, your great mercy and love,
>> for they are from of old.
> Remember not the sins of my youth
>> and my rebellious ways;
> according to your love remember me,
>> for you are good, O LORD.
>
> Good and upright is the LORD;
>> therefore he instructs sinners in his ways.
> He guides the humble in what is right
>> and teaches them his way.
> All the ways of the LORD are loving and faithful
>> for those who keep the demands of his covenant.

P
S
A
L
M

1 Thessalonians 3:9–13 How can we thank God enough for you in return for all the joy we have in the presence of our God because of you? Night and day we pray most earnestly that we may see you again and supply what is lacking in your faith.

Now may our God and Father himself and our Lord Jesus clear the way for us to come to you. May the Lord make your love increase and overflow for each other and for everyone else, just as ours does for you. May he strengthen your hearts so that you will be blameless and holy in the presence of our God and Father when our Lord Jesus comes with all his holy ones.

Luke 21:25–36 Jesus said: "There will be signs in the sun, moon and stars. On the earth, nations will be in anguish and perplexity at the roaring and tossing of the sea. People will faint from terror, apprehensive of what is coming on the world, for the heavenly bodies will be shaken. At that time they will see the Son of Man coming in a cloud with power and great glory. When these things begin to take place, stand up and lift up your heads, because your redemption is drawing near."

He told them this parable: "Look at the fig-tree and all the trees. When they sprout leaves, you can see for yourselves and know that summer is near. Even so, when you see these things happening, you know that the kingdom of God is near.

"I tell you the truth, this generation will certainly not pass away until all these things have happened. Heaven and earth will pass away, but my words will never pass away.

"Be careful, or your hearts will be weighed down with dissipation, drunkenness and the anxieties of life, and that day will close on you unexpectedly like a trap. For it will come upon all those who live on the face of the whole earth. Be always on the watch, and pray that you may be able to escape all that is about to happen, and that you may be able to stand before the Son of Man."

Second Sunday of Advent

Alternative first reading

Either **Baruch 5:1–9**

or **Malachi 3:1–4** "See, I will send my messenger, who will prepare the way before me. Then suddenly the LORD you are seeking will come to his temple; the messenger of the covenant, whom you desire, will come," says the LORD Almighty.

But who can endure the day of his coming? Who can stand when he appears? For he will be like a refiner's fire or a launderer's soap. He will sit as a refiner and purifier of silver; he will purify the Levites and refine them like gold and silver. Then the LORD will have people who will bring offerings in righteousness, and the offerings of Judah and Jerusalem will be acceptable to the LORD, as in days gone by, as in former years.

Canticle: **Benedictus**

Luke 1:68–79   "Praise be to the LORD, the God of Israel,

because he has come and has redeemed his people.

He has raised up a horn of salvation for us

in the house of his servant David,

(as he said through his holy prophets of long ago),

salvation from our enemies

and from the hand of all who hate us –

to show mercy to our fathers

and to remember his holy covenant,

the oath he swore to our father Abraham:

to rescue us from the hand of our enemies,

and to enable us to serve him without fear

in holiness and righteousness before him all our days.

And you, my child, will be called a prophet of the Most High;

for you will go on before the LORD to prepare the way for him,

to give his people the knowledge of salvation

through the forgiveness of their sins,

because of the tender mercy of our God,

by which the rising sun will come to us from heaven

to shine on those living in darkness

and in the shadow of death,

to guide our feet into the path of peace."

C A N T I C L E

Philippians 1:3–11   I thank my God every time I remember you. In all my prayers for all of you, I always pray with joy because of your partnership in the gospel from the first day until now, being confident of this, that he who began a good work in you will carry it on to completion until the day of Christ Jesus.

It is right for me to feel this way about all of you, since I have you in my heart; for whether I am in chains or defending and confirming the gospel, all of you share in God's grace with me. God can testify how I long for all of you with the affection of Christ Jesus.

And this is my prayer: that your love may abound more and more in knowledge and depth of insight, so that you may be able to discern what is best and may be pure and blameless until the day of Christ, filled with the fruit of righteousness that comes through Jesus Christ – to the glory and praise of God.

S R E E C A O D N I N G

Luke 3:1–6   In the fifteenth year of the reign of Tiberius Caesar – when Pontius Pilate was governor of Judea, Herod tetrarch of Galilee, his brother Philip tetrarch of Iturea and Traconitis, and Lysanias tetrarch of Abilene – during the high priesthood of Annas and Caiaphas, the word of God came

G O S P E L

to John son of Zechariah in the desert. He went into all the country around the Jordan, preaching a baptism of repentance for the forgiveness of sins. As is written in the book of the words of Isaiah the prophet:

> "A voice of one calling in the desert,
> 'Prepare the way for the LORD,
>> make straight paths for him.
> Every valley shall be filled in,
>> every mountain and hill made low.
> The crooked roads shall become straight,
>> the rough ways smooth.
> And the whole human race will see God's salvation.'"

Third Sunday of Advent

Zephaniah 3:14–20

> Sing, O Daughter of Zion;
>> shout aloud, O Israel!
> Be glad and rejoice with all your heart,
>> O Daughter of Jerusalem!
> The LORD has taken away your punishment,
>> he has turned back your enemy.
> The LORD, the King of Israel, is with you;
>> never again will you fear any harm.
> On that day they will say to Jerusalem,
>> "Do not fear, O Zion;
>> do not let your hands hang limp.
> The LORD your God is with you,
>> he is mighty to save.
> He will take great delight in you,
>> he will quiet you with his love,
>> he will rejoice over you with singing."
>
> "The sorrows for the appointed feasts
>> I will remove from you;
>> they are a burden and a reproach to you.
> At that time I will deal
>> with all who oppressed you;
> I will rescue the lame
>> and gather those who have been scattered.
> I will give them praise and honour
>> in every land where they were put to shame.
> At that time I will gather you;
>> at that time I will bring you home.
> I will give you honour and praise
>> among all the peoples of the earth
> when I restore your fortunes
>> before your very eyes,"
>>>>> says the LORD.

F
I
R
S
T

R
E
A
D
I
N
G

Canticle:

Isaiah 12:2–6* "Surely God is my salvation;
 I will trust and not be afraid.
The LORD, the LORD, is my strength and my song;
 he has become my salvation."
With joy you will draw water
 from the wells of salvation.
In that day you will say:

"Give thanks to the LORD, call on his name;
 make known among the nations what he has done,
 and proclaim that his name is exalted.
Sing to the LORD, for he has done glorious things;
 let this be known to all the world.
Shout aloud and sing for joy, people of Zion,
 for great is the Holy One of Israel among you."

CANTICLE

Philippians 4:4–7 Rejoice in the Lord always. I will say it again: Rejoice! Let your gentleness be evident to all. The Lord is near. Do not be anxious about anything, but in everything, by prayer and petition, with thanksgiving, present your requests to God. And the peace of God, which transcends all understanding, will guard your hearts and your minds in Christ Jesus.

SECOND READING

Luke 3:7–18 John said to the crowds coming out to be baptised by him, "You brood of vipers! Who warned you to flee from the coming wrath? Produce fruit in keeping with repentance. And do not begin to say to yourselves, 'We have Abraham as our father.' For I tell you that out of these stones God can raise up children for Abraham. The axe is already at the root of the trees, and every tree that does not produce good fruit will be cut down and thrown into the fire."

"What should we do then?" the crowd asked.

John answered, "The person with two tunics should share with him who has none, and the one who has food should do the same."

Tax collectors also came to be baptised. "Teacher," they asked, "what should we do?"

"Don't collect any more than you are required to," he told them.

Then some soldiers asked him, "And what should we do?"

He replied, "Don't extort money and don't accuse people falsely – be content with your pay."

The people were waiting expectantly and were all wondering in their hearts if John might possibly be the Christ. John answered them all, "I baptise you with water. But one more powerful than I will come, the thongs of whose sandals I am not worthy to untie. He will baptise you with the Holy Spirit and with fire. His winnowing fork is in his hand to clear his threshing-floor and to gather the wheat into his barn, but he will burn up the chaff

GOSPEL

with unquenchable fire." And with many other words John exhorted the people and preached the good news to them.

Fourth Sunday of Advent

Micah 5:2–5a

F I R S T   R E A D I N G

"But you, Bethlehem Ephrathah,
though you are small among the clans of Judah,
out of you will come for me
one who will be ruler over Israel,
whose origins are from of old,
from ancient times."

Therefore Israel will be abandoned
until the time when she who is in labour gives birth
and the rest of his people return
to join the Israelites.

He will stand and shepherd his flock
in the strength of the LORD,
in the majesty of the name of the LORD his God.
And they will live securely, for then his greatness
will reach to the ends of the earth.
And he will be their peace.

Alternative Canticle or Psalm

Canticle: **Magnificat**

Luke 1:46b–55

C A N T I C L E

Mary said:

"My soul glorifies the Lord
and my spirit rejoices in God my Saviour,
for he has been mindful
of the humble state of his servant.
From now on all generations will call me blessed,
for the Mighty One has done great things for me –
holy is his name.
His mercy extends to those who fear him,
from generation to generation.
He has performed mighty deeds with his arm;
he has scattered those who are proud in their inmost
thoughts.
He has brought down rulers from their thrones
but has lifted up the humble.
He has filled the hungry with good things
but has sent the rich away empty.
He has helped his servant Israel,
remembering to be merciful
to Abraham and his descendants for ever,
even as he said to our fathers."

or Psalm 80:1–7   Hear us, O Shepherd of Israel,   P
     you who lead Joseph like a flock;   S
you who sit enthroned between the cherubim, shine forth   A
     before Ephraim, Benjamin and Manasseh.   L
Awaken your might;   M
     come and save us.

Restore us, O God;
     make your face shine upon us,
     that we may be saved.

O Lord God Almighty,
     how long will your anger smoulder
     against the prayers of your people?
You have fed them with the bread of tears;
     you have made them drink tears by the bowlful.
You have made us a source of contention to our neighbours,
     and our enemies mock us.

Restore us, O God Almighty;
     make your face shine upon us,
     that we may be saved.

Hebrews 10:5–10   When Christ came into the world, he said: S R

  "Sacrifice and offering you did not desire,   E E
    but a body you prepared for me;   C A
with burnt offerings and sin offerings   O D
    you were not pleased.   N I
Then I said, 'Here I am – it is written about me in the scroll –   D N
    I have come to do your will, O God.'"   G

First he said, "Sacrifices and offerings, burnt offerings and sin offerings
you did not desire, nor were you pleased with them" (although the law
required them to be made). Then he said, "Here I am, I have come to do
your will." He sets aside the first to establish the second. And by that will,
we have been made holy through the sacrifice of the body of Jesus Christ
once for all.

Luke 1:39–45 [46–55]   Mary got ready and hurried to a town in the hill coun-   G
try of Judea, where she entered Zechariah's home and greeted Elizabeth.   O
When Elizabeth heard Mary's greeting, the baby leaped in her womb, and   S
Elizabeth was filled with the Holy Spirit. In a loud voice she exclaimed: P
"Blessed are you among women, and blessed is the child you will bear! But   E
why am I so favoured, that the mother of my Lord should come to me? As   L
soon as the sound of your greeting reached my ears, the baby in my womb
leaped for joy. Blessed is she who has believed that what the Lord has said
to her will be accomplished!"

  [And Mary said:

  "My soul glorifies the Lord
    and my spirit rejoices in God my Saviour,

for he has been mindful
   of the humble state of his servant.
From now on all generations will call me blessed,
   for the Mighty One has done great things for me –
   holy is his name.
His mercy extends to those who fear him,
   from generation to generation.
He has performed mighty deeds with his arm;
   he has scattered those who are proud in their inmost thoughts.
He has brought down rulers from their thrones
   but has lifted up the humble.
He has filled the hungry with good things
   but has sent the rich away empty.
He has helped his servant Israel,
   remembering to be merciful
to Abraham and his descendants for ever,
   even as he said to our fathers."]

CHRISTMAS

Christmas Eve
For text of readings for Years A, B, C see pp 9–11

Christmas Day – 25 December
Any of the sets of readings on pp 11–18 may be used on the evening of Christmas Eve and on Christmas Day. Set III should be used at some service during the celebration.

CHRISTMAS, SET I, YEARS A, B, C

see pp 11–13

CHRISTMAS, SET II, YEARS A, B, C

see pp 13–15

CHRISTMAS, SET III, YEARS A, B, C

see pp 15–18

First Sunday of Christmas
1 Samuel 2:18–20, 26   Samuel was ministering before the LORD – a boy wearing a linen ephod. Each year his mother made him a little robe and took it to him when she went up with her husband to offer the annual sacrifice. Eli would bless Elkanah and his wife, saying, "May the LORD give you children by this woman to take the place of the one she prayed for and gave to the LORD." Then they would go home.

   And the boy Samuel continued to grow in stature and in favour with the LORD and with men.

Psalm 148* Praise the LORD.

Praise the LORD from the heavens,
   praise him in the heights above.
Praise him, all his angels,
   praise him, all his heavenly hosts.
Praise him, sun and moon,
   praise him, all you shining stars.
Praise him, you highest heavens
   and you waters above the skies.
Let them praise the name of the LORD,
   for he commanded and they were created.
He set them in place for ever and ever;
   he gave a decree that will never pass away.

Praise the LORD from the earth,
   you great sea creatures and all ocean depths,
lightning and hail, snow and clouds,
   stormy winds that do his bidding,
you mountains and all hills,
   fruit trees and all cedars,
wild animals and all cattle,
   small creatures and flying birds,
kings of the earth and all nations,
   you princes and all rulers on earth,
young men and maidens,
   old men and children.

Let them praise the name of the LORD,
   for his name alone is exalted;
   his splendour is above the earth and the heavens.
He has raised up for his people a horn,
   the praise of all his saints,
   of Israel, the people close to his heart.
Praise the LORD.

Colossians 3:12–17 As God's chosen people, holy and dearly loved, clothe yourselves with compassion, kindness, humility, gentleness and patience. Bear with each other and forgive whatever grievances you may have against one another. Forgive as the Lord forgave you. And over all these virtues put on love, which binds them all together in perfect unity.

Let the peace of Christ rule in your hearts, since as members of one body you were called to peace. And be thankful. Let the word of Christ dwell in you richly as you teach and admonish one another with all wisdom, and as you sing psalms, hymns and spiritual songs with gratitude in your hearts to God. And whatever you do, whether in word or deed, do it all in the name of the Lord Jesus, giving thanks to God the Father through him.

Luke 2:41–52   Every year Jesus' parents went to Jerusalem for the Feast of G
the Passover. When he was twelve years old, they went up to the Feast, O
according to the custom. After the Feast was over, while his parents were S
returning home, the boy Jesus stayed behind in Jerusalem, but they were P
unaware of it. Thinking he was in their company, they travelled on for a E
day. Then they began looking for him among their relatives and friends. L
When they did not find him, they went back to Jerusalem to look for him.
After three days they found him in the temple courts, sitting among the
teachers, listening to them and asking them questions. Everyone who
heard him was amazed at his understanding and his answers. When his parents saw him, they were astonished. His mother said to him, "Son, why
have you treated us like this? Your father and I have been anxiously
searching for you."

"Why were you searching for me?" he asked. "Didn't you know I had to
be in my Father's house?" But they did not understand what he was saying
to them.

Then he went down to Nazareth with them and was obedient to them.
But his mother treasured all these things in her heart. And Jesus grew in
wisdom and stature, and in favour with God and people.

Second Sunday of Christmas

For text of readings for Years A, B, C see pp 20–22.

EPIPHANY
The Epiphany – 6 January

For text of readings for Years A, B, C see pp 22–24.

The Baptism of Christ

The First Sunday of Epiphany

Isaiah 43:1–7   This is what the LORD says – F
  he who created you, O Jacob, I
  he who formed you, O Israel: R
"Fear not, for I have redeemed you; S
  I have summoned you by name; you are mine. T
When you pass through the waters,
  I will be with you; R
and when you pass through the rivers, E
  they will not sweep over you. A
When you walk through the fire, D
  you will not be burned; I
  the flames will not set you ablaze. N
For I am the LORD, your God, G
  the Holy One of Israel, your Saviour;
I give Egypt for your ransom,
  Cush and Seba in your stead.
Since you are precious and honoured in my sight,
  and because I love you,

I will give men in exchange for you,
and people in exchange for your life.
Do not be afraid, for I am with you;
I will bring your children from the east
and gather you from the west.
I will say to the north, 'Give them up!'
and to the south, 'Do not hold them back.'
Bring my sons from afar
and my daughters from the ends of the earth –
everyone who is called by my name,
whom I created for my glory,
whom I formed and made."

Psalm 29 Ascribe to the LORD, O mighty ones,
ascribe to the LORD glory and strength.
Ascribe to the LORD the glory due to his name;
worship the LORD in the splendour of his holiness.

The voice of the LORD is over the waters;
the God of glory thunders,
the LORD thunders over the mighty waters.
The voice of the LORD is powerful;
the voice of the LORD is majestic.
The voice of the LORD breaks the cedars;
the LORD breaks in pieces the cedars of Lebanon.
He makes Lebanon skip like a calf,
Sirion like a young wild ox.
The voice of the LORD strikes
with flashes of lightning.
The voice of the LORD shakes the desert;
the LORD shakes the Desert of Kadesh.
The voice of the LORD twists the oaks
and strips the forests bare.
And in his temple all cry, "Glory!"

The LORD sits enthroned over the flood;
the LORD is enthroned as King for ever.
The LORD gives strength to his people;
the LORD blesses his people with peace.

Acts 8:14–17 When the apostles in Jerusalem heard that Samaria had accepted the word of God, they sent Peter and John to them. When they arrived, they prayed for them that they might receive the Holy Spirit, because the Holy Spirit had not yet come upon any of them; they had simply been baptised into the name of the Lord Jesus. Then Peter and John placed their hands on them, and they received the Holy Spirit.

Luke 3:15–17, 21–22 The people were waiting expectantly and were all wondering in their hearts if John might possibly be the Christ. John answered

them all, "I baptise you with water. But one more powerful than I will
come, the thongs of whose sandals I am not worthy to untie. He will baptise
you with the Holy Spirit and with fire. His winnowing fork is in his hand to
clear his threshing-floor and to gather the wheat into his barn, but he will
burn up the chaff with unquenchable fire."

When all the people were being baptised, Jesus was baptised too. And as
he was praying, heaven was opened and the Holy Spirit descended on him
in bodily form like a dove. And a voice came from heaven: "You are my Son,
whom I love; with you I am well pleased."

Second Sunday of Epiphany

Isaiah 62:1–5   For Zion's sake I will not keep silent,
   for Jerusalem's sake I will not remain quiet,
till her righteousness shines out like the dawn,
   her salvation like a blazing torch.
The nations will see your righteousness,
   and all kings your glory;
you will be called by a new name
   that the mouth of the LORD will bestow.
You will be a crown of splendour in the LORD's hand,
   a royal diadem in the hand of your God.
No longer will they call you Deserted,
   or name your land Desolate.
But you will be called Hephzibah,
   and your land Beulah;
for the LORD will take delight in you,
   and your land will be married.
As a young man marries a maiden,
   so will your sons marry you;
as a bridegroom rejoices over his bride,
   so will your God rejoice over you.

Psalm 36:5–10   Your love, O LORD, reaches to the heavens,
   your faithfulness to the skies.
Your righteousness is like the mighty mountains,
   your justice like the great deep.
O LORD, you preserve both man and beast.
   How priceless is your unfailing love!
Both high and low among men
   find refuge in the shadow of your wings.
They feast in the abundance of your house;
   you give them drink from your river of delights.
For with you is the fountain of life;
   in your light we see light.

Continue your love to those who know you,
   your righteousness to the upright in heart.

1 Corinthians 12:1–11   About spiritual gifts, brothers, I do not want you to be S E C O N D
ignorant. You know that when you were pagans, somehow or other you
were influenced and led astray to mute idols. Therefore I tell you that no-
one who is speaking by the Spirit of God says, "Jesus be cursed," and
no-one can say, "Jesus is Lord," except by the Holy Spirit.

There are different kinds of gifts, but the same Spirit. There are dif- R E A D I N G
ferent kinds of service, but the same Lord. There are different kinds of
working, but the same God works all of them in all men.

Now to each one the manifestation of the Spirit is given for the common
good. To one there is given through the Spirit the message of wisdom, to
another the message of knowledge by means of the same Spirit, to another
faith by the same Spirit, to another gifts of healing by that one Spirit, to
another miraculous powers, to another prophecy, to another distinguish-
ing between spirits, to another speaking in different kinds of tongues, and
to still another the interpretation of tongues. All these are the work of one
and the same Spirit, and he gives them to each one, just as he determines.

John 2:1–11   On the third day a wedding took place at Cana in Galilee. Jesus' G O S P E L
mother was there, and Jesus and his disciples had also been invited to the
wedding. When the wine was gone, Jesus' mother said to him, "They have
no more wine."

"Dear woman, why do you involve me?" Jesus replied. "My time has not
yet come."

His mother said to the servants, "Do whatever he tells you."

Nearby stood six stone water jars, the kind used by the Jews for ceremonial washing, each holding from twenty to thirty gallons.

Jesus said to the servants, "Fill the jars with water"; so they filled them
to the brim.

Then he told them, "Now draw some out and take it to the master of the
banquet."

They did so, and the master of the banquet tasted the water that had
been turned into wine. He did not realise where it had come from, though
the servants who had drawn the water knew. Then he called the bridegroom aside and said, "Everyone brings out the choice wine first and then
the cheaper wine after the guests have had too much to drink; but you have
saved the best till now."

This, the first of his miraculous signs, Jesus performed at Cana in
Galilee. He thus revealed his glory, and his disciples put their faith in him.

Third Sunday of Epiphany

Nehemiah 8:1–3, 5–6, 8–10   All the Israelite people assembled as one man in F I R S T R E A D
the square before the Water Gate. They told Ezra the scribe to bring out the
Book of the Law of Moses, which the LORD had commanded for Israel.

So on the first day of the seventh month, Ezra the priest brought the Law S T I N G
before the assembly, which was made up of men and women and all who
were able to understand. He read it aloud from daybreak till noon as he
faced the square before the Water Gate in the presence of the men, women

and others who could understand. And all the people listened attentively to the Book of the Law.

Ezra opened the book. All the people could see him because he was standing above them; and as he opened it, the people all stood up. Ezra praised the LORD, the great God; and all the people lifted their hands and responded, "Amen! Amen!" Then they bowed down and worshipped the LORD with their faces to the ground.

The Levites also read from the Book of the Law of God, making it clear and giving the meaning so that the people could understand what was being read.

Then Nehemiah the governor, Ezra the priest and scribe, and the Levites who were instructing the people said to them all, "This day is sacred to the LORD your God. Do not mourn or weep." For all the people had been weeping as they listened to the words of the Law.

Nehemiah said, "Go and enjoy choice food and sweet drinks, and send some to those who have nothing prepared. This day is sacred to our Lord. Do not grieve, for the joy of the LORD is your strength."

Psalm 19* The heavens declare the glory of God;
    the skies proclaim the work of his hands.
Day after day they pour forth speech;
    night after night they display knowledge.
There is no speech or language
    where their voice is not heard.
Their voice goes out into all the earth,
    their words to the ends of the world.

In the heavens he has pitched a tent for the sun,
    which is like a bridegroom coming forth from his pavilion,
    like a champion rejoicing to run his course.
It rises at one end of the heavens
    and makes its circuit to the other;
    nothing is hidden from its heat.

The law of the LORD is perfect,
    reviving the soul.
The statutes of the LORD are trustworthy,
    making wise the simple.
The precepts of the LORD are right,
    giving joy to the heart.
The commands of the LORD are radiant,
    giving light to the eyes.
The fear of the LORD is pure,
    enduring for ever.
The ordinances of the LORD are sure
    and altogether righteous.
They are more precious than gold,
    than much pure gold;

they are sweeter than honey,
than honey from the comb.
By them is your servant warned;
    in keeping them there is great reward.

Who can discern their errors?
    Forgive my hidden faults.
Keep your servant also from wilful sins;
    may they not rule over me.
Then will I be blameless,
    innocent of great transgression.

May the words of my mouth and the meditation of my heart
    be pleasing in your sight,
      O Lord, my Rock and my Redeemer.

1 Corinthians 12:12–31a   The body is a unit, though it is made up of many parts; and though all its parts are many, they form one body. So it is with Christ. For we were all baptised by one Spirit into one body – whether Jews or Greeks, slave or free – and we were all given the one Spirit to drink.

Now the body is not made up of one part but of many. If the foot should say, "Because I am not a hand, I do not belong to the body," it would not for that reason cease to be part of the body. And if the ear should say, "Because I am not an eye, I do not belong to the body," it would not for that reason cease to be part of the body. If the whole body were an eye, where would the sense of hearing be? If the whole body were an ear, where would the sense of smell be? But in fact God has arranged the parts in the body, every one of them, just as he wanted them to be. If they were all one part, where would the body be? As it is, there are many parts, but one body.

The eye cannot say to the hand, "I don't need you!" And the head cannot say to the feet, "I don't need you!" On the contrary, those parts of the body that seem to be weaker are indispensable, and the parts that we think are less honourable we treat with special honour. And the parts that are unpresentable are treated with special modesty, while our presentable parts need no special treatment. But God has combined the members of the body and has given greater honour to the parts that lacked it, so that there should be no division in the body, but that its parts should have equal concern for each other. If one part suffers, every part suffers with it; if one part is honoured, every part rejoices with it.

Now you are the body of Christ, and each one of you is a part of it. And in the church God has appointed first of all apostles, second prophets, third teachers, then workers of miracles, also those having gifts of healing, those able to help others, those with gifts of administration, and those speaking in different kinds of tongues. Are all apostles? Are all prophets? Are all teachers? Do all work miracles? Do all have gifts of healing? Do all speak in tongues? Do all interpret? But eagerly desire the greater gifts.

Luke 4:14–21   Jesus returned to Galilee in the power of the Spirit, and news G about him spread through the whole countryside. He taught in their syna- O gogues, and everyone praised him. S

He went to Nazareth, where he had been brought up, and on the Sabbath P day he went into the synagogue, as was his custom. And he stood up to read. E The scroll of the prophet Isaiah was handed to him. Unrolling it, he found L the place where it is written:

> "The Spirit of the Lord is on me,
>> because he has anointed me
>> to preach good news to the poor.
> He has sent me to proclaim freedom for the prisoners
>> and recovery of sight for the blind,
> to release the oppressed,
>> to proclaim the year of the Lord's favour."

Then he rolled up the scroll, gave it back to the attendant and sat down. The eyes of everyone in the synagogue were fastened on him, and he began by saying to them, "Today this scripture is fulfilled in your hearing."

Fourth Sunday of Epiphany

Ezekiel 43:27 – 44:4   The man said to me: "At the end of seven days, from the F eighth day on, the priests are to present your burnt offerings and fellow- I ship offerings on the altar. Then I will accept you, declares the Sovereign R Lord." S

Then the man brought me back to the outer gate of the sanctuary, the T one facing east, and it was shut. The Lord said to me, "This gate is to remain shut. It must not be opened; no-one may enter through it. It is to R remain shut because the Lord, the God of Israel, has entered through it. E The prince himself is the only one who may sit inside the gateway to eat in A the presence of the Lord. He is to enter by way of the portico of the gate- D way and go out the same way." I

Then the man brought me by way of the north gate to the front of the N temple. I looked and saw the glory of the Lord filling the temple of the G Lord, and I fell face down.

Psalm 48   Great is the Lord, and most worthy of praise, P
    in the city of our God, his holy mountain. S
It is beautiful in its loftiness, A
    the joy of the whole earth. L
Like the utmost heights of Zaphon is Mount Zion, M
    the city of the Great King.
God is in her citadels;
    he has shown himself to be her fortress.

When the kings joined forces,
    when they advanced together,
they saw her and were astounded;
    they fled in terror.

Trembling seized them there,
  pain like that of a woman in labour.
You destroyed them like ships of Tarshish
  shattered by an east wind.

As we have heard,
  so have we seen
in the city of the LORD Almighty,
  in the city of our God:
  God makes her secure for ever.

Within your temple, O God,
  we meditate on your unfailing love.
Like your name, O God,
  your praise reaches to the ends of the earth;
  your right hand is filled with righteousness.
Mount Zion rejoices,
  the villages of Judah are glad
  because of your judgments.

Walk about Zion, go round her,
  count her towers,
consider well her ramparts,
  view her citadels,
  that you may tell of them to the next generation.
For this God is our God for ever and ever;
  he will be our guide even to the end.

1 Corinthians 13:1–13 If I speak in the tongues of men and of angels, but
have not love, I am only a resounding gong or a clanging cymbal. If I have
the gift of prophecy and can fathom all mysteries and all knowledge, and if
I have a faith that can move mountains, but have not love, I am nothing. If
I give all I possess to the poor and surrender my body to the flames, but
have not love, I gain nothing.

  Love is patient, love is kind. It does not envy, it does not boast, it is
not proud. It is not rude, it is not self-seeking, it is not easily angered,
it keeps no record of wrongs. Love does not delight in evil but rejoices
with the truth. It always protects, always trusts, always hopes, always
perseveres.

  Love never fails. But where there are prophecies, they will cease; where
there are tongues, they will be stilled; where there is knowledge, it will
pass away. For we know in part and we prophesy in part, but when perfection comes, the imperfect disappears. When I was a child, I talked like a
child, I thought like a child, I reasoned like a child. When I became a man,
I put childish ways behind me. Now we see but a poor reflection as in a
mirror; then we shall see face to face. Now I know in part; then I shall
know fully, even as I am fully known.

  And now these three remain: faith, hope and love. But the greatest of
these is love.

Luke 2:22–40 When the time of their purification according to the Law of Moses had been completed, Joseph and Mary took Jesus to Jerusalem to present him to the Lord (as it is written in the Law of the Lord, "Every first-born male is to be consecrated to the Lord"), and to offer a sacrifice in keeping with what is said in the Law of the Lord: "a pair of doves or two young pigeons".

Now there was a man in Jerusalem called Simeon, who was righteous and devout. He was waiting for the consolation of Israel, and the Holy Spirit was upon him. It had been revealed to him by the Holy Spirit that he would not die before he had seen the Lord's Christ. Moved by the Spirit, he went into the temple courts. When the parents brought in the child Jesus to do for him what the custom of the Law required, Simeon took him in his arms and praised God, saying:

> "Sovereign Lord, as you have promised,
> you now dismiss your servant in peace.
> For my eyes have seen your salvation,
> which you have prepared in the sight of all people,
> a light for revelation to the Gentiles
> and for glory to your people Israel."

The child's father and mother marvelled at what was said about him. Then Simeon blessed them and said to Mary, his mother: "This child is destined to cause the falling and rising of many in Israel, and to be a sign that will be spoken against, so that the thoughts of many hearts will be revealed. And a sword will pierce your own soul too."

There was also a prophetess, Anna, the daughter of Phanuel, of the tribe of Asher. She was very old; she had lived with her husband seven years after her marriage, and then was a widow until she was eighty-four. She never left the temple but worshipped night and day, fasting and praying. Coming up to them at that very moment, she gave thanks to God and spoke about the child to all who were looking forward to the redemption of Jerusalem.

When Joseph and Mary had done everything required by the Law of the Lord, they returned to Galilee to their own town of Nazareth. And the child grew and became strong; he was filled with wisdom, and the grace of God was upon him.

The Presentation of Christ in the Temple – 2 February

Candlemas

For text of readings for Years A, B, C see pp 33–35.

ORDINARY TIME

Proper 1

Sunday between 3 and 9 February inclusive (if earlier than the Second Sunday before Lent)

Isaiah 6:1–8 [9–13] In the year that King Uzziah died, I saw the Lord seated on a throne, high and exalted, and the train of his robe filled the temple.

Above him were seraphs, each with six wings: With two wings they covered their faces, with two they covered their feet, and with two they were flying. And they were calling to one another:

"Holy, holy, holy is the LORD Almighty;
the whole earth is full of his glory."

At the sound of their voices the doorposts and thresholds shook and the temple was filled with smoke.

"Woe to me!" I cried. "I am ruined! For I am a man of unclean lips, and I live among a people of unclean lips, and my eyes have seen the King, the LORD Almighty."

Then one of the seraphs flew to me with a live coal in his hand, which he had taken with tongs from the altar. With it he touched my mouth and said, "See, this has touched your lips; your guilt is taken away and your sin atoned for."

Then I heard the voice of the LORD saying, "Whom shall I send? And who will go for us?"

And I said, "Here am I. Send me!"

[He said, "Go and tell this people:

"'Be ever hearing, but never understanding;
be ever seeing, but never perceiving.'
Make the heart of this people calloused;
make their ears dull
and close their eyes.
Otherwise they might see with their eyes,
hear with their ears,
understand with their hearts,
and turn and be healed."

Then I said, "For how long, O LORD?"
And he answered:

"Until the cities lie ruined
and without inhabitant,
until the houses are left deserted
and the fields ruined and ravaged,
until the LORD has sent everyone far away
and the land is utterly forsaken.
And though a tenth remains in the land,
it will again be laid waste.
But as the terebinth and oak
leave stumps when they are cut down,
so the holy seed will be the stump in the land."]

Psalm 138 I will praise you, O LORD, with all my heart;
before the "gods" I will sing your praise.
I will bow down towards your holy temple
and will praise your name
for your love and your faithfulness,

for you have exalted above all things
>your name and your word.
When I called, you answered me;
>you made me bold and stout-hearted.

May all the kings of the earth praise you, O Lord,
>when they hear the words of your mouth.
May they sing of the ways of the Lord,
>for the glory of the Lord is great.

Though the Lord is on high, he looks upon the lowly,
>but the proud he knows from afar.
Though I walk in the midst of trouble,
>you preserve my life;
you stretch out your hand against the anger of my foes,
>with your right hand you save me.
The Lord will fulfil his purpose for me;
>your love, O Lord, endures for ever –
>do not abandon the works of your hands.

1 Corinthians 15:1–11 Brothers, I want to remind you of the gospel I preached to you, which you received and on which you have taken your stand. By this gospel you are saved, if you hold firmly to the word I preached to you. Otherwise, you have believed in vain.

For what I received I passed on to you as of first importance: that Christ died for our sins according to the Scriptures, that he was buried, that he was raised on the third day according to the Scriptures, and that he appeared to Peter, and then to the Twelve. After that, he appeared to more than five hundred of the brothers at the same time, most of whom are still living, though some have fallen asleep. Then he appeared to James, then to all the apostles, and last of all he appeared to me also, as to one abnormally born.

For I am the least of the apostles and do not even deserve to be called an apostle, because I persecuted the church of God. But by the grace of God I am what I am, and his grace to me was not without effect. No, I worked harder than all of them – yet not I, but the grace of God that was with me. Whether, then, it was I or they, this is what we preach, and this is what you believed.

Luke 5:1–11 One day as Jesus was standing by the Lake of Gennesaret, with the people crowding round him and listening to the word of God, he saw at the water's edge two boats, left there by the fishermen, who were washing their nets. He got into one of the boats, the one belonging to Simon, and asked him to put out a little from shore. Then he sat down and taught the people from the boat.

When he had finished speaking, he said to Simon, "Put out into deep water, and let down the nets for a catch."

Simon answered, "Master, we've worked hard all night and haven't caught anything. But because you say so, I will let down the nets."

When they had done so, they caught such a large number of fish that their nets began to break. So they signalled to their partners in the other boat to come and help them, and they came and filled both boats so full that they began to sink.

When Simon Peter saw this, he fell at Jesus' knees and said, "Go away from me, Lord; I am a sinful man!" For he and all his companions were astonished at the catch of fish they had taken, and so were James and John, the sons of Zebedee, Simon's partners.

Then Jesus said to Simon, "Don't be afraid; from now on you will catch men." So they pulled their boats up on shore, left everything and followed him.

Proper 2

Sunday between 10 and 16 February inclusive (if earlier than the Second Sunday before Lent)

Jeremiah 17:5–10   This is what the LORD says:

     "Cursed is the one who trusts in man,
       who depends on flesh for his strength
       and whose heart turns away from the LORD.
     He will be like a bush in the wastelands;
       he will not see prosperity when it comes.
     He will dwell in the parched places of the desert,
       in a salt land where no-one lives.

     "But blessed is the man who trusts in the LORD,
       whose confidence is in him.
     He will be like a tree planted by the water
       that sends out its roots by the stream.
     It does not fear when heat comes;
       its leaves are always green.
     It has no worries in a year of drought
       and never fails to bear fruit."

     The heart is deceitful above all things
       and beyond cure.
       Who can understand it?

     "I the LORD search the heart
       and examine the mind,
     to reward everyone according to his conduct,
       according to what his deeds deserve."

(Margin: F I R S T   R E A D I N G)

Psalm 1   Blessed is the man
     who do not walk in the counsel of the wicked
   or stand in the way of sinners
     or sit in the seat of mockers.
   But their delight is in the law of the LORD,
     and on his law he meditates day and night.

(Margin: P S A L M)

He is like a tree planted by streams of water,
   which yields its fruit in season
and whose leaf does not wither.
   Whatever he does prospers.

Not so the wicked!
   They are like chaff
   that the wind blows away.
Therefore the wicked will not stand in the judgment,
   nor sinners in the assembly of the righteous.

For the LORD watches over the way of the righteous,
   but the way of the wicked will perish.

1 Corinthians 15:12–20   If it is preached that Christ has been raised from the dead, how can some of you say that there is no resurrection of the dead? If there is no resurrection of the dead, then not even Christ has been raised. And if Christ has not been raised, our preaching is useless and so is your faith. More than that, we are then found to be false witnesses about God, for we have testified about God that he raised Christ from the dead. But he did not raise him if in fact the dead are not raised. For if the dead are not raised, then Christ has not been raised either. And if Christ has not been raised, your faith is futile; you are still in your sins. Then those also who have fallen asleep in Christ are lost. If only for this life we have hope in Christ, we are to be pitied more than all men.

But Christ has indeed been raised from the dead, the firstfruits of those who have fallen asleep.

Luke 6:17–26   Jesus went down the mountainside with the Twelve and stood on a level place. A large crowd of his disciples was there and a great number of people from all over Judea, from Jerusalem, and from the coast of Tyre and Sidon, who had come to hear him and to be healed of their diseases. Those troubled by evil spirits were cured, and the people all tried to touch him, because power was coming from him and healing them all.

Looking at his disciples, he said:

"Blessed are you who are poor,
   for yours is the kingdom of God.
Blessed are you who hunger now,
   for you will be satisfied.
Blessed are you who weep now,
   for you will laugh.
Blessed are you when men hate you,
   when they exclude you and insult you
   and reject your name as evil,
   because of the Son of Man.

"Rejoice in that day and leap for joy, because great is your reward in heaven. For that is how their fathers treated the prophets.

"But woe to you who are rich,
  for you have already received your comfort.
Woe to you who are well fed now,
  for you will go hungry.
Woe to you who laugh now,
  for you will mourn and weep.
Woe to you when all men speak well of you,
  for that is how their fathers treated the false prophets."

Proper 3

Sunday between 17 and 23 February inclusive (if earlier than the Second Sunday before Lent)

Genesis 45:3–11, 15 Joseph said to his brothers, "I am Joseph! Is my father still living?" But his brothers were not able to answer him, because they were terrified at his presence.

Then Joseph said to his brothers, "Come close to me." When they had done so, he said, "I am your brother Joseph, the one you sold into Egypt! And now, do not be distressed and do not be angry with yourselves for selling me here, because it was to save lives that God sent me ahead of you. For two years now there has been famine in the land, and for the next five years there will not be ploughing and reaping. But God sent me ahead of you to preserve for you a remnant on earth and to save your lives by a great deliverance.

"So then, it was not you who sent me here, but God. He made me father to Pharaoh, lord of his entire household and ruler of all Egypt. Now hurry back to my father and say to him, 'This is what your son Joseph says: God has made me lord of all Egypt. Come down to me; don't delay. You shall live in the region of Goshen and be near me – you, your children and grandchildren, your flocks and herds, and all you have. I will provide for you there, because five years of famine are still to come. Otherwise you and your household and all who belong to you will become destitute.'"

And he kissed all his brothers and wept over them. Afterwards his brothers talked with him.

Psalm 37:1–11, 39–40* Do not fret because of evil men
  or be envious of those who do wrong;
for like the grass they will soon wither,
  like green plants they will soon die away.

Trust in the LORD and do good;
  dwell in the land and enjoy safe pasture.
Delight yourself in the LORD
  and he will give you the desires of your heart.

Commit your way to the LORD;
  trust in him and he will do this:
He will make your righteousness shine like the dawn,
  the justice of your cause like the noonday sun.

Be still before the LORD and wait patiently for him;
>
> do not fret when men succeed in their ways,
> when they carry out their wicked schemes.

Refrain from anger and turn from wrath;
> do not fret – it leads only to evil.

For evil men will be cut off,
> but those who hope in the LORD will inherit the land.

A little while, and the wicked will be no more;
> though you look for them, they will not be found.

But the meek will inherit the land
> and enjoy great peace.

The salvation of the righteous comes from the LORD;
> he is their stronghold in time of trouble.

The LORD helps them and delivers them;
> he delivers them from the wicked and saves them,
> because they take refuge in him.

1 Corinthians 15:35–38, 42–50   Someone may ask, "How are the dead raised? With what kind of body will they come?" How foolish! What you sow does not come to life unless it dies. When you sow, you do not plant the body that will be, but just a seed, perhaps of wheat or of something else. But God gives it a body as he has determined, and to each kind of seed he gives its own body.

So will it be with the resurrection of the dead. The body that is sown is perishable, it is raised imperishable; it is sown in dishonour, it is raised in glory; it is sown in weakness, it is raised in power; it is sown a natural body, it is raised a spiritual body.

If there is a natural body, there is also a spiritual body. So it is written: "The first Adam became a living being"; the last Adam, a life-giving spirit. The spiritual did not come first, but the natural, and after that the spiritual. The first man was of the dust of the earth, the second man from heaven. As was the earthly man, so are those who are of the earth; and as is the man from heaven, so also are those who are of heaven. And just as we have borne the likeness of the earthly man, so shall we bear the likeness of the man from heaven.

I declare to you, brothers, that flesh and blood cannot inherit the kingdom of God, nor does the perishable inherit the imperishable.

Luke 6:27–38   Jesus said: "I tell you who hear me: Love your enemies, do good to those who hate you, bless those who curse you, pray for those who ill-treat you. If someone strikes you on one cheek, turn the other also. If someone takes your cloak, do not stop him from taking your tunic. Give to everyone who asks you, and if anyone takes what belongs to you, do not demand it back. Do to others as you would have them do to you.

"If you love those who love you, what credit is that to you? Even 'sinners' love those who love them. And if you do good to those who are good to you, what credit is that to you? Even 'sinners' do that. And if you lend to those from whom you expect repayment, what credit is that to you? Even 'sinners' lend to 'sinners', expecting to be repaid in full. But love your enemies, do good to them, and lend to them without expecting to get anything back. Then your reward will be great, and you will be sons of the Most High, because he is kind to the ungrateful and wicked. Be merciful, just as your Father is merciful.

"Do not judge, and you will not be judged. Do not condemn, and you will not be condemned. Forgive, and you will be forgiven. Give, and it will be given to you. A good measure, pressed down, shaken together and running over, will be poured into your lap. For with the measure you use, it will be measured to you."

Second Sunday Before Lent

Genesis 2:4b–9, 15–25   When the LORD God made the earth and the heavens – and no shrub of the field had yet appeared on the earth and no plant of the field had yet sprung up, for the LORD God had not sent rain on the earth and there was no man to work the ground, but streams came up from the earth and watered the whole surface of the ground – the LORD God formed the man from the dust of the ground and breathed into his nostrils the breath of life, and the man became a living being.

Now the LORD God had planted a garden in the east, in Eden; and there he put the man he had formed. And the LORD God made all kinds of trees grow out of the ground – trees that were pleasing to the eye and good for food. In the middle of the garden were the tree of life and the tree of the knowledge of good and evil.

The LORD God took the man and put him in the Garden of Eden to work it and take care of it. And the LORD God commanded the man, "You are free to eat from any tree in the garden; but you must not eat from the tree of the knowledge of good and evil, for when you eat of it you will surely die."

The LORD God said, "It is not good for the man to be alone. I will make a helper suitable for him."

Now the LORD God had formed out of the ground all the beasts of the field and all the birds of the air. He brought them to the man to see what he would name them; and whatever the man called each living creature, that was its name. So the man gave names to all the livestock, the birds of the air and all the beasts of the field.

But for Adam no suitable helper was found. So the LORD God caused the man to fall into a deep sleep; and while he was sleeping, he took one of the man's ribs and closed up the place with flesh. Then the LORD God made a woman from the rib he had taken out of the man, and he brought her to the man.

The man said,

"This is now bone of my bones
  and flesh of my flesh;

FIRST READING

she shall be called 'woman',
for she was taken out of man."

For this reason a man will leave his father and mother and be united to his wife, and they will become one flesh.

The man and his wife were both naked, and they felt no shame.

Psalm 65 Praise awaits you, O God, in Zion;
to you our vows will be fulfilled.
O you who hear prayer,
to you all men will come.
When we were overwhelmed by sins,
you forgave our transgressions.
Blessed are those you choose
and bring near to live in your courts!
We are filled with the good things of your house,
of your holy temple.

You answer us with awesome deeds of righteousness,
O God our Saviour,
the hope of all the ends of the earth
and of the farthest seas,
who formed the mountains by your power,
having armed yourself with strength,
who stilled the roaring of the seas,
the roaring of their waves,
and the turmoil of the nations.
Those living far away fear your wonders;
where morning dawns and evening fades
you call forth songs of joy.

You care for the land and water it;
you enrich it abundantly.
The streams of God are filled with water
to provide the people with corn,
for so you have ordained it.
You drench its furrows
and level its ridges;
you soften it with showers
and bless its crops.
You crown the year with your bounty,
and your carts overflow with abundance.
The grasslands of the desert overflow;
the hills are clothed with gladness.
The meadows are covered with flocks
and the valleys are mantled with corn;
they shout for joy and sing.

Revelation 4 I looked, and there before me was a door standing open in heaven. And the voice I had first heard speaking to me like a trumpet said,

"Come up here, and I will show you what must take place after this." At once I was in the Spirit, and there before me was a throne in heaven with someone sitting on it. And the one who sat there had the appearance of a jasper and carnelian. A rainbow, resembling an emerald, encircled the throne. Surrounding the throne were twenty-four other thrones, and seated on them were twenty-four elders. They were dressed in white and had crowns of gold on their heads. From the throne came flashes of lightning, rumblings and peals of thunder. Before the throne, seven lamps were blazing. These are the seven spirits of God. Also before the throne there was what looked like a sea of glass, clear as crystal.

In the centre, around the throne, were four living creatures, and they were covered with eyes, in front and behind. The first living creature was like a lion, the second was like an ox, the third had a face like a man, the fourth was like a flying eagle. Each of the four living creatures had six wings and was covered with eyes all around, even under his wings. Day and night they never stop saying:

> "Holy, holy, holy
> is the Lord God Almighty,
> who was, and is, and is to come."

Whenever the living creatures give glory, honour and thanks to him who sits on the throne and who lives for ever and ever, the twenty-four elders fall down before him who sits on the throne, and worship him who lives for ever and ever. They lay their crowns before the throne and say:

> "You are worthy, our Lord and God,
> to receive glory and honour and power,
> for you created all things,
> and by your will they were created
> and have their being."

Luke 8:22–25 One day Jesus said to his disciples, "Let's go over to the other side of the lake." So they got into a boat and set out. As they sailed, he fell asleep. A squall came down on the lake, so that the boat was being swamped, and they were in great danger.

The disciples went and woke him, saying, "Master, Master, we're going to drown!"

He got up and rebuked the wind and the raging waters; the storm subsided, and all was calm. "Where is your faith?" he asked his disciples.

In fear and amazement they asked one another, "Who is this? He commands even the winds and the water, and they obey him."

Sunday Next Before Lent

Exodus 34:29–35 When Moses came down from Mount Sinai with the two tablets of the Testimony in his hands, he was not aware that his face was radiant because he had spoken with the LORD. When Aaron and all the Israelites saw Moses, his face was radiant, and they were afraid to come near him. But Moses called to them; so Aaron and all the leaders of the community came back to him, and he spoke to them. Afterwards all the Israelites came near him, and he gave them all the commands the LORD had given him on Mount Sinai.

When Moses finished speaking to them, he put a veil over his face. But whenever he entered the LORD's presence to speak with him, he removed the veil until he came out. And when he came out and told the Israelites what he had been commanded, they saw that his face was radiant. Then Moses would put the veil back over his face until he went in to speak with the LORD.

Psalm 99 The LORD reigns,
  let the nations tremble;
he sits enthroned between the cherubim,
  let the earth shake.
Great is the LORD in Zion;
  he is exalted over all the nations.
Let them praise your great and awesome name –
  he is holy.
The King is mighty, he loves justice –
  you have established equity;
in Jacob you have done
  what is just and right.
Exalt the LORD our God
  and worship at his footstool;
  he is holy.

Moses and Aaron were among his priests,
  Samuel was among those who called on his name;
they called on the LORD
  and he answered them.
He spoke to them from the pillar of cloud;
  they kept his statutes and the decrees he gave them.

O LORD our God,
  you answered them;
you were to Israel a forgiving God,
  though you punished their misdeeds.
Exalt the LORD our God
  and worship at his holy mountain,
  for the LORD our God is holy.

2 Corinthians 3:12–4:2 Since we have such a hope, we are very bold. We are not like Moses, who would put a veil over his face to keep the Israelites from gazing at it while the radiance was fading away. But their minds were made dull, for to this day the same veil remains when the old covenant is read. It has not been removed, because only in Christ is it taken away. Even to this day when Moses is read, a veil covers their hearts. But whenever anyone turns to the Lord, the veil is taken away. Now the Lord is the Spirit, and where the Spirit of the Lord is, there is freedom. And we, who with unveiled faces all reflect the Lord's glory, are being transformed into his likeness with ever-increasing glory, which comes from the Lord, who is the Spirit.

Therefore, since through God's mercy we have this ministry, we do not lose heart. Rather, we have renounced secret and shameful ways; we do not use deception, nor do we distort the word of God. On the contrary, by setting forth the truth plainly we commend ourselves to everyman's conscience in the sight of God.

Luke 9:28–36 [37–43a] Jesus took Peter, John and James with him and went up onto a mountain to pray. As he was praying, the appearance of his face changed, and his clothes became as bright as a flash of lightning. Two men, Moses and Elijah, appeared in glorious splendour, talking with Jesus. They spoke about his departure, which he was about to bring to fulfilment at Jerusalem. Peter and his companions were very sleepy, but when they became fully awake, they saw his glory and the two men standing with him. As the men were leaving Jesus, Peter said to him, "Master, it is good for us to be here. Let us put up three shelters – one for you, one for Moses and one for Elijah." (He did not know what he was saying.)

While he was speaking, a cloud appeared and enveloped them, and they were afraid as they entered the cloud. A voice came from the cloud, saying, "This is my Son, whom I have chosen; listen to him." When the voice had spoken, they found that Jesus was alone. The disciples kept this to themselves, and told no-one at that time what they had seen.

[The next day, when they came down from the mountain, a large crowd met him. A man in the crowd called out, "Teacher, I beg you to look at my son, for he is my only child. A spirit seizes him and he suddenly screams; it throws him into convulsions so that he foams at the mouth. It scarcely ever leaves him and is destroying him. I begged your disciples to drive it out, but they could not."

"O unbelieving and perverse generation," Jesus replied, "how long shall I stay with you and put up with you? Bring your son here."

Even while the boy was coming, the demon threw him to the ground in a convulsion. But Jesus rebuked the evil spirit, healed the boy and gave him back to his father. And they were all amazed at the greatness of God.]

LENT

Ash Wednesday

For text of readings for Years A, B, C see pp 48–52.

First Sunday of Lent

Deuteronomy 26:1–11 Moses said: When you have entered the land that the LORD your God is giving you as an inheritance and have taken possession of it and settled in it, take some of the firstfruits of all that you produce from the soil of the land that the LORD your God is giving you and put them in a basket. Then go to the place that the LORD your God will choose as a dwelling for his Name and say to the priest in office at the time, "I declare today to the LORD your God that I have come to the land that the LORD swore to our forefathers to give us." The priest shall take the basket from your hands and set it down in front of the altar of the LORD your God. Then you shall declare before the LORD your God: "My father was a wandering Aramean, and he went down into Egypt with a few people and lived there and became a great nation, powerful and numerous. But the Egyptians ill-treated us and made us suffer, putting us to hard labour. Then we cried out to the LORD, the God of our fathers, and the LORD heard our voice and saw our misery, toil and oppression. So the LORD brought us out of Egypt with a mighty hand and an outstretched arm, with great terror and with miraculous signs and wonders. He brought us to this place and gave us this land, a land flowing with milk and honey; and now I bring the firstfruits of the soil that you, O LORD, have given me." Place the basket before the LORD your God and bow down before him. And you and the Levites and the aliens among you shall rejoice in all the good things the LORD your God has given to you and your household.

Psalm 91:1–2, 9–16*	He who dwells in the shelter of the Most High will rest in the shadow of the Almighty. I will say of the LORD, "He is my refuge and my fortress, my God, in whom I trust."	P S A L M

If you make the Most High your dwelling –
    even the LORD, who is my refuge –
then no harm will befall you,
    no disaster will come near your tent.
For he will command his angels concerning you
    to guard you in all your ways;
they will lift you up in their hands,
    so that you will not strike your foot against a stone.
You will tread upon the lion and the cobra;
    you will trample the great lion and the serpent.

"Because you love me," says the LORD, "I will rescue you;
    I will protect him, for he acknowledges my name.
He will call upon me, and I will answer him;
    I will be with him in trouble,
    I will deliver him and honour him.
With long life will I satisfy him
    and show him my salvation."

Romans 10:8b–13 "The word is near you; it is in your mouth and in your heart," that is, the word of faith we are proclaiming: That if you confess with your mouth, "Jesus is Lord," and believe in your heart that God raised R him from the dead, you will be saved. For it is with your heart that you E believe and are justified, and it is with your mouth that you confess and are A saved. As the Scripture says, "Anyone who trusts in him will never be put D to shame." For there is no difference between Jew and Gentile – the same I Lord is Lord of all and richly blesses all who call on him, for, "Everyone N who calls on the name of the Lord will be saved." G

Luke 4:1–13   Jesus, full of the Holy Spirit, returned from the Jordan and G was led by the Spirit in the desert, where for forty days he was tempted by O the devil. He ate nothing during those days, and at the end of them he was S hungry. P

The devil said to him, "If you are the Son of God, tell this stone to E become bread." L

Jesus answered, "It is written: 'Man does not live on bread alone.'"

The devil led him up to a high place and showed him in an instant all the kingdoms of the world. And he said to him, "I will give you all their authority and splendour, for it has been given to me, and I can give it to anyone I want to. So if you worship me, it will all be yours."

Jesus answered, "It is written: 'Worship the Lord your God and serve him only.'"

The devil led him to Jerusalem and had him stand on the highest point of the temple. "If you are the Son of God," he said, "throw yourself down from here. For it is written:

"'He will command his angels concerning you
  to guard you carefully;
they will lift you up in their hands,
  so that you will not strike your foot against a stone.'"

Jesus answered, "It says: 'Do not put the Lord your God to the test.'"

When the devil had finished all this tempting, he left him until an opportune time.

Second Sunday of Lent

Genesis 15:1–12, 17–18   The word of the Lord came to Abram in a vision: F R

"Do not be afraid, Abram. I E
  I am your shield, R A
your very great reward." S D

But Abram said, "O Sovereign Lord, what can you give me since I T I remain childless and the one who will inherit my estate is Eliezer of Dam- N ascus?" And Abram said, "You have given me no children; so a servant in G my household will be my heir."

Then the word of the Lord came to him: "This man will not be your heir, but a son coming from your own body will be your heir." He took him outside and said, "Look up at the heavens and count the stars – if indeed you can count them." Then he said to him, "So shall your offspring be."

Abram believed the LORD, and he credited it to him as righteousness.

He also said to him, "I am the LORD, who brought you out of Ur of the Chaldeans to give you this land to take possession of it."

But Abram said, "O Sovereign LORD, how can I know that I shall gain possession of it?"

So the LORD said to him, "Bring me a heifer, a goat and a ram, each three years old, along with a dove and a young pigeon."

Abram brought all these to him, cut them in two and arranged the halves opposite each other; the birds, however, he did not cut in half. Then birds of prey came down on the carcasses, but Abram drove them away.

As the sun was setting, Abram fell into a deep sleep, and a thick and dreadful darkness came over him.

When the sun had set and darkness had fallen, a smoking brazier with a blazing torch appeared and passed between the pieces. On that day the LORD made a covenant with Abram and said, "To your descendants I give this land, from the river of Egypt to the great river, the Euphrates.

Psalm 27   The LORD is my light and my salvation –
>   whom shall I fear?
> The LORD is the stronghold of my life –
>   of whom shall I be afraid?
> When evil men advance against me
>   to devour my flesh,
> when my enemies and my foes attack me,
>   they will stumble and fall.
> Though an army besiege me,
>   my heart will not fear;
> though war break out against me,
>   even then will I be confident.
>
> One thing I ask of the LORD,
>   this is what I seek:
> that I may dwell in the house of the LORD
>   all the days of my life,
> to gaze upon the beauty of the LORD
>   and to seek him in his temple.
> For in the day of trouble
>   he will keep me safe in his dwelling;
> he will hide me in the shelter of his tabernacle
>   and set me high upon a rock.
> Then my head will be exalted
>   above the enemies who surround me;
> at his tabernacle will I sacrifice with shouts of joy;
>   I will sing and make music to the LORD.

Hear my voice when I call, O LORD;
  be merciful to me and answer me.
My heart says of you, "Seek his face!"
  Your face, LORD, I will seek.
Do not hide your face from me,
  do not turn your servant away in anger;
  you have been my helper.
Do not reject me or forsake me,
  O God my Saviour.
Though my father and mother forsake me,
  the LORD will receive me.
Teach me your way, O LORD;
  lead me in a straight path
  because of my oppressors.
Do not hand me over to the desire of my foes,
  for false witnesses rise up against me,
  breathing out violence.

I am still confident of this:
  I will see the goodness of the LORD
  in the land of the living.
Wait for the LORD;
  be strong and take heart
  and wait for the LORD.

Philippians 3:17–4:1 Join with others in following my example, brothers, S R
and take note of those who live according to the pattern we gave you. For, E E
as I have often told you before and now say again even with tears, many C A
live as enemies of the cross of Christ. Their destiny is destruction, their O D
god is their stomach, and their glory is in their shame. Their mind is on N I
earthly things. But our citizenship is in heaven. And we eagerly await a D N
Saviour from there, the Lord Jesus Christ, who, by the power that enables   G
him to bring everything under his control, will transform our lowly bodies
so that they will be like his glorious body.

Therefore, my brothers, you whom I love and long for, my joy and
crown, that is how you should stand firm in the Lord, dear friends!

Luke 13:31–35 Some Pharisees came to Jesus and said to him, "Leave this G
place and go somewhere else. Herod wants to kill you."   O

He replied, "Go tell that fox, 'I will drive out demons and heal people S
today and tomorrow, and on the third day I will reach my goal.' In any case, P
I must keep going today and tomorrow and the next day – for surely no E
prophet can die outside Jerusalem!   L

"O Jerusalem, Jerusalem, you who kill the prophets and stone those sent
to you, how often I have longed to gather your children together, as a hen
gathers her chicks under her wings, but you were not willing! Look, your
house is left to you desolate. I tell you, you will not see me again until you
say, 'Blessed is he who comes in the name of the Lord.'"

Third Sunday of Lent

Isaiah 55:1–9 "Come, all you who are thirsty,
come to the waters;
and you who have no money,
come, buy and eat!
Come, buy wine and milk
without money and without cost.
Why spend money on what is not bread,
and your labour on what does not satisfy?
Listen, listen to me, and eat what is good,
and your soul will delight in the richest of fare.
Give ear and come to me;
hear me, that your soul may live.
I will make an everlasting covenant with you,
my faithful love promised to David.
See, I have made him a witness to the peoples,
a leader and commander of the peoples.
Surely you will summon nations you know not,
and nations that do not know you will hasten to you,
because of the LORD your God,
the Holy One of Israel,
for he has endowed you with splendour."

Seek the LORD while he may be found;
call on him while he is near.
Let the wicked forsake their ways
and the unrighteous their thoughts.
Let them turn to the LORD, and he will have mercy on
them,
and to our God, for he will freely pardon.

"For my thoughts are not your thoughts,
neither are your ways my ways,"
declares the LORD.
"As the heavens are higher than the earth,
so are my ways higher than your ways
and my thoughts than your thoughts."

Psalm 63:1–8 O God, you are my God,
earnestly I seek you;
my soul thirsts for you,
my body longs for you,
in a dry and weary land
where there is no water.

I have seen you in the sanctuary
and beheld your power and your glory.
Because your love is better than life,
my lips will glorify you.

I will praise you as long as I live,
  and in your name I will lift up my hands.
My soul will be satisfied as with the richest of foods;
  with singing lips my mouth will praise you.

On my bed I remember you;
  I think of you through the watches of the night.
Because you are my help,
  I sing in the shadow of your wings.
My soul clings to you;
  your right hand upholds me.

1 Corinthians 10:1–13   I do not want you to be ignorant of the fact, brothers, that our forefathers were all under the cloud and that they all passed through the sea. They were all baptised into Moses in the cloud and in the sea. They all ate the same spiritual food and drank the same spiritual drink; for they drank from the spiritual rock that accompanied them, and that rock was Christ. Nevertheless, God was not pleased with most of them; their bodies were scattered over the desert.

Now these things occurred as examples to keep us from setting our hearts on evil things as they did. Do not be idolaters, as some of them were; as it is written: "The people sat down to eat and drink and got up to indulge in pagan revelry." We should not commit sexual immorality, as some of them did – and in one day twenty-three thousand of them died. We should not test the Lord, as some of them did – and were killed by snakes. And do not grumble, as some of them did – and were killed by the destroying angel.

These things happened to them as examples and were written down as warnings for us, on whom the fulfilment of the ages has come. So, if you think you are standing firm, be careful that you don't fall! No temptation has seized you except what is common to man. And God is faithful; he will not let you be tempted beyond what you can bear. But when you are tempted, he will also provide a way out so that you can stand up under it.

Luke 13:1–9   Some people told Jesus about the Galileans whose blood Pilate had mixed with their sacrifices. Jesus answered, "Do you think that these Galileans were worse sinners than all the other Galileans because they suffered this way? I tell you, no! But unless you repent, you too will all perish. Or those eighteen who died when the tower in Siloam fell on them – do you think they were more guilty than all the others living in Jerusalem? I tell you, no! But unless you repent, you too will all perish."

Then he told this parable: "A man had a fig-tree, planted in his vineyard, and he went to look for fruit on it, but did not find any. So he said to the man who took care of the vineyard, 'For three years now I've been coming to look for fruit on this fig-tree and haven't found any. Cut it down! Why should it use up the soil?'

"'Sir,' the man replied, 'leave it alone for one more year, and I'll dig round it and fertilise it. If it bears fruit next year, fine! If not, then cut it down.'"

Fourth Sunday of Lent

Mothering Sunday may be celebrated in preference to the provision for the Fourth Sunday of Lent see pp 62–65.

Joshua 5:9–12 The LORD said to Joshua, "Today I have rolled away the reproach of Egypt from you." So the place has been called Gilgal to this day.

On the evening of the fourteenth day of the month, while camped at Gilgal on the plains of Jericho, the Israelites celebrated the Passover. The day after the Passover, that very day, they ate some of the produce of the land: unleavened bread and roasted grain. The manna stopped the day after they ate this food from the land; there was no longer any manna for the Israelites, but that year they ate of the produce of Canaan.

FIRST READING

Psalm 32

Blessed is he
  whose transgressions are forgiven,
  whose sins are covered.
Blessed is the man
  whose sin the LORD does not count against him
  and in whose spirit is no deceit.

When I kept silent,
  my bones wasted away
  through my groaning all day long.
For day and night
  your hand was heavy upon me;
my strength was sapped
  as in the heat of summer.
Then I acknowledged my sin to you
  and did not cover up my iniquity.
I said, "I will confess my
  transgressions to the LORD" –
and you forgave
  the guilt of my sin.

Therefore let everyone who is godly pray to you
  while you may be found;
surely when the mighty waters rise,
  they will not reach him.
You are my hiding–place;
  you will protect me from trouble
  and surround me with songs of deliverance.

I will instruct you and teach you in the way you should go;
  I will counsel you and watch over you.
Do not be like the horse or the mule,
  which have no understanding
but must be controlled by bit and bridle
  or they will not come to you.
Many are the woes of the wicked,

PSALM

but the LORD's unfailing love
surrounds those who trust in him.

Rejoice in the LORD and be glad, you righteous;
sing, all you who are upright in heart!

Corinthians 5:16–21 From now on we regard no-one from a worldly point of view. Though we once regarded Christ in this way, we do so no longer. Therefore, if anyone is in Christ, he is a new creation: the old has gone, the new has come! All this is from God, who reconciled us to himself through Christ and gave us the ministry of reconciliation: that God was reconciling the world to himself in Christ, not counting men's sins against them. And he has committed to us the message of reconciliation. We are therefore Christ's ambassadors, as though God were making his appeal through us. We implore you on Christ's behalf: Be reconciled to God. God made him who had no sin to be sin for us, so that in him we might become the righteousness of God.

SECOND READING

ke 15:1–3, 11b–32 The tax collectors and "sinners" were all gathering round to hear Jesus. But the Pharisees and the teachers of the law muttered, "This man welcomes sinners, and eats with them."

Then Jesus told them this parable:

"There was a man who had two sons. The younger one said to his father, 'Father, give me my share of the estate.' So he divided his property between them.

GOSPEL

"Not long after that, the younger son got together all he had, set off for a distant country and there squandered his wealth in wild living. After he had spent everything, there was a severe famine in that whole country, and he began to be in need. So he went and hired himself out to a citizen of that country, who sent him to his fields to feed pigs. He longed to fill his stomach with the pods that the pigs were eating, but no-one gave him anything.

"When he came to his senses, he said, 'How many of my father's hired men have food to spare, and here I am starving to death! I will set out and go back to my father and say to him: Father, I have sinned against heaven and against you. I am no longer worthy to be called your son; make me like one of your hired men.' So he got up and went to his father.

"But while he was still a long way off, his father saw him and was filled with compassion for him; he ran to his son, threw his arms around him and kissed him.

"The son said to him, 'Father, I have sinned against heaven and against you. I am no longer worthy to be called your son.'

"But the father said to his servants, 'Quick! Bring the best robe and put it on him. Put a ring on his finger and sandals on his feet. Bring the fattened calf and kill it. Let's have a feast and celebrate. For this son of mine was dead and is alive again; he was lost and is found.' So they began to celebrate.

"Meanwhile, the older son was in the field. When he came near the house, he heard music and dancing. So he called one of the servants and asked him what was going on. 'Your brother has come,' he replied, 'and your father has killed the fattened calf because he has him back safe and sound.'

"The older brother became angry and refused to go in. So his father went out and pleaded with him. But he answered his father, 'Look! All these years I've been slaving for you and never disobeyed your orders. Yet you never gave me even a young goat so I could celebrate with my friends. But when this son of yours who has squandered your property with prostitutes comes home, you kill the fattened calf for him!'

"'My son,' the father said, 'you are always with me, and everything I have is yours. But we had to celebrate and be glad, because this brother of yours was dead and is alive again; he was lost and is found.'"

Mothering Sunday

Mothering Sunday may be celebrated in preference to the provision for the Fourth Sunday of Lent. For text of readings for Years A, B, C see pp 62–65.

Fifth Sunday of Lent

Passiontide begins

Isaiah 43:16–21
This is what the LORD says –
   he who made a way through the sea,
   a path through the mighty waters,
who drew out the chariots and horses,
   the army and reinforcements together,
and they lay there, never to rise again,
   extinguished, snuffed out like a wick:
"Forget the former things;
   do not dwell on the past.
See, I am doing a new thing!
   Now it springs up; do you not perceive it?
I am making a way in the desert
   and streams in the wasteland.
The wild animals honour me,
   the jackals and the owls,
because I provide water in the desert
   and streams in the wasteland,
to give drink to my people, my chosen,
   the people I formed for myself
   that they may proclaim my praise."

Psalm 126
When the LORD brought back the captives to Zion,
   we were like those who dreamed.
Our mouths were filled with laughter,
   our tongues with songs of joy.
Then it was said among the nations,
   "The LORD has done great things for them."

The LORD has done great things for us,
and we are filled with joy.

Restore our fortunes, O LORD,
like streams in the Negev.
Those who sow in tears
will reap with songs of joy.
He who goes out weeping,
carrying seed to sow,
will return with songs of joy,
carrying sheaves with him.

Philippians 3:4b–14 If anyone else thinks he has reasons to put confidence in
the flesh, I have more: circumcised on the eighth day, of the people of
Israel, of the tribe of Benjamin, a Hebrew of Hebrews; in regard to the law,
a Pharisee; as for zeal, persecuting the church; as for legalistic righteousness, faultless.

But whatever was to my profit I now consider loss for the sake of Christ.
What is more, I consider everything a loss compared to the surpassing
greatness of knowing Christ Jesus my Lord, for whose sake I have lost all
things. I consider them rubbish, that I may gain Christ and be found in him,
not having a righteousness of my own that comes from the law, but that
which is through faith in Christ – the righteousness that comes from God
and is by faith. I want to know Christ and the power of his resurrection and
the fellowship of sharing in his sufferings, becoming like him in his death,
and so, somehow, to attain to the resurrection from the dead.

Not that I have already obtained all this, or have already been made perfect, but I press on to take hold of that for which Christ Jesus took hold of
me. Brothers, I do not consider myself yet to have taken hold of it. But one
thing I do: Forgetting what is behind and straining towards what is ahead,
I press on towards the goal to win the prize for which God has called me
heavenwards in Christ Jesus.

SECOND READING

John 12:1–8 Six days before the Passover, Jesus arrived at Bethany, where
Lazarus lived, whom Jesus had raised from the dead. Here a dinner was
given in Jesus' honour. Martha served, while Lazarus was among those
reclining at the table with him. Then Mary took about a pint of pure nard,
an expensive perfume; she poured it on Jesus' feet and wiped his feet with
her hair. And the house was filled with the fragrance of the perfume.

But one of his disciples, Judas Iscariot, who was later to betray him,
objected, "Why wasn't this perfume sold and the money given to the poor?
It was worth a year's wages." He did not say this because he cared about
the poor but because he was a thief; as keeper of the money bag, he used to
help himself to what was put into it.

"Leave her alone," Jesus replied. "It was intended that she should save
this perfume for the day of my burial. You will always have the poor among
you, but you will not always have me."

GOSPEL

Liturgy of the Palms

Luke 19:28–40 Jesus went on ahead, going up to Jerusalem. As he
approached Bethphage and Bethany at the hill called the Mount of Olives,
he sent two of his disciples, saying to them, "Go to the village ahead of
you, and as you enter it, you will find a colt tied there, which no-one has
ever ridden. Untie it and bring it here. If anyone asks you, 'Why are you
untying it?' say, 'The Lord needs it.'"

GOSPEL

Those who were sent ahead went and found it just as he had told them.
As they were untying the colt, its owners asked them, "Why are you untying the colt?"

They replied, "The Lord needs it."

They brought it to Jesus, threw their cloaks on the colt and put Jesus on
it. As he went along, people spread their cloaks on the road.

When he came near the place where the road goes down the Mount of
Olives, the whole crowd of disciples began joyfully to praise God in loud
voices for all the miracles they had seen:

"Blessed is the king who comes in the name of the Lord!"

"Peace in heaven and glory in the highest!"

Some of the Pharisees in the crowd said to Jesus, "Teacher, rebuke your
disciples!"

"I tell you," he replied, "if they keep quiet, the stones will cry out."

Psalm 118:1-2, 19–29★   Give thanks to the LORD, for he is good;
  his love endures for ever.

PSALM

Let Israel say:
  "His love endures for ever."

Open for me the gates of righteousness;
  I will enter and give thanks to the LORD.
This is the gate of the LORD
  through which the righteous may enter.
I will give you thanks, for you answered me;
  you have become my salvation.

The stone the builders rejected
  has become the capstone;
the LORD has done this,
  and it is marvellous in our eyes.
This is the day the LORD has made;
  let us rejoice and be glad in it.

O LORD, save us;
  O LORD, grant us success.
Blessed is he who comes in the name of the LORD.
  From the house of the LORD we bless you.
The LORD is God,
  and he has made his light shine upon us.

With boughs in hand, join in the festal procession
 up to the horns of the altar.

You are my God, and I will give thanks;
 you are my God, and I will exalt you.

Give thanks to the Lord, for he is good;
 his love endures for ever.

Liturgy of the Passion

Isaiah 50:4–9a The Sovereign Lord has given me an instructed tongue, F
 to know the word that sustains the weary. I
He wakens me morning by morning, R
 wakens my ear to listen like one being taught. S
The Sovereign Lord has opened my ears, T
 and I have not been rebellious;
 I have not drawn back. R
I offered my back to those who beat me, E
 my cheeks to those who pulled out my beard; A
I did not hide my face D
 from mocking and spitting. I
Because the Sovereign Lord helps me, N
 I will not be disgraced. G
Therefore have I set my face like flint,
 and I know I will not be put to shame.
He who vindicates me is near.
 Who then will bring charges against me?
 Let us face each other!
Who is my accuser?
 Let him confront me!
It is the Sovereign Lord who helps me.

Psalm 31:9–16* Be merciful to me, O Lord, for I am in distress; P
 my eyes grow weak with sorrow, S
 my soul and my body with grief. A
My life is consumed by anguish L
 and my years by groaning; M
my strength fails because of my affliction,
 and my bones grow weak.
Because of all my enemies,
 I am the utter contempt of my neighbours;
I am a dread to my friends –
 those who see me on the street flee from me.
I am forgotten by them as though I were dead;
 I have become like broken pottery.
For I hear the slander of many;
 there is terror on every side;

they conspire against me
and plot to take my life.

But I trust in you, O LORD;
I say, "You are my God."
My times are in your hands;
deliver me from my enemies
and from those who pursue me.
Let your face shine on your servant;
save me in your unfailing love.

Philippians 2:5–11   Your attitude should be the same as that of Christ Jesus: S

Who, being in very nature God,   E
did not consider equality with God   C
something to be grasped,   O
but made himself nothing,   N
taking the very nature of a servant,   D
being made in human likeness.
And being found in appearance as a man,   R
he humbled himself   E
and became obedient to death – even death on a   A
cross!   D
Therefore God exalted him to the highest place   I
and gave him the name that is above every name,   N
that at the name of Jesus every knee should bow,   G
in heaven and on earth and under the earth,
and every tongue confess that Jesus Christ is Lord,
to the glory of God the Father.

Alternative Gospels

Either **Luke 22:14 – 23:56**   When the hour came, Jesus and his apostles G
reclined at the table. And he said to them, "I have eagerly desired to eat O
this Passover with you before I suffer. For I tell you, I will not eat it again S
until it finds fulfilment in the kingdom of God."   P

After taking the cup, he gave thanks and said, "Take this and divide it E
among you. For I tell you I will not drink again of the fruit of the vine until L
the kingdom of God comes."

And he took bread, gave thanks and broke it, and gave it to them, saying,
"This is my body given for you; do this in remembrance of me."

In the same way, after the supper he took the cup, saying, "This cup is
the new covenant in my blood, which is poured out for you. But the hand of
him who is going to betray me is with mine on the table. The Son of Man will
go as it has been decreed, but woe to that man who betrays him." They
began to question among themselves which of them it might be who would
do this.

Also a dispute arose among them as to which of them was considered to be greatest. Jesus said to them, "The kings of the Gentiles lord it over them; and those who exercise authority over them call themselves Benefactors. But you are not to be like that. Instead, the greatest among you should be like the youngest, and the one who rules like the one who serves. For who is greater, the one who is at the table or the one who serves? Is it not the one who is at the table? But I am among you as one who serves. You are those who have stood by me in my trials. And I confer on you a kingdom, just as my Father conferred one on me, so that you may eat and drink at my table in my kingdom and sit on thrones, judging the twelve tribes of Israel.

"Simon, Simon, Satan has asked to sift you as wheat. But I have prayed for you, Simon, that your faith may not fail. And when you have turned back, strengthen your brothers."

But he replied, "Lord, I am ready to go with you to prison and to death."

Jesus answered, "I tell you, Peter, before the cock crows today, you will deny three times that you know me."

Then Jesus asked them, "When I sent you without purse, bag or sandals, did you lack anything?"

"Nothing," they answered.

He said to them, "But now if you have a purse, take it, and also a bag; and if you don't have a sword, sell your cloak and buy one. It is written: 'And he was numbered with the transgressors'; and I tell you that this must be fulfilled in me. Yes, what is written about me is reaching its fulfilment."

The disciples said, "See, Lord, here are two swords."

"That is enough," he replied.

Jesus went out as usual to the Mount of Olives, and his disciples followed him. On reaching the place, he said to them, "Pray that you will not fall into temptation." He withdrew about a stone's throw beyond them, knelt down and prayed, "Father, if you are willing, take this cup from me; yet not my will, but yours be done." An angel from heaven appeared to him and strengthened him. And being in anguish, he prayed more earnestly, and his sweat was like drops of blood falling to the ground.

When he rose from prayer and went back to the disciples, he found them asleep, exhausted from sorrow. "Why are you sleeping?" he asked them. "Get up and pray so that you will not fall into temptation."

While he was still speaking a crowd came up, and the man who was called Judas, one of the Twelve, was leading them. He approached Jesus to kiss him, but Jesus asked him, "Judas, are you betraying the Son of Man with a kiss?"

When Jesus' followers saw what was going to happen, they said, "Lord, should we strike with our swords?" And one of them struck the servant of the high priest, cutting off his right ear.

But Jesus answered, "No more of this!" And he touched the man's ear and healed him.

Then Jesus said to the chief priests, the officers of the temple guard, and the elders, who had come for him, "Am I leading a rebellion, that you have come with swords and clubs? Every day I was with you in the temple courts, and you did not lay a hand on me. But this is your hour – when darkness reigns."

Then seizing him, they led him away and took him into the house of the high priest. Peter followed at a distance. But when they had kindled a fire in the middle of the courtyard and had sat down together, Peter sat down with them. A servant girl saw him seated there in the firelight. She looked closely at him and said, "This man was with him."

But he denied it. "Woman, I don't know him," he said.

A little later someone else saw him and said, "You also are one of them."

"Man, I am not!" Peter replied.

About an hour later another asserted, "Certainly this fellow was with him, for he is a Galilean."

Peter replied, "Man, I don't know what you're talking about!" Just as he was speaking, the cock crowed. The Lord turned and looked straight at Peter. Then Peter remembered the word the Lord had spoken to him: "Before the cock crows today, you will disown me three times." And he went outside and wept bitterly.

The men who were guarding Jesus began mocking and beating him. They blindfolded him and demanded, "Prophesy! Who hit you?" And they said many other insulting things to him.

At daybreak the council of the elders of the people, both the chief priests and teachers of the law, met together, and Jesus was led before them. "If you are the Christ," they said, "tell us."

Jesus answered, "If I tell you, you will not believe me, and if I asked you, you would not answer. But from now on, the Son of Man will be seated at the right hand of the mighty God."

They all asked, "Are you then the Son of God?"

He replied, "You are right in saying I am."

Then they said, "Why do we need any more testimony? We have heard it from his own lips."

Then the whole assembly rose and led him off to Pilate. And they began to accuse him, saying, "We have found this man subverting our nation. He opposes payment of taxes to Caesar and claims to be Christ, a king."

So Pilate asked Jesus, "Are you the king of the Jews?"

"Yes, it is as you say," Jesus replied.

Then Pilate announced to the chief priests and the crowd, "I find no basis for a charge against this man."

But they insisted, "He stirs up the people all over Judea by his teaching. He started in Galilee and has come all the way here."

On hearing this, Pilate asked if the man was a Galilean. When he learned that Jesus was under Herod's jurisdiction, he sent him to Herod, who was also in Jerusalem at that time.

When Herod saw Jesus, he was greatly pleased, because for a long time he had been wanting to see him. From what he had heard about him, he hoped to see him perform some miracle. He plied him with many questions, but Jesus gave him no answer. The chief priests and the teachers of the law were standing there, vehemently accusing him. Then Herod and his soldiers ridiculed and mocked him. Dressing him in an elegant robe, they sent him back to Pilate. That day Herod and Pilate became friends – before this they had been enemies.

Pilate called together the chief priests, the rulers and the people, and said to them, "You brought me this man as one who was inciting the people to rebellion. I have examined him in your presence and have found no basis for your charges against him. Neither has Herod, for he sent him back to us; as you can see, he has done nothing to deserve death. Therefore, I will punish him and then release him."

With one voice they cried out, "Away with this man! Release Barabbas to us!" (Barabbas had been thrown into prison for an insurrection in the city, and for murder.)

Wanting to release Jesus, Pilate appealed to them again. But they kept shouting, "Crucify him! Crucify him!"

For the third time he spoke to them: "Why? What crime has this man committed? I have found in him no grounds for the death penalty. Therefore I will have him punished and then release him."

But with loud shouts they insistently demanded that he be crucified, and their shouts prevailed. So Pilate decided to grant their demand. He released the man who had been thrown into prison for insurrection and murder, the one they asked for, and surrendered Jesus to their will.

As they led him away, they seized Simon from Cyrene, who was on his way in from the country, and put the cross on him and made him carry it behind Jesus. A large number of people followed him, including women who mourned and wailed for him. Jesus turned and said to them, "Daughters of Jerusalem, do not weep for me; weep for yourselves and for your children. For the time will come when you will say, 'Blessed are the barren women, the wombs that never bore and the breasts that never nursed!' Then

"'they will say to the mountains, "Fall on us!"
and to the hills "Cover us!"'

For if men do these things when the tree is green, what will happen when it is dry?"

Two other men, both criminals, were also led out with him to be executed. When they came to the place called the Skull, there they crucified him, along with the criminals – one on his right, the other on his left. Jesus said, "Father, forgive them, for they do not know what they are doing." And they divided up his clothes by casting lots.

The people stood watching, and the rulers even sneered at him. They said, "He saved others; let him save himself if he is the Christ of God, the Chosen One."

The soldiers also came up and mocked him. They offered him wine vinegar and said, "If you are the king of the Jews, save yourself."

There was a written notice above him, which read: THIS IS THE KING OF THE JEWS.

One of the criminals who hung there hurled insults at him: "Aren't you the Christ? Save yourself and us!"

But the other criminal rebuked him. "Don't you fear God," he said, "since you are under the same sentence? We are punished justly, for we are getting what our deeds deserve. But this man has done nothing wrong."

Then he said, "Jesus, remember me when you come into your kingdom."

Jesus answered him, "I tell you the truth, today you will be with me in paradise."

It was now about the sixth hour, and darkness came over the whole land until the ninth hour, for the sun stopped shining. And the curtain of the temple was torn in two. Jesus called out with a loud voice, "Father, into your hands I commit my spirit." When he had said this, he breathed his last.

The centurion, seeing what had happened, praised God and said, "Surely this was a righteous man." When all the people who had gathered to witness this sight saw what took place, they beat their breasts and went away. But all those who knew him, including the women who had followed him from Galilee, stood at a distance, watching these things.

Now there was a man named Joseph, a member of the Council, a good and upright man, who had not consented to their decision and action. He came from the Judean town of Arimathea and he was waiting for the kingdom of God. Going to Pilate, he asked for Jesus' body. Then he took it down, wrapped it in linen cloth and placed it in a tomb cut in the rock, one in which no-one had yet been laid. It was Preparation Day, and the Sabbath was about to begin.

The women who had come with Jesus from Galilee followed Joseph and saw the tomb and how his body was laid in it. Then they went home and prepared spices and perfumes. But they rested on the Sabbath in obedience to the commandment.

or **Luke 23:1–49**   The whole assembly rose and led Jesus off to Pilate. And they began to accuse him, saying, "We have found this man subverting our nation. He opposes payment of taxes to Caesar and claims to be Christ, a king."

So Pilate asked Jesus, "Are you the king of the Jews?"

"Yes, it is as you say," Jesus replied.

Then Pilate announced to the chief priests and the crowd, "I find no basis for a charge against this man."

But they insisted, "He stirs up the people all over Judea by his teaching. He started in Galilee and has come all the way here."

On hearing this, Pilate asked if the man was a Galilean. When he learned that Jesus was under Herod's jurisdiction, he sent him to Herod, who was also in Jerusalem at that time.

When Herod saw Jesus, he was greatly pleased, because for a long time he had been wanting to see him. From what he had heard about him, he hoped to see him perform some miracle. He plied him with many questions, but Jesus gave him no answer. The chief priests and the teachers of the law were standing there, vehemently accusing him. Then Herod and his soldiers ridiculed and mocked him. Dressing him in an elegant robe, they sent him back to Pilate. That day Herod and Pilate became friends – before this they had been enemies.

Pilate called together the chief priests, the rulers and the people, and said to them, "You brought me this man as one who was inciting the people to rebellion. I have examined him in your presence and have found no basis for your charges against him. Neither has Herod, for he sent him back to us; as you can see, he has done nothing to deserve death. Therefore, I will punish him and then release him."

With one voice they cried out, "Away with this man! Release Barabbas to us!" (Barabbas had been thrown into prison for an insurrection in the city, and for murder.)

Wanting to release Jesus, Pilate appealed to them again. But they kept shouting, "Crucify him! Crucify him!"

For the third time he spoke to them: "Why? What crime has this man committed? I have found in him no grounds for the death penalty. Therefore I will have him punished and then release him."

But with loud shouts they insistently demanded that he be crucified, and their shouts prevailed. So Pilate decided to grant their demand. He released the man who had been thrown into prison for insurrection and murder, the one they asked for, and surrendered Jesus to their will.

As they led him away, they seized Simon from Cyrene, who was on his way in from the country, and put the cross on him and made him carry it behind Jesus. A large number of people followed him, including women who mourned and wailed for him. Jesus turned and said to them, "Daughters of Jerusalem, do not weep for me; weep for yourselves and for your children. For the time will come when you will say, 'Blessed are the barren women, the wombs that never bore and the breasts that never nursed!' Then

"'they will say to the mountains, "Fall on us!"
and to the hills "Cover us!"'

For if men do these things when the tree is green, what will happen when it is dry?"

Two other men, both criminals, were also led out with him to be executed. When they came to the place called the Skull, there they crucified him, along with the criminals – one on his right, the other on his left. Jesus said, "Father, forgive them, for they do not know what they are doing." And they divided up his clothes by casting lots.

The people stood watching, and the rulers even sneered at him. They said, "He saved others; let him save himself if he is the Christ of God, the Chosen One."

The soldiers also came up and mocked him. They offered him wine vinegar and said, "If you are the king of the Jews, save yourself."

There was a written notice above him, which read: THIS IS THE KING OF THE JEWS.

One of the criminals who hung there hurled insults at him: "Aren't you the Christ? Save yourself and us!"

But the other criminal rebuked him. "Don't you fear God," he said, "since you are under the same sentence? We are punished justly, for we are getting what our deeds deserve. But this man has done nothing wrong."

Then he said, "Jesus, remember me when you come into your kingdom."

Jesus answered him, "I tell you the truth, today you will be with me in paradise."

It was now about the sixth hour, and darkness came over the whole land until the ninth hour, for the sun stopped shining. And the curtain of the temple was torn in two. Jesus called out with a loud voice, "Father, into your hands I commit my spirit." When he had said this, he breathed his last.

The centurion, seeing what had happened, praised God and said, "Surely this was a righteous man." When all the people who had gathered to witness this sight saw what took place, they beat their breasts and went away. But all those who knew him, including the women who had followed him from Galilee, stood at a distance, watching these things.

Monday of Holy Week

For text of readings for Years A, B, C see pp 77–79.

Tuesday of Holy Week

For text of readings for Years A, B, C see pp 79–81.

Wednesday of Holy Week

For text of readings for Years A, B, C see pp 81–83.

Maundy Thursday

For text of readings for Years A, B, C see pp 83–85.

Good Friday

For text of readings for Years A, B, C see pp 85–93.

Easter Eve

For text of readings for Years A, B, C see pp 93–95.

EASTER

Easter Vigil

A selection of Old Testament readings and a reading from Romans for Years A, B, C is given on pp 96–112. A minimum of three Old Testament readings (including Exodus 14) must be used, together with the Romans reading and the Gospel which is different for each year. Only the Gospel for Year C appears here as Years A and B have their own Gospel.

Luke 24:1–12 On the first day of the week, very early in the morning, the women took the spices they had prepared and went to the tomb. They found the stone rolled away from the tomb, but when they entered, they did not find the body of the Lord Jesus. While they were wondering about this, suddenly two men in clothes that gleamed like lightning stood beside them. In their fright the women bowed down with their faces to the ground, but the men said to them, "Why do you look for the living among the dead? He is not here; he has risen! Remember how he told you, while he was still with you in Galilee: 'The Son of Man must be delivered into the hands of sinful men, be crucified and on the third day be raised again.'" Then they remembered his words.

GOSPEL YEAR C

When they came back from the tomb, they told all these things to the Eleven and to all the others. It was Mary Magdalene, Joanna, Mary the mother of James, and the others with them who told this to the apostles. But they did not believe the women, because their words seemed to them like nonsense. Peter, however, got up and ran to the tomb. Bending over, he saw the strips of linen lying by themselves, and he went away, wondering to himself what had happened.

Easter Day

Acts 10:34–43 should be read as either the first or second reading.

Alternative first readings

Either **Acts 10:34–43** Peter began to speak: "I now realise how true it is that God does not show favouritism but accepts men from every nation who fear him and do what is right. You know the message God sent to the people of Israel, telling the good news of peace through Jesus Christ, who is Lord of all. You know what has happened throughout Judea, beginning in Galilee after the baptism that John preached – how God anointed Jesus of Nazareth with the Holy Spirit and power, and how he went around doing good and healing all who were under the power of the devil, because God was with him.

FIRST READING

"We are witnesses of everything he did in the country of the Jews and in Jerusalem. They killed him by hanging him on a tree, but God raised him from the dead on the third day and caused him to be seen. He was not seen by all the people, but by witnesses whom God had already chosen – by us who ate and drank with him after he rose from the dead. He commanded us to preach to the people and to testify that he is the one whom God appointed as judge of the living and the dead. All the prophets testify about him that

ALTERNATIVE READING

everyone who believes in him receives forgiveness of sins through his name."

or **Isaiah 65:17–25**

F
I
R
S
T

R
E
A
D
I
N
G

"Behold, I will create
  new heavens and a new earth.
The former things will not be remembered,
  nor will they come to mind.
But be glad and rejoice for ever
  in what I will create,
for I will create Jerusalem to be a delight
  and its people a joy.
I will rejoice over Jerusalem
  and take delight in my people;
the sound of weeping and of crying
  will be heard in it no more.

"Never again will there be in it
  infants who live but a few days,
  or an old man who does not live out his years;
he who dies at a hundred
  will be thought a mere youth;
he who fails to reach a hundred
  will be considered accursed.
They will build houses and dwell in them;
  they will plant vineyards and eat their fruit.
No longer will they build houses and others live in them,
  or plant and others eat.
For as the days of a tree,
  so will be the days of my people;
my chosen ones will long enjoy
  the works of their hands.
They will not toil in vain
  or bear children doomed to misfortune;
for they will be a people blessed by the LORD,
  they and their descendants with them.
Before they call I will answer;
  while they are still speaking I will hear.
The wolf and the lamb will feed together,
  and the lion will eat straw like the ox,
  but dust will be the serpent's food.
They will neither harm nor destroy
  on all my holy mountain,"
                              says the LORD.

Psalm 118:1–2, 14–24*

P
S
A
L
M

Give thanks to the LORD, for he is good;
  his love endures for ever.

  Let Israel say:
    "His love endures for ever."

The LORD is my strength and my song;
    he has become my salvation.

Shouts of joy and victory
    resound in the tents of the righteous:
"The LORD's right hand has done mighty things!
    The LORD's right hand is lifted high;
    the LORD's right hand has done mighty things!"

I will not die but live,
    and will proclaim what the LORD has done.
The LORD has chastened me severely,
    but he has not given me over to death.

Open for me the gates of righteousness;
    I will enter and give thanks to the LORD.
This is the gate of the LORD
    through which the righteous may enter.
I will give you thanks, for you answered me;
    you have become my salvation.

The stone the builders rejected
    has become the capstone;
the LORD has done this,
    and it is marvellous in our eyes.
This is the day the LORD has made;
    let us rejoice and be glad in it.

Alternative second readings

Either **1 Corinthians 15:19–26**   If only for this life we have hope in Christ, we
are to be pitied more than all people.
    But Christ has indeed been raised from the dead, the firstfruits of those
who have fallen asleep. For since death came through a man, the resurrection of the dead comes also through a man. For as in Adam all die, so in
Christ all will be made alive. But each in his own turn: Christ, the firstfruits; then, when he comes, those who belong to him. Then the end will
come, when he hands over the kingdom to God the Father after he has
destroyed all dominion, authority and power. For he must reign until he has
put all his enemies under his feet. The last enemy to be destroyed is death.

or **Acts 10:34–43**   Peter began to speak: "I now realise how true it is that God
does not show favouritism but accepts men from every nation who fear
him and do what is right. You know the message God sent to the people of
Israel, telling the good news of peace through Jesus Christ, who is Lord of
all. You know what has happened throughout Judea, beginning in Galilee
after the baptism that John preached – how God anointed Jesus of
Nazareth with the Holy Spirit and power, and how he went around doing
good and healing all who were under the power of the devil, because God
was with him.

"We are witnesses of everything he did in the country of the Jews and in Jerusalem. They killed him by hanging him on a tree, but God raised him from the dead on the third day and caused him to be seen. He was not seen by all the people, but by witnesses whom God had already chosen – by us who ate and drank with him after he rose from the dead. He commanded us to preach to the people and to testify that he is the one whom God appointed as judge of the living and the dead. All the prophets testify about him that everyone who believes in him receives forgiveness of sins through his name."

Alternative Gospels

Either **John 20:1–18** Early on the first day of the week, while it was still dark, Mary Magdalene went to the tomb and saw that the stone had been removed from the entrance. So she came running to Simon Peter and the other disciple, the one Jesus loved, and said, "They have taken the Lord out of the tomb, and we don't know where they have put him!"

So Peter and the other disciple started for the tomb. Both were running, but the other disciple outran Peter and reached the tomb first. He bent over and looked in at the strips of linen lying there but did not go in. Then Simon Peter, who was behind him, arrived and went into the tomb. He saw the strips of linen lying there, as well as the burial cloth that had been around Jesus' head. The cloth was folded up by itself, separate from the linen. Finally the other disciple, who had reached the tomb first, also went inside. He saw and believed. (They still did not understand from Scripture that Jesus had to rise from the dead.)

Then the disciples went back to their homes, but Mary stood outside the tomb crying. As she wept, she bent over to look into the tomb and saw two angels in white, seated where Jesus' body had been, one at the head and the other at the foot.

They asked her, "Woman, why are you crying?"

"They have taken my Lord away," she said, "and I don't know where they have put him." At this, she turned round and saw Jesus standing there, but she did not realise that it was Jesus.

"Woman," he said, "why are you crying? Who is it you are looking for?"

Thinking he was the gardener, she said, "Sir, if you have carried him away, tell me where you have put him, and I will get him."

Jesus said to her, "Mary."

She turned towards him and cried out in Aramaic, "Rabboni!" (which means Teacher).

Jesus said, "Do not hold on to me, for I have not yet returned to the Father. Go instead to my brothers and tell them, 'I am returning to my Father and your Father, to my God and your God.'"

Mary Magdalene went to the disciples with the news: "I have seen the Lord!" And she told them that he had said these things to her.

or **Luke 24:1–12**   On the first day of the week, very early in the morning, the women took the spices they had prepared and went to the tomb. They found the stone rolled away from the tomb, but when they entered, they did not find the body of the Lord Jesus. While they were wondering about this, suddenly two men in clothes that gleamed like lightning stood beside them. In their fright the women bowed down with their faces to the ground, but the men said to them, "Why do you look for the living among the dead? He is not here; he has risen! Remember how he told you, while he was still with you in Galilee: 'The Son of Man must be delivered into the hands of sinful men, be crucified and on the third day be raised again.'" Then they remembered his words.

When they came back from the tomb, they told all these things to the Eleven and to all the others. It was Mary Magdalene, Joanna, Mary the mother of James, and the others with them who told this to the apostles. But they did not believe the women, because their words seemed to them like nonsense. Peter, however, got up and ran to the tomb. Bending over, he saw the strips of linen lying by themselves, and he went away, wondering to himself what had happened.

Easter 2

Exodus 14:10–31; 15:20–21 As Pharaoh approached the Israelites by the sea, the Israelites looked up, and there were the Egyptians, marching after them. They were terrified and cried out to the LORD. They said to Moses, "Was it because there were no graves in Egypt that you brought us to the desert to die? What have you done to us by bringing us out of Egypt? Didn't we say to you in Egypt, 'Leave us alone; let us serve the Egyptians'? It would have been better for us to serve the Egyptians than to die in the desert!"

Moses answered the people, "Do not be afraid. Stand firm and you will see the deliverance the LORD will bring you today. The Egyptians you see today you will never see again. The LORD will fight for you; you need only to be still."

Then the LORD said to Moses, "Why are you crying out to me? Tell the Israelites to move on. Raise your staff and stretch out your hand over the sea to divide the water so that the Israelites can go through the sea on dry ground. I will harden the hearts of the Egyptians so that they will go in after them. And I will gain glory through Pharaoh and all his army, through his chariots and his horsemen. The Egyptians will know that I am the LORD when I gain glory through Pharaoh, his chariots and his horsemen."

Then the angel of God, who had been travelling in front of Israel's army, withdrew and went behind them. The pillar of cloud also moved from in front and stood behind them, coming between the armies of Egypt and Israel. Throughout the night the cloud brought darkness to the one side and light to the other; so neither went near the other all night long.

Then Moses stretched out his hand over the sea, and all that night the LORD drove the sea back with a strong east wind and turned it into dry land. The waters were divided, and the Israelites went through the sea on dry ground, with a wall of water on their right and on their left.

The Egyptians pursued them, and all Pharaoh's horses and chariots and horsemen followed them into the sea. During the last watch of the night the LORD looked down from the pillar of fire and cloud at the Egyptian army and threw it into confusion. He made the wheels of their chariots come off so that they had difficulty driving. And the Egyptians said, "Let's get away from the Israelites! The LORD is fighting for them against Egypt."

Then the LORD said to Moses, "Stretch out your hand over the sea so that the waters may flow back over the Egyptians and their chariots and horsemen." Moses stretched out his hand over the sea, and at daybreak the sea went back to its place. The Egyptians were fleeing towards it, and the LORD swept them into the sea. The water flowed back and covered the chariots and horsemen – the entire army of Pharaoh that had followed the Israelites into the sea. Not one of them survived.

But the Israelites went through the sea on dry ground, with a wall of water on their right and on their left. That day the Lord saved Israel from the hands of the Egyptians, and Israel saw the Egyptians lying dead on the shore. And when the Israelites saw the great power the Lord displayed against the Egyptians, the people feared the Lord and put their trust in him and in Moses his servant.

Then Miriam the prophetess, Aaron's sister, took a tambourine in her hand, and all the women followed her, with tambourines and dancing. Miriam sang to them:

> "Sing to the Lord,
>   for he is highly exalted.
> The horse and its rider
>   he has hurled into the sea."

Easter 3

Zephaniah 3:14–20

> Sing, O Daughter of Zion;
>   shout aloud, O Israel!
> Be glad and rejoice with all your heart,
>   O Daughter of Jerusalem!
> The Lord has taken away your punishment,
>   he has turned back your enemy.
> The Lord, the King of Israel, is with you;
>   never again will you fear any harm.
> On that day they will say to Jerusalem,
>   "Do not fear, O Zion;
>   do not let your hands hang limp.
> The Lord your God is with you,
>   he is mighty to save.
> He will take great delight in you,
>   he will quiet you with his love,
>   he will rejoice over you with singing."
>
> "The sorrows for the appointed feasts
>   I will remove from you;
>   they are a burden and a reproach to you.
> At that time I will deal
>   with all who oppressed you;
> I will rescue the lame
>   and gather those who have been scattered.
> I will give them praise and honour
>   in every land where they were put to shame.
> At that time I will gather you;
>   at that time I will bring you home.
> I will give you honour and praise
>   among all the peoples of the earth
> when I restore your fortunes
>   before your very eyes,"
>
>   says the Lord.

Genesis 7:1–5, 11–18; 8:6–18; 9:8–13   The LORD said to Noah, "Go into the ark, you and your whole family, because I have found you righteous in this generation. Take with you seven of every kind of clean animal, a male and its mate, and two of every kind of unclean animal, a male and its mate, and also seven of every kind of bird, male and female, to keep their various kinds alive throughout the earth. Seven days from now I will send rain on the earth for forty days and forty nights, and I will wipe from the face of the earth every living creature I have made."

And Noah did all that the LORD commanded him.

In the six hundredth year of Noah's life, on the seventeenth day of the second month – on that day all the springs of the great deep burst forth, and the floodgates of the heavens were opened. And rain fell on the earth for forty days and forty nights.

On that very day Noah and his sons, Shem, Ham and Japheth, together with his wife and the wives of his three sons, entered the ark. They had with them every wild animal according to its kind, all livestock according to their kinds, every creature that moves along the ground according to its kind and every bird according to its kind, everything with wings. Pairs of all creatures that have the breath of life in them came to Noah and entered the ark. The animals going in were male and female of every living thing, as God had commanded Noah. Then the LORD shut him in.

For forty days the flood kept coming on the earth, and as the waters increased they lifted the ark high above the earth. The waters rose and increased greatly on the earth, and the ark floated on the surface of the water.

After forty days Noah opened the window he had made in the ark and sent out a raven, and it kept flying back and forth until the water had dried up from the earth. Then he sent out a dove to see if the water had receded from the surface of the ground. But the dove could find no place to set its feet because there was water over all the surface of the earth; so it returned to Noah in the ark. He reached out his hand and took the dove and brought it back to himself in the ark. He waited seven more days and again sent out the dove from the ark. When the dove returned to him in the evening, there in its beak was a freshly plucked olive leaf! Then Noah knew that the water had receded from the earth. He waited seven more days and sent the dove out again, but this time it did not return to him.

By the first day of the first month of Noah's six hundred and first year, the water had dried up from the earth. Noah then removed the covering from the ark and saw that the surface of the ground was dry. By the twenty-seventh day of the second month the earth was completely dry.

Then God said to Noah, "Come out of the ark, you and your wife and your sons and their wives. Bring out every kind of living creature that is with you – the birds, the animals, and all the creatures that move along the ground – so they can multiply on the earth and be fruitful and increase in number upon it."

So Noah came out, together with his sons and his wife and his sons' wives.

Then God said to Noah and to his sons with him: "I now establish my covenant with you and with your descendants after you and with every living creature that was with you – the birds, the livestock and all the wild animals, all those that came out of the ark with you – every living creature on earth. I establish my covenant with you: Never again will all life be cut off by the waters of a flood; never again will there be a flood to destroy the earth."

And God said, "This is the sign of the covenant I am making between me and you and every living creature with you, a covenant for all generations to come: I have set my rainbow in the clouds, and it will be the sign of the covenant between me and the earth."

Easter 5

Either **Baruch 3:9–15, 32 – 4:4**

or **Genesis 22:1–18**   God tested Abraham. He said to him, "Abraham!" "Here I am," he replied.

Then God said, "Take your son, your only son, Isaac, whom you love, and go to the region of Moriah. Sacrifice him there as a burnt offering on one of the mountains I will tell you about."

Early the next morning Abraham got up and saddled his donkey. He took with him two of his servants and his son Isaac. When he had cut enough wood for the burnt offering, he set out for the place God had told him about. On the third day Abraham looked up and saw the place in the distance. He said to his servants, "Stay here with the donkey while I and the boy go over there. We will worship and then we will come back to you."

Abraham took the wood for the burnt offering and placed it on his son Isaac, and he himself carried the fire and the knife. As the two of them went on together, Isaac spoke up and said to his father Abraham, "Father?"

"Yes, my son?" Abraham replied.

"The fire and wood are here," Isaac said, "but where is the lamb for the burnt offering?"

Abraham answered, "God himself will provide the lamb for the burnt offering, my son." And the two of them went on together.

When they reached the place God had told him about, Abraham built an altar there and arranged the wood on it. He bound his son Isaac and laid him on the altar, on top of the wood. Then he reached out his hand and took the knife to slay his son. But the angel of the LORD called out to him from heaven, "Abraham! Abraham!"

"Here I am," he replied.

"Do not lay a hand on the boy," he said. "Do not do anything to him. Now I know that you fear God, because you have not withheld from me your son, your only son."

Abraham looked up and there in a thicket he saw a ram caught by its horns. He went over and took the ram and sacrificed it as a burnt offering instead of his son. So Abraham called that place The LORD Will Provide.

And to this day it is said, "On the mountain of the LORD it will be provided."

The angel of the LORD called to Abraham from heaven a second time and said, "I swear by myself, declares the LORD, that because you have done this and have not withheld your son, your only son, I will surely bless you and make your descendants as numerous as the stars in the sky and as the sand on the seashore. Your descendants will take possession of the cities of their enemies, and through your offspring all nations on earth will be blessed, because you have obeyed me."

Easter 6

Ezekiel 37:1–14   The hand of the LORD was upon me, and he brought me out by the Spirit of the LORD and set me in the middle of a valley; it was full of bones. He led me to and fro among them, and I saw a great many bones on the floor of the valley, bones that were very dry. He asked me, "Son of man, can these bones live?"

I said, "O Sovereign LORD, you alone know."

Then he said to me, "Prophesy to these bones and say to them, 'Dry bones, hear the word of the LORD! This is what the Sovereign LORD says to these bones: I will make breath enter you, and you will come to life. I will attach tendons to you and make flesh come upon you and cover you with skin; I will put breath in you, and you will come to life. Then you will know that I am the LORD.'"

So I prophesied as I was commanded. And as I was prophesying, there was a noise, a rattling sound, and the bones came together, bone to bone. I looked, and tendons and flesh appeared on them and skin covered them, but there was no breath in them.

Then he said to me, "Prophesy to the breath; prophesy, son of man, and say to it, 'This is what the Sovereign LORD says: Come from the four winds, O breath, and breathe into these slain, that they may live.'" So I prophesied as he commanded me, and breath entered them; they came to life and stood up on their feet – a vast army.

Then he said to me: "Son of man, these bones are the whole house of Israel. They say, 'Our bones are dried up and our hope is gone; we are cut off.' Therefore prophesy and say to them: 'This is what the Sovereign LORD says: O my people, I am going to open your graves and bring you up from them; I will bring you back to the land of Israel. Then you, my people, will know that I am the LORD, when I open your graves and bring you up from them. I will put my Spirit in you and you will live, and I will settle you in your own land. Then you will know that I the LORD have spoken, and I have done it, declares the LORD.'"

Easter 7

Ezekiel 36:24–28   This is what the Sovereign LORD says: "I will take you out of the nations; I will gather you from all the countries and bring you back into your own land. I will sprinkle clean water on you, and you will be clean; I will cleanse you from all your impurities and from all your idols. I will give you a new heart and put a new spirit in you; I will remove from you your heart of stone and give you a heart of flesh. And I will put my Spirit in you and move you to follow my decrees and be careful to keep my laws. You will live in the land I gave your forefathers; you will be my people, and I will be your God."

The Second Sunday of Easter

Acts 5:27–32 Having brought the apostles, the captain of the temple guard and his officers made them appear before the Sanhedrin to be questioned by the high priest. "We gave you strict orders not to teach in this name," he said. "Yet you have filled Jerusalem with your teaching and are determined to make us guilty of this man's blood."

Peter and the other apostles replied: "We must obey God rather than men! The God of our fathers raised Jesus from the dead – whom you had killed by hanging him on a tree. God exalted him to his own right hand as Prince and Saviour that he might give repentance and forgiveness of sins to Israel. We are witnesses of these things, and so is the Holy Spirit, whom God has given to those who obey him."

F R
I E
R A
S D
T I
N
G

Alternative Psalms

P
S
A
L
M

Either **Psalm 118:14–29**
The LORD is my strength and my song;
    he has become my salvation.

Shouts of joy and victory
    resound in the tents of the righteous:
"The LORD's right hand has done mighty things!
    The LORD's right hand is lifted high;
the LORD's right hand has done mighty things!"

I will not die but live,
    and will proclaim what the LORD has done.
The LORD has chastened me severely,
    but he has not given me over to death.

Open for me the gates of righteousness;
    I will enter and give thanks to the LORD.
This is the gate of the LORD
    through which the righteous may enter.
I will give you thanks, for you answered me;
    you have become my salvation.

The stone the builders rejected
    has become the capstone;
the LORD has done this,
    and it is marvellous in our eyes.
This is the day the LORD has made;
    let us rejoice and be glad in it.

O LORD, save us;
    O LORD, grant us success.
Blessed is he who comes in the name of the LORD.
    From the house of the LORD we bless you.
The LORD is God,
    and he has made his light shine upon us.
With boughs in hand, join in the festal procession
    up to the horns of the altar.

You are my God, and I will give thanks;
 you are my God, and I will exalt you.

Give thanks to the LORD, for he is good;
 his love endures for ever.

or **Psalm 150** Praise the LORD.

Praise God in his sanctuary;
 praise him in his mighty heavens.
Praise him for his acts of power;
 praise him for his surpassing greatness.
Praise him with the sounding of the trumpet,
 praise him with the harp and lyre,
praise him with tambourine and dancing,
 praise him with the strings and flute,
praise him with the clash of cymbals,
 praise him with resounding cymbals.

Let everything that has breath praise the LORD.

Praise the LORD.

P S A L M

Revelation 1:4–8 John,

To the seven churches in the province of Asia:

Grace and peace to you from him who is, and who was, and who is to come, and from the seven spirits before his throne, and from Jesus Christ, who is the faithful witness, the firstborn from the dead, and the ruler of the kings of the earth.

To him who loves us and has freed us from our sins by his blood, and has made us to be a kingdom and priests to serve his God and Father – to him be glory and power for ever and ever! Amen.

Look, he is coming with the clouds,
 and every eye will see him,
even those who pierced him;
 and all the peoples of the earth will mourn because of him.
       So shall it be! Amen.

"I am the Alpha and the Omega," says the Lord God, "who is, and who was, and who is to come, the Almighty."

S E C O N D R E A D I N G

John 20:19–31 On the evening of that first day of the week, when the disciples were together, with the doors locked for fear of the Jews, Jesus came and stood among them and said, "Peace be with you!" After he said this, he showed them his hands and side. The disciples were overjoyed when they saw the Lord.

Again Jesus said, "Peace be with you! As the Father has sent me, I am sending you." And with that he breathed on them and said, "Receive the Holy Spirit. If you forgive anyone his sins, they are forgiven; if you do not forgive them, they are not forgiven."

G O S P E L

Now Thomas (called Didymus), one of the Twelve, was not with the disciples when Jesus came. So the other disciples told him, "We have seen the Lord!"

But he said to them, "Unless I see the nail marks in his hands and put my finger where the nails were, and put my hand into his side, I will not believe it."

A week later his disciples were in the house again, and Thomas was with them. Though the doors were locked, Jesus came and stood among them and said, "Peace be with you!" Then he said to Thomas, "Put your finger here; see my hands. Reach out your hand and put it into my side. Stop doubting and believe."

Thomas said to him, "My Lord and my God!"

Then Jesus told him, "Because you have seen me, you have believed; blessed are those who have not seen and yet have believed."

Jesus did many other miraculous signs in the presence of his disciples, which are not recorded in this book. But these are written that you may believe that Jesus is the Christ, the Son of God, and that by believing you may have life in his name.

Third Sunday of Easter

Acts 9:1–6 [7–20] Saul was still breathing out murderous threats against the Lord's disciples. He went to the high priest and asked him for letters to the synagogues in Damascus, so that if he found any there who belonged to the Way, whether men or women, he might take them as prisoners to Jerusalem. As he neared Damascus on his journey, suddenly a light from heaven flashed around him. He fell to the ground and heard a voice say to him, "Saul, Saul, why do you persecute me?"

"Who are you, Lord?" Saul asked.

"I am Jesus, whom you are persecuting," he replied. "Now get up and go into the city, and you will be told what you must do."

[The men travelling with Saul stood there speechless; they heard the sound but did not see anyone. Saul got up from the ground, but when he opened his eyes he could see nothing. So they led him by the hand into Damascus. For three days he was blind, and did not eat or drink anything.

In Damascus there was a disciple named Ananias. The Lord called to him in a vision, "Ananias!"

"Yes, Lord," he answered.

The Lord told him, "Go to the house of Judas on Straight Street and ask for a man from Tarsus named Saul, for he is praying. In a vision he has seen a man named Ananias come and place his hands on him to restore his sight."

"Lord," Ananias answered, "I have heard many reports about this man and all the harm he has done to your saints in Jerusalem. And he has come here with authority from the chief priests to arrest all who call on your name."

But the Lord said to Ananias, "Go! This man is my chosen instrument to carry my name before the Gentiles and their kings and before the people of Israel. I will show him how much he must suffer for my name."

Then Ananias went to the house and entered it. Placing his hands on Saul, he said, "Brother Saul, the Lord – Jesus, who appeared to you on the road as you were coming here – has sent me so that you may see again and be filled with the Holy Spirit." Immediately, something like scales fell from Saul's eyes, and he could see again. He got up and was baptised, and after taking some food, he regained his strength.

Saul spent several days with the disciples in Damascus. At once he began to preach in the synagogues that Jesus is the Son of God.]

Psalm 30

I will exalt you, O LORD,
　　for you lifted me out of the depths
　　and did not let my enemies gloat over me.
O LORD my God, I called to you for help
　　and you healed me.
O LORD, you brought me up from the grave;
　　you spared me from going down into the pit.

Sing to the LORD, you saints of his;
　　praise his holy name.
For his anger lasts only a moment,
　　but his favour lasts a lifetime;
weeping may remain for a night,
　　but rejoicing comes in the morning.

When I felt secure, I said,
　　"I shall never be shaken."
O LORD, when you favoured me,
　　you made my mountain stand firm;
but when you hid your face,
　　I was dismayed.

To you, O LORD, I called;
　　to the Lord I cried for mercy:
"What gain is there in my destruction,
　　in my going down into the pit?
Will the dust praise you?
　　Will it proclaim your faithfulness?
Hear, O LORD, and be merciful to me;
　　O LORD, be my help."

You turned my wailing into dancing;
　　you removed my sackcloth and clothed me with joy,
that my heart may sing to you and not be silent.
　　O LORD my God, I will give you thanks for ever.

Revelation 5:11–14 I looked and heard the voice of many angels, numbering thousands upon thousands, and ten thousand times ten thousand. They encircled the throne and the living creatures and the elders. In a loud voice they sang:

"Worthy is the Lamb, who was slain,
to receive power and wealth and wisdom and strength
and honour and glory and praise!"

Then I heard every creature in heaven and on earth and under the earth and on the sea, and all that is in them, singing:

"To him who sits on the throne and to the Lamb
be praise and honour and glory and power,
for ever and ever!"

The four living creatures said, "Amen", and the elders fell down and worshipped.

John 21:1–19   Jesus appeared again to his disciples, by the Sea of Tiberias. It G
happened this way: Simon Peter, Thomas (called Didymus), Nathanael O
from Cana in Galilee, the sons of Zebedee, and two other disciples were S
together. "I'm going out to fish," Simon Peter told them, and they said, P
"We'll go with you." So they went out and got into the boat, but that night E
they caught nothing. L

Early in the morning, Jesus stood on the shore, but the disciples did not realise that it was Jesus.

He called out to them, "Friends, haven't you any fish?"

"No," they answered.

He said, "Throw your net on the right side of the boat and you will find some." When they did, they were unable to haul the net in because of the large number of fish.

Then the disciple whom Jesus loved said to Peter, "It is the Lord!" As soon as Simon Peter heard him say, "It is the Lord," he wrapped his outer garment around him (for he had taken it off) and jumped into the water. The other disciples followed in the boat, towing the net full of fish, for they were not far from shore, about a hundred yards. When they landed, they saw a fire of burning coals there with fish on it, and some bread.

Jesus said to them, "Bring some of the fish you have just caught."

Simon Peter climbed aboard and dragged the net ashore. It was full of large fish, 153, but even with so many the net was not torn. Jesus said to them, "Come and have breakfast." None of the disciples dared ask him, "Who are you?" They knew it was the Lord. Jesus came, took the bread and gave it to them, and did the same with the fish. This was now the third time Jesus appeared to his disciples after he was raised from the dead.

When they had finished eating, Jesus said to Simon Peter, "Simon son of John, do you truly love me more than these?"

"Yes, Lord," he said, "you know that I love you."

Jesus said, "Feed my lambs."

Again Jesus said, "Simon son of John, do you truly love me?"

He answered, "Yes, Lord, you know that I love you."

Jesus said, "Take care of my sheep."

The third time he said to him, "Simon son of John, do you love me?"

Peter was hurt because Jesus asked him the third time, "Do you love me?" He said, "Lord, you know all things; you know that I love you."

Jesus said, "Feed my sheep. I tell you the truth, when you were younger you dressed yourself and went where you wanted; but when you are old you will stretch out your hands, and someone else will dress you and lead you where you do not want to go." Jesus said this to indicate the kind of death by which Peter would glorify God. Then he said to him, "Follow me!"

Fourth Sunday of Easter

Acts 9:36–43 In Joppa there was a disciple named Tabitha (which, when F translated, is Dorcas), who was always doing good and helping the poor. I About that time she became sick and died, and her body was washed and R placed in an upstairs room. Lydda was near Joppa; so when the disciples S heard that Peter was in Lydda, they sent two men to him and urged him, T "Please come at once!"

Peter went with them, and when he arrived he was taken upstairs to the R room. All the widows stood around him, crying and showing him the robes E and other clothing that Dorcas had made while she was still with them.   A

Peter sent them all out of the room; then he got down on his knees and D prayed. Turning towards the dead woman, he said, "Tabitha, get up." She I opened her eyes, and seeing Peter she sat up. He took her by the hand and N helped her to her feet. Then he called the believers and the widows and G presented her to them alive. This became known all over Joppa, and many people believed in the Lord. Peter stayed in Joppa for some time with a tanner named Simon.

Psalm 23 The LORD is my shepherd, I shall not be in want.   P
    He makes me lie down in green pastures,   S
he leads me beside quiet waters,   A
    he restores my soul.   L
He guides me in paths of righteousness   M
    for his name's sake.
Even though I walk
    through the valley of the shadow of death,
I will fear no evil,
    for you are with me;
your rod and your staff,
    they comfort me.

You prepare a table before me
    in the presence of my enemies.
You anoint my head with oil;
    my cup overflows.
Surely goodness and love will follow me
    all the days of my life,

> and I will dwell in the house of the LORD
> > for ever.

Revelation 7:9–17   I looked and there before me was a great multitude that
no-one could count, from every nation, tribe, people and language, standing before the throne and in front of the Lamb. They were wearing white
robes and were holding palm branches in their hands. And they cried out in
a loud voice:

> "Salvation belongs to our God,
> > who sits on the throne,
> > and to the Lamb."

All the angels were standing round the throne and around the elders and
the four living creatures. They fell down on their faces before the throne
and worshipped God, saying:

> "Amen!
> Praise and glory
> and wisdom and thanks and honour
> and power and strength
> be to our God for ever and ever.
> Amen!"

Then one of the elders asked me, "These in white robes – who are they,
and where did they come from?"

I answered, "Sir, you know."

And he said, "These are they who have come out of the great tribulation;
they have washed their robes and made them white in the blood of the
Lamb. Therefore,

> "they are before the throne of God
> > and serve him day and night in his temple;
> and he who sits on the throne will spread his tent over them.
> Never again will they hunger;
> > never again will they thirst.
> The sun will not beat upon them,
> > nor any scorching heat.
> For the Lamb at the centre of the throne will be their shepherd;
> > he will lead them to springs of living water.
> And God will wipe away every tear from their eyes."

John 10:22-30   The time came for the Feast of Dedication at Jerusalem. It
was winter, and Jesus was in the temple area walking in Solomon's Colonnade. The Jews gathered round him, saying, "How long will you keep us in
suspense? If you are the Christ, tell us plainly."

Jesus answered, "I did tell you, but you do not believe. The miracles I do
in my Father's name speak for me, but you do not believe because you are
not my sheep. My sheep listen to my voice; I know them, and they follow
me. I give them eternal life, and they shall never perish; no-one can snatch

them out of my hand. My Father, who has given them to me, is greater than all; no-one can snatch them out of my Father's hand. I and the Father are one."

Fifth Sunday of Easter

Acts 11:1–18   The apostles and the brothers throughout Judea heard that the Gentiles also had received the word of God. So when Peter went up to Jerusalem, the circumcised believers criticised him and said, "You went into the house of uncircumcised men and ate with them."

Peter began and explained everything to them precisely as it had happened: "I was in the city of Joppa praying, and in a trance I saw a vision. I saw something like a large sheet being let down from heaven by its four corners, and it came down to where I was. I looked into it and saw four-footed animals of the earth, wild beasts, reptiles, and birds of the air. Then I heard a voice telling me, 'Get up, Peter. Kill and eat.'

"I replied, 'Surely not, Lord! Nothing impure or unclean has ever entered my mouth.'

"The voice spoke from heaven a second time, 'Do not call anything impure that God has made clean.' This happened three times, and then it was pulled up to heaven again.

"Right then three men who had been sent to me from Caesarea stopped at the house where I was staying. The Spirit told me to have no hesitation about going with them. These six brothers also went with me, and we entered the man's house. He told us how he had seen an angel appear in his house and say, 'Send to Joppa for Simon who is called Peter. He will bring you a message through which you and all your household will be saved.'

"As I began to speak, the Holy Spirit came on them as he had come on us at the beginning. Then I remembered what the Lord had said: 'John baptised with water, but you will be baptised with the Holy Spirit.' So if God gave them the same gift as he gave us, who believed in the Lord Jesus Christ, who was I to think that I could oppose God?"

When they heard this, they had no further objections and praised God, saying, "So then, God has granted even the Gentiles repentance unto life."

FIRST READING

Psalm 148*   Praise the LORD.

Praise the LORD from the heavens,
   praise him in the heights above.
Praise him, all his angels,
   praise him, all his heavenly hosts.
Praise him, sun and moon,
   praise him, all you shining stars.
Praise him, you highest heavens
   and you waters above the skies.
Let them praise the name of the LORD,
   for he commanded and they were created.

PSALM

He set them in place for ever and ever;
    he gave a decree that will never pass away.

Praise the LORD from the earth,
    you great sea creatures and all ocean depths,
lightning and hail, snow and clouds,
    stormy winds that do his bidding,
you mountains and all hills,
    fruit trees and all cedars,
wild animals and all cattle,
    small creatures and flying birds,
kings of the earth and all nations,
    you princes and all rulers on earth,
young men and maidens,
    old men and children.

Let them praise the name of the LORD,
    for his name alone is exalted;
    his splendour is above the earth and the heavens.
He has raised up for his people a horn,
    the praise of all his saints,
    of Israel, the people close to his heart.

Praise the LORD.

Revelation 21:1–6   I saw a new heaven and a new earth, for the first heaven S
and the first earth had passed away, and there was no longer any sea. I saw E
the Holy City, the new Jerusalem, coming down out of heaven from God, C
prepared as a bride beautifully dressed for her husband. And I heard a O
loud voice from the throne saying, "Now the dwelling of God is with men, N
and he will live with them. They will be his people, and God himself will be D
with them and be their God. He will wipe every tear from their eyes. There
will be no more death or mourning or crying or pain, for the old order of R
things has passed away."   E

He who was seated on the throne said, "I am making everything new!" A
Then he said, "Write this down, for these words are trustworthy and true." D

He said to me: "It is done. I am the Alpha and the Omega, the Beginning I
and the End. To him who is thirsty I will give to drink without cost from the N
spring of the water of life.   G

John 13:31–35   When Judas was gone, Jesus said, "Now is the Son of Man glo- G
rified and God is glorified in him. If God is glorified in him, God will glorify O
the Son in himself, and will glorify him at once.   S

"My children, I will be with you only a little longer. You will look for me, P
and just as I told the Jews, so I tell you now: Where I am going, you cannot E
come.   L

"A new command I give you: Love one another. As I have loved you, so
you must love one another. By this all men will know that you are my disciples, if you love one another."

Sixth Sunday of Easter

Acts 16:9–15 During the night Paul had a vision of a man of Macedonia standing and begging him, "Come over to Macedonia and help us." After Paul had seen the vision, we got ready at once to leave for Macedonia, concluding that God had called us to preach the gospel to them.

From Troas we put out to sea and sailed straight for Samothrace, and the next day on to Neapolis. From there we travelled to Philippi, a Roman colony and the leading city of that district of Macedonia. And we stayed there several days.

On the Sabbath we went outside the city gate to the river, where we expected to find a place of prayer. We sat down and began to speak to the women who had gathered there. One of those listening was a woman named Lydia, a dealer in purple cloth from the city of Thyatira, who was a worshipper of God. The Lord opened her heart to respond to Paul's message. When she and the members of her household were baptised, she invited us to her home. "If you consider me a believer in the Lord," she said, "come and stay at my house." And she persuaded us.

Psalm 67 May God be gracious to us and bless us
 and make his face shine upon us,
that your ways may be known on earth,
 your salvation among all nations.

May the peoples praise you, O God;
 may all the peoples praise you.
May the nations be glad and sing for joy,
 for you rule the peoples justly
 and guide the nations of the earth.
May the peoples praise you, O God;
 may all the peoples praise you.

Then the land will yield its harvest,
 and God, our God, will bless us.
God will bless us,
 and all the ends of the earth will fear him.

Revelation 21:10, 22–22:5 One of the seven angels carried me away in the Spirit to a mountain great and high, and showed me the Holy City, Jerusalem, coming down out of heaven from God.

I did not see a temple in the city, because the LORD God Almighty and the Lamb are its temple. The city does not need the sun or the moon to shine on it, for the glory of God gives it light, and the Lamb is its lamp. The nations will walk by its light, and the kings of the earth will bring their splendour into it. On no day will its gates ever be shut, for there will be no night there. The glory and honour of the nations will be brought into it. Nothing impure will ever enter it, nor will anyone who does what is shameful or deceitful, but only those whose names are written in the Lamb's book of life.

Then the angel showed me the river of the water of life, as clear as crystal, flowing from the throne of God and of the Lamb down the middle of the great street of the city. On each side of the river stood the tree of life, bearing twelve crops of fruit, yielding its fruit every month. And the leaves of the tree are for the healing of the nations. No longer will there be any curse. The throne of God and of the Lamb will be in the city, and his servants will serve him. They will see his face, and his name will be on their foreheads. There will be no more night. They will not need the light of a lamp or the light of the sun, for the Lord God will give them light. And they will reign for ever and ever.

Alternative Gospels

Either **John 14:23–29** Jesus said, "If anyone loves me he will obey my teaching. My Father will love him, and we will come to him and make our home with him. He who does not love me will not obey my teaching. These words you hear are not my own; they belong to the Father who sent me.

"All this I have spoken while still with you. But the Counsellor, the Holy Spirit, whom the Father will send in my name, will teach you all things and will remind you of everything I have said to you. Peace I leave with you; my peace I give you. I do not give to you as the world gives. Do not let your hearts be troubled and do not be afraid.

"You heard me say, 'I am going away and I am coming back to you.' If you loved me, you would be glad that I am going to the Father, for the Father is greater than I. I have told you now before it happens, so that when it does happen you will believe.

or **John 5:1–9** Jesus went up to Jerusalem for a feast of the Jews. Now there is in Jerusalem near the Sheep Gate a pool, which in Aramaic is called Bethesda and which is surrounded by five covered colonnades. Here a great number of disabled people used to lie – the blind, the lame, the paralysed. One who was there had been an invalid for thirty-eight years. When Jesus saw him lying there and learned that he had been in this condition for a long time, he asked him, "Do you want to get well?"

"Sir," the invalid replied, "I have no-one to help me into the pool when the water is stirred. While I am trying to get in, someone else goes down ahead of me."

Then Jesus said to him, "Get up! Pick up your mat and walk." At once the man was cured; he picked up his mat and walked.

The day on which this took place was a Sabbath.

Ascension Day

For text of readings for Years A, B, C see pp 130–133.

Seventh Sunday of Easter

Acts 16:16–34 Once when we were going to the place of prayer, we were met by a slave girl who had a spirit by which she predicted the future. She

earned a great deal of money for her owners by fortune-telling. This girl
followed Paul and the rest of us, shouting, "These men are servants of the
Most High God, who are telling you the way to be saved." She kept this up
for many days. Finally Paul became so troubled that he turned round and
said to the spirit, "In the name of Jesus Christ I command you to come out
of her!" At that moment the spirit left her.

When the owners of the slave girl realised that their hope of making
money was gone, they seized Paul and Silas and dragged them into the market-place to face the authorities. They brought them before the
magistrates and said, "These men are Jews, and are throwing our city into
an uproar by advocating customs unlawful for us Romans to accept or
practise."

The crowd joined in the attack against Paul and Silas, and the magistrates ordered them to be stripped and beaten. After they had been
severely flogged, they were thrown into prison, and the jailer was commanded to guard them carefully. Upon receiving such orders, he put them
in the inner cell and fastened their feet in the stocks.

About midnight Paul and Silas were praying and singing hymns to God,
and the other prisoners were listening to them. Suddenly there was such a
violent earthquake that the foundations of the prison were shaken. At once
all the prison doors flew open, and everybody's chains came loose. The
jailer woke up, and when he saw the prison doors open, he drew his sword
and was about to kill himself because he thought the prisoners had
escaped. But Paul shouted, "Don't harm yourself! We are all here!"

The jailer called for lights, rushed in and fell trembling before Paul and
Silas. He then brought them out and asked, "Sirs, what must I do to be
saved?"

They replied, "Believe in the Lord Jesus, and you will be saved – you and
your household." Then they spoke the word of the Lord to him and to all the
others in his house. At that hour of the night the jailer took them and washed
their wounds; then immediately he and all his family were baptised. The
jailer brought them into his house and set a meal before them; he was filled
with joy because he had come to believe in God – he and his whole family.

salm 97   The LORD reigns, let the earth be glad;
    let the distant shores rejoice.

Clouds and thick darkness surround him;
    righteousness and justice are the foundation of his throne.
Fire goes before him
    and consumes his foes on every side.
His lightning lights up the world;
    the earth sees and trembles.
The mountains melt like wax before the LORD,
    before the LORD of all the earth.
The heavens proclaim his righteousness,
    and all the peoples see his glory.

All who worship images are put to shame,
>> those who boast in idols –
>> worship him, all you gods!

Zion hears and rejoices
>> and the villages of Judah are glad
>> because of your judgments, O LORD.
For you, O LORD, are the Most High over all the earth;
>> you are exalted far above all gods.

Let those who love the LORD hate evil,
>> for he guards the lives of his faithful ones
>> and delivers them from the hand of the wicked.
Light is shed upon the righteous
>> and joy on the upright in heart.
Rejoice in the LORD, you who are righteous,
>> and praise his holy name.

Revelation 22:12–14, 16–17, 20–21 "Behold, I am coming soon! My reward is with me, and I will give to everyone according to what he has done. I am the Alpha and the Omega, the First and the Last, the Beginning and the End.

"Blessed are those who wash their robes, that they may have the right to the tree of life and may go through the gates into the city.

I, Jesus, have sent my angel to give you this testimony for the churches. I am the Root and the Offspring of David, and the bright Morning Star."

The Spirit and the bride say, "Come!" And let him who hears say, "Come!" Whoever is thirsty, let him come; and whoever wishes, let him take the free gift of the water of life.

He who testifies to these things says, "Yes, I am coming soon."

Amen. Come, Lord Jesus.

The grace of the Lord Jesus be with God's people. Amen.

SECOND READING

John 17:20–26 Jesus looked towards heaven and prayed: "My prayer is not for them alone. I pray also for those who will believe in me through their message, that all of them may be one, Father, just as you are in me and I am in you. May they also be in us so that the world may believe that you have sent me. I have given them the glory that you gave me, that they may be one as we are one: I in them and you in me. May they be brought to complete unity to let the world know that you sent me and have loved them even as you have loved me.

"Father, I want those you have given me to be with me where I am, and to see my glory, the glory you have given me because you loved me before the creation of the world.

"Righteous Father, though the world does not know you, I know you, and they know that you have sent me. I have made you known to them, and will continue to make you known in order that the love you have for me may be in them and that I myself may be in them."

GOSPEL

Pentecost – Whit Sunday

(The reading from Acts must be used as either the first or second reading.)

Alternative first readings

Either **Acts 2:1–21**   When the day of Pentecost came, the disciples were all F
together in one place. Suddenly a sound like the blowing of a violent wind I
came from heaven and filled the whole house where they were sitting. R
They saw what seemed to be tongues of fire that separated and came to rest S
on each of them. All of them were filled with the Holy Spirit and began to T
speak in other tongues as the Spirit enabled them.

Now there were staying in Jerusalem God-fearing Jews from every R
nation under heaven. When they heard this sound, a crowd came together E
in bewilderment, because each one heard them speaking in his own lan- A
guage. Utterly amazed, they asked: "Are not all these who are speaking D
Galileans? Then how is it that each of us hears them in our own native lan- I
guage? Parthians, Medes and Elamites; residents of Mesopotamia, Judea N
and Cappadocia, Pontus and Asia, Phrygia and Pamphylia, Egypt and the G
parts of Libya near Cyrene; visitors from Rome (both Jews and converts to
Judaism); Cretans and Arabs – we hear them declaring the wonders of God
in our own tongues!" Amazed and perplexed, they asked one another,
"What does this mean?"

Some, however, made fun of them and said, "They have had too much
wine."

Then Peter stood up with the Eleven, raised his voice and addressed the
crowd: "Fellow Jews and all of you who live in Jerusalem, let me explain
this to you; listen carefully to what I say. These people are not drunk, as you
suppose. It's only nine in the morning! No, this is what was spoken by the
prophet Joel:

"'In the last days, God says,
   I will pour out my Spirit on all people.
Your sons and daughters will prophesy,
   your young men will see visions,
   your old men will dream dreams.
Even on my servants, both men and women,
   I will pour out my Spirit in those days,
   and they will prophesy.
I will show wonders in the heaven above
   and signs on the earth below,
   blood and fire and billows of smoke.
The sun will be turned to darkness
   and the moon to blood
   before the coming of the great and glorious day of the
      Lord.
And everyone who calls
   on the name of the Lord will be saved.'"

or **Genesis 11:1–9**   The whole world had one language and a common
speech. As men moved eastward, they found a plain in Shinar and settled
there.

They said to each other, "Come, let's make bricks and bake them thoroughly." They used brick instead of stone, and bitumen for mortar. Then
they said, "Come, let us build ourselves a city, with a tower that reaches to
the heavens, so that we may make a name for ourselves and not be scattered over the face of the whole earth."

But the Lord came down to see the city and the tower that the men were
building. The Lord said, "If as one people speaking the same language they
have begun to do this, then nothing they plan to do will be impossible for
them. Come, let us go down and confuse their language so they will not
understand each other."

So the Lord scattered them from there over all the earth, and they
stopped building the city. That is why it was called Babel – because there
the Lord confused the language of the whole world. From there the Lord
scattered them over the face of the whole earth.

F I R S T   R E A D I N G

Psalm 104:24–34, 35b*   How many are your works, O Lord!   P
    In wisdom you made them all;   S
    the earth is full of your creatures.   A
There is the sea, vast and spacious,   L
    teeming with creatures beyond number –   M
    living things both large and small.
There the ships go to and fro,
    and the leviathan, which you formed to frolic
      there.

These all look to you
    to give them their food at the proper time.
When you give it to them,
    they gather it up;
when you open your hand,
    they are satisfied with good things.
When you hide your face,
    they are terrified;
when you take away their breath,
    they die and return to the dust.
When you send your Spirit,
    they are created,
    and you renew the face of the earth.

May the glory of the Lord endure for ever;
    may the Lord rejoice in his works –
he who looks at the earth, and it trembles,
    who touches the mountains, and they smoke.
I will sing to the Lord all my life;
    I will sing praise to my God as long as I live.

May my meditation be pleasing to him,
as I rejoice in the LORD.

Praise the LORD, O my soul.

Praise the LORD.

Alternative second readings

Either **Romans 8:14–17**   Those who are led by the Spirit of God are sons of S R
God. For you did not receive a spirit that makes you a slave again to fear, E E
but you received the Spirit of sonship. And by him we cry, "*Abba*, Father." C A
The Spirit himself testifies with our spirit that we are God's children. Now O D
if we are children, then we are heirs – heirs of God and co–heirs with N I
Christ, if indeed we share in his sufferings in order that we may also share D N
in his glory.   G

or **Acts 2:1–21**   When the day of Pentecost came, the disciples were all S R
together in one place. Suddenly a sound like the blowing of a violent wind E E
came from heaven and filled the whole house where they were sitting. C A
They saw what seemed to be tongues of fire that separated and came to rest O D
on each of them. All of them were filled with the Holy Spirit and began to N I
speak in other tongues as the Spirit enabled them.   D N
                                                                             G

Now there were staying in Jerusalem God-fearing Jews from every
nation under heaven. When they heard this sound, a crowd came together
in bewilderment, because each one heard them speaking in his own native
language. Utterly amazed, they asked: "Are not all these who are speaking
Galileans? Then how is it that each of us hears them in our own native language? Parthians, Medes and Elamites; residents of Mesopotamia, Judea
and Cappadocia, Pontus and Asia, Phrygia and Pamphylia, Egypt and the
parts of Libya near Cyrene; visitors from Rome (both Jews and converts to
Judaism); Cretans and Arabs – we hear them declaring the wonders of God
in our own tongues!" Amazed and perplexed, they asked one another,
"What does this mean?"

Some, however, made fun of them and said, "They have had too much
wine."

Then Peter stood up with the Eleven, raised his voice and addressed the
crowd: "Fellow Jews and all of you who live in Jerusalem, let me explain
this to you; listen carefully to what I say. These men are not drunk, as you
suppose. It's only nine in the morning! No, this is what was spoken by the
prophet Joel:

"'In the last days, God says,
  I will pour out my Spirit on all people.
Your sons and daughters will prophesy,
  your young men will see visions,
  your old men will dream dreams.
Even on my servants, both men and women,
  I will pour out my Spirit in those days,
  and they will prophesy.

I will show wonders in the heaven above
and signs on the earth below,
blood and fire and billows of smoke.
The sun will be turned to darkness
and the moon to blood
before the coming of the great and glorious day of the Lord.
And everyone who calls
on the name of the Lord will be saved.'"

John 14:8–17 [25–27]   Philip said, "Lord, show us the Father and that will be
enough for us."

Jesus answered: "Don't you know me, Philip, even after I have been
among you such a long time? Anyone who has seen me has seen the Father.
How can you say, 'Show us the Father'? Don't you believe that I am in the
Father, and that the Father is in me? The words I say to you are not just my
own. Rather, it is the Father, living in me, who is doing his work. Believe me
when I say that I am in the Father and the Father is in me; or at least believe
on the evidence of the miracles themselves. I tell you the truth, anyone
who has faith in me will do what I have been doing. He will do even greater
things than these, because I am going to the Father. And I will do whatever
you ask in my name, so that the Son may bring glory to the Father. You may
ask me for anything in my name, and I will do it.

"If you love me, you will obey what I command. And I will ask the
Father, and he will give you another Counsellor to be with you for ever – the
Spirit of truth. The world cannot accept him, because it neither sees him
nor knows him. But you know him, for he lives with you and will be in you.

["All this I have spoken while still with you. But the Counsellor, the Holy
Spirit, whom the Father will send in my name, will teach you all things and
will remind you of everything I have said to you. Peace I leave with you; my
peace I give you. I do not give to you as the world gives. Do not let your
hearts be troubled and do not be afraid.]"

ORDINARY TIME

Trinity Sunday

Proverbs 8:1–4,   Does not wisdom call out?
22–31   Does not understanding raise her voice?
On the heights along the way,
where the paths meet, she takes her stand;
beside the gates leading into the city,
at the entrances, she cries aloud:

"To you, O men, I call out;
I raise my voice to all mankind.

"The LORD brought me forth as the first of his works,
before his deeds of old;
I was appointed from eternity,
from the beginning, before the world began.

When there were no oceans, I was given birth,
  when there were no springs abounding with water;
before the mountains were settled in place,
  before the hills, I was given birth,
before he made the earth or its fields
  or any of the dust of the world.
I was there when he set the heavens in place,
  when he marked out the horizon on the face of the deep,
when he established the clouds above
  and fixed securely the fountains of the deep,
when he gave the sea its boundary
  so that the waters would not overstep his command,
and when he marked out the foundations of the earth.
  Then I was the craftsman at his side.
I was filled with delight day after day,
  rejoicing always in his presence,
rejoicing in his whole world
  and delighting in mankind."

Psalm 8 O Lord, our Lord,
  how majestic is your name in all the earth!

You have set your glory
  above the heavens.
From the lips of children and infants
  you have ordained praise
because of your enemies,
  to silence the foe and the avenger.

When I consider your heavens,
  the work of your fingers,
the moon and the stars,
  which you have set in place,
what is man that you are mindful of him,
  the son of man that you care for him?
You made him a little lower than the heavenly beings
  and crowned him with glory and honour.

You made him rule over the works of your hands;
  you put everything under his feet:
all flocks and herds,
  and the beasts of the field,
the birds of the air,
  and the fish of the sea,
  all that swim the paths of the seas.

O Lord, our Lord,
  how majestic is your name in all the earth!

Romans 5:1–5 Since we have been justified through faith, we have peace with God through our Lord Jesus Christ, through whom we have gained access by faith into this grace in which we now stand. And we rejoice in the hope of the glory of God. Not only so, but we also rejoice in our sufferings, because we know that suffering produces perseverance; perseverance, character; and character, hope. And hope does not disappoint us, because God has poured out his love into our hearts by the Holy Spirit, whom he has given us.

John 16:12–15   Jesus said: "I have much more to say to you, more than you G can now bear. But when he, the Spirit of truth, comes, he will guide you into O all truth. He will not speak on his own; he will speak only what he hears, and S he will tell you what is yet to come. He will bring glory to me by taking P from what is mine and making it known to you. All that belongs to the E Father is mine. That is why I said the Spirit will take from what is mine and L make it known to you."

If the Sunday between 24 and 28 May inclusive follows Trinity Sunday, Proper 3 (p 411) is used.

Thanksgiving for Holy Communion
Thursday after Trinity Sunday (Corpus Christi)

For text of readings for Years A, B, C see pp 141–142.

Proper 4

Sunday between 29 May and 4 June inclusive (if after Trinity Sunday)
On the Sundays after Trinity, alternative Old Testament readings and Psalms are provided. The first pair of readings headed 'continuous' offer semi-continuous reading of Old Testament texts but allow the Old Testament reading and its complementary Psalm to stand independently of the other readings. The second pair of readings headed 'related' relate the Old Testament reading and the Psalm to the Gospel reading.

It is unhelpful to move from one type of pair to another from week to week. Either 'continuous' or 'related' readings should be followed for the whole sequence of Sundays after Trinity.

CONTINUOUS

1 Kings 18:20–21 [22–29] 30–39   Ahab sent word throughout all Israel and F assembled the prophets on Mount Carmel. Elijah went before the people I and said, "How long will you waver between two opinions? If the LORD is R God, follow him; but if Baal is God, follow him."   S
But the people said nothing.   T
[Then Elijah said to them, "I am the only one of the LORD's prophets left, but Baal has four hundred and fifty prophets. Get two bulls for us. R Let them choose one for themselves, and let them cut it into pieces and E put it on the wood but not set fire to it. I will prepare the other bull and put A it on the wood but not set fire to it. Then you call on the name of your god, D and I will call on the name of the LORD. The god who answers by fire – he is I God."   N
Then all the people said, "What you say is good."   G
Elijah said to the prophets of Baal, "Choose one of the bulls and prepare it first, since there are so many of you. Call on the name of your

god, but do not light the fire." So they took the bull given them and prepared it.

Then they called on the name of Baal from morning till noon. "O Baal, answer us!" they shouted. But there was no response; no-one answered. And they danced around the altar they had made.

At noon Elijah began to taunt them. "Shout louder!" he said. "Surely he is a god! Perhaps he is deep in thought, or busy, or travelling. Maybe he is sleeping and must be awakened." So they shouted louder and slashed themselves with swords and spears, as was their custom, until their blood flowed. Midday passed, and they continued their frantic prophesying until the time for the evening sacrifice. But there was no response, no-one answered, no-one paid attention.]

Then Elijah said to all the people, "Come here to me." They came to him, and he repaired the altar of the LORD, which was in ruins. Elijah took twelve stones, one for each of the tribes descended from Jacob, to whom the word of the LORD had come, saying, "Your name shall be Israel." With the stones he built an altar in the name of the LORD, and he dug a trench round it large enough to hold two seahs of seed. He arranged the wood, cut the bull into pieces and laid it on the wood. Then he said to them, "Fill four large jars with water and pour it on the offering and on the wood."

"Do it again," he said, and they did it again.

"Do it a third time," he ordered, and they did it the third time. The water ran down around the altar and even filled the trench.

At the time of sacrifice, the prophet Elijah stepped forward and prayed: "O LORD, God of Abraham, Isaac and Israel, let it be known today that you are God in Israel and that I am your servant and have done all these things at your command. Answer me, O LORD, answer me, so these people will know that you, O LORD, are God, and that you are turning their hearts back again."

Then the fire of the LORD fell and burned up the sacrifice, the wood, the stones and the soil, and also licked up the water in the trench.

When all the people saw this, they fell prostrate and cried, "The LORD – he is God! The LORD – he is God!"

nd **Psalm 96**	Sing to the LORD a new song;	P
	sing to the LORD, all the earth.	S
	Sing to the LORD, praise his name;	A
	proclaim his salvation day after day.	L
	Declare his glory among the nations,	M
	his marvellous deeds among all peoples.	

For great is the LORD and most worthy of praise;
    he is to be feared above all gods.
For all the gods of the nations are idols,
    but the LORD made the heavens.
Splendour and majesty are before him;
    strength and glory are in his sanctuary.

Ascribe to the LORD, O families of nations,
    ascribe to the LORD glory and strength.
Ascribe to the LORD the glory due to his name;
    bring an offering and come into his courts.
Worship the LORD in the splendour of his holiness;
    tremble before him, all the earth.

Say among the nations, "The LORD reigns."
    The world is firmly established, it cannot be moved;
    he will judge the peoples with equity.
Let the heavens rejoice, let the earth be glad;
    let the sea resound, and all that is in it;
    let the fields be jubilant, and everything in them.
Then all the trees of the forest will sing for joy;
    they will sing before the LORD, for he comes,
    he comes to judge the earth.
He will judge the world in righteousness
    and the peoples in his truth.

Or **RELATED**

1 Kings 8:22–23, 41–43   Solomon stood before the altar of the LORD in front of F R
the whole assembly of Israel, spread out his hands towards heaven and I E
said: R A

    "O LORD, God of Israel, there is no God like you in heaven above or on S D
earth below – you who keep your covenant of love with your servants who T I
continue wholeheartedly in your way.   N

    "As for the foreigner who does not belong to your people Israel but has   G
come from a distant land because of your name – for men will hear of
your great name and your mighty hand and your outstretched arm –
when he comes and prays towards this temple, then hear from heaven,
your dwelling-place, and do whatever the foreigner asks of you, so that
all the peoples of the earth may know your name and fear you, as do your
own people Israel, and may know that this house I have built bears your
Name."

and **Psalm 96:1–9**   Sing to the LORD a new song;   P
    sing to the LORD, all the earth.   S
Sing to the LORD, praise his name;   A
    proclaim his salvation day after day.   L
Declare his glory among the nations,   M
    his marvellous deeds among all peoples.

For great is the LORD and most worthy of praise;
    he is to be feared above all gods.
For all the gods of the nations are idols,
    but the LORD made the heavens.
Splendour and majesty are before him;
    strength and glory are in his sanctuary.

Ascribe to the LORD, O families of nations,
    ascribe to the LORD glory and strength.
Ascribe to the LORD the glory due to his name;
    bring an offering and come into his courts.
Worship the LORD in the splendour of his holiness;
    tremble before him, all the earth.

Galatians 1:1–12   Paul, an apostle – sent not from men nor by man, but by Jesus Christ and God the Father, who raised him from the dead – and all the brothers with me,

To the churches in Galatia:

Grace and peace to you from God our Father and the Lord Jesus Christ, who gave himself for our sins to rescue us from the present evil age, according to the will of our God and Father, to whom be glory for ever and ever. Amen.

I am astonished that you are so quickly deserting the one who called you by the grace of Christ and are turning to a different gospel – which is really no gospel at all. Evidently some people are throwing you into confusion and are trying to pervert the gospel of Christ. But even if we or an angel from heaven should preach a gospel other than the one we preached to you, let him be eternally condemned! As we have already said, so now I say again: If anybody is preaching to you a gospel other than what you accepted, let him be eternally condemned!

Am I now trying to win the approval of men or of God? Or am I trying to please men? If I were still trying to please men, I would not be a servant of Christ.

I want you to know, brothers, that the gospel I preached is not something that man made up. I did not receive it from any man, nor was I taught it; rather, I received it by revelation from Jesus Christ.

SECONDR EADING

Luke 7:1–10   Jesus entered Capernaum. There a centurion's servant, whom his master valued highly, was sick and about to die. The centurion heard of Jesus and sent some elders of the Jews to him, asking him to come and heal his servant. When they came to Jesus, they pleaded earnestly with him, "This man deserves to have you do this, because he loves our nation and has built our synagogue." So Jesus went with them.

GOSPEL

He was not far from the house when the centurion sent friends to say to him: "Lord, don't trouble yourself, for I do not deserve to have you come under my roof. That is why I did not even consider myself worthy to come to you. But say the word, and my servant will be healed. For I myself am a man under authority, with soldiers under me. I tell this one, 'Go', and he goes; and that one, 'Come', and he comes. I say to my servant, 'Do this', and he does it."

When Jesus heard this, he was amazed at him, and turning to the crowd following him, he said, "I tell you, I have not found such great faith even in Israel." Then the men who had been sent returned to the house and found the servant well.

Proper 5

Sunday between 5 and 11 June inclusive (if after Trinity Sunday)
Choose either 'continuous' or 'related' Old Testament and Psalm readings.

CONTINUOUS

1 Kings 17:8–16 [17–24]   The word of the LORD came to Elijah: "Go at once to Zarephath of Sidon and stay there. I have commanded a widow in that place to supply you with food." So he went to Zarephath. When he came to the town gate, a widow was there gathering sticks. He called to her and asked, "Would you bring me a little water in a jar so I may have a drink?" As she was going to get it, he called, "And bring me, please, a piece of bread."

"As surely as the LORD your God lives," she replied, "I don't have any bread – only a handful of flour in a jar and a little oil in a jug. I am gathering a few sticks to take home and make a meal for myself and my son, that we may eat it – and die."

Elijah said to her, "Don't be afraid. Go home and do as you have said. But first make a small cake of bread for me from what you have and bring it to me, and then make something for yourself and your son. For this is what the LORD, the God of Israel, says: 'The jar of flour will not be used up and the jug of oil will not run dry until the day the LORD gives rain on the land.'"

She went away and did as Elijah had told her. So there was food every day for Elijah and for the woman and her family. For the jar of flour was not used up and the jug of oil did not run dry, in keeping with the word of the LORD spoken by Elijah.

[Some time later the son of the woman who owned the house became ill. He grew worse and worse, and finally stopped breathing. She said to Elijah, "What do you have against me, man of God? Did you come to remind me of my sin and kill my son?"

"Give me your son," Elijah replied. He took him from her arms, carried him to the upper room where he was staying, and laid him on his bed. Then he cried out to the LORD, "O LORD my God, have you brought tragedy also upon this widow I am staying with, by causing her son to die?" Then he stretched himself out on the boy three times and cried to the LORD, "O LORD my God, let this boy's life return to him!"

The LORD heard Elijah's cry, and the boy's life returned to him, and he lived. Elijah picked up the child and carried him down from the room into the house. He gave him to his mother and said, "Look, your son is alive!"

Then the woman said to Elijah, "Now I know that you are a man of God and that the word of the LORD from your mouth is the truth."]

and **Psalm 146**   Praise the LORD.

Praise the LORD, O my soul.
   I will praise the LORD all my life;
   I will sing praise to my God as long as I live.

Do not put your trust in princes,
   in mortal man, who cannot save.

When their spirit departs, they return to the ground;
  on that very day their plans come to nothing.

Blessed is he whose help is the God of Jacob,
  whose hope is in the LORD his God,
the Maker of heaven and earth,
  the sea, and everything in them –
  the LORD, who remains faithful for ever.
He upholds the cause of the oppressed
  and gives food to the hungry.
The LORD sets prisoners free,
  the LORD gives sight to the blind,
the LORD lifts up those who are bowed down,
  the LORD loves the righteous.
The LORD watches over the alien
  and sustains the fatherless and the widow,
  but he frustrates the ways of the wicked.

The LORD reigns for ever,
  your God, O Zion, for all generations.

Praise the LORD.

Or RELATED

1 Kings 17:17–24 The word of the LORD came to Elijah: "Go at once to Zarephath of Sidon and stay there. I have commanded a widow in that place to supply you with food." So he went to Zarephath. Some time later the son of the woman who owned the house became ill. He grew worse and worse, and finally stopped breathing. She said to Elijah, "What do you have against me, man of God? Did you come to remind me of my sin and kill my son?"

"Give me your son," Elijah replied. He took him from her arms, carried him to the upper room where he was staying, and laid him on his bed. Then he cried out to the LORD, "O LORD my God, have you brought tragedy also upon this widow I am staying with, by causing her son to die?" Then he stretched himself out on the boy three times and cried to the LORD, "O LORD my God, let this boy's life return to him!"

The LORD heard Elijah's cry, and the boy's life returned to him, and he lived. Elijah picked up the child and carried him down from the room into the house. He gave him to his mother and said, "Look, your son is alive!"

Then the woman said to Elijah, "Now I know that you are a man of God and that the word of the LORD from your mouth is the truth."

and Psalm 30 I will exalt you, O LORD,
    for you lifted me out of the depths
    and did not let my enemies gloat over me.
  O LORD my God, I called to you for help
    and you healed me.

FIRST READING

PSALM

O LORD, you brought me up from the grave;
    you spared me from going down into the pit.

Sing to the LORD, you saints of his;
    praise his holy name.
For his anger lasts only a moment,
    but his favour lasts a lifetime;
weeping may remain for a night,
    but rejoicing comes in the morning.

When I felt secure, I said,
    "I shall never be shaken."
O LORD, when you favoured me,
    you made my mountain stand firm;
but when you hid your face,
    I was dismayed.

To you, O LORD, I called;
    to the LORD I cried for mercy:
"What gain is there in my destruction,
    in my going down into the pit?
Will the dust praise you?
    Will it proclaim your faithfulness?
Hear, O LORD, and be merciful to me;
    O LORD, be my help."

You turned my wailing into dancing;
    you removed my sackcloth and clothed me with joy,
that my heart may sing to you and not be silent.
    O LORD my God, I will give you thanks for ever.

Galatians 1:11–24   I want you to know, brothers, that the gospel I preached is not something man made up. I did not receive it from any man, nor was I taught it; rather, I received it by revelation from Jesus Christ.

For you have heard of my previous way of life in Judaism, how intensely I persecuted the church of God and tried to destroy it. I was advancing in Judaism beyond many Jews of my own age and was extremely zealous for the traditions of my fathers. But when God, who set me apart from birth and called me by his grace, was pleased to reveal his Son in me so that I might preach him among the Gentiles, I did not consult any man, nor did I go up to Jerusalem to see those who were apostles before I was, but I went immediately into Arabia and later returned to Damascus.

Then after three years, I went up to Jerusalem to get acquainted with Peter and stayed with him fifteen days. I saw none of the other apostles – only James, the Lord's brother. I assure you before God that what I am writing to you is no lie. Later I went to Syria and Cilicia. I was personally unknown to the churches of Judea that are in Christ. They only heard the report: "The man who formerly persecuted us is now preaching the faith he once tried to destroy." And they praised God because of me.

Luke 7:11–17 Jesus went to a town called Nain, and his disciples and a large crowd went along with him. As he approached the town gate, a dead person was being carried out – the only son of his mother, and she was a widow. And a large crowd from the town was with her. When the Lord saw her, his heart went out to her and he said, "Don't cry."

Then he went up and touched the coffin, and those carrying it stood still. He said, "Young man, I say to you, get up!" The dead man sat up and began to talk, and Jesus gave him back to his mother.

They were all filled with awe and praised God. "A great prophet has appeared among us," they said. "God has come to help his people." This news about Jesus spread throughout Judea and the surrounding country.

Proper 6

Sunday between 12 and 18 June inclusive (if after Trinity Sunday)
Choose either 'continuous' or 'related' Old Testament and Psalm readings.

CONTINUOUS

1 Kings 21:1–10 [11–14] 15–21a There was an incident involving a vineyard belonging to Naboth the Jezreelite. The vineyard was in Jezreel, close to the palace of Ahab king of Samaria. Ahab said to Naboth, "Let me have your vineyard to use for a vegetable garden, since it is close to my palace. In exchange I will give you a better vineyard or, if you prefer, I will pay you whatever it is worth."

But Naboth replied, "The LORD forbid that I should give you the inheritance of my ancestors."

So Ahab went home, sullen and angry because Naboth the Jezreelite had said, "I will not give you the inheritance of my ancestors." He lay on his bed sulking and refused to eat.

His wife Jezebel came in and asked him, "Why are you so sullen? Why won't you eat?"

He answered her, "Because I said to Naboth the Jezreelite, 'Sell me your vineyard; or if you prefer, I will give you another vineyard in its place.' But he said, 'I will not give you my vineyard.'"

Jezebel his wife said, "Is this how you act as king over Israel? Get up and eat! Cheer up. I'll get you the vineyard of Naboth the Jezreelite."

So she wrote letters in Ahab's name, placed his seal on them, and sent them to the elders and nobles who lived in Naboth's city with him. In those letters she wrote:

"Proclaim a day of fasting and seat Naboth in a prominent place among the people. But seat two scoundrels opposite him and have them testify that he has cursed both God and the king. Then take him out and stone him to death."

[So the elders and nobles who lived in Naboth's city did as Jezebel directed in the letters she had written to them. They proclaimed a fast and seated Naboth in a prominent place among the people. Then two scoundrels came and sat opposite him and brought charges against Naboth before the people, saying, "Naboth has cursed both God and the king." So they took him outside the city and stoned him to death. Then they sent word to Jezebel: "Naboth has been stoned and is dead."]

As soon as Jezebel heard that Naboth had been stoned to death, she said to Ahab, "Get up and take possession of the vineyard of Naboth the Jezreelite that he refused to sell you. He is no longer alive, but dead." When Ahab heard that Naboth was dead, he got up and went down to take possession of Naboth's vineyard.

Then the word of the LORD came to Elijah the Tishbite: "Go down to meet Ahab king of Israel, who rules in Samaria. He is now in Naboth's vineyard, where he has gone to take possession of it. Say to him, 'This is what the LORD says: Have you not murdered a man and seized his property?' Then say to him, 'This is what the LORD says: In the place where dogs licked up Naboth's blood, dogs will lick up your blood – yes, yours!'"

Ahab said to Elijah, "So you have found me, my enemy!"

"I have found you," he answered, "because you have sold yourself to do evil in the eyes of the LORD. 'I am going to bring disaster on you.'"

and **Psalm 5:1–8**

P
S
A
L
M

Give ear to my words, O LORD,
> consider my sighing.
Listen to my cry for help,
> my King and my God,
> for to you I pray.
In the morning, O LORD, you hear my voice;
> in the morning I lay my requests before you
> and wait in expectation.

You are not a God who takes pleasure in evil;
> with you the wicked cannot dwell.
The arrogant cannot stand in your presence;
> you hate all who do wrong.
You destroy those who tell lies;
> those who are bloodthirsty and deceitful
> the LORD abhors.

But I, by your great mercy,
> will come into your house;
in reverence will I bow down
> towards your holy temple.
Lead me, O LORD, in your righteousness
> because of my enemies –
> make straight your way before me.

Or **RELATED**

F
I
R
S
T

2 Samuel 11:26 – 12:10, 13–15 When Uriah's wife, Bathsheba, heard that her husband was dead, she mourned for him. After the time of mourning was over, David had her brought to his house, and she became his wife and bore him a son. But the thing David had done displeased the LORD.

The LORD sent Nathan to David. When he came to him, he said, "There were two men in a certain town, one rich and the other poor. The rich man had a very large number of sheep and cattle, but the poor man had nothing except one little ewe lamb that he had bought. He raised it, and it grew up with him and his children. It shared his food, drank from his cup and even slept in his arms. It was like a daughter to him.

"Now a traveller came to the rich man, but the rich man refrained from taking one of his own sheep or cattle to prepare a meal for the traveller who had come to him. Instead, he took the ewe lamb that belonged to the poor man and prepared it for the one who had come to him."

David burned with anger against the man and said to Nathan, "As surely as the Lord lives, the man who did this deserves to die! He must pay for that lamb four times over, because he did such a thing and had no pity."

Then Nathan said to David, "You are the man! This is what the Lord, the God of Israel, says: 'I anointed you king over Israel, and I delivered you from the hand of Saul. I gave your master's house to you, and your master's wives into your arms. I gave you the house of Israel and Judah. And if all this had been too little, I would have given you even more. Why did you despise the word of the Lord by doing what is evil in his eyes? You struck down Uriah the Hittite with the sword and took his wife to be your own. You killed him with the sword of the Ammonites. Now, therefore, the sword shall never depart from your house, because you despised me and took the wife of Uriah the Hittite to be your own.'"

Then David said to Nathan, "I have sinned against the Lord."

Nathan replied, "The Lord has taken away your sin. You are not going to die. But because by doing this you have made the enemies of the Lord show utter contempt, the son born to you will die."

After Nathan had gone home, the Lord struck the child that Uriah's wife had borne to David, and he became ill.

---

nd **Psalm 32**

> Blessed is he
>> whose transgressions are forgiven,
>> whose sins are covered.
> Blessed is the man
>> whose sin the Lord does not count against him
>> and in whose spirit is no deceit.
>
> When I kept silent,
>> my bones wasted away
>> through my groaning all day long.
> For day and night
>> your hand was heavy upon me;
> my strength was sapped
>> as in the heat of summer.
> Then I acknowledged my sin to you
>> and did not cover up my iniquity.
> I said, "I will confess
>> my transgressions to the Lord" –

P
S
A
L
M

and you forgave
    the guilt of my sin.

Therefore let everyone who is godly pray to you
    while you may be found;
surely when the mighty waters rise
    they will not reach him.
You are my hiding–place;
    you will protect me from trouble
    and surround me with songs of deliverance.

I will instruct you and teach you in the way you should go;
    I will counsel you and watch over you.
Do not be like the horse or the mule,
    which have no understanding
but must be controlled by bit and bridle
    or they will not come to you.
Many are the woes of the wicked,
    but the LORD's unfailing love
    surrounds the man who trusts in him.

Rejoice in the LORD and be glad, you righteous;
    sing, all you who are upright in heart!

Galatians 2:15–21   We who are Jews by birth and not 'Gentile sinners' know that a man is not justified by observing the law, but by faith in Jesus Christ. So we, too, have put our faith in Christ Jesus that we may be justified by faith in Christ and not by observing the law, because by observing the law no-one will be justified.

If, while we seek to be justified in Christ, it becomes evident that we our- selves are sinners, does that mean that Christ promotes sin? Absolutely not! If I rebuild what I destroyed, I prove that I am a law-breaker. For through the law I died to the law so that I might live for God. I have been crucified with Christ and I no longer live, but Christ lives in me. The life I live in the body, I live by faith in the Son of God, who loved me and gave himself for me. I do not set aside the grace of God, for if righteousness could be gained through the law, Christ died for nothing!

Luke 7:36 – 8:3   One of the Pharisees invited Jesus to have dinner with him, so he went to the Pharisee's house and reclined at the table. When a woman who had lived a sinful life in that town learned that Jesus was eating at the Phar- isee's house, she brought an alabaster jar of perfume, and as she stood behind him at his feet weeping, she began to wet his feet with her tears. Then she wiped them with her hair, kissed them and poured perfume on them.

When the Pharisee who had invited him saw this, he said to himself, "If this man were a prophet, he would know who is touching him and what kind of woman she is – that she is a sinner."

Jesus answered him, "Simon, I have something to tell you."

"Tell me, teacher," he said.

"Two men owed money to a certain money-lender. One owed him five hundred denarii, and the other fifty. Neither of them had the money to pay him back, so he cancelled the debts of both. Now which of them will love him more?"

Simon replied, "I suppose the one who had the bigger debt cancelled."

"You have judged correctly," Jesus said.

Then he turned towards the woman and said to Simon, "Do you see this woman? I came into your house. You did not give me any water for my feet, but she wet my feet with her tears and wiped them with her hair. You did not give me a kiss, but this woman, from the time I entered, has not stopped kissing my feet. You did not put oil on my head, but she has poured perfume on my feet. Therefore, I tell you, her many sins have been forgiven – for she loved much. But he who has been forgiven little loves little."

Then Jesus said to her, "Your sins are forgiven."

The other guests began to say among themselves, "Who is this who even forgives sins?"

Jesus said to the woman, "Your faith has saved you; go in peace."

After this, Jesus travelled about from one town and village to another, proclaiming the good news of the kingdom of God. The Twelve were with him, and also some women who had been cured of evil spirits and diseases: Mary (called Magdalene) from whom seven demons had come out; Joanna the wife of Chuza, the manager of Herod's household; Susanna; and many others. These women were helping to support them out of their own means.

Proper 7

Sunday between 19 and 25 June inclusive (if after Trinity Sunday)
Choose either 'continuous' or 'related' Old Testament and Psalm readings.

CONTINUOUS

1 Kings 19:1–4 [5–7] 8–15a   Ahab told Jezebel everything Elijah had done and how he had killed all the prophets with the sword. So Jezebel sent a messenger to Elijah to say, "May the gods deal with me, be it ever so severely, if by this time tomorrow I do not make your life like that of one of them."

Elijah was afraid and ran for his life. When he came to Beersheba in Judah, he left his servant there, while he himself went a day's journey into the desert. He came to a broom tree, sat down under it and prayed that he might die. "I have had enough, LORD," he said. "Take my life; I am no better than my ancestors." [Then he lay down under the tree and fell asleep.

All at once an angel touched him and said, "Get up and eat." He looked around, and there by his head was a cake of bread baked over hot coals, and a jar of water. He ate and drank and then lay down again.

The angel of the LORD came back a second time and touched him and said, "Get up and eat, for the journey is too much for you."] He got up and ate and drank. Strengthened by that food, he travelled for forty days and forty nights until he reached Horeb, the mountain of God. There he went into a cave and spent the night.

And the word of the LORD came to him: "What are you doing here, Elijah?"

He replied, "I have been very zealous for the LORD God Almighty. The Israelites have rejected your covenant, broken down your altars, and put your prophets to death with the sword. I am the only one left, and now they are trying to kill me too."

The LORD said, "Go out and stand on the mountain in the presence of the LORD, for the LORD is about to pass by."

Then a great and powerful wind tore the mountains apart and shattered the rocks before the LORD, but the LORD was not in the wind. After the wind there was an earthquake, but the LORD was not in the earthquake. After the earthquake came a fire, but the LORD was not in the fire. And after the fire came a gentle whisper. When Elijah heard it, he pulled his cloak over his face and went out and stood at the mouth of the cave.

Then a voice said to him, "What are you doing here, Elijah?"

He replied," I have been very zealous for the LORD God Almighty. The Israelites have rejected your covenant, broken down your altars, and put your prophets to death with the sword. I am the only one left, and now they are trying to kill me too."

The LORD said to him, "Go back the way you came, and go to the desert of Damascus."

and **Psalms 42, 43*** As the deer pants for streams of water,
> so my soul pants for you, O God.
My soul thirsts for God, for the living God.
> When can I go and meet with God?
My tears have been my food
> day and night,
while men say to me all day long,
> "Where is your God?"
These things I remember
> as I pour out my soul:
how I used to go with the multitude,
> leading the procession to the house of God,
with shouts of joy and thanksgiving
> among the festive throng.

Why are you downcast, O my soul?
> Why so disturbed within me?
Put your hope in God,
> for I will yet praise him,
> my Saviour and my God.

My soul is downcast within me;
> therefore I will remember you
from the land of the Jordan,
> the heights of Hermon – from Mount Mizar.

Deep calls to deep
　　in the roar of your waterfalls;
all your waves and breakers
　　have swept over me.

By day the LORD directs his love,
　　at night his song is with me –
　　a prayer to the God of my life.

I say to God my Rock,
　　"Why have you forgotten me?
Why must I go about mourning,
　　oppressed by the enemy?"
My bones suffer mortal agony
　　as my foes taunt me,
saying to me all day long,
　　"Where is your God?"

Why are you downcast, O my soul?
　　Why so disturbed within me?
Put your hope in God,
　　for I will yet praise him,
　　my Saviour and my God.

Vindicate me, O God,
　　and plead my cause against an ungodly nation;
　　rescue me from deceitful and wicked men.
You are God my stronghold.
　　Why have you rejected me?
Why must I go about mourning,
　　oppressed by the enemy?
Send forth your light and your truth,
　　let them guide me;
let them bring me to your holy mountain,
　　to the place where you dwell.
Then will I go to the altar of God,
　　to God, my joy and my delight.
I will praise you with the harp,
　　O God, my God.

Why are you downcast, O my soul?
　　Why so disturbed within me?
Put your hope in God,
　　for I will yet praise him,
　　my Saviour and my God.

Or **RELATED**

Isaiah 65:1–9　This is what the LORD says:

　　"I revealed myself to those who did not ask for me;
　　I was found by those who did not seek me.

FRIERASDTING

To a nation that did not call on my name,
    I said, 'Here am I, here am I.'
All day long I have held out my hands
    to an obstinate people,
who walk in ways not good,
    pursuing their own imaginations –
a people who continually provoke me
    to my very face,
offering sacrifices in gardens
    and burning incense on altars of brick;
who sit among the graves
    and spend their nights keeping secret vigil;
who eat the flesh of pigs,
    and whose pots hold broth of unclean meat;
who say, 'Keep away; don't come near me,
    for I am too sacred for you!'
Such people are smoke in my nostrils,
    a fire that keeps burning all day.

"See, it stands written before me;
    I will not keep silent but will pay back in full;
    I will pay it back into their laps –
both your sins and the sins of your ancestors,"
    says the LORD.
"Because they burned sacrifices on the mountains
    and defied me on the hills,
I will measure into their laps
    the full payment for their former deeds."

This is what the LORD says:

"As when juice is still found in a cluster of grapes
    and men say, 'Don't destroy it,
    there is yet some good in it,'
so will I do on behalf of my servants;
    I will not destroy them all.
I will bring forth descendants from Jacob,
    and from Judah those who will possess my mountains;
my chosen people will inherit them,
    and there will my servants live."

and **Psalm 22:** But you, O LORD, be not far off;
19–28   O my Strength, come quickly to help me.
Deliver my life from the sword,
    my precious life from the power of the dogs.
Rescue me from the mouth of the lions;
    save me from the horns of the wild oxen.

I will declare your name to my brothers;
    in the congregation I will praise you.

P
S
A
L
M

You who fear the LORD, praise him!
    All you descendants of Jacob, honour him!
    Revere him, all you descendants of Israel!
For he has not despised or disdained
    the suffering of the afflicted one;
he has not hidden his face from him
    but has listened to his cry for help.

From you comes the theme of my praise in the
    great assembly;
    before those who fear you will I fulfil my vows.
The poor will eat and be satisfied;
    they who seek the LORD will praise him –
    may your hearts live for ever!
All the ends of the earth
    will remember and turn to the LORD,
and all the families of the nations
    will bow down before him,
for dominion belongs to the LORD
    and he rules over the nations.

Galatians 3:23–29   Before faith in Jesus Christ came, we were held prisoners by the law, locked up until faith should be revealed. So the law was put in charge to lead us to Christ that we might be justified by faith. Now that faith has come, we are no longer under the supervision of the law.

You are all sons of God through faith in Christ Jesus, for all of you who were baptised into Christ have clothed yourselves with Christ. There is neither Jew nor Greek, slave nor free, male nor female, for you are all one in Christ Jesus. If you belong to Christ, then you are Abraham's seed, and heirs according to the promise.

SECOND READING

Luke 8:26–39   Jesus and his disciples sailed to the region of the Gerasenes, which is across the lake from Galilee. When Jesus stepped ashore, he was met by a demon–possessed man from the town. For a long time this man had not worn clothes or lived in a house, but had lived in the tombs. When he saw Jesus, he cried out and fell at his feet, shouting at the top of his voice, "What do you want with me, Jesus, Son of the Most High God? I beg you, don't torture me!" For Jesus had commanded the evil spirit to come out of the man. Many times it had seized him, and though he was chained hand and foot and kept under guard, he had broken his chains and had been driven by the demon into solitary places.

Jesus asked him, "What is your name?"

"Legion," he replied, because many demons had gone into him. And they begged him repeatedly not to order them to go into the Abyss.

A large herd of pigs was feeding there on the hillside. The demons begged Jesus to let them go into them, and he gave them permission. When the demons came out of the man, they went into the pigs, and the herd rushed down the steep bank into the lake and was drowned.

GOSPEL

When those tending the pigs saw what had happened, they ran off and reported this in the town and countryside, and the people went out to see what had happened. When they came to Jesus, they found the man from whom the demons had gone out, sitting at Jesus' feet, dressed and in his right mind; and they were afraid. Those who had seen it told the people how the demon-possessed man had been cured. Then all the people of the region of the Gerasenes asked Jesus to leave them, because they were overcome with fear. So he got into the boat and left.

The man from whom the demons had gone out begged to go with him, but Jesus sent him away, saying, "Return home and tell how much God has done for you." So the man went away and told all over the town how much Jesus had done for him.

Proper 8

Sunday between 26 June and 2 July inclusive (if after Trinity Sunday)
Choose either 'continuous' or 'related' Old Testament and Psalm readings.

CONTINUOUS

2 Kings 2:1–2, 6–14 When the LORD was about to take Elijah up to heaven in a whirlwind, Elijah and Elisha were on their way from Gilgal. Elijah said to Elisha, "Stay here; the LORD has sent me to Bethel."

But Elisha said, "As surely as the LORD lives and as you live, I will not leave you." So they went down to Bethel.

Then Elijah said to him, "Stay here; the LORD has sent me to the Jordan."

And he replied, "As surely as the LORD lives and as you live, I will not leave you." So the two of them walked on.

Fifty from the company of the prophets went and stood at a distance, facing the place where Elijah and Elisha had stopped at the Jordan. Elijah took his cloak, rolled it up and struck the water with it. The water divided to the right and to the left, and the two of them crossed over on dry ground.

When they had crossed, Elijah said to Elisha, "Tell me, what can I do for you before I am taken from you?"

"Let me inherit a double portion of your spirit," Elisha replied.

"You have asked a difficult thing," Elijah said, "yet if you see me when I am taken from you, it will be yours – otherwise not."

As they were walking along and talking together, suddenly a chariot of fire and horses of fire appeared and separated the two of them, and Elijah went up to heaven in a whirlwind. Elisha saw this and cried out, "My father! My father! The chariots and horsemen of Israel!" And Elisha saw him no more. Then he took hold of his own clothes and tore them apart.

He picked up the cloak that had fallen from Elijah and went back and stood on the bank of the Jordan. Then he took the cloak that had fallen from him and struck the water with it. "Where now is the LORD, the God of Elijah?" he asked. When he struck the water, it divided to the right and to the left, and he crossed over.

and **Psalm 77:1–2, 11–20***

I cried out to God for help; P
    I cried out to God to hear me. S
When I was in distress, I sought the LORD; A
    at night I stretched out untiring hands L
    and my soul refused to be comforted. M

I will remember the deeds of the LORD;
    yes, I will remember your miracles of long ago.
I will meditate on all your works
    and consider all your mighty deeds.

Your ways, O God, are holy.
    What god is so great as our God?
You are the God who performs miracles;
    you display your power among the peoples.
With your mighty arm you redeemed your people,
    the descendants of Jacob and Joseph.

The waters saw you, O God,
    the waters saw you and writhed;
    the very depths were convulsed.
The clouds poured down water,
    the skies resounded with thunder;
    your arrows flashed back and forth.
Your thunder was heard in the whirlwind,
    your lightning lit up the world;
    the earth trembled and quaked.
Your path led through the sea,
    your way through the mighty waters,
    though your footprints were not seen.

You led your people like a flock
    by the hand of Moses and Aaron.

Or **RELATED**

Kings 19:15–16, 19–21   The LORD said to Elijah, "Go back the way you came, F and go to the Desert of Damascus. When you get there, anoint I Hazael king over Aram. Also, anoint Jehu son of Nimshi king over Israel, R and anoint Elisha son of Shaphat from Abel Meholah to succeed you as S prophet. T

So Elijah went from there and found Elisha son of Shaphat. He was ploughing with twelve yoke of oxen, and he himself was driving the twelfth R pair. Elijah went up to him and threw his cloak around him. Elisha then left E his oxen and ran after Elijah. "Let me kiss my father and mother good- A bye," he said, "and then I will come with you." D

"Go back," Elijah replied. "What have I done to you?" I

So Elisha left him and went back. He took his yoke of oxen and slaugh- N tered them. He burned the ploughing equipment to cook the meat and gave G it to the people, and they ate. Then he set out to follow Elijah and became his attendant.

and **Psalm 16** Keep me safe, O God,
for in you I take refuge.

I said to the LORD, "You are my LORD;
apart from you I have no good thing."
As for the saints who are in the land,
they are the glorious ones in whom is all my delight.
The sorrows of those will increase
who run after other gods.
I will not pour out their libations of blood
or take up their names on my lips.

LORD, you have assigned me my portion and my cup;
you have made my lot secure.
The boundary lines have fallen for me in pleasant places;
surely I have a delightful inheritance.

I will praise the LORD, who counsels me;
even at night my heart instructs me.
I have set the LORD always before me.
Because he is at my right hand,
I shall not be shaken.

Therefore my heart is glad and my tongue rejoices;
my body also will rest secure,
because you will not abandon me to the grave,
nor will you let your Holy One see decay.
You have made known to me the path of life;
you will fill me with joy in your presence,
with eternal pleasures at your right hand.

Galatians 5:1, 13–25 It is for freedom that Christ has set us free. Stand firm, then, and do not let yourselves be burdened again by a yoke of slavery.

You, my brothers, were called to be free. But do not use your freedom to indulge the sinful nature; rather, serve one another in love. The entire law is summed up in a single command: "Love your neighbour as yourself." If you keep on biting and devouring each other, watch out or you will be destroyed by each other.

So I say, live by the Spirit, and you will not gratify the desires of the sinful nature. For the sinful nature desires what is contrary to the Spirit, and the Spirit what is contrary to the sinful nature. They are in conflict with each other, so that you do not do what you want. But if you are led by the Spirit, you are not under law.

The acts of the sinful nature are obvious: sexual immorality, impurity and debauchery; idolatry and witchcraft; hatred, discord, jealousy, fits of rage, selfish ambition, dissensions, factions and envy; drunkenness, orgies, and the like. I warn you, as I did before, that those who live like this will not inherit the kingdom of God.

But the fruit of the Spirit is love, joy, peace, patience, kindness, goodness, faithfulness, gentleness and self-control. Against such things there is no law. Those who belong to Christ Jesus have crucified the sinful nature with its passions and desires. Since we live by the Spirit, let us keep in step with the Spirit.

Luke 9:51–62 As the time approached for Jesus to be taken up to heaven, he resolutely set out for Jerusalem. And he sent messengers on ahead, who went into a Samaritan village to get things ready for him; but the people there did not welcome him, because he was heading for Jerusalem. When the disciples James and John saw this, they asked, "Lord, do you want us to call fire down from heaven to destroy them?" But Jesus turned and rebuked them, and they went to another village.

As they were walking along the road, a man said to him, "I will follow you wherever you go."

Jesus replied, "Foxes have holes and birds of the air have nests, but the Son of Man has nowhere to lay his head."

He said to another man, "Follow me."

But he replied, "Lord, first let me go and bury my father."

Jesus said to him, "Let the dead bury their own dead, but you go and proclaim the kingdom of God."

Still another said, "I will follow you, Lord; but first let me go back and say good-bye to my family."

Jesus replied, "No-one who puts his hand to the plough and looks back is fit for service in the kingdom of God."

Proper 9

Sunday between 3 and 9 July inclusive (if after Trinity Sunday)
Choose either 'continuous' or 'related' Old Testament and Psalm readings.

CONTINUOUS

2 Kings 5:1–14 Naaman was commander of the army of the king of Aram. He was a great man in the sight of his master and highly regarded, because through him the LORD had given victory to Aram. He was a valiant soldier, but he had leprosy.

Now bands from Aram had gone out and had taken captive a young girl from Israel, and she served Naaman's wife. She said to her mistress, "If only my master would see the prophet who is in Samaria! He would cure him of his leprosy."

Naaman went to his master and told him what the girl from Israel had said. "By all means, go," the king of Aram replied. "I will send a letter to the king of Israel." So Naaman left, taking with him ten talents of silver, six thousand shekels of gold and ten sets of clothing. The letter that he took to the king of Israel read: "With this letter I am sending my servant Naaman to you so that you may cure him of his leprosy."

As soon as the king of Israel read the letter, he tore his robes and said, "Am I God? Can I kill and bring back to life? Why does this fellow send someone to me to be cured of his leprosy? See how he is trying to pick a quarrel with me!"

When Elisha the man of God heard that the king of Israel had torn his robes, he sent him this message: "Why have you torn your robes? Make the man come to me and he will know that there is a prophet in Israel." So Naaman went with his horses and chariots and stopped at the door of Elisha's house. Elisha sent a messenger to say to him, "Go, wash yourself seven times in the Jordan, and your flesh will be restored and you will be cleansed."

But Naaman went away angry and said, "I thought that he would surely come out to me and stand and call on the name of the LORD his God, wave his hand over the spot and cure me of my leprosy. Are not Abana and Pharpar, the rivers of Damascus, better than any of the waters of Israel? Couldn't I wash in them and be cleansed?" So he turned and went off in a rage.

Naaman's servants went to him and said, "My father, if the prophet had told you to do some great thing, would you not have done it? How much more, then, when he tells you, 'Wash and be cleansed'?" So he went down and dipped himself in the Jordan seven times, as the man of God had told him, and his flesh was restored and became clean like that of a young boy.

or **Psalm 30**

I will exalt you, O LORD,
    for you lifted me out of the depths
    and did not let my enemies gloat over me.
O LORD my God, I called to you for help
    and you healed me.
O LORD, you brought me up from the grave;
    you spared me from going down into the pit.

Sing to the LORD, you saints of his;
    praise his holy name.
For his anger lasts only a moment,
    but his favour lasts a lifetime;
weeping may remain for a night,
    but rejoicing comes in the morning.

When I felt secure, I said,
    "I shall never be shaken."
O LORD, when you favoured me,
    you made my mountain stand firm;
but when you hid your face,
    I was dismayed.

To you, O LORD, I called;
    to the LORD I cried for mercy:
"What gain is there in my destruction,
    in my going down into the pit?
Will the dust praise you?
    Will it proclaim your faithfulness?
Hear, O LORD, and be merciful to me;
    O LORD, be my help."

P
S
A
L
M

You turned my wailing into dancing;
>> you removed my sackcloth and clothed me with
>>> joy,
> that my heart may sing to you and not be silent.
>> O LORD my God, I will give you thanks for ever.

Or **RELATED**

Isaiah 66:10–14

"Rejoice with Jerusalem and be glad for her,
> all you who love her;
rejoice greatly with her,
> all you who mourn over her.
For you will nurse and be satisfied
> at her comforting breasts;
you will drink deeply
> and delight in her overflowing abundance."

> For this is what the LORD says:

"I will extend peace to her like a river,
> and the wealth of nations like a flooding stream;
you will nurse and be carried on her arm
> and dandled on her knees.
As a mother comforts her child,
> so will I comfort you;
> and you will be comforted over Jerusalem."

When you see this, your heart will rejoice
> and you will flourish like grass;
the hand of the LORD will be made known to his
>> servants,
> but his fury will be shown to his foes.

F
I
R
S
T

R
E
A
D
I
N
G

and **Psalm 66:1–9**

Shout with joy to God, all the earth!
> Sing the glory of his name;
> make his praise glorious!
Say to God, "How awesome are your deeds!
> So great is your power
> that your enemies cringe before you.
All the earth bows down to you;
> they sing praise to you,
> they sing praise to your name."

Come and see what God has done,
> how awesome his works on man's behalf!
He turned the sea into dry land,
> they passed through the waters on foot –
> come, let us rejoice in him.
He rules for ever by his power,
> his eyes watch the nations –
> let not the rebellious rise up against him.

P
S
A
L
M

Praise our God, O peoples,
    let the sound of his praise be heard;
he has preserved our lives
    and kept our feet from slipping.

Galatians 6:[1–6] 7–16 [Brothers, if someone is caught in a sin, you who are ⎫ S
spiritual should restore him gently. But watch yourself, or you also may be   E
tempted. Carry each other's burdens, and in this way you will fulfil the law   C
of Christ. If anyone thinks he is something when he is nothing, he deceives   O
himself. Each one should test his own actions. Then he can take pride in   N
himself, without comparing himself to somebody else, for each one should   D
carry his own load.

    Anyone who receives instruction in the word must share all good things   R
with his instructor.]   E

    Do not be deceived: God cannot be mocked. A man reaps what he sows.   A
The one who sows to please his sinful nature, from that nature will reap   D
destruction; the one who sows to please the Spirit, from the Spirit will reap   I
eternal life. Let us not become weary in doing good, for at the proper time   N
we will reap a harvest if we do not give up. Therefore, as we have opportu-   G
nity, let us do good to all people, especially to those who belong to the
family of believers. See what large letters I use as I write to you with my
own hand!

    Those who want to make a good impression outwardly are trying to
compel you to be circumcised. The only reason they do this is to avoid
being persecuted for the cross of Christ. Not even those who are circumcised obey the law, yet they want you to be circumcised that they may
boast about your flesh. May I never boast except in the cross of our Lord
Jesus Christ, through which the world has been crucified to me, and I to the
world. Neither circumcision nor uncircumcision means anything; what
counts is a new creation. Peace and mercy to all who follow this rule, even
to the Israel of God.

Luke 10:1–11, 16–20 The LORD appointed seventy-two others and sent them   G
two by two ahead of him to every town and place where he was about to go.   O
He told them, "The harvest is plentiful, but the workers are few. Ask the   S
Lord of the harvest, therefore, to send out workers into his harvest field.   P
Go! I am sending you out like lambs among wolves. Do not take a purse or   E
bag or sandals; and do not greet anyone on the road.   L

    "When you enter a house, first say, 'Peace to this house.' If a man of
peace is there, your peace will rest on him; if not, it will return to you. Stay
in that house, eating and drinking whatever they give you, for the worker
deserves his wages. Do not move around from house to house.

    "When you enter a town and are welcomed, eat what is set before you.
Heal the sick who are there and tell them, 'The kingdom of God is near
you.' But when you enter a town and are not welcomed, go into its streets
and say, 'Even the dust of your town that sticks to our feet we wipe off
against you. Yet be sure of this: The kingdom of God is near.'

"He who listens to you listens to me; whoever rejects you rejects me; but he who rejects me rejects him who sent me."

The seventy-two returned with joy and said, "Lord, even the demons submit to us in your name."

He replied, "I saw Satan fall like lightning from heaven. I have given you authority to trample on snakes and scorpions and to overcome all the power of the enemy; nothing will harm you. However, do not rejoice that the spirits submit to you, but rejoice that your names are written in heaven."

Proper 10

Sunday between 10 and 16 July inclusive (if after Trinity Sunday)
Choose either 'continuous' or 'related' Old Testament and Psalm readings.

CONTINUOUS

Amos 7:7–17   This is what the Sovereign LORD showed me: The Lord was standing by a wall that had been built true to plumb, with a plumb-line in his hand. And the LORD asked me, "What do you see, Amos?"

"A plumb-line," I replied.

Then the LORD said, "Look, I am setting a plumb-line among my people Israel; I will spare them no longer.

"The high places of Isaac will be destroyed
and the sanctuaries of Israel will be ruined;
with my sword I will rise against the house of Jeroboam."

Then Amaziah the priest of Bethel sent a message to Jeroboam king of Israel: "Amos is raising a conspiracy against you in the very heart of Israel. The land cannot bear all his words. For this is what Amos is saying:

"'Jeroboam will die by the sword,
and Israel will surely go into exile,
away from their native land.'"

Then Amaziah said to Amos, "Get out, you seer! Go back to the land of Judah. Earn your bread there and do your prophesying there. Don't prophesy any more at Bethel, because this is the king's sanctuary and the temple of the kingdom."

Amos answered Amaziah, "I was neither a prophet nor a prophet's son, but I was a shepherd, and I also took care of sycamore-fig trees. But the LORD took me from tending the flock and said to me, 'Go, prophesy to my people Israel.' Now then, hear the word of the LORD. You say,

"'Do not prophesy against Israel,
and stop preaching against the house of Isaac.'

"Therefore this is what the LORD says:

"'Your wife will become a prostitute in the city,
and your sons and daughters will fall by the sword.
Your land will be measured and divided up,
and you yourself will die in a pagan country.
And Israel will certainly go into exile,
away from their native land.'"

and **Psalm 82**

God presides in the great assembly;
  he gives judgment among the "gods":

"How long will you defend the unjust
  and show partiality to the wicked?
Defend the cause of the weak and fatherless;
  maintain the rights of the poor and oppressed.
Rescue the weak and needy;
  deliver them from the hand of the wicked.

"They know nothing, they understand nothing.
  They walk about in darkness;
  all the foundations of the earth are shaken.

"I said, 'You are "gods";
  you are all sons of the Most High.'
But you will die like mere men;
  you will fall like every other ruler."

Rise up, O God, judge the earth,
  for all the nations are your inheritance.

Or **RELATED**

Deuteronomy 30:9–14 Moses summoned all the Israelites and said to them:
The LORD your God will make you most prosperous in all the work of your
hands and in the fruit of your womb, the young of your livestock and the
crops of your land. The LORD will again delight in you and make you prosperous, just as he delighted in your ancestors, if you obey the LORD your
God and keep his commands and decrees that are written in this Book of
the Law and turn to the LORD your God with all your heart and with all your
soul.

Now what I am commanding you today is not too difficult for you or
beyond your reach. It is not up in heaven, so that you have to ask, "Who will
ascend into heaven to get it and proclaim it to us so that we may obey it?"
Nor is it beyond the sea, so that you have to ask, "Who will cross the sea to
get it and proclaim it to us so that we may obey it?" No, the word is very
near you; it is in your mouth and in your heart so that you may obey it.

and **Psalm 25:1–10**

To you, O LORD, I lift up my soul;
  in you I trust, O my God.
Do not let me be put to shame,
  nor let my enemies triumph over me.
No-one whose hope is in you
  will ever be put to shame,
but they will be put to shame
  who are treacherous without excuse.

Show me your ways, O LORD,
  teach me your paths;
guide me in your truth and teach me,

for you are God my Saviour,
and my hope is in you all day long.
Remember, O Lord, your great mercy and love,
for they are from of old.
Remember not the sins of my youth
and my rebellious ways;
according to your love remember me,
for you are good, O Lord.

Good and upright is the Lord;
therefore he instructs sinners in his ways.
He guides the humble in what is right
and teaches them his way.
All the ways of the Lord are loving and faithful
for those who keep the demands of his covenant.

Colossians 1:1–14   Paul, an apostle of Christ Jesus by the will of God, and
Timothy our brother,

To the holy and faithful brothers in Christ at Colosse:

Grace and peace to you from God our Father.

We always thank God, the Father of our Lord Jesus Christ, when we
pray for you, because we have heard of your faith in Christ Jesus and of the
love you have for all the saints – the faith and love that spring from the
hope that is stored up for you in heaven and that you have already heard
about in the word of truth, the gospel that has come to you. All over the
world this gospel is bearing fruit and growing, just as it has been doing
among you since the day you heard it and understood God's grace in all its
truth. You learned it from Epaphras, our dear fellow-servant, who is a
faithful minister of Christ on our behalf, and who also told us of your love
in the Spirit.

For this reason, since the day we heard about you, we have not stopped
praying for you and asking God to fill you with the knowledge of his will
through all spiritual wisdom and understanding. And we pray this in order
that you may live a life worthy of the Lord and may please him in every
way: bearing fruit in every good work, growing in the knowledge of God,
being strengthened with all power according to his glorious might so that
you may have great endurance and patience, and joyfully giving thanks to
the Father, who has qualified you to share in the inheritance of the saints in
the kingdom of light. For he has rescued us from the dominion of darkness
and brought us into the kingdom of the Son he loves, in whom we have
redemption, the forgiveness of sins.

Luke 10:25–37   On one occasion an expert in the law stood up to test Jesus.
"Teacher," he asked, "what must I do to inherit eternal life?"

"What is written in the Law?" he replied. "How do you read it?"

He answered: "'Love the Lord your God with all your heart and with all your soul and with all your strength and with all your mind'; and, 'Love your neighbour as yourself.'"

"You have answered correctly," Jesus replied. "Do this and you will live."

But he wanted to justify himself, so he asked Jesus, "And who is my neighbour?"

In reply Jesus said: "A man was going down from Jerusalem to Jericho, when he fell into the hands of robbers. They stripped him of his clothes, beat him and went away, leaving him half-dead. A priest happened to be going down the same road, and when he saw the man, he passed by on the other side. So too, a Levite, when he came to the place and saw him, passed by on the other side. But a Samaritan, as he travelled, came where the man was; and when he saw him, he took pity on him. He went to him and bandaged his wounds, pouring on oil and wine. Then he put the man on his own donkey, brought him to an inn and took care of him. The next day he took out two silver coins and gave them to the innkeeper. 'Look after him,' he said, 'and when I return, I will reimburse you for any extra expense you may have.'

"Which of these three do you think was a neighbour to the man who fell into the hands of robbers?"

The expert in the law replied, "The one who had mercy on him."

Jesus told him, "Go and do likewise."

Proper 11

Sunday between 17 and 23 July inclusive (if after Trinity Sunday)
Choose either 'continuous' or 'related' Old Testament and Psalm readings.

CONTINUOUS

Amos 8:1–12   This is what the Sovereign LORD showed me: a basket of ripe fruit. "What do you see, Amos?" he asked.

"A basket of ripe fruit," I answered.

Then the LORD said to me, "The time is ripe for my people Israel; I will spare them no longer.

"In that day," declares the Sovereign LORD, "the songs in the temple will turn to wailing. Many, many bodies – flung everywhere! Silence!"

Hear this, you who trample the needy
  and do away with the poor of the land,

saying,

"When will the New Moon be over
  that we may sell grain,
and the Sabbath be ended
  that we may market wheat?" –
skimping the measure,
  boosting the price
  and cheating with dishonest scales,
buying the poor with silver
  and the needy for a pair of sandals,
selling even the sweepings with the wheat.

The LORD has sworn by the Pride of Jacob: "I will never forget anything they have done.

"Will not the land tremble for this,
and all who live in it mourn?
The whole land will rise like the Nile;
it will be stirred up and then sink
like the river of Egypt.

"In that day," declares the Sovereign LORD,

"I will make the sun go down at noon
and darken the earth in broad daylight.
I will turn your religious feasts into mourning
and all your singing into weeping.
I will make all of you wear sackcloth
and shave your heads.
I will make that time like mourning for an only son
and the end of it like a bitter day.

"The days are coming," declares the Sovereign
LORD,
"when I will send a famine through the land –
not a famine of food or a thirst for water,
but a famine of hearing the words of the LORD.
People will stagger from sea to sea
and wander from north to east,
searching for the word of the LORD,
but they will not find it."

and **Psalm 52** Why do you boast of evil, you mighty man? P
Why do you boast all day long, S
you who are a disgrace in the eyes of God? A
Your tongue plots destruction; L
it is like a sharpened razor, M
you who practise deceit.
You love evil rather than good,
falsehood rather than speaking the truth.
You love every harmful word,
O you deceitful tongue!

Surely God will bring you down to everlasting ruin:
He will snatch you up and tear you from your tent;
he will uproot you from the land of the living.
The righteous will see and fear;
they will laugh at him, saying,
"Here now is the man
who did not make God his stronghold
but trusted in his great wealth
and grew strong by destroying others!"

But I am like an olive tree
    flourishing in the house of God;
I trust in God's unfailing love
    for ever and ever.
I will praise you for ever for what you have done;
    in your name I will hope, for your name is good.
    I will praise you in the presence of your saints.

Or **RELATED**

Genesis 18:1–10a   The LORD appeared to Abraham near the great trees of Mamre while he was sitting at the entrance to his tent in the heat of the day. Abraham looked up and saw three men standing nearby. When he saw them, he hurried from the entrance of his tent to meet them and bowed low to the ground.

He said, "If I have found favour in your eyes, my lord, do not pass your servant by. Let a little water be brought, and then you may all wash your feet and rest under this tree. Let me get you something to eat, so you can be refreshed and then go on your way – now that you have come to your servant."

"Very well," they answered, "do as you say."

So Abraham hurried into the tent to Sarah. "Quick," he said, "get three seahs of fine flour and knead it and bake some bread."

Then he ran to the herd and selected a choice, tender calf and gave it to a servant, who hurried to prepare it. He then brought some curds and milk and the calf that had been prepared, and set these before them. While they ate, he stood near them under a tree.

"Where is your wife Sarah?" they asked him.

"There, in the tent," he said.

Then the LORD said, "I will surely return to you about this time next year, and Sarah your wife will have a son."

and **Psalm 15**   LORD, who may dwell in your sanctuary?
    Who may live on your holy hill?

He whose walk is blameless
    and who does what is righteous,
who speaks the truth from his heart
    and has no slander on his tongue,
who does his neighbour no wrong
    and casts no slur on his fellow-man,
who despises a vile man
    but honours those who fear the LORD,
who keeps his oath
    even when it hurts,
who lends his money without usury
    and does not accept a bribe against the innocent.

He who does these things
    will never be shaken.

Colossians 1:15–28   Christ Jesus is the image of the invisible God, the first-born over all creation. For by him all things were created: things in heaven and on earth, visible and invisible, whether thrones or powers or rulers or authorities; all things were created by him and for him. He is before all things, and in him all things hold together. And he is the head of the body, the church; he is the beginning and the firstborn from among the dead, so that in everything he might have the supremacy. For God was pleased to have all his fulness dwell in him, and through him to reconcile to himself all things, whether things on earth or things in heaven, by making peace through his blood, shed on the cross.

Once you were alienated from God and were enemies in your minds because of your evil behaviour. But now he has reconciled you by Christ's physical body through death to present you holy in his sight, without blemish and free from accusation – if you continue in your faith, established and firm, not moved from the hope held out in the gospel. This is the gospel that you heard and that has been proclaimed to every creature under heaven, and of which I, Paul, have become a servant.

Now I rejoice in what was suffered for you, and I fill up in my flesh what is still lacking in regard to Christ's afflictions, for the sake of his body, which is the church. I have become its servant by the commission God gave me to present to you the word of God in its fulness – the mystery that has been kept hidden for ages and generations, but is now disclosed to the saints. To them God has chosen to make known among the Gentiles the glorious riches of this mystery, which is Christ in you, the hope of glory.

We proclaim him, admonishing and teaching everyone with all wisdom, so that we may present everyone perfect in Christ.

[margin: SECOND READING]

Luke 10:38–42   As Jesus and his disciples were on their way, he came to a village where a woman named Martha opened her home to him. She had a sister called Mary, who sat at the Lord's feet listening to what he said. But Martha was distracted by all the preparations that had to be made. She came to him and asked, "Lord, don't you care that my sister has left me to do the work by myself? Tell her to help me!"

"Martha, Martha," the Lord answered, "you are worried and upset about many things, but only one thing is needed. Mary has chosen what is better, and it will not be taken away from her."

[margin: GOSPEL]

Proper 12

Sunday between 24 and 30 July inclusive (if after Trinity Sunday)
Choose either 'continuous' or 'related' Old Testament and Psalm readings.

CONTINUOUS

Hosea 1:2–10   When the LORD began to speak through Hosea, the LORD said to him, "Go, take to yourself an adulterous wife and children of unfaithfulness, because the land is guilty of the vilest adultery in departing from the LORD." So he married Gomer daughter of Diblaim, and she conceived and bore him a son.

[margin: FIRST READING]

Then the LORD said to Hosea, "Call him Jezreel, because I will soon punish the house of Jehu for the massacre at Jezreel, and I will put an end to the kingdom of Israel. In that day I will break Israel's bow in the Valley of Jezreel."

Gomer conceived again and gave birth to a daughter. Then the LORD said to Hosea, "Call her Lo-Ruhamah, for I will no longer show love to the house of Israel, that I should at all forgive them. Yet I will show love to the house of Judah; and I will save them – not by bow, sword or battle, or by horses and horsemen, but by the LORD their God."

After she had weaned Lo-Ruhamah, Gomer had another son. Then the LORD said, "Call him Lo-Ammi, for you are not my people, and I am not your God.

"Yet the Israelites will be like the sand on the seashore, which cannot be measured or counted. In the place where it was said to them, 'You are not my people', they will be called 'sons of the living God'."

and **Psalm 85***   You showed favour to your land, O LORD;
  you restored the fortunes of Jacob.
You forgave the iniquity of your people
  and covered all their sins.
You set aside all your wrath
  and turned from your fierce anger.

Restore us again, O God our Saviour,
  and put away your displeasure towards us.
Will you be angry with us for ever?
  Will you prolong your anger through all generations?
Will you not revive us again,
  that your people may rejoice in you?
Show us your unfailing love, O LORD,
  and grant us your salvation.

I will listen to what God the LORD will say;
  he promises peace to his people, his saints –
  but let them not return to folly.
Surely his salvation is near those who fear him,
  that his glory may dwell in our land.

Love and faithfulness meet together;
  righteousness and peace kiss each other.
Faithfulness springs forth from the earth,
  and righteousness looks down from heaven.
The LORD will indeed give what is good,
  and our land will yield its harvest.
Righteousness goes before him
  and prepares the way for his steps.

Or **RELATED**

Genesis 18:20–32   The LORD said, "The outcry against Sodom and Gomorrah is so great and their sin so grievous that I will go down and see if what they have done is as bad as the outcry that has reached me. If not, I will know."

The men turned away and went towards Sodom, but Abraham remained standing before the Lord. Then Abraham approached him and said: "Will you sweep away the righteous with the wicked? What if there are fifty righteous people in the city? Will you really sweep it away and not spare the place for the sake of the fifty righteous people in it? Far be it from you to do such a thing – to kill the righteous with the wicked, treating the righteous and the wicked alike. Far be it from you! Will not the Judge of all the earth do right?"

The Lord said, "If I find fifty righteous people in the city of Sodom, I will spare the whole place for their sake."

Then Abraham spoke up again: "Now that I have been so bold as to speak to the Lord, though I am nothing but dust and ashes, what if the number of the righteous is five less than fifty? Will you destroy the whole city because of five people?"

"If I find forty-five there," he said, "I will not destroy it."

Once again he spoke to him, "What if only forty are found there?"

He said, "For the sake of forty, I will not do it."

Then he said, "May the Lord not be angry, but let me speak. What if only thirty can be found there?"

He answered, "I will not do it if I find thirty there."

Abraham said, "Now that I have been so bold as to speak to the Lord, what if only twenty can be found there?"

He said, "For the sake of twenty, I will not destroy it."

Then he said, "May the Lord not be angry, but let me speak just once more. What if only ten can be found there?"

He answered, "For the sake of ten, I will not destroy it."

and **Psalm 138**

I will praise you, O Lord, with all my heart;
　　before the "gods" I will sing your praise.
I will bow down towards your holy temple
　　and will praise your name
　　　for your love and your faithfulness,
for you have exalted above all things
　　your name and your word.
When I called, you answered me;
　　you made me bold and stout-hearted.

May all the kings of the earth praise you, O Lord,
　　when they hear the words of your mouth.
May they sing of the ways of the Lord,
　　for the glory of the Lord is great.

Though the Lord is on high, he looks upon the lowly,
　　but the proud he knows from afar.
Though I walk in the midst of trouble,
　　you preserve my life;

you stretch out your hand against the anger of my foes,
with your right hand you save me.
The LORD will fulfil his purpose for me;
your love, O LORD, endures for ever –
do not abandon the works of your hands.

Colossians 2:6–15 [16–19] Just as you received Christ Jesus as Lord, continue to live in him, rooted and built up in him, strengthened in the faith as
you were taught, and overflowing with thankfulness.

See to it that no-one takes you captive through hollow and deceptive
philosophy, which depends on human tradition and the basic principles of
this world rather than on Christ.

For in Christ all the fulness of the Deity lives in bodily form, and you
have been given fulness in Christ, who is the Head over every power and
authority. In him you were also circumcised, in the putting off of the sinful
nature, not with a circumcision done by the hands of men but with the circumcision done by Christ, having been buried with him in baptism and
raised with him through your faith in the power of God, who raised him
from the dead.

When you were dead in your sins and in the uncircumcision of your sinful nature, God made you alive with Christ. He forgave us all our sins,
having cancelled the written code, with its regulations, that was against us
and that stood opposed to us; he took it away, nailing it to the cross. And
having disarmed the powers and authorities, he made a public spectacle of
them, triumphing over them by the cross.

[Therefore do not let anyone judge you by what you eat or drink, or with
regard to a religious festival, a New Moon celebration or a Sabbath day.
These are a shadow of the things that were to come; the reality, however, is
found in Christ. Do not let anyone who delights in false humility and the
worship of angels disqualify you for the prize. Such a person goes into
great detail about what he has seen, and his unspiritual mind puffs him up
with idle notions. He has lost connection with the Head, from whom the
whole body, supported and held together by its ligaments and sinews,
grows as God causes it to grow.]

Luke 11:1–13 One day Jesus was praying in a certain place. When he finished, one of his disciples said to him, "Lord, teach us to pray, just as John
taught his disciples."

He said to them, "When you pray, say:

"'Father,
hallowed be your name,
your kingdom come.
Give us each day our daily bread.
Forgive us our sins,
for we also forgive everyone who sins against us.
And lead us not into temptation.'"

Then he said to them, "Suppose one of you has a friend, and he goes to him at midnight and says, 'Friend, lend me three loaves of bread, because a friend of mine on a journey has come to me, and I have nothing to set before him."

"Then the one inside answers, 'Don't bother me. The door is already locked, and my children are with me in bed. I can't get up and give you anything.' I tell you, though he will not get up and give him the bread because he is his friend, yet because of the man's boldness he will get up and give him as much as he needs.

"So I say to you: Ask and it will be given to you; seek and you will find; knock and the door will be opened to you. For everyone who asks receives; he who seeks finds; and to him who knocks, the door will be opened.

"Which of you fathers, if your son asks for a fish, will give him a snake instead? Or if he asks for an egg, will give him a scorpion? If you then, though you are evil, know how to give good gifts to your children, how much more will your Father in heaven give the Holy Spirit to those who ask him!"

Proper 13

Sunday between 31 July and 6 August inclusive (if after Trinity Sunday)
Choose either 'continuous' or 'related' Old Testament and Psalm readings.

CONTINUOUS

Hosea 11:1–11   "When Israel was a child, I loved him,
　　　　and out of Egypt I called my son.
　　But the more I called Israel,
　　　　the further they went from me.
　　They sacrificed to the Baals
　　　　and they burned incense to images.
　　It was I who taught Ephraim to walk,
　　　　taking them by the arms;
　　but they did not realise
　　　　it was I who healed them.
　　I led them with cords of human kindness,
　　　　with ties of love;
　　I lifted the yoke from their neck
　　　　and bent down to feed them.

　　"Will they not return to Egypt
　　　　and will not Assyria rule over them
　　　　because they refuse to repent?
　　Swords will flash in their cities,
　　　　will destroy the bars of their gates
　　　　and put an end to their plans.
　　My people are determined to turn from me.
　　　　Even if they call to the Most High,
　　　　he will by no means exalt them.

　　"How can I give you up, Ephraim?
　　　　How can I hand you over, Israel?

(margin: F I R S T   R E A D I N G)

How can I treat you like Admah?
    How can I make you like Zeboiim?
My heart is changed within me;
    all my compassion is aroused.
I will not carry out my fierce anger,
    nor will I turn and devastate Ephraim.
For I am God, and not man –
    the Holy One among you.
    I will not come in wrath.
They will follow the LORD;
    he will roar like a lion.
When he roars,
    his children will come trembling from the west.
They will come trembling
    like birds from Egypt,
    like doves from Assyria.
I will settle them in their homes,"
    declares the LORD.

and **Psalm 107:**
1–9, 43*

Give thanks to the LORD, for he is good;
    his love endures for ever.
Let the redeemed of the LORD say this –
    those he redeemed from the hand of the foe,
those he gathered from the lands,
    from east and west, from north and south.

Some wandered in desert wastelands,
    finding no way to a city where they could settle.
They were hungry and thirsty,
    and their lives ebbed away.
Then they cried out to the LORD in their trouble,
    and he delivered them from their distress.
He led them by a straight way
    to a city where they could settle.
Let them give thanks to the LORD for his unfailing
       love
    and his wonderful deeds for everyone,
for he satisfies the thirsty
    and fills the hungry with good things.

Whoever is wise let him heed these things
    and consider the great love of the LORD.

Or **RELATED**

Ecclesiastes 1:2,
12–14; 2:18–23

"Meaningless! Meaningless!"
    says the Teacher.
"Utterly meaningless!
    Everything is meaningless."

I, the Teacher, was king over Israel in Jerusalem. I devoted myself to study and to explore by wisdom all that is done under heaven. What a heavy burden God has laid on men! I have seen all the things that are done under the sun; all of them are meaningless, a chasing after the wind.

I hated all the things I had toiled for under the sun, because I must leave them to the one who comes after me. And who knows whether he will be a wise man or a fool? Yet he will have control over all the work into which I have poured my effort and skill under the sun. This too is meaningless. So my heart began to despair over all my toilsome labour under the sun. For a man may do his work with wisdom, knowledge and skill, and then he must leave all he owns to someone who has not worked for it. This too is mean-ingless and a great misfortune. What does a man get for all the toil and anxious striving with which he labours under the sun? All his days his work is pain and grief; even at night his mind does not rest. This too is meaning-less.

and **Psalm 49:** Hear this, all you peoples; P
1–12*   listen, all who live in this world, S
both low and high, A
   rich and poor alike: L
My mouth will speak words of wisdom; M
   the utterance from my heart will give understanding.
I will turn my ear to a proverb;
   with the harp I will expound my riddle:

Why should I fear when evil days come,
   when wicked deceivers surround me –
those who trust in their wealth
   and boast of their great riches?
No man can redeem the life of another
   or give to God a ransom for him –
the ransom for a life is costly,
   no payment is ever enough –
that someone should live on for ever
   and not see decay.

For all can see that wise men die;
   the foolish and the senseless alike perish
   and leave their wealth to others.
Their tombs will remain their houses for ever,
   their dwellings for endless generations,
      though they had named lands after themselves. S R

But a man, despite his riches, does not endure; E E
   he is like the beasts that perish. C A

  O D
Colossians 3:1–11   Since you have been raised with Christ, set your hearts on N I
things above, where Christ is seated at the right hand of God. Set your D N
minds on things above, not on earthly things. For you died, and your life is G

now hidden with Christ in God. When Christ, who is your life, appears, then you also will appear with him in glory.

Put to death, therefore, whatever belongs to your earthly nature: sexual immorality, impurity, lust, evil desires and greed, which is idolatry. Because of these, the wrath of God is coming. You used to walk in these ways, in the life you once lived. But now you must rid yourselves of all such things as these: anger, rage, malice, slander and filthy language from your lips. Do not lie to each other, since you have taken off your old self with its practices and have put on the new self, which is being renewed in knowledge in the image of its Creator. Here there is no Greek or Jew, circumcised or uncircumcised, barbarian, Scythian, slave or free, but Christ is all, and is in all.

Luke 12:13–21 Someone in the crowd said to Jesus, "Teacher, tell my brother to divide the inheritance with me." G O S P E L

Jesus replied, "Man, who appointed me a judge or an arbiter between you?" Then he said to them, "Watch out! Be on your guard against all kinds of greed; a man's life does not consist in the abundance of his possessions."

And he told them this parable: "The ground of a certain rich man produced a good crop. He thought to himself, 'What shall I do? I have no place to store my crops.'

"Then he said, 'This is what I'll do. I will tear down my barns and build bigger ones, and there I will store all my grain and my goods. And I'll say to myself, "You have plenty of good things laid up for many years. Take life easy; eat, drink and be merry."'

"But God said to him, 'You fool! This very night your life will be demanded from you. Then who will get what you have prepared for yourself?'

"This is how it will be with anyone who stores up things for himself but is not rich towards God."

Proper 14

Sunday between 7 and 13 August inclusive (if after Trinity Sunday)
Choose either 'continuous' or 'related' Old Testament and Psalm readings.

CONTINUOUS

Isaiah 1:1, 10–20 The vision concerning Judah and Jerusalem that Isaiah son of Amoz saw during the reigns of Uzziah, Jotham, Ahaz and Hezekiah, kings of Judah. F I R S T
R E A D I N G

> Hear the word of the LORD,
>> you rulers of Sodom;
> listen to the law of our God,
>> you people of Gomorrah!
> "The multitude of your sacrifices –
>> what are they to me?" says the LORD.
> "I have more than enough of burnt offerings,
>> of rams and the fat of fattened animals;

I have no pleasure
in the blood of bulls and lambs and goats.
When you come to appear before me,
who has asked this of you,
this trampling of my courts?
Stop bringing meaningless offerings!
Your incense is detestable to me.
New Moons, Sabbaths and convocations –
I cannot bear your evil assemblies.
Your New Moon festivals and your appointed
feasts
my soul hates.
They have become a burden to me;
I am weary of bearing them.
When you spread out your hands in prayer,
I will hide my eyes from you;
even if you offer many prayers,
I will not listen.
Your hands are full of blood;
wash and make yourselves clean.
Take your evil deeds
out of my sight!
Stop doing wrong,
learn to do right!
Seek justice,
encourage the oppressed.
Defend the cause of the fatherless,
plead the case of the widow.

"Come now, let us reason together,"
says the LORD.
"Though your sins are like scarlet,
they shall be as white as snow;
though they are red as crimson,
they shall be like wool.
If you are willing and obedient,
you will eat the best from the land;
but if you resist and rebel,
you will be devoured by the sword."
For the mouth of the LORD has spoken.

nd **Psalm 50:1–8,**
22–23*

The Mighty One, God, the LORD,
speaks and summons the earth
from the rising of the sun to the place where it
sets.
From Zion, perfect in beauty,
God shines forth.

P
S
A
L
M

Our God comes and will not be silent;
    a fire devours before him,
    and around him a tempest rages.
He summons the heavens above,
    and the earth, that he may judge his people:
"Gather to me my consecrated ones,
    who made a covenant with me by sacrifice."
And the heavens proclaim his righteousness,
    for God himself is judge.

"Hear, O my people, and I will speak,
    O Israel, and I will testify against you:
    I am God, your God.
I do not rebuke you for your sacrifices
    or your burnt offerings, which are ever before me.

"Consider this, you who forget God,
    or I will tear you to pieces, with none to rescue:
He who sacrifices thank-offerings honours me,
    and he prepares the way
    so that I may show him the salvation of God."

Or **RELATED**

Genesis 15:1–6   The word of the Lord came to Abram in a vision:

"Do not be afraid, Abram.
    I am your shield,
    your very great reward."

But Abram said, "O Sovereign Lord, what can you give me since I remain childless and the one who will inherit my estate is Eliezer of Damascus?" And Abram said, "You have given me no children; so a servant in my household will be my heir."
    Then the word of the Lord came to him: "This man will not be your heir, but a son coming from your own body will be your heir." He took him outside and said, "Look up at the heavens and count the stars – if indeed you can count them." Then he said to him, "So shall your offspring be."
    Abram believed the Lord, and he credited it to him as righteousness.

and **Psalm 33:12–22***   Blessed is the nation whose God is the Lord,
        the people he chose for his inheritance.
    From heaven the Lord looks down
        and sees all humanity;
    from his dwelling-place he watches
        all who live on earth –
    he who forms the hearts of all,
        who considers everything they do.
    No king is saved by the size of his army;
        no warrior escapes by his great strength.

A horse is a vain hope for deliverance;
    despite all its great strength it cannot save.
But the eyes of the LORD are on those who fear him,
    on those whose hope is in his unfailing love,
to deliver them from death
    and keep them alive in famine.

We wait in hope for the LORD;
    he is our help and our shield.
In him our hearts rejoice,
    for we trust in his holy name.
May your unfailing love rest upon us, O LORD,
    even as we put our hope in you.

Hebrews 11:1–3, 8–16 Faith is being sure of what we hope for and certain of what we do not see. This is what the ancients were commended for.

By faith we understand that the universe was formed at God's command, so that what is seen was not made out of what was visible.

By faith Abraham, when called to go to a place he would later receive as his inheritance, obeyed and went, even though he did not know where he was going. By faith he made his home in the promised land like a stranger in a foreign country; he lived in tents, as did Isaac and Jacob, who were heirs with him of the same promise. For he was looking forward to the city with foundations, whose architect and builder is God.

By faith Abraham, even though he was past age – and Sarah herself was barren – was enabled to become a father because he considered him faithful who had made the promise. And so from this one man, and he as good as dead, came descendants as numerous as the stars in the sky and as countless as the sand on the seashore.

All these people were still living by faith when they died. They did not receive the things promised; they only saw them and welcomed them from a distance. And they admitted that they were aliens and strangers on earth. People who say such things show that they are looking for a country of their own. If they had been thinking of the country they had left, they would have had opportunity to return. Instead, they were longing for a better country – a heavenly one. Therefore God is not ashamed to be called their God, for he has prepared a city for them.

Luke 12:32–40 Jesus said to his disciples: "Do not be afraid, little flock, for your Father has been pleased to give you the kingdom. Sell your possessions and give to the poor. Provide purses for yourselves that will not wear out, a treasure in heaven that will not be exhausted, where no thief comes near and no moth destroys. For where your treasure is, there your heart will be also.

"Be dressed ready for service and keep your lamps burning, like men waiting for their master to return from a wedding banquet, so that when he comes and knocks they can immediately open the door for him. It will be good for those servants whose master finds them watching when he comes. I tell you the truth, he will dress himself to serve, will have them recline at the table and will come and wait on them. It will be good for those servants whose master finds them ready, even if he comes in the second or third watch of the night. But understand this: If the owner of the house had known at what hour the thief was coming, he would not have let his house be broken into, You also must be ready, because the Son of Man will come at an hour when you do not expect him."

Proper 15

Sunday between 14 and 20 August inclusive (if after Trinity Sunday)
Choose either 'continuous' or 'related' Old Testament and Psalm readings.

CONTINUOUS

Isaiah 5:1–7

I will sing for the one I love
　　a song about his vineyard:
My loved one had a vineyard
　　on a fertile hillside.
He dug it up and cleared it of stones
　　and planted it with the choicest vines.
He built a watchtower in it
　　and cut out a winepress as well.
Then he looked for a crop of good grapes,
　　but it yielded only bad fruit.

"Now you dwellers in Jerusalem and men of Judah,
　　judge between me and my vineyard.
What more could have been done for my vineyard
　　than I have done for it?
When I looked for good grapes,
　　why did it yield only bad?
Now I will tell you
　　what I am going to do to my vineyard:
I will take away its hedge,
　　and it will be destroyed;
I will break down its wall,
　　and it will be trampled.
I will make it a wasteland,
　　neither pruned nor cultivated,
　　and briers and thorns will grow there.
I will command the clouds
　　not to rain on it."

The vineyard of the Lord Almighty
　　is the house of Israel,
and the people of Judah
　　are the garden of his delight.
And he looked for justice, but saw bloodshed;
　　for righteousness, but heard cries of distress.

FIRST READING

Hear us, O Shepherd of Israel,
  you who lead Joseph like a flock;
you who sit enthroned between the cherubim,
    shine forth
  before Ephraim, Benjamin and Manasseh.
Awaken your might;
  come and save us.

You brought a vine out of Egypt;
  you drove out the nations and planted it.
You cleared the ground for it,
  and it took root and filled the land.
The mountains were covered with its shade,
  the mighty cedars with its branches.
It sent out its boughs to the Sea,
  its shoots as far as the River.

Why have you broken down its walls
  so that all who pass by pick its grapes?
Boars from the forest ravage it
  and the creatures of the field feed on it.
Return to us, O God Almighty!
  Look down from heaven and see!
Watch over this vine,
    the root your right hand has planted,
    the son you have raised up for yourself.

Your vine is cut down, it is burned with fire;
  at your rebuke your people perish.
Let your hand rest on the man at your right hand,
  the son of man you have raised up for yourself.
Then we will not turn away from you;
  revive us, and we will call on your name.

Restore us, O LORD God Almighty;
  make your face shine upon us,
  that we may be saved.

· RELATED

Jeremiah 23:23–29

"Am I only a God nearby,"
        declares the LORD,
    "and not a God far away?
Can anyone hide in secret places
  so that I cannot see him?"
        declares the LORD.
  "Do not I fill heaven and earth?"
        declares the LORD.

  "I have heard what the prophets say who prophesy lies in my name.
They say, 'I had a dream! I had a dream!' How long will this continue in the

hearts of these lying prophets, who prophesy the delusions of their own minds? They think the dreams they tell one another will make my people forget my name, just as their fathers forgot my name through Baal worship. Let the prophet who has a dream tell his dream, but let the one who has my word speak it faithfully. For what has straw to do with grain?" declares the LORD. "Is not my word like fire," declares the LORD, "and like a hammer that breaks a rock in pieces?"

and **Psalm 82**   God presides in the great assembly;   P
    he gives judgment among the "gods":   S

  "How long will you defend the unjust   A
    and show partiality to the wicked?   L
Defend the cause of the weak and fatherless;   M
    maintain the rights of the poor and oppressed.
Rescue the weak and needy;
    deliver them from the hand of the wicked.

  "They know nothing, they understand nothing.
    They walk about in darkness;
    all the foundations of the earth are shaken.

  "I said, 'You are "gods";
    you are all sons of the Most High.'
But you will die like mere men;
    you will fall like every other ruler."

  Rise up, O God, judge the earth,
    for all the nations are your inheritance.

Hebrews 11:29 – 12:2   By faith the people of Israel passed through the Red   S
Sea as on dry land; but when the Egyptians tried to do so, they were   E
drowned.   C
    By faith the walls of Jericho fell, after the people had marched around   O
them for seven days.   N
    By faith the prostitute Rahab, because she welcomed the spies, was not   D
killed with those who were disobedient.
    And what more shall I say? I do not have time to tell about Gideon,   R
Barak, Samson, Jephthah, David, Samuel and the prophets, who through   E
faith conquered kingdoms, administered justice, and gained what was   A
promised; who shut the mouths of lions, quenched the fury of the flames,   D
and escaped the edge of the sword; whose weakness was turned to   I
strength; and who became powerful in battle and routed foreign armies.   N
Women received back their dead, raised to life again. Others were tortured   G
and refused to be released, so that they might gain a better resurrection.
Some faced jeers and flogging, while still others were chained and put in
prison. They were stoned; they were sawn in two; they were put to death by
the sword. They went about in sheepskins and goatskins, destitute, persecuted and ill-treated – the world was not worthy of them. They wandered in
deserts and mountains, and in caves and holes in the ground.

These were all commended for their faith, yet none of them received what had been promised. God had planned something better for us so that only together with us would they be made perfect.

Therefore, since we are surrounded by such a great cloud of witnesses, let us throw off everything that hinders and the sin that so easily entangles, and let us run with perseverance the race marked out for us. Let us fix our eyes on Jesus, the author and perfecter of our faith, who for the joy set before him endured the cross, scorning its shame, and sat down at the right hand of the throne of God.

Luke 12:49–56   Jesus said to his disciples: "I have come to bring fire on the earth, and how I wish it were already kindled! But I have a baptism to undergo, and how distressed I am until it is completed! Do you think I came to bring peace on earth? No, I tell you, but division. From now on there will be five in one family divided against each other, three against two and two against three. They will be divided, father against son and son against father, mother against daughter and daughter against mother, mother-in-law against daughter-in-law and daughter-in-law against mother-in-law."

He said to the crowd: "When you see a cloud rising in the west, immediately you say, 'It's going to rain,' and it does. And when the south wind blows, you say, 'It's going to be hot,' and it is. Hypocrites! You know how to interpret the appearance of the earth and the sky. How is it that you don't know how to interpret this present time?"

(right margin: GOSPEL)

Proper 16

Sunday between 21 and 27 August inclusive (if after Trinity Sunday)
Choose either 'continuous' or 'related' Old Testament and Psalm readings.

CONTINUOUS

Jeremiah 1:4–10   The word of the LORD came to me, saying,

> "Before I formed you in the womb I knew you,
> before you were born I set you apart;
> I appointed you as a prophet to the nations."

"Ah, Sovereign LORD," I said, "I do not know how to speak; I am only a child."

But the LORD said to me, "Do not say, 'I am only a child.' You must go to everyone I send you to and say whatever I command you. Do not be afraid of them, for I am with you and will rescue you," declares the LORD.

Then the LORD reached out his hand and touched my mouth and said to me, "Now, I have put my words in your mouth. See, today I appoint you over nations and kingdoms to uproot and tear down, to destroy and overthrow, to build and to plant."

(right margin: FIRST READING)

and Psalm 71:1–6   In you, O LORD, I have taken refuge;
> let me never be put to shame.
> Rescue me and deliver me in your righteousness;
> turn your ear to me and save me.

(right margin: PSALM)

Be my rock of refuge,
  to which I can always go;
give the command to save me,
  for you are my rock and my fortress.
Deliver me, O my God, from the hand of the wicked,
  from the grasp of evil and cruel men.

For you have been my hope, O Sovereign LORD,
  my confidence since my youth.
From my birth I have relied on you;
  you brought me forth from my mother's womb.
  I will ever praise you.

Or **RELATED**

Isaiah 58:9b–14

"If you do away with the yoke of oppression,
  with the pointing finger and malicious talk,
and if you spend yourselves on behalf of the hungry
  and satisfy the needs of the oppressed,
then your light will rise in the darkness,
  and your night will become like the noonday.
The LORD will guide you always;
  he will satisfy your needs in a sun-scorched land
  and will strengthen your frame.
You will be like a well-watered garden,
  like a spring whose waters never fail.
Your people will rebuild the ancient ruins
  and will raise up the age-old foundations;
you will be called Repairer of Broken Walls,
  Restorer of Streets with Dwellings.

"If you keep your feet from breaking the Sabbath
  and from doing as you please on my holy day,
if you call the Sabbath a delight
  and the LORD's holy day honourable,
and if you honour it by not going your own way
  and not doing as you please or speaking idle words,
then you will find your joy in the LORD,
  and I will cause you to ride on the heights of the land
  and to feast on the inheritance of your father Jacob."
                    The mouth of the LORD has spoken.

F I R S T R E A D I N G

and **Psalm 103:1–8**

Praise the LORD, O my soul;
  all my inmost being, praise his holy name.
Praise the LORD, O my soul,
  and forget not all his benefits –
who forgives all your sins
  and heals all your diseases,

P S A L M

who redeems your life from the pit
> and crowns you with love and compassion,
who satisfies your desires with good things
> so that your youth is renewed like the eagle's.

The LORD works righteousness
> and justice for all the oppressed.

He made known his ways to Moses,
> his deeds to the people of Israel:
The LORD is compassionate and gracious,
> slow to anger, abounding in love.

Hebrews 12:18–29 You have not come to a mountain that can be touched and that is burning with fire; to darkness, gloom and storm; to a trumpet blast or to such a voice speaking words that those who heard it begged that no further word be spoken to them, because they could not bear what was commanded: "If even an animal touches the mountain, it must be stoned." The sight was so terrifying that Moses said, "I am trembling with fear."

But you have come to Mount Zion, to the heavenly Jerusalem, the city of the living God. You have come to thousands upon thousands of angels in joyful assembly, to the church of the firstborn, whose names are written in heaven. You have come to God, the judge of all men, to the spirits of right-eous men made perfect, to Jesus the mediator of a new covenant, and to the sprinkled blood that speaks a better word than the blood of Abel.

See to it that you do not refuse him who speaks. If they did not escape when they refused him who warned them on earth, how much less will we, if we turn away from him who warns us from heaven? At that time his voice shook the earth, but now he has promised, "Once more I will shake not only the earth but also the heavens." The words "once more" indicate the removing of what can be shaken – that is, created things – so that what cannot be shaken may remain.

Therefore, since we are receiving a kingdom that cannot be shaken, let us be thankful, and so worship God acceptably with reverence and awe, for our "God is a consuming fire."

Luke 13:10–17 On a Sabbath Jesus was teaching in one of the synagogues, and a woman was there who had been crippled by a spirit for eighteen years. She was bent over and could not straighten up at all. When Jesus saw her, he called her forward and said to her, "Woman, you are set free from your infirmity." Then he put his hands on her, and immediately she straightened up and praised God.

Indignant because Jesus had healed on the Sabbath, the synagogue ruler said to the people, "There are six days for work. So come and be healed on those days, not on the Sabbath."

The Lord answered him, "You hypocrites! Doesn't each of you on the Sabbath untie his ox or donkey from the stall and lead it out to give it water? Then should not this woman, a daughter of Abraham, whom Satan has kept bound for eighteen long years, be set free on the Sabbath day from what bound her?"

When he said this, all his opponents were humiliated, but the people were delighted with all the wonderful things he was doing.

Proper 17
Sunday between 28 August and 3 September inclusive (if after Trinity Sunday)
Choose either 'continuous' or 'related' Old Testament and Psalm readings.

CONTINUOUS

Jeremiah 2:4–13   Hear the word of the LORD, O house of Jacob,
    all you clans of the house of Israel.

This is what the LORD says:

"What fault did your fathers find in me,
    that they strayed so far from me?
They followed worthless idols
    and became worthless themselves.
They did not ask, 'Where is the LORD,
    who brought us up out of Egypt
and led us through the barren wilderness,
    through a land of deserts and rifts,
a land of drought and darkness,
    a land where no-one travels and no-one lives?'
I brought you into a fertile land
    to eat its fruit and rich produce.
But you came and defiled my land
    and made my inheritance detestable.
The priests did not ask,
    'Where is the LORD?'
Those who deal with the law did not know me;
    the leaders rebelled against me.
The prophets prophesied by Baal,
    following worthless idols.

"Therefore I bring charges against you again,"
                  declares the LORD.
    "And I will bring charges against your children's
        children.
Cross over to the coasts of Kittim and look,
    send to Kedar and observe closely;
    see if there has ever been anything like this:
Has a nation ever changed its gods?
    (Yet they are not gods at all.)
But my people have exchanged their Glory
    for worthless idols.
Be appalled at this, O heavens,
    and shudder with great horror,"
                   declares the LORD.

FIRST READING

"My people have committed two sins:
They have forsaken me,
   the spring of living water,
and have dug their own cisterns,
   broken cisterns that cannot hold water."

and **Psalm 81:1,**
10–16*

Sing for joy to God our strength;
   shout aloud to the God of Jacob!

I am the LORD your God,
   who brought you up out of Egypt.
   Open wide your mouth and I will fill it.

"But my people would not listen to me;
   Israel would not submit to me.
So I gave them over to their stubborn hearts
   to follow their own devices.

"If my people would but listen to me,
   if Israel would follow my ways,
how quickly would I subdue their enemies
   and turn my hand against their foes!
Those who hate the LORD would cringe before him,
   and their punishment would last for ever.
But you would be fed with the finest of wheat;
   with honey from the rock I would satisfy you."

P
S
A
L
M

Or **RELATED**

Ecclesiasticus 10:12–18

and **Proverbs**
25:6–7c

Do not exalt yourself in the king's presence,
   and do not claim a place among great men;
it is better for him to say to you, "Come up here,"
   than for him to humiliate you before a noble man.

FRIRST
READING

Psalm 112

Praise the LORD.

Blessed is the man who fears the LORD,
   who finds great delight in his commands.

His children will be mighty in the land;
   the generation of the upright will be blessed.
Wealth and riches are in his house,
   and his righteousness endures for ever.
Even in darkness light dawns for the upright,
   for the gracious and compassionate and righteous
      man.
Good will come to him who is generous and lends freely,
   who conducts his affairs with justice.
Surely he will never be shaken;
   a righteous man will be remembered for ever.

P
S
A
L
M

He will have no fear of bad news;
>   his hearts are steadfast, trusting in the LORD.
Their heart is secure, he will have no fear;
>   in the end he will look in triumph on his foes.
They have scattered abroad his gifts to the poor,
>   his righteousness endures for ever;
>   his horn will be lifted high in honour.

The wicked man will see and be vexed,
>   they will gnash their teeth and waste away;
>   the longings of the wicked will come to nothing.

Hebrews 13:1–8, 15–16 Keep on loving each other as brothers. Do not forget to entertain strangers, for by so doing some people have entertained angels without knowing it. Remember those in prison as if you were their fellow-prisoners, and those who are ill-treated as if you yourselves were suffering.

Marriage should be honoured by all, and the marriage bed kept pure, for God will judge the adulterer and all the sexually immoral. Keep your lives free from the love of money and be content with what you have, because God has said,

"Never will I leave you;
>   never will I forsake you."

So we say with confidence,

"The Lord is my helper; I will not be afraid.
>   What can man do to me?"

Remember your leaders, who spoke the word of God to you. Consider the outcome of their way of life and imitate their faith. Jesus Christ is the same yesterday and today and for ever.

Through Jesus, therefore, let us continually offer to God a sacrifice of praise – the fruit of lips that confess his name. And do not forget to do good and to share with others, for with such sacrifices God is pleased.

Luke 14:1, 7–14 One Sabbath, when Jesus went to eat in the house of a prominent Pharisee, he was being carefully watched.

When he noticed how the guests picked the places of honour at the table, Jesus told them this parable: "When someone invites you to a wedding feast, do not take the place of honour, for a person more distinguished than you may have been invited. If so, the host who invited both of you will come and say to you, 'Give this man your seat.' Then, humiliated, you will have to take the least important place. But when you are invited, take the lowest place, so that when your host comes, he will say to you, 'Friend, move up to a better place.' Then you will be honoured in the presence of all your fellow guests. For everyone who exalts himself will be humbled, and he who humbles himself will be exalted."

Then Jesus said to his host, "When you give a luncheon or dinner, do not invite your friends, brothers, relatives, or your rich neighbours; if you do, they may invite you back and so you will be repaid. But when you give a banquet, invite the poor, the crippled, the lame, the blind, and you will be blessed. Although they cannot repay you, you will be repaid at the resurrection of the righteous."

Proper 18

Sunday between 4 and 10 September inclusive (if after Trinity Sunday)
Choose either 'continuous' or 'related' Old Testament and Psalm readings.

CONTINUOUS

Jeremiah 18:1–11 This is the word that came to Jeremiah from the LORD: "Go down to the potter's house, and there I will give you my message." So I went down to the potter's house, and I saw him working at the wheel. But the pot he was shaping from the clay was marred in his hands; so the potter formed it into another pot, shaping it as seemed best to him.

Then the word of the LORD came to me: "O house of Israel, can I not do with you as this potter does?" declares the LORD. "Like clay in the hand of the potter, so are you in my hand, O house of Israel. If at any time I announce that a nation or kingdom is to be uprooted, torn down and destroyed, and if that nation I warned repents of its evil, then I will relent and not inflict on it the disaster I had planned. And if at another time I announce that a nation or kingdom is to be built up and planted, and if it does evil in my sight and does not obey me, then I will reconsider the good I had intended to do for it.

"Now therefore say to the people of Judah and those living in Jerusalem, 'This is what the LORD says: Look! I am preparing a disaster for you and devising a plan against you. So turn from your evil ways, each one of you, and reform your ways and your actions.'"

and Psalm 139: 1–6, 13–18* O LORD, you have searched me
and you know me.
You know when I sit and when I rise;
you perceive my thoughts from afar.
You discern my going out and my lying down;
you are familiar with all my ways.
Before a word is on my tongue
you know it completely, O LORD.

You hem me in – behind and before;
you have laid your hand upon me.
Such knowledge is too wonderful for me,
too lofty for me to attain.

For you created my inmost being;
you knit me together in my mother's womb.
I praise you because I am fearfully and wonderfully made;
your works are wonderful,
I know that full well.

My frame was not hidden from you
>> when I was made in the secret place.
When I was woven together in the depths of the earth,
>> your eyes saw my unformed body.
All the days ordained for me
>> were written in your book
>> before one of them came to be.

How precious to me are your thoughts, O God!
>> How vast is the sum of them!
Were I to count them,
>> they would outnumber the grains of sand.
When I awake,
>> I am still with you.

Or **RELATED**

Deuteronomy 30:15–20 Moses said: "See, I set before you today life and F
prosperity, death and destruction. For I command you today to love the I
LORD your God, to walk in his ways, and to keep his commands, decrees and R
laws; then you will live and increase, and the LORD your God will bless you S
in the land you are entering to possess. T

But if your heart turns away and you are not obedient, and if you are
drawn away to bow down to other gods and worship them, I declare to you R
this day that you will certainly be destroyed. You will not live long in the E
land you are crossing the Jordan to enter and possess. A

This day I call heaven and earth as witnesses against you that I have set D
before you life and death, blessings and curses. Now choose life, so that I
you and your children may live and that you may love the LORD your God, N
listen to his voice, and hold fast to him. For the LORD is your life, and he will G
give you many years in the land he swore to give to your fathers, Abraham,
Isaac and Jacob."

and **Psalm 1**   Blessed is the man   P
>> who does not walk in the counsel of the wicked   S
> or stand in the way of sinners   A
>> or sit in the seat of mockers.   L
But his delight is in the law of the LORD,   M
>> and on his law he meditates day and night.
He is like a tree planted by streams of water,
>> which yields its fruit in season
and whose leaf does not wither.
>> Whatever he does prospers.

Not so the wicked!
>> They are like chaff
>> that the wind blows away.
Therefore the wicked will not stand in the judgment,
>> nor sinners in the assembly of the righteous.

For the L<small>ORD</small> watches over the way of the righteous,
but the way of the wicked will perish.

Philemon 1–21   Paul, a prisoner of Christ Jesus, and Timothy our brother,

To Philemon our dear friend and fellow-worker, to Apphia our sister, to Archippus our fellow-soldier and to the church that meets in your home:

Grace to you and peace from God our Father and the Lord Jesus Christ.

I always thank my God as I remember you in my prayers, because I hear about your faith in the Lord Jesus and your love for all the saints. I pray that you may be active in sharing your faith, so that you will have a full understanding of every good thing we have in Christ. Your love has given me great joy and encouragement, because you, brother, have refreshed the hearts of the saints.

Therefore, although in Christ I could be bold and order you to do what you ought to do, yet I appeal to you on the basis of love. I then, as Paul – an old man and now also a prisoner of Christ Jesus – I appeal to you for my son Onesimus, who became my son while I was in chains. Formerly he was useless to you, but now he has become useful both to you and to me.

I am sending him – who is my very heart – back to you. I would have liked to keep him with me so that he could take your place in helping me while I am in chains for the gospel. But I did not want to do anything without your consent, so that any favour you do will be spontaneous and not forced. Perhaps the reason he was separated from you for a little while was that you might have him back for good – no longer as a slave, but better than a slave, as a dear brother. He is very dear to me but even dearer to you, both as a man and as a brother in the Lord.

So if you consider me a partner, welcome him as you would welcome me. If he has done you any wrong or owes you anything, charge it to me. I, Paul, am writing this with my own hand. I will pay it back – not to mention that you owe me your very self. I do wish, brother, that I may have some benefit from you in the L<small>ORD</small>; refresh my heart in Christ. Confident of your obedience, I write to you, knowing that you will do even more than I ask.

SECOND READING

Luke 14:25–33   Large crowds were travelling with Jesus, and turning to them he said: "If anyone comes to me and does not hate his father and mother, his wife and children, his brothers and sisters – yes, even life itself – he cannot be my disciple. And anyone who does not carry his cross and follow me cannot be my disciple.

"Suppose one of you wants to build a tower. Will he not first sit down and estimate the cost to see if he has enough money to complete it? For if he lays the foundation and is not able to finish it, everyone who sees it will ridicule him, saying, 'This fellow began to build and was not able to finish.'

"Or suppose a king is about to go to war against another king. Will he not first sit down and consider whether he is able with ten thousand men to oppose the one coming against him with twenty thousand? If he is not able, he will send a delegation while the other is still a long way off and will ask

GOSPEL

for terms of peace. In the same way, any of you who does not give up everything he has cannot be my disciple."

Proper 19

Sunday between 11 and 17 September inclusive (if after Trinity Sunday)
Choose either 'continuous' or 'related' Old Testament and Psalm readings.

CONTINUOUS

FIRST READING

Jeremiah 4:11–12, 22–28 At that time the people of Judah and Jerusalem will be told, "A scorching wind from the barren heights in the desert blows towards my people, but not to winnow or cleanse; a wind too strong for that comes from me. Now I pronounce my judgments against them.

"My people are fools;
they do not know me.
They are senseless children;
they have no understanding.
They are skilled in doing evil;
they know not how to do good."

I looked at the earth,
and it was formless and empty;
and at the heavens,
and their light was gone.
I looked at the mountains,
and they were quaking;
all the hills were swaying.
I looked, and there were no people;
every bird in the sky had flown away.
I looked, and the fruitful land was a desert;
all its towns lay in ruins
before the LORD, before his fierce anger.

This is what the LORD says:

"The whole land will be ruined,
though I will not destroy it completely.
Therefore the earth will mourn
and the heavens above grow dark,
because I have spoken and will not relent,
I have decided and will not turn back."

PSALM

and **Psalm 14** The fool says in his heart,
"There is no God."
They are corrupt, their deeds are vile;
there is no-one who does good.

The LORD looks down from heaven
on the sons of man
to see if there are any who understand,
any who seek God.

All have turned aside,
>> they have together become corrupt;
there is no-one who does good,
>> not even one.

Will evildoers never learn –
>> those who devour my people as men eat bread
>> and who do not call on the LORD?
There they are, overwhelmed with dread,
>> for God is present in the company of the righteous.
You evildoers frustrate the plans of the poor,
>> but the LORD is their refuge.

Oh, that salvation for Israel would come out of Zion!
>> When the LORD restores the fortunes of his people,
>> let Jacob rejoice and Israel be glad!

Or **RELATED**

Exodus 32:7–14 The LORD said to Moses, "Go down from the mountain, because your people, whom you brought up out of Egypt, have become corrupt. They have been quick to turn away from what I commanded them and have made themselves an idol cast in the shape of a calf. They have bowed down to it and sacrificed to it and have said, 'These are your gods, O Israel, who brought you up out of Egypt.'

"I have seen these people," the LORD said to Moses, "and they are a stiff-necked people. Now leave me alone so that my anger may burn against them and that I may destroy them. Then I will make you into a great nation."

But Moses sought the favour of the LORD his God. "O LORD," he said, "why should your anger burn against your people, whom you brought out of Egypt with great power and a mighty hand? Why should the Egyptians say, 'It was with evil intent that he brought them out, to kill them in the mountains and to wipe them off the face of the earth'? Turn from your fierce anger; relent and do not bring disaster on your people. Remember your servants Abraham, Isaac and Israel, to whom you swore by your own self: 'I will make your descendants as numerous as the stars in the sky and I will give your descendants all this land I promised them, and it will be their inheritance for ever.'" Then the LORD relented and did not bring on his people the disaster he had threatened.

FIRST READING

nd Psalm 51:1–10 Have mercy on me, O God,
>> according to your unfailing love;
according to your great compassion
>> blot out my transgressions.
Wash away all my iniquity
>> and cleanse me from my sin.

For I know my transgressions,
>> and my sin is always before me.

Against you, you only, have I sinned
   and done what is evil in your sight,
so that you are proved right when you speak
   and justified when you judge.
Surely I was sinful at birth,
   sinful from the time my mother conceived me.
Surely you desire truth in the inner parts;
   you teach me wisdom in the inmost place.

Cleanse me with hyssop, and I shall be clean;
   wash me, and I shall be whiter than snow.
Let me hear joy and gladness;
   let the bones you have crushed rejoice.
Hide your face from my sins
   and blot out all my iniquity.

Create in me a pure heart, O God,
   and renew a steadfast spirit within me.

1 Timothy 1:12–17   I thank Christ Jesus our Lord, who has given me strength, that he considered me faithful, appointing me to his service. Even though I was once a blasphemer and a persecutor and a violent man, I was shown mercy because I acted in ignorance and unbelief. The grace of our Lord was poured out on me abundantly, along with the faith and love that are in Christ Jesus.

Here is a trustworthy saying that deserves full acceptance: Christ Jesus came into the world to save sinners – of whom I am the worst. But for that very reason I was shown mercy so that in me, the worst of sinners, Christ Jesus might display his unlimited patience as an example for those who would believe on him and receive eternal life. Now to the King eternal, immortal, invisible, the only God, be honour and glory for ever and ever. Amen.

Luke 15:1–10   The tax collectors and "sinners" were all gathering round to hear Jesus. But the Pharisees and the teachers of the law muttered, "This man welcomes sinners, and eats with them."

Then Jesus told them this parable: "Suppose one of you has a hundred sheep and loses one of them. Does he not leave the ninety-nine in the open country and go after the lost sheep until he finds it? And when he finds it, he joyfully puts it on his shoulders and goes home. Then he calls his friends and neighbours together and says, 'Rejoice with me; I have found my lost sheep.' I tell you that in the same way there will be more rejoicing in heaven over one sinner who repents than over ninety-nine righteous persons who do not need to repent.

"Or suppose a woman has ten silver coins and loses one. Does she not light a lamp, sweep the house and search carefully until she finds it? And when she finds it, she calls her friends and neighbours together and says, 'Rejoice with me; I have found my lost coin.' In the same way, I tell you, there is rejoicing in the presence of the angels of God over one sinner who repents."

Proper 20

Sunday between 18 and 24 September inclusive (if after Trinity Sunday)
Choose either 'continuous' or 'related' Old Testament and Psalm readings.

CONTINUOUS

Jeremiah 8: 18 – 9:1

O my Comforter in sorrow,
    my heart is faint within me.
Listen to the cry of my people
    from a land far away:
        "Is the LORD not in Zion?
Is her King no longer there?"

"Why have they provoked me to anger
        with their images,
    with their worthless foreign idols?"

"The harvest is past,
    the summer has ended,
    and we are not saved."

Since my people are crushed, I am crushed;
    I mourn, and horror grips me.
Is there no balm in Gilead?
    Is there no physician there?
Why then is there no healing
    for the wound of my people?
Oh, that my head were a spring of water
    and my eyes a fountain of tears!
I would weep day and night
    for the slain of my people.

FIRST READING

and Psalm 79:1–9

O God, the nations have invaded your inheritance;
    they have defiled your holy temple,
    they have reduced Jerusalem to rubble.
They have given the dead bodies of your servants
    as food to the birds of the air,
    the flesh of your saints to the beasts of the earth.
They have poured out blood like water
    all around Jerusalem,
    and there is no-one to bury the dead.
We are objects of reproach to our neighbours,
    of scorn and derision to those around us.

How long, O LORD? Will you be angry for ever?
    How long will your jealousy burn like fire?
Pour out your wrath on the nations
    that do not acknowledge you,

PSALM

on the kingdoms
    that do not call on your name;
for they have devoured Jacob
    and destroyed his homeland.
Do not hold against us the sins of past generations;
    may your mercy come quickly to meet us,
        for we are in desperate need.

Help us, O God our Saviour,
    for the glory of your name;
deliver us and forgive our sins
    for your name's sake.

Or **RELATED**

Amos 8:4–7   Hear this, you who trample the needy
            and do away with the poor of the land,

    saying,

        "When will the New Moon be over
            that we may sell grain,
        and the Sabbath be ended
            that we may market wheat?" –
        skimping the measure,
            boosting the price
            and cheating with dishonest scales,
        buying the poor with silver
            and the needy for a pair of sandals,
        selling even the sweepings with the wheat.

The LORD has sworn by the Pride of Jacob: "I will never forget anything they have done."

and **Psalm 113**   Praise the LORD.

    Praise, O servants of the LORD,
        praise the name of the LORD.
    Let the name of the LORD be praised,
        both now and for evermore.
    From the rising of the sun to the place where it sets,
        the name of the LORD is to be praised.

    The LORD is exalted over all the nations,
        his glory above the heavens.
    Who is like the LORD our God,
        the One who sits enthroned on high,
    who stoops down to look
        on the heavens and the earth?

    He raises the poor from the dust
        and lifts the needy from the ash heap;

he seats them with princes,
    with the princes of their people.
He settles the barren woman in her home
    as a happy mother of children.

Praise the LORD.

1 Timothy 2:1–7 I urge that requests, prayers, intercession and thanksgiving be made for everyone – for kings and all those in authority, that we may
live peaceful and quiet lives in all godliness and holiness. This is good, and
pleases God our Saviour, who wants all men to be saved and to come to a
knowledge of the truth. For there is one God and one mediator between
God and men, the man Christ Jesus, who gave himself as a ransom for all
men – the testimony given in its proper time. And for this purpose I was
appointed a herald and an apostle – I am telling the truth, I am not lying –
and a teacher of the true faith to the Gentiles.

(margin: SECOND READING)

Luke 16:1–13 Jesus told his disciples: "There was a rich man whose manager was accused of wasting his possessions. So he called him in and asked
him, 'What is this I hear about you? Give an account of your management,
because you cannot be manager any longer.'

"The manager said to himself, 'What shall I do now? My master is taking
away my job. I'm not strong enough to dig, and I'm ashamed to beg – I know
what I'll do so that, when I lose my job here, people will welcome me into
their houses.'

"So he called in each one of his master's debtors. He asked the first,
'How much do you owe my master?'

"'Eight hundred gallons of olive oil,' he replied.

"The manager told him, 'Take your bill, sit down quickly, and make it
four hundred.'

"Then he asked the second, 'And how much do you owe?'

"'A thousand bushels of wheat,' he replied.

"He told him, 'Take your bill and make it eight hundred.'

"The master commended the dishonest manager because he had acted
shrewdly. For the people of this world are more shrewd in dealing with
their own kind than are the people of the light. I tell you, use worldly wealth
to gain friends for yourselves, so that when it is gone, you will be welcomed
into eternal dwellings.

"Whoever can be trusted with very little can also be trusted with much,
and whoever is dishonest with very little will also be dishonest with
much. So if you have not been trustworthy in handling worldly wealth,
who will trust you with true riches? And if you have not been trustworthy with someone else's property, who will give you property of your
own?

"No servant can serve to two masters. Either he will hate the one and
love the other, or he will be devoted to the one and despise the other. You
cannot serve both God and Money."

(margin: GOSPEL)

Proper 21

Sunday between 25 September and 1 October inclusive (if after Trinity Sunday)
Choose either 'continuous' or 'related' Old Testament and Psalm readings.

CONTINUOUS

Jeremiah 32:1–3a, 6–15 This is the word that came to Jeremiah from the Lord in the tenth year of Zedekiah king of Judah, which was the eighteenth year of Nebuchadnezzar. The army of the king of Babylon was then besieging Jerusalem, and Jeremiah the prophet was confined in the courtyard of the guard in the royal palace of Judah.

Now Zedekiah king of Judah had imprisoned him there.

Jeremiah said, "The word of the Lord came to me: Hanamel son of Shallum your uncle is going to come to you and say, 'Buy my field at Anathoth, because as nearest relative it is your right and duty to buy it.'

"Then, just as the Lord had said, my cousin Hanamel came to me in the courtyard of the guard and said, 'Buy my field at Anathoth in the territory of Benjamin. Since it is your right to redeem it and possess it, buy it for yourself.'

"I knew that this was the word of the Lord; so I bought the field at Anathoth from my cousin Hanamel and weighed out for him seventeen shekels of silver. I signed and sealed the deed, had it witnessed, and weighed out the silver on the scales. I took the deed of purchase – the sealed copy containing the terms and conditions, as well as the unsealed copy – and I gave this deed to Baruch son of Neriah, the son of Mahseiah, in the presence of my cousin Hanamel and of the witnesses who had signed the deed and of all the Jews sitting in the courtyard of the guard.

"In their presence I gave Baruch these instructions: 'This is what the Lord Almighty, the God of Israel, says: Take these documents, both the sealed and unsealed copies of the deed of purchase, and put them in a clay jar so that they will last a long time. For this is what the Lord Almighty, the God of Israel, says: Houses, fields and vineyards will again be bought in this land.'"

FIRST READING

and **Psalm 91:1–6, 14–16***

Whoever dwells in the shelter of the Most High
    will rest in the shadow of the Almighty.
I will say of the Lord, "He is my refuge
        and my fortress,
        my God, in whom I trust."

Surely he will save you from the fowler's snare
        and from the deadly pestilence.
He will cover you with his feathers,
        and under his wings you will find refuge;
        his faithfulness will be your shield and rampart.
You will not fear the terror of night,
        nor the arrow that flies by day,
    nor the pestilence that stalks in the darkness,
        nor the plague that destroys at midday.

PSALM

"Because he loves me," says the LORD, "I will
    rescue him;
    I will protect him, for he acknowledges my name.
He will call upon me, and I will answer him;
    I will be with him in trouble,
    I will deliver him and honour him.
With long life will I satisfy him
    and show him my salvation."

Or **RELATED**

Amos 6:1a, 4–7   Woe to you who are complacent in Zion,

and to you who feel secure on Mount Samaria.

You lie on beds inlaid with ivory
    and lounge on your couches.
You dine on choice lambs
    and fattened calves.
You strum away on your harps like David
    and improvise on musical instruments.
You drink wine by the bowlful
    and use the finest lotions,
        but you do not grieve over the ruin of Joseph.
Therefore you will be among the first to go into exile;
    your feasting and lounging will end.

and **Psalm 146**   Praise the LORD.

Praise the LORD, O my soul.
    I will praise the LORD all my life;
    I will sing praise to my God as long as I live.

Do not put your trust in princes,
    in mortal men, who cannot save.
When their spirit departs, they return to the ground;
    on that very day their plans come to nothing.

Blessed are those whose help is the God of Jacob,
    whose hope is in the LORD their God,
the Maker of heaven and earth,
    the sea, and everything in them –
    the LORD, who remains faithful for ever.
He upholds the cause of the oppressed
    and gives food to the hungry.
The LORD sets prisoners free,
    the LORD gives sight to the blind,
the LORD lifts up those who are bowed down,
    the LORD loves the righteous.
The LORD watches over the alien
    and sustains the fatherless and the widow,
        but he frustrates the ways of the wicked.

The LORD reigns for ever,
  your God, O Zion, for all generations.
Praise the LORD.

1 Timothy 6:6–19 Godliness with contentment is great gain. For we brought S
nothing into the world, and we can take nothing out of it. But if we have E
food and clothing, we will be content with that. People who want to get rich C
fall into temptation and a trap and into many foolish and harmful desires O
that plunge men into ruin and destruction. For the love of money is a root N
of all kinds of evil. Some people, eager for money, have wandered from the D
faith and pierced themselves with many griefs.

But you, man of God, flee from all this, and pursue righteousness, godli- R
ness, faith, love, endurance and gentleness. Fight the good fight of the E
faith. Take hold of the eternal life to which you were called when you made A
your good confession in the presence of many witnesses. In the sight of D
God, who gives life to everything, and of Christ Jesus, who while testifying I
before Pontius Pilate made the good confession, I charge you to keep this N
command without spot or blame until the appearing of our Lord Jesus G
Christ, which God will bring about in his own time – God, the blessed and
only Ruler, the King of kings and Lord of lords, who alone is immortal and
who lives in unapproachable light, whom no-one has seen or can see. To
him be honour and might for ever. Amen.

Command those who are rich in this present world not to be arrogant
nor to put their hope in wealth, which is so uncertain, but to put their hope
in God, who richly provides us with everything for our enjoyment. Command them to do good, to be rich in good deeds, and to be generous and
willing to share. In this way they will lay up treasure for themselves as a
firm foundation for the coming age, so that they may take hold of the life
that is truly life.

Luke 16:19–31 Jesus told his disciples: "There was a rich man who was G
dressed in purple and fine linen and lived in luxury every day. At his gate was O
laid a beggar named Lazarus, covered with sores and longing to eat what fell S
from the rich man's table. Even the dogs came and licked his sores.   P

"The time came when the beggar died and the angels carried him to E
Abraham's side. The rich man also died and was buried. In hell, where he L
was in torment, he looked up and saw Abraham far away, with Lazarus by
his side. So he called to him, 'Father Abraham, have pity on me and send
Lazarus to dip the tip of his finger in water and cool my tongue, because I
am in agony in this fire.'

"But Abraham replied, 'Son, remember that in your lifetime you
received your good things, while Lazarus received bad things, but now he
is comforted here and you are in agony. And besides all this, between us
and you a great chasm has been fixed, so that those who want to go from
here to you cannot, nor can anyone cross over from there to us.'

"He answered, 'Then I beg you, father, send Lazarus to my father's house, for I have five brothers. Let him warn them, so that they will not also come to this place of torment.'

"Abraham replied, 'They have Moses and the Prophets; let them listen to them.'

"'No, father Abraham,' he said, 'but if someone from the dead goes to them, they will repent.'

"He said to him, 'If they do not listen to Moses and the Prophets, they will not be convinced even if someone rises from the dead.'"

Proper 22

Sunday between 2 and 8 October inclusive (if after Trinity Sunday)
Choose either 'continuous' or 'related' Old Testament and Psalm readings.

CONTINUOUS

Lamentations 1:1–6

How deserted lies the city,
  once so full of people!

How like a widow is she,
  who once was great among the nations!
She who was queen among the provinces
  has now become a slave.

Bitterly she weeps at night,
  tears are upon her cheeks.
Among all her lovers
  there is none to comfort her.
All her friends have betrayed her;
  they have become her enemies.

After affliction and harsh labour,
  Judah has gone into exile.
She dwells among the nations;
  she finds no resting place.
All who pursue her have overtaken her
  in the midst of her distress.

The roads to Zion mourn,
  for no-one comes to her appointed feasts.
All her gateways are desolate,
  her priests groan,
her young women grieve,
  and she is in bitter anguish.

Her foes have become her masters;
  her enemies are at ease.
The LORD has brought her grief
  because of her many sins.
Her children have gone into exile,
  captive before the foe.

All the splendour has departed
  from the Daughter of Zion.

FIRST READING

Her princes are like deer
    that find no pasture;
in weakness they have fled
    before the pursuer.

and Canticle:

Lamentations 3:19–26

I remember my affliction and my wandering,
    the bitterness and the gall.
I well remember them,
    and my soul is downcast within me.
Yet this I call to mind
    and therefore I have hope:

Because of the LORD's great love we are
      not consumed,
    for his compassions never fail.
They are new every morning;
    great is your faithfulness.
I say to myself, "The LORD is my portion;
    therefore I will wait for him."

The LORD is good to those whose hope is in him,
    to the one who seeks him;
it is good to wait quietly for the salvation of the LORD.

C A N T I C L E

or **Psalm 137***

By the rivers of Babylon we sat and wept
    when we remembered Zion.
There on the poplars
    we hung our harps,
for there our captors asked us for songs,
      our tormentors demanded songs of joy;
      they said, "Sing us one of the songs of Zion!"

How can we sing the songs of the LORD
    while in a foreign land?
If I forget you, O Jerusalem,
    may my right hand forget its skill.
May my tongue cling to the roof of my mouth
    if I do not remember you,
if I do not consider Jerusalem
    my highest joy.

Remember, O LORD, what the Edomites did
    on the day Jerusalem fell.
"Tear it down," they cried,
    "tear it down to its foundations!"

O Daughter of Babylon, doomed to destruction,
    happy are those who repay you
    for what you have done to us –

P S A L M

> those who seize your infants
>> and dash them against the rocks.

Or **RELATED**

Habakkuk 1:1–4; The oracle that Habakkuk the prophet received.

2:1–4 How long, O LORD, must I call for help,
>> but you do not listen?
> Or cry out to you, "Violence!"
>> but you do not save?
> Why do you make me look at injustice?
>> Why do you tolerate wrong?
> Destruction and violence are before me;
>> there is strife, and conflict abounds.
> Therefore the law is paralysed,
>> and justice never prevails.
> The wicked hem in the righteous,
>> so that justice is perverted.

> I will stand at my watch
>> and station myself on the ramparts;
> I will look to see what he will say to me,
>> and what answer I am to give to this complaint.

Then the LORD replied:

> "Write down the revelation
>> and make it plain on tablets
>> so that a herald may run with it.
> For the revelation awaits an appointed time;
>> it speaks of the end
>> and will not prove false.
> Though it linger, wait for it;
>> it will certainly come and will not delay.
> "See, he is puffed up;
>> his desires are not upright –
>> but the righteous will live by their faith."

and **Psalm 37:1–9** Do not fret because of evil men
>> or be envious of those who do wrong;
> for like the grass they will soon wither,
>> like green plants they will soon die away.

> Trust in the LORD and do good;
>> dwell in the land and enjoy safe pasture.
> Delight yourself in the LORD
>> and he will give you the desires of your heart.

> Commit your way to the LORD;
>> trust in him and he will do this:

> He will make your righteousness shine like the dawn,
>> the justice of your cause like the noonday sun.

> Be still before the LORD and wait
>> patiently for him;
> do not fret when men succeed in their ways,
>> when they carry out their wicked schemes.

> Refrain from anger and turn from wrath;
>> do not fret – it leads only to evil.
> For those who are evil will be cut off,
>> but those who hope in the LORD will inherit the land.

2 Timothy 1:1–14   Paul, an apostle of Christ Jesus by the will of God, according to the promise of life that is in Christ Jesus,

To Timothy, my dear son:

Grace, mercy and peace from God the Father and Christ Jesus our Lord.

I thank God, whom I serve, as my forefathers did, with a clear conscience, as night and day I constantly remember you in my prayers. Recalling your tears, I long to see you, so that I may be filled with joy. I have been reminded of your sincere faith, which first lived in your grandmother Lois and in your mother Eunice and, I am persuaded, now lives in you also. For this reason I remind you to fan into flame the gift of God, which is in you through the laying on of my hands. For God did not give us a spirit of timidity, but a spirit of power, of love and of self-discipline.

So do not be ashamed to testify about our Lord, or ashamed of me his prisoner. But join with me in suffering for the gospel, by the power of God, who has saved us and called us to a holy life – not because of anything we have done but because of his own purpose and grace. This grace was given us in Christ Jesus before the beginning of time, but it has now been revealed through the appearing of our Saviour, Christ Jesus, who has destroyed death and has brought life and immortality to light through the gospel. And of this gospel I was appointed a herald and an apostle and a teacher. That is why I am suffering as I am. Yet I am not ashamed, because I know whom I have believed, and am convinced that he is able to guard what I have entrusted to him for that day.

What you heard from me, keep as the pattern of sound teaching, with faith and love in Christ Jesus. Guard the good deposit that was entrusted to you – guard it with the help of the Holy Spirit who lives in us.

Luke 17:5–10   The apostles said to the Lord, "Increase our faith!"

He replied, "If you have faith as small as a mustard seed, you can say to this mulberry tree, 'Be uprooted and planted in the sea,' and it will obey you.

"Suppose one of you had a servant ploughing or looking after the sheep. Would he say to the servant when he comes in from the field, 'Come along now and sit down to eat'? Would he not rather say, 'Prepare my supper, get yourself ready and wait on me while I eat and drink; after that you may eat and drink'? Would he thank the servant because he did what he was told to do? So you also, when you have done everything you were told to do, should say, 'We are unworthy servants; we have only done our duty.'"

Proper 23

Sunday between 9 and 15 October inclusive (if after Trinity Sunday)
Choose either 'continuous' or 'related' Old Testament and Psalm readings.

CONTINUOUS

Jeremiah 29:1, 4–7 This is the text of the letter that the prophet Jeremiah sent from Jerusalem to the surviving elders among the exiles and to the priests, the prophets and all the other people Nebuchadnezzar had carried into exile from Jerusalem to Babylon:

This is what the LORD Almighty, the God of Israel, says to all those I carried into exile from Jerusalem to Babylon: "Build houses and settle down; plant gardens and eat what they produce. Marry and have sons and daughters; find wives for your sons and give your daughters in marriage, so that they too may have sons and daughters. Increase in number there; do not decrease. Also, seek the peace and prosperity of the city to which I have carried you into exile. Pray to the LORD for it, because if it prospers, you too will prosper."

and **Psalm 66:1–12** Shout with joy to God, all the earth!
> Sing the glory of his name;
> make his praise glorious!
Say to God, "How awesome are your deeds!
> So great is your power
> that your enemies cringe before you.
All the earth bows down to you;
> they sing praise to you,
> they sing praise to your name."

Come and see what God has done,
> how awesome his works on man's behalf!
He turned the sea into dry land,
> they passed through the waters on foot –
> come, let us rejoice in him.
He rules for ever by his power,
> his eyes watch the nations –
> let not the rebellious rise up against him.

Praise our God, O peoples,
> let the sound of his praise be heard;
he has preserved our lives
> and kept our feet from slipping.
For you, O God, tested us;
> you refined us like silver.
You brought us into prison
> and laid burdens on our backs.

You let men ride over our heads;
we went through fire and water,
but you brought us to a place of abundance.

Or **RELATED**

2 Kings 5:1–3, 7–15c Naaman was commander of the army of the king of F
Aram. He was a great man in the sight of his master and highly regarded, I
because through him the Lord had given victory to Aram. He was a valiant R
soldier, but he had leprosy.   S

Now bands from Aram had gone out and had taken captive a young girl T
from Israel, and she served Naaman's wife. She said to her mistress, "If
only my master would see the prophet who is in Samaria! He would cure R
him of his leprosy." So the king of Aram sent a letter to the king of Israel: E
"With this letter I am sending my servant Naaman to you so that you may A
cure him of his leprosy."   D

As soon as the king of Israel read the letter, he tore his robes and said, I
"Am I God? Can I kill and bring back to life? Why does this fellow send N
someone to me to be cured of his leprosy? See how he is trying to pick a G
quarrel with me!"

When Elisha the man of God heard that the king of Israel had torn his
robes, he sent him this message: "Why have you torn your robes? Make the
man come to me and he will know that there is a prophet in Israel." So
Naaman went with his horses and chariots and stopped at the door of
Elisha's house. Elisha sent a messenger to say to him, "Go, wash yourself
seven times in the Jordan, and your flesh will be restored and you will be
cleansed."

But Naaman went away angry and said, "I thought that he would surely
come out to me and stand and call on the name of the Lord his God, wave
his hand over the spot and cure me of my leprosy. Are not Abana and
Pharpar, the rivers of Damascus, better than any of the waters of Israel?
Couldn't I wash in them and be cleansed?" So he turned and went off in a
rage.

Naaman's servants went to him and said, "My father, if the prophet had
told you to do some great thing, would you not have done it? How much
more, then, when he tells you, 'Wash and be cleansed'?" So he went down
and dipped himself in the Jordan seven times, as the man of God had told
him, and his flesh was restored and became clean like that of a young boy.

Then Naaman and all his attendants went back to the man of God. He
stood before him and said, "Now I know that there is no God in all the world
except in Israel."

and **Psalm 111** Praise the Lord.   P

I will extol the Lord with all my heart   S
in the council of the upright and in the assembly.   A

Great are the works of the Lord;   L
they are pondered by all who delight in them.   M

Glorious and majestic are his deeds,
and his righteousness endures for ever.

He has caused his wonders to be remembered;
the LORD is gracious and compassionate.
He provides food for those who fear him;
he remembers his covenant for ever.
He has shown his people the power of his works,
giving them the lands of other nations.
The works of his hands are faithful and just;
all his precepts are trustworthy.
They are steadfast for ever and ever,
done in faithfulness and uprightness.
He provided redemption for his people;
he ordained his covenant for ever –
holy and awesome is his name.

The fear of the LORD is the beginning of wisdom;
all who follow his precepts have good understanding.
To him belongs eternal praise.

2 Timothy 2:8–15   Remember Jesus Christ, raised from the dead, descended S
from David. This is my gospel, for which I am suffering even to the point E
of being chained like a criminal. But God's word is not chained. Therefore C
I endure everything for the sake of the elect, that they too may obtain the O
salvation that is in Christ Jesus, with eternal glory.   N

Here is a trustworthy saying: D

If we died with him,
we will also live with him;   R
if we endure,   E
we will also reign with him.   A
If we disown him,   D
he will also disown us;   I
if we are faithless,   N
he will remain faithful,   G
for he cannot disown himself.

Keep reminding them of these things. Warn them before God against
quarrelling about words; it is of no value, and only ruins those who listen.
Do your best to present yourself to God as one approved, a workman
who does not need to be ashamed and who correctly handles the word of
truth.

Luke 17:11–19   On his way to Jerusalem, Jesus travelled along the border G
between Samaria and Galilee. As he was going into a village, ten men who O
had leprosy met him. They stood at a distance and called out in a loud voice, S
"Jesus, Master, have pity on us!"   P

When he saw them, he said, "Go, show yourselves to the priests." And as E
they went, they were cleansed.   L

One of them, when he saw he was healed, came back, praising God in a loud voice. He threw himself at Jesus' feet and thanked him – and he was a Samaritan.

Jesus asked, "Were not all ten cleansed? Where are the other nine? Was no-one found to return and give praise to God except this foreigner?" Then he said to him, "Rise and go; your faith has made you well."

Proper 24

Sunday between 16 and 22 October inclusive (if after Trinity Sunday)
Choose either 'continuous' or 'related' Old Testament and Psalm readings.

CONTINUOUS

Jeremiah 31:27–34   "The days are coming," declares the LORD, "when I will plant the house of Israel and the house of Judah with the offspring of men and of animals. Just as I watched over them to uproot and tear down, and to overthrow, destroy and bring disaster, so I will watch over them to build and to plant," declares the LORD. "In those days people will no longer say,

> 'The fathers have eaten sour grapes,
>   and the children's teeth are set on edge.'

Instead, everyone will die for his own sin; whoever eats sour grapes – his own teeth will be set on edge.

> "The time is coming," declares the LORD,
>   "when I will make a new covenant
> with the house of Israel
>   and with the house of Judah.
> It will not be like the covenant
>   I made with their forefathers
> when I took them by the hand
>   to lead them out of Egypt,
> because they broke my covenant,
>   though I was a husband to them,"
>   declares the LORD.
> "This is the covenant that I will make with the house of Israel
>   after that time," declares the LORD.
> "I will put my law in their minds
>   and write it on their hearts.
> I will be their God,
>   and they will be my people.
> No longer will a man teach his neighbour,
>   or a man his brother, saying, 'Know the LORD,'
> because they will all know me,
>   from the least of them to the greatest,"
>   declares the LORD.
> "For I will forgive their wickedness
>   and will remember their sins no more."

FIRST READING

and **Psalm 119:97–104**   Oh, how I love your law!   P
I meditate on it all day long.   S
Your commands make me wiser than my enemies,   A
for they are ever with me.   L
I have more insight than all my teachers,   M
for I meditate on your statutes.
I have more understanding than the elders,
for I obey your precepts.
I have kept my feet from every evil path
so that I might obey your word.
I have not departed from your laws,
for you yourself have taught me.
How sweet are your words to my taste,
sweeter than honey to my mouth!
I gain understanding from your precepts;
therefore I hate every wrong path.

Or **RELATED**

Genesis 32:22–31   At night Jacob got up and took his two wives, his two maid-   F
servants and his eleven sons and crossed the ford of the Jabbok. After he   I
had sent them across the stream, he sent over all his possessions. So Jacob   R
was left alone, and a man wrestled with him till daybreak. When the man   S
saw that he could not overpower him, he touched the socket of Jacob's hip   T
so that his hip was wrenched as he wrestled with the man. Then the man
said, "Let me go, for it is daybreak."   R

But Jacob replied, "I will not let you go unless you bless me."   E
The man asked him, "What is your name?"   A
"Jacob," he answered.   D

Then the man said, "Your name will no longer be Jacob, but Israel, be-   I
cause you have struggled with both God and with men and have overcome."   N
Jacob said, "Please tell me your name."   G
But he replied, "Why do you ask my name?" Then he blessed him there.
So Jacob called the place Peniel, saying, "It is because I saw God face to
face, and yet my life was spared."
The sun rose above him as he passed Peniel, and he was limping because
of his hip.

and **Psalm 121**   I lift up my eyes to the hills –   P
where does my help come from?   S
My help comes from the LORD,   A
the Maker of heaven and earth.   L

He will not let your foot slip –   M
he who watches over you will not slumber;
indeed, he who watches over Israel
will neither slumber nor sleep.

The LORD watches over you –
the LORD is your shade at your right hand;

the sun will not harm you by day,
　　nor the moon by night.

The Lord will keep you from all harm –
　　he will watch over your life;
the Lord will watch over your coming and going
　　both now and for evermore.

2 Timothy 3:14 – 4:5　Continue in what you have learned and have become SECOND READING convinced of, because you know those from whom you learned it, and how from infancy you have known the holy Scriptures, which are able to make you wise for salvation through faith in Christ Jesus. All Scripture is God-breathed and is useful for teaching, rebuking, correcting and training in righteousness, so that the man of God may be thoroughly equipped for every good work.

In the presence of God and of Christ Jesus, who will judge the living and the dead, and in view of his appearing and his kingdom, I give you this charge: Preach the Word; be prepared in season and out of season; correct, rebuke and encourage – with great patience and careful instruction. For the time will come when men will not put up with sound doctrine. Instead, to suit their own desires, they will gather around them a great number of teachers to say what their itching ears want to hear. They will turn their ears away from the truth and turn aside to myths. But you, keep your head in all situations, endure hardship, do the work of an evangelist, discharge all the duties of your ministry.

Luke 18:1–8　Jesus told his disciples a parable to show them that they should GOSPEL always pray and not give up. He said: "In a certain town there was a judge who neither feared God nor cared about men. And there was a widow in that town who kept coming to him with the plea, 'Grant me justice against my adversary.'

"For some time he refused. But finally he said to himself, 'Even though I don't fear God or care about men, yet because this widow keeps bothering me, I will see that she gets justice, so that she won't eventually wear me out with her coming!'"

And the Lord said, "Listen to what the unjust judge says. And will not God bring about justice for his chosen ones, who cry out to him day and night? Will he keep putting them off? I tell you, he will see that they get justice, and quickly. However, when the Son of Man comes, will he find faith on the earth?"

Proper 25　FIRST READING

Sunday between 23 and 29 October inclusive (if after Trinity Sunday)
Choose either 'continuous' or 'related' Old Testament and Psalm readings.

CONTINUOUS

Joel 2:23–32　Be glad, O people of Zion,
　　　　　　　rejoice in the Lord your God,

for he has given you
    the autumn rains in righteousness.
He sends you abundant showers,
    both autumn and spring rains, as before.
The threshing-floors will be filled with grain;
    the vats will overflow with new wine and oil.

"I will repay you for the years the locusts have eaten –
    the great locust and the young locust,
    the other locusts and the locust swarm –
my great army that I sent among you.
You will have plenty to eat, until you are full,
    and you will praise the name of the LORD your God,
    who has worked wonders for you;
never again will my people be shamed.
Then you will know that I am in Israel,
    that I am the LORD your God,
    and that there is no other;
never again will my people be shamed.

"And afterwards,
    I will pour out my Spirit on all people.
Your sons and daughters will prophesy,
    your old men will dream dreams,
    your young men will see visions.
Even on my servants, both men and women,
    I will pour out my Spirit in those days.
I will show wonders in the heavens
    and on the earth,
    blood and fire and billows of smoke.
The sun will be turned to darkness
    and the moon to blood
    before the coming of the great and dreadful day of the
        LORD.
And everyone who calls
    on the name of the LORD will be saved;
for on Mount Zion and in Jerusalem
    there will be deliverance,
    as the LORD has said,
among the survivors
    whom the LORD calls."

nd **Psalm 65***   Praise awaits you, O God, in Zion;
    to you our vows will be fulfilled.
O you who hear prayer,
    to you all people will come.
When we were overwhelmed by sins,
    you forgave our transgressions.

P
S
A
L
M

Blessed are those you choose
  and bring near to live in your courts!
We are filled with the good things of your house,
  of your holy temple.

You answer us with awesome deeds of
      righteousness,
  O God our Saviour,
the hope of all the ends of the earth
  and of the farthest seas,
who formed the mountains by your power,
  having armed yourself with strength,
who stilled the roaring of the seas,
    the roaring of their waves,
    and the turmoil of the nations.
Those living far away fear your wonders;
    where morning dawns and evening fades
    you call forth songs of joy.

You care for the land and water it;
  you enrich it abundantly.
The streams of God are filled with water
    to provide the people with corn,
    for so you have ordained it.
You drench its furrows
    and level its ridges;
you soften it with showers
    and bless its crops.
You crown the year with your bounty,
    and your carts overflow with abundance.
The grasslands of the desert overflow;
    the hills are clothed with gladness.
The meadows are covered with flocks
    and the valleys are mantled with corn;
    they shout for joy and sing.

Or **RELATED**

Ecclesiasticus 35:12–17

or **Jeremiah 14:7–10,**   Although our sins testify against us,   F I
19–22   O LORD, do something for the sake of your name.   I I
    For our backsliding is great;   R A
     we have sinned against you.   S I
    O Hope of Israel,   T I
     its Saviour in times of distress,   I
    why are you like a stranger in the land,   C
     like a traveller who stays only a night?
    Why are you like a man taken by surprise,
     like a warrior powerless to save?

You are among us, O LORD,
    and we bear your name;
    do not forsake us!

This is what the LORD says about this people:

"They greatly love to wander;
    they do not restrain their feet.
So the LORD does not accept them;
    he will now remember their wickedness
    and punish them for their sins."

Have you rejected Judah completely?
    Do you despise Zion?
Why have you afflicted us
    so that we cannot be healed?
We hoped for peace
    but no good has come,
for a time of healing
    but there is only terror.
O LORD, we acknowledge our wickedness
    and the guilt of our ancestors;
    we have indeed sinned against you.
For the sake of your name do not despise us;
    do not dishonour your glorious throne.
Remember your covenant with us
    and do not break it.
Do any of the worthless idols of the nations bring rain?
    Do the skies themselves send down showers?
No, it is you, O LORD our God.
    Therefore our hope is in you,
    for you are the one who does all this.

nd **Psalm 84:1–7**

How lovely is your dwelling-place,
    O LORD Almighty!
My soul yearns, even faints,
    for the courts of the LORD;
my heart and my flesh cry out
    for the living God.

Even the sparrow has found a home,
    and the swallow a nest for herself,
    where she may have her young –
a place near your altar,
    O LORD Almighty, my King and my God.
Blessed are those who dwell in your house;
    they are ever praising you.

Blessed are those whose strength is in you,
    who have set their hearts on pilgrimage.

P
S
A
L
M

As they pass through the Valley of Baca,
    they make it a place of springs;
        the autumn rains also cover it with pools.
They go from strength to strength,
    till each appears before God in Zion.

2 Timothy 4:6–8, 16–18   I am already being poured out like a drink offering, and the time has come for my departure. I have fought the good fight, I have finished the race, I have kept the faith. Now there is in store for me the crown of righteousness, which the Lord, the righteous Judge, will award to me on that day – and not only to me, but also to all who have longed for his appearing.

At my first defence, no-one came to my support, but everyone deserted me. May it not be held against them. But the Lord stood at my side and gave me strength, so that through me the message might be fully proclaimed and all the Gentiles might hear it. And I was delivered from the lion's mouth. The Lord will rescue me from every evil attack and will bring me safely to his heavenly kingdom. To him be glory for ever and ever. Amen.

(margin: SECOND READING)

Luke 18:9–14   To some who were confident of their own righteousness and looked down on everybody else, Jesus told this parable: "Two men went up to the temple to pray, one a Pharisee and the other a tax collector. The Pharisee stood up and prayed about himself: 'God, I thank you that I am not like other men – robbers, evildoers, adulterers – or even like this tax collector. I fast twice a week and give a tenth of all I get.'

"But the tax collector stood at a distance. He would not even look up to heaven, but beat his breast and said, 'God, have mercy on me, a sinner.'

"I tell you that this man, rather than the other, went home justified before God. For everyone who exalts himself will be humbled, and he who humbles himself will be exalted."

(margin: GOSPEL)

Bible Sunday

Bible Sunday may be celebrated in preference to the provision for the Last Sunday after Trinity.

Isaiah 45:22–25   This is what the LORD says:

"Turn to me and be saved,
    all you ends of the earth;
    for I am God, and there is no other.
By myself I have sworn,
    my mouth has uttered in all integrity
    a word that will not be revoked:
Before me every knee will bow;
    by me every tongue will swear.
They will say of me, 'In the LORD alone
    are righteousness and strength.'"
All who have raged against him
    will come to him and be put to shame.

(margin: FIRST READING)

But in the LORD all the descendants of Israel
will be found righteous and will exult.

Psalm 119:129–136   Your statutes are wonderful;   P
therefore I obey them.   S
The unfolding of your words gives light;   A
it gives understanding to the simple.   L
I open my mouth and pant,   M
longing for your commands.
Turn to me and have mercy on me,
as you always do to those who love your name.
Direct my footsteps according to your word;
let no sin rule over me.
Redeem me from the oppression of men,
that I may obey your precepts.
Make your face shine upon your servant
and teach me your decrees.
Streams of tears flow from my eyes,
for your law is not obeyed.

Romans 15:1–6   We who are strong ought to bear with the failings of the   S R
weak and not to please ourselves. Each of us, please his neighbour for   E E
his good, to build him up. For even Christ did not please himself but, as   C A
it is written: "The insults of those who insult you have fallen on me." For   O D
everything that was written in the past was written to teach us, so that   N I
through endurance and the encouragement of the Scriptures we might   D N
have hope.   G

May the God who gives endurance and encouragement give you a spirit
of unity among yourselves as you follow Christ Jesus, so that with one
heart and mouth you may glorify the God and Father of our Lord Jesus
Christ.

Luke 4:16–24   Jesus went to Nazareth, where he had been brought up, and on   G
the Sabbath day he went into the synagogue, as was his custom. And he   O
stood up to read. The scroll of the prophet Isaiah was handed to him.   S
Unrolling it, he found the place where it is written: P

"The Spirit of the Lord is on me,   E
because he has anointed me   L
to preach good news to the poor.
He has sent me to proclaim freedom for the prisoners
and recovery of sight for the blind,
to release the oppressed,
to proclaim the year of the Lord's favour."

Then he rolled up the scroll, gave it back to the attendant and sat down.
The eyes of everyone in the synagogue were fastened on him, and he began
by saying to them, "Today this scripture is fulfilled in your hearing."

All spoke well of him and were amazed at the gracious words that came from his lips. "Isn't this Joseph's son?" they asked.

Jesus said to them, "Surely you will quote this proverb to me: 'Physician, heal yourself! Do here in your home town what we have heard that you did in Capernaum.'"

"I tell you the truth," he continued, "no prophet is accepted in his home town."

Dedication Festival

The First Sunday in October or Last Sunday after Trinity

1 Chronicles 29:6–19   The leaders of families, the officers of the tribes of Israel, the commanders of thousands and commanders of hundreds, and the officials in charge of the king's work gave willingly. They gave towards the work on the temple of God five thousand talents and ten thousand darics of gold, ten thousand talents of silver, eighteen thousand talents of bronze and a hundred thousand talents of iron. Any who had precious stones gave them to the treasury of the temple of the LORD in the custody of Jehiel the Gershonite. The people rejoiced at the willing response of their leaders, for they had given freely and wholeheartedly to the LORD. David the king also rejoiced greatly.

David praised the LORD in the presence of the whole assembly, saying,

"Praise be to you, O LORD,
 God of our father Israel,
 from everlasting to everlasting.
Yours, O LORD, is the greatness and the power
 and the glory and the majesty and the splendour,
 for everything in heaven and earth is yours.
Yours, O LORD, is the kingdom;
 you are exalted as head over all.
Wealth and honour come from you;
 you are the ruler of all things.
In your hands are strength and power
 to exalt and give strength to all.
Now, our God, we give you thanks,
 and praise your glorious name.

"But who am I, and who are my people, that we should be able to give as generously as this? Everything comes from you, and we have given you only what comes from your hand. We are aliens and strangers in your sight, as were all our forefathers. Our days on earth are like a shadow, without hope. O LORD our God, as for all this abundance that we have provided for building you a temple for your Holy Name, it comes from your hand, and all of it belongs to you. I know, my God, that you test the heart and are pleased with integrity. All these things have I given willingly and with honest intent. And now I have seen with joy how willingly your people who are here have given to you. O LORD, God of our fathers Abraham, Isaac and Israel, keep this desire in the hearts of your people for ever, and keep their hearts loyal to you. And give my son Solomon the wholehearted devotion to keep your commands, requirements and decrees and to do everything to build the palatial structure for which I have provided."

Psalm 122
I rejoiced with those who said to me,
    "Let us go to the house of the Lord."
Our feet are standing
    in your gates, O Jerusalem.

Jerusalem is built like a city
    that is closely compacted together.
That is where the tribes go up,
    the tribes of the Lord,
to praise the name of the Lord
    according to the statute given to Israel.
There the thrones for judgment stand,
    the thrones of the house of David.

Pray for the peace of Jerusalem:
    "May those who love you be secure.
May there be peace within your walls
    and security within your citadels."
For the sake of my relatives and friends,
    I will say, "Peace be within you."
For the sake of the house of the Lord our God,
    I will seek your prosperity.

Ephesians 2:19–22   You are no longer foreigners and aliens, but fellow-citizens with God's people and members of God's household, built on the foundation of the apostles and prophets, with Christ Jesus himself as the chief cornerstone. In him the whole building is joined together and rises to become a holy temple in the Lord. And in him you too are being built together to become a dwelling in which God lives by his Spirit.

John 2:13–22   When it was almost time for the Jewish Passover, Jesus went up to Jerusalem. In the temple courts he found people selling cattle, sheep and doves, and others sitting at tables exchanging money. So he made a whip out of cords, and drove all from the temple area, both sheep and cattle; he scattered the coins of the money–changers and overturned their tables. To those who sold doves he said, "Get these out of here! How dare you turn my Father's house into a market!"

His disciples remembered that it is written: "Zeal for your house will consume me."

Then the Jews demanded of him, "What miraculous sign can you show us to prove your authority to do all this?"

Jesus answered them, "Destroy this temple, and I will raise it again in three days."

The Jews replied, "It has taken forty-six years to build this temple, and you are going to raise it in three days?" But the temple he had spoken of was his body. After he was raised from the dead, his disciples recalled what he had said. Then they believed the Scripture and the words that Jesus had spoken.

All Saints' Day

Sunday between 30 October and 5 November or, if this is not kept as All Saint's Sunday, on 1 November itself

Daniel 7:1–3, 15–18 In the first year of Belshazzar king of Babylon, Daniel had a dream, and visions passed through his mind as he was lying on his bed. He wrote down the substance of his dream.

Daniel said: "In my vision at night I looked, and there before me were the four winds of heaven churning up the great sea. Four great beasts, each different from the others, came up out of the sea.

"I, Daniel, was troubled in spirit, and the visions that passed through my mind disturbed me. I approached one of those standing there and asked him the true meaning of all this.

"So he told me and gave me the interpretation of these things: 'The four great beasts are four kingdoms that will rise from the earth. But the saints of the Most High will receive the kingdom and will possess it for ever – yes, for ever and ever.'"

Psalm 149 Praise the Lord.

> Sing to the Lord a new song,
>> his praise in the assembly of the saints.

> Let Israel rejoice in their Maker;
>> let the people of Zion be glad in their King.
> Let them praise his name with dancing
>> and make music to him with tambourine and harp.
> For the Lord takes delight in his people;
>> he crowns the humble with salvation.
> Let the saints rejoice in this honour
>> and sing for joy on their beds.

> May the praise of God be in their mouths
>> and a double-edged sword in their hands,
> to inflict vengeance on the nations
>> and punishment on the peoples,
> to bind their kings with fetters,
>> their nobles with shackles of iron,
> to carry out the sentence written against them.
>> This is the glory of all his saints.

> Praise the Lord.

Ephesians 1:11–23 In Christ we were chosen, having been predestined according to the plan of him who works out everything in conformity with the purpose of his will, in order that we, who were the first to hope in Christ, might be for the praise of his glory. And you also were included in Christ when you heard the word of truth, the gospel of your salvation. Having believed, you were marked in him with a seal, the promised Holy Spirit, who is a deposit guaranteeing our inheritance until the redemption of those who are God's possession – to the praise of his glory.

For this reason, ever since I heard about your faith in the Lord Jesus and your love for all the saints, I have not stopped giving thanks for you, remembering you in my prayers. I keep asking that the God of our Lord Jesus Christ, the glorious Father, may give you the Spirit of wisdom and revelation, so that you may know him better. I pray also that the eyes of your heart may be enlightened in order that you may know the hope to which he has called you, the riches of his glorious inheritance in the saints, and his incomparably great power for us who believe. That power is like the working of his mighty strength, which he exerted in Christ when he raised him from the dead and seated him at his right hand in the heavenly realms, far above all rule and authority, power and dominion, and every title that can be given, not only in the present age but also in the one to come. And God placed all things under his feet and appointed him to be head over everything for the church, which is his body, the fulness of him who fills everything in every way.

Luke 6:20–31 Looking at his disciples, Jesus said:

"Blessed are you who are poor,
  for yours is the kingdom of God.
Blessed are you who hunger now,
  for you will be satisfied.
Blessed are you who weep now,
  for you will laugh.
Blessed are you when men hate you,
  when they exclude you and insult you
  and reject your name as evil,
  because of the Son of Man.

"Rejoice in that day and leap for joy, because great is your reward in heaven. For that is how their fathers treated the prophets.

"But woe to you who are rich,
  for you have already received your comfort.
Woe to you who are well fed now,
  for you will go hungry.
Woe to you who laugh now,
  for you will mourn and weep.
Woe to you when all men speak well of you,
  for that is how their fathers treated the false prophets.

"But I tell you who hear me: Love your enemies, do good to those who hate you, bless those who curse you, pray for those who ill-treat you. If someone strikes you on one cheek, turn to him the other also. If someone takes your cloak, do not stop him from taking your tunic. Give to everyone who asks you, and if anyone takes what belongs to you, do not demand it back. Do to others as you would have them do to you."

On 1 November if the material for All Saint's Day is used on the Sunday, use text of readings for Years A, B, C on pp 221–223.

Fourth Sunday Before Advent

Sunday between 30 October and 5 November inclusive
For use if the Feast of All Saints was celebrated on 1 November and alternative propers are needed.

Isaiah 1:10–18

Hear the word of the LORD,
   you rulers of Sodom;
listen to the law of our God,
   you people of Gomorrah!
"The multitude of your sacrifices –
   what are they to me?" says the LORD.
"I have more than enough of burnt offerings,
   of rams and the fat of fattened animals;
I have no pleasure
   in the blood of bulls and lambs and goats.
When you come to appear before me,
   who has asked this of you,
   this trampling of my courts?
Stop bringing meaningless offerings!
   Your incense is detestable to me.
New Moons, Sabbaths and convocations –
   I cannot bear your evil assemblies.
Your New Moon festivals and your appointed feasts
   my soul hates.
They have become a burden to me;
   I am weary of bearing them.
When you spread out your hands in prayer,
   I will hide my eyes from you;
even if you offer many prayers,
   I will not listen.
Your hands are full of blood;
   wash and make yourselves clean.
Take your evil deeds
   out of my sight!
Stop doing wrong,
   learn to do right!
Seek justice,
   encourage the oppressed.
Defend the cause of the fatherless,
   plead the case of the widow.

"Come now, let us reason together,"
   says the LORD.
"Though your sins are like scarlet,
   they shall be as white as snow;
though they are red as crimson,
   they shall be like wool."

(Marginal note, vertically set: FIRST READING *)*

Psalm 32:1–7   Blessed are those

> whose transgressions are forgiven,
> whose sins are covered.

Blessed is the man

> whose sin the Lord does not count against him
> and in whose spirit is no deceit.

When I kept silent,

> my bones wasted away
> through my groaning all day long.

For day and night

> your hand was heavy upon me;

my strength was sapped

> as in the heat of summer.

Then I acknowledged my sin to you

> and did not cover up my iniquity.

I said, "I will confess

> my transgressions to the Lord" –

and you forgave

> the guilt of my sin.

Therefore let everyone who is godly pray to you

> while you may be found;

surely the rising of the mighty waters

> will not reach them.

You are my hiding-place;

> you will protect me from trouble

and surround me with songs of deliverance.

2 Thessalonians 1:1–12   Paul, Silas and Timothy,

To the church of the Thessalonians in God our Father and the Lord Jesus Christ:

Grace and peace to you from God the Father and the Lord Jesus Christ.

We ought always to thank God for you, brothers, and rightly so, because your faith is growing more and more, and the love every one of you has for each other is increasing. Therefore, among God's churches we boast about your perseverance and faith in all the persecutions and trials you are enduring.

All this is evidence that God's judgment is right, and as a result you will be counted worthy of the kingdom of God, for which you are suffering. God is just: He will pay back trouble to those who trouble you and give relief to you who are troubled, and to us as well. This will happen when the Lord Jesus is revealed from heaven in blazing fire with his powerful angels. He will punish those who do not know God and do not obey the gospel of our Lord Jesus. They will be punished with everlasting destruction and shut out from the presence of the Lord and from the majesty of his power on the day he comes to be glorified in his holy people and to be marvelled at among all those who have believed. This includes you, because you believed our testimony to you.

With this in mind, we constantly pray for you, that our God may count you worthy of his calling, and that by his power he may fulfil every good purpose of yours and every act prompted by your faith. We pray this so that the name of our Lord Jesus may be glorified in you, and you in him, according to the grace of our God and the Lord Jesus Christ.

Luke 19:1–10 Jesus entered Jericho and was passing through. A man was there by the name of Zacchaeus; he was a chief tax collector and was wealthy. He wanted to see who Jesus was, but being a short man he could not, because of the crowd. So he ran ahead and climbed a sycamore-fig tree to see him, since Jesus was coming that way.

When Jesus reached the spot, he looked up and said to him, "Zacchaeus, come down immediately. I must stay at your house today." So he came down at once and welcomed him gladly.

All the people saw this and began to mutter, "He has gone to be the guest of a 'sinner'."

But Zacchaeus stood up and said to the Lord, "Look, Lord! Here and now I give half of my possessions to the poor, and if I have cheated anybody out of anything, I will pay back four times the amount."

Jesus said to him, "Today salvation has come to this house, because this man, too, is a son of Abraham. For the Son of Man came to seek and to save what was lost."

(margin: G O S P E L)

Third Sunday Before Advent

Sunday between 6 and 12 November inclusive

Job 19:23–27a Oh, that my words were recorded,
  that they were written on a scroll,
that they were inscribed with an iron tool on lead,
  or engraved in rock for ever!
I know that my Redeemer lives,
  and that in the end he will stand upon the earth.
And after my skin has been destroyed,
  yet in my flesh I will see God;
I myself will see him
  with my own eyes.

(margin: F I R S T R E A D I N G)

Psalm 17:1–9* Hear, O LORD, my righteous plea;
  listen to my cry.
Give ear to my prayer –
  it does not rise from deceitful lips.
May my vindication come from you;
  may your eyes see what is right.

Though you probe my heart and examine me at night,
  though you test me, you will find nothing;
  I have resolved that my mouth will not sin.

(margin: P S A L M)

As for the deeds of men –
　　by the word of your lips
I have kept myself
　　from the ways of the violent.
My steps have held to your paths;
　　my feet have not slipped.

I call on you, O God, for you will answer me;
　　give ear to me and hear my prayer.
Show the wonder of your great love,
　　you who save by your right hand
　　those who take refuge in you from their foes.
Keep me as the apple of your eye;
　　hide me in the shadow of your wings
from the wicked who assail me,
　　from my mortal enemies who surround me.

2 Thessalonians 2:1–5, 13–17   Concerning the coming of our Lord Jesus s Christ and our being gathered to him, we ask you, brothers, not to become e easily unsettled or alarmed by some prophecy, report or letter supposed to c have come from us, saying that the day of the Lord has already come. Don't o let anyone deceive you in any way, for that day will not come until the n rebellion occurs and the man of lawlessness is revealed, the man doomed d to destruction. He will oppose and will exalt himself over everything that is called God or is worshipped, so that he sets himself up in God's temple, r proclaiming himself to be God.   e

Don't you remember that when I was with you I used to tell you these a things?   d

But we ought always to thank God for you, brothers loved by the Lord, i because from the beginning God chose you to be saved through the sancti- n fying work of the Spirit and through belief in the truth. He called you to g this through our gospel, that you might share in the glory of our Lord Jesus Christ. So then, brothers, stand firm and hold to the teachings we passed on to you, whether by word of mouth or by letter.

May our Lord Jesus Christ himself and God our Father, who loved us and by his grace gave us eternal encouragement and good hope, encourage your hearts and strengthen you in every good deed and word.

Luke 20:27–38   Some of the Sadducees, who say there is no resurrection, g came to Jesus with a question. "Teacher," they said, "Moses wrote for us o that if a man's brother dies and leaves a wife but no children, the man must s marry the widow and have children for his brother. Now there were seven p brothers. The first one married a woman and died childless. The second e and then the third married her, and in the same way the seven died, leaving l no children. Finally, the woman died too. Now then, at the resurrection whose wife will she be, since the seven were married to her?"

Jesus replied, "The people of this age marry and are given in marriage. But those who are considered worthy of taking part in that age and in the resurrection from the dead will neither marry nor be given in marriage, and they can no longer die; for they are like the angels. They are God's children, since they are children of the resurrection. But in the account of the bush, even Moses showed that the dead rise, for he calls the Lord 'the God of Abraham, and the God of Isaac, and the God of Jacob'. He is not the God of the dead, but of the living, for to him all are alive."

Second Sunday Before Advent

Sunday between 13 and 19 November inclusive

Malachi 4:1–2a "Surely the day is coming; it will burn like a furnace. All the arrogant and every evildoer will be stubble, and that day that is coming will set them on fire," says the Lord Almighty. "Not a root or a branch will be left to them. But for you who revere my name, the sun of righteousness will rise with healing in its wings."

Psalm 98 Sing to the Lord a new song,
for he has done marvellous things;
his right hand and his holy arm
have worked salvation for him.
The Lord has made his salvation known
and revealed his righteousness to the nations.
He has remembered his love
and his faithfulness to the house of Israel;
all the ends of the earth have seen
the salvation of our God.

Shout for joy to the Lord, all the earth,
burst into jubilant song with music;
make music to the Lord with the harp,
with the harp and the sound of singing,
with trumpets and the blast of the ram's horn –
shout for joy before the Lord, the King.

Let the sea resound, and everything in it,
the world, and all who live in it.
Let the rivers clap their hands,
let the mountains sing together for joy;
let them sing before the Lord,
for he comes to judge the earth.
He will judge the world in righteousness
and the peoples with equity.

2 Thessalonians 3:6–13 In the name of the Lord Jesus Christ, we command you, brothers, to keep away from every brother who is idle and does not live according to the teaching you received from us. For you yourselves know how you ought to follow our example. We were not idle when we were with you, nor did we eat anyone's food without paying for it. On the contrary, we worked night and day, labouring and toiling so that we would not be a burden to any of you. We did this, not because we do not have the right to such help, but in order to make ourselves a model for you to follow. For even when we were with you, we gave you this rule: "If a man will not work, he shall not eat."

We hear that some among you are idle. They are not busy; they are busybodies. Such people we command and urge in the Lord Jesus Christ to settle down and earn the bread they eat. And as for you, brothers, never tire of doing what is right.

Luke 21:5–19   Some of Jesus' disciples were remarking about how the temple was adorned with beautiful stones and with gifts dedicated to God. But Jesus said, "As for what you see here, the time will come when not one stone will be left on another; every one of them will be thrown down."

"Teacher," they asked, "when will these things happen? And what will be the sign that they are about to take place?"

He replied: "Watch out that you are not deceived. For many will come in my name, claiming, 'I am he,' and 'The time is near.' Do not follow them. When you hear of wars and revolutions, do not be frightened. These things must happen first, but the end will not come right away."

Then he said to them: "Nation will rise against nation, and kingdom against kingdom. There will be great earthquakes, famines and pestilences in various places, and fearful events and great signs from heaven.

"But before all this, they will lay hands on you and persecute you. They will deliver you to synagogues and prisons, and you will be brought before kings and governors, and all on account of my name. This will result in your being witnesses to them. But make up your mind not to worry beforehand how you will defend yourselves. For I will give you words and wisdom that none of your adversaries will be able to resist or contradict. You will be betrayed even by parents, brothers, relatives and friends, and they will put some of you to death. All men will hate you because of me. But not a hair of your head will perish. By standing firm you will gain life."

Christ the King

Sunday between 20 and 26 November inclusive

Jeremiah 23:1–6   "Woe to the shepherds who are destroying and scattering the sheep of my pasture!" declares the LORD. Therefore this is what the LORD, the God of Israel, says to the shepherds who tend my people: "Because you have scattered my flock and driven them away and have not bestowed care on them, I will bestow punishment on you for the evil you have done," declares the LORD. "I myself will gather the remnant of my flock out of all the countries where I have driven them and will bring them back to their pasture, where they will be fruitful and increase in number. I will place shepherds over them who will tend them, and they will no longer be afraid or terrified, nor will any be missing," declares the LORD.

"The days are coming," declares the Lord,
   "when I will raise up to David a righteous Branch,
a King who will reign wisely
   and do what is just and right in the land.
In his days Judah will be saved
   and Israel will live in safety.
This is the name by which he will be called:
   The Lord Our Righteousness."

Psalm 46   God is our refuge and strength,   P
   an ever–present help in trouble.   S
Therefore we will not fear, though the earth give way   A
   and the mountains fall into the heart of the sea,   L
though its waters roar and foam   M
   and the mountains quake with their surging.

There is a river whose streams make glad the city of God,
   the holy place where the Most High dwells.
God is within her, she will not fall;
   God will help her at break of day.
Nations are in uproar, kingdoms fall;
   he lifts his voice, the earth melts.

The Lord Almighty is with us;
   the God of Jacob is our fortress.

Come and see the works of the Lord,
   the desolations he has brought on the earth.
He makes wars cease to the ends of the earth;
   he breaks the bow and shatters the spear,
   he burns the shields with fire.
"Be still, and know that I am God;
   I will be exalted among the nations,
   I will be exalted in the earth."

The Lord Almighty is with us;
   the God of Jacob is our fortress.

Colossians 1:11–20   We pray in order that you may please the Lord Jesus S R
Christ in every way: being strengthened with all power according to his E E
glorious might so that you may have great endurance and patience, and C A
joyfully giving thanks to the Father, who has qualified you to share in the O D
inheritance of the saints in the kingdom of light. For he has rescued us N I
from the dominion of darkness and brought us into the kingdom of the Son D N
he loves, in whom we have redemption, the forgiveness of sins. G

   He is the image of the invisible God, the firstborn over all creation. For
by him all things were created: things in heaven and on earth, visible and
invisible, whether thrones or powers or rulers or authorities; all things
were created by him and for him. He is before all things, and in him all
things hold together. And he is the head of the body, the church; he is the

beginning and the firstborn from among the dead, so that in everything he might have the supremacy. For God was pleased to have all his fulness dwell in him, and through him to reconcile to himself all things, whether things on earth or things in heaven, by making peace through his blood, shed on the cross.

Luke 23:33–43 When they came to the place called the Skull, there they crucified Jesus, along with the criminals – one on his right, the other on his left. Jesus said, "Father, forgive them, for they do not know what they are doing." And they divided up his clothes by casting lots.

The people stood watching, and the rulers even sneered at him. They said, "He saved others; let him save himself if he is the Christ of God, the Chosen One."

The soldiers also came up and mocked him. They offered him wine vinegar and said, "If you are the king of the Jews, save yourself."

There was a written notice above him, which read: THIS IS THE KING OF THE JEWS.

One of the criminals who hung there hurled insults at him: "Aren't you the Christ? Save yourself and us!"

But the other criminal rebuked him. "Don't you fear God," he said, "since you are under the same sentence? We are punished justly, for we are getting what our deeds deserve. But this man has done nothing wrong."

Then he said, "Jesus, remember me when you come into your kingdom."

Jesus answered him, "I tell you the truth, today you will be with me in paradise."

Alternative Psalmody for the Principal Service Lectionary

The purpose of this Alternative Psalmody is, in some cases, to reduce the number of verses of a particular provision and, in others, to simplify the reading. Psalms which are starred* have alternatives listed in this table.

	Year A	Year B	Year C
Advent 1		80:1–7	
Advent 2	72:1–7	85:8–13	
Advent 3			146:5–10
Advent 4	80:1–7	89:1–8	
Christmas 1	148:7–14	148:7–14	148:7–14
Epiphany 2		139:1–10	
Epiphany 3	27:1–9		19:1–6
Proper 1		147:1–11	
Proper 3			37:1–7
Lent 1			91:1–11
Lent 3		19:7–14	
Lent 4		107:1–9	
Palm Sunday	118:19–24	118:19–24	118:19–24
	31:9–18	31:9–18	31:9–18
Tuesday in Holy Week	71:1–8	71:1–8	71:1–8
Maunday Thursday	116:11–19	116:11–19	116:11–19
Good Friday	22:1–11 *or* 1–21	22:1–11 *or* 1–21	22:1–11 *or* 1–21
Easter Eve	31:1–5	31:1–5	31:1–5
Easter Day	118:14–24	118:14–24	118:14–24
Easter 3	116:1–8		
Easter 5	31:1–5		
Easter 7	68:1–10		
Pentecost	104:24–36	104:24–36	104:24–36
Proper 4	31:19–24		
Proper 6	116:11–18	92:1–18	
Proper 7	86:1–10		42 *or* 43
	69:13–18	107:23–32	
Proper 8	89:8–18		77:11–20
Proper 10	65:9–13		
Proper 11	139:1–12		
Proper 12	105:1–11		85:1–7
Proper 13	17:1–7		107:1–9
	145:14–21		49:1–9
Proper 14	105:1–10		50:1–7
			33:12–21
Proper 15			80:8–19
Proper 17	115	45:1–7	81:1–11
Proper 18			139:1–8
Proper 19	103:8–13	19:1–6	
Proper 20	105:37–45		
Proper 21	78:1–7		91:11–16
Proper 22	19:7–14		137:1–6
Proper 23	106:1–6		
Proper 24	99:1–9	104:1–9	
Proper 25	90:1–6	34:1–8	65:1–8
4 before Advent	107:1–8		
3 before Advent			17:1–8
2 before Advent	90:1–8		
Christ the King	95:1–7		

LECTIONARY READINGS FOR FESTIVALS

YEARS A, B, C

The Naming and Circumcision of Jesus – 1 January

Numbers 6:22–27   The LORD said to Moses, "Tell Aaron and his sons, 'This is F R
how you are to bless the Israelites. Say to them: I E

    "'"The LORD bless you   R A
     and keep you;   S D
   the LORD make his face shine upon you   T I
    and be gracious to you;   N
   the LORD turn his face towards you   G
    and give you peace."'

"So they will put my name on the Israelites, and I will bless them."

Psalm 8   O LORD, our LORD,   P
     how majestic is your name in all the earth!   S

   You have set your glory   A
    above the heavens.   L
   From the lips of children and infants   M
    you have ordained praise
   because of your enemies,
    to silence the foe and the avenger.

   When I consider your heavens,
    the work of your fingers,
   the moon and the stars,
    which you have set in place,
   what is man that you are mindful of him,
    the son of man that you care for him?
   You made him a little lower than the heavenly beings
    and crowned him with glory and honour.

   You made him ruler over the works of your hands;
    you put everything under his feet:
   all flocks and herds,
    and the beasts of the field,
   the birds of the air,
    and the fish of the sea,
    all that swim the paths of the seas.

   O LORD, our LORD,
    how majestic is your name in all the earth!

Galatians 4:4–7   When the time had fully come, God sent his Son, born of a woman, born under law, to redeem those under law, that we might receive the full rights of sons. Because you are sons, God sent the Spirit of his Son into our hearts, the Spirit who calls out, "*Abba*, Father." So you are no longer a slave, but a son; and since you are a son, God has made you also an heir.

Luke 2:15–21   When the angels had left them and gone into heaven, the shepherds said to one another, "Let's go to Bethlehem and see this thing that has happened, which the LORD has told us about."

So they hurried off and found Mary and Joseph, and the baby, who was lying in the manger. When they had seen him, they spread the word concerning what had been told them about this child, and all who heard it were amazed at what the shepherds said to them. But Mary treasured up all these things and pondered them in her heart. The shepherds returned, glorifying and praising God for all the things they had heard and seen, which were just as they had been told.

On the eighth day, when it was time to circumcise him, he was named Jesus, the name the angel had given him before he had been conceived.

The Conversion of Paul – 25 January

The Conversion of Paul is celebrated on the Third Sunday of Epiphany (25 January) unless transferred to Monday 26 January.

Alternative first and second readings:

Jeremiah 1:4–10	*or*	Acts 9:1–22
Psalm 67		Psalm 67
Acts 9:1–22		Galatians 1:11–16a
Matthew 19:27–30		Matthew 19:27–30

Jeremiah 1:4–10   The word of the LORD came to me, saying,

> "Before I formed you in the womb I knew you,
>   before you were born I set you apart;
> I appointed you as a prophet to the nations."

"Ah, Sovereign LORD," I said, "I do not know how to speak; I am only a child."

But the LORD said to me, "Do not say, 'I am only a child.' You must go to everyone I send you to and say whatever I command you. Do not be afraid of them, for I am with you and will rescue you," declares the LORD.

Then the LORD reached out his hand and touched my mouth and said to me, "Now, I have put my words in your mouth. See, today I appoint you over nations and kingdoms to uproot and tear down, to destroy and overthrow, to build and to plant."

Psalm 67   May God be gracious to us
      and bless us and make his face shine upon us,

that your ways may be known on earth,
　　your salvation among all nations.

May the peoples praise you, O God;
　　may all the peoples praise you.
May the nations be glad and sing for joy,
　　for you rule the peoples justly
　　and guide the nations of the earth.
May the peoples praise you, O God;
　　may all the peoples praise you.

Then the land will yield its harvest,
　　and God, our God, will bless us.
God will bless us,
　　and all the ends of the earth will fear him.

Acts 9:1–22 Saul was still breathing out murderous threats against the
Lord's disciples. He went to the high priest and asked him for letters to the
synagogues in Damascus, so that if he found any there who belonged to the
Way, whether men or women, he might take them as prisoners to
Jerusalem. As he neared Damascus on his journey, suddenly a light from
heaven flashed around him. He fell to the ground and heard a voice say to
him, "Saul, Saul, why do you persecute me?"

"Who are you, Lord?" Saul asked.

"I am Jesus, whom you are persecuting," he replied. "Now get up and go
into the city, and you will be told what you must do."

The men were travelling with Saul stood there speechless; they heard
the sound but did not see anyone. Saul got up from the ground, but when he
opened his eyes he could see nothing. So they led him by the hand into Damascus. For three days he was blind, and did not eat or drink anything.

In Damascus there was a disciple named Ananias. The Lord called to
him in a vision, "Ananias!"

"Yes, Lord," he answered.

The Lord told him, "Go to the house of Judas on Straight Street and ask
for a man from Tarsus named Saul, for he is praying. In a vision he has seen
a man named Ananias come and place his hands on him to restore his
sight."

"Lord," Ananias answered, "I have heard many reports about this man
and all the harm he has done to your saints in Jerusalem. And he has come
here with authority from the chief priests to arrest all who call on your
name."

But the Lord said to Ananias, "Go! This man is my chosen instrument to
carry my name before the Gentiles and their kings and before the people
of Israel. I will show him how much he must suffer for my name."

Then Ananias went to the house and entered it. Placing his hands on
Saul, he said, "Brother Saul, the Lord – Jesus, who appeared to you on the
road as you were coming here – has sent me so that you may see again and
be filled with the Holy Spirit." Immediately, something like scales fell from

Saul's eyes, and he could see again. He got up and was baptised, and after taking some food, he regained his strength.

Saul spent several days with the disciples in Damascus. At once he began to preach in the synagogues that Jesus is the Son of God. All those who heard him were astonished and asked, "Isn't he the man who caused havoc in Jerusalem among those who call on this name? And hasn't he come here to take them as prisoners to the chief priests?" Yet Saul grew more and more powerful and baffled the Jews living in Damascus by proving that Jesus is the Christ.

Matthew 19:27–30   Peter said to Jesus, "We have left everything to follow G
you! What then will there be for us?" O

Jesus said to them, "I tell you the truth, at the renewal of all things, when S
the Son of Man sits on his glorious throne, you who have followed me will P
also sit on twelve thrones, judging the twelve tribes of Israel. And every- E
one who has left houses or brothers or sisters or father or mother or L
children or fields for my sake will receive a hundred times as much and
will inherit eternal life. But many who are first will be last, and many who
are last will be first."

Or
Acts 9:1–22   *For text of first reading see second reading p 557.*

Psalm 67   May God be gracious to us P
  and bless us and make his face shine upon us, S
that your ways may be known on earth, A
  your salvation among all nations. L

May the peoples praise you, O God; M
  may all the peoples praise you.
May the nations be glad and sing for joy,
  for you rule the peoples justly
  and guide the nations of the earth.
May the peoples praise you, O God;
  may all the peoples praise you.

Then the land will yield its harvest,
  and God, our God, will bless us.
God will bless us,
  and all the ends of the earth will fear him.

Galatians 1:11–16a   I want you to know, brothers, that the gospel I preached S R
is not something that man made up. I did not receive it from any man, nor E E
was I taught it; rather, I received it by revelation from Jesus Christ. C A

For you have heard of my previous way of life in Judaism, how intensely O D
I persecuted the church of God and tried to destroy it. I was advancing in N I
Judaism beyond many Jews of my own age and was extremely zealous for D N
the traditions of my fathers. But when God, who set me apart from birth G
and called me by his grace, was pleased to reveal his Son in me so that I
might preach him among the Gentiles.

Matthew 19:27–30   *For text of the Gospel see p 558.*

Joseph – 19 March

2 Samuel 7:4–16   The word of the Lord came to Nathan, saying: F

"Go and tell my servant David, 'This is what the Lord says: Are you the   I
one to build me a house to dwell in? I have not dwelt in a house from the day   R
I brought the Israelites up out of Egypt to this day. I have been moving   S
from place to place with a tent as my dwelling. Wherever I have moved   T
with all the Israelites, did I ever say to any of their rulers whom I commanded to shepherd my people Israel, "Why have you not built me a house   R
of cedar?"'   E

"Now then, tell my servant David, 'This is what the Lord Almighty says: A
I took you from the pasture and from following the flock to be ruler over   D
my people Israel. I have been with you wherever you have gone, and I have   I
cut off all your enemies from before you. Now I will make your name   N
great, like the names of the greatest men of the earth. And I will provide a   G
place for my people Israel and will plant them so that they can have a home
of their own and no longer be disturbed. Wicked people shall not oppress
them any more, as they did at the beginning and have done ever since the
time I appointed leaders over my people Israel. I will also give you rest
from all your enemies.

"'The Lord declares to you that the Lord himself will establish a house
for you: When your days are over and you rest with your ancestors, I will
raise up your offspring to succeed you, who will come from your own body,
and I will establish his kingdom. He is the one who will build a house for my
Name, and I will establish the throne of his kingdom for ever. I will be his
father, and he shall be my son. When he does wrong, I will punish him with
the rod of men, with floggings inflicted by men. But my love will never be
taken away from him, as I took it away from Saul, whom I removed from
before you. Your house and your kingdom shall endure for ever before me;
your throne shall be established for ever.'"

Psalm 89:27–36   I will also appoint him my firstborn,   P
the most exalted of the kings of the earth.   S
I will maintain my love to him for ever,   A
and my covenant with him will never fail.   L
I will establish his line for ever,   M
his throne as long as the heavens endure.

"If his sons forsake my law
and do not follow my statutes,
if they violate my decrees
and fail to keep my commands,
I will punish their sin with the rod,
their iniquity with flogging;
but I will not take my love from him,
nor will I ever betray my faithfulness.

I will not violate my covenant
    or alter what my lips have uttered.
Once for all, I have sworn by my holiness –
    and I will not lie to David –
that his line will continue for ever
    and his throne endure before me like the sun.

Romans 4:13–18 It was not through law that Abraham and his offspring received the promise that he would be heir of the world, but through the righteousness that comes by faith. For if those who live by law are heirs, faith has no value and the promise is worthless, because law brings wrath. And where there is no law there is no transgression.

Therefore, the promise comes by faith, so that it may be by grace and may be guaranteed to all Abraham's offspring – not only to those who are of the law but also to those who are of the faith of Abraham. He is the father of us all. As it is written: "I have made you a father of many nations." He is our father in the sight of God, in whom he believed – the God who gives life to the dead and calls things that are not as though they were.

Against all hope, Abraham in hope believed and so became the father of many nations, just as it had been said to him, "So shall your offspring be."

SECOND READING

Matthew 1:18–25 This is how the birth of Jesus Christ came about: His mother Mary was pledged to be married to Joseph, but before they came together, she was found to be with child through the Holy Spirit. Because Joseph her husband was a righteous man and did not want to expose her to public disgrace, he had in mind to divorce her quietly.

But after he had considered this, an angel of the Lord appeared to him in a dream and said, "Joseph son of David, do not be afraid to take Mary home as your wife, because what is conceived in her is from the Holy Spirit. She will give birth to a son, and you are to give him the name Jesus, because he will save his people from their sins."

All this took place to fulfil what the Lord had said through the prophet: "The virgin will be with child and will give birth to a son, and they will call him Immanuel" – which means, "God with us."

When Joseph woke up, he did what the angel of the Lord had commanded him and took Mary home as his wife. But he had no union with her until she gave birth to a son. And he gave him the name Jesus.

GOSPEL

The Annunciation – 25 March

Isaiah 7:10–14 The Lord spoke to Ahaz, "Ask the Lord your God for a sign, whether in the deepest depths or in the highest heights."

But Ahaz said, "I will not ask; I will not put the Lord to the test."

Then Isaiah said, "Hear now, you house of David! Is it not enough to try the patience of men? Will you try the patience of my God also? Therefore the Lord himself will give you a sign: The virgin will be with child and will give birth to a son, and will call him Immanuel."

FIRST READING

Psalm 40:5–10   Many, O Lᴏʀᴅ my God,
are the wonders you have done.
The things you planned for us
no-one can recount to you;
were I to speak and tell of them,
they would be too many to declare.

Sacrifice and offering you did not desire,
but my ears you have pierced;
burnt offerings and sin offerings
you did not require.
Then I said, "Here I am, I have come –
it is written about me in the scroll.
I desire to do your will, O my God;
your law is within my heart."

I proclaim righteousness in the great assembly;
I do not seal my lips,
as you know, O Lᴏʀᴅ.
I do not hide your righteousness in my heart;
I speak of your faithfulness and salvation.
I do not conceal your love and your truth
from the great assembly.

P
S
A
L
M

Hebrews 10:4–10   It is impossible for the blood of bulls and goats to take away sins.

Therefore, when Christ came into the world, he said:

"Sacrifice and offering you did not desire,
but a body you prepared for me;
with burnt offerings and sin offerings
you were not pleased.
Then I said, 'Here I am – it is written about me in the scroll –
I have come to do your will, O God.'"

First he said, "Sacrifices and offerings, burnt offerings and sin offerings you did not desire, nor were you pleased with them" (although the law required them to be made). Then he said, "Here I am, I have come to do your will." He sets aside the first to establish the second. And by that will, we have been made holy through the sacrifice of the body of Jesus Christ once for all.

S
E
C
O
N
D

R
E
A
D
I
N
G

Luke 1:26–38   In the sixth month, God sent the angel Gabriel to Nazareth, a town in Galilee, to a virgin pledged to be married to a man named Joseph, a descendant of David. The virgin's name was Mary. The angel went to her and said, "Greetings, you who are highly favoured! The Lord is with you."

Mary was greatly troubled at his words and wondered what kind of greeting this might be. But the angel said to her, "Do not be afraid, Mary, you have found favour with God. You will be with child and give birth to a son, and you are to give him the name Jesus. He will be great and will be

G
O
S
P
E
L

called the Son of the Most High. The Lord God will give him the throne of his father David, and he will reign over the house of Jacob for ever; his kingdom will never end."

"How will this be," Mary asked the angel, "since I am a virgin?"

The angel answered, "The Holy Spirit will come upon you, and the power of the Most High will overshadow you. So the holy one to be born will be called the Son of God. Even Elizabeth your relative is going to have a child in her old age, and she who was said to be barren is in her sixth month. For nothing is impossible with God."

"I am the Lord's servant," Mary answered. "May it be to me as you have said." Then the angel left her.

George – 23 April

Alternative first readings

Either **1 Maccabees 2:59–64**

or **Revelation 12:7–12**   There was war in heaven. Michael and his angels fought against the dragon, and the dragon and his angels fought back. But he was not strong enough, and they lost their place in heaven. The great dragon was hurled down – that ancient serpent called the devil, or Satan, who leads the whole world astray. He was hurled to the earth, and his angels with him.

Then I heard a loud voice in heaven say:

"Now have come the salvation and the power and the
    kingdom of our God,
  and the authority of his Christ.
For the accuser of our brothers,
  who accuses them before our God day and night,
  has been hurled down.
They overcame him
  by the blood of the Lamb
  and by the word of their testimony;
they did not love their lives so much
  as to shrink from death.
Therefore rejoice, you heavens
  and you who dwell in them!
But woe to the earth and the sea,
  because the devil has gone down to you!
He is filled with fury,
  because he knows that his time is short."

Psalm 126   When the Lord brought back the captives to Zion,
    we were like those who dreamed
  Our mouths were filled with laughter,
    our tongues with songs of joy.

Then it was said among the nations,
    "The LORD has done great things for them."
The LORD has done great things for us,
    and we are filled with joy.

Restore our fortunes, O LORD,
    like streams in the Negev.
Those who sow in tears
    will reap with songs of joy.
Those who go out weeping,
    carrying seed to sow,
will return with songs of joy,
    carrying sheaves with them.

2 Timothy 2:3–13   Endure hardship with us like a good soldier of Christ Jesus. No-one serving as a soldier gets involved in civilian affairs – he wants to please his commanding officer. Similarly, if anyone competes as an athlete, he does not receive the victor's crown unless he competes according to the rules. The hardworking farmer should be the first to receive a share of the crops. Reflect on what I am saying, for the Lord will give you insight into all this.

Remember Jesus Christ, raised from the dead, descended from David. This is my gospel, for which I am suffering even to the point of being chained like a criminal. But God's word is not chained. Therefore I endure everything for the sake of the elect, that they too may obtain the salvation that is in Christ Jesus, with eternal glory.
Here is a trustworthy saying:

If we died with him,
    we will also live with him;
if we endure,
    we will also reign with him.
If we disown him,
    he will also disown us;
if we are faithless,
    he will remain faithful,
    for he cannot disown himself.

SECOND READING

John 15:18–21   Jesus said to his disciples: "If the world hates you, keep in mind that it hated me first. If you belonged to the world, it would love you as its own. As it is, you do not belong to the world, but I have chosen you out of the world. That is why the world hates you. Remember the words I spoke to you: 'No servant is greater than his master.' If they persecuted me, they will persecute you also. If they obeyed my teaching, they will obey yours also. They will treat you this way because of my name, for they do not know the One who sent me."

GOSPEL

Alternative first reading

Either **Proverbs 15:28–33**

The heart of the righteous weighs its answers,
  but the mouth of the wicked gushes evil.

The LORD is far from the wicked
  but he hears the prayer of the righteous.

A cheerful look brings joy to the heart,
  and good news gives health to the bones.

Whoever listens to a life-giving rebuke
  will be at home among the wise.

He who ignores discipline despises himself,
  but whoever heeds correction gains understanding.

The fear of the LORD teaches a man wisdom,
  and humility comes before honour.

F R I E R A S D T I N G

or **Acts 15:35–41**   Paul and Barnabas remained in Antioch, where they and many others taught and preached the word of the Lord.
  Some time later Paul said to Barnabas, "Let us go back and visit the brothers in all the towns where we preached the word of the Lord and see how they are doing." Barnabas wanted to take John, also called Mark, with them, but Paul did not think it wise to take him, because he had deserted them in Pamphylia and had not continued with them in the work. They had such a sharp disagreement that they parted company. Barnabas took Mark and sailed for Cyprus, but Paul chose Silas and left, commended by the brothers to the grace of the Lord. He went through Syria and Cilicia, strengthening the churches.

F R I E R A S D T I N G

Psalm 119:9–16

How can a young man keep his way pure?
  By living according to your word.

I seek you with all my heart;
  do not let me stray from your commands.

I have hidden your word in my heart
  that I might not sin against you.

Praise be to you, O LORD;
  teach me your decrees.

With my lips I recount
  all the laws that come from your mouth.

I rejoice in following your statutes
  as one rejoices in great riches.

I meditate on your precepts
  and consider your ways.

I delight in your decrees;
  I will not neglect your word.

P S A L M

Ephesians 4:7–16 To each one of us grace has been given as Christ apportioned it. This is why it says:

> "When he ascended on high, he led captives in his train and gave gifts to men."

(What does "he ascended" mean except that he also descended to the lower, earthly regions? He who descended is the very one who ascended higher than all the heavens, in order to fill the whole universe.) It was he who gave some to be apostles, some to be prophets, some to be evangelists, and some to be pastors and teachers, to prepare God's people for works of service, so that the body of Christ may be built up until we all reach unity in the faith and in the knowledge of the Son of God and become mature, attaining to the whole measure of the fulness of Christ.

Then we will no longer be infants, tossed back and forth by the waves, and blown here and there by every wind of teaching and by the cunning and craftiness of men in their deceitful scheming. Instead, speaking the truth in love, we will in all things grow up into him who is the Head, that is, Christ. From him the whole body, joined and held together by every supporting ligament, grows and builds itself up in love, as each part does its work.

Mark 13:5–13 Jesus said to his disciples: "Watch out that no-one deceives you. Many will come in my name, claiming, 'I am he,' and will deceive many. When you hear of wars and rumours of wars, do not be alarmed. Such things must happen, but the end is still to come. Nation will rise against nation, and kingdom against kingdom. There will be earthquakes in various places, and famines. These are the beginning of birth-pains.

"You must be on your guard. You will be handed over to the local councils and flogged in the synagogues. On account of me you will stand before governors and kings as witnesses to them. And the gospel must first be preached to all nations. Whenever you are arrested and brought to trial, do not worry beforehand about what to say. Just say whatever is given you at the time, for it is not you speaking, but the Holy Spirit.

"Brother will betray brother to death, and a father his child. Children will rebel against their parents and have them put to death. All men will hate you because of me, but those who stand firm to the end will be saved."

Philip and James – 1 May

Isaiah 30:15–21 This is what the Sovereign LORD, the Holy One of Israel, says:

> "In repentance and rest is your salvation,
>   in quietness and trust is your strength,
>   but you would have none of it.
> You said, 'No, we will flee on horses.'
>   Therefore you will flee!
> You said, 'We will ride off on swift horses.'
>   Therefore your pursuers will be swift!

A thousand will flee
  at the threat of one;
at the threat of five
  you will all flee away,
till you are left
    like a flagstaff on a mountaintop,
    like a banner on a hill."

Yet the LORD longs to be gracious to you;
  he rises to show you compassion.
For the LORD is a God of justice.
  Blessed are all who wait for him!

O people of Zion, who live in Jerusalem, you will weep no more. How gracious he will be when you cry for help! As soon as he hears, he will answer you. Although the Lord gives you the bread of adversity and the water of affliction, your teachers will be hidden no more; with your own eyes you will see them. Whether you turn to the right or to the left, your ears will hear a voice behind you, saying, "This is the way; walk in it."

Psalm 119:1–8   Blessed are they whose ways are blameless,
              who walk according to the law of the LORD.
          Blessed are they who keep his statutes
              and seek him with all their heart.
          They do nothing wrong;
              they walk in his ways.
          You have laid down precepts
              that are to be fully obeyed.
          Oh, that my ways were steadfast
              in obeying your decrees!
          Then I would not be put to shame
              when I consider all your commands.
          I will praise you with an upright heart
              as I learn your righteous laws.
          I will obey your decrees;
              do not utterly forsake me.

Ephesians 1:3–10   Praise be to the God and Father of our Lord Jesus Christ, who has blessed us in the heavenly realms with every spiritual blessing in Christ. For he chose us in him before the creation of the world to be holy and blameless in his sight. In love he predestined us to be adopted as his sons through Jesus Christ, in accordance with his pleasure and will – to the praise of his glorious grace, which he has freely given us in the One he loves. In him we have redemption through his blood, the forgiveness of sins, in accordance with the riches of God's grace that he lavished on us with all wisdom and understanding. And he made known to us the mystery of his will according to his good pleasure, which he purposed in Christ, to be put into effect when the times will have reached their fulfilment – to bring all things in heaven and on earth together under one head, even Christ.

John 14:1–14   Jesus said: "Do not let your hearts be troubled. Trust in God; G trust also in me. In my Father's house are many rooms; if it were not so, I O would have told you. I am going there to prepare a place for you. And if I go S and prepare a place for you, I will come back and take you to be with me P that you also may be where I am. You know the way to the place where I am E going." L

Thomas said to him, "Lord, we don't know where you are going, so how can we know the way?"

Jesus answered, "I am the way and the truth and the life. No-one comes to the Father except through me. If you really knew me, you would know my Father as well. From now on, you do know him and have seen him."

Philip said, "Lord, show us the Father and that will be enough for us."

Jesus answered: "Don't you know me, Philip, even after I have been among you such a long time? Anyone who has seen me has seen the Father. How can you say, 'Show us the Father'? Don't you believe that I am in the Father, and that the Father is in me? The words I say to you are not just my own. Rather, it is the Father, living in me, who is doing his work. Believe me when I say that I am in the Father and the Father is in me; or at least believe on the evidence of the miracles themselves. I tell you the truth, anyone who has faith in me will do what I have been doing. He will do even greater things than these, because I am going to the Father. And I will do whatever you ask in my name, so that the Son may bring glory to the Father. You may ask me for anything in my name, and I will do it."

Matthias – 14 May

Alternative first and second readings:

Isaiah 22:15–25	*or*	Acts 1:15–26
Psalm 15		Psalm 15
Acts 1:15–26		1 Corinthians 4:1–7
John 15:9–17		John 15:9–17

Isaiah 22:15–25   This is what the LORD, the LORD Almighty, says: F R

> "Go, say to this steward, I E
>> to Shebna, who is in charge of the palace: R A
> What are you doing here and who gave you permission S D
>> to cut out a grave for yourself here, T I
> hewing your grave on the height N
>> and chiselling your resting place in the rock? G

> "Beware, the LORD is about to take firm hold of you
>> and hurl you away, O you mighty man.

He will roll you up tightly like a ball
    and throw you into a large country.
There you will die
    and there your splendid chariots will remain –
    you disgrace to your master's house!
I will depose you from your office,
    and you will be ousted from your position.

"In that day I will summon my servant, Eliakim son of Hilkiah. I will clothe him with your robe and fasten your sash around him and hand your authority over to him. He will be a father to those who live in Jerusalem and to the house of Judah. I will place on his shoulder the key to the house of David; what he opens no-one can shut, and what he shuts no-one can open. I will drive him like a peg into a firm place; he will be a seat of honour for the house of his father. All the glory of his family will hang on him: its offspring and offshoots – all its lesser vessels, from the bowls to all the jars.

"In that day," declares the LORD Almighty, "the peg driven into the firm place will give way; it will be sheared off and will fall, and the load hanging on it will be cut down." The LORD has spoken.

Psalm 15   LORD, who may dwell in your sanctuary?
    Who may live on your holy hill?

He whose walk is blameless
    and who does what is righteous,
who speaks the truth from his heart
    and has no slander on his tongue,
who does his neighbour no wrong
    and casts no slur on his fellow-man,
who despises a vile man
    but honours those who fear the LORD,
who keeps his oath
    even when it hurts,
who lends his money without usury
    and does not accept a bribe against the innocent.

He who does these things
    will never be shaken.

Acts 1:15–26   Peter stood up among the believers (a group numbering about a hundred and twenty) and said, "Brothers, the Scripture had to be fulfilled which the Holy Spirit spoke long ago through the mouth of David concerning Judas, who served as guide for those who arrested Jesus – he was one of our number and shared in this ministry."

(With the reward he got for his wickedness, Judas bought a field; there he fell headlong, his body burst open and all his intestines spilled out. Everyone in Jerusalem heard about this, so they called that field in their language Akeldama, that is, Field of Blood.)

"For," said Peter, "it is written in the Book of Psalms,

"'May his place be deserted;
let there be no-one to dwell in it,'
and,

"'May another take his place of leadership.'

Therefore it is necessary to choose one of the men who have been with us the whole time the Lord Jesus went in and out among us, beginning from John's baptism to the time when Jesus was taken up from us. For one of these must become a witness with us of his resurrection."

So they proposed two men: Joseph called Barsabbas (also known as Justus) and Matthias. Then they prayed, "Lord, you know everyone's heart. Show us which of these two you have chosen to take over this apostolic ministry, which Judas left to go where he belongs." Then they cast lots, and the lot fell to Matthias; so he was added to the eleven apostles.

John 15:9–17   Jesus said: "As the Father has loved me, so have I loved you. G
Now remain in my love. If you obey my commands, you will remain in O
my love, just as I have obeyed my Father's commands and remain in his S
love. I have told you this so that my joy may be in you and that your joy P
may be complete. My command is this: Love each other as I have loved E
you. Greater love has no-one than this, that he lay down his life for his L
friends. You are my friends if you do what I command. I no longer call you
servants, because a servant does not know his master's business. Instead,
I have called you friends, for everything that I learned from my Father I
have made known to you. You did not choose me, but I chose you and
appointed you to go and bear fruit – fruit that will last. Then the Father will
give you whatever you ask in my name. This is my command: Love each
other."

Or

Acts 1:15–26   Peter stood up among the believers (a group numbering about F
a hundred and twenty) and said, "Brothers, the Scripture had to be fulfilled I
which the Holy Spirit spoke long ago through the mouth of David concern- R
ing Judas, who served as guide for those who arrested Jesus – he was one S
of our number and shared in this ministry." T

(With the reward he got for his wickedness, Judas bought a field; there
he fell headlong, his body burst open and all his intestines spilled out. R
Everyone in Jerusalem heard about this, so they called that field in their E
language Akeldama, that is, Field of Blood.) A

"For," said Peter, "it is written in the Book of Psalms, D

"'May his place be deserted; I
let there be no-one to dwell in it,'
and, N
G

"'May another take his place of leadership.'

Therefore it is necessary to choose one of the men who have been with us
the whole time the Lord Jesus went in and out among us, beginning from

John's baptism to the time when Jesus was taken up from us. For one of these must become a witness with us of his resurrection."

So they proposed two men: Joseph called Barsabbas (also known as Justus) and Matthias. Then they prayed, "Lord, you know everyone's heart. Show us which of these two you have chosen to take over this apostolic ministry, which Judas left to go where he belongs." Then they cast lots, and the lot fell to Matthias; so he was added to the eleven apostles.

Psalm 15 *For text of Psalm see p 568.*

1 Corinthians 4:1–7 Men ought to regard us as servants of Christ and as those entrusted with the secret things of God. Now it is required that those who have been given a trust must prove faithful. I care very little if I am judged by you or by any human court; indeed, I do not even judge myself. My conscience is clear, but that does not make me innocent. It is the Lord who judges me. Therefore judge nothing before the appointed time; wait till the Lord comes. He will bring to light what is hidden in darkness and will expose the motives of men's hearts. At that time each will receive his praise from God.

Now, brothers, I have applied these things to myself and Apollos for your benefit, so that you may learn from us the meaning of the saying, "Do not go beyond what is written." Then you will not take pride in one man over against another. For who makes you different from anyone else? What do you have that you did not receive? And if you did receive it, why do you boast as though you did not?

John 15:9–17 *For text of the Gospel see p 569.*

The Visit of Mary to Elizabeth – 31 May

Zephaniah 3:14–18

Sing, O Daughter of Zion;
  shout aloud, O Israel!
Be glad and rejoice with all your heart,
  O Daughter of Jerusalem!
The Lord has taken away your punishment,
  he has turned back your enemy.
The Lord, the King of Israel, is with you;
  never again will you fear any harm.
On that day they will say to Jerusalem,
  "Do not fear, O Zion;
  do not let your hands hang limp.
The Lord your God is with you,
  he is mighty to save.
He will take great delight in you,
  he will quiet you with his love,
  he will rejoice over you with singing."

> "The sorrows for the appointed feasts
>> I will remove from you;
>> they are a burden and a reproach to you."

Psalm 113 Praise the LORD.

> Praise, O servants of the LORD,
>> praise the name of the LORD.
> Let the name of the LORD be praised,
>> both now and for evermore.
> From the rising of the sun to the place where it sets,
>> the name of the LORD is to be praised.

> The LORD is exalted over all the nations,
>> his glory above the heavens.
> Who is like the LORD our God,
>> the One who sits enthroned on high,
> who stoops down to look
>> on the heavens and the earth?

> He raises the poor from the dust
>> and lifts the needy from the ash heap;
> he seats them with princes,
>> with the princes of their people.
> He settles the barren woman in her home
>> as a happy mother of children.

> Praise the LORD.

Romans 12:9–16 Love must be sincere. Hate what is evil; cling to what is good. Be devoted to one another with brotherly love. Honour one another above yourselves. Never be lacking in zeal, but keep your spiritual fervour, serving the Lord. Be joyful in hope, patient in affliction, faithful in prayer. Share with God's people who are in need. Practise hospitality.

Bless those who persecute you; bless and do not curse. Rejoice with those who rejoice; mourn with those who mourn. Live in harmony with one another. Do not be proud, but be willing to associate with people of low position. Do not be conceited.

Luke 1:39–49 [50–56] Mary got ready and hurried to a town in the hill country of Judea, where she entered Zechariah's home and greeted Elizabeth. When Elizabeth heard Mary's greeting, the baby leaped in her womb, and Elizabeth was filled with the Holy Spirit. In a loud voice she exclaimed: "Blessed are you among women, and blessed is the child you will bear! But why am I so favoured, that the mother of my Lord should come to me? As soon as the sound of your greeting reached my ears, the baby in my womb leaped for joy. Blessed is she who has believed that what the Lord has said to her will be accomplished!"

And Mary said:

"My soul glorifies the Lord
  and my spirit rejoices in God my Saviour,
for he has been mindful
  of the humble state of his servant.
From now on all generations will call me blessed,
  for the Mighty One has done great things for me –
  holy is his name."
["His mercy extends to those who fear him,
  from generation to generation.
He has performed mighty deeds with his arm;
  he has scattered those who are proud in their inmost thoughts.
He has brought down rulers from their thrones
  but has lifted up the humble.
He has filled the hungry with good things
  but has sent the rich away empty.
He has helped his servant Israel,
  remembering to be merciful
to Abraham and his descendants for ever,
  even as he said to our ancestors."

Mary stayed with Elizabeth for about three months and then returned home.]

Barnabas – 11 June

Alternative first and second readings:

Job 29:11–16 *or*	Acts 11:19–30
Psalm 112	Psalm 112
Acts 11:19–30	Galatians 2:1–10
John 15:12–17	John 15:12–17

Job 29:11–16 Whoever heard me spoke well of me,
            and those who saw me commended me,
          because I rescued the poor who cried for help,
            and the fatherless who had none to assist him.
          The man who was dying blessed me;
            I made the widow's heart sing.
          I put on righteousness as my clothing;
            justice was my robe and my turban.
          I was eyes to the blind
            and feet to the lame.
          I was a father to the needy;
            I took up the case of the stranger.

Psalm 112   Praise the LORD.

P
S
A
L
M

Blessed is the man who fears the LORD,
  who finds great delight in his commands.

His children will be mighty in the land;
  the generation of the upright will be blessed.
Wealth and riches are in his house,
  and his righteousness endures for ever.
Even in darkness light dawns for the upright,
  for the gracious and compassionate and righteous man.
Good will come to him who is generous and lends freely,
  who conducts his affairs with justice.
Surely he will never be shaken;
  a righteous man will be remembered for ever.
He will have no fear of bad news;
  his heart is steadfast, trusting in the LORD.
His heart is secure, he will have no fear;
  in the end he will look in triumph on their foes.
He has scattered abroad his gifts to the poor,
  his righteousness endures for ever;
  his horn will be lifted high in honour.

The wicked man will see and be vexed,
  he will gnash his teeth and waste away;
  the longings of the wicked will come to nothing.

Acts 11:19–30   Those who had been scattered by the persecution in connec- S
tion with Stephen travelled as far as Phoenicia, Cyprus and Antioch, telling E
the message only to Jews. Some of them, however, men from Cyprus and C
Cyrene, went to Antioch and began to speak to Greeks also, telling them O
the good news about the Lord Jesus. The Lord's hand was with them, and a N
great number of people believed and turned to the Lord. D

News of this reached the ears of the church at Jerusalem, and they sent
Barnabas to Antioch. When he arrived and saw the evidence of the grace of R
God, he was glad and encouraged them all to remain true to the Lord with E
all their hearts. He was a good man, full of the Holy Spirit and faith, and a A
great number of people were brought to the Lord. D

Then Barnabas went to Tarsus to look for Saul, and when he found him, I
he brought him to Antioch. So for a whole year Barnabas and Saul met with N
the church and taught great numbers of people. The disciples were called G
Christians first at Antioch.

During this time some prophets came down from Jerusalem to Antioch.
One of them, named Agabus, stood up and through the Spirit predicted
that a severe famine would spread over the entire Roman world. (This
happened during the reign of Claudius.) The disciples, each according
to his ability, decided to provide help for the brothers living in Judea. This
they did, sending their gift to the elders by Barnabas and Saul.

John 15:12–17 Jesus said: "My command is this: Love each other as I have G loved you. Greater love has no-one than this, that he lay down his life for O his friends. You are my friends if you do what I command. I no longer call S you servants, because a servant does not know his master's business. P Instead, I have called you friends, for everything that I learned from my E Father I have made known to you. You did not choose me, but I chose you L and appointed you to go and bear fruit – fruit that will last. Then the Father will give you whatever you ask in my name. This is my command: Love each other."

Or

Acts 11:19–30 Those who had been scattered by the persecution in connec- F tion with Stephen travelled as far as Phoenicia, Cyprus and Antioch, telling I the message only to Jews. Some of them, however, men from Cyprus and R Cyrene, went to Antioch and began to speak to Greeks also, telling them S the good news about the LORD Jesus. The LORD's hand was with them, and a T great number of people believed and turned to the LORD.

News of this reached the ears of the church at Jerusalem, and they sent R Barnabas to Antioch. When he arrived and saw the evidence of the grace of E God, he was glad and encouraged them all to remain true to the LORD with A all their hearts. He was a good man, full of the Holy Spirit and faith, and a D great number of people were brought to the LORD. I

Then Barnabas went to Tarsus to look for Saul, and when he found him, N he brought him to Antioch. So for a whole year Barnabas and Saul met with G the church and taught great numbers of people. The disciples were called Christians first at Antioch. During this time some prophets came down from Jerusalem to Antioch. One of them, named Agabus, stood up and through the Spirit predicted that a severe famine would spread over the entire Roman world. (This happened during the reign of Claudius.) The disciples, each according to his ability, decided to provide help for the believers living in Judea. This they did, sending their gift to the elders by Barnabas and Saul.

Psalm 112 *For the text of the Psalm see p 573.*

Galatians 2:1–10 Fourteen years later I went up again to Jerusalem, this S time with Barnabas. I took Titus along also. I went in response to a revela- E tion and set before them the gospel that I preach among the Gentiles. But I C did this privately to those who seemed to be leaders, for fear that I was run- O ning or had run my race in vain. Yet not even Titus, who was with me, was N compelled to be circumcised, even though he was a Greek. This matter D arose because some false believers had infiltrated our ranks to spy on the freedom we have in Christ Jesus and to make us slaves. We did not give in to them for a moment, so that the truth of the gospel might remain with you.

As for those who seemed to be important – whatever they were makes no difference to me; God does not judge by external appearance – these men added nothing to my message. On the contrary, they saw that I had been entrusted with the task of preaching the gospel to the Gentiles, just as Peter had been to the Jews. For God, who was at work in the ministry of Peter as an apostle to the Jews, was also at work in my ministry as an apostle to the Gentiles. James, Peter and John, those reputed to be pillars, gave me and Barnabas the right hand of fellowship when they recognised the grace given to me. They agreed that we should go to the Gentiles, and they to the Jews. All they asked was that we should continue to remember the poor, the very thing I was eager to do.

John 15:12–17 *For the text of the Gospel see p 574.*

The Birth of John Baptist – 24 June

Isaiah 40:1–11

Comfort, comfort my people,
    says your God.
Speak tenderly to Jerusalem,
    and proclaim to her
that her hard service has been completed,
    that her sin has been paid for,
that she has received from the Lord's hand
    double for all her sins.

A voice of one calling:
"In the desert prepare
    the way for the Lord;
make straight in the wilderness
    a highway for our God.
Every valley shall be raised up,
    every mountain and hill made low;
the rough ground shall become level,
    the rugged places a plain.
And the glory of the Lord will be revealed,
    and all people will see it together.
    For the mouth of the Lord has spoken."

A voice says, "Cry out."
    And I said, "What shall I cry?"

"All men are like grass,
    and all their glory is like the flowers of the field.
The grass withers and the flowers fall,
    because the breath of the Lord blows on them.
    Surely the people are grass.
The grass withers and the flowers fall,
    but the word of our God stands for ever."

You who bring good tidings to Zion,
    go up on a high mountain.
You who bring good tidings to Jerusalem,
    lift up your voice with a shout,

(marginal vertical text:) FIRST READING

lift it up, do not be afraid;
    say to the towns of Judah,
    "Here is your God!"
See, the Sovereign LORD comes with power,
    and his arm rules for him.
See, his reward is with him,
    and his recompense accompanies him.
He tends his flock like a shepherd:
    He gathers the lambs in his arms
and carries them close to his heart;
    he gently leads those that have young.

Psalm 85:7–13   Show us your unfailing love, O LORD,
    and grant us your salvation.

I will listen to what God the LORD will say;
    he promises peace to his people, his saints –
    but let them not return to folly.
Surely his salvation is near those who fear him,
    that his glory may dwell in our land.

Love and faithfulness meet together;
    righteousness and peace kiss each other.
Faithfulness springs forth from the earth,
    and righteousness looks down from heaven.
The LORD will indeed give what is good,
    and our land will yield its harvest.
Righteousness goes before him
    and prepares the way for his steps.

Alternative second reading

Either **Acts 13:14b–26**   On the Sabbath Paul and his companions entered the synagogue and sat down. After the reading from the Law and the Prophets, the synagogue rulers sent word to them, saying, "Brothers, if you have a message of encouragement for the people, please speak."

Standing up, Paul motioned with his hand and said: "Men of Israel and you Gentiles who worship God, listen to me! The God of the people of Israel chose our fathers; he made the people prosper during their stay in Egypt, with mighty power he led them out of that country, he endured their conduct for about forty years in the desert, he overthrew seven nations in Canaan and gave their land to his people as their inheritance. All this took about 450 years.

"After this, God gave them judges until the time of Samuel the prophet. Then the people asked for a king, and he gave them Saul son of Kish, of the tribe of Benjamin, who ruled for forty years. After removing Saul, he made David their king. He testified concerning him: 'I have found David son of Jesse a man after my own heart; he will do everything I want him to do.'

"From this man's descendants God has brought to Israel the Saviour Jesus, as he promised. Before the coming of Jesus, John preached repentance and baptism to all the people of Israel. As John was completing his work, he said: 'Who do you think I am? I am not that one. No, but he is coming after me, whose sandals I am not worthy to untie.'

"Brothers, children of Abraham, and you God-fearing Gentiles, it is to us that this message of salvation has been sent."

or **Galatians 3:23–29** Before faith in Jesus Christ came, we were held prisoners by the law, locked up until faith should be revealed. So the law was put in charge to lead us to Christ that we might be justified by faith. Now that faith has come, we are no longer under the supervision of the law.

You are all sons of God through faith in Christ Jesus, for all of you who were baptised into Christ have clothed yourselves with Christ. There is neither Jew nor Greek, slave nor free, male nor female, for you are all one in Christ Jesus. If you belong to Christ, then you are Abraham's seed, and heirs according to the promise.

SECOND READING

Luke 1:57–66, 80 When it was time for Elizabeth to have her baby, she gave birth to a son. Her neighbours and relatives heard that the Lord had shown her great mercy, and they shared her joy.

On the eighth day they came to circumcise the child, and they were going to name him after his father Zechariah, but his mother spoke up and said, "No! He is to be call John."

GOSPEL

They said to her, "There is no–one among your relatives who has that name."

Then they made signs to his father, to find out what he would like to name the child. He asked for a writing tablet, and to everyone's astonishment he wrote, "His name is John." Immediately his mouth was opened and his tongue was loosed, and he began to speak, praising God. The neighbours were all filled with awe, and throughout the hill country of Judea people were talking about all these things. Everyone who heard this wondered about it, asking, "What then is this child going to be?" For the Lord's hand was with him.

And the child grew and became strong in spirit; and he lived in the desert until he appeared publicly to Israel.

Peter and Paul – 29 June

Alternative first and second readings:

Zechariah 4:1–6a, 10b–14	*or*	Acts 12:1–11
Psalm 125		Psalm 125
Acts 12:1–11		2 Timothy 4:6–8, 17–18
Matthew 16:13–19		Matthrew 16:13–19

FIRST READING

Zechariah 4:1–6a, 10b–14 The angel who talked with me returned and wakened me, as one is wakened from his sleep. He asked me, "What do you see?"

I answered, "I see a solid gold lampstand with a bowl at the top and seven lights on it, with seven channels to the lights. Also there are two olive trees by it, one on the right of the bowl and the other on its left."

I asked the angel who talked with me, "What are these, my lord?"

He answered, "Do you not know what these are?"

"No, my lord," I replied.

So he said to me, "Men will rejoice when they see the plumb-line in the hand of Zerubbabel.

"(These seven are the eyes of the LORD, which range throughout the earth.)"

Then I asked the angel, "What are these two olive trees on the right and the left of the lampstand?"

Again I asked him, "What are these two olive branches beside the two gold pipes that pour out golden oil?"

He replied, "Do you not know what these are?"

"No, my lord," I said.

So he said, "These are the two who are anointed to serve the Lord of all the earth."

Psalm 125
Those who trust in the LORD are like Mount Zion,
    which cannot be shaken but endures for ever.
As the mountains surround Jerusalem,
    so the LORD surrounds his people
    both now and for evermore.

The sceptre of the wicked will not remain
    over the land allotted to the righteous,
for then the righteous might use
    their hands to do evil.

Do good, O LORD, to those who are good,
    to those who are upright in heart.
But those who turn to crooked ways
    the LORD will banish with the evildoers.

Peace be upon Israel.

Acts 12:1–11
King Herod arrested some who belonged to the church, intending to persecute them. He had James, the brother of John, put to death with the sword. When he saw that this pleased the Jews, he proceeded to seize Peter also. This happened during the Feast of Unleavened Bread. After arresting him, he put him in prison, handing him over to be guarded by four squads of four soldiers each. Herod intended to bring him out for public trial after the Passover.

So Peter was kept in prison, but the church was earnestly praying to God for him.

The night before Herod was to bring him to trial, Peter was sleeping between two soldiers, bound with two chains, and sentries stood guard at the entrance. Suddenly an angel of the Lord appeared and a light shone in the cell. He struck Peter on the side and woke him up. "Quick, get up!" he said, and the chains fell off Peter's wrists.

Then the angel said to him, "Put on your clothes and sandals." And Peter did so. "Wrap your cloak around you and follow me," the angel told him. Peter followed him out of the prison, but he had no idea that what the angel was doing was really happening; he thought he was seeing a vision. They passed the first and second guards and came to the iron gate leading to the city. It opened for them by itself, and they went through it. When they had walked the length of one street, suddenly the angel left him.

Then Peter came to himself and said, "Now I know without a doubt that the Lord sent his angel and rescued me from Herod's clutches and from everything the Jewish people were anticipating."

Matthew 16:13–19   When Jesus came to the region of Caesarea Philippi, he asked his disciples, "Who do people say the Son of Man is?"

They replied, "Some say John the Baptist; others say Elijah; and still others, Jeremiah or one of the prophets."

"But what about you?" he asked. "Who do you say I am?"

Simon Peter answered, "You are the Christ, the Son of the living God."

Jesus replied, "Blessed are you, Simon son of Jonah, for this was not revealed to you by flesh and blood, but by my Father in heaven. And I tell you that you are Peter, and on this rock I will build my church, and the gates of Hades will not overcome it. I will give you the keys of the kingdom of heaven; whatever you bind on earth will be bound in heaven, and whatever you loose on earth will be loosed in heaven."

Or

Acts 12:1–11   *For text of first reading see second reading p 578.*

Psalm 125   *For the text of the Psalm see p 578.*

2 Timothy 4:6–8, 17–18   I am already being poured out like a drink offering, and the time has come for my departure. I have fought the good fight, I have finished the race, I have kept the faith. Now there is in store for me the crown of righteousness, which the Lord, the righteous Judge, will award to me on that day – and not only to me, but also to all who have longed for his appearing.

The Lord stood at my side and gave me strength, so that through me the message might be fully proclaimed and all the Gentiles might hear it. And I was delivered from the lion's mouth. The Lord will rescue me from every evil attack and will bring me safely to his heavenly kingdom. To him be glory for ever and ever. Amen.

Matthew 16:13–19   *For the text of the Gospel see above.*

Alternative first and second readings:

Ezekiel 3:22–27	*or*	Acts 12:1–11
Psalm 125		Psalm 125
Acts 12:1–11		1 Peter 2:19–25
Matthew 16:13–19		Matthew 16:13–19

Ezekiel 3:22–27 The hand of the LORD was upon me, and he said to me, "Get up and go out to the plain, and there I will speak to you." So I got up and went out to the plain. And the glory of the LORD was standing there, like the glory I had seen by the Kebar River, and I fell face down.

Then the Spirit came into me and raised me to my feet. He spoke to me and said: "Go, shut yourself inside your house. And you, son of man, they will tie with ropes; you will be bound so that you cannot go out among the people. I will make your tongue stick to the roof of your mouth so that you will be silent and unable to rebuke them, though they are a rebellious house. But when I speak to you, I will open your mouth and you shall say to them, 'This is what the Sovereign LORD says.' Whoever will listen let him listen, and whoever will refuse let him refuse; for they are a rebellious house."

Psalm 125 Those who trust in the LORD are like Mount Zion,
  which cannot be shaken but endures for ever.
As the mountains surround Jerusalem,
  so the LORD surrounds his people
both now and for evermore.

The sceptre of the wicked will not remain
  over the land allotted to the righteous,
for then the righteous might use
  their hands to do evil.

Do good, O LORD, to those who are good,
  to those who are upright in heart.
But those who turn to crooked ways
  the LORD will banish with the evildoers.

Peace be upon Israel.

Acts 12:1–11 King Herod arrested some who belonged to the church, intending to persecute them. He had James, the brother of John, put to death with the sword. When he saw that this pleased the Jews, he proceeded to seize Peter also. This happened during the Feast of Unleavened Bread. After arresting him, he put him in prison, handing him over to be guarded by four squads of four soldiers each. Herod intended to bring him out for public trial after the Passover.

So Peter was kept in prison, but the church was earnestly praying to God for him.

The night before Herod was to bring him to trial, Peter was sleeping between two soldiers, bound with two chains, and sentries stood guard at the entrance. Suddenly an angel of the Lord appeared and a light shone in the cell. He struck Peter on the side and woke him up. "Quick, get up!" he said, and the chains fell off Peter's wrists.

Then the angel said to him, "Put on your clothes and sandals." And Peter did so. "Wrap your cloak around you and follow me," the angel told him. Peter followed him out of the prison, but he had no idea that what the angel was doing was really happening; he thought he was seeing a vision. They passed the first and second guards and came to the iron gate leading to the city. It opened for them by itself, and they went through it. When they had walked the length of one street, suddenly the angel left him.

Then Peter came to himself and said, "Now I know without a doubt that the Lord sent his angel and rescued me from Herod's clutches and from everything the Jewish people were anticipating."

Matthew 16:13–19   When Jesus came to the region of Caesarea Philippi, he G asked his disciples, "Who do people say the Son of Man is?" O

They replied, "Some say John the Baptist; others say Elijah; and still S others, Jeremiah or one of the prophets." P

"But what about you?" he asked. "Who do you say I am?" E

Simon Peter answered, "You are the Christ, the Son of the living God." L

Jesus replied, "Blessed are you, Simon son of Jonah, for this was not revealed to you by flesh and blood, but by my Father in heaven. And I tell you that you are Peter, and on this rock I will build my church, and the gates of Hades will not overcome it. I will give you the keys of the kingdom of heaven; whatever you bind on earth will be bound in heaven, and whatever you loose on earth will be loosed in heaven."

Or

Acts 12:1–11   *For text of first reading see second reading p 580.*

Psalm 125   *For text of the Psalm see p 580.*

1 Peter 2:19–25   It is commendable if a man bears up under the pain of unjust S R suffering because he is conscious of God. But how is it to your credit if you E E receive a beating for doing wrong and endure it? But if you suffer for C A doing good and you endure it, this is commendable before God. To this you O D were called, because Christ suffered for you, leaving you an example, that N I you should follow in his steps. D N

> "He committed no sin, G
>   and no deceit was found in his mouth."

When they hurled their insults at him, he did not retaliate; when he suffered, he made no threats. Instead, he entrusted himself to him who judges justly. He himself bore our sins in his body on the tree, so that we might die to sins and live for righteousness; by his wounds you have been healed. For you were like sheep going astray, but now you have returned to the Shepherd and Overseer of your souls.

Matthew 16:13–19   *For the text of the Gospel see p 580.*

Thomas – 3 July

Habbakuk 2:1–4   I will stand at my watch
  and station myself on the ramparts;
I will look to see what he will say to me,
  and what answer I am to give to this complaint.

Then the Lord replied:

"Write down the revelation
  and make it plain on tablets
  so that a herald may run with it.
For the revelation awaits an appointed time;
  it speaks of the end
  and will not prove false.
Though it linger, wait for it;
  it will certainly come and will not delay.

"See, he is puffed up;
  his desires are not upright –
  but the righteous will live by his faith."

Psalm 31:1–6   In you, O Lord, I have taken refuge;
  let me never be put to shame;
  deliver me in your righteousness.
Turn your ear to me,
  come quickly to my rescue;
be my rock of refuge,
  a strong fortress to save me.
Since you are my rock and my fortress,
  for the sake of your name lead and guide me.
Free me from the trap that is set for me,
  for you are my refuge.
Into your hands I commit my spirit;
  redeem me, O Lord, the God of truth.

I hate those who cling to worthless idols;
  I trust in the Lord.

Ephesians 2:19–22   You are no longer foreigners and aliens, but fellow-citizens with God's people and members of God's household, built on the foundation of the apostles and prophets, with Christ Jesus himself as the chief cornerstone. In him the whole building is joined together and rises to become a holy temple in the Lord. And in him you too are being built together to become a dwelling in which God lives by his Spirit.

John 20:24–29   Thomas (called Didymus), one of the Twelve, was not with the disciples when Jesus came. So the other disciples told him, "We have seen the Lord!"

But he said to them, "Unless I see the nail marks in his hands and put my finger where the nails were, and put my hand into his side, I will not believe it."

A week later his disciples were in the house again, and Thomas was with them. Though the doors were locked, Jesus came and stood among them and said, "Peace be with you!" Then he said to Thomas, "Put your finger here; see my hands. Reach out your hand and put it into my side. Stop doubting and believe."

Thomas said to him, "My Lord and my God!"

Then Jesus told him, "Because you have seen me, you have believed; blessed are those who have not seen and yet have believed."

G
O
S
P
E
L

Mary Magdalene – 22 July

Song of Solomon 3:1–4

All night long on my bed
    I looked for the one my heart loves;
    I looked for him but did not find him.
I will get up now and go about the city,
    through its streets and squares;
I will search for the one my heart loves.
    So I looked for him but did not find him.
The watchmen found me
    as they made their rounds in the city.
    "Have you seen the one my heart loves?"
Scarcely had I passed them
    when I found the one my heart loves.
I held him and would not let him go
    till I had brought him to my mother's house,
    to the room of the one who conceived me.

F
I
R
S
T

R
E
A
D
I
N
G

Psalm 42:1–7

As the deer pants for streams of water,
    so my soul pants for you, O God.
My soul thirsts for God, for the living God.
    When can I go and meet with God?
My tears have been my food
    day and night,
while men say to me all day long,
    "Where is your God?"
These things I remember
    as I pour out my soul:
how I used to go with the multitude,
    leading the procession to the house of God,
with shouts of joy and thanksgiving
    among the festive throng.

P
S
A
L
M

Why are you downcast, O my soul?
    Why so disturbed within me?
Put your hope in God,
    for I will yet praise him,
      my Saviour and my God.

My soul is downcast within me;
    therefore I will remember you
from the land of the Jordan,
    the heights of Hermon – from Mount Mizar.
Deep calls to deep
    in the roar of your waterfalls;
all your waves and breakers
    have swept over me.

2 Corinthians 5:14–17   Christ's love compels us, because we are convinced S R that one died for all, and therefore all died. And he died for all, that those E E who live should no longer live for themselves but for him who died for C A them and was raised again. O D

So from now on we regard no-one from a worldly point of view. Though N I we once regarded Christ in this way, we do so no longer. Therefore, if D N anyone is in Christ, he is a new creation; the old has gone, the new has G come!

John 20:1–2, 11–18   Early on the first day of the week, while it was still dark, G Mary Magdalene went to the tomb and saw that the stone had been O removed from the entrance. So she came running to Simon Peter and the S other disciple, the one Jesus loved, and said, "They have taken the Lord out P of the tomb, and we don't know where they have put him!" E

Mary stood outside the tomb crying. As she wept, she bent over to look L into the tomb and saw two angels in white, seated where Jesus' body had been, one at the head and the other at the foot.

They asked her, "Woman, why are you crying?"

"They have taken my Lord away," she said, "and I don't know where they have put him." At this, she turned round and saw Jesus standing there, but she did not realise that it was Jesus.

"Woman," he said, "why are you crying? Who is it you are looking for?"

Thinking he was the gardener, she said, "Sir, if you have carried him away, tell me where you have put him, and I will get him."

Jesus said to her, "Mary."

She turned towards him and cried out in Aramaic, "Rabboni!" (which means Teacher).

Jesus said, "Do not hold on to me, for I have not yet returned to the Father. Go instead to my brothers and tell them, 'I am returning to my Father and your Father, to my God and your God.'"

Mary Magdalene went to the disciples with the news: "I have seen the Lord!" And she told them that he had said these things to her.

Alternative first and second readings

Jeremiah 45:1–5	*or*	Acts 11:27–12:2
Psalm 126		Psalm 126
Acts 11:27–12:2		2 Corinthians 4:7–15
Matthew 20:20–28		Matthew 20:20–28

Jeremiah 45:1–5   This is what Jeremiah the prophet told Baruch son of Neriah in the fourth year of Jehoiakim son of Josiah king of Judah, after Baruch had written on a scroll the words Jeremiah was then dictating: "This is what the LORD, the God of Israel, says to you, Baruch: You said, 'Woe to me! The LORD has added sorrow to my pain; I am worn out with groaning and find no rest.'"

> The LORD said, "Say this to him: 'This is what the LORD says: I will overthrow what I have built and uproot what I have planted, throughout the land. Should you then seek great things for yourself? Seek them not. For I will bring disaster on all people, declares the LORD, but wherever you go I will let you escape with your life.'"

Psalm 126   When the LORD brought back the captives to Zion,
  we were like men who dreamed.
Our mouths were filled with laughter,
  our tongues with songs of joy.
Then it was said among the nations,
  "The LORD has done great things for them."
The LORD has done great things for us,
  and we are filled with joy.

Restore our fortunes, O LORD,
  like streams in the Negev.
Those who sow in tears
  will reap with songs of joy.
Those who go out weeping,
  carrying seed to sow,
will return with songs of joy,
  carrying sheaves with them.

Acts 11:27 – 12:2   Some prophets came down from Jerusalem to Antioch. One of them, named Agabus, stood up and through the Spirit predicted that a severe famine would spread over the entire Roman world. (This happened during the reign of Claudius.) The disciples, each according to his ability, decided to provide help for the brothers living in Judea. This they did, sending their gift to the elders by Barnabas and Saul.

> It was about this time that King Herod arrested some who belonged to the church, intending to persecute them. He had James, the brother of John, put to death with the sword.

Matthew 20:20–28   The mother of Zebedee's sons came to Jesus with her
sons and, kneeling down, asked a favour of him.

"What is it you want?" he asked.

She said, "Grant that one of these two sons of mine may sit at your right
and the other at your left in your kingdom."

"You don't know what you are asking," Jesus said to them. "Can you
drink the cup I am going to drink?"

"We can," they answered.

Jesus said to them, "You will indeed drink from my cup, but to sit at my
right or left is not for me to grant. These places belong to those for whom
they have been prepared by my Father."

When the ten heard about this, they were indignant with the two brothers. Jesus called them together and said, "You know that the rulers of the
Gentiles lord it over them, and their high officials exercise authority over
them. Not so with you. Instead, whoever wants to become great among you
must be your servant, and whoever wants to be first must be your slave –
just as the Son of Man did not come to be served, but to serve, and to give
his life as a ransom for many."

Or

Acts 11:27 – 12:2   *For text of first reading see second reading p 585.*

Psalm 126   *For text of the Psalm see p 585.*

2 Corinthians 4:7–15   We have this treasure in jars of clay to show that this
all-surpassing power is from God and not from us. We are hard pressed on
every side, but not crushed; perplexed, but not in despair; persecuted, but
not abandoned; struck down, but not destroyed. We always carry around in
our body the death of Jesus, so that the life of Jesus may also be revealed
in our body. For we who are alive are always being given over to death for
Jesus' sake, so that his life may be revealed in our mortal body. So then,
death is at work in us, but life is at work in you.

It is written: "I believed; therefore I have spoken." With that same spirit
of faith we also believe and therefore speak, because we know that the one
who raised the LORD Jesus from the dead will also raise us with Jesus and
present us with you in his presence. All this is for your benefit, so that the
grace that is reaching more and more people may cause thanksgiving to
overflow to the glory of God.

Matthew 20:20–28   *For text of the Gospel see above.*

The Transfiguration – 6 August

Daniel 7:9–10, 13–14   Daniel said: "As I looked,

"thrones were set in place,
   and the Ancient of Days took his seat.
His clothing was as white as snow;
   the hair of his head was white like wool.

His throne was flaming with fire,
  and its wheels were all ablaze.
A river of fire was flowing,
  coming out from before him.
Thousands upon thousands attended him;
  ten thousand times ten thousand stood before him.
The court was seated,
  and the books were opened.

"In my vision at night I looked, and there before me was one like a son of man, coming with the clouds of heaven. He approached the Ancient of Days and was led into his presence. He was given authority, glory and sovereign power; all people, nations and men of every language worshipped him. His dominion is an everlasting dominion that will not pass away, and his kingdom is one that will never be destroyed."

Psalm 97 The LORD reigns, let the earth be glad;
    let the distant shores rejoice.

Clouds and thick darkness surround him;
    righteousness and justice are the foundation of his throne.
Fire goes before him
    and consumes his foes on every side.
His lightning lights up the world;
    the earth sees and trembles.
The mountains melt like wax before the LORD,
    before the Lord of all the earth.
The heavens proclaim his righteousness,
    and all the peoples see his glory.

All who worship images are put to shame,
    those who boast in idols –
    worship him, all you gods!

Zion hears and rejoices
    and the villages of Judah are glad
    because of your judgments, O LORD.
For you, O LORD, are the Most High over all the earth;
    you are exalted far above all gods.

Let those who love the LORD hate evil,
    for he guards the lives of his faithful ones
    and delivers them from the hand of the wicked.
Light is shed upon the righteous
    and joy on the upright in heart.
Rejoice in the LORD, you who are righteous,
    and praise his holy name.

2 Peter 1:16–19 We did not follow cleverly invented stories when we told you about the power and coming of our Lord Jesus Christ, but we were eye-witnesses of his majesty. For he received honour and glory from God the Father when the voice came to him from the Majestic Glory, saying, "This is my Son, whom I love; with him I am well pleased." We ourselves heard this voice that came from heaven when we were with him on the sacred mountain.

And we have the word of the prophets made more certain, and you will do well to pay attention to it, as to a light shining in a dark place, until the day dawns and the morning star rises in your hearts.

Luke 9:28–36   Jesus took Peter, John and James with him and went up onto a mountain to pray. As he was praying, the appearance of his face changed, and his clothes became as bright as a flash of lightning. Two men, Moses and Elijah, appeared in glorious splendour, talking with Jesus. They spoke about his departure, which he was about to bring to fulfilment at Jerusalem. Peter and his companions were very sleepy, but when they became fully awake, they saw his glory and the two men standing with him. As the men were leaving Jesus, Peter said to him, "Master, it is good for us to be here. Let us put up three shelters – one for you, one for Moses and one for Elijah." (He did not know what he was saying.)

While he was speaking, a cloud appeared and enveloped them, and they were afraid as they entered the cloud. A voice came from the cloud, saying, "This is my Son, whom I have chosen; listen to him." When the voice had spoken, they found that Jesus was alone. The disciples kept this to themselves, and told no-one at that time what they had seen.

The Blessed Virgin Mary – 15 August

Alternative first readings

Either **Isaiah 61:10, 11**   I delight greatly in the LORD;
     my soul rejoices in my God.
For he has clothed me with garments of salvation
     and arrayed me in a robe of righteousness,
as a bridegroom adorns his head like a priest,
     and as a bride adorns herself with her jewels.
For as the soil makes the young plant come up
     and a garden causes seeds to grow,
so the Sovereign LORD will make
     righteousness and praise
spring up before all nations.

or **Revelation 11:19 – 12:6, 10**   God's temple in heaven was opened, and within his temple was seen the ark of his covenant. And there came flashes of lightning, rumblings, peals of thunder, an earthquake and a great hailstorm.

A great and wondrous sign appeared in heaven: a woman clothed with the sun, with the moon under her feet and a crown of twelve stars on her head. She was pregnant and cried out in pain as she was about to give birth. Then another sign appeared in heaven: an enormous red dragon with seven heads and ten horns and seven crowns on his heads. His tail swept a third of the stars out of the sky and flung them to the earth. The dragon stood in front of the woman who was about to give birth, so that he might devour her child the moment it was born. She gave birth to a son, a male child, who will rule all the nations with an iron sceptre. And her child was snatched up to God and to his throne. The woman fled into the desert to a place prepared for her by God, where she might be taken care of for 1,260 days.

Then I heard a loud voice in heaven say:

"Now have come the salvation and the power and the
    kingdom of our God,
  and the authority of his Christ.
For the accuser of our brothers,
  who accuses them before our God day and night,
  has been hurled down."

Psalm 45:10–17   Listen, O daughter, consider and give ear:
    Forget your people and your father's house.
  The king is enthralled by your beauty;
    honour him, for he is your lord.
  The Daughter of Tyre will come with a gift,
    people of wealth will seek your favour.

  All glorious is the princess within her chamber;
    her gown is interwoven with gold.
  In embroidered garments she is led to the king;
    her virgin companions follow her
    and are brought to you.
  They are led in with joy and gladness;
    they enter the palace of the king.

  Your sons will take the place of your fathers;
    you will make them princes throughout the land.
  I will perpetuate your memory through all
      generations;
    therefore the nations will praise you for ever and
      ever.

Galatians 4:4–7   When the time had fully come, God sent his Son, born of a woman, born under law, to redeem those under law, that we might receive the full rights of sons. Because you are sons, he sent the Spirit of his Son into our hearts, the Spirit who calls out, "*Abba*, Father." So you are no longer a slave, but a son; and since you are a son, God has made you also an heir.

Luke 1:46–55   Mary said: G
O
S
P
E
L

> "My soul glorifies the LORD
>> and my spirit rejoices in God my Saviour,
> for he has been mindful
>> of the humble state of his servant.
> From now on all generations will call me blessed,
>> for the Mighty One has done great things for me –
>> holy is his name.
> His mercy extends to those who fear him,
>> from generation to generation.
> He has performed mighty deeds with his arm;
>> he has scattered those who are proud in their inmost
>>> thoughts.
> He has brought down rulers from their thrones
>> but has lifted up the humble.
> He has filled the hungry with good things
>> but has sent the rich away empty.
> He has helped his servant Israel,
>> remembering to be merciful
> to Abraham and his descendants for ever,
>> even as he said to our ancestors."

Bartholomew – 24 August

Alternative first and second readings.

Isaiah 43:8–13	*or*	Acts 5:12–16
Psalm 145:1–7		Psalm 145:1–7
Acts 5:12–16		1 Corinthians 4:9–15
Luke 22:24–30		Luke 22:24–30

Isaiah 43:8–13   Lead out those who have eyes but are blind,   F
I
R
S
T

> who have ears but are deaf.
> All the nations gather together
>> and the peoples assemble.
> Which of them foretold this
>> and proclaimed to us the former things?
> Let them bring in their witnesses to prove they were **right**,   R
E
A
D
I
N
G
>> so that others may hear and say, "It is true."
> "You are my witnesses," declares the LORD,
>> "and my servant whom I have chosen,
> so that you may know and believe me
>> and understand that I am he.
> Before me no god was formed,
>> nor will there be one after me.
> I, even I, am the LORD,
>> and apart from me there is no saviour.

I have revealed and saved and proclaimed –
I, and not some foreign god among you.
You are my witnesses," declares the LORD, "that I am
God.
Yes, and from ancient days I am he.
No-one can deliver out of my hand.
When I act, who can reverse it?"

Psalm 145:1–7   I will exalt you, my God the King; P
I will praise your name for ever and ever. S
Every day I will praise you A
and extol your name for ever and ever. L
M
Great is the LORD and most worthy of praise;
his greatness no-one can fathom.
One generation will commend your works to
another;
they will tell of your mighty acts.
They will speak of the glorious splendour of your
majesty,
and I will meditate on your wonderful works.
They will tell of the power of your awesome works,
and I will proclaim your great deeds.
They will celebrate your abundant goodness
and joyfully sing of your righteousness.

Acts 5:12–16   The apostles performed many miraculous signs and wonders S R
among the people. And all the believers used to meet together in Solomon's E E
Colonnade. No-one else dared join them, even though they were highly C A
regarded by the people. Nevertheless, more and more men and women O D
believed in the Lord and were added to their number. As a result, people N I
brought the sick into the streets and laid them on beds and mats so that at D N
least Peter's shadow might fall on some of them as he passed by. Crowds G
gathered also from the towns around Jerusalem, bringing their sick and
those tormented by evil spirits, and all of them were healed.

Luke 22:24–30   A dispute arose among the disciples as to which of them was G
considered to be greatest. Jesus said to them, "The kings of the Gentiles O
lord it over them; and those who exercise authority over them call them- S
selves Benefactors. But you are not to be like that. Instead, the greatest P
among you should be like the youngest, and the one who rules like the one E
who serves. For who is greater, the one who is at the table or the one who L
serves? Is it not the one who is at the table? But I am among you as one who
serves. You are those who have stood by me in my trials. And I confer on
you a kingdom, just as my Father conferred one on me, so that you may eat
and drink at my table in my kingdom and sit on thrones, judging the twelve
tribes of Israel."

Or

Acts 5:12–16   *For text of first reading see second reading p 591.*

Psalm 145:1–7   *For text of the Psalm see p 591.*

1 Corinthians 4:9–15   It seems to me that God has put us apostles on display S R
at the end of the procession, like men condemned to die in the arena. We E E
have been made a spectacle to the whole universe, to angels as well as to C A
men. We are fools for Christ, but you are so wise in Christ! We are weak, O D
but you are strong! You are honoured, we are dishonoured! To this very N I
hour we go hungry and thirsty, we are in rags, we are brutally treated, we D N
are homeless. We work hard with our own hands. When we are cursed, we   G
bless; when we are persecuted, we endure it; when we are slandered, we
answer kindly. Up to this moment we have become the scum of the earth,
the refuse of the world.

   I am not writing this to shame you, but to warn you, as my dear children. Even though you have ten thousand guardians in Christ, you do not
have many fathers, for in Christ Jesus I became your father through the
gospel.

Luke 22:24–30   *For text of the Gospel see p 591.*

Holy Cross Day – 14 September

Numbers 21:4–9   The Israelites travelled from Mount Hor along the route to F R
the Red Sea, to go round Edom. But the people grew impatient on the way; I E
they spoke against God and against Moses, and said, "Why have you R A
brought us up out of Egypt to die in the desert? There is no bread! There is S D
no water! And we detest this miserable food!"   T I

   Then the LORD sent venomous snakes among them; they bit the people N
and many Israelites died. The people came to Moses and said, "We sinned G
when we spoke against the LORD and against you. Pray that the LORD will
take the snakes away from us." So Moses prayed for the people.

   The LORD said to Moses, "Make a snake and put it up on a pole; anyone
who is bitten can look at it and live." So Moses made a bronze snake and put
it up on a pole. Then when anyone was bitten by a snake and looked at the
bronze snake, that person lived.

Psalm 22:23–28   You who fear the LORD, praise him!   P
            All you descendants of Jacob, honour him!   S
            Revere him, all you descendants of Israel!   A
            For he has not despised or disdained   L
                the suffering of the afflicted one;   M
            he has not hidden his face from him
                but has listened to his cry for help.

From you comes the theme of my praise in the
great assembly;
before those who fear you will I fulfil my vows.
The poor will eat and be satisfied;
they who seek the LORD will praise him –
may your hearts live for ever!
All the ends of the earth
will remember and turn to the LORD,
and all the families of the nations
will bow down before him,
for dominion belongs to the LORD
and he rules over the nations.

SECOND READING

Philippians 2:6–11 Christ Jesus, being in very nature God,
did not consider equality with God something to be
grasped,
but made himself nothing,
taking the very nature of a servant,
being made in human likeness.
And being found in appearance as a man,
he humbled himself
and became obedient to death – even death on a
cross!
Therefore God exalted him to the highest place
and gave him the name that is above every name,
that at the name of Jesus every knee should bow,
in heaven and on earth and under the earth,
and every tongue confess that Jesus Christ is LORD,
to the glory of God the Father.

GOSPEL

John 3:13–17 Jesus said: "No-one has ever gone into heaven except the one who came from heaven – the Son of Man. Just as Moses lifted up the snake in the desert, so the Son of Man must be lifted up, that everyone who believes in him may have eternal life.

For God so loved the world that he gave his one and only Son, that whoever believes in him shall not perish but have eternal life. For God did not send his Son into the world to condemn the world, but to save the world through him."

Matthew – 21 September

FIRST READING

Proverbs 3:13–18 Blessed is the man who finds wisdom,
the man who gains understanding,
for she is more profitable than silver
and yields better returns than gold.

She is more precious than rubies;
  nothing you desire can compare with her.
Long life is in her right hand;
  in her left hand are riches and honour.
Her ways are pleasant ways,
  and all her paths are peace.
She is a tree of life to those who embrace her;
  those who lay hold of her will be blessed.

Psalm 119:65–72   Do good to your servant
  according to your word, O LORD.
Teach me knowledge and good judgment,
  for I believe in your commands.
Before I was afflicted I went astray,
  but now I obey your word.
You are good, and what you do is good;
  teach me your decrees.
Though the arrogant have smeared me with lies,
  I keep your precepts with all my heart.
Their hearts are callous and unfeeling,
  but I delight in your law.
It was good for me to be afflicted
  so that I might learn your decrees.
The law from your mouth is more precious to me
  than thousands of pieces of silver and gold.

2 Corinthians 4:1–6   Since through God's mercy we have this ministry of the
Spirit, we do not lose heart. Rather, we have renounced secret and shameful ways; we do not use deception, nor do we distort the word of God. On the
contrary, by setting forth the truth plainly we commend ourselves to every
man's conscience in the sight of God. And even if our gospel is veiled, it is
veiled to those who are perishing. The god of this age has blinded the minds
of unbelievers, so that they cannot see the light of the gospel of the glory of
Christ, who is the image of God. For we do not preach ourselves, but Jesus
Christ as Lord, and ourselves as your servants for Jesus' sake. For God,
who said, "Let light shine out of darkness," made his light shine in our
hearts to give us the light of the knowledge of the glory of God in the face
of Christ.

Matthew 9:9–13   Jesus saw a man named Matthew sitting at the tax collector's booth. "Follow me," he told him, and Matthew got up and followed
him.
  While Jesus was having dinner at Matthew's house, many tax collectors
and "sinners" came and ate with him and his disciples. When the Pharisees
saw this, they asked his disciples, "Why does your teacher eat with tax
collectors and 'sinners'?"

On hearing this, Jesus said, "It is not the healthy who need a doctor, but the sick. But go and learn what this means: 'I desire mercy, not sacrifice.' For I have not come to call the righteous, but sinners."

Michael and All Angels (Michaelmas) – 29 September

Alternative first and second readings:

Genesis 28:10–17	*or*	Revelation 12:7–12
Psalm 103:19–22		Psalm 103:19–22
Revelation 12:7–12		Hebrews 1:5–14
John 1:47:51		John 1:47:51

Genesis 28:10–17   Jacob left Beersheba and set out for Haran. When he reached a certain place, he stopped for the night because the sun had set. Taking one of the stones there, he put it under his head and lay down to sleep. He had a dream in which he saw a stairway resting on the earth, with its top reaching to heaven, and the angels of God were ascending and descending on it. There above it stood the LORD, and he said: "I am the LORD, the God of your father Abraham and the God of Isaac. I will give you and your descendants the land on which you are lying. Your descendants will be like the dust of the earth, and you will spread out to the west and to the east, to the north and to the south. All peoples on earth will be blessed through you and your offspring. I am with you and will watch over you wherever you go, and I will bring you back to this land. I will not leave you until I have done what I have promised you."

When Jacob awoke from his sleep, he thought, "Surely the LORD is in this place, and I was not aware of it." He was afraid and said, "How awesome is this place! This is none other than the house of God; this is the gate of heaven."

Psalm 103:19–22   The LORD has established his throne in heaven,
  and his kingdom rules over all.

Praise the LORD, you his angels,
  you mighty ones who do his bidding,
  who obey his word.
Praise the LORD, all his heavenly hosts,
  you his servants who do his will.
Praise the LORD, all his works
  everywhere in his dominion.

Praise the LORD, O my soul.

Revelation 12:7–12   There was war in heaven. Michael and his angels fought against the dragon, and the dragon and his angels fought back. But he was not strong enough, and they lost their place in heaven. The great dragon was hurled down – that ancient serpent called the devil, or Satan, who leads

The margin text reads vertically: FIRST READING (Genesis), PSALM (Psalm), SECOND READING (Revelation).

the whole world astray. He was hurled to the earth, and his angels with him.

Then I heard a loud voice in heaven say:

"Now have come the salvation and the power and the
    kingdom of our God,
  and the authority of his Christ.
For the accuser of our brothers,
  who accuses them before our God day and night,
  has been hurled down.
They overcame him
  by the blood of the Lamb
  and by the word of their testimony;
they did not love their lives so much
  as to shrink from death.
Therefore rejoice, you heavens
  and you who dwell in them!
But woe to the earth and the sea,
  because the devil has gone down to you!
He is filled with fury,
  because he knows that his time is short."

John 1:47–51   When Jesus saw Nathanael approaching, he said of him, "Here G
is a true Israelite, in whom there is nothing false."   O

  "How do you know me?" Nathanael asked.   S

  Jesus answered, "I saw you while you were still under the fig-tree P
before Philip called you."   E

  Then Nathanael declared, "Rabbi, you are the Son of God; you are the L
King of Israel."

  Jesus said, "You believe because I told you I saw you under the fig-tree.
You shall see greater things than that." He then added, "I tell you the truth,
you shall see heaven open, and the angels of God ascending and descending on the Son of Man."

Or
Revelation 12:7–12   *For text of first reading see second reading p 595.*

Psalm 103:19–22   *For text of the Psalm see p 595.*

Hebrews 1:5–14   To which of the angels did God ever say,   S R

  "You are my Son;   E E
    today I have become your Father"?   C A
                                                                             O D
Or again,   N I

  "I will be his Father,   D N
    and he will be my Son"?   G

And again, when God brings his firstborn into the world, he says,

  "Let all God's angels worship him."

In speaking of the angels he says,

"He makes his angels winds,
his servants flames of fire."

But about the Son he says,

"Your throne, O God, will last for ever and ever,
and righteousness will be the sceptre of your kingdom.
You have loved righteousness and hated wickedness;
therefore God, your God, has set you above your companions
by anointing you with the oil of joy."

He also says,

"In the beginning, O LORD, you laid the foundations of the earth,
and the heavens are the work of your hands.
They will perish, but you remain;
they will all wear out like a garment.
You will roll them up like a robe;
like a garment they will be changed.
But you remain the same,
and your years will never end."

To which of the angels did God ever say,

"Sit at my right hand
until I make your enemies
a footstool for your feet"?

Are not all angels ministering spirits sent to serve those who will inherit salvation?

John 1:47–51   *For text of the Gospel see p 596.*

Luke – 18 October

Alternative first reading

Either **Isaiah 35:3–6**	Strengthen the feeble hands,	F
	steady the knees that give way;	I
	say to those with fearful hearts,	R
	"Be strong, do not fear;	S
	your God will come,	T
	he will come with vengeance;	
	with divine retribution	R
	he will come to save you."	E
	Then will the eyes of the blind be opened	A
	and the ears of the deaf unstopped.	D
	Then will the lame leap like a deer,	I
	and the mute tongue shout for joy.	N
	Water will gush forth in the wilderness	G
	and streams in the desert.	

or **Acts 16:6–12a** Paul and his companions travelled throughout the region of Phrygia and Galatia, having been kept by the Holy Spirit from preaching the word in the province of Asia. When they came to the border of Mysia, they tried to enter Bithynia, but the Spirit of Jesus would not allow them to. So they passed by Mysia and went down to Troas. During the night Paul had a vision of a man of Macedonia standing and begging him, "Come over to Macedonia and help us." After Paul had seen the vision, we got ready at once to leave for Macedonia, concluding that God had called us to preach the gospel to them.

From Troas we put out to sea and sailed straight for Samothrace, and the next day on to Neapolis. From there we travelled to Philippi, a Roman colony and the leading city of that district of Macedonia.

F R I E R A S D T I N G

Psalm 147:1–7 Praise the LORD.

> How good it is to sing praises to our God,
>> how pleasant and fitting to praise him!

> The LORD builds up Jerusalem;
>> he gathers the exiles of Israel.
> He heals the broken-hearted
>> and binds up their wounds.

> He determines the number of the stars
>> and calls them each by name.
> Great is our LORD and mighty in power;
>> his understanding has no limit.
> The LORD sustains the humble
>> but casts the wicked to the ground.

> Sing to the LORD with thanksgiving;
>> make music to our God on the harp.

P S A L M

2 Timothy 4:5–17 Keep your head in all situations, endure hardship, do the work of an evangelist, discharge all the duties of your ministry.

For I am already being poured out like a drink offering, and the time has come for my departure. I have fought the good fight, I have finished the race, I have kept the faith. Now there is in store for me the crown of righteousness, which the Lord, the righteous Judge, will award to me on that day – and not only to me, but also to all who have longed for his appearing.

Do your best to come to me quickly, for Demas, because he loved this world, has deserted me and has gone to Thessalonica. Crescens has gone to Galatia, and Titus to Dalmatia. Only Luke is with me. Get Mark and bring him with you, because he is helpful to me in my ministry. I sent Tychicus to Ephesus. When you come, bring the cloak that I left with Carpus at Troas, and my scrolls, especially the parchments.

Alexander the metalworker did me a great deal of harm. The Lord will repay him for what he has done. You too should be on your guard against him, because he strongly opposed our message.

S R E E C A O D N I D N G

At my first defence, no-one came to my support, but everyone deserted me. May it not be held against them. But the Lord stood at my side and gave me strength, so that through me the message might be fully proclaimed and all the Gentiles might hear it. And I was delivered from the lion's mouth.

Luke 10:1–9 The L<small>ORD</small> appointed seventy-two others and sent them two by two ahead of him to every town and place where he was about to go. He told them, "The harvest is plentiful, but the workers are few. Ask the L<small>ORD</small> of the harvest, therefore, to send out workers into his harvest field. Go! I am sending you out like lambs among wolves. Do not take a purse or bag or sandals; and do not greet anyone on the road.

"When you enter a house, first say, 'Peace to this house.' If anyone there loves peace, your peace will rest on that person; if not, it will return to you. Stay in that house, eating and drinking whatever they give you, for workers deserve their wages. Do not move around from house to house.

"When you enter a town and are welcomed, eat what is set before you. Heal the sick who are there and tell them, 'The kingdom of God is near you.'"

Simon and Jude – 28 October

Isaiah 28:14–16 Hear the word of the L<small>ORD</small>, you scoffers
  who rule this people in Jerusalem.
You boast, "We have entered into a covenant with death,
  with the grave we have made an agreement.
When an overwhelming scourge sweeps by,
  it cannot touch us,
for we have made a lie our refuge
  and falsehood our hiding-place."
So this is what the Sovereign L<small>ORD</small> says:

"See, I lay a stone in Zion,
  a tested stone,
a precious cornerstone for a sure foundation;
  the one who trusts will never be dismayed."

Psalm 119:89–96 Your word, O L<small>ORD</small>, is eternal;
  it stands firm in the heavens.
Your faithfulness continues through all generations;
  you established the earth, and it endures.
Your laws endure to this day,
  for all things serve you.
If your law had not been my delight,
  I would have perished in my affliction.
I will never forget your precepts,
  for by them you have preserved my life.
Save me, for I am yours;
  I have sought out your precepts.

The wicked are waiting to destroy me,
 but I will ponder your statutes.
To all perfection I see a limit;
 but your commands are boundless.

Ephesians 2:19–22 You are no longer foreigners and aliens, but fellow-citizens with God's people and members of God's household, built on the foundation of the apostles and prophets, with Christ Jesus himself as the chief cornerstone. In him the whole building is joined together and rises to become a holy temple in the Lord. And in him you too are being built together to become a dwelling in which God lives by his Spirit.

SECOND READING

John 15:17–27 Jesus said: "This is my command: Love each other.
 If the world hates you, keep in mind that it hated me first. If you belonged to the world, it would love you as its own. As it is, you do not belong to the world, but I have chosen you out of the world. That is why the world hates you. Remember the words I spoke to you: 'No servant is greater than his master.' If they persecuted me, they will persecute you also. If they obeyed my teaching, they will obey yours also. They will treat you this way because of my name, for they do not know the One who sent me. If I had not come and spoken to them, they would not be guilty of sin. Now, however, they have no excuse for their sin. He who hates me hates my Father as well. If I had not done among them what no-one else did, they would not be guilty of sin. But now they have seen these miracles, and yet they have hated both me and my Father. But this is to fulfil what is written in their Law: 'They hated me without reason.'
 "When the Counsellor comes, whom I will send to you from the Father, the Spirit of truth who goes out from the Father, he will testify about me. And you also must testify, for you have been with me from the beginning."

GOSPEL

Andrew – 30 November

Isaiah 52:7–10 How beautiful on the mountains
 are the feet of those who bring good news,
who proclaim peace,
 who bring good tidings,
 who proclaim salvation,
who say to Zion,
 "Your God reigns!"
Listen! Your watchmen lift up their voices;
 together they shout for joy.
When the LORD returns to Zion,
 they will see it with their own eyes.
Burst into songs of joy together,
 you ruins of Jerusalem,
for the LORD has comforted his people,
 he has redeemed Jerusalem.

FIRST READING

The LORD will lay bare his holy arm
in the sight of all the nations,
and all the ends of the earth will see
the salvation of our God.

Psalm 19:1–6   The heavens declare the glory of God;
the skies proclaim the work of his hands.
Day after day they pour forth speech;
night after night they display knowledge.
There is no speech or language
where their voice is not heard.
Their voice goes out into all the earth,
their words to the ends of the world.

In the heavens he has pitched a tent for the sun,
which is like a bridegroom coming forth from his pavilion,
like a champion rejoicing to run his course.
It rises at one end of the heavens
and makes its circuit to the other;
nothing is hidden from its heat.

Romans 10:12–18   There is no difference between Jew and Gentile – the same Lord is Lord of all and richly blesses all who call on him, for, "Everyone who calls on the name of the Lord will be saved."

How, then, can they call on the one they have not believed in? And how can they believe in the one of whom they have not heard? And how can they hear without someone preaching to them? And how can they preach unless they are sent? As it is written, "How beautiful are the feet of those who bring good news!"

But not all the Israelites accepted the good news. For Isaiah says, "Lord, who has believed our message?" Consequently, faith comes from hearing the message, and the message is heard through the word of Christ. But I ask: Did they not hear? Of course they did:

"Their voice has gone out into all the earth,
their words to the ends of the world."

Matthew 4:18–22   As Jesus was walking beside the Sea of Galilee, he saw two brothers, Simon called Peter and his brother Andrew. They were casting a net into the lake, for they were fishermen. "Come, follow me," Jesus said, "and I will make you fishers of men." At once they left their nets and followed him.

Going on from there, he saw two other brothers, James son of Zebedee and his brother John. They were in a boat with their father Zebedee, preparing their nets. Jesus called them, and immediately they left the boat and their father and followed him.

Alternative first and second readings:

2 Chronicles 24:20–22	*or*	Acts 7:51–60
Psalm 119:161–168		Psalm 119:161–168
Acts 7:51–60		Galatians 2:16b–20
Matthew 23:34–39		Matthew 23:34–39

2 Chronicles 24:20–22 The Spirit of God came upon Zechariah son of Jehoiada the priest. He stood before the people and said, "This is what God says: 'Why do you disobey the LORD's commands? You will not prosper. Because you have forsaken the LORD, he has forsaken you.'"

But they plotted against him, and by order of the king they stoned him to death in the courtyard of the LORD's temple. King Joash did not remember the kindness Zechariah's father Jehoiada had shown him but killed his son, who said as he lay dying, "May the LORD see this and call you to account."

Psalm 119:161–168 Rulers persecute me without cause,
but my heart trembles at your word.
I rejoice in your promise
like one who finds great spoil.
I hate and abhor falsehood
but I love your law.
Seven times a day I praise you
for your righteous laws.
Great peace have they who love your law,
and nothing can make them stumble.
I wait for your salvation, O LORD,
and I follow your commands.
I obey your statutes,
for I love them greatly.
I obey your precepts and your statutes,
for all my ways are known to you.

Acts 7:51–60 "You stiff-necked people, with uncircumcised hearts and ears!" said Stephen. "You are just like your ancestors: You always resist the Holy Spirit! Was there ever a prophet your ancestors did not persecute? They even killed those who predicted the coming of the Righteous One. And now you have betrayed and murdered him – you who have received the law that was put into effect through angels but have not obeyed it."

When the Sanhedrin heard this, they were furious and gnashed their teeth at him. But Stephen, full of the Holy Spirit, looked up to heaven and saw the glory of God, and Jesus standing at the right hand of God. "Look," he said, "I see heaven open and the Son of Man standing at the right hand of God."

At this they covered their ears and, yelling at the top of their voices, they all rushed at him, dragged him out of the city and began to stone him. Meanwhile, the witnesses laid their clothes at the feet of a young man named Saul.

While they were stoning him, Stephen prayed, "Lord Jesus, receive my spirit." Then he fell on his knees and cried out, "Lord, do not hold this sin against them." When he had said this, he fell asleep.

Matthew 10:17–22 Jesus said: "Be on your guard against men; they will hand you over to the local councils and flog you in their synagogues. On my account you will be brought before governors and kings as witnesses to them and to the Gentiles. But when they arrest you, do not worry about what to say or how to say it. At that time you will be given what to say, for it will not be you speaking, but the Spirit of your Father speaking through you.

"Brother will betray brother to death, and a father his child; children will rebel against their parents and have them put to death. All men will hate you because of me, but he who stands firm to the end will be saved."

Or

Acts 7:51–60 *For text of first reading see second reading p 602.*

Psalm 119:161–168 *For text of the Psalm see p 602.*

Galatians 2:16b–20 We, too, have put our faith in Christ Jesus that we may be justified by faith in Christ and not by observing the law, because by observing the law no-one will be justified.

If, while we seek to be justified in Christ, it becomes evident that we ourselves are sinners, does that mean that Christ promotes sin? Absolutely not! If I rebuild what I destroyed, I prove that I am a law-breaker. For through the law I died to the law so that I might live for God. I have been crucified with Christ and I no longer live, but Christ lives in me. The life I live in the body, I live by faith in the Son of God, who loved me and gave himself for me.

Matthew 23:34–39 *For text of the Gospel see above.*

John – 27 December

Exodus 33:7–11a Moses used to take a tent and pitch it outside the camp some distance away, calling it the "tent of meeting". Anyone enquiring of the LORD would go to the tent of meeting outside the camp. And whenever Moses went out to the tent, all the people rose and stood at the entrances to their tents, watching Moses until he entered the tent. As Moses went into the tent, the pillar of cloud would come down and stay at the entrance, while the LORD spoke with Moses. Whenever the people saw the pillar of cloud standing at the entrance to the tent, they all stood and worshipped, each at the entrance to his tent. The LORD would speak to Moses face to face, as a man speaks with his friend.

Praise the LORD, all you nations;
extol him, all you peoples.
For great is his love towards us,
and the faithfulness of the LORD endures for ever.
Praise the LORD.

1 John 1 That which was from the beginning, which we have heard, which we have seen with our eyes, which we have looked at and our hands have touched – this we proclaim concerning the Word of life. The life appeared; we have seen it and testify to it, and we proclaim to you the eternal life, which was with the Father and has appeared to us. We proclaim to you what we have seen and heard, so that you also may have fellowship with us. And our fellowship is with the Father and with his Son, Jesus Christ. We write this to make our joy complete.

This is the message we have heard from him and declare to you: God is light; in him there is no darkness at all. If we claim to have fellowship with him yet walk in the darkness, we lie and do not live by the truth. But if we walk in the light, as he is in the light, we have fellowship with one another, and the blood of Jesus, his Son, purifies us from all sin.

If we claim to be without sin, we deceive ourselves and the truth is not in us. If we confess our sins, he is faithful and just and will forgive us our sins and purify us from all unrighteousness. If we claim we have not sinned, we make him out to be a liar and his word has no place in our lives.

John 21:19b–25 Jesus said to Peter, "Follow me!"

Peter turned and saw that the disciple whom Jesus loved was following them. (This was the one who had leaned back against Jesus at the supper and had said, "Lord, who is going to betray you?") When Peter saw him, he asked, "Lord, what about him?"

Jesus answered, "If I want him to remain alive until I return, what is that to you? You must follow me." Because of this, the rumour spread among the brothers that this disciple would not die. But Jesus did not say that he would not die; he only said, "If I want him to remain alive until I return, what is that to you?"

This is the disciple who testifies to these things and who wrote them down. We know that his testimony is true.

Jesus did many other things as well. If every one of them were written down, I suppose that even the whole world would not have room for the books that would be written.

Holy Innocents – 28 December

Jeremiah 31:15–17 This is what the LORD says:

"A voice is heard in Ramah,
mourning and great weeping,

> Rachel weeping for her children
>> and refusing to be comforted,
>> because her children are no more."

This is what the LORD says:

> "Restrain your voice from weeping
>> and your eyes from tears,
>> for your work will be rewarded,"
>>>> declares the LORD.
> "They will return from the land of the enemy.
> So there is hope for your future,"
>>>> declares the LORD.
> "Your children will return to their own land.

Psalm 124   If the LORD had not been on our side –
>> let Israel say –
> if the LORD had not been on our side
>> when men attacked us,
> when their anger flared against us,
>> they would have swallowed us alive;
> the flood would have engulfed us,
>> the torrent would have swept over us,
> the raging waters
>> would have swept us away.

> Praise be to the LORD,
>> who has not let us be torn by their teeth.
> We have escaped like a bird
>> out of the fowler's snare;
> the snare has been broken,
>> and we have escaped.
> Our help is in the name of the LORD,
>> the Maker of heaven and earth.

P
S
A
L
M

Corinthians 1:26–29   Brothers, think of what you were when you were called. Not many of you were wise by human standards; not many were influential; not many were of noble birth. But God chose the foolish things of the world to shame the wise; God chose the weak things of the world to shame the strong. He chose the lowly things of this world and the despised things – and the things that are not – to nullify the things that are, so that no-one may boast before him.

S R
E E
C A
O D
N I
D N
G

Matthew 2:13–18   When the Magi had gone, an angel of the Lord appeared to Joseph in a dream. "Get up," he said, "take the child and his mother and escape to Egypt. Stay there until I tell you, for Herod is going to search for the child to kill him." So he got up, took Jesus and his mother during the night and left for Egypt, where he stayed until the death of Herod. And so

G
O
S
P
E
L

was fulfilled what the Lord has said through the prophet: "Out of Egypt I called my son."

When Herod realised that he had been outwitted by the Magi, he was furious, and he gave orders to kill all the boys in Bethlehem and its vicinity who were two years old and under, in accordance with the time he had learned from the Magi. Then what was said through the prophet Jeremiah was fulfilled:

> "A voice is heard is Ramah,
>   weeping and great mourning,
> Rachel weeping for her children
>   and refusing to be comforted,
> because they are no more."

YEAR A HARVEST

Alternative first reading

Either **Deuteronomy 8:7-18** For the LORD your God is bringing you into a F
good land - a land with streams and pools of water, with springs flowing in I
the valleys and hills; a land with wheat and barley, vines and fig-trees, R
pomegranates, olive oil and honey; a land where bread will not be scarce S
and you will lack nothing; a land where the rocks are iron and you can dig T
copper out of the hills.

When you have eaten and are satisfied, praise the LORD your God for the R
good land he has given you. Be careful that you do not forget the LORD your E
God, failing to observe his commands, his laws and his decrees that I am A
giving you this day. Otherwise, when you eat and are satisfied, when you D
build fine houses and settle down, and when your herds and flocks grow I
large and your silver and gold increase and all you have is multiplied, then N
your heart will become proud and you will forget the LORD you God, who G
brought you out of Egypt, out of the land of slavery. He led you through the
vast and dreadful desert, that thirsty and waterless land, with its venomous snakes and scorpions. He brought you water out of hard rock. He
gave you manna to eat in the desert, something your fathers had never
known, to humble and to test you so that in the end it might go well with
you. You may say to yourself, "My power and the strength of my hands
have produced this wealth for me." But remember the LORD your God, for
it is he who gives you the ability to produce wealth, and so confirms his
covenant, which he swore to your forefathers, as it is today.

or **Deuteronomy 28:1-14** If you fully obey the LORD your God and carefully F
follow all his commands that I give you today, the LORD your God will set I
you high above all the nations on earth. All these blessings will come upon R
you and accompany you if you obey the LORD your God: S

> You will be blessed in the city and blessed in the country. T
> The fruit of your womb will be blessed, and the crops of your land
> and the young of your livestock - the calves of your herds and the lambs R
> of your flocks. E
> Your basket and your kneading trough will be blessed. A
> You will be blessed when you come in and blessed when you go out. D

The LORD will grant that the enemies who will rise up against you will be I
defeated before you. They will come at you from one direction but flee N
from you in seven. G

The LORD will send a blessing on your barns and on everything you
put your hand to. The LORD your God will bless you in the land he is giving
you.

The LORD will establish you as his holy people, as he promised you on
oath, if you keep the commands of the LORD your God and walk in his ways.
Then all the peoples on the earth will see that you are called by the name of

the LORD, and they will fear you. The LORD will grant you abundant prosperity - in the fruit of your womb, the young of your livestock and the crops of your ground - in the land he swore to your forefathers to give you.

The LORD will open the heavens, the storehouse of his bounty, to send rain on your land in season and to bless all the work of your hands. You will lend to many nations but will borrow from none. The LORD will make you the head, not the tail. If you pay attention to the commands of the LORD your God that I give you this day and carefully follow them, you will always be at the top, never at the bottom. Do not turn aside from any of the commands I give you today, to the right or to the left, following other gods and serving them.

Psalm 65 Praise awaits you, O God, in Zion;
  to you our vows will be fulfilled.
O you who hear prayer,
  to you all men will come.
When we were overwhelmed by sins,
  you forgave our transgressions.
Blessed are those you choose
  and bring near to live in your courts!
We are filled with the good things of your house,
  of your holy temple.

You answer us with awesome deeds of righteousness,
  O God our Saviour,
the hope of all the ends of the earth
  and of the farthest seas,
who formed the mountains by your power,
  having armed yourself with strength,
who stilled the roaring of the seas,
  the roaring of their waves,
  and the turmoil of the nations.

Those living far away fear your wonders;
  where morning dawns and evening fade
  you call forth songs of joy.

You care for the land and water it;
  you enrich it abundantly.
The streams of God are filled with water
  to provide the people with corn,
  for so you have ordained it.
You drench its furrows
  and level its ridges;
you soften it with showers
  and bless its crops.
You crown the year with your bounty,
  and your carts overflow with abundance.

The grasslands of the desert overflow;
   the hills are clothed with gladness.
The meadows are covered with flocks
   and the valleys are mantled with corn;
   they shout for joy and sing.

Corinthians 9:6-15   Remember this: Whoever sows sparingly will also reap sparingly, and whoever sows generously will also reap generously. Each man should give what he has decided in his heart to give, not reluctantly or under compulsion, for God loves a cheerful giver. And God is able to make all grace abound to you, so that in all things at all times, having all that you need, you will abound in every good work. As it is written:

   "He has scattered abroad his gifts to the poor;
      his righteousness endures for ever."

Now he who supplies seed to the sower and bread for food will also supply and increase your store of seed and will enlarge the harvest of your righteousness. You will be made rich in every way so that you can be generous on every occasion, and through us your generosity will result in thanksgiving to God.

   This service that you perform is not only supplying the needs of God's people but is also overflowing in many expressions of thanks to God. Because of the service by which you have proved yourselves, men will praise God for the obedience that accompanies your confession of the gospel of Christ, and for your generosity in sharing with them and with everyone else. And in their prayers for you their hearts will go out to you, because of the surpassing grace God has given you. Thanks be to God for his indescribable gift!

SECOND READING (margin)

Alternative Gospel

Either **Luke 12:26-30**   Since you cannot do this very little thing, why do you worry about the rest?

   Consider how the lilies grow. They do not labour or spin. Yet I tell you, not even Solomon in all his splendour was dressed like one of these. If that is how God clothes the grass of the field, which is here today, and tomorrow is thrown into the fire, how much more will he clothe you, O you of little faith! And do not set your heart on what you will eat or drink; do not worry about it. For the pagan world runs after all such things, and your Father knows that you need them. But seek his kingdom, and these things will be given to you as well.

GOSPEL (margin)

Luke 17:11-19   Now on his way to Jerusalem, Jesus travelled along the border between Samaria and Galilee. As he was going into a village, ten men who had leprosy met him. They stood at a distance and called out in a loud voice, "Jesus, Master, have pity on us!"

   When he saw them, he said, "Go, show yourselves to the priests." And as they went, they were cleansed.

GOSPEL (margin)

One of them, when he saw he was healed, came back, praising God in a loud voice. He threw himself at Jesus' feet and thanked him - and he was a Samaritan.

Jesus asked, "Were not all ten cleansed? Where are the other nine? Was no-one found to return and give praise to God except this foreigner?" Then he said to him, "Rise and go; your faith has made you well."

YEAR B HARVEST

Joel 2 :21-27
Be not afraid, O land;
   be glad and rejoice.
Surely the Lord has done great things.
   Be not afraid, O wild animals,
    for the open pastures are becoming green.
The trees are bearing their fruit;
   the fig-tree and the vine yield their riches.
Be glad, O people of Zion,
   rejoice in the Lord your God,
for he has given you
   the autumn rains in righteousness.
He sends you abundant showers,
   both autumn and spring rains, as before.
The threshing-floors will be filled with grain;
   the vats will overflow with new wine and oil.

"I will repay you for the years the locusts have eaten -
   the great locust and the young locust,
   the others locusts and the locust swarm -
my great army that I sent among you.
You will have plenty to eat, until you are full,
   and you will praise the name of the Lord your God,
   who has worked wonders for you;
never again will my people be shamed.
Then you will know that I am in Israel,
   that I am the Lord your God,
   and that there is no other;
never again will my people be shamed."

(margin: F I R S T   R E A D I N G)

Psalm 126
When the Lord brought back the captives to Zion,
   we were like men who dreamed.
Our mouths were filled with laughter,
   our tongues with songs of joy.
Then it was said among the nations,
   "The Lord has done great things for them."
The Lord has done great things for us,
   and we are filled with joy.

(margin: P S A L M)

Restore our fortunes, O LORD,
like streams in the Negev.
Those who sow in tears
will reap with songs of joy.
He who goes out weeping,
carrying seed to sow,
will return with songs of joy,
carrying sheaves with him.

Alternative second reading

Either **1 Timothy 2:1-7**   I urge, then, first of all, that requests, prayers, inter- S R
cession and thanksgiving be made for everyone - for kings and all those E E
in authority, that we may live peaceful and quiet lives in all godliness C A
and holiness. This is good, and pleases God our Saviour, who wants all O D
men to be saved and to come to a knowledge of the truth. For there is one N I
God and one mediator between God and men, the man Christ Jesus, who D N
gave himself as a ransom for all men - the testimony given in its proper   G
time. And for this purpose I was appointed a herald and an apostle - I
am telling the truth, I am not lying - and a teacher of the true faith to the
Gentiles.

or **1 Timothy 6:6-10**   But godliness with contentment is great gain. For we S R
brought nothing into the world, and we can take nothing out of it. But if we E E
have food and clothing, we will be content with that. People who want to get C A
rich fall into temptation and a trap and into many foolish and harmful O D
desires that plunge men into ruin and destruction. For the love of money is N I
a root of all kinds of evil. Some people, eager for money, have wandered D N
from the faith and pierced themselves with many griefs.   G

Matthew 6:25-33   "Therefore I tell you, do not worry about your life, what G
you will eat or drink; or about your body, what you will wear. Is not O
life more important than food, and the body more important than clothes? S
Look at the birds of the air; they do not sow or reap or store away in P
barns, and yet your heavenly Father feeds them. Are you not much more E
valuable than they? Who of you by worrying can add a single hour to his L
life?

"And why do you worry about clothes? See how the lilies of the field
grow. They do not labour or spin. Yet I tell you that not even Solomon in all
his splendour was dressed like one of these. If that is how God clothes the
grass of the field, which is here today and tomorrow is thrown into the fire,
will he not much more clothe you, O you of little faith? So do not worry, saying, 'What shall we eat?' or 'What shall we drink?' or 'What shall we wear?'
for the pagans run after all these things, and your heavenly Father knows
that you need them. But seek first his kingdom and his righteousness, and
all these things will be given to you as well."

YEAR C HARVEST

Deuteronomy 26:1-11 When you have entered the land that the LORD your F
God is giving you as an inheritance and have taken possession of it and settled I
in it, take some of the firstfruits of all that you produce from the soil of the R
land that the LORD your God is giving you and put them in a basket. Then go to S
the place that the LORD your God will choose as a dwelling for his Name and T
say to the priest in office at the time, "I declare today to the LORD your God
that I have come to the land that the LORD swore to our forefathers to give us." R
The priest shall take the basket from your hands and set it down in front of the E
altar of the LORD your God. Then you shall declare before the LORD your God: A
"My father was a wandering Aramean, and he went down into Egypt with a D
few people and lived there and became a great nation, powerful and numer- I
ous. But the Egyptians ill-treated us and made us suffer, putting us to hard N
labour. Then we cried out to the LORD, the God of our fathers, and the LORD G
heard our voice and saw our misery, toil and oppression. So the LORD brought
us out of Egypt with a mighty hand and an outstretched arm, with great terror and with miraculous signs and wonders. He brought us to this place and
gave us this land, a land flowing with milk and honey; and now I bring the firstfruits of the soil that you, O LORD, have given me." Place the basket before the
LORD your God and bow down before him. And you and the Levites and the
aliens among you shall rejoice in all the good things the LORD your God has
given to you and your household.

Psalm 100 Shout for joy to the LORD, all the earth, P
Worship the LORD with gladness; S
come before him with joyful songs. A

Know that the LORD is God. L
It is he who made us, and we are his; M
we are his people, the sheep of his pasture.

Enter his gates with thanksgiving
and his courts with praise;
give thanks to him and praise his name.
For the LORD is good and his love endures for ever;
his faithfulness continues through all generations.

Alternative second reading

Either **Philippians 4:4-9** Rejoice in the LORD always. I will say it again: S
Rejoice! Let your gentleness be evident to all. The LORD is near. Do not be E
anxious about anything, but in everything, by prayer and petition, with C
thanksgiving, present your requests to God. And the peace of God, which O
transcends all understanding, will guard your hearts and your minds in N
Christ Jesus. D
Finally brothers, whatever is true, whatever is noble, whatever is right,
whatever is pure, whatever is lovely, whatever is admirable - if anything is

excellent or praiseworthy - think about such things. Whatever you have learned or received or heard from me, or seen in me - put it into practice. And the God of peace will be with you.

or **Revelation 14:14-18** I looked, and there before me was a white cloud, and seated on the cloud was one "like a son of man" with a crown of gold on his head and a sharp sickle in his hand. Then another angel came out of the temple and called in a loud voice to him who was sitting on the cloud. "Take your sickle and reap, because the time to reap has come, for the harvest of the earth is ripe." So he who was seated on the cloud swung his sickle over the earth, and the earth was harvested.

Another angel came out of the temple in heaven, and he too had a sharp sickle. Still another angel, who had charge of the fire, came from the altar and called in a loud voice to him who had the sharp sickle, "Take your sharp sickle and gather the clusters of grapes from the earth's vine, because its grapes are ripe."

S R
E E
C A
O D
N I
D N
G

John 6:25-35 When they found him on the other side of the lake, they asked him, "Rabbi, when did you get here?"

Jesus answered, "I tell you the truth, you are looking for me, not because you saw miraculous signs but because you ate the loaves and had your fill. Do not work for food that spoils, but for food that endures to eternal life, which the Son of Man will give you. On him God the Father has placed his seal of approval."

Then they asked him, "What must we do to do the works God requires?"

Jesus answered, "The work of God is this; to believe in the one he has sent."

So they asked him. "What miraculous sign then will you give that we may see it and believe you? What will you do? Our forefathers ate the manna in the desert; as it is written: 'He gave them bread from heaven to eat.'"

Jesus said to them, "I tell you the truth, it is not Moses who has given you the bread from heaven, but it is my Father who gives you the true bread from heaven. For the bread of God is he who comes down from heaven and gives life to the world."

"Sir," they said, "from now on give us this bread."

Then Jesus declared, "I am the bread of life. He who comes to me will never go hungry, and he who believes in me will never be thirsty."

G
O
S
P
E
L

NOTES

NOTES

NOTES

NOTES

NOTES

NOTES

NOTES

NOTES

NOTES

NOTES

NOTES

NOTES

NOTES

NOTES

NIV BIBLES AT LOW PRICES
FOR BULK PURCHASE
Ideal for Church or School Use

The NEW INTERNATIONAL VERSION
of the Bible is the most popular modern English Bible
translation in the world. It is acclaimed for its accurate
scholarship and its lucid dignified English making it the ideal
edition for general use in churches and schools today.

The ECONOMY EDITIONS, available in
two different hardback bindings, have been produced to the
highest specification making them not only attractive but
durable. (The PEW EDITION is suitable for gold blocking
with your logo/crest. We can supply details on
orders for 100 copies of more).

The COMPETITIVE PRICES of these editions have been
made possible by our bulk production and distribution methods
which allow us to pass the saving on to your organisation,
church or school. The only conditions are that they are bought
in packs of twenty copies and are not for resale.

OTHER EDITIONS of the NIV Bible are also available at
considerable savings for bulk purchase.

For full details and a scale of prices, please contact:
The Religious Books Division
Hodder & Stoughton Publishers
338 Euston Road
London NW1 3BH
Phone: 0171 873 6060
Fax: 0171 873 6059
Email: religious-sales@hodder.co.uk